Digitalization, New Media, and Education for Sustainable Development

Lars Keller
University of Innsbruck, Austria

Gerd Michelsen
Leuphana University, Germany

Martin Dür
University of Innsbruck, Austria

Syamsul Bachri
Universitas Negeri Malang, Indonesia

Michaela Zint
University of Michigan, USA

IGI Global
PUBLISHER of TIMELY KNOWLEDGE

A volume in the Advances in Educational Technologies and Instructional Design (AETID) Book Series

Published in the United States of America by
IGI Global
Information Science Reference (an imprint of IGI Global)
701 E. Chocolate Avenue
Hershey PA, USA 17033
Tel: 717-533-8845
Fax: 717-533-8661
E-mail: cust@igi-global.com
Web site: http://www.igi-global.com

Library of Congress Cataloging-in-Publication Data

Names: Keller, Lars, editor. | Michelsen, Gerd, 1948- editor. | Dür, Martin, 1974- editor. | Bachri, Syamsul, 1983- editor. | Zint, Michaela T. (Michaela Theresia), editor.
Title: Digitalization, new media, and education for sustainable development / Lars Keller, Gerd Michelsen, Martin Dür, Syamsul Bachri, and Michaela Zint, editors.
Description: Hershey PA : Information Science Reference, [2023] | Includes bibliographical references and index. | Summary: "This book will examine all aspects related to and interconnections between digitalization, new media, and educational sustainable development, offering perspectives from primary to tertiary education, from formal to informal education, from global to local education, from scientific findings to political strategies, and highlighting exceptional "best practice" examples and case studies"-- Provided by publisher.
Identifiers: LCCN 2022027232 (print) | LCCN 2022027233 (ebook) | ISBN 9781799850335 (hardcover) | ISBN 9781668424971 (paperback) | ISBN 9781799850342 (ebook)
Subjects: LCSH: Educational technology--Social aspects. | Educational technology--Environmental aspects. | Educational equalization. | Sustainable development--Study and teaching.
Classification: LCC LB1028.3 .D559 2023 (print) | LCC LB1028.3 (ebook) | DDC 371.33--dc23/eng/20220815
LC record available at https://lccn.loc.gov/2022027232
LC ebook record available at https://lccn.loc.gov/2022027233

This book is published in the IGI Global book series Advances in Educational Technologies and Instructional Design (AE-TID) (ISSN: 2326-8905; eISSN: 2326-8913)

British Cataloguing in Publication Data
A Cataloguing in Publication record for this book is available from the British Library.

For electronic access to this publication, please contact: eresources@igi-global.com.

Advances in Educational Technologies and Instructional Design (AETID) Book Series

Lawrence A. Tomei
Robert Morris University, USA

ISSN:2326-8905
EISSN:2326-8913

Mission

Education has undergone, and continues to undergo, immense changes in the way it is enacted and distributed to both child and adult learners. In modern education, the traditional classroom learning experience has evolved to include technological resources and to provide online classroom opportunities to students of all ages regardless of their geographical locations. From distance education, Massive-Open-Online-Courses (MOOCs), and electronic tablets in the classroom, technology is now an integral part of learning and is also affecting the way educators communicate information to students.

The **Advances in Educational Technologies & Instructional Design (AETID) Book Series** explores new research and theories for facilitating learning and improving educational performance utilizing technological processes and resources. The series examines technologies that can be integrated into K-12 classrooms to improve skills and learning abilities in all subjects including STEM education and language learning. Additionally, it studies the emergence of fully online classrooms for young and adult learners alike, and the communication and accountability challenges that can arise. Trending topics that are covered include adaptive learning, game-based learning, virtual school environments, and social media effects. School administrators, educators, academicians, researchers, and students will find this series to be an excellent resource for the effective design and implementation of learning technologies in their classes.

Coverage

- Educational Telecommunications
- Classroom Response Systems
- Higher Education Technologies
- Game-Based Learning
- Instructional Design
- Curriculum Development
- Social Media Effects on Education
- Collaboration Tools
- Web 2.0 and Education
- Instructional Design Models

The Advances in Educational Technologies and Instructional Design (AETID) Book Series (ISSN 2326-8905) is published by IGI Global, 701 E. Chocolate Avenue, Hershey, PA 17033-1240, USA, www.igi-global.com. This series is composed of titles available for purchase individually; each title is edited to be contextually exclusive from any other title within the series. For pricing and ordering information please visit http://www.igi-global.com/book-series/advances-educational-technologies-instructional-design/73678. Postmaster: Send all address changes to above address.

Titles in this Series

For a list of additional titles in this series, please visit: http://www.igi-global.com/book-series/advances-educational-technologies-instructional-design/73678

Implementing Rapid E-Learning Through Interactive Materials Development
Mohammad Issack Santally (University of Mauritius, Mauritius) Yousra Rajabalee (Mauritius Institute of Education, Mauritius) and Ravi Rajputh (University of Mauritius, Mauritius)
Information Science Reference • © 2023 • 300pp • H/C (ISBN: 9781668449400) • US $215.00

Exploring Social Emotional Learning in Diverse Academic Settings
Regina Rahimi (Georgia Southern University, USA) and Delores Liston (Georgia Southern University, USA)
Information Science Reference • © 2023 • 330pp • H/C (ISBN: 9781668472279) • US $215.00

New Approaches to the Investigation of Language Teaching and Literature
Aitor Garcés-Manzanera (University of Murcia, Spain) and María Encarnacion Carrillo García (University of Murcia, Spain)
Information Science Reference • © 2023 • 325pp • H/C (ISBN: 9781668460207) • US $215.00

Agricultural Education for Development in the Arab Countries
Mohamed M. Samy (Independent Researcher, USA) and R. Kirby Barrick (University of Florida, USA (retired))
Information Science Reference • © 2023 • 364pp • H/C (ISBN: 9781668440506) • US $215.00

Fostering Diversity and Inclusion Through Curriculum Transformation
Cily Elizabeth Mamatle Tabane (University of South Africa, South Africa) Boitumelo Molebogeng Diale (University of Johannesburg, South Africa) Ailwei Solomon Mawela (University of South Africa, South Africa) and Thulani Vincent Zengele (University of South Africa, South Africa)
Information Science Reference • © 2023 • 315pp • H/C (ISBN: 9781668469958) • US $215.00

Supporting Self-Regulated Learning and Student Success in Online Courses
Danny Glick (University of California, Irvine, USA) Jeff Bergin (General Assembly, USA) and Chi Chang (Michigan State University, USA)
Information Science Reference • © 2023 • 382pp • H/C (ISBN: 9781668465004) • US $215.00

Strategies and Considerations for Educating the Academically Gifted
Tia Neal (University of Louisiana at Monroe, USA)
Information Science Reference • © 2023 • 384pp • H/C (ISBN: 9781668466773) • US $215.00

IGI Global
PUBLISHER of TIMELY KNOWLEDGE

701 East Chocolate Avenue, Hershey, PA 17033, USA
Tel: 717-533-8845 x100 • Fax: 717-533-8661
E-Mail: cust@igi-global.com • www.igi-global.com

Table of Contents

Detailed Table of Contents

This paper intends to illustrate the role of geography education concerning sustainability in a digital age. In current everyday life, (non-)sustainability and digitalization are closely linked to each other, including societal issues beyond technology and ecology. For instance, digitalization may be a key to solve certain sustainability problems and is the source for challenges to sustainability at the same time. Geography education has both strong links with an education for digitalization and with an education for sustainable development. Therefore, it is an ideal learning environment to teach about the complexity of the linkages between both fields, and the necessity of thinking them together. Alongside with specific thematic examples for the classroom this chapter provides a number of didactic approaches that are a starting point to design subject-oriented classroom settings, appropriate to the complexity of the issue, and aimed at an emancipatory education for sustainable development.

The chapter explores the risks of the platform society to sustainability and how education for sustainability (ESD) can address these risks. The platform society is built on a business model that depends on network effects and user productivity. It, therefore, with the help of algorithms, bots, and AI, maintains the kind of content that can stimulate user engagement. This content is often related to the polarization of society, the deepening of political conflicts, and the diffusion of biased opinions. The response of ESD can be the concept of devalorisation of society, which means the orientation of the development of society toward the reduction of the ecological costs of human and social habitation. Pedagogical approaches that can embody the concept of devalorisation in ESD include the widespread use in teaching of triple bottom line, meta-analysis of social media information, elaboration of transition scenarios between different futures, and the nurturing of ecological solidarity.

COVID-19 has impacted the East Kalimantan, Indonesia, community market, especially for indigenous food and non-food souvenirs. These conditions threaten the global pursuit of SDGs. The University of Mulawarman and PT Aplikasi Karya Anak Bangsa, a subsidiary of Gojek Indonesia, identified social concerns for matching program. Our university team's experience integrating the tridharma led us to offer a five-stage framework: (1) vision internalization, (2) persistence learning, (3) technology adaption, (4) collaboration growth, and (5) outcomes integration. Multi-stakeholder cooperation starts with mutual benefits, ideas, agreements, and program designs. Learning aspects are integrated through final assignments, practical experiences, and organized assignments related to learning outcomes on specific course areas (embedded learning). The emancipated learning of the Independent Campus (MBKM) was implemented at the university level. Outcome-based education for higher education multi-stakeholder matching program is an approach for addressing education SDG.

Digital storytelling and participatory video (PV) are closely linked since they share common objectives, development tools, and methodologies. They are not just informative but purposefully aim to empower, educate, and activate people toward building a more sustainable and just society. This chapter describes both digital storytelling as a tool and as a teaching and learning methodology applied in an Erasmus+ project in Southeast Asia. It has been revealed that the interaction between digital technology and education for sustainability creates new opportunities to address sustainability, as well as new challenges. The teachers trained produced digital storytelling/PV applications that can be categorized as "authentic" learning activities addressing issues in the "real world." It was widely assumed that teachers involved in this process learned to view teaching and learning from alternative ways, feeling ownership and control of their own learning and experiencing a sense of contribution to society and the environment.

This chapter discusses the role of education and sustainable development in Pakistan, especially in tribal areas. Forty-six teachers and 28 parents from 15 primary schools were interviewed for this study, and data has also been collected via observational technique. A mixed methods approach employs both qualitative and quantitate techniques. To achieve quality education at any level, especially at primary level, teachers and students should aim at creating the link between culture, pedagogy, and digitalization. Teachers should be competent in the implementation of technology, that is, the use of computers, and have multimedia skills in order to find and adopt pedagogies relevant to class environments. This chapter looks at the current situation Pakistan, and especially in the tribal areas of Pakistan, and suggests recommendations for the incorporation of ESD goals in the single national curriculum, the development of teacher education programs, incentives for teachers and (female) students, and the facilitation of electricity, computer technology, and internet access for all schools.

This chapter reviews recent research related to students' educational device use, online content consumption, and students' understanding of content providers' algorithmic targeting practices to make the case for a new information literacy content area that encompasses a comprehensive and responsive education initiative focused on maintaining students' autonomy and wellbeing. By examining the great extent to which online content providers' large-scale switch to algorithmic, responsive, individualized content provision proliferates, this chapter makes the case that students' (and teachers') lack of engagement in this regard makes for a crisis of sustainability. The chapter situates the need for systemic adaptation to this new reality as overdue and urgent.

The chapter is concerned with the use of digital games in educating about societal challenges connected to the Sustainable Development Goals (SDG) in geography classes. The first part of the chapter summarizes the potentials of the medium and answers the question of why bringing games into the classroom is worth the effort. Subsequently, the chapter offers guidelines to aid teachers in making this step, including guidance on how to choose the right game for the given purpose, how to integrate the game into the lesson, and most importantly, how to reflect on the playing experience with the students.

Preface

In this day and age, climate change, biodiversity loss, resource depletion, armed conflicts, violence, authoritarian rule, lack of political participation, and growing inequality, are just a few aspects of unsustainable development. To address these Grand Challenges, societies have to undergo substantial transformations. The Sustainable Development Goals (SDGs) are an attempt by the United Nations to define appropriate goals and targets to be reached by 2030, to ensure quality of life for all, now and in the future. Whether or to what extent these goals will be reached will depend in part on how successfully education strategies will empower learners of all ages with the knowledge, skills, attitudes, and, perhaps most importantly of all, values to transform themselves, their communities, and their societies. Educational institutions have critical roles to play in facilitating and supporting the necessary transitions. To fulfill this vision and be truly transformational, however, education and educational institutions themselves will have to undergo profound change. Education for Sustainable Development can play an essential role in achieving necessary processes and outcomes.

In order for Education for Sustainable Development to realize its potential, it must engage with a range of current societal challenges. This is most definitely the case in light of the growing role of digitization and associated widespread adoption of new media. The latter permeates virtually all aspects of our lives, from the individual through to societal levels and is already bringing about fundamental changes. The global climate protests by predominantly young adolescents, driven by digital networking to demand implementation of the Paris agreement, make it clear that youth are ready to take on the challenges associated with sustainable development. This trend illustrates how the transformation toward a sustainable society must take into account developments associated with digitization and in particular, new forms of communication. Importantly, digitization cannot be adopted and accepted as purely being a technological process. Rather, digitization is actively shaped by individual and societal actions, including powerful interests. The SDGs, the biodiversity initiative and Paris agreement are interconnected by political, societal and economic actions. The question therefore arises as to how to shape digitization and the use of new media in ways that result in positive rather than negative contributions toward these goals. There can be no doubt that educational processes will be required at different levels and in a range of settings to ensure learners master the competencies they will need in order to navigate these complexities. Against this backdrop, Education for Sustainable Development offers guidance on how to manage digitization and use new media within the broader context of education including what content to include and which pedagogies to use to advance systems thinking and collective knowledge creation and application.

Sincedigitization and the use of new media are strongly driven by a range of powerful profit motives, critical reflection about their possible applications and scientific debate about unanticipated consequences often fall short. Automated algorithms developed by private providers, which are not transparent and therefore elude societal deliberation and democratic political legitimation, influence the content of digital media and play major roles in shaping public opinion. In addition, the growing dominance of a small number of powerful new media providers (e.g., Meta with Whatsapp, Facebook, Instagram, and Messenger) increases the potential for abuse and shaping of public opinion in ways that do not benefit society at large.

It must also be highlighted that digitalization and new media are already and will continue to shape the transformation of education systems globally. The COVID-19 pandemic has demonstrated that massive digitalization in education is possible. Although much remains to be learned about its effects on learning and societal outcomes, home schooling and distance learning have illustrated that formal education does not necessarily have to be restricted to traditional classrooms, and that learners can learn from and with each other across geographical distances. Furthermore, digitalization seems to hold the potential to support self-regulated, situated, and informal learning, which fundamentally changes the way individuals can access, process, and use information, ultimately changing the way individuals think and act. Digitization offers opportunities, particularly in the area of communication and the management of ever larger bodies of knowledge, by enabling new forms of interaction and inspiring creativity for societal transformation. It provides opportunities to make educational processes more collaborative and supports learning independent of time and place. Realizing the positive potential of digitization, however, will need fundamental changes to our education systems.

One question that must be addressed is to what extent the potential of digitalization and new media is actually unlocked in learning settings. Associated processes, resources and tools are only likely to make valuable contributions to empower individuals to actively shape the process of transformation toward sustainability, if teachers and students have acquired the competencies to link digitalization and Education for Sustainable Development. Moreover, the processes on which digitalization and the use of new media depend can have many negative consequences and unanticipated effects. Concerns include, for example, the energy used to produce and store digital content and to power digital devices as well as the risk of spreading distortion and fake news. Additional troubling aspects are the gaps between those who have access to digital infrastructures and the skills to use these effectively and mindfully –and- those who are denied access to them and experience reduced meaningful physical social interactions.

As already suggested, digitization and the use of new media involve many social as well as ecological, economic, legal, political, and educational challenges that will need to be addressed. Within the context of education, differences in living and learning conditions and the associated (lack of) access to digital resources and networks can reinforce educational inequalities. Moreover, data privacy concerns raise questions about the use of learning and communication platforms within the context of protecting learners' fundamental and personal rights. Children and young people may be at particular high risk as a result of uncontrolled use of digital media. The production and operation of information technologies also prove problematic. Both aspects require a lot of energy and as such, represent a considerable burden on the climate. Electronic devices contain precious metals and other valuable non-renewable resources. The extraction of these resources will need to be assessed critically from both a social and ecological perspective, especially if only a small proportion of these can be reused, recycled, or repurposed.

If Education for Sustainable Development is to be successful, these aspects of digitization and its negative societal impacts must be taken into account. There will have to be a willingness to accept the necessity for fundamental changes in education and a commitment to developing, implementing, and evaluating new strategies. Development is sustainable when all individuals from across the world, both in the present and in the future, can live with dignity, meet their needs, and develop their talents while respecting planetary boundaries. Through Education for Sustainable Development individuals can be empowered to understand the impact of their own actions on the world and to make more responsible, sustainable choices. Such a societal transformation requires strong institutions, participatory decision-making and conflict resolution, knowledge, technologies, as well as new patterns of thinking and acting.

Education for Sustainable Development aims to enable individuals to master the competencies they need to think and act in ways that will ensure a sustainable future. Education for Sustainable Development is a holistic and transformative educational approach that focuses on content and learning outcomes as well as learning process and environments. Teaching and learning for sustainability development takes place interactively, and enables inquiry-based, action-oriented as well as transformative learning. It is not only about addressing sustainability issues, but also about using participatory methods to promote critical and networked thinking as well as the skills to work toward solutions in teams. Education for Sustainable Development also aims to help learners develop worldviews that makes it possible for them to recognize themselves as global citizens. Local actions are seen as contributing to global sustainable development.

Networking in the digital world has the potential to generate and bring together knowledge from across the world to allow individuals to interact more easily with others and to develop solutions collectively. When digital competencies are strengthened through educational processes, they can support individuals' decision making and action competence with regard to sustainable development. Digitization can also be used to make it easier for youth as well as adults to participate in sustainable development through opportunities that support learning along with civic engagement.

Education and learning within the contexts of both sustainable development and digitization can also be examined from the perspective of data literacy education. Data literacy has the primary goal of addressing and solving real-world problems in ways that take ethical and contextual considerations into account. Without going into them in greater detail, the competency models underlying these concepts, with the exception of application-related competencies, enable the development of critical attitudes based on these ethical and contextual considerations. Such critical examination of one's attitudes and values, as part of Education for Sustainable Development, leads to reflecting on one's own behaviors in terms of "ethically justifiable action" against the backdrop of guiding sustainability principles. Data literacy tends to look at questions surrounding information and data procurement and evaluation. Taking into account ethical and context-related considerations when exploring these questions, can subsequently improve decision-making processes. One of the main desired competencies is to be able to reflect on which values can, and should, guide data-driven decisions and actions.

Education for Sustainable Development is about finding solutions to the most complex societal challenges of our time. Data literacy can support such educational processes, in part by enabling learners to draw on competencies that facilitate their ability to critically apply (technological) opportunities - as well as providing, analyzing, and interpreting data and information. Education for Sustainable Development with its key competencies emphasizes the links between the current state of affairs and desired future targets, and explores potential pathways to facilitate the transition between the two. The resulting deeper understanding of evidence-based processes and decision-making, in turn, contributes to more informed questions and discussions surrounding sustainability challenges in a digitalized world. It offers the opportunity to develop and test potential concrete contributions for shaping a more sustainable future.

Against the background of the necessity of transformation toward sustainability and the certainty that the process of digitization cannot be reversed or stopped, education faces the challenge to develop effective learning settings which, on the one hand, make the most of new possibilities, and on the other, minimize associated risks. The individual contributions in this book examine different aspects of digitization and new media within the context of Education for Sustainable Development. They come from authors from countries in different regions of the world, informed by a range of perspectives derived from diverse settings and conditions.

In "Theoretical reflections on Education for Sustainable Development and Digital technologies," Ute Stoltenberg and Gerd Michelsen provide an overview of the diverse relationships between digitization and Education for Sustainable Development. They explain that the starting point of all considerations must be the focus of educational processes on the goal of social transformation toward sustainable development. In this paper, based on this concept of education they show both the potential and the limitations of the use of digital technologies for the design of educational processes and discuss the role of data literacy in this context.

Kate Maloney Williams and Jehad Halawani's "The Impact of Biased Design and Hegemony on Sustainable Future-Ready Learning: Digital Transformation Challenges" draws attention to defining and measuring the goal of 'Quality Education', particularly in the face of an increasingly digitized future, fueled by emergencies and the need for quality distance learning. In order to achieve SDG 4 in a digital era, they claim that societies must undergo substantial reforms in conceptualizing teaching, learning, and assessment as well as designing and exporting technology. The authors argue that effective technology-based interventions must include awareness of the externalities that impact digital design, providing examples from the Global South.

In "The Role of Geography Education in Sustainability in a Digital Age," Inga Gryl looks at current everyday life, where (non-)sustainability and digitalization are closely linked to each other, including societal issues beyond technology and ecology. For instance, digitalization may be a key to solve certain sustainability problems and is the source for challenges to sustainability at the same time. Geography education has both strong links with an education for digitalization and with Education for Sustainable Development. Therefore, it is an ideal learning environment in which to teach the complexity of the links between both fields, and the necessity of thinking about them together in tandem.

Maxim Shatkin explores both the risks of the platform society to sustainability and how education for sustainability can address these risks in his chapter "Education for Sustainable Development and the Platform Society." The platform society, building on algorithms, bots, and AI, maintains the kind of content that can stimulate user engagement, yet is often related to the polarization of society, the deepening of political conflicts and the diffusion of biased opinions. The response of Education for Sustainable Development could include the widespread use in teaching of triple bottom line, meta-analysis of social media information, elaboration of transition scenarios between different futures, and the nurturing of ecological solidarity.

Ilja Steffelbauer and others look at "Complexity Literacy for a Sustainable Digital Transition: Cases and Arguments From Transdisciplinary Education Programs." Educational measures, they claim, should go far beyond traditional educational means and require the integration of systems thinking, complexity understanding, knowledge integration across disciplines and between science and practice together with supporting communication patterns and strategies. Complexity literacy as a core component of sustainability literacy thus becomes indispensable in any educational program that aims to enable students to actively shape the process of digital transition.

In "Digital Literacy Among Teacher Educators in Ethiopia: Implications to the Achievement of SDG4 and (Education for) Sustainable Development," Aklilu Dalelo, Anteneh Gebremariam, and Kedir Gebi provide interesting insights. The findings of a questionnaire indicate that teacher educators demonstrate marked strengths in certain domains of competence, and have serious limitations in others. With regard to factors that affect the utilization of digital technologies, teacher educators identify the lack of facilities supporting resources, and training as being the most decisive. The chapter ends by making recommendations based on the findings of the study.

Kanako N. Kusanagi examines in "Holistic Learning and Education for Sustainable Development: Building a Virtual Community of Engaged and Responsible Learners by Tokkatsu" the implementation of holistic learning in virtual space and presents it as a humanistic approach to ensure students' democratic participation in online and distance learning. While Education for Sustainable Development envisions active and engaged learners, students struggled to engage in online and distance learning during the COVID-19 pandemic. This chapter examines the holistic learning curriculum, Tokkatsu – which originated in Japan – and discusses its prospect for nurturing responsible and active learners.

Anton Rahmadi et al. examine the "COVID-19 Impacts on the Traditional Indonesian Community Market: The Global Pursuit of SDGs and Outcome-Based Higher Education in a Multi-Stakeholder Matching Program." This is carried out in the context of the SDGs and the integration of the Tridharma, with a particular focus on learning processes among the students involved. The authors can show that a multi-stakeholder matching program in terms of outcome-based education for higher education is a suitable approach to address the SDGs in the context.

In "Enabling Education for Sustainable Development Through Digital Storytelling," Vassilios Makrakis and Nelly Kostoulas-Makrakis discuss digital storytelling as a tool and as a teaching and learning methodology. They show that the interaction between digital technology and Education for Sustainable Development can create new opportunities to address sustainability issues. The teachers who were trained in an international project produced digital storytelling applications that can be categorized as authentic learning activities addressing issues in the real world.

Khalida Nasreen and Muhammad Tanveer Afzal embrace "Linking Culture, Pedagogy, and Digitalization for Education and Sustainable Development in Tribal Areas: A Perspective From Pakistan." Teachers and parents from primary schools in tribal areas in Pakistan were interviewed for this study, and data was also collected via observational technique in the participating schools. The authors suggest recommendations for the incorporation of Education for Sustainable Development goals in the single national curriculum, the development of teacher education programs, and the facilitation of electricity, computer technology, and internet access for all schools.

In "Updating the US K-12 Information Technology Curriculum," Cristofer G. Sloteroff examines the increasing influence of algorithms that analyze personal user behavior on the content consumers are confronted with on the Internet. Since content from the Internet is used in more and more areas of life and even in childhood, Cristofer G. Sloteroff calls for increased support for modern information literacy in schools in order to raise awareness of this development and to enable a reflective handling of it. Only through a better understanding of these developments is it possible for a society to deal with the ethical and moral questions associated with these technological developments.

Alexandra Budke gives "Guidelines for Teachers on the Use of Digital Games on SDG-Relevant Topics in Geography Classes" in her chapter. It not only describes the potential of such media to deal with complex social and socio-ecological topics, but also offers guidelines for assessing digital games with regard to their suitability for teaching. Therefore, this chapter has the potential to improve teachers' competences in dealing with this medium and to incorporate it in a constructive and efficient manner.

In "Promoting Education for Sustainable Development Using Blended Learning and Digital Tools: Two University Courses – One Case Study," Helga Mayr presents two interdisciplinary blended learning project-based Master's courses. Both use the SDGs as a framework and design thinking as an approach, while one also uses digital tools beyond the digital media necessary for collaboration. The students' reflections on their learning processes are described, and the chapter concludes with considerations regarding the further potential developments of the course.

Marlene Kollmayer and Selma Korlat Ikanovic in their chapter "Digital Learning During COVID-19: An Intersectional Perspective on Secondary Students' Motivation and Perceived Teacher Support" deal with the expectation that increasing digitization in the educational sector will bring decisive progress for the empowerment of individuals in terms of sustainable development. For their reasoning, the authors draw on a study that examines the effects of distance learning during the COVID-19 pandemics in connection with perceived teacher support. Their results show the importance of teachers and schools to specifically design digital learning environments in a way that all social groups can gain advantage.

Nicole Raschke, Lisa Wey, and Thomas Arendt in "Smart Energy Smart Schools: Project-Based Learning About Energy Transition and Digitalization" present a project dealing with energy in public school buildings. In this chapter, three different educational modules, the environmental measuring station, the history of light sources, and the planetarium are dealt with in more detail. They show a useful connection between Education for Sustainable Development and digitalization or digital media. Another focus is the evaluation of feedback from the participating students and teachers, and the opportunities and challenges that arose on an individual and institutional level during the implementation of the project.

In their chapter "Sustainability Online? Actors, Hierarchies, and Communication Patterns in Collaborative Development of Open Educational Resources," Jana Dlouhá and others analyze the role of digital media in the context of processes, if different actors, including students, are involved in co-creating learning content. The question raised in this chapter is whether these changes in the "metabolism" of information could contribute to the transformations foreseen by Education for Sustainable Development, and how. The authors focus on open educational resources used in higher education, specifically wiki systems, and explore mutual relationships/ hierarchies of actors involved in its development.

Martin Dür and Lars Keller ask, "Will Social Media Replace Face-to-Face Interactions in International Collaboration Discussions?" Within the project AustrIndia-4QOL, teenagers from Austria and India jointly conducted research on the topics of quality of life and sustainability. While the collaboration was mainly carried out via social media, some of the teenagers took part in an additional one-week face-to-face collaboration. Examinations of the AustrIndia-4QOL project show that social media collaborations have their own limitations and that the total removal of the opportunity for live face-to-face interactions is questionable.

In conclusion. it can be said that the individual contributions differ greatly in their conception, methods, and design, as well as in their understandings and views of Education for Sustainable Development. Our aim is to reflect these unique diversities to feature associated strengths as well as a range of views from across the world, to give them a voice through this book. We have gained new, valuable, and surprising insights from the contributing chapters. We hope that you, the reader, will have the same meaningful experience.

Lars Keller
University of Innsbruck, Austria

Gerd Michelsen
Leuphana University, Germany

Martin Dür
University of Innsbruck, Austria

Syamsul Bachri
Universitas Negeri Malang, Indonesia

Michaela Zint
University of Michigan, USA

Section 1
Theoretical Reflections

Chapter 1
Theoretical Reflections on Education for Sustainable Development and Digital Technologies

Ute Stoltenberg
Leuphana University Lueneburg, Germany

Gerd Michelsen
Leuphana University Lueneburg, Germany

ABSTRACT

In this chapter the author discusses the relationship between digitalization and education from the perspective of the concept of education for sustainable development. The aim is to counter a development that sees digitalization as a natural phenomenon or as inevitable technological "progress" to which education must respond. The starting point of the discussion cannot be the many possible applications of digital technologies and the question of how they can best support current educational practice, but instead an understanding of education that needs to be made explicit along with the educational goals associated with it. The international as well as national education policy benchmark for an education that prepares us to meet the challenges of the future is the concept of education for sustainable development. In this chapter is it shown, based on this concept of education, both the potential and the limitations of the use of digital technologies for the design of educational processes.

DOI: 10.4018/978-1-7998-5033-5.ch001

INTRODUCTION

Education in the Face of Societal Challenges

Since Agenda 21 was endorsed by nations in 1992, education has been understood as a prerequisite for a societal transformation toward sustainable development, one that requires far-reaching changes in how we treat nature as the foundation of life and how we realize human dignity and justice in our societies. An understanding of how educational processes and institutions can advance this transformation has taken place nationally and in international cooperation, especially with the support of UNESCO (e.g. Vare, Lausselet & Rieckmann 2022).

Today, we can describe goals, working methods, content-related tasks and perspectives that are regarded worldwide as fundamental elements of the concept of (ESD). Every individual should be empowered to participate together with others in shaping sustainable development: in everyday life, in an educational institution, at the workplace, in the community, as well as in the context of civil society and political activities. ESD aims at both individual and social learning. Such education and learning processes include the acquisition of knowledge, skills and perspectives needed to promote sustainable development. Transformative potential is developed by making both the critical analysis of non-sustainable practices and the opportunities to experience and shape real challenges and tasks of sustainable development an integral part of educational processes.

Perspectives on the world, values, subject matter and methods that are grounded in the concept of ESD underlie further discussion on the relationship between digitalization and education. Although many considerations will apply to any particular educational opportunity, a special focus is placed here on schools. After all, school is the place where values and world views are engaged and reproduced, thus stabilizing societal conditions. It should become a place that further opens perspectives for the future – in contrast to positions seeking to reduce the concept of ESD to simply adding new content to the curriculum, proclaiming their addition simply for economic and technological reasons.

EDUCATION FOR SUSTAINABLE DEVELOPMENT AND DIGITAL EDUCATION – TWO UNEQUAL PARTNERS

The concept of ESD is a response to societal processes that are not sustainable (Hopkins et al. 2020). However, this tension makes a discussion of the relationship between education and digitalization difficult, because the massive impact of digitalization – its focus on economic growth, high resource and energy consumption, the priority of efficiency as a goal – reinforces the very developments that underpin the need for sustainable development. Development based on digitalization[1] aims at speed, mass data processing and networking, and the implementation of short-term economic interests (e.g., promoting consumption of short-lived goods, replacing jobs through digitalization). It is used to screen and assess preferences, needs and life practices – which can serve as a type of control – as well as to influence political movements and decision-making, including elections, in a non-transparent way. For the individual, this development results in a loss of control of one's own data, a shifting of work to consumers, or even imperceptible influence through the allocation of information online (Lange & Santarius 2018), a list which by no means covers all aspects of the consequences of digitalization.

Technologies change society – and thus also education – in fundamental ways, as Weizenbaum, a leading computer scientist of his time, vividly described already in 1976. He understands "the rejection of direct experience" to be a central feature of modern natural science and its accomplishments. Tools "constitute a kind of language for the society that employs them, a language of social action" (Weizenbaum 1976, p. 36). Reckwitz (2019) sees, compared to previous technologies, a new quality in this interrelationship: "Technology is less and less a tool, and becomes more and more a technological environment in which subjects move" (p. 237).[2] He analyzes digital technologies as a "cultural machine" that produces new "cultural formats" that always touch people emotionally. Through the possibility of programmatically designing, reshaping, reproducing and transmitting all media formats (text, image, sound), messages on the Internet become affectively charged. "The digital objects that captivate recipients and producers do not, to a large extent, have a merely cognitive character, but a narrative, aesthetic, creative, or ludic one" (p. 235). Young people, and even children, are shaped by this culture and help to produce and shape it.

Particularly relevant for educational processes is the tendency toward "de-informatization and emotionalization" on the web and the orientation toward the topicality of the moment, with the tendency that "topics and reflections that are of long-term importance [tend] to fall through the topicality filter" (p. 269). In addition, digital networking promotes communication communities defined by social exclusion. "Self-referential worlds" are formed in which communication takes place on self-defined topics, with "specific perspectives on the world and one's own actions" (Stalder 2016, p. 135ff.).

The discussion about digitalization and ESD is also difficult because digitalization is considered "modern," "innovative," "progressive" and more or less indispensable. Almost everyone is now digitally networked – even if only by cellphone. The speed and range of communication, networking and access to information influence personal and social behavior. Since one can break off any communication on the Internet at will, there is no need to tolerate the inadequacy of real people (Stoll 1996). Extensive use of so-called "social media" instead of face-to-face communication and relationships makes people susceptible to conspiracy theories, aggressiveness and radical ideologies (Kaczinski, Hennig-Thurau & Sattler 2019). Many functions of digitalization are already changing cultural patterns – such as shared meals in restaurants, which are hardly ever taken without a cell phone. Young people have grown into this world, so that a critical distance to the everyday use of technologies cannot be taken for granted.

With the goal of exploiting its potential, digitalization is communicated as a necessary contribution to the transformation of society as a whole. This objective is hardly surprising, since the main drivers of this communication (closely followed by a number of politicians) are the large Californian media corporations and, in Germany, its leading media companies as well as the Bertelsmann Foundation (Rolf 2018; Stalder 2016). "Control and decision-making processes that should be subject to public and democratic discussion are thus increasingly taken by actors from the private sector, as they promise 'development'" (Magilchrist 2019, p. 19). The German Digital Pact for Schools, for example, reveals itself as an "investment program for digital corporations," promoting "novel forms of interconnectedness between the public sector and corporations, many of which have a global presence and which now have almost oligarchic structures" (Scheller 2019, p. 17). This understanding of transformation collides with the value-oriented understanding of a Great Transformation for sustainable development to preserve life's chances of survival on earth (WBGU 2012). Against this background of society's need for sustainable development, digitalization itself "requires creating appropriate frameworks and demarcations. Unless it is actively shaped global digital change additionally runs the risk of further increasing the threat to humankind's natural life-support systems (WBGU 2019).

Stalder makes it clear that there is a tension in the development of digitalization: "those developments ... that preserve opportunities for participation or even create new ones ... [can] at the same time strengthen decision-making capacities at levels where joint decision-making is excluded" (Stalder 2016, p. 209). This trend toward a "culture of digitality" is clearly dominant today. Examples include the delegation "of issues affecting the polity to 'autonomous IT systems'" (p. 241) or the increasing technocratic argument that there is no alternative to this development – resulting in "post-democratic processes and structures" in all areas of life. As an alternative, Stalder describes approaches that use the "community of practice" on the Internet to develop and implement initiatives promoting the common good.

However, in education policy today, technological development is met with a more reactive attitude. The most often cited goal is that we should be prepared and qualified for the digitalized world (KMK 2016). "In political position papers the acquisition of digital competence is directly linked to social participation" (Macgilchrist 2019, p. 19) which is primarily understood to mean an individual's qualification during their "educational and vocational path" (KMK 2016, p. 6). "The question of what needs to be done today in order to be economically successful in the future should become the guiding theme for all of us" (vbw 2018, p. 7).

New Learning, together with related competencies, is thereby thought to begin with the possibilities technologies offer: individual and personalized learning paths by means of online learning, with large corporations in control by providing education concepts and specialized technology. By applying criteria determined by technological structures, digitalization makes it possible to control learning processes to an extent not possible before.

Since the 2000s there has been broader acceptance of the concept of ESD in Germany. But only a few federal states, where responsibility for the formal education system lies, have so far adopted it as a fundamental orientation for the design of educational institutions and educational processes (Stoltenberg & Fischer 2018).[3] Its task of contributing to a transformation toward sustainable development by implementing structural changes in the education system is instead obscured by the prevailing understanding that the concept can be reduced to introducing new topics to the curriculum and shifting the need for action to the individual.

Against this background, it is an urgent task to enter into the recently begun discussion on sustainability and digitalization and bring together ESD and education for digital literacy (Lange & Santarius 2018; WBGU 2019). In view of the "culture of digitality," it can no longer be a matter of viewing digital technologies in education merely as "tools" that support or replace previous didactic arrangements, but instead understanding them as something that should be developed to extend educational processes to include digital literacy.

Digital technologies have the potential to enable and promote ESD, but there are also indications as to which features and possible uses of digitalization in educational processes need critical attention (Döbeli Honegger 2017). Creative and responsible approaches to digitalization are already found in educational practice – albeit often merely as digital media education, and usually without reference to the concept of ESD.

Education and learning processes for sustainable development and digitalization can also be viewed from the perspective of data literacy education (Schüller et al. 2019; Ridsdale et al. 2015), whereby data literacy primarily pursues the goal of learning to address and solve real-world problems while taking into account ethical and contextual considerations. In particular, the competencies targeted by this concept enable the development of a critical stance based on ethical and contextual considerations. While ESD pursues a reflection of one's own actions in the sense of "ethically responsible action" against the background of the guiding principle of sustainability (Wiek, Withycombe & Redman 2011), data literacy rather considers questions of information and data procurement and evaluation, also from a perspective of ethical and context-related considerations. The competence consists of being able to reflect on which values can and should guide data-driven actions. ESD aims at the search, learning and design process for solutions advancing sustainable development. The data literacy approach supports this process and takes into account the corresponding competencies for the critical and adequate application of the (technical) possibilities as well as for the design of the entire process of providing, evaluating and interpreting information and data. Such an understanding of the process of knowledge and decision making with data contributes to a more informed engagement with issues of sustainability in a digitized world and offers the opportunity to develop and test the potentials of concrete contributions for shaping a more sustainable future (Weiser, van Deest & Barth 2022). The project "Sustainability and Digitalization – a European Perspective" addresses the necessary prerequisites and framework conditions for transformation processes towards a sustainable digitalized future from different perspectives. It looks at individual, organizational and societal learning processes, focusing in particular on the interface between sustainability and digitalization (Cieslewicz, Lang & Barth 2022).

EDUCATION FOR SUSTAINABLE DEVELOPMENT AS A FRAMEWORK FOR ORIENTATION

ESD enables systemic knowledge, orientation knowledge and action knowledge (Stoltenberg 2007). The term "transformation knowledge" (WBGU 2011) focuses action knowledge even more on the task of sustainable development. In the following, these three dimensions serve to structure considerations on the potential of digitalization in educational processes based on the concept of ESD.

The focus of ESD is not on providing the best possible support for individuals in competition with others, but on educational processes that are geared toward social responsibility and the ability to act, as well as opportunities for participation. They enable collaborative learning, the collaborative acquisition of knowledge and reflection on experiences as well as on educational processes themselves. In this context, media spaces such as Internet platforms can certainly be opportunities for exchange on jointly formulated problem areas and issues. However, in addition to the self-organized search for knowledge and evaluation in communities on the Internet, they depend on personal encounters and communication – with all the opportunities for perceiving different points of view – as well as on the diversity of knowledge and experiences and the chance for personal negotiation and conflict resolution.

Learning with and from each other in a group of learners is just as much in view as the role of teachers. Teachers can make knowledge accessible through the media at the moment the collaborative learning process requires it. The personality of teachers offers young people opportunities for identification and for critical debate; teachers can motivate and draw attention to social contexts; they can provide an occasion for as well as the experience of learning across generations. Such social relationships cannot be easily replaced by technologies, especially since not all human communication can be translated into algorithms. Weizenbaum echoes Polanyi when he writes, "we know more than we can tell" (Weizenbaum 1976, p. 71) and demands "that certain acts of thought should be reserved exclusively for humans" (p. 13).

Learning systems, on the other hand, that aim at the effective acquisition of knowledge with predetermined objectives and corresponding controls do not meet the requirements of learning for social cohesion under the guiding principle of sustainable development. If, in addition, learning is personalized, it hardly opens the chance for learners to step out of their previous enculturation. Learning systems that are open and flexible, on the other hand, can certainly play a meaningful role in educational processes in the context of sustainable development.

Systemic Knowledge and Digitalization

Based on the insight that the ecological, social, economic and cultural aspects of a social problem and action for sustainable development must be seen in relation to each other, systemic thinking and thinking in relations play a central role. The process of knowledge acquisition is not simply adding up available knowledge, but reflecting on and questioning its interrelationships and contradictions. This allows a confrontation with complexity to take place, whereby different perspectives and discourses are brought together – in schools, this would be all subjects related to cultural knowledge; in universities, this would be all the individual disciplines. This can be organized in working groups, in projects involving several subjects, or in collaborative team teaching. Digital media can help reveal the different contributions of the individual subjects or academic disciplines.

In order to decide what traditional subject matter and mindsets should be questioned and which new ones should be part of advancing sustainable development, it is necessary to determine what individual subjects or disciplines can contribute to understanding social transformation and overcoming obstacles along the way. Access to a topic, engagement with that topic as well as an awareness of perspectivity in the sense of a broader perception of problems – which are important for being able to experience the change of perspective necessary for acquiring systemic knowledge – can be initiated and supported by a search on the Internet oriented toward sustainability issues.

In addition to basic knowledge of an issue, which can be reflected on as shaping culture, ESD aims at generating new knowledge in order to follow alternative paths, such as in the use of natural resources, in the organization of human societies, in dealing with ecosystems or in individual consumer behavior. For this reason, young people should be given the opportunity to participate in negotiating concrete solutions to problems so that they can experience how new knowledge is gained: by reviewing state-of-the-art knowledge, by formulating new criteria for knowledge and by searching for new solutions. An essential step in this process is communication among learners – also on shared learning platforms or in networks. Learner memberships in different networks and platforms also play a role and can be made fruitful in discussions.

The same applies to the field of technology development and use itself: On the basis of experience of previous technology development and its use, a deeper understanding of technology can be acquired that enables, among other things, practical participation in the development of small transparent networks, data security and the provision of digital technologies for the common good. Systemic knowledge about digitalization thus includes understanding technological contexts and knowledge as well as its social, cultural and ecological consequences.

Since the starting point for educational processes in ESD are real-world problems and issues, it generally makes sense not only to bring together different academic perspectives, but also include the knowledge and perspectives of social actors from different areas for action in order to better understand the context of knowledge and to discover possibilities for shaping it. Against this background, we can determine how digitalized information and communication can support the acquisition of systemic knowledge.

Knowledge resources from multiple current sources are quickly and abundantly accessible via digital media – both for teachers and learners. Quality information on sustainability issues is readily available on the Internet. This enables users to learn to question the origin of the material they find along with the interests and goals behind it, especially as accessing content on the Internet brings with it the "risk of manipulation or selective perception of facts" (WBGU 2019). Work with search engines in ESD depends on having transparent and trustworthy information services.

Transparent dialogue can emerge in a protected space by networking groups of people who trust each other. Networking also enables groups to gather information using a division of labor and sharing responsibility – which allows the value and difficulties of complex issues to be jointly recognized and reflected upon. It becomes clear what a subject, a discipline or a specific area of social practice can contribute to understanding and solving problems. Likewise, it enables an examination of the structure and mindset of a subject, a discipline or specific social perspectives. By involving actors from different social areas relevant to a topic, different and possibly also controversial perspectives can be shown.

Education packages (comprising hardware, software, training, instruction materials) provided by large corporations should first of all be viewed critically. Incidentally, they are already routinely offered at scientific conferences as an innovative development, on the same level as, for example, presentations by professional organizations on state-of-the-art teaching. It almost goes without saying that given the amount of information and learning programs available today, individual teachers can hardly make informed choices; and an evaluation from the perspective of a single subject would not be sufficient anyway. This is a broad area needing development. Criteria for evaluating knowledge sources, learning programs, and digital tools must be developed and made available that are comprehensibly oriented as far as possible to the concept of ESD.

Orientation Knowledge and Digitalization

In the discourse on ESD, different perspectives play a key role in building up orientation knowledge: value orientation, an understanding of nature, a one-world perspective and sustainability strategies. They have the potential to develop the mindset, knowledge and skills for shaping the future in a responsible way. Teachers can use these perspectives as benchmarks when designing educational processes, just as educational institutions can use them for selecting educational content and how it is presented, as well as for deciding on appropriate working methods. Unlike core sustainability content, these perspectives of the concept of ESD apply to all subjects and underline once again that all subjects can contribute to forming orientation knowledge for sustainable development. Reflection is needed on the role of digital media in developing these perspectives, both in terms of positive and negative effects.

ESD is based on the values of human dignity and justice as well as the preservation of natural life processes and the basis of life for all living beings. Based on evidence concerning the economic and social conditions resulting from prevalent business practices and lifestyle choices, the world community has agreed on this guiding principle. Agenda 2030 is the exemplary achievement of international efforts to take joint steps towards sustainable development. This normative perspective specifies areas for action and tasks that are also relevant for educational processes. Value orientation means becoming aware of and engaging with these values and, at the same time, reaching a common understanding of what this fundamental value orientation means for the concrete problems at hand. The Internet offers access to different value systems and to the results of global communication processes such as the Earth Charter – the creation of which, incidentally, would hardly have been conceivable without digital exchange crossing geographic and cultural distances. The Earth Charter can be drawn upon when – in different teaching contexts and embedded in a personal discourse – implicit values, ethical standards or social norms are consciously addressed in order to promote sensitivity for their significance in shaping the future and one's own orientation.

For educational institutions, the goal of justice poses a new challenge. Not only the technical equipment of learners, but also the way in which digital technologies are used, prevents equitable participation for all. An Austrian study identified a "new form of communicative elite" (Stalder 2016, p. 39), in which digitally and technically savvy actors exchange information and exert influence among themselves. That this statement also holds for children and adolescents can be assumed, since "televisions and stationary game consoles (are) significantly more often owned by adolescents with a lower formal educational background, while adolescents with higher formal education more often own laptops or computers" (Feierabend, Rathgeb & Reuter 2018, p. 588).

Orientation to the values of sustainable development is also a sound benchmark for evaluating technology developments and for using technology both in the classroom and in the experiential space outside of school. Evaluation and orientation competence as a central element of digital literacy (WBGU 2019) can be built up by such means as:

- engaging in an analysis of technology development (also historically) and its drivers, which makes digitalization visible not only as a technical constraint or advantage, but as a result of social relations shaped by power structures driving technologies,
- analyzing economic, social, ecological and cultural aspects of digital technologies,
- making decisions about the use of technical devices and technologies in one's own experiential spaces, including teaching and school,
- by making decisions participatory and involving the perspectives and knowledge of the different actors in a school,
- questioning the individual use of technology, and
- reflecting on the access and uses of digital technologies by people in other regions of the world.

An understanding and appreciation of nature that does justice to the idea of sustainable development includes the insight that nature is the sum of all interrelationships among living creatures, including humans, and at the same time is their basis of life. The ability to perceive this interconnectedness presupposes, first of all, sensory-emotional possibilities of experience. Nonverbal experiences of the world remain the foundation of any understanding of nature. Landscapes are wonderful places to approach the world of things in a playful, probing way, in symbols, in gestures as well as in language. There are approaches that use the affinity of children and young people to digital media as a means to introduce them to nature. The extent to which digital technology makes nature accessible, or perhaps only provides an instrumental experience, is largely an open question. Promising approaches use apps as a source of information – not as a substitute for experience – in nature, for example, to identify flora and fauna found and to make knowledge about them accessible.

Intellectually engaging with the meaning of nature requires different levels of reflection that allow one's own understanding of nature to be made conscious and reflected upon. This process is encouraged by the perspectives of other learners, as well as by views of nature in other cultures, which through the use of digital technologies are more readily accessible. In principle the connection between nature and cultural artifacts, processes and decisions can become a topic in any school subject. The social relevance of different understandings of nature can be investigated, for example, by researching the communicated and the actual understandings of nature in political statements or on the websites of companies – which would be much more difficult and less up-to-date without Internet research. Nevertheless, central to educational processes for sustainable development is the question how natural resources are endangered by digitalization or how they can be put to good use – a question that reveals conflicting goals, contradictions and dilemmas, which must then be weighed up. Emotional engagement and compassion are necessary elements not often found in a digital format.

Sustainable development cannot be realized on a regional level, but as a rule only on a global one – just as many non-sustainable developments can be traced back to problems of global change. The emergence of Agenda 2030 as a global action program eloquently demonstrates this. ESD therefore also includes an examination of global interdependencies, which promotes an understanding of the planetary boundaries of "one world" and the notion of global citizenship. The use of media plays a very important role in the perspective of living together in one world because digital media overcome space and time and thus make possible experiences of global interdependencies, of cultural diversity as well as of unequal life chances. Virtual travelers learn about culture as well as about the animal and plant world. Digital media also enable schools to engage in direct exchange with each other in a global classroom. This diversity of cultural forms of expression leads to the discovery of common perspectives, needs and interests – which can also lead to collaborative work projects for participation in sustainable development.

In sustainability discourse the question of how to deal responsibly with the natural foundations of life is pursued by means of three strategies: efficiency, consistency and sufficiency strategies (Stoltenberg & Michelsen 1999). In educational processes, they can be used as an orientation for teaching and as a perspective that opens up new views and possibilities for action. Digitalization benefits use of the efficiency strategy. Processing large volumes of data helps to achieve the most efficient use of energy, for example, the best possible mobility infrastructures or the most efficient reuse of resources. However, focusing or even relying on this strategy alone because of its good predictability is often not enough. The efficient use of resources can easily lead to a so-called rebound effect if the other strategies are not considered at the same time.

Regarding the consistency strategy, which aims to make the use of technology consistent with nature, digital media would even be counterproductive for recreational purposes, as an appreciation of the rhythms and times of nature would be obstructed by the incomprehensible speed of digital apps.

With regard to the sufficiency strategy, digitalization has two sides. On the one hand, resources can be saved through a digitally supported culture of sharing, for example. At the same time, however, when looking at the resource consumption of these technologies as well as their social, cultural and political consequences, the question arises as to how much digitalization is enough. Langer & Santarius (2018) justify technology sufficiency (through long useful life, easy maintenance and repair), as well as data sufficiency and usage sufficiency – both strategies that require behavioral changes of the user or user group – as meaningful sustainability strategies. They can serve as orientation for educational processes as well as for equipping educational institutions.

Knowledge for Action and Digitalization

A goal of ESD is to empower people to participate in shaping sustainable development. Experience and knowledge are required to make systemic knowledge and orientation knowledge fruitful for transformative processes realizing sustainable development. How educational processes can achieve this will be discussed under the headings "learning from real problems, tasks, phenomena," "participation" and "transformative thinking."

Choosing real problems, tasks or phenomena as the starting point of educational processes corresponds to an understanding of learning that is fed by curiosity, intrinsic motivation and the willingness to engage in new things. Such processes do not only create systemic knowledge and orientation knowledge, but also stimulate motivation and action strategies. The integration of experiences and creative possibilities in educational processes is therefore an important element of the concept of ESD. Self-organized and collaborative learning can be enriched by digital media (Barth 2007; Barth & Michelsen 2013; Birkelbach, Preglau & Rammel 2019).

Commercial providers can now be bypassed by free communication infrastructures, the use of which at the same time allows for critical reflection on one's own data use (Macgilchrist 2019). Digital media can be used to document learning processes, make them available for discussion and communicate findings. Young people at school or university can thus let others share their insights and questions about sustainable development. Although citizen science, service learning or student startups make effective use of digital media as tools, learning culture is primarily determined by experiences of personal exchange, cooperation, participation and the assumption of responsibility in a meaningful, future-oriented task. Such face-to-face encounters with people can also lead to changed perspectives and practices on both sides.

When sustainable development is understood as a search, learning and development process, the ability to participate is a key competence. Participation processes should be in an easily understandable concrete context of action in the school and in the local or regional environment, in which people or institutions with different perspectives, interests and different contributions take part. Digital media offer the opportunity to practice participation and learning at the same time – by supporting self-organized exchange among children and young people. The "transmission of information and communication via the web, which makes texts, images, videos and multimedia content possible via blogs, wikis, podcasts and social media, [encourages] exchange as well as interactive learning" (Rolf 2018, p. 152). Instead of instruction-oriented design (with all its possibilities of direction and control), digital media make possible action-oriented and production-oriented learning, which correspond to the goals of ESD to contribute to competencies that enable individuals to work towards implementing sustainable development.

The Fridays for Future movement shows how in a short period of time global networking can grow awareness, knowledge and public advocacy for effective action in the face of the climate crisis. Digital media enable the timely inclusion of such processes in a classroom that takes children and young people seriously, including by enabling and encouraging their participation. For example, the school class that made contact with the boat on which Greta Thunberg crossed the Atlantic to New York (The Guardian, Aug. 19, 2019) will certainly value this experience not as "learning material" but as a life experience. Participatory learning – especially in serious tasks of local sustainability policy, for example, in the municipal environment – can be encouraged and supported when digital platforms for major tasks of sustainable development, such as the development of a mobility concept, or participation on so-called citizen platforms are set up on the local level for the participation of young people.

Digital media have great potential for use in the development of transformative thinking – the willingness and ability to go beyond traditional individual and social practices and find new solutions for shaping the relationship between people and nature, and people among each other. Rethinking issues, creative thinking and hypothetical thinking, supported by risk assessment, can benefit from the use of digital media: Various apps are able to illustrate different future scenarios, simulations can be used to broaden the basis for risk assessment, and virtual simulation games can be used to discover decision-making spaces. However, the task of transformative thinking cannot be handed over to technology. We can imagine futures that contradict all previous experience, but an algorithm simply cannot come up with such ideas (Grunwald 2018). This is impossible when artificial intelligence is fed solely by previous experience. Thus, to encourage and empower transformative thinking, methods that do not require digital technologies at all remain relevant: For example, by having young people take their future hopes and visions as a starting point and consider together what they can already do to achieve this today.

CONCLUSION

ESD – most recently reaffirmed by the Transforming our World: the 2030 Agenda for Sustainable Development – is a vital element of sustainable development worldwide. Digitalization can be designed and used to meet and enrich its goals.

However, in view of the power and speed with which digitalization is being pushed into society – and into education systems – intensified efforts of addressing this issue within education policy are indispensable. Even though the number of publications on the relationship between education and digitalization is increasing, conferences on this complex issue are becoming more frequent, and public funds seem to be flowing, especially for equipping schools with digital media, there is still no consensus on what role digitalization should play in education in the future, especially in schools. What remains missing is the role of digitalization and ESD which itself is unique from traditional education pursuits. What is urgently needed is a broad discourse that is not exhausted by a comparison of "opportunities and threats" but also reveals the different interests and social values that are currently at odds with each other. Decisions about the use of digital media in schools and the classroom should be, as a matter of principle, participatory because they are not a neutral tool, but are capable of restructuring the participants' culture, learning environment and educational processes. The current practice of purchasing complete digitalized packages for educational content and methods should, given this context, be rejected. In order to adopt a cogent position toward the use of digital media, educational institutions must create and reflect on experiences that show how educational processes can take place both with and without digitalization. However, many teachers and school administrators do not have the knowledge, skills or experience to confidently meet the challenge of digitalization on the basis of a well-reasoned educational concept. They need professional consultation, assistance and training to understand the potential of ESD and, at the same time, they need the support of independent media experts so that they can find their way through the digital jungle and become digitally literate. They themselves need "orientation competence about the fundamentals of digital transformation" (Rolf 2018, p. 16) as well as sustainability competence to know how to meaningfully use digital media. In order to be able to participate in shaping the future, these needs and recommendations must be integrated in professional development offerings for education policymakers and practitioners and placed in the center of a broad public discourse.

REFERENCES

Barth, M. (2007). *Gestaltungskompetenz durch Neue Medien? Die Rolle des Lernens mit Neuen Medien in der Bildung für eine nachhaltige Entwicklung*. Berliner Wissenschaftsverlag.

Barth, M., & Michelsen, G. (2013). Learning for change: An educational contribution to sustainability. *Science Sustain Science*, *8*(1), 103–119. doi:10.100711625-012-0181-5

Birkelbach, L., Preglau, D., & Rammel, Ch. (2019). *BNE im Zeitalter der Digitalisierung.* Regional Centre of Expertise on Education for Sustainable Development Wien. openscience4sustainability.at.

Cieslewicz, K., Lang, D., & Barth, M. (2022). Der europäische Weg. In: Ökologisches Wirtschaften, 37(1), 8–9. doi:10.14512/OEW370108

Döbeli Honegger, B. (2017). Mehr als 0 und 1. Schule in einer digitalisierten Welt. 2. Auflage, Bern.

Feierabend, S., Rathgeb, Th., & Reuter, Th. (2018). Jugend, Information, Medien. Ergebnisse der JIM-Studie 2018. In: Media Perspektiven.

Grunwald, A. (2018). *Der unterlegene Mensch. Die Zukunft der Menschheit im Angesicht von Algorithmen, künstlicher Intelligenz und Robotern.* Riva.

Hopkins, Ch., Michelsen, G., Salite, I., Siegmund, A., Wagner, D., Yokoi, A., Fischer, D., Kohl, K., Razak, D., & Tilleczek, K. (2020). Sustainability as a Purpose on the Path of Learning. In: *Humanistic Futures of Learning. Perspectives from UNESCO Chairs and UNITWIN Networks* (pp. 58–62). UNESCO.

Kaczinski, A., Hennig-Thurau, Th. & Sattler, H. (2019). *Wie Deutschland soziale Medien nutzt und was das für unsere Gesellschaft bedeutet.* Social Media & Society Report.

KMK – Kultusministerkonferenz (2016). Bildung in der digitalen Welt. *Beschluss der Kultusministerkonferenz vom 8.12.2016.*

Lange, St. & Santarius, T. (2018): Smarte Grüne Welt? Digitalisierung zwischen Überwachung. *Konsum und Nachhaltigkeit. oekom Verlag.*

Macgilchrist, F. (2019). Digitale Bildungsmedien im Diskurs. In: Aus Politik und Zeitgeschichte: Bildung und Digitalisierung. (Vol. 69). Bildung und Digitalisierung.

Politische Ökologie. (2018). Smartopia. Geht Digitalisierung auch nachhaltig? 36.

Reckwitz, A. (2019). Die Gesellschaft der Singularitäten. *edition suhrkamp.*

Ridsdale, C., Rothwell, J., Smit, M., Bliemel, M., Irvine, D., Kelley, D., Matwin, S., Wuetherick, B. & Ali-Hassan, H. (2015). Strategies and Best Practices for Data Literacy Education. *Knowledge Synthesis Report.*

Rolf, A. (2018). *Weltmacht Vereinigte Daten. Die Digitalisierung und Big Data verstehen.* Metropolis.

Scheller, H. (2019). "Digitalpakt Schule." Föderale Kulturhoheit zulasten der Zukunftsfähigkeit des Bildungswesens? In: Aus Politik und Zeitgeschichte: Bildung und Digitalisierung. (Vol. 69).

SchüllerK.BuschP.HindingerC. (2019): Future Skills: Ein Framework für Data Literacy – Kompetenzrahmen und Forschungsbericht. Arbeitspapier Nr. 47. Berlin: Hochschulforum Digitalisierung. doi:10.5281/zenodo.3349

Stalder, F. (2016): Kultur der Digitalität. *edition suhrkamp.*

Stoll, C. (1996). *Die Wüste Internet. Geisterfahrten auf der Datenautobahn.* Fischer.

Stoltenberg, U. (2007). Gesellschaftliches Lernen und Partizipation. In: H. Jonuschat, E. Baranek, M. Behrendt, K. Dietz, B. Schlussmeier, H. Walk, & A. Zehm (Eds.), *Partizipation und Nachhaltigkeit – Vom Leitbild zur Umsetzung. Ergebnisse sozial-ökologischer Forschung. oekom Verlag.*

Stoltenberg, U., & Fischer, D. (2018). Bildung für eine nachhaltige Entwicklung in Deutschland: vom Projekt zur Struktur? In: *Perspektive wechseln. In: Jahrbuch Bildung für nachhaltige Entwicklung.* Forum Umweltbildung Vienna.

Stoltenberg, U., & Michelsen, G. (1999): Lernen nach der Agenda 21: Überlegungen zu einem Bildungskonzept für eine nachhaltige Entwicklung. In: NNA-Berichte, 12. Jg., H.1.

Stoltenberg, U., & Michelsen, G. (2020). Digitalisierung im Kontext von Bildung für eine nachhaltige Entwicklung. In: M. von Hauff & A. Reller (Eds.): *Nachhaltige Digitalisierung – eine noch zu bewältigende Zukunftsaufgabe Wiesbaden.*

Sühlmann-Saul, F. & Rammler, St. (2018): Der blinde Fleck der Digitalisierung. *oekom Verlag.*

United Nations (2015): Transforming our World: The 2030 Agenda for Sustainable Development. UN.

Vare, P., Lausselet, N., & Rieckmann, M. (2022): *Competences in Education for Sustainable Development.* Springer International Publishing.

VBW - Vereinigung der bayerischen Wirtschaft e.V. (2018). *Digitae Souveränität und Bildung.* White paper

WBGU – German Advisory Council on Global Change (2011). *World in Transition. A Social Contract for Sustainability.* WGBU. https://www.wbgu.de/fileadmin/user_upload/wbgu/publikationen /hauptgutachten/hg2011/pdf/wbgu_jg2011_en.pdf

WBGU – German Advisory Council on Global Change (2019). *Towards our Common Digital Future.* WBGU. https://www.wbgu.de/en/publications/publication/towards-our-common-digital-future

Weiser, A., van Deest, J., & Barth, M. (2022): Transformation verstehen lernen: Nachhaltigkeitsbildung und Data Literacy Education in der Studieneingangsphase. In: Weselek, J., Kohler, F. & Siegmund, A. (Hrsg., 2022): Digitale Bildung für nachhaltige Entwicklung. Springer.

Weizenbaum, J. (1976). *Computer Power and Human Reason.* W.H. Freeman and Company.

Wiek, A., Keeler, L., & Redman, C. (2011): Key Competencies in Sustainability: A Reference Framework for Academic Program Development. In: Sustainability Science. 6. doi:10.100711625-011-0132-6

ENDNOTES

1 Digitization is the transformation of analog content or processes into a digital form or mode of operation that permeates all areas of business, government, society and everyday life.

2 Quotes from German-language sources, here and in the following, are translations.

3 See also the results of national monitoring of the implementation of education for sustainable development at https://www.bne-portal.de/bne/de/news/monitoring-zur-veranke rung-von-ndschaft-mit-neuen-ergebnissen.

Chapter 2
The Impact of Biased Design and Hegemony on Sustainable Future-Ready Learning:
Digital Transformation Challenges

Kate Maloney Williams
University of Maryland, College Park, USA

Jehad Halawani
George Mason University, USA

ABSTRACT

The UN 2030 Agenda for Sustainable Development is committed to "quality education." However, little actionable strategy remains on how to define and measure this goal, particularly in the face of an increasingly digitized future, fueled by emergencies and the need for quality distance learning. Additionally, to achieve SDG 4 in a digital era, societies must undergo substantial reforms in 1) conceptualizing teaching, learning, and assessment, and 2) designing and exporting technology. The successful uptake of new technology is frustrated by a complex array of ecological conditions, hegemonic power structures, and multifaceted digital divides. Through a systems approach, this chapter explores how digital environments function and create barriers. The authors argue that effective technology-based interventions must include awareness of the externalities that impact digital design, providing examples from the Global South. The chapter concludes with recommendations on the transformation needed for successful implementation and sustainable integration.

DOI: 10.4018/978-1-7998-5033-5.ch002

INTRODUCTION

One of the central pillars of the United Nations' 2030 Agenda for Sustainable Development is a commitment to "Quality Education." To this end, it hopes to achieve basic education delivery that is equitable, accessible, and inclusive. However, there remains little actionable strategy as to how to define, measure, and meet these goals, particularly in the face of an increasingly digitized future – one that is further fueled by pandemics and other emergencies and the need for quality distance learning.

Additionally, in order to achieve SDG 4 in a globalized digital era, we must undergo substantial reforms to our education systems. Primarily, these reforms need to include 1) how we design and export technology and 2) how we conceptualize teaching, learning, and assessment (towards more critical, collaborative, and problem-based practices). New technology does hold great potential to advance educational opportunities; however, its successful uptake is frustrated by a complex array of ecological conditions, hegemonic power structures, and multifaceted digital divides.

All of these conditions fuel biased design – or the ways in which both intentional and unintentional prejudices get built into our user experiences and the media we consume. Most often, these biases occur unintentionally – internalized by our lived experiences in a problematic world. However, they can also be fueled subversively by geopolitical, racial, and patriarchal forces, trying to exploit or disenfranchise the other. This chapter will further describe the ways in which these forces can operate, how they impact our education systems, and how this should shape future initiatives for sustainable education.

BACKGROUND

For nearly two decades, user-generated ('Web 2.0') technologies have been heralded for their built-in architecture that allegedly fosters creativity and horizontal models of participation. Consequently, many development practitioners invest in the diffusion of Information and Communication Technologies for Development (ICT4D), mistakenly believing that increased access to ICTs serves as *development per se* and that all communities will interact with the technology in similar manners. Thus, hoping to drive low-index countries towards a more sustainable, knowledge-based economy, they overlook how computer usage may be affected by the message of another medium: the classroom. This is particularly important as educational technologies and online platforms become increasingly prevalent across schools.

MAIN FOCUS OF THE CHAPTER

Through a systems approach, this chapter will explore how digital environments function, drawing on a complex interplay of fields and theories, including but not limited to international development, Social Construction of Technology (SCOT), media ecology, algorithmic bias, and surveillance capitalism. We will argue that successful technology-based interventions for a sustainable education must include strategic awareness of the externalities that impact digital design and will describe those externalities here. The chapter will conclude with recommendations on the transformation needed for successful implementation and integration.

Issues, Controversies, Problems

The phrase "the medium is the message" was coined by one of the founding theorists of the media ecology approach, Marshall McLuhan, to illustrate the ways in which technology inherently carries values and influence. He believed that "our conventional response to all media, namely that it is how they are used that counts, is the numb stance of the technological idiot" (McLuhan, 1964, p. 31). Rather, media – any tools and channels of communication that can be used to reach or influence people – define and constitute our base behaviors and life environments, providing affordances and constraints to how we navigate and understand the world. In turn, media influence our patterns of thought and response, habits of mind, and conceptualizations of culture, complicating our perceptions and how we interact and form relationships with others.

Media ecologists often reference McLuhan's analogy on media environments: a fish being unaware of water in the same way that a person is oblivious to the technologies that shape and influence daily life. Just as fish have no "anti-environment" which would enable them to perceive the opposite of water – people have no element of coping with media bombardment – unless a critical education steps in to challenge that space and raise consciousness. This is necessary for all sustainable, future-ready classrooms.

As Bird (2003) argues, "we really cannot isolate the role of the media in culture, because the media are firmly anchored into the web of culture, although articulated by individuals in different ways" (p. 3). One could look at how the components of any device fundamentally shape the options available to its user; "embedded in every tool is an ideological bias, a predisposition to construct the world as one thing rather than another, to value one thing over another, to amplify one sense or skill or attitude more loudly than another" (Postman, 1992, p. 13). ICTs serve as an essential part of the social reproduction of knowledge and culture, not only as mediators of media consumption but as consumables themselves (Silverstone et al., 1992). The inseparability of culture and communication allows certain priorities and reinforces hegemonic values. Those priorities and values subtly interfere with the minds of their audiences, making them receptive to embedded messages. This premise undergirds additional theories, such as *social construction of technology* and *communication power*, which counter technological determinism with constructivism. These argue that human behavior shapes technology and that media have become the space where power strategies are played out (see Additional Reading).

Further, digital products are also undercut by micro and macro problems in design – the result of a tech culture and industry built on white, male values and the deterministic idea that the products are "brilliant" enough to serve everyone in the same way – which they most often do not (O'Neil, 2016). Standard design practices, such as *pattern recognition*, would be seen as profiling or stereotyping behaviors in other contexts. Also, the ways in which technology offers tracking opportunities of its users play into Foucault's definition of power and actor-networks, which are exercised through techniques of surveillance in which people are constantly watched and disciplined -- 'the object of information, never a subject of communication' (Foucault, 1975).

Several digital media scholars also explore the social construct of "whiteness" as a context for understanding how race and identity are specifically engaged in online environments. Daniels (2009) explores the concept of cyber-racism, arguing that Internet culture is built to protect perpetrators of racial hostilities more than the targets of race-based hate. Benjamin (2019) refers to what she calls *New Jim Code,* or "the employment of new technologies that reflect and reproduce existing inequities but that are promoted and perceived as more objective or progressive than the discriminatory systems of a previous era" (p. 5-6). This can be read as an extension of the *Matrix of Domination* (Collins, 1990) that explains systems of oppression through the interaction of social categories, such as race, class, and gender, particularly in how they play out against problematic concepts like *meritocracy ideology* and *bootstrap ethics*.

According to O'Neil (2016), the meritocracy myth fuels "a sort of techno-paternalism: when a group of mostly white guys from mostly the same places believes it deserves to be at the top, it's also quick to assume that it has all the perspective … to make decisions for everyone else" (p. 175-176). *Data feminism* tries to better understand power relations through the social relations of technology, particularly that technology itself cannot be fully understood without reference to gender, especially in how it may disenfranchise female identities. It asserts that "data are not neutral or objective. They are the products of unequal social relations, and this context is essential for conducting accurate, ethical analysis" (D'Ignazio & Klein, 2020, p. 149).

Although during the early Internet ('Web 1.0'), it was theorized that the emergence of virtual environments and an accompanying culture of fantasy would mean an escape from the boundaries of race and the experience of racism, this has not proven to be the case with racist tensions playing out across platforms. Historically, Goffman (1959) upheld that humans have a special drive for social contact and companionship, manifested around both the need for an audience before which to try out one's vaunted self and a need for teammates with whom to enter into more private or "backstage" comradery. This continues to play out on social platforms albeit in different ways. However, evidence indicates that user anonymity and the ability to forge new identities online have not actually allowed people to look past race (Bird, 2003). Rather, we have been embroiled in data mining and tracking, algorithmic bias, disinformation, and other trappings of short-sighted design – perpetuating exploitation.

According to Silverstone et al. (1992), "media disengage the location of action and meaning from experience, and at the same time (and through the same displaced spaces) claim action and meaning for the modern world system of capitalist social and economic (and moral) relations" (p. 20). In other words, the group that controls the institutions controls the distribution and embeds its racial bias into the fabric of society. Within digital life, the literature indicates that these hierarchies are mostly perpetuated through algorithmic bias. This is further problematized by preexisting structural discrimination: the policies of dominant race, ethnic, and gender institutions and how the implementers use these policies to control certain situations.

This means that bias becomes baked into the technologies themselves, inheriting traits from its creators and users. For example, Google's algorithms aggregate and optimize the racially discriminating patterns of past users who have clicked on ads, learning the racist preferences of some users and perpetuating feedback loops, also known as "echo chambers." This is not usually intentional but centered on source code – where errors or biases could reside and can reproduce or amplify existing prejudices (Amoore, 2020). Costanza-Chock (2020) particularly outlines the intersection of algorithmic bias and AI and how they play out in the application of bots. In their book *Design Justice*, they discuss the phenomenon of *emergent bias* – or how a system that may not have been originally biased becomes biased based on shifting contexts and users (Costanza-Chock, 2020). Unfortunately, the literature also shows problems that are either separate or compounded by algorithmic biases. These include the rise of mis- and disinformation, sometimes fueled by international information warfare, surveillance capitalism, and a media illiterate population.

Additionally, "research has extended the study of microaggressions to online interactions, such as in chat rooms, on social media platforms, and in real-time online multiplayer games'' (Costanza-Chock, 2020, p. 44). This generates *dysaffordances*, a subcategory of disaffordances, that refers to moments when users are forced to misidentify themselves to gain access and engage with the online platform/

community. Evidence shows that this form of discriminatory (reactive) design, the antithesis of universal (proactive) design, remains particularly disenfranchising for marginalized groups, such as people of color, the disabled, and LGBTQ+.

Further still, lies the practice of *digital redlining*, the practice of actively perpetuating existent inequities between marginalized groups. In education, this includes the use of policies that regulate and track students' engagement with information technology. Additionally, these policies create boundaries that not only control information access and filtering but determine methods of data collection and retention to third parties.

More Issues, Controversies, Problems

The question then arises – what is the most effective way to cope with this new world order? How can we better promote the critical literacies needed to navigate life in our heavily digitized, mediated, and polarized environments, especially when the future consists of being at the receiving end of these technologies? A media ecology approach fundamentally argues that "when you plug something into a wall, someone is getting plugged into you. Which means you need new patterns of defense, perception, understanding, evaluation. You need a new kind of education" (Postman & Weingarter, 1971, p. 20). This is where digital transformation becomes the central foundation for any delivery of sustainable, quality education and future-ready learning.

Yet, limited work has been done on approaching the classroom as a media environment or anti-environment. Moreover, "educational institutions often treat learners as consumers, fostering in students a mindset of consumerism rather than of ownership of problems, which they carry with them for the rest of their lives" (Fischer, 2011, p. 42). When we talk about the problems of social media and digital design, we often look at the symptoms rather than the causes (Buckingham, 2021). Often the debate is too narrow, dealing with particular symptoms one by one – rather than looking at bigger systemic and social changes needed. To this end, our education systems fail us in sustainable reforms toward a critical education for these realities. The medium of the classroom ends up diffused no differently than other technological devices, such as televisions, mobile phones, and computers, as was thrust upon the Global South by the Global North during the "dominant paradigm of development" (Rogers, 1976). As argued, there is "no evidence that consideration has been given to … how the learners … are to incorporate their access to the laptops and associated learning resources (local or global) into their everyday lives or … ways in which this might empower them" (Mansell, 2006, p. 907).

In recent years, funders and policymakers have looked at "media literacy" campaigns as a kind of quick fix investment solution – one that can be alleviated through grassroots campaigns, particularly short-term "upskilling" initiatives (Buckingham, 2021). This is misguided, short-sighted, and counter-productive. Governments are wary of regulating media, and companies likewise resist regulation. Often, this translates to education policies falling short of sustainable reform.

There has been a very particular kind of modernization of the education system – one that does not effectively extend to the teaching of new critical literacies. For one, comprehensive media literacy education is still marginal across international curricula. It should also not fundamentally be about instrumental educational technology; it needs to be centered on critical understanding – the main objective often most lost in the discussion. As has been argued on behalf of many technological devices, its mechanisms carry over multifaceted values:

a curriculum, educationists tell us, is more than the constituent courses. It is also the teaching methods, the course materials and aids, the facilities, and in truth the entire experience that the students undergo in the learning environment. All of these components embody values that consciously or unconsciously shape the learners. (Quebral, 1988, p. 53)

In countries like the United States, media environments have cyclically fueled opposition within education between traditional and progressive pedagogies. For neoconservatives, it is not about conserving what exists but a restoration of the past (Buckingham, 2021). However, we need to rethink how we teach with educational technology. We need to put technology back in the context of culture and politics. Future-ready learning is not an instrumental view – or about a set of tools or skills. Rather, digital literacy should be synonymous with literacy, digital culture with culture (Buckingham, 2021).

The challenges of educational delivery during the COVID-19 pandemic compounded these issues and the ways in which quality online education is collectively viewed and understood. Emergency response teaching largely failed to take into account many key considerations for social-emotional wellness, cognitive loading, accessibility, and usability. Instead, it should be remembered that there are a unique set of design principles needed for effective digital classrooms. Unhelpfully, these are largely conceptualized and implemented separately from the general Internet technology previously discussed.

Online classroom spaces, particularly vis-à-vis learning management systems, provide their own set of challenges and affordances for structuring a meaningful, interactive, and inclusive learning environment. There is an overt tension between the benefits and challenges that accompany technology-enabled learning that is important to comprehending its impact on instructors and course designers. Further, several key considerations impact the design of online teaching and the accompanying roles and workload of the instructor. Zhu et al. (2018) align these considerations into three categories: 1) *pedagogical considerations* (including learning objectives, assessment methods, course length, course content, flexibility, and collaborative learning support, 2) *resource considerations* (including platform affordances, institutional support, and available intellectual and hardware resources), and 3) *logistical considerations* (including the time spent designing the online environment). Unfortunately, the ways that lessons and classrooms are developed, do not take into account the problematic design of technologies and their influence on student thinking and behavior as discussed.

SOLUTIONS AND RECOMMENDATIONS

From here, it is worth exploring whether any practical strategies exist to serve as a panacea – to show how to lessen growing disparities, tensions, and polarizations within our global communities through more applied guidance. As Costanza-Chock (2020) laments, "unfortunately, most design processes do not yet systematically interrogate how the unequal distribution of user experiences might be structured by the user's position within intersecting fields of race, class, gender, and disability" (p. 59). As such, there is a growing need in this field for additional study, particularly in the production of peer-reviewed empirical data and analysis.

However, the literature strongly upholds that while biased design is a serious problem that impacts our critical understanding and navigation of the contemporary world, "it should not be viewed as something that can be fixed after the fact" (D'Ignazio & Klein, 2020, p. 63). Rather, we need to utilize proactive and inclusive design principles, such as User Interface/User Experience (UI/UX) engineering and/or

Universal Design from concept origination. To support this process, D'Ignazio & Klein (2020) argue that "we must look to understand and design systems that address the source of the bias: structural oppression. In truth, oppression is itself an outcome, one that results from the matrix of domination" (p. 63). This awareness needs to be equally built into course planning and lesson development.

To fully address structural oppression, we need to reform our classrooms, curriculum, and instructional practices, particularly for *future-ready learning* (Tan et al., 2017). This concept is generally used to refer to a range of core competencies, which include collaboration, digital literacy, critical thinking, and problem-solving, such as being supported through inquiry-based learning and project-based work (see Additional Reading). In many ways, they may not focus on *what* we think but on *how* we think. As a start, we must find new critical pedagogies to help transform citizen consciousness and support students in living fuller, more inclusive lives. This should be bolstered by more content on diversity and citizenship education, particularly as supported through such frameworks of *cura personalis, holistic education, maker education,* and *digital empathy.* Critical pedagogy as a fundamental teaching approach should undergird how we transfer all subject curricula to learners.

Additionally, the Universal Design for Learning (UDL) framework offers several strategies for designing and managing online instruction beyond improving accessibility for disabilities and cognitive differences. Universal Design first emerged as an architectural movement in the mid-twentieth century, aimed at reducing barriers to access for those with physical disabilities. The main idea was that good design was proactive and inclusive – that it could be made to benefit the community equally without having to specifically be tailored to the individual. Over the years, general Universal Design principles spilled into a framework, UDL, geared towards the effective design of classrooms. It holds that instruction can be designed upfront to be inclusive of different abilities and modalities – whether in physical or virtual spaces. Further, it acknowledges a "hidden curriculum of online teaching" and argues that educational systems can serve specific goals and objectives, such as equity, diversity, and flexibility, by underlying design. Thus, it aims to reduce barriers in instruction through an intentional and systematic approach, striving to circumvent the need for individualized accommodation. Evidence has shown that "thoughtfully designed online instruction has proven to enhance learner's engagement with course material, the instructor, and with one another" (Hollingshead & Carr-Chellman, 2019, n.p.) Although there are generally seven principles that UDL utilizes, these are framed by three overlying concepts – that online classrooms must provide 1) multiple means of representation, 2) multiple means of expression, and 3) multiple means of engagement.

Fundamentally, each learner varies in the ways they perceive and comprehend information, whether or not it is related to any underlying sensory or learning disabilities, as well as language, gender, or cultural differences. This requires that instructors and course designers assume online pedagogies or strategies for assisting students with the "going online" process, as well as the learning outcomes as assigned by the instructor. Digital learning and teaching require a narrower focus on educational goals and outcomes-based approaches, demonstrating that the nature of assessment cannot stay the same for all online courses. Rather, quality digital education requires a learner-centered pedagogy, built on meaning making, where students should have some autonomy in creating final products that utilize different forms of multimedia. These new media provide the greater opportunity to construct and make meaning through ongoing reflection and discourse, which requires instructors to utilize a more critical pedagogy. There is also the question of usability -- an effective online classroom needs to be designed from origination to be scaffolded, navigable, and conceptually demonstrated.

Borrowing from the literature on Massive Open Online Classroom (MOOC) development, there are several considerations that online instructors need to note to foster better learner outcomes and bolster student retention. These include connectivist strategies, perceived effectiveness of content, high instructor-student interaction, personalization, and an array of instructional practices and technology tools (Hone & El Said, 2016; Zhu et al., 2018). However, when it comes to technology tools, there are several additional frameworks and models to consider for meaningful integration, each one needing to be defined with intention. For example, as Wood and Joicus (2014) state, "we must remember that digital devices are not magic wands that instantly turn literary responses into critical responses. Like paper and pencils, technology is a tool, and it's what teachers and students do with the tool that matters" (p. 133). Similarly, digital technology is ubiquitous in students' everyday lives, and they must be prepared in how to navigate it. In this vein, there are several comprehensive frameworks for the integration of technology in the classroom, the most prominent being the TPACK Framework developed by Mishra and Koehler (2006).

TPACK is intended to guide teachers through their own strengths and weaknesses in three domains: 1) technological knowledge, 2) pedagogical knowledge, and 3) content knowledge. Ultimately, reflection in these areas comes together to drive more innovative teaching and learning. Part of this framework is not new to curriculum development – considerations towards the content, instructional strategies, teaching models, and assessments used are important for successfully designing scaffolded environments in general. However, the digital tools and platforms incorporated are what really foster future-ready learning skills by forcing educators to specifically think about the digital tools for learning and their affordances.

As a supplement to TPACK, the SAMR Model (Puentedura, 2009) further prompts teachers to not just consider the ways that different technologies and media may enhance lessons through augmentation and substitution but, rather, how the right selection can *transform* lessons through redefinition and modification. It is important to remember that for better learning outcomes, substitution is not adequate – yet substitution is a tactic that has prolifically popped up in order to address emergency remote teaching during the COVID-19 pandemic. Good online instruction requires selecting, monitoring, and evaluating the right digital extensions.

Further, the Community of Inquiry (COI) conceptual framework (Garrison et al., 2000) is a social connectivist model of learning used for assessing both online and blended learning environments. It is essentially defined by three dimensions: 1) teaching presence, 2) social presence, and 3) cognitive presence. It holds that through this intersection a meaningful educational experience occurs. Under these dimensions, "teaching presence" refers to the ways in which instructors design their syllabi, course objectives, and methods. It is the instructional design and organization of the course – the activities, the facilitation thereof, and the direct instruction. "Social presence" involves the extent to which students feel they are perceived as real people. In the online classroom, increased anonymity can lead to less accountability, retention, and engagement (Hone & El Said, 2016). The COI Framework upholds that online classrooms require open communication, affective expression, and group cohesion or "team building" as the groundwork for fostering deep learning and student engagement. This requires instructors to focus on quality student-tutor and student-student communication as a means of supporting not just student engagement but also psycho social well-being. The role of instructors in structuring and monitoring online discussions is especially key. They must utilize strategies for online community building, including reaching out to students often, limiting the time spent lecturing, using video and chat as modes of engagement, and allowing class time to be used for both personal and professional updates.

As the U.S. Department of Education (2010) notes, "modern online learning includes offerings that run the gamut from conventional didactic lectures or textbook-like information delivered over the Web to Internet-based collaborative role-playing in social simulations and highly interactive multiplayer strategy games" (p. 3). COI takes into consideration the type of learning experience, which can be defined through the amount of control that the student has over content and the nature of the learning activity. Rather than traditional didactic or expository learning experiences (i.e., transmission models, banking models, or rote learning), technologies better afford for means of both active and interactive learning. Under these tenants, an active learner builds knowledge through inquiry-based exploration of digital production. Technology is intended as the mediator for human interaction with real learning hinging on those generative activities. In turn, this works to realign the role of teachers as co-learners and facilitators – with different accountabilities toward workload and evaluation. These frameworks help us to better understand the unique demands, opportunities, and challenges of sustainably digitizing course design.

There are also additional considerations towards fostering SDG 4, equally shared between traditional, hybrid, and online classrooms. Thus far, we have already discussed several key factors that have implications for quality education achievement: economic, socio-cultural, and hegemonic forces. Few frameworks have been integrated successfully to have a significant impact on educational reform. However, evidence shows some promise with the *Whole Institutional Approach (WIA), learner-centered pedagogy, and action-oriented transformative pedagogy* (see Additional Reading). We call on practitioners to further align these approaches with those of digital learning.

While a singular or comprehensive definition of WIA is not available in the literature, we define it as a multilevel system that addresses change for sustainable development at various levels: macro, meso, and micro. WIA transcends beyond the classroom to institutional operations and external communications. Key elements of WIA include the involvement of all stakeholders as partners in the reform process: targeting when and where support is needed throughout the development process and mobilizing and enhancing all existing resources and working practices. The macro level (or "government level") relates to policy- and decision-making, financial management and budgeting, and outcomes. The meso and micro levels intersect closely to support these macro initiatives. For example, schools' decisions on curriculum, teaching and learning, and building human capital with local partnerships stem from macro visioning and mandates. This rhetoric has become popular in development and educational planning as of late but may pose some risks if not defined intentionally and executed mindfully. Two cases are presented below (see Tables 1 and 2).

Table 1. Kenya's policy framework for reforming education, training, and research for sustainable development (2019)

In 2019, the Kenya Ministry of Education (MoE) published a report, describing the structure of its education system and its vision for implementing sustainable and systemic reforms across all levels (Republic of Kenya, 2019). On the surface, its mission is laid out as achieving "holistic quality and inclusive education and training for transformation to a knowledge economy, social cohesion and sustainable development" (Republic of Kenya, 2019, p. 13), advocating values such as "inclusive and equitable quality education and training" and "lifelong learning opportunities for all," especially "the most disadvantaged" (Republic of Kenya, 2019, p. 3). However, it does not define these terms or what they look like with many of its trappings falling into the same short-sighted upskilling and public-private partnerships currently espoused throughout the aid sector. Like many national development agendas, much emphasis is put on aspirational goals, such as digital transformation and achieving a knowledge-based economy – yet little actionable strategy is articulated in how to measure, evaluate, or achieve progress toward those outcomes. Although the report claims to take a WIA, little is targeted or defined in terms of a Theory of Change, particularly a lack of SMART (Specific, Measurable, Achievable, Results-Based, Time-bound) goals. Further, action steps have included the decentralization of school operations to regions, counties, and sub-counties.

Our stance would argue that this fails to account for an interplay in macro, meso, and micro levels. It is also not incorporating critical digital literacy or the soft skills needed for digitalization. Instead, the report actively compartmentalizes each level of education to its own set of goals while merely hoping for a cumulative change. In doing so, it undercuts the ecological factors that impact its students: a lack of scaffolding across the educational lifespan, the interdisciplinary aspects of a critical and holistic curriculum, or the critical skills needed for self-actualization and autonomy in a fundamentally mediated (and user commodified) world.

For example, goals such as "integrate Science, Technology and Innovation (ST&I) into all sectors" (Republic of Kenya, 2019, p. 3) fail to address how this can tangibly be achieved. It also does not seemingly recognize how technology already undergirds other subject matter, particularly as either an instructional/learning tool or an alternative medium of expression.

Too much emphasis in the primary grades is put exclusively on traditional literacy and numeracy through the continued bearing down on rote instruction. There is arguably no reason that "the labour market demand for graduates with knowledge and competencies … can only start to be acquired at the secondary education and beyond" (Republic of Kenya, 2019, p. 37), especially when a future-ready workforce is constantly evolving and requires the lifelong adaptive skills of how to think, collaborate, and problem-solve toward that end. Rather than seeing technology as a vehicle for more reciprocal learning and enhanced cognitive processing in young children, it uses low rates as an excuse to exclude it. The MoE also tries to pander to negative parental views rather than using technology as a way to partner with parents for more transparency, dialogue, and co-teaching.

In its section on special needs education, nothing is said about technology as an innovative vehicle for accessibility and stimulating multimodal expression. The dedicated exposition on *Integration of ICT in Education, Training and Research* focuses almost exclusively on infrastructural barriers, telecommunications, and techno-determinism. It shows no integration on how any of this fits within the education system and impacts teachers and students – treating these realities as parallel, yet siloed, issues.

Further, it states that culturally there are negative attitudes towards STEM subjects but tries to push for more opportunities in areas, such as computing and engineering, rather than finding ways to change these perceptions through technology's relevance to everyday life and its ability to innovate other areas of arts, business, and the humanities. One objective is to promote open and distance education and research at the tertiary level – yet there is little lead up through blended learning in the lower grades to make this a smooth transition for adult students. Both areas require a different set of instructional design skills and study/communication skills for the best execution and impact.

Ultimately, if one of the final outcomes is "better educated citizens," there is no sign the curricula has built this result, needed through critical pedagogy. The concern over "harmonized" national assessment also does not seem to dive into the granularity needed for meaningful review. It has only "shuffled the deck," unsustainably focusing on quantity over quality. Defining what one intends to measure, as well as establishing a consistent system to define the magnitude of what is being measured are crucial to assessment; these choices are often straightforward for rote learning but not for measures of higher-order thinking.

Table 2. Zambia Kids Online: a global kids online study (2022)

Global Kids Online is an international research project that aims to generate and sustain a rigorous cross-national evidence base about children's use of the Internet. Its work has produced a global research toolkit for educators and policymakers to use in conducting standardized national research with children and their parents on the opportunities, risks, and protective factors of children's Internet use. In partnership with several funders, Save the Children published a report in April 2022, containing the latest evidence on children's Internet usage, risks, and learning opportunities online in Zambia. As the Burton et al. (2022) report argues:

While much of the growth in the use of ICTs over the past decade has taken place in developed countries, there is exponential growth taking place in developing countries as more and more children, in particular, come online. The internet offers a wealth of opportunities for children to learn, to play, to develop new skills and to expand their interests and circle of friends. At the same time, it may also present a number of risks and dangers. To date, there is little written on online risks and harms to children within the Zambian context. (p. 1)

The data shows a high level of Internet access for Zambian children in peri-urban areas; however, it also argues that it is important to assume that every child has some Internet access rather than working from the too commonly erred assumption that many do not. Personal devices, such as smart or feature phones, guarantee access whether at the familial or individual level. Yet, despite increases in access and MoE aspirations, children were determined to exhibit "a very rudimentary understanding of their privacy online, their data footprint and how to protect their data" (Burton et al., 2022, p. 78).

Within the school environment, teachers were reported to generally restrict, rather than promote, Internet use. The report attributes most of the disparity to these behaviors rather than the usual scapegoat of emerging infrastructure. Just one quarter of the children reported that their teachers sometimes encouraged and supported them to learn new things online - with approximately another one in ten of the children reporting that their teachers did this very often or often. As a matter of safeguarding, girls' access was also more often restricted in the schools than boys' access – contributing to gendered digital and educational disparity.

When asked about different steps that they take to keep their data and identity safe online, Zambian children generally reflected a very low level of understanding of data privacy and protection. The sample (of 999 parents and caregivers and 988 children) engaged in a wide range of activities online although many of these were concentrated on content consumption and communication rather than content creation. Children also commonly engaged in, and were exposed to, several risky online activities. Additionally, the report found that:

Digital citizenship, literacy, and media literacy should be integrated into core curriculums [sic], across all grade levels, where possible. This is particularly important in a context where it is common for children to be online while their parents or caregivers are not. It is important that teachers learn how they can instill values that positively affect online safety. (Burton et al., 2022, p. xiv)

These types of studies are crucial digital landscapes, sorely missing from the design of most aid-based project implementation, rendering the projects unsustainable. Although an intervention is not currently in place here, the findings support our arguments surrounding the gaps in sustainable education and ICT4E, such as we see in the Kenyan strategy. Similarly, the Zambian MoE aims to increase access to and the use of technology within the classroom, particularly correlating with the shift to online learning and resources that has been a result of COVID-19 and emergency response teaching.

Consequently, the report calls on the schools and the MoE to increase access to computers and tablets at schools across Zambia:

This must be accompanied by digital literacy and online safety training for teachers and school staff, including the provision of school data protection systems and guidance for schools on acceptable use policies, the use of EdTech, the integration of online safety into school safety policies and on the provision of support and referral systems within schools. (Burton et al., 2022, p. xiv)

All areas that too often fail to be defined and quantified. The report further calls for specific measures to ensure that children with disabilities have equitable access, as well as the integration of online safety and child online protection measures into existing child protection policies and legislation, ranging from the national-level child protection systems and mechanisms down to the district- and local-level child protection systems and mechanisms.

Schools should encourage very clear guidelines for teachers on the use of personal devices (what can be used and how it can be used and what is acceptable use), including the acceptable use of school hardware and the Internet, arguing that model guidelines can be developed by the MoE on a consultative basis.

FUTURE RESEARCH DIRECTIONS

Our goal has been to demonstrate the complex intersection between technology usage and hegemonic power – and how those implications should impact educational delivery, especially as it pertains to the achievement of sustainable future-ready learning. Especially when contextualized within development initiatives, the ways in which digital environments create barriers – beyond barriers of access – are too often overlooked. The ways in which biases get baked into the technologies we use exacerbates how technologies are diffused across marginalized groups, particularly gender, racial, socio-economic, and cultural divides. The most effective project implementation should include awareness of these externalities, but too often the fields of international, education, and technology development remain siloed and exclude the important theories tied to communications and media theory. This same exclusion roots the hegemonic structures placed on cultures and societies that have been historically colonized and exploited by the Global North.

Without more interdisciplinary dialogue and collaborative research into these fields, future interventions and reform attempts will be doomed to fail – falling short of the aims of SDG 4. There also needs to be more precision in both academia and development in how we discuss *sustainable education* versus *education for sustainability*. Too often in the literature, the terms are used interchangeably and/or conflated -- when they should denote very different meanings and functions. Sustainable education is not fully or specifically about promoting action towards climate change and environmentalism within education – although this content can most assuredly be incorporated into the curricula of sustainable education and complement its delivery. However, sustainable education must foremost focus on the long-term, ongoing delivery of education – the learning, outcomes, and impact. This includes meaningful and ongoing reform to improve quality, access, and equity. The rote education models and content of the past will not prepare the students of today and tomorrow with the critical skills needed to navigate the new age of life and work, including solving “wicked problems” like climate change. Our literacies are changing, and we need to adapt to thrive as people. During the last few years of public health emergency and extensive digitization, there is ample space for additional study and evaluation.

Moving forward, we also recommend that educational policy planning and instructional design take into account the frameworks outlined and include multi-level stakeholders. The different models highlighted hold promise of improved learning outcomes if digitization is structured by clear criteria and SMART goals. For example, coupling action-oriented transformative pedagogy, which focuses on learning at the micro and meso levels, with WIA, which offers holistic vertical design, would help lessen the problems that both impact digital design and perpetuate disenfranchisement amongst vulnerable groups, particularly in the Global South.

CONCLUSION

This chapter has served as a platform for us to share critical aspects, often neglected, in the discussion of sustainable education. As experienced educators and development practitioners, we have personally experienced the disconnect between design, practice, and results. Too often global partnerships are forged solely at the macro level – conducting needs assessments or funding hardware without being process-oriented. Sustainable change then does not occur, particularly when evaluation is ignored and baseline, mid-line, or endline data are not collected. This top-down approach to reform excludes the systemic issues that pervade the environments in which schools and daily life operate, including the hegemonic forces and problematic values baked into technology and media – some of the largest influences on culture, behavior, and psychology. For the achievement of SDG 4, there needs to be more focus on critical literacy, as well as meaningful technology usage, problem-centric approaches, and integrated subject matter across the curriculum. The hegemonic forces and biases laden in information and communication technologies must be brought to the forefront of educational design, reform, and curricula if digitization is to successfully provide sustainable future-ready learning.

REFERENCES

Amoore, L. (2020). *Cloud ethics: Algorithms and the attributes of ourselves and others*. Duke UP.

Benjamin, R. (2019). Race after technology: Abolitionist tools for the new Jim Code. *Polity*.

Bird, S. E. (2003). *The audience in everyday life: Living in a media world*. Routledge.

Buckingham, D. (2021, May 12). *Media literacy and media education in the age of digital capitalism* [Paper Presentation]. *4th International Conference on Literacy and Contemporary Society*, Cyprus.

Burton, P., Bwalya, M., & Sihubwa, S. (2022). *Zambia Kids Online: A Global Kids online study*. Save the Children.

Collins, P. H. (1990). *Black feminist thought: Knowledge, consciousness, and the politics of empowerment*. Hyman.

Costanza-Chock, S. (2020). *Design justice: Community-led practices to build the worlds we need*. MIT Press. doi:10.7551/mitpress/12255.001.0001

D'Ignazio, C., & Klein, L. F. (2020). *Data Feminism*. MIT Press. doi:10.7551/mitpress/11805.001.0001

Daniels, J. (2009). *Cyber racism: White supremacy online and the new attack on civil rights*. Rowman & Littlefield.

Fischer, G. (2011). Understanding, fostering, and supporting cultures of participation. *Interaction*, *18*(3), 42–53. doi:10.1145/1962438.1962450

Foucault, M. (1975). *Discipline and punish: The birth of the prison*. Vintage.

Garrison, D. R., Anderson, T., & Archer, W. (2000). Critical inquiry in a text-based environment: Computer conferencing in higher education model. *The Internet and Higher Education*, *2*(2-3), 87–105. doi:10.1016/S1096-7516(00)00016-6

Goffman, E. (1959). *The presentation of self in everyday life*. Doubleday.

Hollingshead, A., & Carr-Chellman, D. (2019, Feb). Engaging learners in online environments utilizing Universal Design for Learning principles. *eLearn Magazine.* https://elearnmag.acm.org/featured.cfm?aid=3310383

Hone, K. S., & El Said, G. R. (2016). Exploring the factors affecting MOOC retention: A survey study. *Computers & Education*, *98*, 157–168. doi:10.1016/j.compedu.2016.03.016

Kenya Ministry of Education. (2019). *A policy framework for reforming education and training for sustainable development in Kenya: Towards realizing quality, relevant and inclusive education and training for sustainable development.* Republic of Kenya.

Mansell, R. (1982). The 'new dominant paradigm' in communication: Transformation versus adaptation. *Canadian Journal of Communication*, *8*(3), 42–60. doi:10.22230/cjc.1982v8n3a278

McLuhan, M. (1964). *Understanding media: The extensions of man* (2nd ed.). Mentor.

Mishra, P., & Koehler, M. J. (2006). Technological pedagogical content knowledge: A new framework for teacher knowledge. *Teachers College Record*, *108*(6), 1017–1054. doi:10.1111/j.1467-9620.2006.00684.x

O'Neil, C. (2016). *Weapons of math destruction: How Big Data increases inequality and threatens democracy*. Crown.

Postman, N. (1992). *Technopoly: The surrender of culture to technology*. Alfred A. Knopf.

Postman, N., & Weingarter, C. (1971). *Teaching as a subversive activity*. Delta.

Puentedura, R. R. (2009). SAMR: First steps. *Hippasus.* http://hippasus.com/resources/tte/

Quebral, N. (1988). *Development communication*. UPLB College of Agriculture.

Rogers, E. (1976). Communication and development: The passing of the dominant paradigm. *Communication Research*, *3*(2), 213–240. doi:10.1177/009365027600300207

Silverstone, R. (1992). *Consuming technologies: Media and information in domestic spaces*. Psychology Press.

Tan, J. P. L., Choo, S. S., Kang, T., & Liem, G. A. D. (2017). Educating for twenty-first century competencies and future-ready learners: Research perspectives from Singapore. *Asia Pacific Journal of Education*, *37*(4), 425–436. doi:10.1080/02188791.2017.1405475

U.S. Department of Education. (2010). *Evaluation of evidence-based practices in online learning*. USDE. www.ed.gov/about/offices/list/opepd/ppss/reports.html

Wood, S., & Joicus, R. (2014). Beyond fun and games: Using an iPad as a tool for critical response. *The Reading Teacher*, *68*(2), 129–133. doi:10.1002/trtr.1309

Zhu, M., Bonk, C. J., & Sari, A. R. (2018). Instructor experiences designing MOOCs in higher education: Pedagogical, resource, and logistical considerations and challenges. *Online Learning*, *22*(4), 203–241. doi:10.24059/olj.v22i4.1495

ADDITIONAL READING

Berger, P. L., & Luckman, T. (1966). *The social construction of reality: A treatise in the sociology of knowledge*. Anchor.

CAST. (2018). Universal design for learning guidelines. http://udlguidelines.cast.org

Castells, M. (2009). *Communication power*. Oxford UP.

Helsper, E. (2021). The digital disconnect: The social causes and consequences of digital inequalities. *Sage (Atlanta, Ga.)*. doi:10.4135/9781526492982

Moyo, D. (2009). *Dead Aid: Why aid is not working and how there is a better way for Africa*. Farrar, Straus & Giroux.

Pedler, M., & Abbott, C. (2013). *Facilitating action learning: A practitioner's guide*. Open UP.

Pinch, T. J., & Bijker, W. E. (1984). The social construction of facts and artefacts: Or how the sociology of science and the sociology of technology might benefit each other. *Social Studies of Science*, *14*(3), 399–441. doi:10.1177/030631284014003004

Rieckmann, M. (2018). Learning to transform the world: Key competencies in education for sustainable development. In A. Leicht, J. Heiss, & W. J. Byun (Eds.), *Issues and trends in education for sustainable development* (pp. 39–59). UNESCO.

United Nations Economic Commission for Europe (UNECE). (n.d.). *Whole Institutional Approach (WIA) to ESD: Institutions as communities of transformational learning*. UNECE. https://unece.org/fileadmin/DAM/env/esd/14thMeet_SC/Doc/Presentations/STRAND_1_Whole_Institution_Approach_P.Pace.pdf

Zuboff, S. (2019). *The age of surveillance capitalism: The fight for a human future at the new frontier of power*. PublicAffairs.

Chapter 3
The Role of Geography Education in Sustainability in a Digital Age

Inga Gryl
University of Duisburg-Essen, Germany

ABSTRACT

This paper intends to illustrate the role of geography education concerning sustainability in a digital age. In current everyday life, (non-)sustainability and digitalization are closely linked to each other, including societal issues beyond technology and ecology. For instance, digitalization may be a key to solve certain sustainability problems and is the source for challenges to sustainability at the same time. Geography education has both strong links with an education for digitalization and with an education for sustainable development. Therefore, it is an ideal learning environment to teach about the complexity of the linkages between both fields, and the necessity of thinking them together. Alongside with specific thematic examples for the classroom this chapter provides a number of didactic approaches that are a starting point to design subject-oriented classroom settings, appropriate to the complexity of the issue, and aimed at an emancipatory education for sustainable development.

INTRODUCTION

In 2018, a youth movement emerged that gained visibility due to its physical presence – and absence. Following the example of Greta Thunberg, a remarkable number of youngsters decided to use one of the rare weapons their generation has: cutting school time to demonstrate for climate protection, thus, breaking the institutional regulations of socialization that adults have set for them. Empty classrooms should convince adults to reflect on their role in the global catastrophe of climate change. Furthermore, they should also reflect on their demands towards the youngsters in contrast to the world they have prepared for them. The school strike symbolized a deep intergenerational conflict on the mistakes young generations convincingly claim adults are responsible for. During the Corona pandemic, the school strike weapon was blunted, but the struggle went on with active web and social media communication. Hashtags, tweets,

DOI: 10.4018/978-1-7998-5033-5.ch003

and images kept the discourse alive (at least more than it would have been without those communication channels), particularly at a time the world was facing pressing crises such as old and new wars. Using social media, and thus, digitalization, for participatory issues is nothing new. However, this example, among many others, illustrates that the pursuit of sustainable development goals and digitalization meet at several points. However, they can also clash with many others.

Both digitalization and sustainability are complex concepts, full of promises and problems. Sustainability will help to shape human-human and human-environmental relations in a way that assures global justice and preserves the world for future generations, working to stop and compensate for the overexploitation of the Anthropocene. However, sustainability cannot fulfill all promises of reaching economic prosperity, social equality, cultural protection and development, and ecological protection at the same time (Hasse 2006). Digitalization is a technological revolution that permeates every aspect of human life and comes with many side effects. For instance, Stalder (2017) illustrates the social consequences and changed everyday practices in his reflections on *The digital condition* (A *Culture of digitality*) (e.g. support and control of human actions by algorithms). Digitalization can also be a part of the technological solution for certain problems around sustainability, for instance, aiming at digital education, dislocated communication, and efficient production and distribution. With this, resources and energy might be saved and carbon dioxide production reduced. On the other side, digitalization comes with other side effects that challenge sustainability, in particular *accelerated* energy and resource usage. Thus, and as always, there is only a thin line between sustainability and non-sustainability. Didactically, both concepts face the problem of invisibility of their phenomena, which makes them difficult to comprehend: For instance, algorithms are a complex 'black box' while CO_2 cannot be 'seen'.

This paper reflects on the links between sustainability and digitalization in educational contexts. A certain emphasis is placed on geographical education as this subject has strong links to and roots in both concepts, and as both concepts have spatial linkages (e.g. bridging distances with digitalization; global impacts of unsustainability). The paper highlights different aspects of this complex relation. Firstly, the relation of sustainability and digitalization is analyzed briefly on an everyday basis, outside the educational context, to provide a background and subject knowledge basis and, as a sideline, examples that can be useful in class (2). Afterwards, the role of geography education concerning sustainability on the one side and digitalization on the other side is presented (3). Then, different approaches of geography education are presented that can be used to teach competences related to digitalization and sustainability in the classroom, using adequate examples from tech companies to overtourism (4). This chapter involves approaches aimed at teaching competences to reflect and analyze (un)sustainability, but also to act politically and participate in sustainability processes with the help of digital tools. Finally, additional pedagogical implications are sketched to enrich the conclusion and round-up the whole picture (5).

DIGITALIZATION: HOPES AND THREATS FOR SUSTAINABILITY

The Corona Pandemic has at least shown that mankind *can* – under certain circumstances – produce less carbon dioxide (Liu et al. 2022). A lot of the savings came from a shutdown of certain industries that caused significant economic backslash in some regions. But in everyday life, another factor was omnipresent: people were less mobile. Many did not fly away on vacation (and used local alternatives, when possible), and most importantly, many could work from home and were prevented from going to the office. Digital communication (mainly video conference applications), replaced personal meetings and connected colleagues around the corner as well as between continents. Notwithstanding the side effects of video conferences (not being able to make eye-contact, challenging replacement of spontaneous communication etc.) they seem to save ecological (and economical) costs of mobility. It is likely that at least a certain number of meetings will remain purely digital or at least hybrid – perhaps only for the reason that it saves a lot of money on traveling costs for firms and institutions.

However, this is just one side of the coin. Energy and infrastructure never come without side effects on sustainability. Video conferences, like all digital applications, need energy. While these apps require local hardware, the Internet servers also require large amounts of electricity to run and cool their systems. Different estimations are available: The Shift Project (cit. in: Parrisius 2019), for instance, estimates that all information and communication technology together produce 3,7% of the global carbon dioxide emissions – twice as much as civil aviation does. Companies such as Google claim that they are carbon neutral. However, this is currently only possible through investment in compensation programs. Renewable energy won't run all Google's systems before 2030 (Clifford 2022). Furthermore, there are extremely energy-consuming applications on the web, such as blockchain technologies, crypto currencies and, last but not least, streaming services. Streaming alone makes up 80% of the Internet's data traffic, resulting in a carbon dioxide production comparable to Spain (Parrisius 2019). When one uses a smart home, the usage of all the devices on the Wi-Fi network might consume more energy than energy saved through smart heating regulation and light management (Parrisius 2019). An autonomous driving car produces 3 to 5 GB of data per second, resulting in remarkable energy costs (Parrisius 2019) – which is one of the limitations of these technologies that basically could promise a more rational distribution of individual travel by limiting the number of cars needed, when they can navigate autonomously towards the next user.

Additionally, digitalization requires hardware. In a market-driven economy where software updates often require hardware updates, and gadgets are a symbol of lifestyle, sustainability is not yet at the center. Computer hardware is made from materials that are difficult to acquire, such as rare earths and minerals. The conditions of production are often both unfair and unecological: The example of a simple computer mouse whose developers have set the target of creating a sustainably and fairly produced product shows how difficult this undertaking actually is (Nager IT 2022). In contrast, e-waste is delicate to recycle and waste exports to other countries illustrate how the problem is shifted on a global dimension. Although technology is partly helpful to become more sustainable, history has shown that not everything that is possible is realized on a market level. This is because interests may be affected (c.f. profit and jobs in the automobile industry) – and, in some cases, side effects may occur that are difficult to predict to their full extent (e.g. the impact of wind power plants on certain bird species). Furthermore, there are highly innovative concepts that further push the possibilities of technology and, at the same time, come with massive consequences in different fields of sustainability. Star Link is an example of such an issue. With tens of thousands of satellites in the earth's orbit, Star Link brings internet connection to every corner of the earth. In a highly digitalized world, internet access is particularly valuable in remote and poorly developed regions (and was also recently used to support Ukrainian forces in the war). However, rocket launches obviously produce a lot of carbon dioxide, and the satellites' space debris (seeing as they only have a limited life span) is a threat to unmanned and manned space travel for future generations, with effects on current and future technologies that might play their own role in the complex (un)sustainability system.

The view of sustainability has widened. When discourse around sustainability first emerged, it was mainly an ecological-economical problem related to forestry. Later social-ecological and social problems were included, putting the term justice on the agenda, and resulting in a broader range of issues:

For instance, video conferences may not only limit ecological costs of mobility, but *may* also have an – positive or negative – impact on gender equality by providing options or bringing up new challenges for the compatibility of (family) care work and careers (Lott 2019). A further look at the United Nations' SDGs supports this broadening of perspectives (e.g. gender equality, quality education) that can be also linked to societal issues of digitalization.

THE ROLE OF GEOGRAPHY EDUCATION CONCERNING SUSTAINABILITY UND DIGITALIZATION

Geography Education and Sustainability

The last paragraph has shown that sustainability is a highly interdisciplinary issue, one that requires endeavors from all fields and subject areas. Consequently, when it comes to education, no subject can claim sustainability as their own. Rather, all subjects need to take their part and look for links with one another. Nevertheless, geography education plays a fruitful and important role towards sustainability education (Haubrich et al. 2007; Gryl et al. 2016; DGfG 2020).

In school, Geography is mainly regarded as an interdisciplinary subject. Concerning the discipline, the gap between physical and human geography is remarkable, which also has an influence on the school subject. For instance, Kersting (2015) reflects on the theoretical and methodological limitations of integrating approaches. However, in the Anthropocene, an era in that humans change the world irreversibly, there is a strong need for integrating research, and with environmental and problem-orientation at school, the subsequent challenges need to be subject of teaching and learning. One of the earlier supporters of this practice was the educational theorist Klafki (2007) with his notion of *key problems* (which are, among others, maintaining peace, environment, human rights, democracy, transl. by author) that should be an environmentally-relevant starting point for learning. Beyond ancient, encyclopedic or dichotomous approaches to the human-environment-relations in geography education, systemic approaches have proven to be fruitful to handle such (key) problems in educational settings. Thus, one of the basic concepts of geography education is the term *system* (DGfG 2020). As a result, geography education is a core subject for education for sustainable development, as the Luzern Declaration on Education for Sustainable Development and others underline (Haubrich et al. 2007).

Systemic approaches as used in geography have a strong advantage. Firstly, they uncover causalities and contingencies in sustainability problems. Secondly, they allow a shift from a solely individually-centered perspective on parts of sustainability education: For a long time, education and particularly ESD has been focusing on teaching young people how to become responsible, conscientious but dutiful citizens. This practice may lead to an overload, but also to a lack of understanding and outright rejection when they realize the failure of adults' and older generations to act sustainably (Hasse 2006). A compensatory personal responsibility (Bröckling 2007), to name only one of the critics on ESD, is a seemingly easy but ineffective way to teach education for sustainability when the world stays unsustainable at the same time. In contrast to systemic approaches, it will not necessarily result in people who act in a sustainable manner on a larger scale in their future lives.

Related to the focus on the systemic approach, different concepts of space (Massey 1998; Wardenga 2002) also contribute to the role of geography education in the field of education for sustainable development. On the level of absolute (Euclidian) space, geography works on different, interconnected local and global spatial scales, which is particularly meaningful in understanding the global impact of unsustainability. Regarding socially constructed space, geography helps to illustrate how the construction of meaning based on power imbalances and interests may lead to seemingly irrational and unsustainable actions (e.g. automobile industry and lobbying influences on policy, supported by parts of the public). Hence, education for sustainable development is not only about human-environment relations, but also about relations between people in society. Thus, it is about political education including a normative background, e.g. regarding the central term of justice and the ability to participate beyond conventional paths.

Boehn's and Hamann's (2011) research illustrates that this dimension was, at least in Germany, not yet the focus in those days. In their analysis of lesson plans, sustainable development education was mainly focused on ecology without a focus on the economic and social (and cultural) aspects of sustainability. With the renewal of SDGs in 2016 including aims such as gender equality, the social realm of sustainability was strengthened, leading to adequate educational endeavors (UNESCO 2017). This also supports approaches such as "emancipatory education for sustainable development" (Pettig 2021). This approach enables students to not only rationally understand sustainability issues and potential solutions, it also allows for a reflection of the tensions and contradictions between and within SDGs and involved actors with their interests and power relations, and thus supports a political subject in an emancipated manner (Mitchell 2018).

Geography education has, starting from general critical thinking, a number of methods and approaches that can support such an emancipatory education for sustainable development, such as political ecology, actor networks, aesthetic approaches, and multi-perspective, holistic thinking, and inter- and transdisciplinary thinking (Bojie 2020). It also supports subject matter related approaches such as the syndrome concept and climate change education. The Luzern Declaration also names information and communication technologies as an important contribution for education in sustainable development. Haubrich et al. (2007, 248-249) argue that those technologies help a.o. "to acquire up-to-date knowledge easily, to compare contradicting information, (…) to gain direct insight into the attitudes and perspectives of people who are personally affected by issues of sustainability, (…) to visualize multidimensional environmental issues related to sustainable development." This follows a certain tradition of geography education aimed at using digital technologies as a tool to improve learning. However, today's story of digitalization in geography education is more complex than ever before.

Geography Education and Digitalization

Nowadays, geography education identifies itself as a subject interwoven with digitalization (HGD 2020), which many other subjects do too. However, there are some good arguments for this.

Geography education has a long tradition of including digital technologies into its curriculum. Since the 1990s Geographic Information Systems, (GIS) have been part of geography education on the secondary level, mainly in order to teach methodological competences that might be fruitful for a geospatial workforce that had and has an increasing importance in many fields of industry (science, administration, planning, logistics, trading etc.). GIS allow us to model spaces beyond the map, to collect and sort data spatially and to quantify spatial relations in order to optimize allocations and mobility. However, they are still complicated to navigate and the challenge to become fluent in their usage might – in the limited time of geography classes – even cover up the geographical problems one would like to teach using GIS.

Nevertheless, GIS have increasingly become the backbone of everyday digitalization. While it remains barely visible to the user, it plays a key role in a vast amount of mobile internet applications. Navigation services, car sharing, delivery services and even dating platforms use the base of an underlying GIS that is fed with the users' big data. Furthermore, political analysis, insurance calculation, police work, infrastructural planning – and its everyday consequences – all require GIS. Social media is also highly related to space, as the *instagramability* of places, discussed on social media illustrates (meaning the potential of a place to be photogenic). At the same time, social media picks up and creates worlds in a manner of everyday constructions of spaces (Kanwischer & Schlottmann 2017). Everyday geospatial technology applications (e.g. navigation apps, webmapping, augmented reality) have led to a broader focus of geography education on digitalization. More specifically, they have resulted in a broader focus regarding the geospatial world as a topic of education, as an environment to learn about geographies and as an everyday condition where one requires adequate competences to overcome challenges. Simple geo-communication systems that are much more user-friendly than complex GIS provide chances to participate via the simple usage of geospatial technologies (Gryl & Jekel 2012) and simultaneously highlight the challenges concerning the opaque backend of human-made algorithms (Dorsch 2022).

There are several models to sort the relations of the subject of geography and digitalization. Beginning with GIS competences (Milson et al. 2012) to *learning about, with, and through geomedia* (Schulze & Gryl 2022) to a recent model (Pettig & Gryl, in press) that identifies three cornerstones and integrates several didactical approaches: (a) geographical learning with, about and through digital media, (b) digital geographies as subject knowledge, and (c) geographical education in digital media. (a) Means teaching geographical knowledge with the help of geotechnologies, teaching digitally-related competences, and gaining personal competences (such as reflection), preferably all at the same time. It is a competence-oriented view. (b) Refers to identifying the geographical dimensions of digitalization and analyzing them as geographical phenomena. As geography education is closely related to contemporary issues, new topics such as smart cities and gig economy have to find their way into the curriculum. This view is content-oriented. (c) Is a dimension that clearly goes beyond digitally-related competences of usage, as Jörissen and Marotzki (2009) claim in their structural media education. With life-structuring and life-changing impacts, digitalization is an issue in education that helps the subject to find its way between appropriation and alienation to shape its individual self-world relations in the most emancipated way possible. This viewpoint is pedagogically and educationally centered.

A DIGITALLY ROOTED GEOGRAPHY EDUCATION FOR SUSTAINABILITY

As the previous section has shown, when it comes to education for sustainable development and education in a culture of digitality, geography education aims at different sets of competences as well as education beyond. The following section presents four examples that utilize four approaches from geography education – immanent critique, political ecology, viral construction of space, spatial citizenship – in order to link the fields within geography learning and show how inseparably connected sustainability issues and digitalization are.

E-Mobility in Cities: Immanent Contradictions

E-mobility, a product of technological progress involving innovative hardware such as electric engines and powerful batteries, and compatible steering software, is regarded as a solution for the remarkable amounts of carbon dioxide and fine dust that is produced by conventional individual traffic. Therefore, the e-mobility economy as well as individual customers are supported politically with subsidies in several states around the world. The interlinking of technology, everyday social practices of mobility, environmental impact, policymaking and the observation of transformation processes makes e-mobility a great topic for geography and sustainability education.

It becomes even more valuable when a learning environment discussing this topic considers the side effects that can be made visible by immanent critique (Jaeggi 2014). Immanent critique is a form of critique that not only criticizes a certain situation as contradicting external or internal norms (offense against environmental law, for instance), but also identifies the paradoxes within a norm (Lehner et al. in press). It uncovers the ambivalences and conflicts of sustainable solutions, showing the sustainable and unsustainable sides at the same time. In the case of e-mobility, it is not only the production and disposal of batteries and the origin of the electric power used that raise certain questions, but also the side effects of the often unquestioned background of individual mobility. Thus, immanent critique widens the view and encourages students to question underlying conditions. One important method is to find contrary terms to normalized ones (e.g. personal freedom of mobility – limitations to others, traffic jam etc.). Cars don't only raise questions about emissions, but also questions about space, which makes them a particular geographical issue. E-mobility does not solve the problem of a car-friendly rather than pedestrian-friendly city. Pedestrians and cyclists are still in a space-usage conflict with cars and are still in danger of being involved in accidents. Individual cars require so much space for moving and parking that, even if the air quality is better without emissions, surfaces are still sealed up and green areas remain limited. This results in a lower quality of life, overheating in cities, less carbon dioxide decomposition and less space for other pressing issues such as housing (Lehner et al. in press). Methodologically, immanent critique enables students to question the seemingly normal, identify different forms of critique, and encourages teachers to be transparent with paradoxes in the subject matter as well as in sustainability issues that reflect the complexity of the world.

Greenwashing in Tech-Companies: Political Ecology

Apple is famous for its up-to-date innovations regarding gadgets for end users. Part of their business model is the mass-like releases of new products that enforce the users' belief that they really need the newest visionary products to be part of the digital avant-garde. Though this is a motor for innovation, it is also undoubtedly an unsustainable strategy. Therefore, Apple dedicates a certain amount of effort to transparently communicate its struggle for sustainability. As transparent as this may seem, is also profitable to maintain an image of a green company. An Apple environmental report from 2014 (cit. in Wölbert 2014) used green pie charts to show that the company's offices and servers run on green energy, which makes up 30% of its total emissions. The report does not say anything about the 70% emissions of the manufacturing part. A report on Heise (Wölbert 2014) illustrates that production is mainly located with subcontractors in China that rely 97% on fossil fuels. Later, Apple announced that they will sell their new iPhones without headphones or power adapters. They claimed that this would save resources, avoid e-waste, and require less space for transportation and thus lower carbon dioxide emissions (Calma

2020). While they were not necessarily wrong, it was also the perfect strategy to increase profit margins as they began to sell accessories separately. Recently, links between the company and stakeholders and groups that lobby against a climate saving policy have become public, highly contradicting the firm's official communication (Költzsch 2022). Apple's strategy can be subsumed under the term greenwashing (Emrich 2015), referring to corporate practices (often related to marketing on social media) that use the guise of sustainability to hide greater problems of unsustainability within a company, and even interests related to unsustainability.

Political ecology (Krings 2018) is an approach that can help in understanding actor networks and actors' interests as the basis for their actions in sustainable and unsustainable processes. The main idea behind the approach is that an environmental analysis has to be enriched with a social analysis. Environmental problems are always reshaped by social constructions, and the environment is regarded as a "battlefield of divergent interests" (Krings 2008, 8, transl. by author). Political ecology uses a multitude of theories and methods (to name a few. actor-centered analysis, discourse theory, field studies etc.) and addresses different dimensions of those problems. It includes symptoms of unsustainability as well as the power relations and inequalities between actors and institutions. In the case of greenwashing, compatible and conflicting interests are to be analyzed in the classroom, e.g. with a simulation game after searching the press and social media for different perspectives on green(washing) marketing. Average customers require sustainable products in coherence with their own conscientiousness and the law, but also want to consume at a reasonable price and style. The company seeks to fulfill the sustainability requirements of policy and the market (one can only speculate about the main decision makers' personal interest in sustainability, but the indicated closeness to particular groups at least illustrates a certain ambivalence) but also tries to keep costs low and profit margins high. Contributing subcontractors keep to their *local* political standards concerning sustainability (and probably also of social 'wellbeing' of workers), and Apple profits from their limited costs within those long-established structures. One of the main challenges is that interests, particularly those that are unpopular, are often not communicated openly and remain covered (Emrich 2015), as this greenwashing example illustrates. Thus, a careful analysis of different sources as well as a deconstruction of actors' limited communication is necessary in order to identify (un)sustainable interests and processes.

Insta-Triggered Over Tourism: Viral Construction of Spaces

The construction of spaces (Werlen 1993) is a classical approach in geographical analysis and is also more or less established in geography education. It refers to the attribution of meaning to physical spaces based on everyday action and communication. Those meanings structure further action (by defining socially accepted action), institutionalize spaces and make other meanings less visible. While physical conditions set a certain benchmark for action, social constructions limit it even more while triggering certain practices. When it comes to digital communication on the internet and on social media, a new form of the production of space emerges: the viral construction of space (Kanwischer & Schlottmann 2017).

Pictures of places are shared via social media and commented on with stories and hashtags on platforms such as Instagram. Photo angles, filters and suitable texts construct new worlds full of meanings and feelings the students can analyze using these categories. On Instagram, the main form of communication portrays positive feelings and aesthetics. These new worlds have a certain link to the physical place but are also independent new constructions, creating a bridge between the physical location and imagination. The image and the construction may be shared and altered on the web, creating a vague, limited, idealistic idea of what it is like at a certain place. Furthermore, this construction is also relevant to the construction of the identity of those who have made it there and who share the image. The term *viral* illustrates that some meanings are spread vastly and quickly thanks to social media (Kanwischer & Schlottmann 2017). However, even if the construction has gained a life of its own on the web, consequences have a physically-bound component as well. The images, still linked with hashtags and/or coordinates to a certain location, trigger people to include those spots into their range of mobility and to travel and see the places with their own eyes. Finally, they produce and communicate their own, often quite similar, photographs with slight alterations to illustrate their individuality. The web "is part of the world and provider of the world, too" (Kanwischer & Schlottmann 2017, 63, transl. by author) and at the same time, the meanings cannot be separated between physical action and online communication. The term "socially hyped locations" (Paul, in press) illustrates the potential consequences. Many Instagram-highlighted spots such as the Königsbach pools in the German Alps face serious overtourism which is, among others, triggered by viral communication on the web that makes the images iconic (Merkle 2021). The reproduction and communication of those pictures, often supplemented with one's own face and body, becomes desirable for many. Overtourism, a form of mass tourism a place is not prepared for, however, is a condition with widely unsustainable dimensions, including emissions of mobility, waste, degradation, and the disturbance of wildlife. This example is particularly interesting not only to let students analyze social media communication but also to include their own experiences and let them reflect on their own social media spatial constructions.

Web Communication With Fridays for Future and Others: Spatial Citizenship

As mentioned in the introduction, an important pillar of Fridays for Future is web communication. It is used to organize protests, mobilize protesters and to communicate their message to a wider audience, including public and political stakeholders. As the concept of the viral construction of spaces highlights, social media communication can be a powerful and potentially far-reaching tool. Concerning geography, the approach of spatial citizenship (Gryl & Jekel 2012) is an educational program that enables competences which are useful to such geomedia web communication platforms. The approach was established to shift the focus from complex GIS usage to the utilization of simple web mapping in order to enable everybody to communicate spatially without technical barriers that might cover the social realm or hinder its communication. In recent years, forms of usable geomedia have increased and go beyond the map image, and now include pictures and hashtags, too. Spatial citizenship consists of the deconstruction of limited spatial communications (such as greenwashing maps, or posts of seemingly green production plants), based on powerful constructions of space. It also enables us to communicate alternative forms of geomedia (e.g. contrasting images and new hashtags that uncover unsustainable practices, suggesting options for more sustainable practices, and organizing protests as in Fridays for Future) and to negotiate new constructions with other forms of web communication. The last point is particularly important because the complexity of sustainability problems requires interdisciplinary knowledge. At this, students can use existing collaborative mapping platforms (e.g. ReUse Revolution, Wheelmap) or create their own map (e.g. umap) or social media communication to inform others about unsustainability issues. In-depth competencies to communicate adequately and successfully (e.g. sharing stories, using hashtags, addressing media and experts) can be tried and learnt while doing so.

CONCLUSION

Geography education is a subject with a high potential to link education with both sustainability and digitalization. It has the capacity to include both fields as subject matter on a meta level, and at the same time supports corresponding competences. However, both digitalization and sustainability involve remarkable challenges, requiring an emancipatory approach to education. Digitalization comes with a promising potential to solve environmental problems and to push us all into an ever-developing future, but also comes with many side effects concerning surveillance, privacy issues, marketing strategies, and limitations to sustainability. Sustainability is complex as well, marked by the corners of the sustainability rectangle and the conflicting interests that tug at them. The complexity includes side effects such as communication strategies to obscure interests (c.f. greenwashing). If we want to enable students to contribute to a sustainable society – not only on a level of personal responsibility, but also as political subjects – and if we want them to use technology in a sustainable manner, we have to teach a number of competences, particularly emancipatory competences as mentioned above. Emancipatory education for sustainable development, immanent critique, spatial citizenship and other concepts are all necessary in bringing about meaningful sustainable change – but we have to go even further into general pedagogical fields as the following section illustrates.

An "mature-oriented education" (Mündigkeit) by Dorsch (2022, based on Adorno 1971) is closely linked to the structural media education by Jörissen and Marotzki (2009), which relates it to the third corner of the model of Pettig & Gryl (2023) and an emancipatory ESD. It addresses the importance of the interlinkages between the self and the world when it comes to (media) education. Only then, learners can understand interests involved in sustainability and reflect on the responsibilities of different actors, including themselves. Dorsch defines three dimensions of maturity: reflection/reflexivity, being aware of oneself, and autonomy. The upper examples – except spatial citizenship – place a certain emphasis on reflection/reflexivity in order to gain in-depth-insights into sustainability issues. Concerning self-awareness, we can add additional approaches from practice. Hintermann et al. (2018) reflect with students on digitalization and social media issues related to their construction of identity, particularly the role of social media in constructing views on the self and the planet as highly important. This must be part of educational reflection, with the aim of empowering students while remaining critical towards unhealthy structures (c.f. facebook papers). Mohring and Brendel (in press) reflect on the necessity of awareness when it comes to digitally mediated communication and learning (for instance in VR). When one is aware of the impact and distinctiveness of such digitally permeated experiences, they can then assess and classify the gained insights related to human-environmental relations and understand the complexity of the connection between the self and sustainability. Autonomy is a component that stands in certain contrast to institutionalized educational systems, but should rather be one of its aims. It refers mainly to the actions and practices of students, and their decision to start, share, or reject certain (perhaps unsustainable) actions. With the action-oriented component, it can be linked to the spatial citizenship approach named above. Furthermore, autonomy has a strong, multidimensional moral component that intervenes with self-awareness and reflexivity.

Thus, Geography education needs to be enriched with emancipatory perspectives when it comes to competences additional to and beyond subject knowledge on sustainability and digitalization. To gain these competences, we need to actively and closely involve students in the learning processes, especially when those processes become less transparent due to ed-tech options such as adaptive learning environments (Allen et al. 2016). We as teachers need to talk with the learners about the negative consequences of inequality, surveillance, limited terms of education, and the potential benefits of measurability and adaptability by KI in learning contexts. We need to learn and teach to negotiate openly with them on ways to gain emancipation and balances between personal autonomy, participation, eligible interests, justice and a sustainable planet. Therefore, an education that combines deep systemic knowledge and one that is taught at eye-level with those who inherit urgent sustainability challenges as current and future actors is absolutely necessary. This might enable students to stand up against unsustainable practices, utilize digitalization to fight for sustainability, and feel the impact of their personal options and responsibility.

REFERENCES

Adorno, T. W. (1971). *Erziehung zur Mündigkeit. Vorträge und Gespräche mit Hellmut Becker*. Suhrkamp.

Allen, M., Webb, A. W., & Matthews, C. E. (2016). Adaptive teaching in STEM: Characteristics for effectiveness. *Theory into Practice*, *55*(3), 217–224. doi:10.1080/00405841.2016.1173994

Boehn, D., & Hamann, B. (2011). Approaches to sustainability. Examples from geography textbook analysis in Germany. *European Journal of Geography*, *2*(1). http://www.eu-rogeographyjournal.eu/articles/2_1_APPROACHES%20TO%20SUSTAINABILITY_BOEHN_HAMANN.pdf

Bojie, F. (2020). Promoting Geography for Sustainability. *Geography and Sustainability*, *2020*(1), 1–7.

Bröckling, U. (2007). *Das unternehmerische Selbst: Soziologie einer Subjektivierungsform* [The entrepreneurial self: Sociology of a form of subjectivation]. Suhrkamp.

Calma, J. (2020). Apple ditching chargers saves costs but not the planet. *The Verge*. https://www.theverge.com/2020/10/16/21519466/apple-iphone-12-chargers-airpods-greenhouse-gas-emissions-e-waste

Cliffford, C. (2022). How Google plans to use 100% carbon-free energy in its data centers by 2030. *CNBC*. https://www.cnbc.com/2022/04/13/google-data-center-goal-100percent-green-energy-by-2030.html

DGfG (Deutsche Gesellschaft für Geographie) (2020). *Bildungsstandards im Fach Geographie für den mittleren Schulabschluss [Educational standards in the subject of geography for the middle school graduation]*. DGfG.

Dorsch, C. (2022). *Mündigkeit und Digitalität: E-Portfolioarbeit in der geographischen Lehrkräftebildung (= Praxis Neue Kulturgeographie, 16) [Maturity and Digitality: E-Portfolio in geography teacher education (= Praxis of New Cultural Geography, 16)]*. Lit.

Emrich, C. (2015). *Nachhaltigkeits-Marketing-Management. Konzept, Strategien, Beispiele* [Sustainability Marketing Management. Concept, strategies, examples]. De Gryter. doi:10.1515/9783110376302

Gryl, I., & Jekel, T. (2012). Re-centering geoinformation in secondary education: Toward a spatial citizenship approach. *Cartographica*, *47*(1), 18–28. doi:10.3138/carto.47.1.18

Gryl, I., Schlottmann, A., & Kanwischer, D. (2016). Mensch:Umwelt:System. Zur Einbettung naturwissenschaftlichen Lernens. [Human:Environment:System. On the embedding of science learning] In K.-H. Otto (Ed.), *Geographie und naturwissenschaftliche Bildung – Der Beitrag des Fachs für Schule, Lernlabor und Hochschule* [Geography and science education – The subject's contribution to school, learning lab and university]. (pp. 188–205). Monsenstein und Vannerdat.

Hasse, J. (2006). Bildung für Nachhaltigkeit statt Umweltbildung? Starke Rhetorik – schwache Perspektiven. [Education for sustainability instead of environmental education? Strong rhetoric – weak perspectives] In B. Hiller & M. Lange (Eds.), *Bildung für nachhaltige Entwicklung. Perspektiven für die Umweltbildung (= Vorträge und Studien. Zentrum für Umweltforschung der Westfälischen Wilhelms-Universität, 16)* [Education for Sustainable Development. Perspectives for Environmental Education (= Lectures and Studies. Centre for Environmental Research of the Westphalian Wilhelms University, 16)]. (pp. 29–43). Zentrum für Umweltforschung.

Haubrich, H., Reinfried, S., & Schleicher, Y. (2007). Lucerne Declaration on Geographical Education for Sustainable Development. In S. Reinfried, Y. Schleicher, & A. Rempfler (Eds.), *Geographical Views on Education for Sustainable Development (= Geographiedidaktische Forschungen, 42)* [Geography education research, 42]. (pp. 243–250). HGD.

HGD. (2020). *Der Beitrag des Fachs Geographie zur Bildung in einer durch Digitalisierung und Mediatisierung geprägten Welt. Positionspapier des Hochschulverbands für Geographiedidaktik (HGD) e.V. [The contribution of the subject of geography to education in a world shaped by digitalisation and mediatisation. Position paper of the Association for Geography Education (HGD) e.V.]* Geographie Didaktik. https://geographiedidaktik.org/download/der-beitrag-des-fachs-geographie-zur-bildung-in-einer-durch-digitalisierung-und-mediatisierung-gepraegten-welt/

Hintermann, C., Bergmeister, F., Kessel, V., Pichler, H., & Raithofer, D. (2018). Hybride Identitaten im Kopf. Nachlese zur Abschlussveranstaltung des Sparkling Science Projekts MiDENTITY [Hybrid identities on the mind. Follow-up to the closing event of the Sparkling Science project MiDENTITY]. *GW-Unterricht*, *1*(151), 59–62. doi:10.1553/gw-unterricht151s59

Jaeggi, R. (2014). *Kritik von Lebensformen* [Critique of life forms]. Suhrkamp.

Jorissen, B., & Marotzki, W. (2009). *Medienbildung – Eine Einführung: Theorie – Methoden – Analysen* [Media Education - An introduction: theory - methods – analyses]. UTB. doi:10.36198/9783838531892

Kanwischer, D., & Schlottmann, A. (2017). Virale Raumkonstruktionen – Soziale Medien und Mündigkeit im Kontext gesellschaftswissenschaftlicher Medienbildung [Viral constructions of space – social media and maturity in the context of social science media education]. *Zeitschrift für Didaktik der Gesellschaftswissenschaften*, *8*(2), 60–78. doi:10.46499/979.1232

Kersting, P. (2015). Ein kritischer Überblick systemtheoretisch geprägter Ansätze in der Geographie [A critical overview of system theoretical approaches in geography]. In I. Gryl, A. Schlottmann, & D. Kanwischer (Eds.): Mensch:Umwelt:System. Theoretische Grundlagen und praktische Beispiele für den Geographieunterricht [Human:Environment:System. Theoretical foundations and practical examples for geography education] (43-60). Lit.

Klafki, W. (2007). *Neue Studien zur Bildungstheorie und Didaktik: Zeitgemäße Allgemeinbildung und kritisch-konstruktive Didaktik [New studies in educational theory and didactics: Contemporary general education and critical-constructive didactics]*. Beltz.

Költzsch, T. (2022). Apple soll klimafeindliche Gruppierungen unterstützen [Apple is said to support anti-climate groups]. *Golem.de.* https://www.golem.de/news/greenwashing-apple-soll-klimafeindliche-gruppierungen-unterstuetzen-2206-165818.html

Krings, T. (2008). Politische Ökologie. Grundlagen und Arbeitsfelder eines geographischen Ansatzes der Mensch-Umwelt-Forschung [Political Ecology. Basics and fields of a geographical approach of human-environment research]. *Geographische Rundschau*, *60*(12), 4–9.

Lehner. (n.d). Widersprüche und Ambivalenzen als Impulse für eine Bildung für Nachhaltige Entwicklung. [Contradictions and ambivalences as impulses for an education for sustainability]. *GW Unterricht.*

Liu, Z., Deng, Z., Zhu, B., Ciais, P., Davis, S. J., Tan, J., Andrew, R. M., Boucher, O., Arous, S. B., Canadell, J. G., Dou, X., Friedlingstein, P., Gentine, P., Guo, R., Hong, C., Jackson, R. B., Kammen, D. M., Ke, P., Le Quéré, C, & Schellnhuber, H. J. (2022). Global patterns of daily CO2 emissions reductions in the first year of COVID-19. *Nature Geoscience*, *15*(8), 615–620. Advance online publication. doi:10.103841561-022-00965-8

Lott, Y. (2019). Weniger Arbeit, mehr Freizeit? [Less work, more leisure time?]. *WSI Report*, (47), 1–16.

Massey, D. (1998). Power geometries and the politics of space-time. Hettner Lectures, University of Heidelberg.

Merkle, J. (2021). Reisen für „Likes". Wie Instagram den Tourismus verändert. *Geographische Rundschau*, *2021*(1), 16–20.

Milson, A., Kerski, J., & Demirci, A. (2012). The world at their fingertips. GIS in secondary education. In A. Milson, J. Kerski, & A. Demirci (Eds.), *International Perspectives on Teaching and Learning with GIS in Secondary Schools* (pp. 1–11). Springer. doi:10.1007/978-94-007-2120-3_1

Mitchell, K. (2018). *Making Workers: Radical Geographies of Education*. Pluto Press.

Mohring, K., & Brendel, N. (in press). Erkenntnisse aus einer körpersensiblen Lehre mit und zu dem digitalen Medium VR – Potentiale für eine nachhaltigkeitsbezogene geographische Bildung. [Findings from a body-sensitive teaching with and about the digital medium VR – Potentials for a sustainability-related geographical education] In F. Pettig & I. Gryl (Eds.), *Geographische Bildung in einer Kultur der Digitalität* [Geographical education in a culture of digitality]. Springer.

Nager, I. T. (2022). *Die faire Maus. [The fair mouse]* https://www.nager-it.de/maus

Parrisius, A. (2019). Stromfresser Internet. Was unser Digitalkonsum an Energie kostet [Internet as an energy guzzler. What our digital consumption costs in energy]. *Tagesspiegel.* https://www.tagesspiegel.de/wirtschaft/stromfresser-internet-wie-viel-strom-wir-im-einzelnen-verbrauchen/25182828-2.html

Paul, J. (in press). Socially Hyped Locations. *Wochenschau.*

Pettig, F. (2021). Transformative Lernangebote kritisch-reflexiv gestalten. Fachdidaktische Orientierungen einer emanzipatorischen BNE [Designing transformative learning opportunities critically and reflectively. Subject didactic orientations of an emancipatory ESD]. *GW Unterricht*, *162*(2), 5–17. doi:10.1553/gw-unterricht162s5

Pettig, F., & Gryl, I. (in press). Diskursive Orientierungen geographischer Bildung in digitalen Kulturen. [Discursive orientations of geographical education in digital cultures] In F. Pettig & I. Gryl (Eds.), *Geographische Bildung in einer Kultur der Digitalität* [Geographical education in a culture of digitality]. Springer.

Schulze, U., & Gryl, I. (2022). Geographische Bildung in der digitalen Welt. Die digitale Transformation im Fokus der Geographiedidaktik - Theorie, Empirie, Praxis. [Geographical education in the digital world. The digital transformation in the focus of geography didactics - theory, empiricism, practice] In V. Frederking & R. Romeike (Eds.), *Fachliche Bildung im Zeichen von Digitalisierung, Big Data und KI* [Professional education under the sign of digitalisation, big data and AI]. (pp. 143–173). Waxmann.

Stalder, F. (2017). The digital condition. *Polity*.

UNESCO. (2017). *Education for Sustainable Development Goals. Learning Objectives*. UNESCO. https://www.unesco.de/sites/default/files/2018-08/unesco_education_for_sustainable_development_goals.pdf

Wardenga, U. (2002). Alte und neue Raumkonzepte für den Geographieunterricht [Old and new spatial concepts for geography education]. *Geographie heute, 23*(200), 8-11.

Werlen, B. (1993). *Society, action, and space: An alternative human geography*. Routledge.

Wölbert, C. (2014). Apple ist ganz groß im Greenwashing [Apple is big on greenwashing]. *Heise online*. https://www.heise.de/mac-and-i/meldung/Kommentar-Apple-ist-ganz-gross-im-Greenwashing-2253419.html

Chapter 4
Education for Sustainable Development and the Platform Society

Max Shatkin
Povolzhsky Institute of Management Named After P.A. Stolypin, RANEPA, Russia

ABSTRACT

The chapter explores the risks of the platform society to sustainability and how education for sustainability (ESD) can address these risks. The platform society is built on a business model that depends on network effects and user productivity. It, therefore, with the help of algorithms, bots, and AI, maintains the kind of content that can stimulate user engagement. This content is often related to the polarization of society, the deepening of political conflicts, and the diffusion of biased opinions. The response of ESD can be the concept of devalorisation of society, which means the orientation of the development of society toward the reduction of the ecological costs of human and social habitation. Pedagogical approaches that can embody the concept of devalorisation in ESD include the widespread use in teaching of triple bottom line, meta-analysis of social media information, elaboration of transition scenarios between different futures, and the nurturing of ecological solidarity.

INTRODUCTION

In the 2010s, the rapid proliferation of Internet platforms, defined as "more or less extensive, rule-based and strongly technically mediated social action spaces" (Dolata and Schrape, 2022), and their infiltration into all areas of society—economics, politics, health care, and also education—was an important stage in the organizational design of digitalization into a coherent architecture. Digital platforms, which require investments in hardware and software infrastructure for their development, are primarily an economic phenomenon. Scholars (Evans and Gawer, 2016; Rolf et al., 2022) define platforms as assemblages of digital and physical infrastructures, controlled by a firm, which intermediate transactions between discrete user groups (a 'multi-sided market') and depend on network effects: "platforms become more valuable as more users use them" (Evans and Gawer, 2016, p. 6). The expansion of digital platforms has been

DOI: 10.4018/978-1-7998-5033-5.ch004

correlated with the emergence of the so-called "gig economy" or "sharing economy" associated with new labor models. The fact that digital platforms are central to this new economy, and that the terms "gig economy" and "sharing economy" do not cover all forms of labor possible through platforms, led to the term "platform economy" (Nielsen et al. 2022).

However, platforms play a role in society far beyond economic interactions. They transform social practices and public values in culture (Nieborg and Poell, 2018), healthcare, public administration and also in education (van Dijck et al., 2018). The significant impact of online platforms on social structures and public values has been epitomized in the "controversial concept" of "platform society" (Ibid., pp. 2-3, 8, 21). Given the emerging nature of platform society, there is no universally accepted clear definition of the concept. Today, this concept is used in academic literature in competition with such concepts as "digital society" "information society" and "algorithmic society" (Schuilenburg and Peeters, 2020). The argument for the term "the platform society" over the above is that it reflects not only the prevailing technology of value creation and power, but also the model of social and economic interactions made possible by information (digital) technology. Based on the literature, the platform society (PS) can be briefly defined as a society in which private and public (state) digital platforms enable and make cheaper (through digital infrastructure), regulate (through algorithms), and extract political or economic profit from (through data collection and processing (Perrotta et al., 2020) any form of interaction and transaction between individuals, corporations, and public institutions.

Thus, the platform society is a society based on a consciously used business model, the key characteristics of which are cost reduction through the network effect and algorithmic regulation of social interactions. The dialectical contradiction at the core of the thus defined platform society is obvious: privately owned platforms support (including by reducing transaction costs) and regulate public processes, while public platforms collect information about citizens, which can be used in the private interests of politicians (or can be sold to private parties by corrupt officials). Meanwhile, the line between private and public interests in the platform society is more blurred than in previous stages and forms of human society. Platforms promote private interests under the banner of (but often at odds with) public values (van Dijck, 2020). This contradiction reaches not only social and economic relations, but also the values and goals of sustainable development. Platforms contribute to reducing the carbon footprint and the pollution of the environment (by the sharing economy), but at the same time, they have made possible a significant increase in individual consumption through the provision of global transactions that allow cheap goods to be ordered on the other side of the world. Platforms of the on-demand economy allow users to get cheap services and find part-time work, but this leads to an overall lower cost of labor and increased poverty.

Educational platforms significantly expand access to knowledge, but they also contribute to the commodification and privatization of knowledge, which has traditionally been seen as a public good. Social media can spread keywords (tags) related to the goals and values of sustainable development, but by making them "trendy," platforms contribute to their simplification and blurring of the original meaning. For example, under the influence of social networks for the last few years in the Russian language, the adjective "ecological" ("eco-friendly") has acquired the basic meaning of "polite", "balanced (style of communication)", "made with (good) taste". Finally, social media recommendation systems can help find like-minded people and address social and cultural needs, but they can also replace an individual's traditional socialization with constant immersion in engaging content (Gilbert et al., 2022, pp. 27-30) and thereby possibly reduce the individual's receptivity to the values and goals of sustainable development.

The contradictory impact of digital platforms on different domains of society, including sustainable development and education for sustainable development, is due to the following: Platforms, while embodying a specific business model of a multi-sided market regulated by private platform owners, are at the same time a tool for communications and transactions that can be used for almost any purpose, including sustainable development. The academic literature focuses mainly on the second side of this controversy, namely, how to use digital platforms as a tool to support democratic values and sustainable development (Guo et al., 2022). "If societies want to create a platform structure that reflects and constructs a democratic order, they need to strive to implement public values and collective interests in the ecosystem's design" (van Dijck, 2020, p.139).

However, despite the great opportunities that platforms offer to disseminate the ideas of sustainable development, collaborative consumption, and circular economy, platforms remain capitalist enterprises with their logic of growth. Nowadays, the first steps have been made in the academic literature to conceptualize a "platform theory" reflecting the main elements of the logic of the development of platforms as a business model (Gawer, 2021). Now, this theory does not reflect the issues of the impact of platforms on sustainable development. Meanwhile, understanding the risks of a platform society for achieving the Sustainable Development Goals (SDGs) is a prerequisite for constructing the goals and content of education for sustainable development in the platform society.

Thus, the main goal of this chapter is to explore how education for sustainable development can affect the transformation of the platform society in the context of reducing the latter's risks to sustainable development. Accordingly, this chapter proposes to discuss the following questions:

1) What risks does the emergence of the platform society entail for sustainable development?
2) How can education for sustainable development (ESD) influence the development of the platform society to make it more compatible with the goals of sustainable development?

METHODS

Currently, the platform society (as well as platform economy and platform capitalism) is in its early stages. Digital platforms, private and public, are in no hurry to share information about their organization, governance, and problems with the public. Therefore, despite the diversity of empirical and theoretical methods for studying the platform society, they can be reduced to a synthesis of two main methods: phenomenological methods (describing the experience of interaction and perception of users and society of digital platforms) and inductive methods (generalizing knowledge about platforms based on relatively few known facts). Given these circumstances—the infant state of platform society and limited information about its functioning—not all relationships and interdependencies between the various elements of platform society have been identified and theorized. For example, what is the connection between the business model of social media platforms and the fact that social media contributes to the involvement of civilians in military conflicts through the posting of information about combat encounters and troop movements?

To achieve the goals of our chapter, we will complement these methods by elaborating a scenario for the development of the platform society very soon through the extrapolation of current trends and current (2022) events. A key requirement for the scenario is to consider the development of artificial intelligence (AI) technologies, which are common to all kinds of platforms today. It is not our goal to systematically analyze the different aspects of the platform society, but only those that may become a threat to the achievement of sustainable development goals.

Further, it will be concluded about the general features of these threats, which will allow us to grasp that characteristic of the platform society, which produces risks for sustainable development. Accordingly, the content of ESD that responds to the threats of the platform society must be based on concepts that are the opposite of those on which the platform society is rooted. The next step is to discuss the concept that can affect minimizing the negative impact of platform society on sustainable development, and the pedagogical approaches through which this concept can be translated into curricula.

THE DEVELOPMENT OF THE PLATFORM SOCIETY: A SCENARIO FOR THE NEAR FUTURE

The inner logic of the platform society is determined by two key features of the business model of digital platforms (Sadowski, 2020): 1) the attractiveness of platforms for users is based on the ability of the former to significantly reduce the transaction costs of the latter; 2) since platforms extract rents from user actions and transactions and/or data about these transactions, platforms are interested in the continuous growth of these actions and transactions, i.e. user productivity, and growth of user numbers to achieve network effects.

Cusumano et al. (2019) identified two main types of platforms: transaction platforms and innovation platforms, as well as a hybrid type that combines features of both. Transaction platforms (Airbnb, Facebook, Alibaba, WeChat, etc.) facilitate exchange or transaction across sides; innovation platforms (Apple IOS, Steam. Google Android) facilitate innovation (i.e. creating new products) on the platform; hybrid platforms (Apple, Google, Microsoft) both provide tools for transactions of existing products and creating new ones. Today we should add to this list AI service platforms, which provide the ability to use pre-trained AI “models,” or to train user models (Sundberg and Holmström, 2022). Here, platforms act as a direct seller (service provider), since AI training requires significant computing power and training data, which are now being accumulated by platforms.

The specifics of the business model, according to which the cost of platforms is higher the more users it has and the more products (goods, services, content) they offer, make platforms depend on the productivity of users and the demand for the products they offer. And “productivity” includes not only creating content or offering goods and services, but also any user actions in the platform’s user interface that turn into data for AI learning (Perrotta et al., 2020). Therefore, it is justified to say that today the digital frontier offers platforms, and through platforms their users, machine learning and AI as a performance boosting tool.

In the proposed scenario, the platform society evolves as a set of several global, pervasive platforms that integrate different forms of social and economic activity of individuals. The constant growth of transactions processed by the platforms requires increasingly intelligent systems for regulating user behavior. The following phenomena are regulated: 1) relationships between users (stimulating interest in interacting with each other, limiting toxic content, etc.); 2) user productivity (facilitating the creation of new content using AI); 3) user activity (continually offering them engaging content, including AI-generated content). The key direction of platform development is the transition from interfaces on laptop screens and mobile devices to three-dimensional virtual worlds, “metaverses” (Dwivedi et al., 2022), where users get additional tools to influence the external environment — “superpowers” (Strickland,

2022). Metaverses created nowadays do not fully reproduce reality: some cut off lower body parts to avoid their indecent use, and others cut off images and phenomena that do not fit the ideological picture of the world (Gandolfo and Hamilton, 2022). Instead of solving social, environmental, and also educational problems, metaverses create spaces that are immersive in terms of form, but distorted in terms of content, supporting the illusion that these problems do not exist or are easily solved with virtual superpowers.

Metaverses, like their predecessors—social media and trading platforms—are depending on the network effect: their competitiveness is determined by the number of users and their activity. Accordingly, the main challenge in the development of metaverses will be the continued expansion of the physical space adapted for immersive connection to the virtual one. This will naturally lead to an emphasis on the technocratic tasks of filling the planet's surface with a new generation of technological devices. Correspondingly, the development of the platform society requires a growth in the output of the traditional industry. This will increase the technogenic burden on the environment through the greater need for energy for these devices, rare earth minerals for their production, and the filling of the biosphere with new alien elements. The uneven global distribution of production of chips and batteries for digital devices increases their value as instruments of geopolitical confrontation, and facilitates, on the one hand, opportunities for indirect conflicts and economic pressure, and, on the other hand, calls for the construction of excess productive forces to ensure the security of regional economies.

Social media stimulate user engagement through personalized recommendations of those people, communities, and ideas that users are expected to be interested in from their prior preferences. This leads to echo chambers in which users encounter only those opinions that they support, and the polarization and radicalization of opinions (Haroon et al., 2022). Extrapolating this trend to future metaverse environments, where an unlimited number of "rooms" can be created, this polarization will be intensified through the filtering of visual content, which will reduce the diversity of the user's perceived world. For example, the prohibition of creating full-length avatars to avoid objectionable actions may prevent people with disabilities, who move around in wheelchairs in real life, from reflecting their features in the virtual environment.

Currently, social media and some users use bots to increase the presence of a topic in the information space. Training increasingly skillful AI models capable of having seemingly meaningful dialogue, and potentially visualizing bots in metaverse would give platforms a more powerful tool to force their agenda. Early on, platforms claimed to unite people around the world. However, unlike oceans and open seas, which give room for movement and food for representatives of all views and political systems, platforms claiming global distribution are not neutral. They follow the goals and values of their societies and political parties and, in the case of geopolitical conflicts, tend to support only one side, depriving the other side of the opportunity to make its point. This has led to the banning of certain social media platforms that support the views of Western society in some countries. The result has been an artificial increase in the value of certain content (ideas, news, people, products) that is proclaimed to be true only because it reflects the interests of one of the opposing sides.

Given that in the platform society interactions between people from different parts of the world are enabled by platforms, reciprocal actions by states and platforms to limit each other's ability to broadcast their ideas lead to the fragmentation of the platform society into several clusters that interact poorly with each other. Given the tendency of platforms to polarize opinions, the disappearance of platforms' ability to express certain ideas (deplatformization, van Dijck et al., 2021) and the intense presence of other ideas may, over time, lead to different segments of platform society relying on an increasingly radical understanding of their values.

The ubiquitous proliferation of digital platforms means that, in times of conflict, fault lines between peoples reach edges they have never reached before, and sanctions decisions quickly impact entire industries and national economies. Financial platforms raise funds for weapons, making warfare more protracted and more damaging to people, wildlife, and cultural heritage. The same effect is achieved by social media, through which civilians can relay information about troop concentrations (the information may be false, and the war is used by residents for revenge or to harm personal rivals). It can be said that platforms make conflicts and wars more destructive and prolonged. In our view, this is because the business model of platforms is built on the network effect, which requires the constant attention of users, and war is an event that attracts ongoing attention. Therefore, wars and conflicts have a positive effect on the activity and "performance" of platform users and thereby on the well-being of the platforms themselves.

We need to remember that the content posted on platforms and the manipulation of it by users is data for AI learning. The radicalization of views supported by platforms leads to learning AI models that will support and reinforce biases and translate them into automatically generated content. Assuming that AI will be used in education (creating educational programs, tailoring them to students, and monitoring academic performance), social welfare, entertainment (creating multimedia content that matches the interests and expectations of the public), and forecasting political, social, and economic processes, AI trained on the content presented in social media can become a source of wrong and unfair decisions and a transmitter of a distorted and biased picture of the world. With Western countries and especially the EU leading the way in promoting sustainable development (Franc and Bilas, 2016), the rejection of Western world values in social media may include a rejection of sustainability goals in education. While in Western platform societies the goals and values of sustainable development will be subordinate to the content generated by AI, in non-Western platform societies they may be associated with hostile Western values.

Broadcasting these views through educational platforms, and potentially creating educational content by AI models trained on biased opinions, will contribute to an emotional engagement in education that may cultivate support or rejection of certain political views instead of critical thinking. The positive value of such skewed education for platforms is that emotional engagement will encourage users to rush to share their support or disapproval of different people, ideas, and countries on social media.

In the scenario presented, risks to the following sustainability goals can be identified:

SDG4 "Quality Education". Education provided by digital platforms, where educational content is generated by AI trained on biased data, can convey distorted data about the world, people, society, history, and culture to students.

SDG9: "Industry, Innovation, and Infrastructure" and SDG12: "Responsible Consumption and Production". The development of the platform society toward virtual worlds requires an increasingly complex infrastructure that involves filling the environment with an increasing number of digital devices and their power sources. The production of these devices, on the one hand, requires an increase in the number of factories, and on the other hand, an increase in their sales to return the investment in the expansion of production.

SDG8: "Decent Work and Economic Growth". The platformization of industrial, trade, and financial ties ensures economic growth on a global scale. But in times of geopolitical conflicts, sanctions, and blockades, platforms reinforce the separation of different segments of the world, shrinking markets, provoking rising prices and unemployment.

SDG16 "Peace and Justice Strong Institutions". Platforms contribute to the intensification and duration of military and economic conflicts by promoting biased judgments, fake news, and fundraising for military action.

SDG17 "Partnerships to achieve the Goal". Platforms stimulate the creation and dissemination of content that can attract the attention of users. In times of geopolitical conflict, social media platforms that support one side emphasize negative news about the other side. By remaining in the collective memory, this news can have a delayed effect in the form of a lack of willingness to partner to solve any problems, including sustainable development.

SDGs were a response to the threats posed by human productivity growth, which in turn was driven by the pursuit of wealth, power, and prestige (of individuals, countries, ideologies). Platforms directly or indirectly exploit these pursuits to accelerate user productivity to sustain the business model. Dependence on network effects encourages platforms to alternately give exaggerated value and idealization to certain ideas (e.g., turning the world into one community unified by social media), events (social media hypes), lifestyles, and behaviors (e.g., Kirkpatrick and Lee, 2022), etc. This should capture users' attention and encourage them to generate, evaluate, and share relevant content. In addition, if we look at the many products owned by prestigious brands and advertised through social media around the world, the high prices of these products encourage customers to increase their productivity to generate enough income to purchase them.

Boltanski and Esquerre (2017) referred to the process and result of enriching certain objects (historical sites, medieval manufactured household items, wines, perfumes, works of art) with an additional market value that does not reflect the real costs of making them in the term "valorization". This term can be applied to platform-initiated or platform-supported overvaluation of certain phenomena to boost user performance. Content valorization helps platforms reach more users, which increases the flow of data for AI training and audience size for advertisers.

ESD has two possibilities for exploiting platforms' reliance on content valorization. The first, straightforward, focuses on the inclusion of sustainability issues in the category of valorized content. In this case, ESD would have to compete with the many ideas, brands, and events that also claim to overvalue, as well as support a platform business model that contributes to exacerbating sustainability issues. The second possibility involves the development and dissemination of ideas opposed to valorization, that is, the removal of excess value from any objects in exchange within human society. This process may be called "devalorisation". This concept has not been conceptualized in contemporary academic literature and is used without discussion to refer to the devaluation of tangible assets (Saka, 2014), labor (Farrugia, 2020), and symbolic structures (Andrews, 1995). In our view, it is useful to distinguish between "devaluation", referring in everyday language to the loss of value by objects, and "devalorisation", meaning the removal of excess value that is not justified by costs to the producer and benefits to the consumer. This general notion of devalorisation requires adaptation to the tasks of education for sustainable development in a platform society, which will be carried out in the next section.

THE CONCEPT OF DEVALORIZATION IN EDUCATION FOR SUSTAINABLE DEVELOPMENT

First, it is necessary to define devalorisation in the context of the SDGs and ESD. In our view, this concept should refer to the reduction of the excess cost of human society to the biosphere and the well-being of society and individuals. In this sense, the concept of devalorisation epitomizes the UN Sustainable Development Goals, but in contrast to the latter, it is aimed at undermining the social and economic preconditions of environmental, economic, and social problems.

The term "devalorisation" as action requires an indication of the object to which this action is directed. According to this definition, such an object is human society, with the beneficiaries being the biosphere, society itself, and individuals. This clarification is important because it emphasizes that devalorisation cannot take place at the expense of the biosphere, society, or the well-being of individuals. Devalorisation, as the deprivation of any ideas of surplus value, cannot itself become a totalitarian super-value that requires the sacrifice of the well-being of any social group or individuals.

Devalorisation of society can be presented as a philosophical or visionary paradigm, which not only forms the conceptual basis for today's ESD but also determines the direction of technological and social development of human society. Devalorisation can become a theoretical framework for ESD, which includes the following main aspects:

First, the concept of devalorisation replaces the popular thesis that "humanity must live in harmony with nature" with the thesis that "the goal of human development is to take as little as possible from the environment and to influence it as little as possible". This goal links society's social, scientific, and cultural development more closely to living nature, which now serves as a reference point by which humanity can assess its development, rather than a circumstantial factor to be considered in developing strategies and plans.

Second, devalorisation determines the goals of humanity's scientific and technological development. Instead of creating artificial or augmented intelligence systems, science should focus on deeper digitalization, creating new materials and biotechnologies with which humans can depend as little as possible on environmental resources. In addition to reducing the environmental costs on our planet, in the long term, this will contribute to the colonization of the nearest planets. In the short term, this direction of development will solve the problem of food scarcity and hunger.

Third, devalorisation corresponds to the logic of platform society in terms of the constant reduction of production, logistical and transaction costs and counteracts the late-capitalist logic of excessive and demonstrative consumption of rare goods to express social status, and the related exploitation of historical memory and cultural heritage described by Boltanski and Esquerre (2017). In this aspect, devalorisation supports greater social equality and wide access to culture and education, which cease to be a tool for emphasizing social differences. Philosophically, devalorisation would be close to the ideas of classical philosophy about reducing human dependence on nature—not by dominating it, but by reducing the need to intrude on it.

Fourth, the forced or voluntary reduction of production and consumption and the introduction of basic income raises the question of the social, professional, and creative self-realization of people. Devalorisation implies that this self-realization will seek to reduce the ecological value, i.e., will be predominantly intangible (which in the modern world means "digital"), aimed at solving local problems, not requiring long-distance travel, and not involving "new value creation". For the curriculum, this will mean more time to master cultural heritage and cultural creativity skills through digital technologies, and possibly more time for general and higher education in general.

The practical implementation of the concept of devalorisation in educational programs will differ in STEM and social sciences. The goal of ESD in natural sciences and engineering will be to train individuals who are able and willing to create and apply technologies that:

- reduce the human body's need for nutrients and water, and dependence on external temperature conditions without compromising human dignity and freedom;
- enhance human cognitive abilities, namely the ability to hold more objects in our attention;

- make it possible to adjust the properties of materials, such as resistance to wear and tear and malleability to biodegradation;
- the platformization of things, i.e., the ability of purchased goods to be automatically renewed and reassembled according to the users' needs.

The promising technologies presented are not directly related to the platform society, and their elaboration would be humanity's task anyway, but they also contribute to counteracting the negative impact of platforms. The development of cognitive abilities is designed to reduce the power of viral and fake content. Reducing the dependence of the human body on external resources, regulating the durability of materials, and the platformization of things would reduce society's dependence on global trading platforms. At the same time, it will require the construction of new models of profit creation that do not depend on network effects.

In teaching the social sciences, the goal of ESD will need to be the cultivation of a mindset resistant to attempts to impose values that reflect a polarized, simplistic view of the world. On a formal level, therefore, ESD is not meant to replace some values with others ("environmental"), but to form in students a picture of the world that will be too diverse and multi-component for any single value to dominate it. In our opinion, the achievement of this goal today can be achieved through the transformation of the educational program through the following methodological and pedagogical approaches:

Triple Bottom Line. In the last decade, the term "triple bottom line" (TBL) has gained acceptance in the academic literature, meaning that "environmental conservation, social justice, and economic growth should be balanced" (Zhang and Tavitiyaman 2022). Today, TBL is predominantly used in the context of the hospitality industry and manufacturing. However, this approach could be used more broadly and extended to the teaching of history, philosophy, sociology, and the arts, in which the habit of viewing historical events, worldview constructions, social phenomena, and works of art from at least three perspectives would be ingrained.

Meta-analysis. Today, social media has become one of the main channels for the dissemination of information, but this channel is subject to manipulation by viral content and bots that create a false picture of the world and the value of information. When studying contemporary society, economy, and culture, the analysis of real processes needs to be supplemented by a meta-analysis of the dissemination of information about these processes, to separate reliable information from viral and fake information. In July 2022, the Social Media Observatory at Indiana University introduced tools that enable interactive 3D mapping of social media distribution, identifying viral topics, and determining how popular a topic is due to bot support (Indiana University, 2022). Skills in the meta-analysis of information from social media will help students avoid overestimating it and participating in commenting and spreading biased and fake information.

Transition Scenarios. One of ESD's competencies is anticipatory or future thinking (UNESCO, 2018). A key tool for developing such thinking is the development of scenarios for the future (Imara and Altinay, 2021). Although students learn the differences between a possible, probable, and desirable future, they are usually asked to construct a linear scenario (present-to-future or future-to-present) that promotes individual values as guides for development. Therefore, a devalorisation-oriented ESD proposes to bring students' learning to the point of acquiring the skills to develop more complex multilevel scenarios. The first level will include the formulation of several scenarios (models) for the development of different spheres of society — social, technological, cultural, political, etc. At the second level, it will be proposed to develop scenarios for the transition from one development model to another. For example, a scenario of transition from a future technocratic society to an idyll of agricultural communities or a world in which mythological narratives describe social problems as the cultural norm. Recursively, these scenarios can also imagine a transition from different models of the future to a model built on the devalorisation of society. In this way, the adoption of this approach can contribute to the accumulation of data for the development of a holistic theory of devalorisation.

Ecological Solidarity. The propaganda of simplistic views and values often serves the purpose of strengthening political solidarity. This solidarity is a necessary condition for politicians to come to power, retain power, channel public funds into various projects. Today, platforms are a suitable means of creating and maintaining such solidarity. The downside of political solidarity is polarization and conflicts between communities, which makes it less likely that they will cooperate to achieve the SDGs. Usually, environmental issues do not participate in the creation and maintenance of solidarity, except in the face of natural disasters. Attempts by individual activists to become wildlife ambassadors, as recent history has shown, result only in short-term increases in interest in environmental issues, which then give way to political and economic crises.

Devalorisation as a consideration of the interests of wildlife implies the creation of a type of solidarity in which the biosphere acts as a full-fledged participant in society. Methods of fostering such solidarity, which can be called "ecological solidarity," require further reflection. In this chapter, we propose only one technique for the formation of ecological solidarity in the context of ESD. It is a game simulating the implementation of various economic and social projects. Participants, representing different areas of society and economy, exchange among themselves a conventional currency that can be invested in the projects. This notional currency also correlates with environmental costs. One of the participants represents living nature (preferably, this role should be played by each participant in turn), whose peculiarity is that it has no voice and other participants can arbitrarily take from it and give it conventional currency in different amounts. By stepping into the shoes of wildlife, which has no voice and is usually left to lose, students will experience interacting with wildlife as an equal actor who is initially in a vulnerable position. While various oppressed minorities and despised social groups may tell their stories sooner or later, wildlife will remain voiceless forever. It can be assumed that by going through a cycle of such business games, graduates will bring elements of ecological solidarity into economics, politics, and culture, which will thus become a social norm.

Environmental solidarity, which implies considering the interests of those parties who will never be able to speak, could potentially reduce the value of discursive content that fills social media. The reciprocal exchange of matter and energy in nature is older and wiser than digital platforms and capitalism as such, and ecological solidarity is designed not to allow this fact to be forgotten or "canceled".

The presented approaches are only a first approximation to creating full-fledged theoretical and methodological lenses that re-interpret the content and instructional design of ESD in the context of devalorisation. The development of the theoretical framework and the accumulation of practical experience in applying the concept of devalorisation will very likely allow the development of new, more advanced approaches.

CONCLUSION

The emergence of new technologies and business models poses new risks to the sustainability and well-being of human communities. The platform society, which promises humanity previously unimaginable possibilities for communication and resource sharing, has become another risk. Based on capitalist logic and dependent on network effects, the platform society needs constant expansion and growth of user productivity. Lacking (yet) the resources of administrative, military, and economic coercion, platforms manipulate users by hyping the values to be found in their networks. Platforms do not "make the world a better place," but parasitize on social, economic, and political conflicts, increasing their duration and destructive impact.

ESD's response to the challenge of platforms cannot be an attempt to "tame the dragon". The platform society and economy is a new round in the evolution of capitalism, and the history of capitalism has demonstrated its amazing ability to absorb everything that tried to overcome and limit it, and thus become stronger. The only way out of this stalemate can be to move beyond just society and turn to a new actor—living nature—and its interests and needs. The devalorisation of society means finding a benchmark for the true valorization of those phenomena that usually become illusory values — power, wealth, and prestige.

This chapter has attempted a general description of devalorisation and the first possible steps toward its implementation in ESD curricula. The author hopes that these suggestions will prove useful to theorists and practitioners of education for sustainable development and will contribute to the emergence of ecological solidarity, uniting people across the feuding segments of the platform society.

REFERENCES

Andrews, D. R. (1995). Subjective Reactions to Two Regional Pronunciations of Great Russian: A Matched-Guise Study. *Canadian Slavonic Papers*, *37*(1–2), 89–106. doi:10.1080/00085006.1995.11092083

Boltanski, L., & Esquerre, A. (2017). *Enrichissement: Une critique de la merchandise*. Gallimard.

Cusumano, M. A., Gawer, A., & Yoffie, D. B. (2019). *The Business of Platforms: Strategy in the Age of Digital Competition, Innovation, and Power*. Harper Business.

Dolata, U., & Schrape, J. F. (2022). Platform Architectures. The Structuration of Platform Companies on the Internet. SSRN *Electronic Journal*. doi:10.2139/ssrn.4018396

Dwivedi, Y. K., Hughes, L., Baabdullah, A. M., & Wamba, S. F. (2022). Metaverse beyond the hype: Multidisciplinary perspectives on emerging challenges, opportunities, and agenda for research, practice and policy. *International Journal of Information Management*, *66*, 102542. doi:10.1016/j.ijinfomgt.2022.102542

Evans, P. C., & Gawer, A. (2016). *The Rise of the Platform Enterprise: A Global Survey*. The CGE. https://www.thecge.net/app/uploads/2016/01/PDF-WEB-Platform-Survey_01_12.pdf

Farrugia, D. (2020). Youth, work and global capitalism: New directions. *Journal of Youth Studies*, 1–16. doi:10.1080/13676261.2020.1729965

Franc, S., & Bilas, V. (2016). Financing Sustainable Development: The Role of the European Union. *Global Journal of Business Social Sciences Review*, *4*(4), 79–86. doi:10.35609/gjbssr.2016.4.4(9)

Gandolfo, R., & Hamilton, M. (2022). How China will censor the metaverse. *SupChina*. https://supchina.com/2022/04/13/how-china-will-censor-the-metaverse/

Gawer, A. (2021). Digital platforms' boundaries: The interplay of firm scope, platform sides, and digital interfaces. *Long Range Planning*, *54*(5), 102045. doi:10.1016/j.lrp.2020.102045

Gilbert, T. K., Dean, S., Zick, T., & Lambert, N. (2022). *Choices, Risks, and Reward Reports: Charting Public Policy for Reinforcement Learning Systems*. University of California.

Guo, Y., Zhang, Y., Boulaksil, Y., Qian, Y., & Allaoui, H. (2022). Modelling and analysis of online ride-sharing platforms–A sustainability perspective. *European Journal of Operational Research*. doi:10.1016/j.ejor.2022.04.035

HaroonM. (2022). *YouTube, The Great Radicalizer? Auditing and Mitigating Ideological Biases in YouTube Recommendations*. Arxiv. https://arxiv.org/abs/2203.10666v2

Imara, K., & Altinay, F. (2021). Integrating Education for Sustainable Development Competencies in Teacher Education. *Sustainability*, *13*(22), 12555. doi:10.3390u132212555

Indiana University. (2022). *New social media tools help public assess viral posts, check for bots*. IU News. https://news.iu.edu/stories/2022/07/iub/releases/27-social-media-tools-bots-viral-posts.html

Kirkpatrick, C. E., & Lee, S. (2022). Comparisons to picture-perfect motherhood: How Instagram's idealized portrayals of motherhood affect new mothers' well-being. *Computers in Human Behavior*, *107417*, 107417. doi:10.1016/j.chb.2022.107417

Nieborg, D. B., & Poell, T. (2018). The platformization of cultural production: Theorizing the contingent cultural commodity. *New Media & Society*, *20*(11), 4275–4292. doi:10.1177/1461444818769694

Nielsen, M. L., Laursen, C. S., & Dyreborg, J. (2022). Who takes care of safety and health among young workers? Responsibilization of OSH in the platform economy. *Safety Science*, *149*, 105674. doi:10.1016/j.ssci.2022.105674

Perrotta, C., Gulson, K. N., Williamson, B., & Witzenberger, K. (2020). Automation, APIs and the distributed labour of platform pedagogies in Google Classroom. *Critical Studies in Education*, *62*(1), 97–113. doi:10.1080/17508487.2020.1855597

Rolf, S., O'Reilly, J., & Meryon, M. (2022). Towards privatized social and employment protections in the platform economy? Evidence from the UK courier sector. *Research Policy*, *51*(5), 104492. doi:10.1016/j.respol.2022.104492

Sadowski, J. (2020). The Internet of Landlords: Digital Platforms and New Mechanisms of Rentier Capitalism. *Antipode*, *52*(2), 562–580. doi:10.1111/anti.12595

Saka, B. (2014). Petty commodity production in the neoliberal phase of global capitalism. *Research in Rural Sociology and Development*, *20*, 93–113. doi:10.1108/S1057-192220140000020004

Schuilenburg, M., & Peeters, R. (2020). *The Algorithmic Society*. Routledge. doi:10.4324/9780429261404

Strickland, E. (2022). Are You Still Using Real Data to Train Your AI? *IEEE Spectrum*. https://spectrum.ieee.org/synthetic-data-ai

Sundberg, L. T., & Holmström, J. (2022). Towards 'Lightweight' Artificial Intelligence: A Typology of AI Service Platforms. *AMCIS 2022 Proceedings*. AMC. https://aisel.aisnet.org/amcis2022/sig_odis/sig_odis/13

UNESCO. (2018). *Issues and Trends in Education for Sustainable Development*. UNESCO.

van Dijck, J. (2020). Governing digital societies: Private platforms, public values. *Computer Law & Security Review, 36*, 105377.. doi:10.1016/j.clsr.2019.105377

van Dijck, J., de Winkel, T., & Schäfer, M. T. (2021). Deplatformization and the governance of the platform ecosystem. *New Media & Society*, *23*(9). doi:10.1177/14614448211045662

van Dijck, J., Poell, T., & de Waal, M. (2018). *The Platform Society: Public Values in a Connective World*. Oxford University Press. doi:10.1093/oso/9780190889760.001.0001

Zhang, X., & Tavitiyaman, P. (2022). Sustainability courses in hospitality and tourism higher education: Perspectives from industry practitioners and students. *Journal of Hospitality, Leisure, Sport and Tourism Education*, *31*, 100393. doi:10.1016/j.jhlste.2022.100393

ADDITIONAL READINGS

Akasaki, H., Ishizawa, F., Sakamoto, M., & Nakajima, T. (2017). Building a Platform Society Towards Sustainability Based on Internet-of-Things. *Distributed, Ambient and Pervasive Interactions*, 235–251. . doi:10.1007/978-3-319-58697-7_17

Plantin, J. C., Lagoze, C., Edwards, P., & Sandvig, C. (2018). Infrastructure studies meet platform studies in the age of Google and Facebook. *New Media & Society*, *20*(1), 293–310. doi:10.1177/1461444816661553

Sefton-Green, J. (2021). *Platform Pedagogies–Toward a Research Agenda Algorithmic Rights and Protections for Children*. shttps://wip.mitpress.mit.edu/pub/platform-pedagogies/release/1?readingCollection=646d0673

Srnicek, N. (2016). *Platform capitalism*. Polity Press.

Chapter 5

Complexity Literacy for a Sustainable Digital Transition: Cases and Arguments From Transdisciplinary Education Programs

Gerald Steiner
University for Continuing Education Krems, Austria

Ilja Steffelbauer
University for Continuing Education Krems, Austria

Manfred Laubichler
Arizona State University, USA

Lukas Zenk
University for Continuing Education Krems, Austria

Eva Schernhammer
Medical University of Vienna, Austria

Brenda M. Birmann
Brigham and Women's Hospital, USA & Harvard Medical School, USA

Martin Bertau
TU Bergakademie Freiberg, Germany

Guido Caniglia
Konrad Lorenz Institute for Evolution and Cognition Research, Austria

Kay Mühlmann
University for Continuing Education Krems, Austria

Liliya Satalkina
University for Continuing Education Krems, Austria

Jakob Weitzer
Medical University of Vienna, Austria

ABSTRACT

Educational measures in line with challenges related to increasing complexity need to go beyond traditional educational means and require the integration of the basic competences of systems thinking and complexity understanding. In addition, the chapter argues for a transdisciplinary approach, based on

DOI: 10.4018/978-1-7998-5033-5.ch005

knowledge integration across disciplines and between science and practice together with supporting communication patterns and strategies. In order to train current and future generations for this kind of transition process, with the aim of making this emergent digital environment ecologically and socially sustainable, we must consequently adopt digital literacy as well as complexity understanding and systems thinking in sustainability education more consistently.

INTRODUCTION

The argument and exemplary cases put forward in this paper follow a transdisciplinary approach that considers knowledge integration between science and practice a key success factor for dealing with the kind of wicked, multi-stakeholder, multi-perspective problems that are typical of sustainability issues. Coming from a planning background with its tradition of stakeholder involvement, sustainability education integrated processes of negotiation and knowledge integration early on (Caniglia et al., 2016). Systems thinking and complexity understanding in this context were also already established as necessary prerequisites for dealing with the inherently complex and systemic nature of sustainability challenges (R. W. Scholz & Binder, 2011; R. W. Scholz & Steiner, 2015a, 2015b). This seems to be less the case in digitalization education, where the predominant paradigm still seems to hold, that the main purpose of education is to bring anyone who lags behind up to standards (Buckingham, 2020) and expert expectations of qualification remain uncontested. This has further implications beyond demands for a voice for those affected by digitalization: A major one being expert group think. In combination with the fast pace and potentially divisive quality of digitalization, disciplinary and expert forms of knowledge on their own are likely to miss important unseen side effects, as shown paradigmatically by the DiDaT-Project on the unseen side effects of digitalization in Germany ('Responsible Use of Digital Data as the Subject of a Transdisciplinary Process'). Also, closed discourses within the "tech" bubble amount to ideal growing conditions for group think (Pedersen, 2019). Thus forms of knowledge integration, tapping the situational knowledge of practice partners and giving voice to stakeholders, are more likely to produce comprehensive, fair and sustainable orientations for societal or political interventions (R. W. Scholz et al., 2021) than the kind of closed discourse that still predominates digitalization.

Our contribution builds on experiences from two sustainability and transition oriented higher education programs: First, the Global Classroom Project (Showcase 1), a transnational experiment in curriculum reform for undergraduate education in sustainable development (i.e. Bachelor students, US and Germany) which focused on the need to combine complexity understanding and digital literacy in the creation of innovative teaching-learning environments and curricula for the education of future change agents who can contribute critically and creatively to sustainable development.

Second, the European Erasmus Mundus Project Transition, Innovation, and Sustainability Environments (TISE) (Showcase 2), which, as a transdisciplinary higher education study program reaching out to undergraduate students from all over the world, provides a holistic and intercultural perspective on transitional processes from various stakeholder perspectives.

The two cases span a period of almost a decade and offer insights from before, during, and after the pandemic and the accompanying surge in digitization in academia and beyond. This long time span, regrettably, also shows that the struggle to incorporate complexity literacy into sustainability education has been going on for quite some time and it has not yet become mainstream in the contemporary education landscape. The same is true for Education for Sustainable Development (ESD), that has been promulgated by various international and national bodies for decades and implemented into national frameworks for education in the DACH-countries in the first decade of the new millennium.

The two education programs also show two different stages of development and execution: The Global Classroom Project was successfully concluded and developed into a theoretical framework under the title of the Glocal Curriculum as well as in different spin-offs in the development of innovative masters programs and curricula in different parts of the world such as (REF). TISE was developed under the influenceafter of a more societally oriented preliminary series of transdisciplinary international expert round tables on digitalization and an extensive project on the unintended side-effects of digitalization in various cultural settings from Japan, to Europe, South America, and North America (Sugiyama et al., 2017; R. Scholz et al., 2018; Viale Pereira et al., 2020)., b But a As of now TISE still is in its first iteration and undergoing all the rigors and excitement of practical testing as we write this chapter. Insights and results from this project are consequently tentative and prone to revision.

Both education programs approach the question of digitazation in relation to sustainability from different angles, but both also show that complexity understanding based on systems thinking and a collaborative approach (transdisciplinary in name or not) should be reinforced and strengthened in sustainability education.

Furthermore, both cases are not only interdisciplinary and transdisciplinary in their teaching and learning approach and staff but also in their student body: They are both intercultural and intersectional in both aspects. This is important as digitalization is an inherently global phenomenon that has both the potential to level and to divide the playing field for diverse stakeholder groups. Even within the world of academic education that endeavors to prepare students for participating in that very process, different levels of financial endowment and access to digital resources can create division where digitazation was programmatically intended to further cooperation (Caniglia et al., 2018). At the same time, sustainability issues are characterized by wicked problems with the involvement of multiple stakeholders necessitating a high degree of interpersonal - and in a pluralistic globalized world - increasingly intercultural (both within and between cultures) competences.

By building on the experiences from these two showcase projects we summarize in our conclusion why complexity understanding and systems thinking are necessary to improve our conception of a successful transition to a sustainable digital environment. To this purpose we endeavor to showcase a past successful and a current innovative approaches to teaching this indispensable competences.

BACKGROUND

The higher degree of complexity and dynamics that result from digital transformation and its sustainability implications increases the need for students' empowerment through training and education. In order to "em-power", the first question to be asked is, what kind of "powers" (skills and competencies) are best suited to meet the dual challenges of digital transformation and sustainability. By their very nature, the skills and competences demanded by both phenomena are quite unlike those promulgated by traditional systems of education. These essentially prepared consecutive generations for reiterations of the socio-economic and environmental realities that past generations have created. As Luhmann (Luhmann, 2018) put it: "culture being the continuation of successful action". This is no longer true since the slow process of social learning (Henrich, 2016) that traditionally enabled societies to adapt to environmental and technological change by distilling the life experiences of one generation into learnings for the next

- the basis of all systems of education - has increasingly been falling behind since the advent of mass society in the 20th century. With seminal transitions happening once or even several times within one human generation, social learning has been replaced by a constant state of "future shock" (Toffler, 2022).

It is not only the accelerating pace of digital transformation and increasing stress on the human-environmental system that make established models obsolete. While historic technological transformations permeated the social and geographic space incrementally and following a center-periphery logic that gave late adopters time and the advantage of observing the experiences of forerunners (Wehler 1987), this holds less true in the case of digitalization. Digitalization processes have shown a tendency to outrun earlier digital technologies, for example cell phones arriving in remote locations before desktop computers become wide-spread, agribusinesses collecting and using data on land use long before farmers are even aware that this data exists, and they are helping to produce it (Zscheischler et al., 2022).

Furthermore, digitalization tends to create quickly shifting landscapes of stark digital divides (both within and between societies) with the accompanying power imbalances and disruptions following in step (Skog et al., 2018). To boot, a globalized economy running on the highest output of energy and resources in human history is virtually drenching the global market in digital products branching out into every aspect of human activity. The underlying law of quantity and quality is part of the unprecedented impact of digitalization on all aspects of global society and the heightened level of disruption accompanying this technological transformation in comparison to past ones, regardless of the positive impacts and potentials it shows in diverse fields – from "greening" production processes and supply chains to using remote sensing to optimize fertilizer and pesticide use (Mondejar et al., 2021).

At the same time the environmental crises are increasingly showing their effects not in the shape of flat increases or decreases in relevant indicators – temperature, precipitation, soil fertility, biodiversity – over long time periods. This was the case, for instance, of historic shifts in global temperature or weather patterns e.g., the Little Ice Age. Rather, the current crises are characterized by an increase in extreme values and short-term catastrophic events and – increasingly – by the triggering of irreversible tipping points that shift the whole system into a new mode (Pachauri & Meyer, 2015).

So, both developments are by their very nature highly disruptive and largely impermeable to traditional systems of learning that emphasize teaching following generations established means and methods to deal with challenges, originally developed, tried and tested by generations before and sieved through established processes of curriculum development.

Furthermore, digitization and sustainability have a global dimension, yet their effects are increasingly felt on the local level, so purely local experiential and purely global abstract solutions are bound to miss out on parts of the positive and negative as well as intended and unintended (side)effects. Both regular education – from primary to higher education – as well as institutions of life-long learning thus face the challenge to train for addressing multiple parallel crises and processes of transition.

Education systems are not unacquainted with the demand to stem the tide of future shock while it is still rising. Past experience of various "media literacy" education schemes of the earlier decades of the 21st century from primary to higher education (Khan et al., 2022), that were often already outdated when they made their appearance in the classroom, show that a reactive approach, that tries to educate students about the potentials and pitfalls of emergent digital technologies after they have become apparent and made their way through the various layers of public discourse and expert assessment into the curriculum, is woefully inadequate (Buckingham, 2020). This previously observed lag is still felt both in the classroom and in practice. In several propositions of a series of international expert round tables on digitazation organized by some of the co-authors (Steiner et al., 2023), the importance of adjusting to a faster pace of change was emphasized, including cybersecurity education and workforce development. As technologies will remain changing, there is no particular set of new digital technologies to adapt to and to train for, instead, greater adaptability as such is needed.

The same holds true for sustainability education (Risopoulos-Pichler et al., 2020). In the past, specific sustainability issues in various fields – from biodiversity loss through pesticide application in agriculture to urban traffic collapse due to commuter culture – were potential future or emergent risks. Their effects would concern future generations of academic experts and practitioners, who could be prepared well in advance through the curricula of sustainability education programs. Today, the global human-environmental system is hurtling along its trajectory into the decade that will show the first marked effects of resource depletion and environmental degradation (Meadows, 1972; Herrington, 2021), including cascading economic, societal and political effects. The time between the emergence of critical sustainability issues and the necessity to address them in order to preserve a humane standard of living for those affected, now shrinks well below the time frame that would be necessary to integrate these specific challenges into any meaningful sustainability education curriculum. As unsustainable practices with increasing frequency begin to affect human livelihoods, there is no particular set of new sustainable strategies to adapt to and to train for, instead, greater adaptability as such is needed.

These similar observations in both fields demand new and adequate educational offers that continuously identify lead indicators, reduce temporary skill shortages, and build long-term competences. "The jobs that new technologies help create or augment tend to require much more education than those that new technologies substitute for" (Nedelkoska et al., 2018). Similarly, the sustainability issues that will crop up in the diverse real world's real-life settings of groups and individuals everywhere will require new strategies and the necessary knowledge bases and skill sets to implement them; many of which will have to be developed on the fly.

For example, at the juncture between digitazation in agriculture and the sustainability of our system of food production, farmers will have to become savvy in collecting, accessing and analyzing digital data to optimize irrigation, fertilizer and pesticide use towards securing reliable yields in times of less predictable weather patterns. At the same time, they act as crucial agents for implementing measures to secure indispensable ecosystem services – like pollination by insects, threatened by biodiversity loss – that are equally important for the sustained operation of the global system of agricultural production but were as of now taken for granted. Consequently, no strategies towards these aims exist in practice and the necessary skill sets are lacking.

In both fields and even more so at their juncture we tread a thin line that makes the transdisciplinary call for an integration of academic and practical knowledge and experience so crucial: A one-sided increase in training and education programs for those already involved in some form of training or education shows the flip sides of the coin. Nedelkoska (Nedelkoska et al., 2018) show that in the last decades, the younger generation tends to attend more training programs during the summer months, obviously feeling that increased formal training and qualification will benefit them. Yet, at the same time they fail to get early work experience, which in turn affects important on-the-job skills and valuable professional networks that would help to launch their careers. So, an increased emphasis on formal education may be detrimental to bridging the gap between academically acquired knowledge and practice experience. It may also increase the gap between those who are educated, motivated, and used to learning and have the necessary skills to move in a globalized, digital environment and those who are less well educated and/or motivated and beholden to more regional or local social contexts (Goodhart, 2017). In both cases, transdisciplinarity or other forms of science society collaboration and knowledge integration including the competences necessary for these processes become increasingly important. As the pressure to adapt quickly – both to new digital technologies and sustainability strategies – increases, either the individual ability and willingness to learn or the readiness to participate in collaborative processes that enable one to co-create sustainable and fair solutions for concrete real-world problems, offer a way out of potentially fatal individual and collective dead ends.

MAIN FOCUS

The arguments presented above show that comprehensive education programs are needed which aim at competency building for tackling complex real-world problems. Given the diverse background of the individuals interested in contributing to addressing both digitalization and sustainability challenges – and who are thus in need of education and training in suitable competences to master them – learners' cognitive, emotional, and motivational capabilities under specific social, cultural, economic, and technological environmental conditions have to be taken into account and have to factor prominently in any curricular design. This in turn requires appropriately trained teachers (respectively coaches) with less of a focus on simple knowledge transfer but instead on learner centered competency building, sensitive to the intersectional situatedness of their students (e.g., such as by transdisciplinary case study approaches (Kubisch et al., 2021; Posch & Scholz, 2006; Posch & Steiner, 2006; Steiner & Laws, 2006).

With the processes of digital transition and sustainability challenges continuously evolving and new challenges continuously emerging, continuing education and life-long learning are at the forefront to meet these societal needs at present. Consequently, this implies a major challenge for the development of suitable and adaptable further education and training in the sense of lifelong learning. Additionally, to basic schooling, incremental education and to a lesser degree long-training programs for re-qualifications are needed to train very heterogeneous target groups.

Besides technical skills, socio-ethical topics and the interaction between man and technology will be increasingly important, but the concrete subject matter will be defined by the emergent properties of the ongoing transition processes and are thus nearly impossible to predict: So, if, for example, digitalization leads to a situation where artificial intelligence systems are used as a basis for substantial decisions in e.g., politics or health care, knowledge about human bias in data input, understanding of algorithm design up to the point of the interpretation of automated results are crucial. The global increase in digital transformations has long passed the point where only experts in the field interact with digital systems, instead the whole of society – or on a global level "societies" – interact routinely with digital systems that were designed to be expert systems but have become fixtures of daily life on a local and personal level. E.g., the tastes, shopping behavior and spending of consumers worldwide are being monitored and subtly shaped by algorithms (Linden et al., 2003; Smith & Linden, 2017).

In a similar way, if urban heating becomes a relevant sustainability issue, teaching legal and administrative experts occupied with formulating building codes the basics and systemic interrelations between built environment, facility management and thermal physics becomes a relevant issue for sustainability education programs.

Further training is therefore not only relevant for individual target groups, but rather a societal transition towards a public educated in digital and sustainability knowledge is necessary to enable a broad population to accept and profit from digitalization and the transition to a more sustainable society. Here the advantages of knowledge integration come into their own. To avert potential risks, a workforce and broader populace involved in and experienced in transdisciplinary processes could provide broad support to deal with the unexpected and unseen side effects of digital transformation and the transition to a sustainable society. To that purpose education in basic systems thinking, complexity literacy and the necessary interpersonal skills to participate in processes of knowledge integration and science society collaboration become not only an issue for higher education but particularly for continuing education (to reach the already active workforce) and also for primary and secondary education (to reach the future workforce) (Curwen et al., 2018). In this chapter, given the background and focus of the contributors, we focus on the former, while still emphasizing the point that teaching these competences in a life long education framework amounts to patching over the failings of the past, while it is high time to include these indispensable competences into primary education.

SHOWCASE 1: FROM THE GLOBAL CLASSROOM PROJECT TO THE GLOCAL CURRICULUM

The Global Classroom

Under the "The Global Classroom: Liberal Arts Education in the 21st Century", a project between Leuphana University of Lüneburg, Germany and Arizona State University, USA funded by Stiftung Mercator researchers and instructors developed educational settings that allow students to actively engage with real-world sustainability problems. An important assumption in the project is that exposure to real-world problems is essential to enable students to develop systems thinking, normative, anticipatory, strategic and inter- as well as transdisciplinary collaborative competences necessary for engaging in problem-solving efforts in sustainability education.

The program ran the course of the academic years 2013 and 2014, encompassing two cohorts of 70 students in total, roughly half in Germany and the United States, from diverse disciplinary backgrounds ranging from urban planning and the natural sciences to the humanities and business administration. By gathering feedback from the first cohort, the instructors were able to improve the framework from its first implementation in 2013 to the second round of implementation in 2014. The teaching experience has been presented in several articles (Caniglia et al., 2016; Caniglia et al., 2017) with the results presented here in condensed form. In pre-pandemic times, when it was almost inconceivable that most parts of the population would be isolated and using only online communication, the Global Classroom project elaborated a novel way of conceiving of the curriculum as well as of the teaching-learning environment that can be still useful today. Indeed, the use of hybrid virtual-digital approaches as well as the person-centered approach anticipated many of the collaboration forms that we have then seen spreading rapidly in the last couple of years of the COVID pandemic.

The Global Classroom had a modular structure that spanned three semesters. In the first semester the experience-based learning framework was used to introduce sustainability concepts, perspectives and frameworks to the students. In the remaining two semesters of The Global Classroom, the students engaged in joint projects in small groups. The experiential and conceptual introductions became the basis for the further development of team projects in the following modules. In the following, we present first the experience-based learning framework (EBL) and then the Glocal Curriculum, which resulted from the Global Classroom project. We emphasize how in both cases digitalization and sustainability have been critically addressed and constructively leveraged with the goal of supporting students' competency development for sustainability.

Figure 1. The experience-based learning framework

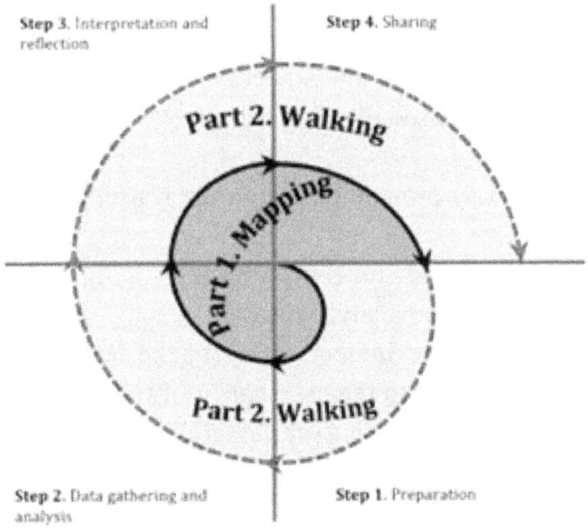

Note: The experience-based learning framework as a spiral consisting of two main parts (mapping and walking) each of which is divided in four steps (preparation, data gathering and analysis, interpretation and reflection and sharing)

For the initial stage, a student-centered and experience-based framework was developed for the novice-level development of the above-mentioned competences in introductory-level sustainability courses that were specifically aimed at students from different disciplinary, social and cultural backgrounds, e.g., in international education settings. To further student engagement, they were confronted with experiences of (un)sustainability in local urban contexts through mental mapping and exploratory walking interwoven with theoretical and methodological inputs as well as with reflections and discussions.

Unlike the so-called pull-concept for mutual learning (Posch & Steiner, 2006) that first provides input and then confronts students with interactions between societal stakeholders, the experience-based learning framework offers students the opportunity to explore and experience sustainability issues in the real world, without prior sustainability knowledge or commitment. To this purpose students were allowed to build an experiential image of urban spaces through the aforementioned mental mapping and exploratory walking techniques. The experience of walking exposed the students to the complexity of the urban environment while promoting curiosity, creativity and critical thinking. They learned first-hand that addressing the complexity of (un)sustainability is not only about understanding order but also disharmony and uncertainty. By walking and collecting data, students experienced different domains (i.e., society, environment, economy) and different scales (local to global) in which sustainability issues emerge. Sharing the experience of the walk among the students allowed for in-depth discussions of social, environmental, economic and cultural dimensions of urban sustainability.

In the experience-based learning (Kolb 1984, Moore 2010, Wurdinger & Carlson 2010) framework students are supported by teaching staff, but generally self-organizing, going through a four-step spiral (Caniglia et al., 2017). In all the steps, the curriculum involved the use of digital technologies used to allow for collaboration and sharing of ideas. At each of the steps the sensorial and experiential were interwoven with the digitally mediated and linguistic communication and collaboration. It was the hybrid format that made the experience-based learning framework an effective way to start the program.

(1) Step 1 – Preparation: Instructors provide inputs on the learning methodology and its theoretical background.
(2) Step 2 – Data gathering and analysis: Students perform mapping and walking activities (data gathering), as well as organize, store and analyze the data.
(3) Step 3 – Interpretation and reflection: Students reflect on the data collected in light of sustainability. They apply sustainability principles in the assessment of (un)sustainability and situate their own social and cultural background in relation to sustainability in local contexts.
(4) Step 4 – Sharing: Students share their data and interpretations.

Indeed, the initial mapping and walking experience had a formative impact on the later modules of the program. Students often relied on their projects on what they had learnt, for instance on the lessons about teamwork during the mapping and walking activities. Also, when it came to assessing sustainability issues within their projects, students often referred to the way they had identified and started appraising sustainability issues both in the mapping and in the walking activities. Students also made use of the mental mapping and walking as methods for their own research or in some projects, asked stakeholders to draw mental maps of specific neighborhoods to capture different perceptions of the urban environment.

Concerning the learning targets of basic systems thinking, normative and collaborative competences, students used the mental maps with their different elements (paths, nodes, etc.) to visualize the urban environment as a complex unit composed of many interacting components. Coming from concrete issues like mobility as expressed in the highway infrastructure of Phoenix, AR, students began to develop an understanding of feedback loops and non-linear cause– effect relations. The walking experience in particular encouraged students to think about urban spaces as coupled social, ecological and economic domains. Normative competences showed particularly well in students' ability to connect quality of ecosystem services in different neighborhoods to equity issues, as experienced through their walking exercises.

By sharing the results of the mapping and walking activities at Leuphana and at ASU, students could not rely on previous knowledge of each other's local contexts. They had to add explanations about habits and lifestyles as well as basic information about infrastructures and urban form, developing basic skills in intercultural communication, up to the point of translating metric to US measurement systems. Building both communicative and collaborative competences prepared students for the final projects in The Global Classroom where they engaged in transnational teams composed of both Leuphana and ASU students.

The Global Classroom Project provided an exemplary model that could potentially be applied more broadly in higher education and even in learning projects for advanced primary education (high school) settings. It also holds great potential for transdisciplinary projects in general, providing, through the mapping and walking exercises, a means for different experiences and perceptions in stakeholders to emerge gradually through common confrontation with the environment in question. Reflecting upon these differences could lead to a shared understanding of the local environment as well as of the sustainability issues that need attention. With its focus on collaboration, the framework could also facilitate communication and collaboration between professional academics, local communities, and societal stakeholders.

The Global Curriculum

The Global Classroom also provided the basis and practical experience for the formulation of the Global Curriculum (John et al., 2017) defined as an "intentional imaging and ordering of educational experiences" which engages students' knowledge, skills, and mindsets. The Global Curriculum rethinks the engagement of these three dimensions through the demands posed by learning about sustainability problems and solutions on global and local scales and across geographical and cultural contexts.

The Global Curriculum conceives of sustainable development in terms of problems and solutions in local and global contexts. It does so in a transnational teaching learning environment where competency can be developed within the context of the different cultures and practices of knowing, doing, and being. The curriculum engages knowing, acting, and being to prepare and empower students to become agents of transformation. Yet, it also supports the development of knowledge, skills, and mindsets to think critically about processes of knowledge production, power relations as well as about historical and current drivers that resulted in an unsustainable world.

Figure 2. Engaging knowing, acting, and being (the triangle) in different learning areas(the lines inside of the triangle) in teaching-learning environments that are local and global as well as virtual and real (the bubble surrounding the triangle)

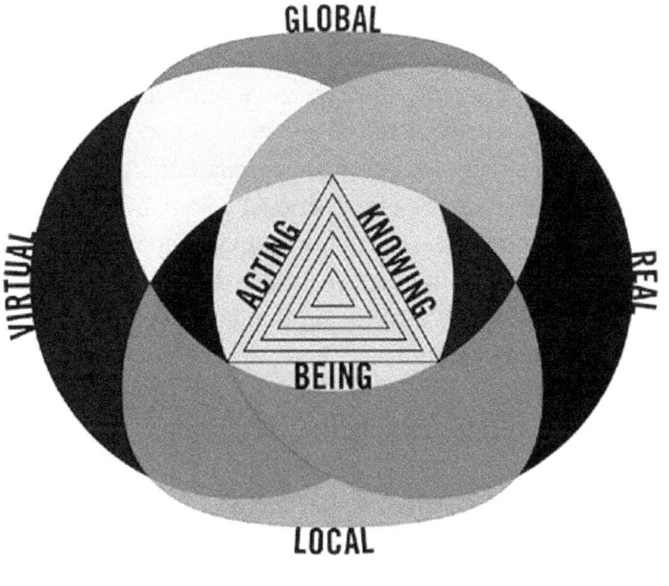

Fig. 1. Engaging knowing, acting, and being (the triangle) in different learning areas (the lines inside the triangle) in teaching-learning environments that are local and global as well as virtual and real (the bubble surrounding the triangle).

1. It fosters inter- and transdisciplinary knowledge production and competency generation (Lang et al., 2012): Global knowing
2. It prepares students with skills to collaborate and work together across cultural, social, national, and geographical contexts: Global acting
3. It empowers students to contribute to social change across cultural and geographical contexts: Global being.

The implementation of a global curriculum requires a global teaching-learning environment. Such a global teaching-learning environment expands both locally and globally. Locally, it includes communities, businesses and governments as well as multiple relationships among the students, instructors, and different social actors. Globally, it enables connection, communication, and collaboration across different local contexts through the use of digital technologies.

The experiences from the Global Classroom Project provided a sound foundation for aligning local experiences and engagement with global collaboration and intercultural exchange. It helped to develop four core dimensions of the Global Curriculum:

1. Direction: A student-centered teaching-learning environment encompasses features of responsibility, and self-management.
2. Place: Local and global refers to methods, contents, and activities explicitly rooted and engaged on the global and local scale.
3. Space: Virtual and Real refers to the physical space that expands from real to digitally enhanced, virtual spaces.
4. People: Collaborations and relationships refers to collective learning as students, instructors, and social actors are part of the learning experience.

The global model relies less on mobility and more on domestic and digitally-mediated environments to support international and intercultural learning (i.e. internationalization at home). The use of digital technologies to communicate and collaborate across different contexts can complement in-person meetings and collaborations that usually take place in expensive study-abroad programs and create a global imbalance founded on the material endowments of universities and students (Caniglia et al., 2017). It allows students to connect with international peers and communities and to recognize local needs. Students have the opportunity to collaborate in an international community of scholars on projects that aim to positively impact their local communities. In this way, global approaches can contribute not only to the education of citizens who are able to think and act from local to global scales, but also allow for an immediate impact of educational programs towards sustainability, making institutions of higher learning active participants in local sustainability efforts.

Digitization And Complexity Sustainability in The Global Curriculum

The blended learning space of the Global Classroom challenges conventional ways of conceiving of the classroom as well as of the teaching and learning processes that take place in it. Overall, it is important to create an awareness of possibly different degrees of digital literacy and provide opportunities for students as well as teachers to continue to learn and improve their individual digital literacy (such as through a targeted approach to the selection of software and digital media), from digital critical thinking (such as when learning how to find and scrutinize information) to find and evaluate information, which might be defined as) to higher levels of digital literacy (such as when learning how to publish content, e.g. videos and blogs). These different degrees of literacy imply different levels of access and participation in the digital knowledge community of the information age, but require careful planning to translate contents into the right environment, to choose appropriate tools, and to make use of technology for meaningful publication of contents.

More specifically, thinking about the aspects related to the delivery of the technologies is not sufficient for competency development. The use of digital technologies invites reflections about how the space affects the direction of the teaching-learning environment as well as the kind of relationships that it is possible to build in it, such as among students or between students and instructors. First, inhabiting blended teaching-learning environments requires combining the development of digital literacy, the creation of a learning environment that fosters students' learning process, and a critical mindset to find personalized ways of using and organizing digital platforms and content in relation to the sustainability topics addressed (from local to global). Second, a blended learning space has the potential to enable an extension of the cultural and social contexts for students' learning. It allows for connecting to a global context while keeping the connection to a multiplicity of specific places. Yet, specific pedagogies are required (such as those dealing with collaborative and interpersonal competences in Higher Education for Sustainability) in order for this to happen and to be useful for the students. Finally, managing digitally-mediated environments requires care and time, such as including considerations about how students and instructors can communicate and collaborate through the technology, how roles and responsibilities are divided and how class activities are planned and implemented. The potential of digitally-mediated environments and curricula to support sustainability competency thus depends on our capacities to critically and thoughtfully articulate and manage the complexities that characterize such environments.

SHOWCASE 2: ERASMUS MUNDUS JOINT MASTER'S DEGREE IN TRANSITION, INNOVATION AND SUSTAINABILITY ENVIRONMENTS – TISE

Transition, Innovation and Sustainability Environments (TISE) is a European Master of Excellence / Erasmus Mundus Joint Master initiated by the University of Continuing Education Krems (UWK) in cooperation with the Universidade Nova de Lisboa (NOVA), University College Dublin (UCD) and Poznan University of Economics and Business (PUEB) (Mühlmann et al., 2022). The program was inaugurated in the fall term of 2021 at Lisbon, where the first international student cohort of twenty-seven spent its first semester, afterwards going for consecutive semesters to the other participating universities. According to the curriculum of the program, the mobility scheme is the same for every cohort, starting with the first semester at NOVA, followed with the second semester at UCD, third semester at PUEB and last semester at UWK. Unlike the Global Classroom discussed above, TISE is thus still in its first iteration, having reached the end of its second semester as of the writing of this chapter and preparing for the second intake of another roughly thirty students. Thus, while some experiences from ongoing teaching are tentatively included, without claiming conclusive results, the focus in this showcase is on the original design of the teaching program and the role of complexity education and digitalization in this context.

The focus of TISE is on sustainable and resilient societal, business and industry processes and structures. The structure of applicants during the two application periods shows that a significant number of candidates have economic (including business administration) and technical backgrounds. However, the consortium aims for a disciplinary diverse cohort from the over four hundred applicants, achieving also a high cultural diversity by including students from approximately 20 countries from all over the world. Through its strong transdisciplinary approach (i.e. a method guided by mutual learning processes between science and practice), students on this program gain a comprehensive understanding of relevant coupled human-nature-technology systems (respectively 'human environment systems'), positive and negative mechanisms and effects of transitional processes (including underlying obvious and hidden rebound effects), and interventions together with the innovation potential therein.

Using a hierarchical system perspective, the program encompasses the individual agents, teams, organizations, networks, and clusters, within regional, national, and supranational systems, and ultimately global implications. Building on a complexity science foundation the program presents an inter- and cross-disciplinary view of socio-cultural studies, social sciences, economics, technology, and design, but also integrating communities of practice and the tacit knowledge of practitioners in order to address real-world complex problems. The program promotes transdisciplinarity as an innovative approach towards the challenges encountered by social systems today. To this purpose it delivers a holistic take on transitional processes and innovation strategies, educating students to be change agents for challenges in complex human-environment systems (socio-cultural/socio-technical/socio-economic).

TISE has five main program objectives, of which objectives 1 and 2 apply to complexity and technological innovation (i.e. digitalization) in particular. These are consequently at the heart of the program and feature prominently in the modular curriculum (https://www.donau-uni.ac.at/en/studies/transition-innovation-and-sustainability-environments-tise/content-dates.html).

Insert

Objective 1: To educate change agents for institutions and organizations, who are capable of utilizing diverse sets of tools and competences from the different disciplines (socio-cultural studies, social sciences, economics and technology). Complexity sciences functions as an umbrella to enable the interdisciplinary discourse as base for transdisciplinary approaches to address complex challenges respond to processes of transition and thus increase resilience and sustainability of organizations and institutions.

Objective 2: To foster the ability to assess the impact of socio-technological and transitional processes on culture and society, through a deeper system understanding (in context of multiplex-coupled system environments), especially concerning system vulnerabilities, and, furthermore, to recognize the correlations/interrelations on the different spheres of human action.

Objective 3: To improve the initiation and management of transdisciplinary initiatives for complex problem areas by equipping graduates with managerial and decision-making competences to develop innovation and leadership concepts and instruments for institutions and organizations.

Objective 4: To foster cross-border and cross-boundary collaboration by providing alumni with tools and competences using transdisciplinary approaches to initiate multidimensional knowledge integration for problem and solution-oriented innovation strategies.

Objective 5: To promote an innovation supporting mind-set and strengthen science-society relationships by equipping graduates with entrepreneurial competences and the ability to facilitate the transfer of scientific knowledge and foster science – society relations embedded in sustainable environments.

TISE stretches over four semesters, each focused on the specific disciplinary strong points of the hosting institutions. The final term at the University for Continuing Education Krems is dedicated to writing the master thesis and transdisciplinary field research training (that starts already in the mid of the third semester). Similarly, to the Global Classroom, the question, when to confront students with systems and complexity content – before or after specific input and practice experience – arose during the design phase of the curriculum. TISE has solved this issue by making systems science, complexity science, systems modeling and theory and practice of transdisciplinary processes a "continuous parallel curriculum". So, while immersing themselves in the specific subject matters provided by the consortium partners – from socio-cultural studies in Lisbon over ethics and information systems in Dublin to transitions in economics in Poznań – students receive introductions to these foundational competences during the workshops with guest lecturers and focused teaching interventions. So before entering the final semester dedicated to writing master thesis, over the course of the first–three semesters, students build up a basic understanding of interrelated societal systems; specific methods for reflecting and analyzing complex systems (e.g., methods of system dynamics); transdisciplinarity as part of a solution-oriented perspective which fosters socially robust orientation in the decision-making process instead of providing only solutions (Satalkina et al., 2022).

The rationale behind this approach follows from the principle that sound disciplinary foundations and focused instruction in specialized knowledge are the prerequisite for successful inter- and transdisciplinary work. At the same time, in order to create the mindset required for the master thesis, students are fed introductory material and assignments with the expectation that the systemic and complexity-oriented perspective will inform their choices and approach when it comes to finally formulating a research question and project idea for their thesis, that will then be written in a teaching and mentoring environment fully steeped in these concepts. In order to facilitate this final stage of the program, hybrid learning spaces are being developed. They allow for examining how digital, physical and hybrid spaces can improve the modeling of complex relations in order to enhance the quality of decision-making. In the transdisciplinary collaborative project-work, the learning spaces are used for workshops by the mixed teams (science-society), where practical and relevant challenges are identified and systemically analyzed (combined stakeholder and system analyses), statistical data and network analyses are carried out and the results are consolidated and interpreted. Consequently, a comprehensive knowledge integration is the ultimate goal.

Still being in its first iteration, it remains to be seen how well this teaching strategy works out. The point to assess the impact of the "parallel curriculum" on the perspectives and choices taken by the students is still in the future, roughly at the end of the third semester when they have to decide on the content of their master theses. Still, by May 2022 the students of TISE, as part of their study program, organized their first CSS (Collaboration for Sustainable Solutions) online conference (https://www.css-conference.com/) from their location in Dublin, with the aim to bringing people engaged in best practices for solving complex problems together to share their knowledge and expertise. The success and professional execution of this conference gives high hopes that the transdisciplinary and knowledge integration aspect of the curriculum has successfully taken root. As of now, the program coordinators are deliberating to make no changes to the content of the curriculum in that respect. The only adaptation for the second intake – starting in fall 2022 – will be an earlier start for the parallel workshops and interventions compared to the first round, giving students more time to engage with these issues and to digest the content presented. TISE is flanked by an ongoing program of accompanying research (Mühlmann et al., 2022), evaluating the expected results and considering the perspectives and experiences of students in terms of the TISE program.

CONCLUSION

We have presented different approaches to the implementation of systems thinking and complexity understanding in programs of higher and continuing education with conclusive and tentative results on their efficacy and outcome. Within each showcase and the accompanying documentation and publications there is ample argument for the importance of these indispensable competences within the specific study programs and – by extension – within curricula dealing with digital transition and sustainability in general. Our argument not only extends to the proposed advantages academically schooled (regardless, if in an initial higher education or later in life) experts derive from these skills. We also argue that spreading these competences by whatever means suitable within the general populace and workforce (either by means of or in preparation for participation in transdisciplinary processes) would help to increase societal adaptability that will be crucial in coming times of accelerating digitalization and mounting sustainability challenges. competences

RECOMMENDATIONS

The above argument leads to four core recommendations:

Firstly: Systems thinking and complexity understanding need to become generic competences and educators on all levels are called upon to implement them in curricula. Early access to these skills should be an agenda for reforms in primary education. Continuing, lifelong education is called upon to do its part in spreading these competences in the adult population. Compartmentalization without appropriate interlinkages between the various phases of education (from primary to life-long education) need to be overcome and replaced by a more comprehensive and systemic orientation, which will require adapted structures, organizations, and processes.

Secondly: Transdisciplinary methodology combined with the experiential character of transdisciplinary processes when implemented in a learning environment has been shown to greatly improve student competences in systems thinking and complexity understand as well as beyond that in social, self-organizational and interactional competences. We thus recommend implementing elements of science/education practice collaboration and stakeholder integration as part of experiential learning environments.

Thirdly: The range of competences acquired through these approaches has been shown – in our showcase programs – to greatly improve the ability of students to come up with viable proposals for socially and environmentally sustainable solutions, considering the complex and wicked nature of challenges posed by digital transition and environmental crises. We therefor recommend the integration of systems thinking, complexity understanding and transdisciplinary methodology as integral to further curriculum development in sustainability education, particularly pertaining to the highly disruptive field of digitalization.

Fourth: Concerning digitalization we highly recommend the active embrace of digital technologies as means of teaching and collaboration, both within the student body and the faculty as well as with outside partners and stakeholders. Digital collaboration and the creative use of digital tools have to be adopted, utilized and spread by educational programs. A defensive stance as practiced by decades of failed media education has proven untenable. As a strategy of empowerment vis-à-vis the growing digital divide the integration of digital competences in any education program his highly commendable, always under the caveat that digital technologies must be inclusive, not pose additional hurdles.

But we way also tentatively take this argument beyond reasoned recommendation and add a strong emphasis from current research. Over the course of the COVID 19-crisis, several of the contributors to this chapter under the auspices of the recently founded Transatlantic Research Lab on Complex Societal Challenges, have contributed to a number of surveys and research articles dealing with public acceptance of anti-COVID-measures, trust in government measures, vaccination hesitancy and believe in conspiracy theories (Schernhammer et al., 2022; Weitzer et al., 2022; Caniglia et al., 2021; Weitzer, Laubichler, et al., 2021; Weitzer, Papantoniou, et al., 2021). In the latter survey, complexity thinking was correlated with the likelihood to accept conspiracy theories (publication forthcoming). The result was a resounding negative. The ability to accept, cogitate and understand the systemic nature and complexity of real-world problems, seems to have an immunizing effect against falling into the specific mental pitfalls of conspiracy thinking. In a society likely to suffer increasing stress from societal transitions and disruptions of the human-environmental system, it seems our best bet to attain "herd immunity" against destructive forms of group-thinking as embodied by conspiracy theories by a program of "inoculation" with systems thinking and complexity understanding in combination with science-practice collaboration that – like any inoculation program – not only increases personal resistance against harmful ideas, but also heightens societal resilience and helps protect those who cannot be easily reached.

FUTURE DIRECTIONS

Developing and implementing curricula and didactic strategies for systems and complexity literacy in a transdisciplinary context are and will remain on the agenda not only of the contributors but of science and practice in general (Steiner, 2013; Bates et al., 2022). A critical factor for empowerment and competency building is the institutional and strategic setting of the educational system. We are looking forward to further research and practice projects in this respect. Also, we are aware that the issue of teaching systems thinking and complexity understanding at an early stage has been around for quite a while (e.g., Cabrera & Cabrera, 2012; Goleman & Senge, 2015), it has made progress only under specific conditions. We are interested in finding out more about the necessary preconditions that enabled that and the potential to transplant them to other sectors of the education system at large.

Coming from the highly diverse background of our student bodies, we are very aware that different demographics face different challenges in obtaining the skillset and competences we recommend. We expect that programs tailored to the needs of specific groups will have to be developed and we are looking forward to developments in this area, specifically programs aiming at vulnerable and minority groups that are most likely to be affected negatively by the (side)effects of both digitalization and environmental degradation.

REFERENCES

Bates, R., Brenner, B., Schmid, E., Steiner, G., & Vogel, S. (2022). Towards meta-competences in higher education for tackling complex real-world problems - a cross disciplinary review. *International Journal of Sustainability in Higher Education*, *24*(1), 290–308. doi:10.1108/IJSHE-06-2021-0243

Buckingham, D. (2020). Epilogue: Rethinking digital literacy: Media education in the age of digital capitalism. *Digital Education Review*, (37), 230–239. doi:10.1344/der.2020.37.230-239

Cabrera, D., & Cabrera, L. (2012). *Thinking at every desk: Four simple skills to transform your classroom. Norton books in education.* W.W. Norton & Company.

Caniglia, G., Jaeger, C., Schernhammer, E., Steiner, G., Russo, F., Renn, J., Schlosser, P., & Laubichler, M. D. (2021). Covid-19 heralds a new epistemology of science for the public good. *History and Philosophy of the Life Sciences*, *43*(2), 59. doi:10.100740656-021-00413-7 PMID:33864155

Caniglia, G., John, B., Bellina, L., Lang, D., & Laubichler, M. (2018). Digital Technologies for Transnational Collaboration: A Glocal Approach from Sustainability Education.

Caniglia, G., John, B., Kohler, M., Bellina, L., Wiek, A., Rojas, C., Laubichler, M. D., & Lang, D. (2016). An experience-based learning framework. *International Journal of Sustainability in Higher Education*, *17*(6), 827–852. doi:10.1108/IJSHE-04-2015-0065

Caniglia, G., Luederitz, C., Groß, M., Muhr, M., John, B., Withycombe Keeler, L., von Wehrden, H., Laubichler, M., Wiek, A., & Lang, D. (2017). Transnational collaboration for sustainability in higher education: Lessons from a systematic review. *Journal of Cleaner Production*, *168*, 764–779. doi:10.1016/j.jclepro.2017.07.256

Curwen, M. S., Ardell, A., MacGillivray, L., & Lambert, R. (2018). Systems Thinking in a Second Grade Curriculum: Students Engaged to Address a Statewide Drought. *Frontiers in Education*, *3*, 90. doi:10.3389/feduc.2018.00090

Goleman, D., & Senge, P. M. (2015). *The triple focus: A new approach to education*. More Than Sound.

Goodhart, D. (2017). *The road to somewhere: The populist revolt and the future of politics*. Hurst & Company.

Henrich, J. (2016). *The secret of our success: How culture is driving human evolution, domesticating our species, and making us smarter*. Princeton University Press. https://www.degruyter.com/isbn/9781400873296, doi:10.1515/9781400873296

Herrington, G. (2021). Update to limits to growth: Comparing the World3 model with empirical data. *Journal of Industrial Ecology*, *25*(3), 614–626. doi:10.1111/jiec.13084

John, B., Caniglia, G., Bellina, L., J. Lang, D., & Laubichler, M. (2017). The Global Curriculum: A Practical Guide to Teaching and Learning in an Interconnected World tredition.

Khan, N., Sarwar, A., Chen, T. B., & Khan, S. (2022). Connecting digital literacy in higher education to the 21st century workforce. Knowledge Management & E-Learning. *International Journal (Toronto, Ont.)*, 46–61. doi:10.34105/j.kmel.2022.14.004

Kolb, D. A. (1984). *Experiential learning: Experience as the source of learning and development*. Prentice-Hall.

Kubisch, S., Parth, S., Deisenrieder, V., Oberauer, K., Stötter, J., & Keller, L. (2021). From Transdisciplinary Research to Transdisciplinary Education—The Role of Schools in Contributing to Community Well-Being and Sustainable Development. *Sustainability*, *13*(1), 306. doi:10.3390u13010306

Linden, G., Smith, B., & York, J. (2003). Amazon.com recommendations: Item-to-item collaborative filtering. *IEEE Internet Computing*, *7*(1), 76–80. doi:10.1109/MIC.2003.1167344

Luhmann, N. (2018). Soziale Systeme: Grundriß einer allgemeinen Theorie (17. Auflage). Suhrkamp-Taschenbuch Wissenschaft: Vol. 666. Suhrkamp.

Meadows, D. H. (Ed.). (1972). *A Potomac Associates book. The limits to growth: A report for the club of rome's project on the predicament of mankind*. Earth Island Limited.

Mondejar, M. E., Avtar, R., Diaz, H. L. B., Dubey, R. K., Esteban, J., Gómez-Morales, A., Hallam, B., Mbungu, N. T., Okolo, C. C., Prasad, K. A., She, Q., & Garcia-Segura, S. (2021). Digitalization to achieve sustainable development goals: Steps towards a Smart Green Planet. *The Science of the Total Environment*, *794*, 148539. doi:10.1016/j.scitotenv.2021.148539 PMID:34323742

Moore, D. T. (2010). Forms and issues in experiential learning. In D. M. Qualters (Ed.), *New Directions for Teaching and Learning* (pp. 3–13). Wiley.

Mühlmann, K., Satalkina, L., Zenk, L., & Steiner, G. (2022). Transition, Innovation and Sustainability Environments, TISE: A Showcase of Education Geared Towards Societal Challenges and Future Orientation. In M. E. Auer, H. Hortsch, O. Michler, & T. Köhler (Eds.), *Lecture Notes in Networks and Systems. Mobility for Smart Cities and Regional Development - Challenges for Higher Education* (Vol. 390, pp. 879–887). Springer International Publishing. doi:10.1007/978-3-030-93907-6_94

Nedelkoska, L., Diodato, D., & Neffke, F. (2018). Is Our Human Capital General Enough to Withstand the Current Wave of Technological Change? Pachauri, R. K., & Meyer, L. (Eds.). (2015). Climate change 2014: Synthesis report: [longer report]. Intergovernmental Panel on Climate Change.

Pedersen, C. L. (2019). Is Silicon Valley Diverse Enough to Resist Reduction? *Journal of Design and Science*.

Posch, A., & Scholz, R. W. (2006). Transdisciplinary case studies for sustainability learning. *International Journal of Sustainability in Higher Education*, *7*(3). doi:10.1108/ijshe.2006.24907caa.001

Posch, A., & Steiner, G. (2006). Integrating research and teaching on innovation for sustainable development. *International Journal of Sustainability in Higher Education*, *7*(3), 276–292. doi:10.1108/14676370610677847

Risopoulos-Pichler, F., Daghofer, F., & Steiner, G. (2020). Competences for Solving Complex Problems: A Cross-Sectional Survey on Higher Education for Sustainability Learning and Transdisciplinarity. *Sustainability*, *12*(15), 6016. doi:10.3390u12156016

Satalkina, L., Zenk, L., Mühlmann, K., & Steiner, G. (2022). Beyond Simple: Entrepreneurship as a Driver for Societal Change. In M. E. Auer, H. Hortsch, O. Michler, & T. Köhler (Eds.), *Mobility for Smart Cities and Regional Development—Challenges for Higher Education* (Vol. 390, pp. 888–896). Springer International Publishing. doi:10.1007/978-3-030-93907-6_95

Schernhammer, E., Weitzer, J., Laubichler, M. D., Birmann, B. M., Bertau, M., Zenk, L., Caniglia, G., Jäger, C. C., & Steiner, G. (2022). Correlates of COVID-19 vaccine hesitancy in Austria: Trust and the government. *Journal of Public Health (Oxford, England)*, *44*(1), e106–e116. doi:10.1093/pubmed/fdab122 PMID:33948665

Scholz, R., Bartelsman, E., Diefenbach, S., Franke, L., Grunwald, A., Helbing, D., Hill, R., Hilty, L., Höjer, M., Klauser, S., Montag, C., Parycek, P., Prote, J., Renn, O., Reichel, A., Schuh, G., Steiner, G., & Viale Pereira, G. (2001). [Gerald], & Viale Pereira, G. (2018). Unintended Side Effects of the Digital Transition: European Scientists' Messages from a Proposition-Based Expert Round Table. *Sustainability (New Rochelle, N.Y.)*, *10*(6), 2001. Advance online publication. doi:10.3390u10062001

Scholz, R. W., Beckedahl, M., Noller, S., & Renn, O. (2021). DiDaT Weißbuch. Nomos Verlagsgesellschaft mbH & Co. KG. doi:10.5771/9783748924111

Scholz, R. W., & Binder, C. R. (2011). *Environmental literacy in science and society: From knowledge to decisions*. Cambridge University Press. doi:10.1017/CBO9780511921520

Scholz, R. W., & Steiner, G. (2015a). The real type and ideal type of transdisciplinary processes: Part II—what constraints and obstacles do we meet in practice? *Sustainability Science*, *10*(4), 653–671. doi:10.100711625-015-0327-3

Scholz, R. W., & Steiner, G. (2015b). The real type and ideal type of transdisciplinary processes: Part I—theoretical foundations. *Sustainability Science*, *10*(4), 527–544. doi:10.100711625-015-0326-4

Skog, D. A., Wimelius, H., & Sandberg, J. (2018). Digital Disruption. *Business & Information Systems Engineering*, *60*(5), 431–437. doi:10.100712599-018-0550-4

Smith, B., & Linden, G. (2017). Two Decades of Recommender Systems at Amazon.com. *IEEE Internet Computing*, *21*(3), 12–18. doi:10.1109/MIC.2017.72

Steiner, G. (2013). Competences for Complex Real-World Problems: Toward an Integrative Framework. *Working Paper 2013-0002, Weatherhead Center for International Affairs.* Harvard University.

Steiner, G. (2023). *Turning digital vulnerability spaces into innovation niches. Results from the Transdisciplinary USA Expert Round Table Series on sustainable digital transformation.* Working Paper.

Steiner, G., & Laws, D. (2006). How appropriate are two established concepts from higher education for solving complex real-world problems? *International Journal of Sustainability in Higher Education*, *7*(3), 322–340. doi:10.1108/14676370610677874

Sugiyama, M., Deguchi, H., Ema, A., Kishimoto, A., Mori, J., Shiroyama, H., & Scholz, R. (2017). Unintended Side Effects of Digital Transition: Perspectives of Japanese Experts. *Sustainability*, *9*(12), 2193. doi:10.3390u9122193

Toffler, A. (2022). *Future Shock. Random House Publishing Group.* EBook Central. https://ebookcentral.proquest.com/lib/kxp/detail.action?docID=6829200

Viale Pereira, G., Estevez, E., Cardona, D., Chesñevar, C., Collazzo-Yelpo, P., Cunha, M. A., Diniz, E. H., Ferraresi, A. A., Fischer, F. M., Cardinelle Oliveira Garcia, F., Joia, L. A., Luciano, E. M., de Albuquerque, J. P., Quandt, C. O., Sánchez Rios, R., Sánchez, A., Da Damião Silva, E., Silva-Junior, J. S., & Scholz, R. W. (2020). South American Expert Roundtable: Increasing Adaptive Governance Capacity for Coping with Unintended Side Effects of Digital Transformation. *Sustainability*, *12*(2), 718. doi:10.3390u12020718

Wehler, H.-U. (1987). *Deutsche Gesellschaftsgeschichte. Erster Band Vom Feudalismus des alten Reiches bis zur defensiven Modernisierung der Reformära. 1700-1815*. C.H. Beck.

Weitzer, J., Birmann, B. M., Steffelbauer, I., Bertau, M., Zenk, L., Caniglia, G., Laubichler, M. D., Steiner, G., & Schernhammer, E. S. (2022). Willingness to receive an annual COVID-19 booster vaccine in the German-speaking D-A-CH region in Europe: A cross-sectional study. The Lancet Regional Health. *Europe*, *18*, 100414. doi:10.1016/j.lanepe.2022.100414 PMID:35651957

Weitzer, J., Laubichler, M. D., Birmann, B. M., Bertau, M., Zenk, L., Caniglia, G., Jäger, C. C., & Steiner, G [Gerald], & Schernhammer, E. (. (2021). Comment on Alley, S.J., et al. As the Pandemic Progresses, How Does Willingness to Vaccinate against COVID-19 Evolve? Int. J. Environ. Res. Public Health 2021, 18, 797. *International Journal of Environmental Research and Public Health*, *18*(6). doi:10.3390/ijerph18062809 PMID:33801986

Weitzer, J., Papantoniou, K., Seidel, S., Klösch, G., Caniglia, G., Laubichler, M., Bertau, M., Birmann, B. M., Jäger, C. C., Zenk, L., Steiner, G., & Schernhammer, E. (2021). Working from home, quality of life, and perceived productivity during the first 50-day COVID-19 mitigation measures in Austria: A cross-sectional study. *International Archives of Occupational and Environmental Health*, *94*(8), 1823–1837. doi:10.100700420-021-01692-0 PMID:33877416

Wurdinger, D. D., & Carlson, J. A. (2010). *Teaching for experiential learning: Five approaches that work*. Rowman & Littlefield Education.

Zscheischler, J., Brunsch, R., Rogga, S., & Scholz, R. W. (2022). Perceived risks and vulnerabilities of employing digitalization and digital data in agriculture – Socially robust orientations from a transdisciplinary process. *Journal of Cleaner Production*, *358*, 132034. doi:10.1016/j.jclepro.2022.132034

Section 2
Cases and Perspectives

Chapter 6
Digital Literacy Among Teacher Educators in Ethiopia:
Implications to the Achievement of SDG4 and (Education for) Sustainable Development

Aklilu Dalelo
Addis Ababa University, Ethiopia

Anteneh Gebremariam
Hawassa College of Teacher Education, Ethiopia

Kedir Gebi
Robe College of Teacher Education, Ethiopia

ABSTRACT

This study was initiated to assess the status of digital competencies among teacher educators in Ethiopia. A questionnaire, adopted from an instrument previously developed to measure teachers' preparedness to use digital technology has been used to gather information. Findings indicate that teacher educators demonstrated marked strength in certain domains of competence (e.g., preparedness to use digital technologies; and attitude towards use of digital technologies); and had serious limitations in others (e.g., awareness about the shortcomings of digital technologies). With regard to factors that affect the utilization of digital technologies, teacher educators identified three factors as most important: lack of facilities, supporting resources, and training. The chapter ends by making recommendations based on the findings of the study.

DOI: 10.4018/978-1-7998-5033-5.ch006

INTRODUCTION

Ethiopia gives due recognition to the value of digital literacy. The country's Information and Communications Technology (ICT) Policy and Strategy acknowledges that ICT is crucial in addressing access and quality of education as the vast majority of the Ethiopian population still live in remote areas where there is a severe shortage of teachers (FDRE, 2016). The ICT Policy therefore sets the following goals with regard to education: "Ensure that ICT is equally available across all levels of the school system and across all levels of the country, is an integral part of the educational system, and is used to extensively deliver quality online education" (FDRE, 2016, p.17). It is striking that the aforementioned policy doesn't make any reference to teachers and teacher educators in its objectives. However, three of the nine strategies carry provisions related to teachers, namely, achieving a critical mass of computer literate teachers, devising affordable schemes for teachers and students to acquire ICT products and services, and linking academic institutions and libraries electronically to enable both teachers and students to access information resources (FDRE, 2016).

The ICT Policy of Ethiopia also lists what it calls "key challenges" faced in deploying ICT in schools. These include the problem of maintenance, the inability of rural schools to afford the price of an internet connection, and ICT being not widely implemented across the curriculum. With regard to the preparation and development of teachers, the policy seems to be quite uncertain and admits that "teachers may not have been trained properly". This seems awkward as policy of this kind is expected to be based on a sound assessment of the situation. This was also one of the reasons why the present-study was planned and executed. In other words, the absence of any statement directly related to teachers and teacher educators in the objectives of the ICT Policy, and the uncertainty about the level of training of teachers in Ethiopia (not to mention teacher educators) are taken as adequate justification to carry out a study that explores the level of digital literacy among teacher educators.

The specific objectives of the study are to a) explore the level of digital literacy among teacher educators in Ethiopia, b) examine factors that enhance and/or limit the competence of teacher educators in using digital technologies for educational purposes, c) analyze the implications of the current level of use of digital technologies in view of achieving SDG4, and d) provide recommendations to improve digital literacy, also in the context of Education for Sustainable Development, among teacher educators in Ethiopia.

BACKGROUND

Definition, Scope, and Benefits of Digital Literacy

Digital literacy has been defined as the ability to "access, manage, understand, integrate, communicate, evaluate, and create information safely and appropriately through digital technologies for employment, decent jobs and entrepreneurship" (UNESCO, 2018, p.6). Beyond the ability to handle computers, it involves skills such as use and production of digital media, information processing and retrieval, participation in social networks for creating and sharing knowledge, and a much wider range of professional computing skills.

Digital literacy is believed to have a significant impact on education, ranging from curriculum development to classroom practice. Digitalization of education radically changes how course content and curricula are developed and delivered to students. The potential for greater flexibility, standardization, and even globalization of curricula will increase equitability and provide greater choice. Hence an interesting assertion: "No longer will the best outcomes be provided by the 'best schools'; there is no reason why an engineer from sub-Saharan Africa will be any less competent than one from the USA or Japan" (TWI2050, 2019, p.38).

The potential impact of digital technologies on activities of teachers (the same could be said for teacher educators) is quite massive (Kitchenham, 2008; Alemu, 2017; TWI2050, 2019). Teachers will have to develop "a radically different skill set to be able to deliver engaging 'lessons' via new technologies" (TWI2050, 2019, p.38). Although the approaches used to deploy digital technologies in schools take various forms, one can group them into three broad categories; technology for instructional preparation, technology for instructional delivery, and technology as a learning tool (Jonassen *et al.* 2008).

There are also subject-specific benefits of use of digital technologies. In Geography and other Earth Science-related disciplines, for instance, the new geo-technologies "have made the world 'virtually accessible' to the individual Internet user in ways that were not feasible until relatively recently" (Fargher, 2019, p.176). Evidence on the ground also indicates that use of digital technologies is bringing a marked change in teachers' practices. Sharma (2017) suggests, for instance, that most of the teaching and learning processes in the classroom these days are changing from autocratic style to democratic or participatory style where learners play an active role. Another study that investigated the changing role of the teacher in ICT-supported foreign language instruction shows that the teachers' "focus shifted from teacher to student-centred instruction, the relationship between the teachers and the students was more relaxed than in a usual class" (Podgoršek, 2020, p.346).

Digital Technologies, SDG4, and Sustainable Development

ICT, as related to sustainability, has been subdivided into "sustainability in ICT" and "sustainability by ICT" (Hilty and Aebischer, 2015 cited in Ruchi, Suresh, Zubkov and Shariq, 2020, p.435). Sustainability in ICT refers to making ICT goods and services more sustainable over their whole life cycle (mainly by reducing the energy and material flows they invoke), whereas sustainability by ICT refers to creating, enabling, and encouraging sustainable patterns of production and consumption by means of ICT. It has been strongly argued that teachers (and teacher educators by implication) play an indispensable role both in the promotion of sustainability in ICT and sustainability by ICT. For instance, the document entitled "Incheon Declaration and Framework for Action for the Implementation of Sustainable Development Goal 4" clearly admits not only that teachers are "the key to achieving all of the SDG4-Education 2030 agenda", but also restates the fact that "teachers are a fundamental condition for guaranteeing quality education" (Unesco, 2016, p.54).

SDG4 aims at ensuring an "inclusive and equitable quality education and promote lifelong learning opportunities for all". It has seven targets including the one which calls for ensuring that all learners acquire the knowledge and skills needed to promote sustainable development (SD), including, among others, through education for sustainable development and sustainable lifestyles, human rights, gender equality, promotion of a culture of peace and non-violence, global citizenship and appreciation of cultural diversity and of culture's contribution to sustainable development.

Besides the seven targets, three means of implementation have been specified under SGD4. These are (1) building and upgrading education facilities and providing safe, non-violent, inclusive and effective learning environments for all, (2) substantially expanding the number of scholarships available to developing countries for enrolment in higher education, including vocational training and information and communications technology, technical, engineering and scientific programmes, and (3) substantially increasing the supply of qualified teachers, including through international cooperation for teacher training in developing countries. It is therefore interesting to see a direct reference to teacher education and an aspect of digital literacy has been made in SDG4 albeit at the level of means of implementation, not that of the seven targets.

A strong call has been made to empower teachers and educators so that they play their expected role effectively. In relation to this, it is important to note that the findings of the 6th Consultation on (among others) how countries across the world are progressing towards Target 4.7 (Education for Sustainable Development (ESD)) of SDG4 show positive development in most of the indicators except teacher training, which was presented as a "stumbling block" (Unesco, 2018, p.9). This is indeed a grim assessment with far reaching implications. Given the role teachers play in meeting the SDG4 targets, poor training will have a serious impact. This chapter aims specifically at assessing the digital literacy among teacher educators (those who are in charge of training teachers) in Ethiopia; and the implication of this to the achievement of SDG4 and ESD.

Factors Affecting the Use of Digital Technologies

Preparedness of Teachers and Teacher Educators

Viberg *et al.* (2020) underscore that teachers' preparedness to use digital technology in education is a key for the construction of useful pedagogical knowledge thereby improving students' learning. This, in turn, shows that the "benefits of digital technology can be best realized when strategically introduced and used by skilled and confident teachers" (ILO, 2021, p.7). The problem, however, is that many of the approximately 80 million teachers worldwide (as of 2019) have had no formal pedagogical training, and that the vast majority have no experience or expertise in information and communication technologies (TWI2050, 2019, p.38). The problem is even more rampant in Sub-Saharan Africa (SSA) where the lack of trained teachers and the low level of teachers' ICT knowledge and skills are believed to be "major impediments to effectively introducing technology into schools" (Harrison, 2010, P.67). The situation is not any different in Ethiopia. A recently completed doctoral research (Jang, 2020) shows, for instance, that teacher educators at Addis Ababa University and Kotebe Metropolitan University (KMU) have a good knowledge of the technology, but inadequate skill as to how to integrate technology in teaching.

Knowledge About and Skills in Ethical and Critical Use of Digital Technology

A research conducted by ILO (2021, p.11) suggests that, in all of the participating countries, the ethical and critical dimensions of the use of digital technologies was often overlooked. Ethical and critical concerns here relate to assessing the validity of digital sources and data, including distinguishing between reliable and unreliable information, ensuring academic integrity in coursework, establishing and protecting copyright over materials produced, ensuring data protection and online safety and security, and preventing health and mental risks.

STATUS OF DIGITAL LITERACY IN ETHIOPIA

In Ethiopia, there have been efforts, albeit limited and in most cases ineffective, to use digital technologies in teaching and learning. In 2003, for instance, the Ethiopian Government initiated the Satellite Plasma TV Project with a hope to improve the quality of secondary education by utilizing educational media (Temtim, 2017; Genet, 2018; Mogus, 2021). Through the project, pre-recorded course content had been delivered by a remote teacher via the plasma screen, with the classroom teacher monitoring and explaining content. Dr Genet Zewde, former Minister of Education, seems to paint a very positive picture as to the impact of the then new technology in alleviating some of the critical problems facing the country's education system:

"This program helped minimize the shortage of teachers and laboratories since the same standard of education is transmitted throughout the country .... Moreover, (...) English is strictly used which helps students to improve their language proficiency. Furthermore, it enabled students to observe lab demonstrations through ICT." (in Genet, 2018, p.100)

Subsequent initiatives in Ethiopia included the national SchoolNet, which was launched in 2004 and focused on the deployment and use of ICT to facilitate teaching and learning in secondary schools and aimed to develop a wide-area network linking all secondary schools in the country by making internet and online education accessible. As a follow-up to the SchoolNet Initiative, another project was launched in 2013 under the General Education Quality Improvement Programme II (GEQIP II) (ILO, 2021; Mogus, 2021).

An empirical study that assessed the benefits of and challenges encountered during the use of Satellite Plasma (Temtim, 2017) seems to substantiate some of the arguments by Dr Genet Zewdie. It was found that the project brought some benefits for the students, including attracting their attention for learning, simplifying complex concepts by visual demonstration, and helping teachers to upgrade their pedagogical skills by watching the plasma teacher. The study also singled out a number of problems related to the use of plasma. As the instructional delivery was quite fast and used advanced English, students often had difficulty to keep pace with the plasma teacher. Besides, as much of the class time was allocated for the plasma teacher, classroom teachers acted more like "classroom managers rather than source of knowledge to their students" (Temtim, 2017, p.413). Other challenges include frequent power interruption, and failure of the plasma TVs.

A more recent study on students' social media literacy in Bahir Dar University (Behailu, 2021) shows that students' social media literacy is generally low. Their performance in media access, awareness and production is relatively better whereas students performed the least on ethical awareness and media evaluation, which are both critical for a responsible utilization of ICT. Yet another study that assesses the determinants of instructors' educational ICT use in Ethiopian higher education institutions (Bekalu *et al.*, 2021) shows that instructors perceived that they had limited knowledge and skills (which they had developed through self-learning) in using ICT for teaching and learning purposes.

The review of literature indicates that no systematic study has been conducted to assess the digital competencies of teacher educators in Ethiopia. The study, the results of which will be reported in this chapter, was therefore initiated to bridge this gap.

PROBLEM AND RATIONALE

"Teachers who do not have a chance to develop professionally in the use of emerging technologies and acquire modern computer literacy and skills are under threat" (Harrison, 2010, P.69).

The warning quoted here seems somehow exaggerated. However, the reality in the classroom indicates that teachers who struggle to use emerging technologies are already being left back. Harrison also argues that the "relevance of a teacher in the 21st century is determined by the will to develop professionally and appropriately" (Harrison, 2010, P.69). In Sub-Saharan Africa, the role of the teacher in developing ICT use in schools is said to be "utterly critical" as there are many obstacles to be faced, in addition to those that emerge more generally anyway, like a shortage of resources. In Ethiopia, the recently launched Education Roadmap (ERM), covering the period from 2018-2030, clearly presents the problems related to the utilization of ICT for educational purposes, and the limitations related to the competences of teachers (MOE, 2018). The ERM states, for instance, that ICT is "not well utilized mainly due to inaccessibility of ICT facilities and poor infrastructure, and inadequate preparation of teacher candidates to use ICT" (MOE, 2018, p.38).

A more recent study reveals that the present status of ICT materials "in teacher training institutes discourages trainees from integrating ICT into their teaching" (Jang, 2020, p.247). Another study conducted to assess the use of digital technology in secondary schools (Berhanu, 2017) shows that school teachers lack appropriate training in ICT. Related challenges include a lack of interest and motivation on the part of some teachers to adopt new technologies; and a lack of commitment on the part of the school leadership.

In its policy recommendations, the Ethiopian Education Roadmap, provides two suggestions directly related to the use of ICT for education: (1) enabling pre-service teachers to not only understand how to use a computer, but also how to design high quality technology-enhanced lessons, and (2) providing adequate access to ICT infrastructure (MOE, 2018). The implementation of the first recommendation requires a good understanding about the state of digital literacy among the teacher educators currently serving in the various colleges of teacher education. The aim of this chapter is therefore to report the findings on the status of digital literacy among teacher educators in Ethiopia along with the implications thereof to the achievement of SDG4 and (E)SD.

METHODS

This study was conducted in two colleges of teacher education. A questionnaire was applied in both colleges. The questionnaire was adopted from an instrument developed by Viberg et al. (2020) to measure Teachers' "Preparedness to Use Digital Technology in their Teaching". It has five sections aimed at gathering information on the following issues: a) personal and academic profile, type and duration of use of computer/mobile, purpose for which computers/mobiles are used, and the way the respondent got introduced to a computer, b) competence in the use of computer skills, c) competence in various aspects of digital technologies, d) factors affecting use of digital technologies for teaching-learning purposes, and views about the use of digital technologies for teaching-learning activities.

The part of the questionnaire that tries to seek information about teacher educators' preparedness in the use of digital learning technologies or ICT in education has 23 items. For each of the statements, the respondents were requested to indicate their level of agreement in a five-point Likert scale ranging from "strongly agree" to "strongly disagree". The 23 items were put under seven headings (see table 2): Teacher educators' preparedness to use ICT in education, social influence and support, usefulness and efficiency, intention of use, pedagogical potential, assistance awareness, and limitation awareness. An eight- A five-point Likert scale (see table 3) was used to assess the views of teacher educators about the use of digital technologies for teaching and learning.

The questionnaire has been given to randomly selected teacher educators in the two colleges either in hard copy or as an email attachment. A total of 78 questionnaires were completed, 40 from Hawassa College of Teacher Education and 38 from Robe College of Teacher Education. Data analysis was done using SPSS Version 26.

RESULTS AND DISCUSSION

Background of the Participants

A total of 78 teacher educators took part in the study, of which 74 were male and only 4 female. The low representation of females is a reflection of the bigger picture as the proportion of female teacher educators is still quite low in Ethiopia (Almaz, 2003). The situation has not changed much over the past two decades. The current proportion of female teacher educators is 15.6% in Hawassa College of Teacher Education and 5.6% in Robe College of Teacher Education. The age of participants ranges from 28 to 59 years, the average age being 40. Close to 90% of the responds hold a masters degree (table 1). More than 80% have experiences as teachers or teacher educators for longer than ten years. The shortest and longest experiences were found to be 3 and 36 years, respectively, the average experience being 17 years.

Table 1. Background of the 78 teacher educators involved in this study

Item	Category	Frequency	Percentage
Gender	Female	4	5.1
	Male	74	94.9
Age	≤30	6	7.7
	31-40	41	52.5
	41-50	23	29.5
	≥51	8	10.3
Qualification	BA/BSc	9	11.5
	MA/MSc	69	88.5
Experience	≤10	15	19.2
	11-20	40	51.3
	≥21	23	29.5

Preparedness to Use ICT in Education

As indicated in the methodology section, 23 items statements have been included in the instrument to measure the degree of preparedness of teacher educators to use ICT in education. The items have been classified and ordered into seven categories (table 2). All four statements related to the abilities to use digital technologies have been rated positively by more than 60% of the respondents. The statement: "I feel comfortable using digital technology in education" received the highest degree of endorsement (89.7%). This is quite a remarkable finding as confidence in the use of such technologies is often believed to be an important factor with a potential to determine the use of the technologies for educational purposes.

A mixed view is to be seen with regard to social influence and support. Close to three-fourth of the respondents indicated agreement to the statement: "Colleagues in my work place think I should use digital technology". However, more than half (59%) of the respondents were either not sure or did not believe that the infrastructure in their college could support the actual use of digital technology. On the other hand, the two statements related to intentions to use digital technology have been positively rated by more than 60% of the respondents (table 2).

Participants of this study demonstrated the highest rate of agreement to statements related to usefulness and efficiency of digital technologies. All the six statements were agreed on by more than 80% of the participants. Two of the statements ("Digital technology increases my work and productivity" and "I believe that digital technology may enable a new and more diversified production of knowledge") drew the highest rates of agreement, i.e. 98.7% and 96.2%, respectively. This shows that the respondents seem to put massive trust in digital technologies in terms of capacity to boost productivity and production of new knowledge (table 2).

Table 2. Teacher educators' preparedness to use ICT in education, frequencies and percentages of answers given by 78 teacher educators involved in this study

Code	Statements	Result in	Strongly Disagree	Disagree	Not sure	Agree	Strongly agree
	Abilities to use DLT						
S1	I find digital technology easy to use for my purposes.	Freq.	2	13	6	30	27
		%	2.6	16.7	7.7	38.5	34.6
S2	I can use digital tools in my teaching.	Freq.	1	15	3	40	19
		%	1.3	19.2	3.8	51.3	24.4
S3	I have sufficient skills to teach my pupils to use digital technology as a tool for knowledge search, communication, creativity and learning.	Freq.	2	17	10	32	17
		%	2.6	21.8	12.8	41.0	21.8
S4	I feel comfortable using digital technology in education.	Freq.	-	3	5	44	26
		%	-	3.8	6.4	56.4	33.3
	Social influence and support						
S5	Colleagues in my work place think I should use digital technology.	Freq.	-	5	15	39	19
		%	-	6.4	19.2	50.0	24.4
S6	The college infrastructure has, generally, supported the use of digital technology.	Freq.	11	24	11	28	4
		%	14.1	30.8	14.1	35.9	5.1
	Intention of use						
S7	I plan to use digital technology in the coming year.	Freq.	-	5	23	33	17
		%	-	6.4	29.5	42.3	21.8
S8	I believe that the available supply of digital technology supports my teaching.	Freq.	1	6	9	38	24
		%	1.3	7.7	11.5	48.7	30.8
	Usefulness & efficiency						
S9	I have found digital technology that is useful in my work.	Freq.	1	3	8	41	25
		%	1.3	3.8	10.3	52.6	32.1
S10	Digital technology increases my work and productivity.	Freq.	-	1	-	43	34
		%	-	1.3	-	55.1	43.6
S11	I believe that digital technology may enable a new and more diversified production of knowledge.	Freq.	1	1	1	35	40
		%	1.3	1.3	1.3	44.9	51.3
S12	The digital tools in teaching help students achieve their learning goals.	Freq.	-	1	8	33	36
		%	-	1.3	10.3	42.3	46.2
S13	The digital tools facilitate my efforts to assess pupils' learning.	Freq.	-	2	10	38	28
		%	-	2.6	12.8	48.7	35.9
S14	I think the digital tools that I have found, or been introduced to, support my pedagogical ideas.	Freq.	-	1	15	37	25
		%	-	1.3	19.2	47.4	32.1
	Pedagogical potential						
S15	I understand the potential of digital technology and how this can be used differently, depending on the purpose and course content.	Freq.	-	1	15	39	23
		%	-	1.3	19.2	50.0	29.5

Continued on following page

Table 2. Continued

Code	Statements	Result in	Strongly Disagree	Disagree	Not sure	Agree	Strongly agree
	Abilities to use DLT						
S16	I'm actively looking for digital technology that I can use to facilitate student learning.	Freq.	-	8	4	40	26
		%	-	10.3	5.1	51.3	33.3
S17	I am aware of the possibilities and limitations of digital technology in my teaching and how it may affect the pedagogical design in my subject area.	Freq.	-	1	14	37	26
		%	-	1.3	17.9	47.4	33.3
	Assistance awareness						
S18	I have access to the necessary resources to be able to use digital technology.	Freq.	3	24	5	31	15
		%	3.8	30.8	6.4	39.7	19.2
S19	I know where I can get help if I encounter a problem with digital technology.	Freq.	5	10	16	32	15
		%	6.4	12.8	20.5	41.0	19.2
S20	I can find useful digital tools that can be easily integrated into my teaching.	Freq.	3	10	17	35	13
		%	3.8	12.8	21.8	44.9	16.7
	Limitation awareness						
S21	I believe that there are limitations to what the available digital technology can be used to teach in certain areas of my subject.	Freq.	1	9	14	38	16
		%	1.3	11.5	17.9	48.7	20.5
S22	I believe that some choices of knowledge content can limit the type of digital technology I can use.	Freq.	1	4	19	41	13
		%	1.3	5.1	24.4	52.6	16.7
S23	I believe that digital technology can limit representations of knowledge content.	Freq.	3	17	18	28	12
		%	3.8	21.8	23.1	35.9	15.4

The three statements related to the pedagogical potential of digital technologies have been endorsed by more than three-fourth of the respondents. For instance, 84.6% of the teacher educators who took part in the study agree to the statement: "I'm actively looking for digital technology that I can use to facilitate student learning" (table 2). This is indeed encouraging given the actual and potential role of digital technology in enhancing students' learning and achievement. In relation to statements pertaining to "assistance awareness", there is a moderate agreement. More than one third of the respondents were either unsure about the assistances available or didn't agree that they existed. It is interesting to see that more than one third (34.6%) of the respondents expressed their disagreement to the statement: "I have access to the necessary resources to be able to use digital technology" showing that a good proportion of teacher educators are keen to use the technology, but have no access to it.

The last category of statements of the preparedness measure relate to limitation awareness. Here again, there is a general agreement to the three statements but not that strong. Close to one third of the respondents expresses that they are unsure or disagree with the statements (Table 2). For instance, 25.6% of the respondents disagree with the statement which relates to one of the potential limitations of digital technology, i.e. limiting the representation of content knowledge. Close to one fourth of the respondents are not sure about the view that "some choices of knowledge content can limit the type of digital technology" teachers/teacher educators can use. Almost an equal proportion (23.1%) of the respondents expressed their hesitation to support or reject the view "that digital technology can limit representations of knowledge content". The findings thus clearly indicate that teacher educators lack an in-depth understanding about the shortcomings of digital technologies. As awareness about the limitations of educational technologies is necessary for a critical choice and application of such technologies for instructional purposes, this area of digital literacy seems to require a closer attention during capacity building programs meant to improve competencies of teacher educators.

Views on Use of Digital Technologies for Teaching and Learning

Assessing teachers' attitude about ICT innovations could provide valuable information for educational managers dealing with the adoption and use of ICT in teaching/learning (Pucer, Vičič, and Žvanut, 2020). This study uses an eight-item Likert scale to assess the views of teacher educators about the use of digital technologies for teaching and learning (table 3). In general, the teacher educators involved in this study seem to hold a highly desirable view with regard to the use of digital technologies. Close to 90% said that they enjoyed using digital technologies; and even a greater proportion (93.6%) expressed that they "feel comfortable using digital devices". On the other hand, 44.9% of the respondents indicated that they "feel threatened when others talk about digital technologies". One can see a bit of a contradiction here: If the overwhelming majority are comfortable using the technology, how can they feel threatened when others talk about it? One can only assume that some people might be well skilled in using but still uncomfortable talking about it with others. The responses to the third, fifth and sixth statements seem to lend credence to this assumption.

Almost equal proportions of the respondents (42.3%) felt that they lie behind "fellow teacher educator in using digital technologies". This is probably why they feel threated to talk about the technology. The great desire to learn more (statement 3) and improve digital fluency (statement 5) could also be taken as important clues to explain the apparent contradiction indicated above. Close to ninety percent (87.2%) of the respondents agree to the statement: "I think that it is important for me to improve my digital fluency" whereas two-thirds expressed willingness to "learn more about digital technologies".

Table 3. Views on the use of digital technologies for teaching and learning, frequencies and percentages of answers given by 78 teacher educators involved in this study

Code	Statement	Strongly disagree		Disagree		Not sure		Agree		Strongly agree	
		Freq.	%	Freq.	%	Freq.	%	Freq.	%	Freq.	%
V1	I enjoy using digital devices.	-	-	-	-	8	10.3	31	39.7	39	50.0
V2	I feel comfortable using digital devices.	-	-	-	-	5	6.4	30	38.5	48	55.1
V3	I am willing to learn more about digital technologies.	1	1.3	11	14.1	15	19.2	28	35.9	23	29.5
V4	I feel threatened when others talk about digital technologies.	19	24.4	16	20.5	8	10.3	30	38.5	5	6.4
V5	I feel that I am behind my fellow teacher educators in using digital technologies.	16	20.5	17	21.8	9	11.5	34	43.6	2	2.6
V6	I think that it is important for me to improve my digital fluency.	-	-	-	-	10	12.8	27	34.6	41	52.6
V7	I think that my learning can be enhanced by using digital tools and resources.	-	-	-	-	4	5.1	34	43.6	40	51.3
V8	I think that training in technology-enhanced teaching and learning should be included in teacher education programs.	-	-	1	1.3	10	12.8	25	32.1	42	53.8

Table 3 also shows that almost all respondents (94.9%) thought that their learning could be "enhanced by using digital tools and resources". This could be the decisive factor why 84.9% of the respondents endorse the suggestion that "training in technology-enhanced teaching and learning should be included in teacher education programs". On the whole, the study shows that teacher educators have a positive attitude toward the use of digital technologies, and feel a need to integrate it into teacher education programs. This implies that there is a great chance for digital technologies to be used for achieving the goals of ESD and SD, provided that some of the most important shortcomings (e.g. poor facility) are addressed.

CONCLUSION AND RECOMMENDATIONS

It is widely acknowledged that digital technologies play an important role in achieving Sustainable Development Goals (SDGs) in general and SDG4 in particular. Digital literacy makes a significant contribution to quality education through its impact on both curriculum development and classroom practice. It is a well-established fact that digitalization of education radically changes (and is already changing) how course content and curricula are developed and delivered to students. It has also been strongly argued that well prepared teachers (and teacher educators by implication) play an indispensable role both in the promotion of sustainability in ICT and sustainability by ICT.

One should also stress that making use of digital technologies to bring about quality in education requires having the necessary infrastructure like broadband internet connection and reliable energy supply. Besides, the level of teachers' preparedness determines the degree to which digital technologies could be used for instructional purposes. Among the factors that contribute to teachers' preparedness is the extent of digital literacy among teacher educators. Therefore, this study sought to assess digital literacy among teacher educators in Ethiopia, and the findings shade light on both areas of strengths and weaknesses.

Among the strengths identified by the study is a loud and clear recognition policy documents give to the value of digital literacy. The Ethiopian Information and Communications Technology (ICT) Policy and Strategy acknowledges that ICT is crucial in addressing access and quality of education as the vast majority of the Ethiopian population still live in remote areas where there is a severe shortage of teachers (FDRE, 2016). At policy level, the country took a bold step towards the integration of digital technologies to improve both access and quality of education (Hare, 2007; Genet, 2018). It is hence argued that unlike many African countries “where educationalists are still grappling with policy issues and trying to formulate strategies for adoption of ICT within their education sector, Ethiopia has done well in developing a detailed strategy and an accompanying implementation plan all with action plans and timelines” (Hare, 2007, p.7).

The practice related to the application of digital technologies for educational purposes in Ethiopia does not seem as encouraging as the policy provisions. There is, for instance, a serious shortage of infrastructure and resources. The opportunities for teachers and students to get appropriate training are also limited. With regard to the digital literacy among teacher educators, this study comes up with mixed results.

On the positive side, teacher educators reported a generally high level of preparedness to use digital technologies, more than 60% felt they had both the ”abilities” and ”intentions” to use digital technologies, more than 80% appreciated the ”usefulness and efficiency of digital technologies”; and more than three-fourth valued the ”pedagogical potential of digital technologies.” Teacher educators also expressed a positive attitude towards the use of digital technologies and the need to integrate it into the teacher education programs.

On the other hand, the participants of the study indicated areas that need further improvement. For instance, respondents exhibited a limited awareness about the shortcomings of digital technologies. With regard to factors that affect the utilization of digital technologies, teacher educators identified three as most important: lack of facilities, supporting resources and training. For instance, more than one third of the participants expressed their disagreement to the statement: “I have access to the necessary resources to be able to use digital technology” thereby indicating that a good proportion of teacher educators are keen to use the technology, but have no access to it.

One can also infer that teacher educators lack an in-depth understanding about the shortcomings of digital technologies. As awareness about the limitations of educational technologies is necessary for a critical choice and application of such technologies for instructional purposes, this area of digital literacy seems to require a closer attention during capacity building programs meant to improve competencies of teacher educators.

On the whole, the study shows that teacher educators have a positive attitude toward the use of digital technologies, and feel a need to integrate it into teacher education programs. This implies that there is a great chance for digital technologies to be used for achieving the goals of ESD and SD, provided that some of the most important shortcomings are duly addressed. The chapter therefore ends by suggesting three points that could address the gaps identified.

First, improving accessibility and affordability of professional development programs. Training and professional development should be not only affordable and accessible to all teacher educators but should also take the role of digital literacy to achieving the goals of ESD and SD into account. *Second*, equip colleges of teacher education with appropriate infrastructure and facilities. In addition to providing more equipment and facilities, the existing facilities for development of digital literacy must be significantly improved and regularly monitored and maintained. *Third*, and finally, design and implement a long-term plan. Studies indicate that shifts in the teaching as well as in the learning paradigm are gradual and challenging processes (Podgoršek, 2020). Efforts to integrate digital technologies should therefore be carefully planned and supported over a longer period of time. One can think, for instance, of establishing a national ”Center of Excellence” aimed at improving the digital literacy of teachers and teacher educators.

REFERENCES

Alemu, B. M. (2017). Transforming Educational Practices of Ethiopia into Development and the Knowledge Society through Information and Communication Technology. *American Educational Research Journal*, *5*(1), 1–14.

Assefa, T. (2017). Educational Technology Implementation in Ethiopian High Schools: Benefits and Challenges of the Instructional Plasma TV. In A. Marcus-Quinn & T. Hourigan (Eds.), *Handbook on Digital Learning for K-12 Schools*. Springer International Publishing. doi:10.1007/978-3-319-33808-8_25

Eshete, A. (2003). Women in Faculties of Teacher Training Institutions in Ethiopia. Addis Ababa: UNESCO International Institute for Capacity Building in Africa .

Behailu, A. (2021). Higher Education Students' Social Media Literacy in Ethiopia: A Case of Bahir Dar University. *The Journal of Media Literacy Education*, *13*(3), 86–96.

Fargher, M. (2019). The Role of Geography and Geospatial Technologies. In González R. D., Donert, K. and Koutsopoulos, K. (eds.), Geospatial Technologies in Geography Education. Cham: Springer Nature Switzerland AG

FDRE (The Federal Democratic Republic of Ethiopia). (2016). *The National Information and Communication Technology (ICT) Policy and Strategy: Final Draft. Addis Ababa Genet Zewde (2018). No One Left Behind: Redesigning the Ethiopian Education System*. Mega Publishing and Distribution PLC.

Ferede, B., Elen, J., Van Petegem, W., Hunde, A. B., & Goeman, K. (2022). Determinants of instructors' educational ICT use in Ethiopian higher education. *Education and Information Technologies*, *27*(1), 917–936. doi:10.100710639-021-10606-z PMID:34230802

Hare, H. (2007). ICT in Education in Ethiopia, https://documents1.worldbank.org/curated/en/9955414682561428 02/pdf/463910BRI0Box31ia010ICTed0Survey111.pdf (accessed on 23 March, 2022)

Harrison, D. (2010). Teacher Factors Influencing Classroom ICT Use. In *Sara Hennessy et al., Developing Use of ICT to Enhance Teaching and Learning in East African Schools: A Review of the Literature*. University of Cambridge and DFID.

ILO. (2021). *Digitalization in Teaching and Education in Ethiopia, Kenya, Malawi, Rwanda and the United Republic of Tanzania: Digitalization, the Future of Work and the Teaching Profession Project, A Synthesis Report*. International Labour Office.

Jang, C. 1. (2020). *Teachers' Beliefs and Practices of ICT Use in Secondary Schools in Addis Ababa, Ethiopia*. [Thesis Submitted for the Degree of Doctor of Philosophy to the School of International Development of the University of East Anglia].

Jonassen, D. (2008). *Meaningful Learning with Technology*. Pearson, Merrill Prentice Hall.

Kim, S.-W., & Bogale, G. (2014). Does Satellite Program Satisfy Ethiopian Secondary School Education? In *International Conference e-Learning 2014*, (p. 79–86).

Kitchenham, H. (2008). One-to-One Computing and Teacher Transformation. In *Hansson, T. Handbook of Research on Digital Information Technologies: Innovations, Methods, and Ethical Issues*. Information Science Reference. doi:10.4018/978-1-59904-970-0.ch007

MOE (Ministry of Education). (2018). Ethiopian Education Development Roadmap (2018-30): An Integrated Executive Summary. Addis Ababa: Education Strategy Center (ESC)

Podgoršek, S. (2020). The Changing Role of the Teacher in ICT-Supported Foreign Language Instruction: A Multiple-Case Study. In *Eva Podovšovnik, Examining the Roles of Teachers and Students in Mastering New Technologies*. IGI Global. doi:10.4018/978-1-7998-2104-5.ch018

Pucer, P., Vičič, Š. G., & Žvanut, B. (2020). ICT Adoption among Higher Education Teachers: A Case Study of a University in the Awareness/Exploration Stage of Blended Learning Adoption. In *Eva Podovšovnik, Examining the Roles of Teachers and Students in Mastering New Technologies*. IGI Global. doi:10.4018/978-1-7998-2104-5.ch016

Ruchi, T., Suresh, V., Zubkov, S. A., & Shariq, M. (2020). ICT Skills for Sustainable Development Goal 4. In W. Leal Filh (Eds.), *Quality Education, Encyclopedia of the UN Sustainable Development Goals*. Springer Nature Switzerland AG.

Sharma, M. (2017). Teacher in a Digital Era. *Global Journal of Computer Science and Technology (G), 17*(3).

Tjoa, A., & Simon, T. (2016). The Role of ICT to Achieve the UN Sustainable Development Goals (SDG). *6th IFIP World Information Technology Forum (WITFOR),* (pp.3-13).

TWI2050. (2019). The Digital Revolution and Sustainable Development: Opportunities and Challenges. *Report Prepared by The World in 2050 Initiative. International Institute for Applied Systems Analysis (IIASA),* Laxenburg, Austria. www.twi2050.org

UNESCO (2018). A Global Framework of Reference on Digital Literacy Skills for Indicator 4.4.2. *Information Paper No. 51*. UNESCO.

UNESCO. (2016). *Incheon Declaration and Framework for Action for the Implementation of Sustainable Development Goal 4: Ensure Inclusive and Equitable Quality Education and Promote Lifelong Learning Opportunities For All.* UNESCO.

Unesco (2018). *Progress on Education for Sustainable development and Global Citizenship*. UNESCO.

Viberg, O., Mavroudi, A., Khalil, M., & Bälter, O. (2020). Validating an Instrument to Measure Teachers' Preparedness to Use Digital Technology in their Teaching. *Nordic Journal of Digital Literacy*, *15*(1), 38–54. doi:10.18261/issn.1891-943x-2020-01-04

Yigezu, M. (2021). Digitalization in Teaching and Education in Ethiopia. In *ILO, Digitalization, the Future of Work and the Teaching Profession Project, Background Report*. International Labour Office.

Chapter 7

Holistic Learning and Education for Sustainable Development:

Building a Virtual Community of Engaged and Responsible Learners by Tokkatsu

Kanako N. Kusanagi
Graduate School of Education and Human Development, Nagoya University, Japan

ABSTRACT

This chapter examines the implementation of holistic learning in virtual space and presents it as a humanistic approach to ensure students' democratic participation in online and distance learning. While education for sustainable development (ESD) envisions active and engaged learners, students struggled to engage in online and distance learning (ODL) during the Coronavirus disease (COVID-19) pandemic. This study examines the holistic learning curriculum, tokkatsu—which originated in Japan—and discusses its prospect for nurturing responsible and active learners. In tokkatsu, students participate in nonacademic activities where they learn to take the initiative, have dialogue, and collaborate as responsible members of the community. This chapter presents an application of the tokkatsu in virtual space, taking a case from Indonesia. It describes the contextualized case of tokkatsu to build a community of learners in the crisis of the COVID-19 pandemic and how challenges in the digitalization of the classroom were overcome.

INTRODUCTION

Education for Sustainable Development (ESD) encourages learners to embody knowledge, skills, values, and attitudes to transform themselves for a more sustainable and just society for all. To take up unforeseen challenges in the complex and rapidly changing society in the VUCA (volatile, uncertain, complex, ambiguous) era, learning needs to be transformative to cope with rapidly changing societies (Pavlova, 2013). ESD targets:

DOI: 10.4018/978-1-7998-5033-5.ch007

To empower learners to transform themselves and the society they live in by developing knowledge, skills, attitudes, competences, and values required for addressing global citizenship and local contextual challenges of the present and the future, such as critical and systemic thinking, analytical problem-solving, creativity, working collaboratively and making decisions in the face of uncertainty, and understanding of the interconnectedness of global challenges and responsibilities emanating from such awareness. (UNESCO, 2015a)

For learners to be active and engaging citizens, they need a learning experience that is beyond the traditional concept of narrowly defined academic learning and top-down dissemination of knowledge. Their democratic participation in building a relationship, involvement in decision-making, and taking active roles in their communities are essential.

The school shut down by the COVID-19 pandemic posed many challenges to students and teachers. In a difficult time, students needed more support from their teachers and peers. In reality, the traditional way of teaching and learning was reinforced in the online and distance learning (ODL) situation, and many students could not accommodate learning individually from the home environment. Learning loss encompassed not only academic learning but also students' social and character development. They were deprived of the experience of being a part of the classroom and school community. People realize that school serves a role of a social place where "students can learn and develop social competencies, such as self-confidence, friendship, empathy, participation, respect, gratitude, compassion, and responsibility" (Colao et al., 2020). There were concerns about taking care of mental health issues during social isolation and the need for social and emotional care of students (Adegboye et al., 2021).

In fact, ESD recognizes learning to be social and holistic and anticipates its experience to be more engaging and participatory. Learning for sustainability is defined by UNESCO experts by five pillars (Combes, 2005, pp. 216–217; Delors et al., 1996).

- **Learning to Know**, so as to acquire a taste for learning throughout life and for understanding the world. This concerns cognitive skills and reasoning.
- **Learning to Do**, so as to be able to deal with many situations and be an actor as well as a thinker. This focuses on practical skills and knowing how to act.
- **Learning to Be**, so as to better develop one's personality and be able to act with greater autonomy, judgment, and personal responsibility. This relates to personal skills and dignity.
- **Learning to Live Together**, so as to develop an understanding of other people and their own history, traditions, and spirituality, in order to participate and cooperate with others in all human activities. This has to do with social skills and social capital.
- **Learning to Transform Oneself and Society**, so as to develop respect for the environment, social solidarity, and a non-discriminatory, gender-sensitive world. This reflects a synergy of cognitive, practical, personal, and social skills to bring about sustainability.

However, this is not easy since such learning activities have not been structured within the traditional school system and require a systematic change. Especially in collectivistic societies such as Japan and Indonesia, people's well-being is greatly influenced by how well they can work with one another and with those who surround them. For a sustainable society, the integration of independent and interdependent dimensions is important; thus, the ability to work with others is essential, not limited to Asia but in other parts of the world (Kjell, 2011).

This chapter examines the holistic learning curriculum in Japanese education—tokkatsu—and its adaptation in an Indonesian context as an activity system for holistic learning needed in ESD. In the Japanese curriculum, there are designated periods of nonacademic educational activities called tokkatsu. The definition of tokkatsu by the Ministry of Education, Culture, Sports, and Technology (MEXT, 2017) is as follows:

The period of Special Activities ("Tokkatsu") provides educational activities in which the school and classrooms are considered "societies ." Through group activities conducted there, independent and practical attitudes are cultivated in children to enable them to build better group life and make better personal selves.

Through engagement in the tokkatsu activities, students acquire various skills and competencies that are essential to living their school lives as well as living in society. Tokkatsu embeds collaboration and learning by doing activities in daily school activities and builds a learning community essential for ESD.

This chapter discusses tokkatsu as an approach for ESD to transforming learning activities to accommodate the needs of learners and provide social and emotional support needed in ODL. It presents the contextualized case of employing tokkatsu to build a community of learners in the crisis of the COVID-19 pandemic and the digitalization of the classroom.

1. How did tokkatsu facilitate structuring holistic learning activities in ODL in Indonesia?
2. What were the impacts of tokkatsu on ensuring student participation in virtual learning?
3. What are the implications of tokkatsu for ESD?

Tokkatsu and Education for Sustainable Development

In Japan, the ESD concept is stated in the current Course of Study (MEXT, 2019; Tanaka, 2017). On the other hand, the discussions in ESD mainly focused on the societal need for globalization, valuing individual character, and creating a lifelong learning system (Fredriksson et al., 2021). The cases of ESD in Japan concentrated on the topic of environmental and development education. ESD was rarely discussed in relation to the holistic philosophy of learning embedded in Japanese schools. One of the few studies by Clark et al. (2020) points out that Japan's engagement with ESD is underlined by the philosophy of *zenjin*-education (whole-person education). One characteristic of Japanese education has been its emphasis on students' holistic development on students and how various activities are structured to realize this goal. The holistic philosophy of education is represented in tokkatsu, where 35 hours per year are designated for nonacademic social activities.

There has been international attention to the holistic approach to Japanese education. This is due to the emerging interest in attending to the social and emotional dimensions of student learning (Tsuneyoshi et al., 2019). The strength of the Japanese curriculum is that cognitive and noncognitive learning are integrated (Tsuneyoshi et al. 2019, v.). The core principle in the Japanese curriculum is "Competencies for Living" (*Ikiru chikara*). Schools are expected to develop a healthy body, healthy life habits, and rich personalities/good ethics needed for future citizens, as shown in Figure 1. The feature of Japanese education is community-building activities and the emphasis on bond—*Kizuna*—in achieving holistic education (Le Tendre, 1999; Sato, 2003). Tokkatsu provides such an opportunity for community-building that is the foundation of the collaborative learning experience.

Tokkatsu consists of four types of activities: 1) class activities, 2) student council, 3) club activities, and 4) school events. School cleaning, school lunch, and sports festivals are well-known internationally. However, the purpose of these activities is often misunderstood. Tokkatsu focuses not on the implementation of these activities per se but provides students opportunities for community-building, democratic participation in decision-making, and fostering a positive attitude and ability to make the most of one's life (MEXT, 2019). Its bottom-up structure for embedding holistic learning into daily school activities has caught international attention (Tsuneyoshi et al., 2019).

Figure 1. Holistic approach in Japanese education (MEXT, 2019)

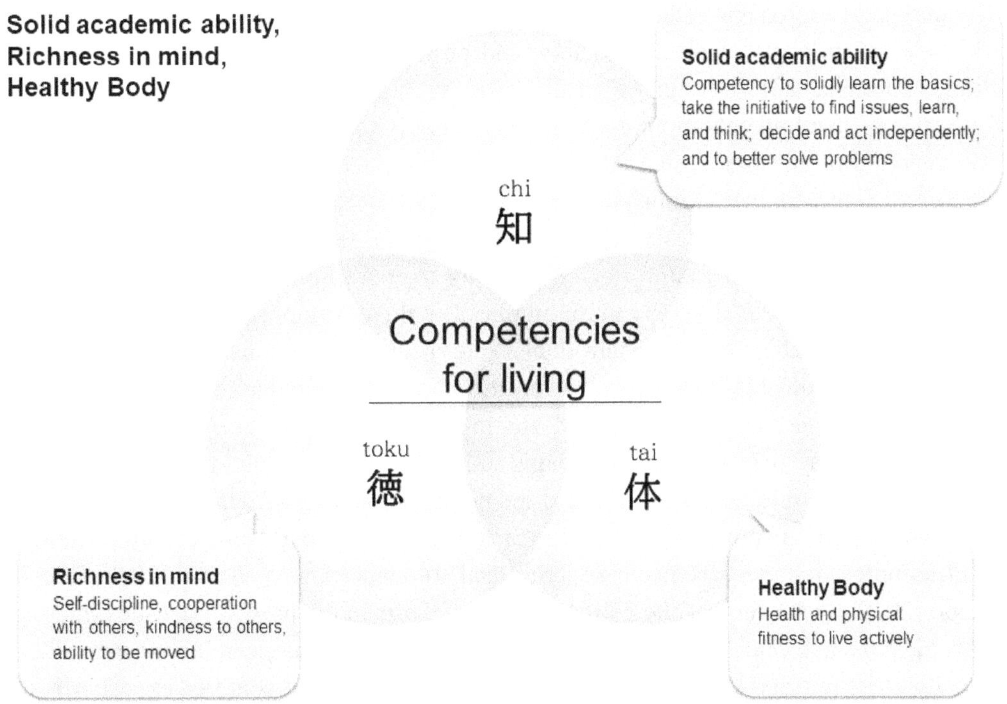

Tokkatsu embeds the egalitarian philosophy of the Japanese schooling system. The curriculum aims to instill social and emotional competencies in every member of the community. For example, every student takes a turn to be a class leader, and every student belongs to a school management committee. Various educational activities are structured in schools for students to take responsibility for collaborative problem-finding and problem-solving. These learning experiences provide students necessary competencies and skills to be responsible citizens. There are limited studies on tokkatsu implemented in foreign contexts because it was not available in English until 2012 (Tsuneyoshi, 2019). The Egyptian government has been implementing tokkatsu since 2015, supported by the Japan International Cooperation Agency (Tanaka, 2019). There are also some cases of grass-root initiatives in Indonesia (Kusanagi, 2020), but no study has been focused on the holistic learning model in the ODL situation.

Indonesian Contexts for Holistic Learning

The holistic and humanistic philosophy of education has existed in Indonesia since the establishment of the national education system. Ki Hajar Dewantara, an influential educational philosopher and the first minister of national education of the Republic of Indonesia—known as the father of Indonesian education—promoted such an idea. According to Dewantara, education should be humanistic and aim for character building to develop unity in three aspects: *cipta* (reasoning/logical thinking), *rasa* (feeling), and *karsa* (inner motivation) (Musolin, 2021). His principle of *Tut Wuri Handayani*—to follow from behind and give moral support in Javanese—impacted Indonesian education ideology and remained to be the motto of the Ministry of Education and Culture (Claramita, 2016). Education was understood to explore individual student potential and see the world from their perspective (Dewantara, 1962). Dewantara's educational approach—establishing the dialogic relationship between teachers and students, situating knowledge in local culture and society, and promoting individualized process and meaning of education (Claramita, 2016)—aligns with the underlying philosophy of tokkatsu. This case study uses tokkatsu not as an implementation of a foreign concept but as a structure to realize the humanistic approach envisioned by the Indonesian education philosophy represented by Dewantara—especially incorporating social aspects in designing student learning.

The challenge in ESD in Indonesia reflects a challenge in general education. It is how to transform from teacher-centered and exam-oriented learning to more holistic and learner-centered learning (Tristananda, 2018). The 2013 curriculum emphasizes the development of character-building and moral education across subjects. It also introduced interdisciplinary thematic learning and promoted hands-on learning activities for students. However, the studies suggest that top-down and bureaucratic cultures demotivate Indonesian teachers from designing student-centered activities due to their lack of confidence and autonomy (Bjork, 2005; Kusanagi, 2021). The government launched a program called *Merdeka Belajar* (freedom to learn) in 2019 and the new curriculum—*Curriculum Merdeka* (freedom curriculum)—in 2022. It encourages teachers to teach innovatively, pay more attention to the learning process in classrooms, and meet the needs of individual students (Anis & Anwar, 2020; Jannah, 2019; Kemendikbud, 2019). However, despite all these reform efforts in the past two decades, there has been little improvement (Chang et al., 2013; MONE, 2007); a recurrent challenge in Indonesian education has been how to alter teaching and learning to be a more holistic and student-centered experience. There are thematic ESD studies in Indonesia, especially on environmental education (Nomura, 2009; Kusanagi, 2021); however, the cases of ESD are project-based, and these project-based studies do not discuss how to promote holistic learning and democratic student participation.

School Background

St. Ann is a private Catholic school in Bandung City, Indonesia. It was founded by a Dutch missionary around 110 years ago. The vision of St. Ann—attractive cross—reflects holistic learning goals. It places the heart at the center, and there are four targets for educational goals: 1) growth, 2) care, 3) thinking, and 4) creativity. This study focuses on an elementary school, but a kindergarten and junior high school are located in the same complex and also implement tokkatsu. There are 22 teachers in the elementary school, and there are 12 classes (two classes for each grade), and each class has 27 to 28 students.

Like many other schools in Indonesia, one of the challenges at St. Ann was to shift away from teacher-centered pedagogy and implement student-centered learning. For this, the school envisioned altering its reward and punishment approach based on Catholic values to a holistic learning approach, including character development. St. Ann started school reform in July 2017 with the support of an external advisor, Tatang Suratno, from the Indonesia University of Education. In the beginning, lesson study, a bottom-up professional development model that originated in Japan, was introduced to facilitate collaborative teacher learning. Lesson study is "a system for building and sharing practitioner knowledge that involves teachers in learning from colleagues as they research, plan, teach, observe and discuss a classroom lesson" (Lewis et al., 2009, p. 142). In addition, the school started to implement tokkatsu in 2019. This was intended to shift the teachers' focus to student learning rather than on teaching. The process of this transition is discussed in the previous study (Kusanagi & Suratno, 2020).

Prior to the COVID-19 pandemic, tokkatsu activities such as school cleaning and school lunch duties had been introduced. However, it was an add-on to the existing activities rather than achieving a holistic education. The school experienced school closure and hybrid learning for two years, from March 2020 to May 2022 (Table 1). When Mrs. Dee became the principal in July 2020, the school faced many challenges in adjusting to the ODL situation. During the school closure, the teachers had 3 to 4 hours of online meetings with students. Students worked on assignments with the support of their parents.

From November 2020 to October 2022, the school participated in the Toyota Foundation International Program led by the author. In the program, Indonesian, Malaysian, and Japanese teachers exchanged their holistic learning practice and had dialogues about how to support student learning during the pandemic. It enhanced the understanding of tokkatsu among St. Ann teachers and encouraged them to share their practice with the international community.

Table 1. Online and hybrid learning at St. Ann

Date	Type of Student Learning
1st Semester 2020/2021 (July–December 2020)	Online and distance learning
2nd Semester 2020/2021 (January 2021–May 2021)	Online and distance learning
1st Semester 2021/2022 (July–December 2021)	Online and distance learning (November to December) & Hybrid
2nd Semester 2021/2022 (January–May 2022)	Hybrid

METHODOLOGY

The study examines the educational activities at St. Ann Elementary School during the pandemic guided by the following research questions.

1. How did tokkatsu facilitate structuring holistic learning activities in ODL in Indonesia?
2. What were the impacts of tokkatsu on ensuring student participation in virtual learning?
3. What are the implications of tokkatsu for ESD?

The collected data include recordings of online lessons, monthly school reports (written by a principal and an external school adviser), and semi-structured interviews with teachers and two school advisors. The use of multiple sources facilitated the illustration of the process of tokkatsu and the understanding of flexible, and adaptable nature of holistic learning promoted by it. The interview respondents were selected based on their experience with tokkatsu. A principal, six teachers, and three parents were interviewed. The semi-structured interviews were conducted in August and December 2022.[1] The questions focused on teachers' understanding of tokkatsu, the contents of tokkatsu-related activities, and their impacts on student learning. All the interviews were audio recorded and transcribed. These data were analyzed qualitatively and coded into themes to illuminate the experiences of holistic learning to understand the process of education transformation. All names used in this study (school, teachers, and students) are pseudonyms.

The list of activities introduced by tokkatsu is shown in Table 2. The case of St. Ann is unique because tokkatsu was contextualized to fit the school context rather than imposing the model; this was helpful in overcoming challenges posed by the pandemic. This study examines how St. Ann teachers adapted tokkatsu to support the holistic learning of students, especially in providing social and emotional support.

Table 2. List of holistic learning activities introduced by tokkatsu

	Started in	**Frequency**
Daily teacher dialogue	July 2020	Every day
Orientation activities	July 2021, July 2022	The first month of the academic year
Student projects	July 2021	Once a semester
After-school activities	August 2021	Once a week
Leader dialogue	November 2021	Every 2 weeks
Tokkatsu Circle	February 2022	Every 2 weeks

Discussion of Findings

Finding 1: Promoting Teacher Dialogue for Holistic Learning

In the pedagogical transformation for ESD, creating a space for reflection, dialogue, and action is important (Moore, 2005). Tokkatsu facilitated teacher dialogue to transform their pedagogy to support the holistic learning of students.

When Mrs. Dee became the principal in July 2020, the school was going through a transition period due to the ODL situation; thus, there were many issues. Mrs. Dee prioritized building a holistic learning culture centered on the well-being of students. While St. Ann has envisioned holistic learning and engaged in tokkatsu since 2017, these activities were implemented as additional activities to daily classroom teaching and learning. The principal first held a "supervision café," where she had informal consultations with individual teachers to discuss their students and practice. In addition, all teachers met daily to hold a reflective meeting at the end of the school day. In the beginning, it was difficult to hold teacher dialogue. Although teachers were empathetic to their students who faced many challenges in the ODL situation, they were less empathetic to each other and did not know how to show support (from the Activity Report, November 2020). Gradually, they started to share observations and challenges in ODL.

The challenges teachers faced by the school closure pushed them to experiment with new pedagogy and collaborate with one another. At the initial stage of ODL, the teachers were reluctant to give students space to grow. They feared that students might make mistakes and that there would not be enough time to teach the curriculum. The principal encouraged teachers to give time and opportunity for students to take the initiative in their learning. Through daily reflection, the teachers realized that they face common challenges in ODL, such as a decline in student's motivation to learn and a lack of experience in using Information and Communication Technology (ICT). They expressed sympathy and exchanged ideas to improve class management. Through these collegial exchanges, teachers developed listening skills, and later they applied them in their classrooms.

To promote further holistic learning, the principal assigned a group of teachers to initiate what they called the "Tokkatsu Circle" in February 2022. There were 12 teachers that met biweekly, exchanged their practices, and deepened their understanding of holistic learning. The principal envisioned those teachers—who had 10 to 20 years of experience in teaching—to be active agents in promoting holistic learning at St. Ann. They read the handbook on tokkatsu, *The World of Tokkatsu* (Tsuneyoshi, 2012), to study how to design tokkatsu activities. They also shared the issues in ODL and anticipated challenges in reopening the school. Gradually, the topic of discussion shifted from sharing the issues in the classroom to share stories about their students. For example, Mrs. Ais shared a case where a student's suggestion helped her. When students were noisy during lunchtime, one student suggested playing calm music. When Mrs. Ais tried it, students became quiet and sat properly to eat. Mrs. Ais reflected that she was happy she listened to her student's suggestions rather than yelling at her students (interview with Mrs. Ais, August 9, 2022). This kind of exchange of stories helped teachers realize the importance of listening to students and giving students space to grow.

Finding 2: Rapport-Building in Virtual Space and Fostering a Sense of Community

In tokkatsu, rapport-building is considered the foundation of active and collaborative learning. During the school closure, it was difficult for the teachers to build a relationship with students due to the limited online meeting time. To build a sense of community in virtual space, St. Ann teachers restructured the orientation period, inspired by tokkatsu. Indonesian schools generally hold an orientation program called "Introduction to School Environment" (*Masa Pengenalan Lingkungan Sekolah*: MPLS) at the beginning of the academic year. In the program, students are generally informed of school rules and facilities to prepare for their adjustment to a new school environment. St. Ann restructured MPLS and introduced fun and interactive nonacademic activities to: 1) take care of the mental and physical aspects of students, 2) build social relationships, 3) foster student leadership, and 4) align the school curriculum with these goals. The relationship building was considered a foundation to engage students in democratizing the classroom culture and building a caring community. Students needed a safe environment where they were not judged based on correct or incorrect answers, and engagement in nonacademic activities created such an environment.

After they engaged in game-like activities in the first week, students were given two assignments in the second week. First, they designed home learning activities, such as cooking or exercising, for their own well-being. Secondly, they were asked to make a self-introduction video to show their peers. It was part of an effort to build a community by getting to know each other and fostering their skills to express themselves and see themselves as community members.

(In the orientation period), we engaged students through various playful activities and class discussions. We learned how to manage their thoughts, heart, and body in order to nurture an authentic relationship,

a relationship without JUDGMENT. Students were able to see themselves and their peers as human. We (teachers) believe that if we can do that, we can have reflective dialogue and learn much from the students and from ourselves. (November Activity Report, 2022)

In addition, the school organized two types of after-school club activities modeled after tokkatsu. This was to deal with a concern raised by parents and to provide social support to students. Parents were worried that students had shorter learning time and considerably longer free time. Students longed for more social interactions with their classmates; after the online lessons, they often stayed online to chitchat with one another. Students could participate in two types of club activities. The first club activity was intraclass club activities like basketball, music, dance, knitting, and computer programming. Teachers and students discussed what kind of after-school program they wanted to have, and each grade decided on a different menu based on their personal interests. The second type of club activity was peer support groups for subject learning. In each class, students met after online classes to tutor one another. These activities were managed by student volunteers. They communicated through Telegram and arranged their meetings. Teachers only offered help when students asked for it. Club activities were organized to enable students to have a fun time socializing and supporting one another in a virtual space.

Finding 3: Cultivating Good Habits Based on Collective Responsibility

In ODL, students needed to cultivate new habits and rules in joining lessons online and from home. Teachers used a classroom community to hold students accountable to nurture learning habits and responsibility. Some students could not get up on time to join online lessons, and parents had difficulty supporting them. A parent expressed:

Mrs. Sally: The challenge is in an online school; because my child was still five years old during the pandemic, there was no motivation to learn yet; it's hard for him to learn to face a laptop because he's not used to it. During the learning session, he lifted the laptop up and down and walked around. After being reminded, then he wanted to study again. So, the challenge was between me dividing my time between work and accompanying my child because there was no desire for my child to study at the age of 5. I also understand that. I had to constantly remind him and accompany him to finish (homework). (Interview with Mrs. Sally, August 15, 2022)

For this, teachers encouraged students to take care of one another. Mrs. Nuria described:

There were often some students who were late to a class. I asked the students in the same group to contact her/him. Eventually, students started to tell me who was not in the class, and they contacted those who were not there to join the class. I did not have to make sure they were present or call everyone. (Interview with Mrs. Nuria, August 8, 2022)

Mrs. Ais explained why the participation of every student and delegating authority to students to manage their classrooms are important:

Yes, because they [students] are there, well, they all have to be involved. The class belongs to twenty children, not to one or two people. That's why when I'm around, I have a list [to check]. Has this kid spoke? So those who haven't said anything yet, I'm asking. Or, ask their friends. Kids, who we haven't heard their voice so far?...so their presence must be acknowledged. Everyone must feel they are a member of the community. (Interview with Mrs. Ais, August 8, 2022).

However, ensuring every student's participation in ODL was a challenge. Many students were noisy and did not have the patience to listen to their classmates. St. Ann's teachers realized that they could not manage students well with a teacher-centered approach (interview with the school advisor, December 2, 2022). The first-grade teacher, Mrs. Ais, said it was especially challenging for the first graders who had a big adjustment to make entering elementary school. They were not used to formal classroom learning, and they did not know the basic rules for classrooms. She encouraged students to make classroom rules. They came up with rules like don't be noisy, take turns to talk, and listen attentively when someone is talking. She also set up a student facilitator. In the end, students could facilitate classroom discussions by themselves. They listened to each other attentively, made sure everyone had a turn to talk and helped their classmates when someone could not answer.

Mr. Sebastian stated that classroom rules taught students to be considerate of their peers.

Mr. Sebastian: This year, compared to last year, students understood the purpose (of making classroom rules), and they were more engaged. They understand rules are not only for himself/herself but it is for others. They realize if they break the rule, it will impact others in the class. (Interview with Mr. Sebastian, August 8, 2022)

By delegating more authority to students, teachers realized students could manage more than they initially assumed and changed their view toward students. Mrs. Nuria said she felt less pressure to be the one in control and perfect for their students.

I can be a friend or mom, not just a teacher. I become a child when I work with them. I can be one of them and feel like them. Students need to be heard, and students can make their own choice in daily life. (Interview with Mrs. Nuria, August 8, 2022)

Finding 4: Student Project to Promote the Holistic Learning Process

Student projects in ODL also allowed students to have more autonomy and were implemented to facilitate a holistic learning process. Previously, the topic of projects was assigned by teachers, and students worked individually. After the introduction of tokkatsu, teachers encourage students to take the initiative to design their projects and to collaborate with one another. For example, first graders had a wall bulletin/magazine project in 2021. At the time, Mrs. Ais asked students to suggest how they wanted to present what they had learned in the semester (interview with Mrs. Ais, August 10, 2022; and an interview with the school advisor, December 2, 2022). The students decided to do a learning wall project. Students worked in groups to make a wall newspaper on the topic of their choices, such as local weather, religion, stories, and writing.

The teacher also changed the form of the end-of-semester assessment to make it a more process-orientated and collaborative effort. Previously, students were given individual grades, and parents were handed report cards at the end of each semester. But instead, the first graders held an exhibition event and presented their project to their classmates and their parents. After the presentations, the students and parents commented on the projects. They wrote comments on the Post-it notes and put these on each student's body. Altering the form of assessment enabled teachers and parents to embrace the process of holistic learning. These dialogic opportunities supported parents in having a better understanding of the teachers' intention to foster holistic learning. They appreciated the students' creativity, communication and collaboration skills, and courage to present in front of people.

Prior to the pandemic, parents met teachers only twice a year when their children's semester report cards were handed out. After the school closure, parental support became crucial. They had to set up their children's online meeting accounts and help manage their homework. This allowed them to understand the value of their children's educational activities. At the beginning of the academic year, some parents were worried that their children were falling behind in the curriculum (interview with Mrs. Dee, August 9, 2022; and an interview with a school advisor, December 2, 2022). There were also some complaints about the noise level in online meetings or they wanted special attention on their own children. Some parents wanted to have traditional academic learning, and they were opposed to an assessment in the form of student projects. However, after joining the student presentations, parents realized how students were able to gain communication and collaboration skills and appreciate the value of holistic learning activities. One parent said:

Mrs. Cecilia: I'm so amazed by what she (her child) did. I was doing that (project and presentation) when I was in high school. But she was doing it in the second grade... maybe two days before her presentation, she said, "mom, I'm so afraid. What if my friends laugh at me because I cannot say anything." This six-year-old girl was worried, but I got her to practice her presentation, and she did it very well. I loved her presentation. (...) When her teacher sent photos (of her presentation) to me, I saw a really big smile on her face. And she said to me, "Mommy, I did it." And I was so proud of her. (Interview with Mrs. Cecilia, August 15, 2022)

The parental response to the process-oriented assessment was not always positive. In fact, one parent preferred the traditional assessment:

Mrs. Sally: I prefer the formal assessment over a project. I understand it's not just memorizing and answering questions asked by the teacher, but it focuses on the development, the way a student thinks of ideas, what he thinks about, and what to put into words. (...) In my opinion, it can be pursued in other ways, not necessarily in school. (Interview with Mrs. Sally, August 15, 2022)

Nevertheless, student projects enabled parents to share in the process of student learning. Student projects allowed students to take the initiative in their own learning design and express the process and result of their learning in their own words. When parents saw how their children expressed their excitement to learn and they could collaborate with their classmates, parents thanked the teachers for developing their potential for both academic skill and social skills.

DISCUSSIONS AND CONCLUSION

This chapter examined the holistic learning process in the virtual learning situation facilitated by tokkatsu. Figure 2 summarizes holistic learning activities as an activity system for a whole-school engagement at St. Ann. The case showed that tokkatsu activities provided a support system for both teachers and students. This became a foundation for realizing holistic learning.

Firstly, tokkatsu enabled to shift teacher dialogue from classroom problems to the exchange of practice in holistic learning activities. This was possible since teachers faced challenges in the pandemic and felt the lecturing style no longer worked in ODL. The case of teachers showed that establishing dialogue among teachers needed time until they felt safe to disclose the issues in their classrooms. Also, the nonacademic nature of tokkatsu activities allowed teachers to focus on social and emotional aspects of learning where previously they focused on academic aspects only.

Secondly, tokkatsu activities facilitated the building of a learning community in the virtual space where students could support one another. Without physical contact time, keeping up the motivation of students was an issue. Tokkatsu activities allowed students space to build a sense of community at the beginning of the academic year. Club activities also gave a space for students to gain the social and emotional support they lacked in ODL.

Thirdly, the engagement with tokkatsu supported students in building good habits to participate in ODL. Without physical contact and direct guidance from teachers, students struggle to be punctual and respect classroom rules. Tokkatsu facilitated students to adjust to the new learning environment in ODL. By setting up their own rules and supporting one another to keep up with these rules, students built a sense of responsibility as a member of the community.

Fourthly, a student project was used to nurture students' social and emotional skills, such as confidence, communication, and collaboration. This enabled students to enjoy taking the initiative to design their own learning and collaborate on student projects. In addition, the student presentation of the project at the end of the semester altered the way of assessment to more process—oriented and participative. The COVID-19 pandemic facilitated the introduction of digital technologies and a partnership between parents and teachers. This new triadic partnership between students, teachers, and parents provided enjoyable and meaningful learning experiences, emotional support, and the care parents, students, and teachers need.

St. Ann provided a unique case of contextualizing tokkatsu into a virtual space and local school context. There are several implementations of this study for holistic learning and ESD. The case showed how an activity system facilitated building new learning routines and collective effort to support the well-being of students based on the holistic ideal. Understanding this, teachers restructured the existing educational activities and created new ones based on the needs of each classroom. Under the leadership of a new principal, each teacher came up with ways to give more autonomy to students to overcome the challenges under the difficult circumstance in ODL. Both classroom management and lesson design became more bottom-up and democratic. Students made their own class rules and decided the topic of learning and how they presented the result of their projects. This is in contrast with other schools that could not cope with the dramatic change brought in by the COVID-19 pandemic and continued to employ traditional teacher-centered learning. Building a learning community is essential for ESD.

The case of tokkatsu showed that attending to the social and emotional needs of students is crucial in ODL. Teachers faced challenges in working with students who were struggling to adjust to learning from home in ODL. Students struggled to adjust to the new way of classroom participation in ODL, keep up with motivation for learning, and collaborate with their classmates. Tokkatsu provided fun social activities that supported students to enjoy their learning activities with their peers.

Tokkatsu approach facilitates the learning goals envisioned by ESD. Its activity system enabled to embed holistic educational activities in the daily classroom, where students gradually learn to take the initiative, dialogue, and collaborate as responsible members of the community. It provided opportunities for students to experience the five pillars of learning stated in the beginning, learning to know, learning to do, learning to be, learning to live together, and learning to transform oneself and society. Tokkatsu is not a recipe for holistic learning; it merely provides an activity system. Its success depends on its application—especially how to recontextualize its activities to meet the school context and overcome the challenges a school is facing. In fact, tokkatsu could merely reinforce the current school problems if its practice is not updated to meet the current needs of education. In Japan, schools are facing their own challenge to build more diverse and inclusive schools under the current collectivistic and conforming school culture (Tsuneyoshi & Nukaga, 2021).

There are several limitations to this study. While the school envisioned building a learning community involving teachers, students, and parents, the activities were largely designed by teachers. The parent-teacher dialogue was limited to the end-of-semester event. While teachers employed a humanistic approach and wanted students to take ownership of their learning, it was still at the initial stage. There was a variation among teachers as to what extent students' autonomy was embraced.

Despite the limitations, the case showed how tokkatsu activities contribute to ESD through its approach to establishing holistic learning and overcoming challenges for democratic participation of students in the ODL situation. This case showed that holistic learning is possible and especially needed in virtual space and digitized learning. It also presented that tokkatsu should not be implemented as a "Japanese model" or "best practice," but its role is in building a learning community where students support one another socially and emotionally to be responsible and engaged learners. This shows a possibility of further adaptation and other cases of implementation in the future. St. Ann resumed their face-to-face classroom activities in the academic year of 2022/2023, and tokkatsu activities are continuing in a non-virtual classroom setting. A future study might track the progress of tokkatsu activities to explore its role in promoting transformative learning by ESD.

Figure 2. Activity system for holistic learning at St. Ann

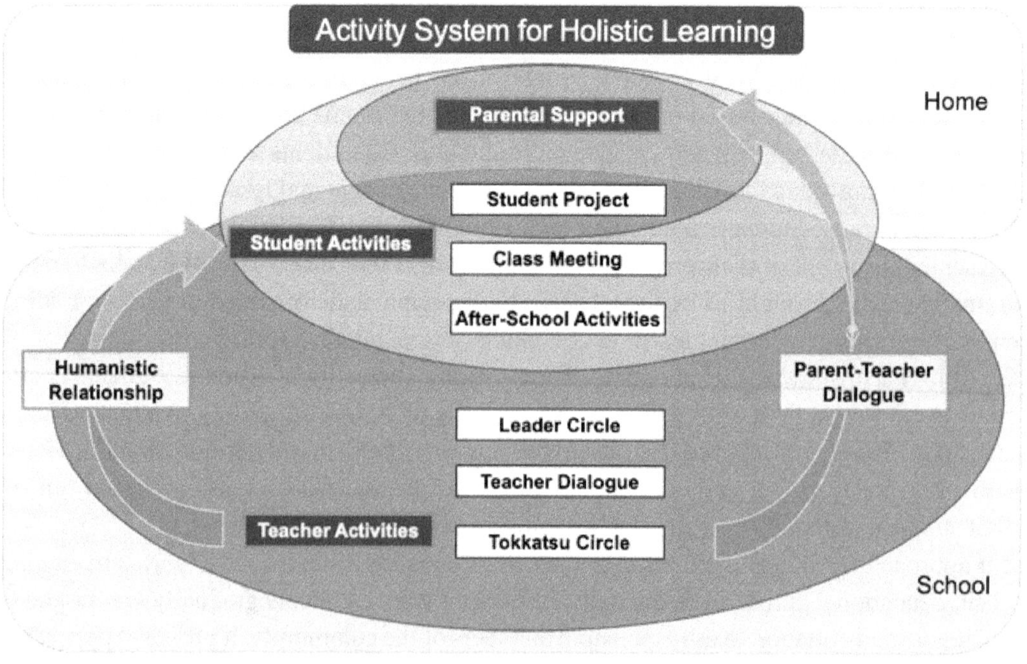

ACKNOWLEDGMENT

I would like to thank Mr. Tatang Suratno, Mr. Andrian Rizki Ajie, and the teachers of St. Ann for their collaboration in the project. I would also like to thank the Toyota Foundation (D20-N-0084) for the financial support of the program.

REFERENCES

Adegboye, D., Williams, F., Collishaw, S., Shelton, K., Langley, K., Hobson, C., Burley, D., & van Goozen, S. (2021). Understanding why the COVID-19 pandemic-related lockdown increases mental health difficulties in vulnerable young students. *JCPP Advances*, *1*(1), e12005. doi:10.1111/jcv2.12005 PMID:34485985

Anis, M., & Anwar, C. (2020). Self-organized learning environment teaching strategy for ELT in Merdeka Belajar concept for high school students in Indonesia. [Journal of English Educators Society]. *JEES*, *5*(2), 199–204. doi:10.21070/jees.v5i2.869

Bjork, C. (2005). *Indonesian education: Teachers, schools, and central bureaucracy*. Routledge. doi:10.4324/9780203959015

Chang, M. C., Al-Samarrai, S., Ragatz, A. B., Shaeffer, S., De Ree, J., & Stevenson, R. (2013). *Teacher reform in Indonesia: The role of politics and evidence in policymaking*. World Bank Publications.

Claramita, M. (2016). Revealing "Tut Wuri Handayani": A student-centered learning approach-by Ki Hajar Dewantara from the early 20th century: A literature review. *Jurnal Pendidikan Kedokteran Indonesia*, *5*(1), 14. doi:10.22146/jpki.25295

Clark, I., Nae, N., & Arimoto, M. (2020). *Education for sustainable development and the "Whole Person" curriculum in Japan*. ORE. doi:10.1093/acrefore/9780190264093.013.935

Colao, A., Piscitelli, P., Pulimeno, M., Colazzo, S., Miani, A., & Giannini, S. (2020). Rethinking the role of the school after COVID-19. *The Lancet. Public Health*, *5*(7), e370. doi:10.1016/S2468-2667(20)30124-9 PMID:32464100

Combes, B. P. (2005). The United Nations decade of education for sustainable development (2005–2014): Learning to live together sustainably. *Applied Environmental Education and Communication*, *4*(3), 215–219. doi:10.1080/15330150591004571

Delors, J., Mufti, I. A., Amagi, I., Carneiro, R., Bronislaw, C., Gorham, W., Kornhauser, A., Manley, M., Quero, P. M., Savane, M.-A., Singh, K., Stavenhagen, R., Suhr, M. W., & Nanzhao, Z. (1996). *Learning: The treasure within: Report to Unesco of the International Commission on Education for the 21st century*. UNESCO.

Dewantara, K. H. (1962). *Karja Ki Hadja Dewantara. Bagian Pertama: Pendidikan* (M. L. P. T. Siswa, Ed.; 1st ed.).

Fredriksson, U. N., Kusanagi, K., Gougoulakis, P., Matsuda, Y., & Kitamura, Y. (2020). A comparative study of curriculums for education for sustainable development (ESD) in Sweden and Japan. *Sustainability*, *12*(3), 1123. doi:10.3390u12031123

Jannah, C. (2019). *Merdeka Belajar: Kebijakan Lompat-lompat ala Nadiem Makarim,* Muslimahnews. https://www.muslimahnews.com/2019/12/23/merdeka-belajar-kebijakan-lompat-lompat-ala-nadiem-makarim/

Kemendikbud. (2019). *Merdeka Belajar: Pokok-Pokok Kebijakan Merdeka Belajar.* Jakarta: Makalah Rapat Koordinasi Kepala Dinas Pendidikan Seluruh Indonesia.

Kjell, O. N. (2011). Sustainable well-being: A potential synergy between sustainability and well-being research. *Review of General Psychology*, *15*(3), 255–266. doi:10.1037/a0024603

Kusanagi, K. (2021). Indonesia ni okeru sogo gakushu to ESD—Sogo karikyuramu to kankyo kyoiku puroguramu Adiwiyata no jissen. *Musashi University In-service Education Bulletin*, *35*, 203–211.

Kusanagi, K., & Suratno, T. (2020). Kodomo no manabi wo chushin to shita jyugyo kenkyu to manabi no kyodotai zukuri. *Tokyo Future University Bulletin*, *14*, 63–68.

Kusanagi, K. N. (2020). Education for sustainable development and the implementation of "tokkatsu" in Indonesia. In *International Conference on Social Studies and Environmental Issues (ICOSSEI 2019)* (pp. 69–74). Atlantis Press. 10.2991/assehr.k.200214.013

Le Tendre, G. K. (1999). Community-building activities in Japanese schools: Alternative paradigms of the democratic school. *Comparative Education Review*, *43*(3), 283–310. doi:10.1086/447564

Lewis, C., Perry, R., & Friedkin, S. (2009). Lesson study as action research. In *The SAGE handbook of educational action research* (pp. 142–154). Sage Publications Ltd. doi:10.4135/9780857021021.n14

Ministry of Education. (2017). *Culture, Sports, Science and Technology (MEXT).* Basic Education in Japan. https://www.eduport.mext.go.jp/epsite/wp-content/uploads/2021/03/educa2017_pamphlet.pdf

Ministry of Education. (2019). Culture, Sports, Science and Technology (MEXT). *The Ministry of Education, Culture, Sports, Science and Technology (MEXT) website.* http://www.mext.go.jp/a_menu/shotou/new-cs/1383986.htm#section4

MONE. (2007). *Reforming teachers: Towards educational equality and quality.* Ministry of National Education.

Moore, J. (2005). Seven recommendations for creating sustainability education at the university level: A guide for change agents. *International Journal of Sustainability in Higher Education*, *6*(4), 326–333. doi:10.1108/14676370510623829

Musolin, M., & Nisa', K. (2021). Pendidikan Masa Pandemik Covid 19: Implementasi Konsep Tri Pusat Pendidikan Ki Hajar Dewantara. *Edukatif: Jurnal Ilmu Pendidikan*, *3*(6), 4134–4144. doi:10.31004/edukatif.v3i6.1316

Pavlova, M. (2013). Towards using transformative education as a benchmark for clarifying differences and similarities between environmental education and education for sustainable development. *Environmental Education Research*, *19*(5), 656–672. doi:10.1080/13504622.2012.736476

Rieckmann, M. (2018). Learning to transform the world: Key competencies in education for sustainable development. *Issues and Trends in Education for Sustainable Development*, *39*, 39–59.

Sato, N. (2003). *Inside Japanese classrooms: The heart of education*. Routledge. doi:10.4324/9780203465707

Tanaka, H. (2017). Current state and future prospects of education for sustainable development (ESD) in Japan. *Educational Studies in Japan*, *11*(0), 15–28. doi:10.7571/esjkyoiku.11.15

Tanaka, S. (2019). Tokkatsu plus in Egypt: Extending the tokkatsu concept. In *Tokkatsu: The Japanese educational model of holistic education* (pp. 225–250). World Scientific. doi:10.1142/9789813232679_0017

Tristananda, P. W. (2018). Membumikan education for sustainable development (ESD) di Indonesia dalam menghadapi isu–isu global. *Purwadita: Jurnal Agama dan Budaya, 2*(2), 42–49.

Tsuneyoshi, R. (Ed.). (2012). *The World of Tokkatsu*. Tsune Lab. http://www.p.u.-tokyo.ac.jp/~tsunelab/tokkatsu/

Tsuneyoshi, R., & Nukaga, M. (2021). *Shin gurōbaru jidai ni idomu Nihon no kyōiku: Tabunka shakai o kangaeru hikaku kyōikugaku no shiza* [Japanese education in the new global era: A comparative education perspective on a multicultural society]. Tokyo University Press.

Tsuneyoshi, R., Sugita, H., Kusanagi, K., & Takahashi, F. (Eds.). (2019). *Tokkatsu: The Japanese educational model of holistic education*. World Scientific. doi:10.1142/10781

UNESCO. (2015b). *Rethinking education: Towards a global common good?* UNESCO.

ENDNOTE

1 Prior to this study, the researcher interviewed teachers in February 2020 at the initial stage of tokkatsu implementation. The data are not explicitly used but facilitated the author's understanding of the process of educational transformation at St. Ann.

Chapter 8
Implementation of eSDG Framework Involving Multi Stakeholders Matching Program Engagement:
Digitalization of Traditional Community Market

Anton Rahmadi
Universitas Mulawarman, Indonesia

Miftakhur Rohmah
University of Mulawarman, Indonesia

Kartika Sari
University of Mulawarman, Indonesia

Nur Amaliah
University of Mulawarman, Indonesia

Masayu Widiastuti
University of Mulawarman, Indonesia

Uni Wahyuni Sagena
University of Mulawarman, Indonesia

Dina Lusiana Setyowati
University of Mulawarman, Indonesia

Swandari Paramita
University of Mulawarman, Indonesia

Zainal Arifin
University of Mulawarman, Indonesia

Malta Nur Doa
PT Aplikasi Karya Anak Bangsa, Indonesia

Mikael Onny Setiawan
PT Aplikasi Karya Anak Bangsa, Indonesia

Hadi Pranoto
University of Mulawarman, Indonesia

Rusliansyah Rusliansyah
University of Mulawarman, Indonesia

ABSTRACT

COVID-19 has impacted the East Kalimantan, Indonesia, community market, especially for indigenous food and non-food souvenirs. These conditions threaten the global pursuit of SDGs. The University of

DOI: 10.4018/978-1-7998-5033-5.ch008

Mulawarman and PT Aplikasi Karya Anak Bangsa, a subsidiary of Gojek Indonesia, identified social concerns for matching program. Our university team's experience integrating the tridharma led us to offer a five-stage framework: (1) vision internalization, (2) persistence learning, (3) technology adaption, (4) collaboration growth, and (5) outcomes integration. Multi-stakeholder cooperation starts with mutual benefits, ideas, agreements, and program designs. Learning aspects are integrated through final assignments, practical experiences, and organized assignments related to learning outcomes on specific course areas (embedded learning). The emancipated learning of the Independent Campus (MBKM) was implemented at the university level. Outcome-based education for higher education multi-stakeholder matching program is an approach for addressing education SDG.

INTRODUCTION

The government of Indonesia defines policy framework to increase human related sustainable development goals (SDGs) on six areas, namely (1) educational access, (2) educational quality (3) synergy between governmental agencies, (4) higher education and industry; (5) industry linkages; and (6) educational incentives (Indrawati & Kuncoro, 2021). Higher education in Indonesia is required by law to have three pillars (*tridharma*): (a) to achieve competence in a particular field, (b) to research with multiple stakeholders, and (c) to aid in the resolution of societal issues (Irawan et al, 2021).

However, from early 2020 until mid 2022, education SDG (eSDG) achievement suffers a setback. Higher education faced a transformational problem regarding COVID-19 as a significant disruptive agent, disabling the benefit of laboratory hands-on and face-to-face classrooms and tutorials (Martha et al, 2021). Students are not able to conduct industrial internships as the industries also cut expenses to survive during the pandemic era (Wagiran et al, 2022).

From higher education perspective, in this age of pandemics, the final pillar of *tridharma* is the most important. Referring to the government strategy on leveraging higher education with support from external actors (Rosser, 2022), outstanding teamwork with multiple stakeholders is required for mankind to prosper in the face of the many different facets of social problems produced by the COVID-19 pandemic. Outcome-based education with reference to multi-stakeholder public participation in higher education becomes a paradigm for actively addressing the linked SDGs agenda.

As a case study of industrial survival in East Kalimantan, Indonesia, the traditional market was at stake due to market embracement from conventional face-to-face and in-store showrooms to digital platforms (Astari, 2021). Moreover, in the current condition, inter-islands and international barriers erected to suppress the spread of COVID-19 have taken a heavy toll on the community market, especially for tourism-linked products, i.e., indigenous food and non-food souvenirs (Ketter & Avraham, 2021). These conditions directly challenge the global pursuance of achieving SDGs, particularly decent work, economic growth, and sustainable communities. Limited face to face transaction requires a bridging to provide online offerings and online transactions.

An opportunity was offered by PT Aplikasi Karya Anak Bangsa (PT AKAB), a subsidiary of a well-known unicorn company of Gojek Indonesia. AKAB that has a platform to integrate traditional market to digital economy, but the human resources behind traditional markets need to learn how it works and to provide qualified products to sustain their business. These situations can be mutually solved by a matching program between university and Gojek Indonesia, giving students from universities can educate MSME operators to enter digital market, while also improving the souvenir and food standards. This also directly addresses the issue of loss of quality education through conventional ways. Providing students with real case problems and solutions facing the community and traditional markets was equivalent to an entrepreneurial study by student conducted in bench class (Blesia et al, 2021).

This matching program is best fit with emancipated learning (*merdeka belajar*), partly defined as a participatory learning model initiated by the Ministry of Education, Culture, Research, and Technology (MoECRT) as a main agenda in 2019-2024 (Purwanti, 2021). For the matching program scheme that was initiated by the MoECRT, the University of Mulawarman and PT AKAB collaborated to identify several social issues. The societal issues are assisting (1) the digitalization of souvenir businesses, (2) the improvement of the availability, quality, and certification of online ghost kitchens, and (3) the initiation of Food Bank as a meeting platform to solve food waste and food rationing for individuals who are in need. To successfully implement the eSDG framework, the solutions are crafted and put into action with the participation of multiple stakeholders. For the higher education, direct feedback of the program was to invest in student competences and skills, hence preparing them for better job in the future (Ollivaud, 2021).

ESDG FRAMEWORK INVOLVING MULTI STAKEHOLDERS' ENGAGEMENT

The process of translating the findings of public participation into excellent teaching must be carried out in stages. We present the idea of translation of emancipated learning within the framework of five stages, based on the seven years of experience that our university team has had integrating the *tridharma*. The framework consists of the following components: (1) the internalization of the vision; (2) the transmission of persistence; (3) the adaption of new technologies; (4) the extension of the partnership; and (5) the integration of results. The vision internalization phase's successful implementation led to improved comprehension of the situation as a whole and more methodical approaches to problem resolution. The most obvious result of its implementation is the enhancement of laboratory capabilities and the increased involvement of students in real-world activities.

Framework 1: Internalization of Learning Vision by Taking Realistic Examples in the Community

The vision of education for a just and equitable society is one of the SDGs. The educational mission of University of Mulawarman is closely related to community economic empowerment. Activities involving Multi stakeholders' Public Engagement are also carried out to touch on aspects of gender equity and social inclusion, positively impacting women and marginalized groups affected by COVID-19 (Sukmawati and Maryanti, 2022). In our previous program, about 60-69% of the MSMEs from the three sectors were operated by women. Financial literacy affects MSME and traditional market survivability (Raza et al, 2022).

In the COVID-19 pandemic, the educational requirements for the digitalization of the traditional community market are as follows: (1) the ability to produce goods or services to specific standards; (2) the ability to read the practical needs of the market for the product being developed, such as product size, price, segmentation, and packaging; and (3) the ability to promote the product. The learning context is divided into courses that include both structured and innovative (free form) learning scenarios. This vision can be applied in a variety of classes that are directly related to the educational specifications required by the community, as well as in fieldwork practices and final assignments. The mission of mobilizing students to directly help improve the quality of MSME products as part of innovative learning in the *merdeka belajar* (emancipated learning) program scenario is to support the government in improving product quality in terms of standardization and product legalization. Internalization of the learning vision in higher education is accomplished through listening to the needs of stakeholders during the hearing process and generating opinions to obtain curriculum agreement. On a practical level, these activities are carried out through the matching program activity between industry and university.

Framework 2: Developing Resilience in Societal Problem-Solving That Relates to Theories in Learning

The core of this second framework is resilience, with two attitudes expected to grow in students: (1) higher education students' resilience to solve community problems and (2) the spirit of not giving up easily and lifelong learning to develop and progress (Bento et al, 2021). The matching program is rich in learning and provides direct practice in resolving community problems, with a focus on improving the economy of MSMEs. Students learn about food production techniques, thermal processing, sanitation and hygiene, packaging techniques, types of packaging, measuring shelf life, and product design in lectures based on the literature they have read. In this matching program, students are given the opportunity to apply the theory they have learned. The opportunity to express opinions and develop the ability to analyze problems and find alternative solutions will alter students' perspectives. Following the implementation of this program, for example, several students chose a specific final project theme to develop the food industry with stakeholders.

Students develop an attitude that connects with the community's relevant problems by observing them (Guzman-Valenzula et al, 2021). For example, they will gain the ability to converse with others and resolve problems through new ideas or simple improvements. Many MSMEs, for example, have only considered survival. Interacting with students can help them gain new perspectives while also improving their product (Trespalacios et al, 2021). As a result, positive vibes pervade the teaching classroom.

Framework 3: Adaptation of New and Relevant Technologies in Problem-Solving-Based Learning Processes in The Community

Louis Pasteur and Claude Bernard successfully tested thermal processing for food preservation in 1862. This technology is then developed and studied in textbooks and novel studies, such as combining temperature and pressure to obtain specific food properties. Ironically, most of the food sold in Indonesia is produced by people with little knowledge of food processing. What students learn about the pasteurization process and how they are introduced to the community, particularly MSMEs, demonstrates that technology that existed hundreds of years ago is still relevant and needs to be reintroduced today.

MIT (Massachusetts Institute of Technology) has recently launched an online bootcamp called Innovation Leadership. The courses are also available from any online provider, with varying emphasis on learning materials. We conducted practical ecommerce and digital market onboarding, taught students, and delivered to MSME partners as part of this matching program.

Students apply relevant knowledge and technology in the classroom by reviewing the literature to answer a specific problem-based task based on the examples (Maftuna, 2022). In another case, the lecturer may instruct students to create an improved product based on their observations and to incorporate appropriate technology for the problem at hand. Students must present their findings to the class and receive feedback from their peers (Sanchez-Carraced et al, 2021). The process is repeated in several courses, most notably in the latter stages of study, i.e., semesters seven and eight for undergraduate students. As a result, they are developing an innate ability to learn new things for their future career.

The University of Mulawarman thrives on improving educational quality through the reintroduction of established technology. The learning materials are always infused with the technology presented in class as theories. Students in integrated practicum classes, industry teaching, and business incubators practice a variety of technological adaptations (Susilawati, 2021). This matching program allows MSME products to adopt new technologies from the leading partner, PT AKAB, which has advantages in market integration into the digital world. University collaborations with key partners allow students and lecturers to gain hands-on experience with developing technologies as well as practical experiences integrating MSME partners on platforms owned by the key partner.

Framework 4: Develop Collaboration with Other Parties, Such as Government Partners and The Community, As Learning Resources

Teamwork is an important factor in problem-solving efforts even in virtual activities (Watson et al, 2022). Multisectoral roles necessitate an effective and efficient system to maximize potential and achieve common goals. Collaborative learning creates a distinct personality in a team and aims to improve problem-solving abilities, work efficiency, and effectiveness (Richter et al, 2021). Improving the quality and quantity of MSME production, which requires the participation of all parties, is one of the cooperative learning implementations, integrated into the form of emancipated learning activities.

For example, efforts to standardize and legalize products necessitate multidisciplinary collaboration among universities, key partner companies, government, and the community. As a result, the University of Mulawarman and PT AKAB collaborate with a variety of stakeholders, including the Provincial Health Office, a bank, local government, the Tax Registration Service Office, the Occupational Health and Safety Office, and the Association of Indonesian Food Technologists.

These extensive collaborations give the university an advantage in enriching learning material with actual community conditions. Because the learning material is relevant to the real world, it provides an excellent opportunity for students to learn and develop their problem-solving skills that often require interdisciplinary knowledge (Corbacho et al, 2021). Furthermore, this collaboration introduces new research and community service topics to the local community.

Framework 5: Integrating the Results of Problem-Solving in The Community Into Learning

The pattern of integrating research and public engagement in the role of empowered teachers is reciprocal between universities and multi-stakeholder elements as indicated by three institutional functions, including 1) as an umbrella for research and public engagement; 2) collaborative research, public engagement, and learning; and 3) commercialization and policy brief. A learning method is based on semester learning designs and lesson plans called context learning to achieve the vision, mission, and learning outcomes. Context learning is a learning method that links the material being taught with real-world situations (Budiman et al, 2021).

We involve over 250 MSMEs in the digitalization of traditional community markets program, implemented in 2021. These businesses range from new micro-commercial entities spurred by the COVID-19 pandemic to established small businesses. Since face-to-face interaction was restricted, the situation was dire, and they needed to survive by transforming into a new business or increasing business efficiency. Field supervisors and students work to improve their situation by assisting with product development and, in many cases, developing a distinguishing identity that can be easily identified in the digital market. Prior to the pandemic, several artisan groups may not have needed an identity because tourists flocked to their traditional shops. However, the pandemic hampered business. They sell products on the internet and expand their market reach with the assistance of lecturers and students. This is not an easy transition. For example, they must register as a business entity, differentiate their products, and organize their digital presence and transactions. Examples of improved learning based on real-life problem solving and research are written in books used as references in formal undergraduate courses, such as Food Preservation, Food Packaging, and Entrepreneurship.

THE ESDG FRAMEWORK IMPLEMENTATION IN A CASE STUDY OF DIGITALIZATION OF TRADITIONAL COMMUNITY MARKET

The matching program with industry is a type of curriculum transformation launched by the Ministry of Education, Culture, Research, and Technology. The partnership has prioritized eight Key Performance Indicators (KPIs) to encourage the implementation of emancipated learning on campuses. Learning theory in higher education and implementing direct practice in the industry can help to accelerate the development of science and technology. Matching is accomplished through the processes of initiation, integration, program negotiation, and program implementation. The matching program's implementation yields solutions to problems in science as well as social, economic, and political agendas such as democracy, sustainable development, and cultural understanding (Diana and Hakim 2020).

The matching program between the University of Mulawarman and PT AKAB arose as a form of trust between universities and industry in resolving industry problems, namely jointly developing the potential of MSME partners on a platform built by key partners. Multi-stakeholder collaboration begins with cooperation that provides mutual benefits, solicits ideas, builds agreements, and implements program designs.

The Initial Stage of Mutually Beneficial Cooperation

Prior to the matching program, the collaboration with the critical partner was based on a research scheme concerning the pandemic's impact. The virus's behavior and the risk to drive-sharing workers are largely unknown. Vaccinations for productive workers were not guaranteed. Measuring compliance and the impact on the welfare of productive workers on this ride-sharing platform yields results that critical partner consider necessary.

Health application education provided by accompanying lecturers and students provides insight into related industries. It demonstrates the importance of universities in expanding the reach of crash program socialization during a pandemic and implementing public health theories (Setyowati et al., 2021). The collaboration with critical partners was continued by defining ideas and expanding program beneficiaries, namely communities affected by the COVID-19 pandemic and MSME actors who experienced transaction setbacks, particularly those who relied on transactions from the tourism sector.

Idea Screening Stage

The Digital Souvenir Business Sector

The selection stage of presenting ideas relevant to the purpose of collaboration activities is known as idea screening. Since the COVID-19 pandemic, the tourism industry, including souvenir business groups or souvenir centers in Samarinda, has been one of the most impactful sectors (Purba et al., 2021). Unfortunately, since the COVID-19 pandemic, the business turnover of souvenir shops has dropped by 80% and is on the verge of closing. Several studies have found that the COVID pandemic has reduced sales of souvenir crafts (Novitasari et al., 2021; Wiliyanto et al., 2022). Profitability and sales at the Citra Niaga Souvenir Center in Samarinda were also down. According to Adam and Alarifi (2021), external support assistance could boost the positive impact of SME innovation practices on business continuity. Serious efforts are required to save one of Samarinda's cultural centers. We thrive on resolving the issue by digitizing the souvenir business group via the assistance program and preparing supporting facilities for the souvenir business group via digital access facilities such as a website, ecommerce, online payment gateway, business chat facility, training facilities, and promotional facilities.

The Food Business Sector

The COVID pandemic has caused paralysis in several sectors, including the performance of the business supply chain, which includes the food sector (Hasanat et al., 2020; Papadopoulos et al., 2017). During the COVID-19 pandemic, ghost kitchens emerged as an impact felt by food and beverage industry actors who were forced to downsize or as a survival step to continue living life. The ghost kitchen industry is growing in response to the economic crisis caused by the pandemic and the growing public demand for food that is easily accessible. According to a survey conducted by Bilali et al. (2021), during the pandemic in Morocco, there was an increase in the consumption of local goods as well as an increase in online grocery shopping, so the ghost and cloud kitchen concepts are currently in high demand by global culinary business players and have begun to penetrate in Indonesia (Fridayani et al., 2010).

The ghost kitchen comes in two varieties. First and foremost, the restaurant is in survival mode. Second, after losing their jobs, newcomers must support their daily lives. Because of the economic conditions impacted by the COVID-19 pandemic, unemployment in Samarinda City has increased. As a result, many restaurants were unable to provide on-site dining because most activities were halted. Delivery service is a popular feature in restaurants during the pandemic.

The second type of ghost kitchen flourished in Indonesian households. The number of non-restaurant ghost kitchens or online culinary businesses has grown (Purnama et al., 2022). The home-based online culinary movement is required as one of the income-generating solutions.

Ghost kitchen actors find digital marketing to be both appealing and challenging. This company's presentation, packaging, marketing, price, and product quality are all summarized in the popularity rating by consumers. As a result, businesses must have strategies and innovations in place to compete in the digitalization era and survive this pandemic (Agustriyana et al., 2021).

Our strategy is to launch a home-based online culinary movement in each neighborhood unit (RT), with a goal of reaching 5 RTs in Samarinda via an assistance program and the construction of supporting facilities.

Initiating the Food Share Platform

Germany has a food waste problem during COVID-19 pandemic, stating food service sector could not operate in conventional way (Strotmann et al, 2022). In lieu of global condition, unsold food products in Indonesia contribute to an undesired waste problem. To put a number in the context, Samarinda has more than 2500 eateries and food sellers. On the other hand, Samarinda City is home to almost 10,000 individuals who lack food daily. These two conditions must be linked together. The food share program is a communal obligation carried out together by the government, colleges, important industry, and business partners. This endeavor tries to connect philanthropists with economically disadvantaged individuals in need of direct aid, particularly food. This program was motivated by government initiatives, including as food rations for homeless groups and other forms of social support during the pandemic. On the one side, The Food Share

targets food producer merchants, while on the other, it screens for low-income family and orphanage groups. The food bank support system includes an expanded program for food preparation, as well as online communities for carpooling and ridesharing. Students and instructors establish and apply food safety guidelines.

Agreement Building Stage

PT AKAB has a digital infrastructure for commercialization that relies on partner contributions of content. Universities can educate partners, so they are qualified to join the platform developed by important partners. MSME partners require a business continuity solution, as well as an active and transactional marketplace, so that the general public can acquire MSME products.

The government then assists these intersecting interests between universities, the digital business, and producers (MSMEs) in matching programs incorporated into emancipated learning situations to enhance the capabilities of accompanying instructors and students.

The program agreement was developed by incorporating each party's best practices and areas of expertise, including onboarding services to the commercialization platform by key partners (PT AKAB) and university support for MSMEs to make them commercially viable (Figure 1). The two primary features of this agreement are described in three sectors: digitizing the souvenir industry, bolstering the resilience of ghost kitchens, and assisting those severely impacted by the epidemic through the food bank program.

Figure 1. Action model for the matching program

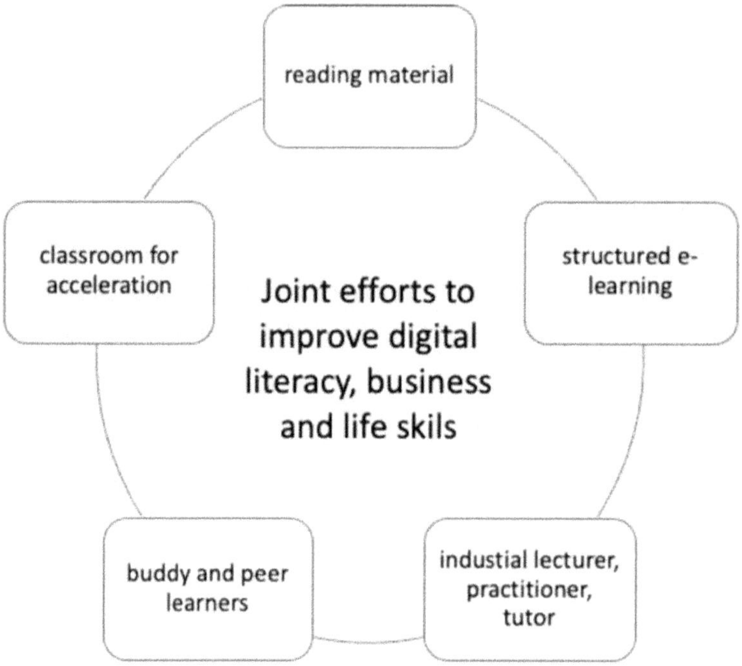

Program Implementation

Digitizing the Souvenir Business

Souvenir digitization activities are conducted to increase the empowerment of MSMEs through the MSME digitization program gradually, periodically, and continuously (sustainability) and to improve infrastructure tools for MSME actors such as IT infrastructure (hardware and software applications) to accelerate the expansion of marketing, product presentations, and MSME services, as well as increasing the number and quality of Human Resources (HR) of MSME actors through familiarization.

During the pandemic, the rate of growth in online product sales rose dramatically. This initiative incorporates University of Mulawarman students, alumni, and adjunct faculties. Students do market research and participate in the selection of MSMEs to be involved. They also aid in various market segmentation and product positioning training and contribute to the opening of the e-commerce market for crafters and souvenir sellers. Students then document their knowledge in fieldwork practice reports or short projects as an alternative to test scores in specific courses.

Table 1. Onboarding selection criteria for souvenir business entity

General Requirements	Special Recruitment Requirements			
	Featured Class	Potential Class	Beginner Class	Idea Class
Traders/Sellers only				
• Actively trading in the last three months • Complete business identity	• Already have a digital payment point/QRIS • Already have a showroom/ display/ shop • Complete business legality • Already have employees	• Already have a showroom/ display/ shop • Business legality exists but it's not complete • Have seasonal workers	• Active trading • Not registered as an MSME unit • Having seasonal workers/not having employees	• sales by order/ request • Do not have registration as an MSME unit • Don't have employees
Sellers and Artisan				
• Active in production in the last 1/2 year • Complete identity business	• Have own production machine • Have a regular production schedule • Already have a showroom/ display/ shop • Already have employees • Complete business legality	• Have/don't have own production machine • Don't have a regular production schedule • Either have /yet to have a showroom/ display/ store • Have seasonal workers • Business legality exists but it's not complete	• Don't have own production machine • Production by way of offshore/ by order • Don't have a showroom/ display/ shop • Having seasonal workers/not having employees • Do not have registration as an MSME unit	• Don't have own production machine • Production by order • Don't have a showroom/ display/ shop • Don't have employees • Do not have registration as an MSME unit •

MSME classification data viewed from multiple factors, including firm ownership, number of employees, production facilities, production frequency, permits held, and sales volume prior to the pandemic, provide some of the insights for this sector. In accordance with the onboarding selection criteria for souvenir business entities, the estimated proportions of new, potential, and advanced entities are 60%, 35%, and 15%, respectively (Table 1). This information is then used as instructional material in classes such as marketing management. In addition, it is discovered that not all MSMEs feel the necessity to seek complete licenses. This demonstrates that there are non-technical impediments to adopting theories in the actual world that cannot always be learnt through reading references alone.

Ghost Kitchen Companionship

This approach to increase the quality of ghost kitchen actors is carried out in multiple phases, beginning with a business actor survey. Initial data was collected from recipients of presidential assistance through the Department of Industry and Trade, visually confirmed, and validated by student interviews. According to the early categorizations, the actual percentages of ghost kitchen entities in the beginning, potential, and advanced stages are 65, 28, and 7 percent, respectively (Table 2). The ghost kitchen players were then asked if they would be willing to participate in mentoring, training, and easy certification programs, such as those for food safety handlers. This individual certification is the first step in getting a local government business license. Each ghost kitchen actor is thus involved in the identification and determination of business entities with potentially distinct expectations. The purpose of artificial exclusivity is to prevent business actors from competing. This company's physical identity is represented by a business license number and a taxpayer identification number. Finally, e-banking and online transactions were implemented in coordination with banks that have formed partnerships with universities.

Participating in this activity provides students with the opportunity to practice all stages of legally owning a business, knowledge that can increase their future options as young entrepreneurs. In addition, the actual thinking scope of ghost kitchen firms is illuminating for accompanying teachers, particularly in terms of presenting real-world examples for subjects such as entrepreneurship, product creation, and occupational health.

Table 2. Onboarding selection criteria for ghost kitchen entity

General requirements	Special Recruitment Requirements		
	Featured Class	Potential Class	Beginner Class
• Actively have sales in the last three months • Complete business identity	• Have partnered with local/ online platform • Have a fixed/ unique product • Sustainable production • Already have a production group	• Have partnered with local/ online platform • Have a fixed/ unique product • Production by order/ not sustainable/sales are still small • Either have or yet to have a production group	• Not partnered with any local/ online platform • Don't have a fixed/ unique product • Production by order/ not sustainable/sales are still small • don't have a production group

Food Share

This food bank's embryos are arranged in a situation where there are still compassionate individuals amid a devastating pandemic. This circumstance necessitates the provision of evidence and services by parties with a good reputation for honesty, notably educational institutions. This social function is organized through the collection and distribution of edible food. Students verify the viability of consumption after receiving training from the authorities and employing pertinent theories. Universities and the government provide all philanthropists, in this case, large restaurants, with business development help. Meanwhile, the recipient communities receive growth and development counseling.

Every Friday, the food bank is open, hence the name Friday benefit activity. Over 3,200 individuals have benefited from this initiative. After being begun, philanthropic organizations in the food bank scheme continue this Friday's benefit activities autonomously. The institution must develop the concept of multifaceted social services, including scholarships, blood donations, health services, food banks, and counseling, particularly for underprivileged students and the surrounding community.

LESSON LEARNED FROM THE CASE STUDY OF DIGITALIZATION OF TRADITIONAL COMMUNITY MARKET

Measuring Impact by Achieving Primary Key Indicators

Digitalization of Traditional Community Market establishes four primary key indicators with multi-stakeholder strategic partnership (Table 3), namely (1) updating the curriculum of higher education institutions, (2) enhancing access to facilities and infrastructure through resource sharing with partners, (3) enabling lecturers and students to solve real-world cases in the community, and (4) fostering future collaboration. The participation of multiple stakeholders is summarized in Table 3.

Internships, research, autonomous assignments, and humanitarian endeavors categorized as major projects are examples of curricular enrichment activities. These activities serve to improve the connection between theories and implementations.

A plan for resource sharing makes possible the improvement of access to amenities and infrastructure. Higher education can exploit their lack of facilities through partnerships with government, other universities, and business and community organizations. The cooperation includes a win-win solution, such as a collaborative publication using an inter-university center, an industrial internship in the partner's workshop, and a joint certification and training program in government-owned training facilities.

The matching program enables professors and students to tackle actual community situations. Real-world problem solving sharpens the lecturers' and students' capacity to produce feasible approaches for tackling difficulties faced by MSMEs. For instance, packaging design theory must balance production costs at suboptimal production levels, such as too few items, which results in high production costs. One of the recommended solutions is the use of a shared packaging design by multiple MSMEs so that costs can be reduced to a level that enables the adoption of enhanced packaging for similar products.

Existing between academics, students, alumni, and MSMEs partners is a positive rapport that generates chances for future collaboration. Students may, for instance, choose a prospective MSME as the subject of their final project, which would include a feasibility analysis and advanced problem-solving incorporating hygiene and product quality analysis, market re-segmentation, product refreshment, and product differentiation.

Table 3. Digitalization of Traditional Community Market Multi stakeholders' involvement in figures

Indicator	Target (entity)	Achievement	
		Number (entity)	Percentage
Study programs involvement	7	7	100%
Students Gaining Off-Campus Experience	60	70	116%
Lecturers with Off-Campus Activities	20	24	120%
Practitioners Teaching On-Campus	25	25	100%
Key Partners (big industry, government)	7	20	285%
Alumni involvement	20	20	100%
MSMEs	250	260	104%
Community	3200	3243	101%

Recognition of the Involved Human Resources

The matching program is implemented by planning for the human resource needs of universities, corporations, and governments to support the program's operation. In this instance, universities are academic institutions that assist with design thinking, production process improvement, packaging, and labeling, business actor development, business funding, human resource certification, community group formation, and aggregating growth chances.

Human Resources departments inside postsecondary institutions must be acknowledged as the curriculum's implementers. Lecturers, students, alumni, and partners (business, industry, government, and society). Lecturers are responsible for leading students through their final assignments or significant projects, including internships, research, autonomous assignments, and humanitarian missions. In addition, lecturers direct courses with learning outcomes that undergo pedagogical content enrichment and replacement (Cam and Erdamar, 2021). Students and alumni participate in the available programs, while partners are a part of the corporate digital upgrade program.

The recognition of professors is based on the instruction delivered to students, alumni, and business partners (Figure 2). Partner recognition of lecturer contributions appears as an Industrial lecturer certificate, which is subsequently evaluated as community service credit. Depending on the type of sub-program executed and the duration of execution, student contributions are acknowledged as unit credits or accomplishments documented on the accompanying certificate for diplomas. Business partners provide alumni with a certificate of honor. Government and industry partners receive university collaboration documents as a means of achieving key performance indicators.

The recognition of human resources involved in the program is an illustration of the three framework implementations: the internalization of the vision (framework 1), collaboration with multiple stakeholders (framework 4), and the incorporation of community service results into research and teaching (framework 5).

Figure 2. Recognition of the involved resources

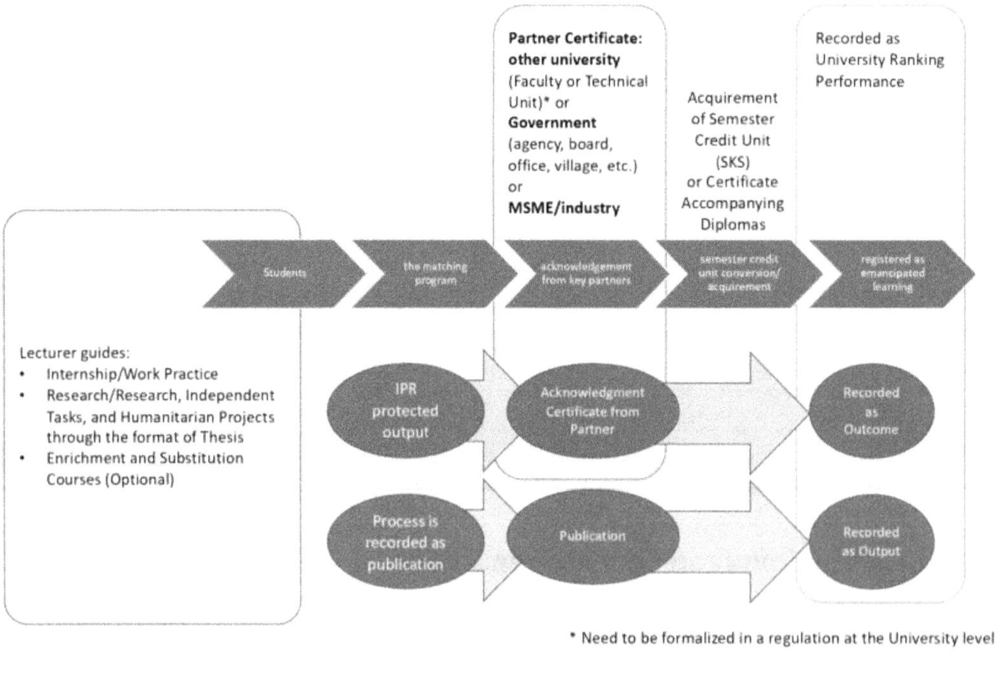

Established Definition and Implementation of Emancipated Learning Student Credit Recognition

At the university level, the merdeka belajar – kampus merdeka (MBKM) or translated into emancipated learning integration of the independent campus, was implemented. The program and recruitment team consulted with the academic the vice rector for the first-time regarding student recruitment. The matching program team, along with the vice rector for academics, the vice rector for student affairs and alumni, the vice rector for cooperation, the head of the Institute for Educational Development and Quality Assurance, and the chairperson of the drafter of guidelines for emancipated learning, conducted the second consultation regarding the implementation of the university-wide program. Lastly, the implementing team and the head of the Institute for Educational Development and Quality Assurance conducted the third consultation. Students enrolled in the MBKM Program are permitted to engage in academically-recognized extracurricular learning to satisfy course requirements.

The MBKM program intends to execute and achieve activities, which are specified as activities based on quantifiable learning objectives through the quantification of credits that students apply and get. The basis for quantifying MBKM credits is the conversion of hours spent on MBKM activities; one credit is equivalent to 45.3 hours. This citation is based on the definition of a single credit unit (170 minutes) in accordance with Article 19 Paragraph (4) of Regulation No. 3/2020 of the Minister of Education and Culture, as well as the determination that a semester consists of 16 program weeks. Credit is awarded for a variety of activities, including internships, research, and entrepreneurship. The MBKM recognition is tailored to the program's graduate learning outcomes (LO). The form of activity output is issued in a certificate of acknowledgement or will be formally acknowledged by a certificate accompanying diplomas. The MBKM credit recognition consultation is included in the first and fourth frameworks of the program framework, namely internalizing the learning vision by utilizing realistic examples from the community and cooperating with multiple stakeholders. Implementing the MBKM Semester Credit Units (SCU) recognized consultation in the matching program is properly coordinated by the program team and academics in the linked study programs.

Quantifying Semester Credit Units for Emancipated Learning

The application of learning credit quantification in the matching program is conducted in accordance with the three primary programs that students pursue. Each program includes sub-activities that are planned and quantifiable to achieve learning outcomes. Under the supervision of the instructor, students do MBKM based on the program in which they are enrolled. Students can convert credits based on the learning outcomes of each program if there is coordination between study programs.

Credits for emancipated learning must be quantified in accordance with the curriculum of a home study program. To translate student actions into emancipated learning unit credits, the acquired skills, materials, and learning experiences must be calculated. Each activity is comprised of multiple meetings with learning objectives. SCU quantification is based on two mechanisms: (1) equalization of courses based on LO, and (2) free form structure, tailored to the activities performed by estimating the activity time (according to the Regulation of the Minister of Education and Culture number 3 of 2020). The majority of program implementation by students is turned into unit credits that are applied to the study program's internal optional courses. Conversion is performed to guarantee that the weight of MBKM credits corresponds with the learning outcomes for each subject in the study program (Figure 3). As a result, the student earned credit and gained experience with actual cases. The MBKM activity to SCU conversion can be quantified based on the outputs created by the involved students in the form of reports, publications, and intellectual property rights (IPRs).

Frameworks of creating resilience in tackling societal challenges associated to learning theories (framework 2) and adopting new technologies in the learning process include credit quantification of student-initiated learning units (framework 3).

Matching Platform between Academics and Industrial Entities

The need for a workforce relevant with the field's qualifications is increasing. This is supported by changes in the business world and faster technological advances. Based on this, universities must be more adaptive and flexible to the needs of the new technology, business, and industry, as well as various other advances, by utilizing and allocating their resources. Therefore, a collaboration between universities and the business world needs to be done. The goal of implementing the collaboration is to prepare prospective workers who meet the demand of qualified workers in the respective sectors. Ivascu et al. (2016) mention that collaboration between academia and the business world can be established in activities such as research collaboration, knowledge sharing, and other collaborations. Indicators of achievement of matching platforms and collaboration between academia and the business world can be measured through the number of research collaborations and knowledge-sharing activities. In the emancipated learning university scheme, the implementation of cooperation can be measured through the achievement of the key performance indicators (KPI) implemented. The KPIs that can be achieved include graduates getting decent jobs (KPI 1), students getting experience outside of campus (KPI 2), lecturers having activities outside campus (KPI 3), practitioners teaching on campus (KPI 4), number of partnership (KPI 6), and collaborative classrooms (KPI 7). Through activities in the cooperation program between universities and the business world, it is also expected to realize three sustainable development goals, namely quality education (SDG 4), decent education and economic growth (SDG 8), and partnerships to achieve goals (SDG 17), summarized in developing collaboration with other parties (framework 4), such as partners and the community as learning resources (Table 4).

The implementation of the matching program is set as an integrated program within the university environment and is hosted in a business incubator institution. Al-Mubaraki (2015) describe a describe a business incubator is initiatives to stimulate and support economic growth by promoting the creation and development of innovative companies. In addition, the business incubator is also referred to an innovation center, company center, and business enterprise center or technology center.

The competencies achieved by University of Mulawarman include developing lab-scale products to slow rate production, certifying partner business institutions, developing production management, SOPs, and financial management. These activities are conducted in collaboration with recruiters, trainers, and assessors from business and government sectors. Coaching was conducted within the teaching industry facility as a form of agreed collaboration to create innovative solutions. Post-training and alumni engagement are established with the help of digital platforms. All these collaborations create an industrial ecosystem within the university environment.

Figure 3. Mapping alignment of emancipated learning curriculum applied for the matching program

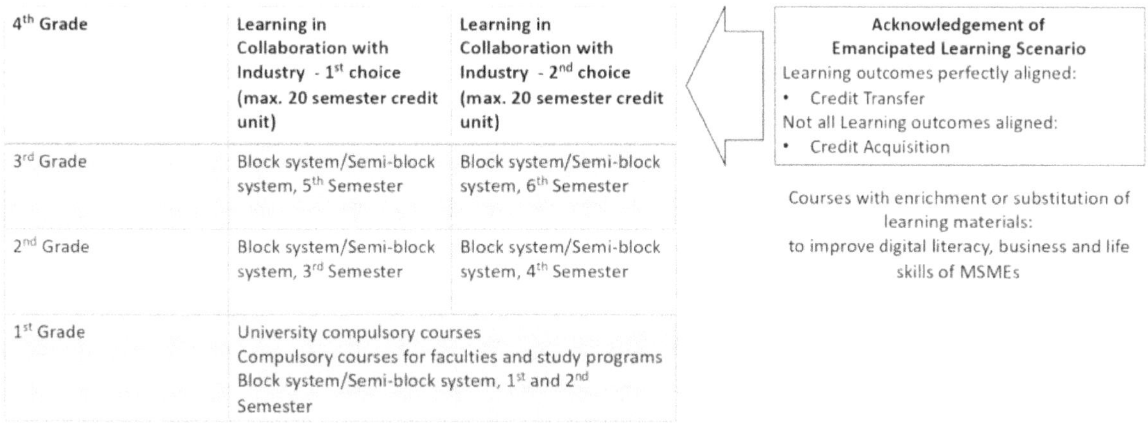

Converting Lesson Learnt to Publications

The COVID-19 epidemic in Indonesia has the potential to reduce economic growth by much to 3.5 percent annually. The epidemic quickly increased the poverty rate from 9.7 percent in September 2019 to 16.6 percent by the end of 2020 (Suryahadi et al., 2020). Due to economic shocks, theoretical concepts, and thoughts to boost economic growth are urgently required. The publication is a means of disseminating information that can contribute to the advancement of scientific understanding, particularly in community service activities. This lesson is judged by the number of publications produced and the number of individuals involved in creating publications covering university performance indicators and the achievement of sustainable development goals.

The activities of the matching program are a kind of service in the sphere of MSME development including academic actors such as students, professors, and campus institutions, as well as MSME partners and industry players. The results are reported in scientific article submissions that will be published in numerous service journals, as well as in written reports and intellectual property rights. In the face of economic shocks such as the current COVID-19 epidemic, the information and data offered in the paper contain pictures of sustainable development successes in frameworks 1 through 5.

Table 4. Agreed expertise sharing between industry and academics

<table>
<tr><th>University</th><th>Competence of University</th><th>Agreed Cooperation</th><th>Competence of partner</th><th>industry partner</th></tr>
<tr><td rowspan="4">Business Incubation</td><td>Lab-scale product development toward slow-rate production</td><td>human resources aspect</td><td>Developing Startups (Institutional Business Development)</td><td rowspan="4">Real world Industrial Business</td></tr>
<tr><td>Improvement of production management, standard operating procedures, and financial management</td><td>Recruiter, Coach, Assessor</td><td>The process of sharing best practices</td></tr>
<tr><td>Licensing; coaching</td><td>Sharing facility aspect</td><td>Creating innovative solutions</td></tr>
<tr><td>Post-training activities; alumni engagement</td><td>Classroom (physical/ virtual), Case Study (PBL material), Assessment material</td><td>Digital power
Digital platform</td></tr>
</table>

The MSMEs have challenges in executing their businesses, such as implementing support in operating an internet business and acquiring online communication skills. In addition, through the University of Mulawarman and PT AKAB's partnership program, MSME empowerment is achieved by introducing and selling items through the Gojek Business (GoBiz) marketing digitalization system. Assisting MSMEs has resulted in the conceptual findings produced and reported in scientific publications on the operations conducted. It is anticipated that the final publication will serve as a resource for devising adaptations to the effects of economic shocks.

Expertise and Resource Sharing of Facilities and Infrastructure Achieving Common Goals

The most fundamental problems MSME actors face are additional resource skills, access to product marketing, and facilities and infrastructure. The availability of facilities and infrastructure is one of the factors that support the implementation of a program, increasing the growth and development of the MSME economic sector.

In the development of human, institutional, facility, and financial resources for MSMEs, each stakeholder group—Academics, Business, Government, and Community—plays a unique role. For instance, University of Mulawarman as academics can serve as accelerators for design thinking, production process improvement, packaging, and labeling, business unit design, step-by-step and certification document preparation assistance, commercial production scaling in pilot facility (teaching industry), preparation of funding proposals, funding scenarios, step-by-step financial development, and verification of MSMEs. PT AKAB become market leaders by leveraging their business platforms can contribute to the creation of business development, business funding, business unit design, business development partnership systems, and core and plasma systems. The government plays a crucial role for HR certification (example: food safety extension), certification funding and training (example: small business certification, halal), business protection (example: IPR conflict), provision of a common room, workshop, or joint production site, provision of micro financing, and social assistance. In the meantime, the MSMEs community can contribute to group certification applications, community formation, the aggregation of development chances, and cooperative actions (Table 5).

Table 5. Collaboration matrix between academics, business actors, governments, and communities

	Academics (University of Mulawarman)	Business (PT Aplikasi Karya Anak Bangsa)	Government (Various governmental agencies)	Community (MSMEs)
Human Resources	design thinking, production process improvement, packaging, and labeling	business development, business funding	HR certification (example: food safety extension)	community formation, aggregation of development opportunities
Institutional Resources	business unit design, stepping and certification document preparation assistance,	business unit design	certification funding and training (e.g. small business certification, halal), business protection (e.g. IPR conflict)	group certification application
Facility Resources	commercial production scaling in pilot facility (teaching industry)	business development	provision of a common room/ workshop/ joint production site	community formation, aggregation of development opportunities
Financial Resources	preparation of funding proposals, funding scenarios, stepping financial development, verification of MSMEs	partnership system, core and plasma system	provision of micro financing, social assistance	cooperative actions

One of the activities of the matching program is the improvement of infrastructure and facilities for the development of MSMEs. Through the Department of Agricultural Product Technology, University of Mulawarman also offers MSME clinic services. This clinic enables and offers business assistance services to community members or owners of MSMEs. In addition, the MSMEs were given access to product development training and basic equipment to enhance the quality of their products.

Osoba (2003) contends that the government-provided infrastructure facilities aid the expansion of small companies by easing the charging of necessary inputs. These amenities constitute vital infrastructure that facilitates and encourages investment. The priority scale serves as the foundation for providing facilities and infrastructure for HR development training activities and institutions, as well as for enhancing partner cooperation. The timely execution of programs, objectives, and goals is one indication of a functioning supporting infrastructure. Strengthening facilities and infrastructure is an example of a resilience framework for addressing community issues (framework 2), adapting technology (framework 3), and fostering partnerships (framework 4).

Institutional Strengthening of the MSME Development Team

Strengthening institutional units plays a crucial role in the MSMEs program development capabilities. The University of Mulawarman business incubator is an institution for MSME development. As part of the implementation of the agreement, the University of Mulawarman Incubator joined the Indonesian Business Incubator Association (AIBI). Another institution is the education sector, which has 24 products with PIRT certification and 23 with halal certification. National Standardization Agency (2015), PT Bank Syariah Mandiri (2020), PT Bank Syariah Indonesia (2021), Gojek-Indonesia (2020-2021), The ministry of education, culture, research, and technology (2020), The board of national research agency (2021), The Ministry of Cooperation and MSME (2021), National Narcotics Agency (2021), and various provincial and local governments have collaborated with University of Mulawarman for MSMEs development (2014-2021).

In the period of globalization, business actors must satisfy the fundamental requirements of expanding product innovation, developing human resource capabilities, and advancing technology. Business incubation is a requirement of the new global economy, which is the result of rapid and significant changes in technology, telecommunications, and digitalization; the existence of deregulation and globalization (Wajdi et al., 2020). Therefore, it is necessary to strengthen business incubator institutions in order to enhance the quality of continuous incubation. With the 7S functions of space, shared resources, service, support, skill development, seed money, and synergy, business incubators are at the forefront of increasing MSME development. University of Mulawarman business incubator adds HR training activities, hard and soft skills, and organizational management to the matching program.

Network cooperation aspect is achieved by the number of partners in the implementation of a series of activities. Implementation of integrated business incubator activities on sustainable development goals suits all proposed framework.

CONCLUSION

During the COVID-19 epidemic, traditional markets' viability has reduced. This research proposes five frameworks for achieving eSDG in the implementation of problem-solving (Table 6): 1) internalization of the vision, 2) propagation of persistence, 3) adaption of new technologies, 4) extension of collaboration, and 5) integration of results. For the matching program scheme created by the government, the University of Mulawarman and PT Aplikasi Karya Anak Bangsa, a subsidiary of a well-known unicorn company of Gojek Indonesia, together identified certain societal concerns. Integrated learning elements are implemented for the three programs, (1) Souvenir business Digitization, (2) Ghost Kitchen Online, and (3) Food Bank, through the completion of final assignments, lectures on real-world problem solving, fieldwork practices, and structured assignments tied to the learning outcomes of specific course topics (embedded learning).

The most significant lessons learned in the implementation of the proposed eSDG framework in digitalization of traditional community market were: (1) the design of the MSME Development Curriculum requires the identification of factors that influence MSME development models; (2) case studies of MSME development models show that the design of the MSME development curriculum needs to be adapted to the nature of MSME business and the readiness of MSMEs to receive guidance; (3) MSME development models can be used as a benchmark in the design of the MSME development curriculum; (4) integration of matching program models like this into the ministry of education flagship emancipated learning program – the independent campus (MBKM) is very possible, so that cross-sectoral cooperation in developing MSMEs will be a win-win solution.

Table 6. Tabulated Matrix of the proposed eSDG framework implementation in Digitalization of Traditional Community Market

The proposed eSDG framework	Lesson learned	Involvement of Stakeholders
Framework 1: Internalization of the learning vision by taking realistic examples in the community	expertise and resource sharing of facilities and infrastructure achieving common goals (7) institutional strengthening of the MSME development team (8)	The university Academic Community Key Partners
Framework 2: Developing resilience in problem solving in society that relates to theories in learning	recognition of the involved human resources (2) established definition and implementation of emancipated learning student credit recognition (3) quantifying semester credit units for emancipated learning (4) converting activities to publications (6)	The university Academic Community Key Partners Government agencies
Framework 3: Adaptation of new technologies in problem-solving-based learning processes in the community	matching platform between academics and industrial entities (5) institutional strengthening of the MSME development team (8)	The university Academic Community Key Partners Government agencies
Framework 4: Develop collaboration with other parties, such as partners and the community as learning resources	matching platform between academics and industrial entities (5) institutional strengthening of the MSME development team (8)	The university Academic Community Key Partners Government agencies Certification Body
Framework 5: Integrating the results of problem solving in the community into learning	established definition and implementation of emancipated learning student credit recognition (3) quantifying semester credit units for emancipated learning (4) converting lesson learned to publications (6)	The university Academic Community Key Partners

REFERENCES

Adam, N. A., & Alarifi, G. (2021). Innovation practices for the survival of small and medium enterprises (SMEs) in the COVID-19 times: The role of external support. *Journal of Innovation and Entrepreneurship, 10*(15), 1–22. doi:10.118613731-021-00156-6 PMID:34075328

Agustriyana, D., Ramadhan, N., Oktavien, S., & Sofyandi, H. R. (2021). Keeping Business in SMEs in the Midst of the COVID-19 Pandemic. *Journal of Devotion Dharma Laksana Serving the Nation, 3*(2), 93–99.

Al-Mubaraki, H. M. (2015). The Importance of business incubation in developing countries: Case study approach. *International Journal of Foresight and Innovation Policy, 10*(1), 17–28. doi:10.1504/IJFIP.2015.070054

Astari, N. (2021). A Literature Review: Digital Marketing Trends in Indonesia During the COVID-19 Pandemic. *CHANNEL: Jurnal Komunikasi, 9*(2), 125–134. doi:10.12928/channel.v9i2.20836

Bento, F., Giglio Bottino, A., Cerchiareto Pereira, F., Forastieri de Almeida, J., & Gomes Rodrigues, F. (2021). Resilience in higher education: A complex perspective to lecturers' adaptive processes in response to the COVID-19 pandemic. *Education Sciences, 11*(9), 492. doi:10.3390/educsci11090492

Bilali, H. E., Ben Hassen, T., Baya Chatti, C., Abouabdillah, A., & Alaoui, S. B. (2021). Exploring Household Food Dynamics During the COVID-19 Pandemic in Morocco. *Frontiers in Nutrition*, *8*, 724803. doi:10.3389/fnut.2021.724803 PMID:34646850

Blesia, J. U., Iek, M., Ratang, W., & Hutajulu, H. (2021). Developing an Entrepreneurship Model to Increase Students' Entrepreneurial Skills: An Action Research Project in a Higher Education Institution in Indonesia. *Systemic Practice and Action Research*, *34*(1), 53–70. doi:10.100711213-019-09506-8

Budiman, A., Samani, M., & Setyawan, W. H. (2021). The Development of Direct-Contextual Learning: A New Model on Higher Education. *International Journal of Higher Education*, *10*(2), 15–26. doi:10.5430/ijhe.v10n2p15

Çam, Ş. S., & Erdamar Koç, G. (2021). Technological pedagogical content knowledge practices in higher education: First impressions of preservice teachers. *Technology. Knowledge and Learning*, *26*(1), 123–153. doi:10.100710758-019-09430-9

Corbacho, A. M., Minini, L., Pereyra, M., González-Fernández, A. E., Echániz, R., Repetto, L., Cruz, P., Fernández-Damonte, V., Lorieto, A., & Basile, M. (2021). Interdisciplinary higher education with a focus on academic motivation and teamwork diversity. *International Journal of Educational Research Open*, *2*, 100062. doi:10.1016/j.ijedro.2021.100062

Diana, H. L. (2020). Collaborative Strategy Between Universities, Industry and Government: A Conceptual Review in Efforts to Improve Educational Innovation and Learning Creativity in Higher Education. *Proceedings of the National Conference on Management Economics and Accounting*. Master Program in Accounting, Faculty of Economics, Universitas Islam Indonesia, Yogyakarta.

Fridayani, H. D., Iqbal, M., & Atmojo, M. E. (2021). Cloud Kitchen: Strategy for Indonesian Culinary Business (SMEs) Growth During and Post Pandemic Era. *Management Research and Behavior Journal*, *1*(2), 41–46.

Guzmán-Valenzuela, C., Gómez-González, C., Rojas-Murphy Tagle, A., & Lorca-Vyhmeister, A. (2021). Learning analytics in higher education: A preponderance of analytics but very little learning? *International Journal of Educational Technology in Higher Education*, *18*(1), 1–19. doi:10.118641239-021-00258-x PMID:34778523

Hasanat, M. W., Hoque, A., Shikha, F. A., Anwar, M., Hamid, A. B. A., & Tat, H. H. (2020). The impact of coronavirus (COVID-19) on E-business in Malaysia. *Asian Journal of Multidisciplinary Studies*, *3*(1), 85–90.

Indrawati, S. M., & Kuncoro, A. (2021). Improving competitiveness through vocational and higher education: Indonesia's vision for human capital development in 2019–2024. *Bulletin of Indonesian Economic Studies*, *57*(1), 29–59. doi:10.1080/00074918.2021.1909692

Irawan, A. P., Supriyatna, E., Widjaja, I., & Lin, L. L. C. (2021). The Implementation of Basic Principles of Financial Management to Improve Higher Education Reputation. In *International Conference on Economics, Business, Social, and Humanities (ICEBSH 2021)* (pp. 1510-1514). Atlantis Press. 10.2991/assehr.k.210805.238

Ivascu, L., Cirjaliu, B., & Draghici, A. (2016). Business Model for the University-industry Collaboration in Open Innovation. *Procedia Economics and Finance*, *39*, 674–678. doi:10.1016/S2212-5671(16)30288-X

Ketter, E., & Avraham, E. (2021). # StayHome today so we can# TravelTomorrow: Tourism destinations' digital marketing strategies during the Covid-19 pandemic. *Journal of Travel & Tourism Marketing*, *38*(8), 819–832. doi:10.1080/10548408.2021.1921670

Maftuna, G. (2022). Methodology of Organizing Problem Lessons in Higher Education. *International Journal of Culture and Modernity*, *14*, 72–77.

Martha, A. S. D., Junus, K., Santoso, H. B., & Suhartanto, H. (2021). Assessing Undergraduate Students' e-Learning Competencies: A Case Study of Higher Education Context in Indonesia. *Education Sciences*, *11*(4), 189. doi:10.3390/educsci11040189

Novitasari, A. T., Wijayanti, R., & Sholeh, Y. (2021). Socialization of Souvenir Craft Marketing Strategy Using Online Media in the Era of the COVID-19 Virus Pandemic. *Journal of Community Service*, *4*(2), 190–196.

Ollivaud, P. (2021). Investing in competences and skills and reforming the labour market to create better jobs in Indonesia. *OECD Economics Department Working Papers*. No. 1670, OECD Publishing, Paris, doi:10.1787/18151973

Papadopoulos, T., Gunasekaran, A., Dubey, R., Altay, N., Childe, S., & Fosso-Wamba, S. (2017). The role of big data in explaining disaster resilience for sustainability. *Journal of Cleaner Production*, *142*, 1108–1118. doi:10.1016/j.jclepro.2016.03.059

Purba, J.H., Fathiah, R. & Steven, S. 2021. The impact of covid-19 pandemic on the tourism sector in indonesia. *Jurnal Aplikasi Ekonomi Akuntansi dan Bisnis*, *3*(1), 389 - 401. DOI:. doi:10.37641/riset.v3i1.82

Purnama, S., Bangun, C. S., Panjaitan, A. R. S., & Sampoerna, S. T. (2022). The Effect Of Digitalization On Culinary MSMEs On Increasing Sales Turnover During COVID 19 Pandemic. [ATT]. *Artist Transactions on Technopreneurship*, *4*(1), 59–68. doi:10.34306/att.v4i1.228

Purwanti, E. (2021). Preparing the implementation of merdeka belajar–kampus merdeka policy in higher education institutions. *In 4th International Conference on Sustainable Innovation 2020–Social, Humanity, and Education, Atlantis Press. (ICoSIHESS 2020)*. ACM. 10.2991/assehr.k.210120.149

Raza, H., Saputra, J., & Muhammad, Z. (2022). The effect of the implementation of financial accounting standards on MSMEs. *Accounting*, *8*(2), 209–216. doi:10.5267/j.ac.2021.6.018

Richter, U. M., Veerabhatla, S., & Zasiekina, L. (2021). Managing and facilitating student learning in teams in higher education. In *Cases on Active Blended Learning in Higher Education* (pp. 149–171). IGI Global. doi:10.4018/978-1-7998-7856-8.ch008

Rosser, A. (2022). Higher Education in Indonesia: The political economy of institution-level Governance. *Journal of Contemporary Asia*, 1–26.

Sánchez-Carracedo, F., Moreno-Pino, F. M., Romero-Portillo, D., & Sureda, B. (2021). Education for sustainable development in Spanish university education degrees. *Sustainability, 13*(3), 1467. doi:10.3390u13031467

Setyowati, D. L., Paramita, S., Ifroh, R. H., Asrianti, T., Fitriani, E., & Rahman, W. (2021). Work readiness during COVID-19 among taxibike online drivers in Samarinda, Indonesia. *International Journal of Public Health Science, 10*(13), 617. doi:10.11591/ijphs.v10i3.20870

Strotmann, C., Baur, V., Börnert, N., & Gerwin, P. (2022). Generation and prevention of food waste in the German food service sector in the COVID-19 pandemic–Digital approaches to encounter the pandemic related crisis. *Socio-Economic Planning Sciences, 82*, 101104. doi:10.1016/j.seps.2021.101104 PMID:35721382

Sukmawati, D., & Maryanti, R. (2022). Development of education and economic circulation in supporting local potential as community empowerment efforts amid the Covid-19 pandemic. *Indonesian Journal of Multidiciplinary Research, 1*(2), 235–250. doi:10.17509/ijomr.v1i2.37598

Suryahadi, A., Al Izzati, R., & Suryadarma, D. (2020). The Impact of COVID-19 Outbreak on Poverty: An Estimation for Indonesia (Draft). *SMERU Working Paper*, 1–20. https://smeru.or.id/en/content/impact-COVID-19-outbreak-poverty-estimation-indonesia

Susilawati, E., Khaira, I., & Pratama, I. (2021). Antecedents to student loyalty in Indonesian higher education institutions: The mediating role of technology innovation. *Educational Sciences: Theory and Practice, 21*(3), 40–56.

Trespalacios, J., Snelson, C., Lowenthal, P. R., Uribe-Flórez, L., & Perkins, R. (2021). Community and connectedness in online higher education: A scoping review of the literature. *Distance Education, 42*(1), 5–21. doi:10.1080/01587919.2020.1869524

Wagiran, W., Suharjana, S., Nurtanto, M., & Mutohhari, F. (2022). Determining the e-learning readiness of higher education students: A study during the COVID-19 pandemic. *Heliyon, 8*(10), e11160. doi:10.1016/j.heliyon.2022.e11160 PMID:36276754

Wajdi MF, Mangifera L, Isa M. 2020. Strategy for strengthening business incubators in developing small and medium enterprises. *Competitiveness Journal of resource management economics. 22*(2): 101-107.

Watson, S., Fulton, K. A., Carpio, C., & Boonsaeng, T. (2022). Virtual Student Teamwork in Higher Education: Is There a Secret Recipe for Productivity? *American Journal of Distance Education*, 1–13. doi:10.1080/08923647.2022.2143700

Wiliyanto, R., Mahirah, A., & Firmansyah, F. I. (2022). Determining the Promotion Strategy of MSME Fashion and Souvenirs with the Market Basket Analysis Method. *INISTA: Journal of Informatics, Information Systems. Software Engineering and Applications, 4*(2), 46–54. doi:10.20895/inista.v4i2.559

Chapter 9
Enabling Education for Sustainable Development Through Digital Storytelling

Vassilios Makrakis
University of Crete, Greece & Frederick University, Cyprus

Nelly Kostoulas-Makrakis
University of Crete, Greece

ABSTRACT

Digital storytelling and participatory video (PV) are closely linked since they share common objectives, development tools, and methodologies. They are not just informative but purposefully aim to empower, educate, and activate people toward building a more sustainable and just society. This chapter describes both digital storytelling as a tool and as a teaching and learning methodology applied in an Erasmus+ project in Southeast Asia. It has been revealed that the interaction between digital technology and education for sustainability creates new opportunities to address sustainability, as well as new challenges. The teachers trained produced digital storytelling/PV applications that can be categorized as "authentic" learning activities addressing issues in the "real world." It was widely assumed that teachers involved in this process learned to view teaching and learning from alternative ways, feeling ownership and control of their own learning and experiencing a sense of contribution to society and the environment.

INTRODUCTION

Storytelling is a powerful way that enables students and adults to communicate experiences and to explore ideas (Skouge & Ra, 2009). Digital storytelling can be seen both as a teaching method and a learning resource that has been applied in many creative and innovative ways at all levels of education (Rahiem, 2021; Ketelle, 2017). Digital storytelling merges a number of media such as image, video, sound and music to contextualise a story that may convey messages cutting across the four pillars of sustainable development (Makrakis, 2018; Makrakis & Kostoulas-Makrakis, 2012a). Humanity is living in a crisis

DOI: 10.4018/978-1-7998-5033-5.ch009

of sustainability that reflects not only environmental issues such as climate change and biodiversity loss, but also economic and social issues, pertaining to poverty, social exclusion, violation of human rights, unequal trade, gender inequalities, and so forth.

Education for Sustainable Development (ESD) or Education for Sustainability (EfS) is usually used interchangeably across all education levels and types from formal to non-formal and informal. It represents a new vision of teaching and learning, a vision that helps people reconnect with nature, by addressing the complexity and interconnectedness of sustainability issues facing humanity. Education for sustainability is described as "overtly transformative" (Huckle & Sterling, 1999, p.1) whereby student learning moves from a focus on "doing things better [to] doing better things [to] seeing things differently" (Sterling, 2004, p. 56). Participatory video/digital storytelling has been used extensively as a pedagogical tool for empowerment and emancipation (George et al., 2021; Lunch & Lunch, 2006). In general, PV (Participatory Video) is an activity that is used with disadvantaged or vulnerable groups for empowerment, visibility and raising critical awareness.

ESD themes could provide a worthwhile context for ICTs and digital tools in teaching, learning and curriculum development across all educational levels and types (Makrakis & Kostoulas-Makrakis, 2017). For example, social, economic, and environmental issues can provide meaningful and challenging contexts for developing a wide range of ICT/Digital skills.

- ESD methods are conducive to constructivist and transformative learning theories, which can provide a context and rationale for using ICT-based learning tools such as concept mapping, modeling, and social networking.
- When considering areas such as cultural diversity and intercultural understanding, health, governance, natural resources, climate change, rural development, sustainable urbanisation, poverty reduction, corporate responsibility and accountability, there is potential to assess the impact of ICTs in these key sustainable development areas.

The telling of stories provides the context within which they convey meaning while the beneficiaries of digital storytelling can simultaneously acquire and cultivate digital skills. Digital storytelling is considered a strategy for meaningful learning that can becontrasted to surface learning as following (cf. Makrakis & Kostoulas-Makrakis, 2020; Makrakis, 2018):

- **Reflective:** Learning that involves students in a process to a self-critical assessment of their learning experiences, identifying areas that require improvement and proceeding in constructing new knowledge that makes a difference.
- **Active:** Learning that involves students in a process that requires them to play an active role to construct knowledge and understanding.
- **Experiential:** Learning that involves students in a process whereby they reflect on, learn from, develop new knowledge, and take new action based on experience.
- **Constructive:** Learning that involves students in a process of experiencing things and reflecting on those experiences to constructing understanding, knowledge and meaning of the world.
- **Transformative:** Learning that involves students in a critical self-reflecting process of deconstructing, constructing, and reconstructing themselves and social realities.
- **Collaborative:** Learning that involves students constructing meaning and knowledge collectively and collaboratively.

- **Dialogical:** Learning that involves two or more students in a process of structured, purposeful egalitarian dialogue with a shared goal of raising their critical consciousness about an issue that concerns them.
- **Political:** Learning that involves students in a process of reflecting and acting on themselves and the world in order to transform it.
- **Ethical:** Learning that involves students in a process of reflection and action toward the common good driven by moral principles and values.
- **Authentic:** Learning that involves students in a process that allows them to explore, discuss, and meaningfully construct concepts and relationships in contexts that involve real-life problems.
- **Problem-Posing:** Learning that involves students in a process of identifying, coding and decoding real-life issues through critical discursive reflection and acting to change realities.
- **Subversive:** Learning that involves students in a process of raising critical questions about teaching, learning and curriculum and their role and underlying assumptions about these processes.

Figure 1. The meaningful learning constituencies

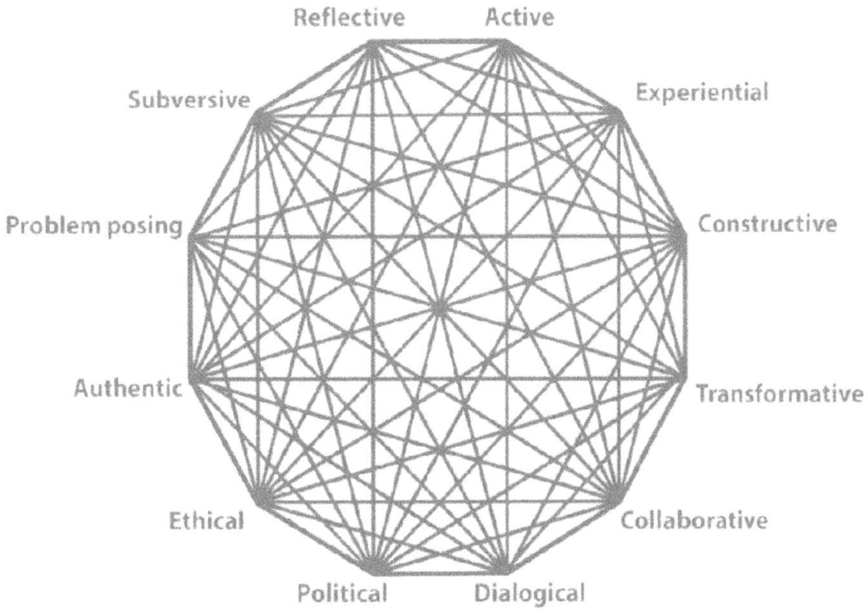

Digital storytelling infused with sustainability issues can be also considered a new teaching, learning and curriculum approach that promotes learners' experiential, constructivist and transformative knowledge construction. The ExConTra (Experiential-Constructivist-Transformative) learning paradigm provides a context for digital learning design (Makrakis & Kostoulas-Makrakis, 2012b). In this approach, the pre-specified sustainability content is viewed not as an end in itself, but as a process, praxis and context to promote sustainability justice, a concept advanced by Makrakis (2017a). The concept of "sustainability justice" reflects the four pillars of sustainable development, namely: environment, society, economy and culture. Environmental justice implies that all people on the planet have the right to enjoy an equitable, clean, safe, fairly treated and healthy environment as well as the right to social, economic and cultural well-being. The social justice component addresses inequalities and injustices of all kinds, from poverty to racism, and violation of human rights. The economic justice addresses issues, such as unfair trade, economic exploitation, the unequal distribution of wealth, racism and poverty. In an integrative way, cultural justice encompasses all the other three components of sustainability justice in the same way as it does the three sustainable development pillars (Makrakis, 2017b). Sustainability justice enabled by digital storytelling and participatory video is viewed as a process and praxis. As a process, the focus is on interactions, interpretation and meaning-making, while as a praxis it goes a step further by making more explicit the interests it serves and a commitment to emancipation through the dynamic interaction of action and reflection. Unlocking the potentiality and actuality of digital storytelling for sustainability justice is not a matter of technology per se, but it has to do more with the way we perceive technology, teaching, learning, curriculum and human agency (Makrakis, 2017b).

According to theories of agency and empowerment, the concept of agency can be defined as one's ability to see and to make strategic life choices based on his/her vision of what is possible and in pursuit of what she/he desires (Mochizuki & Fadeeva, 2010). But the agency is not a power that one possesses; it is not an individual capacity. Rather, it is something that one achieves through action competence, critical consciousness and reflection (Makrakis, 2017a, 2017b). In addition, agency is at once endogenous and exogenous, engendered from within and without; it is both individual and relational. In other words, it depends on the quality or meaningfulness of relationships with peers, facilitators, mentors, parents, and other significant individuals (Waltner et al., 2019).

The interaction between digital technology and education for sustainability creates new opportunities to address sustainability, as well as new challenges. Digital technologies and ICTs can function both as empowering and disempowering forces. Video activism has also been given attention in recent times (Miranda et al., 2016; Wilson & Serisier, 2010). However, it has to be noted that technologies and digital media can function as emancipatory affordances in one setting and manipulative in another. Thus, we should be conscious on the multiple uses of technology and the driving forces and interests behind them.

In the context of an evolving paradigm in pedagogy enabled by ICTs and digital storytelling, teachers have to see themselves functioning as facilitators and mentors, as resources and as curriculum developers (Makrakis, 2006) as well as transformative intellectuals (Giroux & McLaren, 1996). Each of these roles is connected with specific tasks. Teachers as "facilitators and mentors" will guide and facilitate learners' creativity and critical thinking in a collaborative learning environment enabled by new technology. This can be extended to all the 10Cs (critical transversal skills) as they have been explored by Makrakis (2017b). Teachers as "resources" will have to develop learners' capacities for active local/global citizenship and to contribute to their fellow teachers' professional development enabled by new technology. As "curriculum developers", teachers are critically engaged to deconstruct, construct and reconstruct school knowledge and enrich the curriculum. Teachers as "transformative intellectuals" are involved in developing a discourse that unites the language of critique with the language of possibility (Giroux, 1988). Teachers functioning as "transformative intellectuals" are giving students an active voice, making the political more pedagogical and the latter more political (Giroux, n.d.). In other words, teachers have the potential to functioning as change agents of reorienting what they teach and how they teach for promoting a key goal for 21st Century education that is, learning to transform oneself and society.

The ICTeEfS Project

The ICTeEfS project focuses on contextualizing ICT to EfS and vice versa through a capacity-building program funded by the European Commission Erasmus+ for the period 2019-2023 targeting teacher educators, ICT coordinators, other school leaders and subject teachers in Indonesia, Malaysia and Vietnam. The project is led by Frederick University (Cyprus), in collaboration with the University of Crete (Greece), RCE Crete (Greece), Universiti Teknologi Malaysia (UTM), Universiti Sains Malaysia, Open University Malaysia, Universitas Pendidikan (Education) Indonesia (UPI), University Gadjah Mada Indonesia (UGM), Ho Chi Minh City International University (IU) and University of Social Sciences and Humanities (USSH) in Vietnam.

Malaysia, Indonesia and Vietnam are among the Asian countries, whose teaching force demand training to address the sustainability challenges faced locally and regionally. On the one hand, faculties of education need to reorganise their curricula in line with the new pedagogical trends aiming to embed sustainability and especially SDGs in teaching, learning and curriculum. Education for Sustainability enabled by ICTs opens new opportunities for quality education. Our needs analysis showed that training programs in the partner countries often focus on teacher-centred approaches that make it difficult to take advantage of the potential of ICT to bring about changes in the teaching and learning process and the curriculum. The objectives of the ICTeEfS program were first to support the development of the faculties of education in the three partner countries to align curriculum, teaching, learning and research with the area of education for sustainability. It was also to build the capacity of academic staff to turn them able to contribute towards the implementation of the UN Agenda on SDGs. Developing a Euro-Asian Network of ICT-enabled Education for Sustainability was also conceived as a driver to strengthen cooperation in the field of ICTeEfS, nationally, regionally and globally. The in-service training aimed to engender an environment in which teachers and learners, finding their own voice, can transform ideas focusing on SDGs and projects into concrete action, showing motivation and engagement for building a more sustainable and just society. The program has been conducted in a series of hybrid workshops combining face-to-face and online modes of delivery training, especially during the COVID-19 pandemic. As part of the in-service teacher training program, participants were asked to develop participatory community-based digital storytelling videos infused with SDGs. Teacher capacity building has proved to be a critical driver for embedding sustainability in course curricula (Biasutti et al., 2018; Barth & Rieckmann, 2016; Makrakis, 2014a, 2014b).

Steps in Implementing the PV/Digital Storytelling Intervention

The steps are structured on the four interlinked stages, named the PV4Ps: 1) pre-planning, 2) planning, 3) production, and 4) publication.

Pre-Planning

Step 1: Starting With an Idea While Being Trained: The first point is to start with an idea referring to a sustainability issue as part of the capacity-building programme. Humanity is made and driven through ideas. People's ability to have ideas, and process them by coming up with meaningful solutions or actions, is what makes humanity distinct from the rest of other species. Ideas in the context of education for sustainability enabled by ICTs give us the impetus to make the world more sustainable and just for everyone. They give us the power and the means to overcome the obstacles and enable the drivers and the reason to take action against sustainability injustices.

The question is where do I find an idea to start developing a digital storytelling or a participatory video? Our experience through the ICTeEfS project shows that as a starting point, one can search for a local issue that has drawn attention to the community and connect it with SDGs. Usually, sustainability issues, as real-life issues, capture our attention and imagination or unlock a powerful emotional reaction to sustainability justice. In the context of the ICTeEfS capacity-building intervention, about,3,000 in-service teachers with sufficient knowledge on ICTs have been trained to infuse sustainability issues elicited from SDGs across all school subjects. The teachers trained provided in-house training for more than,6,000 teachers. Participatory video and digital storytelling were used as an instructional, learning and curriculum approach. Hundreds of such applications were developed by trainees, which besides training purposes, are used as useful resource in enriching school curricula.

Step 2: Searching and Looking Into Good Examples: During the in-service training, teachers were encouraged to search PV/Digital storytelling clips from the Web, preferably dealing with education for sustainability issues and go into a thorough analysis of the inherent goals, objectives and messages conveyed. Teacher trainers were also asked to develop an example to be used as a model for trainees.

Step 3: Looking for Participants: The issues or problems reflecting the initial ideas revealed who will be the actors of the application to be developed. The task of each teacher trainee was to look for participants facing the problems/issues chosen, in order to involve them in the Digital storytelling/PV process. Intergenerational learning was encouraged, bringing together younger and older generations for a common purpose.

Step 4: Building Participatory Communication: In forming the Digital storytelling/PV group, particular emphasis was placed: 1) on creating friendly, trustful and egalitarian relationships among the people to be involved in the project and 2) on the need to sensitise the community members to experience their own realities and the potential for transforming these realities. Throughout the capacity-building intervention, trainees were engendered in creating a dynamic, interactional, and transformative process of dialogue about the significance of the Digital storytelling/PV application to be developed and providing trainees with the knowledge to actively participate in the completion of the application.

Planning

The planning stage is perhaps the most critical step to producing a successful and meaningful Digital storytelling/PV, using the following steps.

Step 5: Setting Goals, Objectives, and Strategies: Before setting goals, objectives and strategies, trainees were encouraged to reflect on meanings behind these terms. Through this exercise, trainees recall their own conceptualisation on the meanings and through dialoguing they started setting goals, objectives, and strategies conducive to the Digital storytelling/PV application to be developed. Two techniques are worth pointing out: 1) the S.M.A.R.T. strategy that stands for Specific, Measurable, Achievable (or "Actionable"), Realistic and Time-Bound objectives and 2) the use of SWOT Analysis to explore the Strengths, Weaknesses, Opportunities and Threats as you build a roadmap from where you are today to where you want to be tomorrow. As you develop your strategy and set your goals, make strategic choices about what to do and not to do.

Step 6: Deepening Inquiry: Through the capacity building intervention, teacher trainees were encouraged to discuss that they may have many ideas but realising them, that is putting them to real life makes all the difference. The investigative process that started in the pre-planning stage continued to ensure that the ideas behind the video to be produced are based not only on sound and credible information and resources but also on the fact that the group members have deepened their capacity to carry out the task effectively.

Step 7: Scheduling: There was a need to establish realistic timelines for the entire project in order to keep track. This proved very critical in monitoring and assessing the progress of the project.

Step 8: Writing/Revising Script: Digital storytelling/PV teams were encouraged to complete scripting that will be taken into consideration in the development of the storyboard. The script was not perceived as a fixed product, but as a process, leaving space for revisions. Trainees were guided to find out film/video scripts online and get ideas about the structure, format, action, dialogues, and characters developed in the script. A "What if?" strategy seems very effective in writing/revising a script. Through this strategy, we can make important decisions about the text, the dialogues, the characters, and their interactions in the plot of the story. In addition to that, two important tools can be used in writing and organising the script of the story: a) the treatment, that is the plotting and b) the step-outline, that is the sequence or the roadmap of the events taking place in the plot. More specifically, the step-outline helps to define the content, function, and placement of each individual scene of the video, while the treatment is a narrative summation of the story, written in the present tense. The visualisation and dramatization of the scenes are important in the script-writing process. In other words, a Step-Outline is a scene-by-scene template of what happens in the screenplay.

Step 9: Storyboarding: Storyboards can visually and graphically depict and describe the action that will take place in each scene of the Digital storytelling/PV project through the use of a template. Teacher trainees were asked to develop their storyboards and discuss them with those involved, including teacher trainers. Structuring the beginning, the middle, and the end of the story through the storyboarding technique is the most important part of the process. In a way, the beginning reflects the exposition of the characters, introducing the issue of the story and its context, the middle reflects the confrontation that leads toward a solution by overcoming the barriers, and the end reflects the resolution. As in the previous step (writing the script), the strategy of "What if?" allows the team to explore all the possible dramatic situations that can develop from the original idea. Through this process, the narrative of the digital storytelling/PV starts progressing in the desired direction.

During the project planning phase, teacher trainers discussed how the trainees would organise their storyboards and the footage. It was important in the project design phase to stress that PV/Digital storytelling was designed in an ethical and respectful way. The training instructions clearly presented this issue and in particular, issues concerned with data privacy and copyright. This process also allowed the trainees an opportunity to voice concerns about these issues in their own culture.

Production

Step 10: Editing: The editing process was one of the most demanding tasks that required special care and skills. Teacher trainees were trained to make appropriate decisions in the division of tasks according to the skills acquired and the resources available. Once the footage in each project had been captured, it needed to be put together in a meaningful way based on the script and storyboard. In the editing process issues related to privacy and ethics were also raised and discussed.

Step 11: Titles, Text, Credits: Although this may be part of the editing step, this can also be done as a separate step. Particular emphasis was placed on the intellectual rights of the resources used, copyrights and the credits to be used. The titles of the projects were also refined to reflect the messages conveyed and examine the need for narrations.

Step 12: Logging and Capturing Footage: Once the footage had been shot, it was viewed and then captured into the computer using the appropriate software tools. Discussions were held during the teacher training sessions so they cooperatively determined which footage should be used in the final product.

Step 13: Formative Assessment: Across all the stages and included steps, there was a need to provide the teacher trainees an opportunity to give feedback on the video planning and production process. As the video process moved towards its end, it was important that sufficient time was available to react to the feedback from the discussions. The final video was compared with the goals/objectives of the project the Digital storytelling/PV group decided on in the earlier steps of the process and reflected those as closely as possible.

Publication

Step 14: Print to CD/DVD/Export for Web: Once the project is complete and validated, it was exported as a movie for use on the web (YouTube) and/or CD. Not all PV-clips were uploaded to the Web due to privacy issues raised by group members.

Step 15: Dissemination: A common goal in a Digital storytelling/PV project is to use the final product as an advocacy tool. Thus, dissemination of a video to the public and decision-makers is very critical according to the rules and ethics.

DISCUSSION AND CONCLUSION

This paper examined the role of Digital storytelling/PV as a tool and a product, process and praxis in advancing education for sustainability. It is important to point out that within the digital storytelling/PV concept the process of production rather than the end product is central to its function for advocacy, empowerment and emancipation. Such a medium enables people to produce and distribute content that is authentic and meaningful. It has been found that digital storytelling can provide a quality teaching and learning tool underpinned by modern constructive–collaborative learning theories, in both formal and non-formal forms of education (Karantalis & Koukopoulos, 2022). Such applications provide opportunities for participants to not only engage with real-life issues but also to participate in collaborative inquiry and discourse with other people. Digital storytelling/PV could help in challenging established values, norms and practices as well as empower people to act for building a more sustainable and just society.

Teachers trained, produced digital storytelling/PV applications that can be categorized as "authentic" learning activities because they take place in the "real world". It was widely assumed that teachers involved in this process were feeling ownership and control of their own learning and experienced a sense of contribution to society and the environment. This has been revealed by individual and group testimonials collected during the training process and post-training. In a testimonial, it was stated that "Competencies such as critical thinking, envisioning future scenarios and making collaborative decisions.... empowered us to change practices and think differently. Involving various people, especially of different generations in developing such digital artifacts promotes intergenerational learning" (e.g., Kaplan & Larking, 2021) and active citizenship. Indeed, giving younger and older citizens the opportunity to reflect on community-based issues, relevant to SDGs, and the reasons behind their engagement makes it possible to boost the debate on the critical importance of SDGs on citizens' daily lives and initiating an intergenerational dialogue for climate action.

This capacity-building programme was perceived as a process that leads to transformative praxis as it involves participants in the process of defining what to do, why to do and how to do digital artifacts that can empower them to transform their personal and social realities. Preliminary results of an assessment revealed that this training intervention helps to question the reproduction of the dominant ideology and existing power relations, as it strengthens advocacy skills and promotes alternatives to norms and practices that reproduce sustainability injustices.

The challenge of turning teachers becoming transformative intellectuals, as Giroux (1988) pointed out, resides in their emancipation from viewing their profession as technicians and transmitters of prescribed knowledge, carrying out dictates and objectives decided by experts far removed from the realities they face in their classrooms.

Contextualising digital storytelling/PV with education for Sustainability seems to promote a participatory culture by combining beneficiaries' imagination skills, editing skills, problem-solving skills, creativity and ideas they want to tell or share, enabled by ICT tools and digital media. Such interventions will make possible not only to develop collaborative and communication skills but also to disseminate the digital product widely through various communication tools and platforms. Communication empowers people, allows for dialogue and expression and provides outward reflection while increasing awareness of social and structural problems (Kuşay, 2019). More importantly, addressing sustainability issues of local, regional and global concern, turns dissemination into an effective means for building a more sustainable and just society.

By establishing a Euro-Asian network of teachers in the field of ICT-enabled Education for Sustainability we envision being a leading network to:

- Serve as a multi-stakeholder platform between its members and partner organisations.
- Share knowledge, experiences, resources and good practices for building teachers' capacity in the field of ICTeEfS.
- Foster and promote an ongoing dialogue on issues related to ICTeEfS.
- Support the professional development of teachers and teacher educators to align curriculum, teaching, learning and research in the area of ICT-enabled Education for Sustainability.
- Support teachers in designing, developing, and disseminating innovative teaching and learning activities dealing with the infusion of SDGs in course curricula.
- Help teachers develop appropriate and effective instructional materials that infuse sustainability issues and SDGs across all education levels.
- Organise webinars and annual conferences to disseminate innovative teaching and learning practices in the field of ICT-enabled Education for Sustainability.

A major challenge of the 21st century for institutions of higher education is to train teachers to function as change agents. This challenge implies major shifts in the ways teachers are approaching curriculum, learning, and teaching, but also in viewing their own role in society in light of their responsibility for creating a sustainable future and lifestyle.

The project was implemented during the Covid-19 pandemic that has turned our partners to make significant changes not only in the delivery of training but also in keeping the target group on board. Due to the financing of ICT labs and videoconferencing equipment along with the internal response to such technologies due to Covid-19, it was possible to keep work activities running. Distributed leadership was also a critical strategy for ensuring the motivation of both local project team leaders and also to the trainers involved. There was also a need to develop a shared understanding and acceptance of managerial principles among all partner countries' institutional coordinators and teacher trainers. Visibility was another challenge we faced that was effectively tackled by defining clear and measurable objectives, encouraging regular project status updates, warning of possible risks, organising community events, involving local educational leadership, and scheduling frequent communication. To encourage and motivate teachers, we have organised special days for awarding certifications and special prizes to good practices.

This participatory process has led both teacher trainers and trainees to experience new ways of teaching, learning and curriculum development. They have also uncovered their own potentialities and actualities as well as important insights into the reality of work with digital tools and platforms as well as in a period of the COVID-19 pandemic. Among other things, they learned to set clear expectations during the process of developing a digital application and to be realistic.

The modern era is characterized by the explosion of digital ICTs and their multiple applications in formal, non-formal and informal education. Digital storytelling is one of the most enabling learning technologies in promoting education for sustainable development. Digital storytelling and Participatory Video (PV) closely linked should empower, educate and activate people toward building a more sustainable and just society. It is envisioned that the use of digital storytelling will contribute to developing environmental and sustainability-justice awareness while at the same time enhancing the digital literacy of those involved.

ACKNOWLEDGMENT

This work has been developed in the context of an Erasmus+ CBHE-funded project entitled ICT-enabled Education for Sustainability (Ref. No. 598244-EPP-1-2018-1-CY-EPPKA2-CBHE-JP (2018-3907-001-001). The content in this Chapter expresses the views of the authors and does not necessarily reflect the views of the European Commission. The European Commission is not liable for any use that may be made of the information contained herein.

REFERENCES

Barth, M., & Rieckmann, M. (2016). State of the art in research on higher education for sustainable development. In M. Barth, G. Michelsen, M. Rieckmann, & I. Thomas (Eds.), *Routledge Handbook of Higher Education for Sustainable Development* (pp. 100–113). Routledge.

Biasutti, M., Makrakis, V., Concina, E., & Frate, S. (2018). Educating academic staff to reorient curricula in ESD. *International Journal of Sustainability in Higher Education*, *19*(1), 179-196. doi:10.1108/IJSHE-11-2016-0214

George, J., George, T., & Moquin, R. (2021). I can't breathe: How digital video becomes an emancipatory technology. *Proceedings of the 54th Hawaii International Conference on System Sciences*. https://scholarspace.manoa.hawaii.edu/server/api/core/bitstreams/515c6a80-29f7-4731-94a3-f856f55b39ea/content

Giroux, H. (1988). *Teachers as intellectuals*. Bergin & Garvey.

Giroux, H. (n.d.). Teachers as transformative intellectuals. Symposium on understanding quality education. *Conference on Re-envisioning Quality Education*. http://www.afed.itacec.org/document/henry_giroux_2_ok.pdf

Giroux, H. A., & Mclaren, P. (1996). Teacher education and the politics of engagement: The case for democratic schooling. In P. Leistyna, A. Woodrum, & S. A. Sherblom (Eds.), *Breaking free: The transformative power of critical pedagogy* (pp. 301–331). Harvard Educational Review.

Huckle, J., & Sterling, S. (1999). *Education for sustainability: An invitation to join a debate*. https://john.huckle.org.uk/download/2106/Education%20for%20Sustainability,%20an%20invitation%20to%20join%20a%20debate.do
c

Kaplan, M., & Larkin, E. (2021). Building community: Intergenerational projects with young children. In M. Renck Jalongo & P. A. Crawford (Eds.), *Intergenerational Bonds. Educating the Young Child, 18*. Springer., doi:10.1007/978-3-030-81965-1_12

Karantalis, N., Koukopoulos, D. (2022). Utilizing digital storytelling as a tool for teaching literature through constructivist learning theory. *SN Soc Sci, 2*, 109. doi:10.1007/s43545-022-00412-w

Ketelle, D. (2017). Introduction to the special issue: What is storytelling in the higher education classroom? *Storytelling, Self, Society*, *13*(2), 143–150. doi:10.13110torselfsoci.13.2.0143

Kuşay, Y. (2019). Digital storytelling as a part of participatory culture in communication and public relation practices. In R. Yilmaz, N. Erdem, & F. Resuloglu (Eds.), *Handbook of Research on Transmedia Storytelling and Narrative Strategies* (pp. 271–291). IGI Global. doi:10.4018/978-1-5225-5357-1.ch014

Lunch, N., & Lunch, C. (2006). *Insights into participatory video: A handbook for the field*. Insight.

Makrakis, V. (2006). *Preparing United Arab Emirates teachers for building a sustainable society, E-Media Publications*. University of Crete.

Makrakis, V. (2014a). ICTs as transformative enabling tools in education. In R. Huang, Kinshuk, & J. Price (Eds.), ICT in Education in Global Context (pp. 101-119). Springer Verlag.

Makrakis, V. (2014b). Transforming university curricula towards sustainability: A Euro-Mediterranean initiative. In K. Tomas & H. Muga (Eds.), *Handbook of research on pedagogical innovations for sustainable development* (pp. 619–640). IGI Global. doi:10.4018/978-1-4666-5856-1.ch032

Makrakis, V. (2017a). Developing and validating a sustainability justice instrument to transform curriculum, Learning and Teaching. *9th International Conference in Open & Distance Learning – November 2017, Athens, Greece–Proceedings*. https://eproceedings.epublishing.ekt.gr/index.php/openedu/article/viewFile/1368/1303

Makrakis, V. (2017b). Unlocking the potentiality and actuality of ICTs in developing sustainable–justice curricula and society. *Knowledge Cultures*, *5*(2), 103–122. doi:10.22381/KC5220177

Makrakis, V. (2018). *From STEM to STEAM and to STREAM enabled through meaningful critical reflective learning*. Paper presented at the 2nd International Conference on Innovating STEM Education. 24-28 June 2018, Deutsch School Athens.

Makrakis, V., & Kostoulas-Makrakis, N. (2012a). Course curricular design and development of the M.Sc. programme in the field of ICT in education for sustainable development. *Journal of Teacher Education for Sustainability*, *14*(2), 5–40. doi:10.2478/v10099-012-0007-7

Makrakis, V., & Kostoulas-Makrakis, N. (2012b). The challenges of ICTs to online climate change education for sustainable development: The ExConTra learning paradigm. In S. A. Anwar (Ed), *Proceedings of the 5th Conference on eLearning Excellence in the Middle East - Sustainable Innovation in Education* (pp. 594–605). Hamdan Bin Mohammed e-University.

Makrakis, V., & Kostoulas-Makrakis, N. (2017). Paradigm shift in higher education teaching and learning: Practices towards education for sustainability. In G. Mickelsen & P. J. Wells (Eds.), *A Decade of Progress on Education for Sustainable Development Reflections from the UNESCO Chairs Programme* (pp. 94–102). UNESCO.

Makrakis, V., & Kostoulas-Makrakis, N. (2020). The quest for meaningful learning. In *Humanistic Futures of Learning. Perspectives from UNESCO Chairs and UNITWIN networks* (pp. 143–147). UNESCO.

Miranda, S. M., Young, A., & Yetgin, E. (2016). Are social media emancipatory or hegemonic? Societal effects of mass media digitization. *Management Information Systems Quarterly*, *40*(2), 303–329. doi:10.25300/MISQ/2016/40.2.02

Mochizuki, Y., & Fadeeva, Z. (2010). Competences for sustainable development and sustainability: Significance and challenges for ESD. *Int. J. Sustain. High. Educ.*, *1*, 391–403. doi:10.118640723-021-00081-x

Rahiem, M.D.H. (2021). Storytelling in early childhood education: Time to go digital. *ICEP*, *15*, 4. doi:10.118640723-021-00081-x

Skouge, J., & Ra, K. (2009). Digital storytelling in teacher education: Creating transformations through narrative. *Educational Perspectives*, *42*(1&2), 54–60.

Sterling, S. (2004). Higher education, sustainability and the role of systemic thinking. In P. B. Corcoran & A. E. J. Wals (Eds.), *Higher education and the challenge of sustainability: problematics, promise, and practice* (pp. 49–70). Kluwer Academic Publishers. doi:10.1007/0-306-48515-X_5

Waltner, E.-M., Rieß, W., & Mischo, C. (2019). Development and validation of an instrument for measuring student sustainability competencies. *Sustainability*, *11*(6), 1717. doi:10.3390u11061717

Wilson, D. J., & Serisier, T. (2010). Video activism and the ambiguities of counter-surveillance. *Surveillance & Society*, *8*(2), 166–180. doi:10.24908s.v8i2.3484

Chapter 10
Linking Culture, Pedagogy, and Digitalization for Education and Sustainable Development in Tribal Areas:
A Perspective From Pakistan

Khalida Nasreen
Government of Pakistan, Pakistan

Muhammad Tanveer Afzal
Allama Iqbal Open University, Pakistan

ABSTRACT

This chapter discusses the role of education and sustainable development in Pakistan, especially in tribal areas. Forty-six teachers and 28 parents from 15 primary schools were interviewed for this study, and data has also been collected via observational technique. A mixed methods approach employs both qualitative and quantitate techniques. To achieve quality education at any level, especially at primary level, teachers and students should aim at creating the link between culture, pedagogy, and digitalization. Teachers should be competent in the implementation of technology, that is, the use of computers, and have multimedia skills in order to find and adopt pedagogies relevant to class environments. This chapter looks at the current situation Pakistan, and especially in the tribal areas of Pakistan, and suggests recommendations for the incorporation of ESD goals in the single national curriculum, the development of teacher education programs, incentives for teachers and (female) students, and the facilitation of electricity, computer technology, and internet access for all schools.

DOI: 10.4018/978-1-7998-5033-5.ch010

INTRODUCTION

Education plays a great role in the development of individuals, societies, and countries. Sustainable development is necessary to meet human needs and improve quality of life, but at the same time it should also beneficial for present and future generations. In this regard the sustainable development goals (SDGs) developed by the UN are important landmarks in order to achieve peace and sustainable prosperity on our planet (UNESCO, 2017). The 17 SDGs are interlinked, and the improvement (or deterioration) in one area will affect all other areas of development. Quality Education is itself a central sustainability goal (SDG4), and it is also necessary in order to achieve all other goals (UNESCO, 2017). In this context, the role of technology and digitalization must not be underestimated.

The same is true for the actual quality of education, which is mainly influenced by the quality of teaching and the teachers' understanding of what learning actually means. Quality teaching makes an important difference to students' learning, their achievements, and their life chances (Smith, 2003). Thus, teacher quality matters a lot, in fact, it is reported to be the most important school-related factor influencing student achievement (Rice, 2003). Students and teachers play a vital role in creating an academic, social, cultural, intellectual, spiritual, and, most importantly, a supportive environment adapted to students' interests, motivations, needs, and abilities. However, the question remains what exactly should teachers do to create such a positive environment? How should lessons be constructed and what methods of instruction should be used to deliver the content/curriculum in the classrooms? Which communication technologies should teachers use to interact with their students?

Here, technology related pedagogy is among the players entering the stage. In this current moment of history, the scope of new technologies, knowledge, and learning is emphasized by digital learning environments. Digital learning is defined as technology-related methods used to support learning (Wheeler, 2012), and to provide learners with more control over pace, time, place etc. Overall, this type of pedagogy demands a highly digitally competent teacher.

Discourses on teaching, learning, and pedagogy, however, are shaped not only by the decisions made by teachers, but also by school values and organization, by local pressures, national policies, and the balance of political control, as well as by the tensions and ambiguities of the democratic ideal, and by culture and history in general (Alexander, 2001). Classrooms themselves are also considered to be of a complex nature. So, a classroom is not only a static picture of a room filled with 20 or 30 students, chairs, desks, books etc. On the contrary, classrooms are always in motion, and the atmosphere is influenced by immediacy, publicness, multidimensionality, unpredictability, history, and also by simultaneity (Doyle, 1980). In a classroom, students do not share the same lifestyles, IQ-/EQ-levels, color, even languages, customs, and family backgrounds.

At the same time, we might consider teachers to be the central change agents in implementing education for sustainable development in the classroom (J. K and O' Neil, 2019). Good teachers recognize both individual and cultural differences and translate them into a positive digital learning environment. Now if we look at teacher education programs in Pakistan, they all seem to be made for an average homogenous culture – a 'one size fits all'. What is sorely missing, however, is what teachers should do in classrooms with students of different cultures i.e., which type of pedagogy will be useful for urban, rural, and also the tribal areas of Pakistan. If there is a cultural gap between a student's everyday world and the world of the school, it can result in an inauthentic and ineffective teaching and learning process, be it digital or not.

As to digitalization, however, one more important point is that the technological and digital competence of teachers is frequently also ignored or at least not taken as seriously as it should in these educational programs. It is the need of the hour that such types of competencies and pedagogical techniques be developed so that teachers are empowered to work in a digital world whilst also considering the context of different cultural backgrounds of learners. The connection between culture, history, and technology-related pedagogies should be a central consideration here. Digitally competent teachers are more than that though: they are individuals who are data and communication literate, who understand and can deal with complex interconnections between safety, problem solving, and productivity. They aim at empowering learners, guiding their students, being the source and transmitter of relevant information, and facilitating learning. They need such personal characteristics as being open to change and development, versatile in using technology effectively, creatively and innovatively (Aycca & Reisoglu, 2022). In this way digital quality education will indeed contribute to achieving all SDGs, and not just be yet another add-on in the classroom.

The Multifaceted Situation in Urban, Rural, and Tribal Areas of Pakistan in This Time and Age

Pakistan is a culturally diverse country, and it has many unequal, dissimilar, and just very different urban, rural, and tribal areas. The culture(s) of tribal areas in particular is (are) quite distinct from other areas of Pakistan.

Worldwide, tribal areas are those areas which are considered backward from the point of view of other areas. They often reflect a lack of basic necessities of life and education, especially when it comes to female education. Often the living conditions of tribal people are reported to be worse than those in urban areas, and their participation in the economic, social, and political development is frequently very little. Due to the language differences and also the lack of education, especially female education, they cannot compete with the other citizens of their own country and/or the world. India has the largest tribal population in the world after Africa. Their peoples are often deprived of basic human rights and violated in every step of life. They frequently live in remote areas (hills and forests) and are devoid of basic facilities of life, i.e., roads, means of communication, health, education, or even clean drinking water (Purhottan & Dhingra, 2017).

The same situation is true for the tribal areas of Pakistan. They are divided in to provincially administered and federally administered tribal areas (the latter are also called FATA). Yet, all of these have a difficult geographical situation and/or topography, i.e., they lie in mountainous/ hilly areas, often connected with only unpaved and winding roads. There is a considerable lack of the basic facilities, e.g., of good food, clean water, medicines and doctors, transport, electricity etc. There is no reliable data, but the population of tribal areas in Pakistan is estimated to comprise more than 10 million people. As opposed to urban and many rural areas, people in tribal areas frequently do not have computers/ laptops, and even cell phones are still rare and often available only to men, especially in the tribal areas of Dera Ghazi Khan These areas have different cultures and legal systems. Tribal areas remain among the poorest regions of Pakistan. People in these areas have to travel long distances to achieve basic health care. Tribal areas are among the most underdeveloped regions of Pakistan. Its people are poorly educated and inadequately skilled, and also deprived of the fundamental necessities of life. The majority of people live below the poverty line. The unemployment rate is between 60 and 80 percent. Net primary school enrollment for children in FATA is 52.1 percent as compared to 65 percent in mainstream Pakistan (all numbers from Ali, 2018).

A look at the situation of women paints an even darker picture: Before and directly after the 9/11 attacks in the USA, Pakistan was providing routes to Afghanistan, and tribal areas were infamous for sheltering Al Qaeda leaders. With the emergence of militant terrorist groups, the economic, cultural, and social conditions in tribal areas became badly affected, which is particularly true for the lives of women. Availability of basic resources like health and education were further reduced, and women were not permitted to see a doctor, attend school or social gatherings. In tribal areas, more than half of the girls from the first to the twelfth grade have never been to school, and only one in ten girls can read (Naveed, 2018).

Moreover, military operations from both the joint United States and Pakistani forces until 2014 affected 3 million people of FATA. As a result, schools were destroyed, poverty reached extreme levels, and thousands of girls either dropped out or never attended school (Naveed, 2018). The Shaoor Foundation issued a report in 2014 stating that 14.7% girls have never been enrolled in any school. In 2017, the FATA annual education census reported that only 37% girls were enrolled at primary level and 5% at secondary level compared to 49% and 17% of boys. Alif Ailaan (2016) reported that the dropout rate of girls was at 77% (Wadood Afridi, 2020), Dawn (2018) reported that 97% of girls were leaving primary schools in the tribal districts. The primary level net enrolment rate for both sexes is 52.1% in FATA compared to 65% in Pakistan (FATA Development Indicators HouseHold Survey, 2013-14).

The tribal areas are also facing many problems with regards to educational institutions. Lack of teachers, zero enrolment, vacant teacher posts, local disputes, and military operations are some of the causes for the institutions becoming non- functional. Statistics show at least 307 schools in tribal districts have remained non-functional for more than a decade. The vast majority of the girls schools are non-functional, and their buildings have been destroyed (Mehsud, 2018).

Thus, today there is also a huge gender gap in the literacy rate in FATA. The literacy rate of men is currently at 45 percent. For women it is a meagre 7.8 percent, which is far below the national average (Afridi, 2020). Women from Pakistan tribal areas face a life lacking in basic education and health care, are bound by socio cultural taboos, and are thus denied basic human rights. The overall literacy rate here is 39.9%, with the literacy rate for boys at nearly 34.2 percent and just 5.75 for girls (ANI, 2022).

Women are continuously disadvantaged by a lack of education as well as by cultural and legal systems (Ali, 2018). Values are an important element of every culture, and they also decide what is good or bad in the society (Steven, 2010). As opposed to the urban areas of Pakistan, women in the rural and especially in the tribal areas are not allowed to have a job, leave their own home without permission, and do not even have the right to choose their own husband. If these rules are broken, it is considered to be an act of dishonor, and especially in the tribal areas of Pakistan, women/ girls have been murdered for such "disrespectful" behavior. Women have been the prime victims of patriarchal tribal traditions. For example, in tribal areas women are (ab)used as a tool for the settlement of disputes between two families or tribes. Pre-pubescent girls are even married to older men for this. "Honor killing" is yet another inhumane crime against women (Ali, 2018). Another consequence of poor literacy levels in tribal areas is that most of the teachers who work in these areas come from distant, often urban areas of Pakistan, and thus have a very different culture and lifestyle than those of their students, which is expressed in different customs, social values, beliefs, manners and behaviors. In many cases, they even speak a different language. Teachers are confronted with many major cultural differences in their day to day lives in the classroom, which obviously affects the culture within these classrooms as well.

More than that, within tribal areas digitalization faces many multifaceted problems beyond the average situation in Pakistan, especially a lack or shortage of electricity, coverage of mobile phone services, internet access, and the actual hardware (computers, laptops internet etc.) (Saed,2018), and, last but not least the lack of digitally competent teachers willing to deal with all these difficulties.

Consequently, this chapter takes a very critical perspective on culture, pedagogy, and digitalization in the context of ESD, which, it is hoped, might be helpful for government authorities, policy makers, and other societal stakeholders when developing policies to strengthen quality education in Pakistan in general and ESD in connection with digitalization in particular.

METHODS USED: OBSERVATIONS AND INTERVIEWS

In the following, insights into some of the results from observations and interviews will be presented, which confirm many of the statements given above. The objective of the study is to analyze the present situation of education and its underlying basic conditions in tribal areas of Pakistan.

This study uses a mixed method research approach, using both qualitative and quantitative techniques (Tashakkori & Cresswell, 2007).

Observation was scheduled and structured. All the constructs of the observation had been developed according to the background and needs of the study: physical facilities available in schools and classrooms (especially the availability and/or use of digital technology), teaching methods/pedagogies, the language of teachers, the content of textbooks in connection with students' culture/language, and other relevant factors. Teachers had been informed about the team of researchers visiting the schools, and that the information from the observations and interviews would be kept confidential, and used for research purposes only.

In order to further explore external and internal factors responsible for today's situation of education in the tribal areas of Pakistan (beyond those observed on site), structured interviews (Zhang & Wildemuth, 2009) were conducted with both teachers and parents. As all attempts to get into contact with teachers from a distance, and make them fill in an online questionnaire failed, face-to-face interviews were conducted with 50 teachers at primary school level. The interview was structured in nature, and the following questions were asked:

1. What is your current status of employment and qualification?
2. What is the distance between your school and place of residence?
3. What is the language of your students and the language you use in your lessons?
4. How many students come to school regularly?
5. Why do you think parents do not send their daughters to school?
6. How many times do officers visit the schools for check-ups?
7. What are the particular problems of teachers in tribal areas?
8. What do you as a teacher demand from the Government of Pakistan (and the Department of Education in particular)?

Interviews were also conducted with the parents of the students of tribal areas, many of whom are illiterate, so the questions had to be read aloud. The following questions were asked:

1. What is your occupation?
2. How many children do you have?
3. What is your point of view as to customs and traditions?
4. Do you send your children to school?
5. Why do you prefer to send your son to school?
6. (Why) Do you (not) send your daughters to school? What are the reasons?
7. What do you as a parent demand from the Government of Pakistan (and the Department of Education in particular)?

Only those parents who voluntarily agreed to take part were interviewed.

Altogether, 86 participants from 25 different primary schools took part in this study. Interviews were collected from 46 teachers and 28 parents.

RESULTS FROM OBSERVATIONS IN SCHOOLS AND CLASSROOMS

Out of 25 school buildings, only 15 were functional, six school buildings were non-functional, and four schools did not even have a school building. So, 15 schools could be included in the actual study and these were where the observations took place. Ten schools had one classroom, four schools had two rooms, and one school actually had three rooms. As Table 1 shows, 11 out of 15 schools had functional toilets, four had none. The access to clean drinking water was only given in seven out of 25 schools. Libraries and playgrounds did not exist in a single school. At least one working tablet or mobile device was available for every school, upon which all the records were saved, i.e. students' enrollment, the total number and names of teachers, teachers' status, students' status, total number in each class etc. However, the teachers often kept it locked in their homes in the cities they come from, because at the actual schools there is hardly any electricity or internet available, so they cannot use them. A connection to the grid or a solar charger for electricity supply was available in three and ten schools respectively. This also means, that digital devices for educating students do not exist, and that even if they were, they would not be fully functional because electrical power and internet access are often absent. The same problem can be derived from Table 2.

Table 1. Characteristics of physical facilities available in the 15 functional primary schools selected for this study

Facilities	Number of Schools	Percentage (%)
Functional Toilets	11	73
Clean Drinking Water	7	47
Library	0	0
Playground	0	0
Boundary wall	10	67
Working tablet/ mobile device (belonging to teacher)	15	100
Connected to power grid (electricity)	3	20
Solar charger (electricity)	10	67
Internet Access	0	0

Table 2. Physical facilities available in the classrooms in the 15 primary schools selected for this study

Physical Facilities	Number of Schools	Percentage (%)
Desks (for students to sit at)	8	53
Chairs for teacher	11	73
Tables (for teachers)	9	60
Carpets	11	73
Blackboards	8	53
Textbooks	6	40
Computers (laptops/ PCs) (for students)	0	0

Table 2 describes the physical facilities available in the classrooms of the 15 primary schools selected for this study. While observing lessons, various other important points could be identified. Desks for students to sit at existed in only 8 classrooms, chairs in eleven classrooms, and tables for teachers in nine classrooms. Students were sitting on carpets in eleven classrooms, only 8 classrooms had a blackboard. Observing the situation, it seemed that these blackboards were also seldomly used in these classrooms. Textbooks were available in six classrooms. With regards digital education, there was not a single computer in any school able to be used by students. As previously mentioned, these are the hard facts of education in tribal areas in Pakistan, digitalization is simply not available to any of the students, be they male or female.

Table 3. Teaching/learning methods/pedagogy in the classrooms in the 15 primary schools selected for this study

Teaching Method	Number of Schools	Percentage (%)
Didactical Lecture Method	7	47
Demonstration Method	3	20
Culturally Related Method	5	33
Multimedia Projector Technique	0	0

Table 3 looks at the pedagogy and or teaching/ learning methods adopted by the teachers in the classrooms of the 15 selected schools in this study. It shows that 7 teachers used a didactical lecture method to teach students in a rather classical way of frontal teaching. Only 3 teachers applied a demonstration method. A pedagogy related to the culture of the students was used by 5 teachers in the sampled classroom (e.g., the lecture was held in the language of students and was relevant to cultural issues). There was not a single school in which a multimedia projector technique or any such facility was used or available.

Table 4. Language of teachers spoken in the classrooms in 15 lessons observed in the 15 primary schools (one per school) selected for this study

Language of Teacher	Number of Lessons	Percentage (%)
Pashto	4	27
Urdu	7	47
Balochi	3	20
English	1	7

Table 4 gives more detailed information about the languages used by the teachers in 15 lessons observed in the 15 primary schools (one per school) selected for this study. The languages spoken by the students are Pashto, Balochi and other local languages, yet the teachers often speak in Urdu. Only four teachers in the observed lessons were using Pashto language, only three were speaking Balochi. One teacher was using English, and three teachers used Urdu, which means that more than half of the lessons were held in a language the that students neither actually speak or fully understand.

Table 5. Textbooks (ir)relevant to students' language and culture in the 15 primary schools selected for this study

Relevancy	Number	Percentage
Textbooks in tribal language and following special syllabus relevant to students' own culture	0	0
Textbooks in Urdu and or English used for all students in Pakistan following the National Curriculum	15	100%

Table 5 shows that in 100% of lessons, the content dealt with was not related to students' culture and/or language, but it was exactly the same in all other areas of Pakistan (urban and rural).

RESULTS FROM INTERVIEWS WITH TEACHERS

Before some of the qualitative results are presented, it should be stated that some of the teachers were not allowed to take part in the interview because of security issues or cultural issues (mostly veiling). All in all, interviews were conducted with 46 teachers (with four out of 50 teachers not willing to take part in this research process due to customs and traditions). In the interviews, it was identified that most of the teachers working in this tribal area were primary school teachers, and their qualifications were not high i.e. F.A/F.SC, B.A/B.SC. The teachers of one particular tribal region, Dera Ghazi Khan, however, were highly qualified, i.e. M.A, M.SC, M.PHIL. Most teachers were not local, and came from distant places. That is why they are not at the schools on a regular basis, and this could be one of the most important factors of low female literacy rate in the tribal areas of Pakistan. Just as in the observation results presented above, most of the teachers in the interviews did not to speak or teach in the local language of learners (Pashto, Balochi, etc.), but in Urdu, which is the national and official language of Pakistan (although only 7% speak Urdu as mother-tongue language). They also report transportation problems because of the difficult geographical location of their school(s), low salaries, and a lack of the availability of textbooks in time. Most of the teachers stated the low attendance of students in rather low numbers.

The majority of teachers also reported that the parents do not give any importance to their daughters' education due to many reasons, mostly poverty, preference of son over daughter, early marriage, help in household work, school distance, and especially because of security issues. The majority of teachers demanded that the government provide transport facilities, scholarships for students, increases in salaries, appointments in their nearest locations, and that an awareness scheme about daughters' education should be started in order to finally eliminate the customs, traditions and prejudice surrounding female education. This interview also indicated that the monitoring system is not running on regular basis. Lack of monitoring officers worsens the situation. The majority of teachers said that the Government has not provided either them personally or the schools they teach at, with any kind of modern technology like laptops, multimedia projectors etc. The fundamentals of digital education, i.e., the reliable supply of power and internet access must be provided in schools in the future, does not yet exist.

RESULTS FROM INTERVIEWS WITH PARENTS

An interview was also conducted with the parents of the students. In these areas, women are not permitted to take part in such activities, so the students' fathers took part. 28 people agreed to be interviewed in this research process.

Most of the parents of this area were poor and illiterate, most of them worked in farming (grazing cattle), in small grocery stores and the army etc. They reported that they did not to send their daughters to school as these were either too far away from their home, for security issues and because many teachers were not at the school regularly. Many parents also stated that they sent their son(s) to school, not their daughter(s), because daughters would be marrying soon anyway. They would leave the family home, whereas their sons were regarded to be the only breadwinners for the remaining family. Some parents told their daughters to stay at home because they had to help in the household and take care of their brothers and sisters.

The majority of the parents participating in the study were also worried about the customs and traditions of their tribal culture, which does not allow them to send their daughters to schools. In this area, customs even lead to the killing of girls/women in the name of "honor". During the war on terrorism, the area where our study was conducted was badly affected, and the girls' schools in particular were targeted and destroyed by terrorists. That is why parents expressed they were also very conscious and worried about the safety and health of their daughters. Currently, however, many reforms are being implemented in this area, but in education, especially in matters concerning female education, progress is very slow to pretty much non-existent. Most of the parents also blamed the teachers as being the reason for their not sending their daughters to school. The majority of the parents demanded from the Government of Pakistan and the governmental officials of the Department of Education that they should provide funds and scholarships for their children, send regular teachers to the area, and most of all, to provide security for their daughters, especially when schools are at a distance from their homes. The number of girls' schools they said should be increased and the provision of functioning toilets should be improved. Many parents expressed that they would be willing to send their daughters to school, if the teachers were present on a regular basis and if they took real interest in the education of their children. However, a majority of the parents involved reported that they were, at the same time, very worried about customs and traditions of this tribal culture, which does simply not allow sending females to schools. The researchers consider this circumstance as the darkest side of the tribal culture, and demand it should be eliminated at any cost.

CONCLUSIONS AND RECOMMENDATIONS

Education can play a vital role in the development, and especially the sustainable development of countries or regions. Yet, it can only be successful, if the access to education is provided to all the people regardless of their age, gender, color, ethical or cultural background, or geographical location. It is a bitter fact that in Pakistan the access to education is not at all equal for all people. Pakistan is a culturally diverse country, and in many aspects divided when it comes to similarities and differences in urban, rural, and tribal areas. In urban areas, the situation of male and female education is satisfactory, and in rural areas it is somewhat better than in tribal areas. In tribal areas, however, the situation of education, and particularly female education, has to be described as both unsatisfactory and insufficient.

Men and women are equally important for the development of any country, especially for achieving the SDGs. However, it is a tough realization that women are still lagging behind men in many fields and respects, and especially in education globally, nationally, and particularly in tribal areas. Despite the continuous rise in literacy rates over the past 50 years, there are still 773 million illiterate adults in the world, most of them women (UIS, 2022). This study also found that the female education situation in tribal areas of Pakistan is not satisfactory. Many internal and external factors are responsible, and they have been mentioned above. Yet, there is also another factor which simply cannot be ignored any longer, i.e. the lack of digital technology infrastructure available to students in rural and, above all, in tribal areas of Pakistan, where students do not have any access to laptops, multimedia technology, the internet or even electricity. How can we even think about digital learning environments – which could be highly relevant to finding out and discussing students' own culture and give glimpses into other cultures and cultural thinking not only within Pakistan, but also on an international level. Digital technologies have emerged as being essential to achieve the targets of SDG4 and can contribute strongly to ESD environments as well. The introduction of new technology-assisted learning tools, e.g., mobile phones, laptops, tablets, smart boards, open online courses, dynamic visualizations, or virtual laboratories have changed education in schools and institutions worldwide (Haleem et al., 2022). During the Covid19-years, online teaching has often been the only access to schooling and education in general, and helped to prevent a total loss of education time for the young generation.

The author suggests that it should not be the destiny of the tribal (male and female) students to always remain behind in all fields of education, and, ultimately, in life. If such a large percentage of a country's population lags behind, it will not be possible to achieve any development, and especially sustainable development, for today's and future generations.

In conclusion, this chapter recommends the following:

1. The implementation of the goals of Quality Education and ESD in the Single National Curriculum and in Special Syllabi respecting the positive aspects of different cultural backgrounds in tribal areas,

2. The development of teacher education programs considering heterogeneous cultures and diverse cultural accesses to education and sustainability contents in urban, rural, and tribal areas of Pakistan,
3. Language courses for particular regions where teachers could be trained to understand and speak the locally relevant language(s),
4. Regular monitoring visits by governmental officers in tribal areas,
5. Taking positive action against non- functional schools,
6. Digital equipment and digital education courses for teachers,
7. The provision of schools with local and/or permanent teachers,
8. The increase of salaries and special incentives for teachers in tribal or otherwise disadvantaged areas,
9. The provision of fully functioning school buildings, and more and more new school buildings (these also being closer to the students' homes),
10. The tackling of security issues (especially for female students),
11. The development of official schemes for improving parents' attitudes on female education,
12. And, last but not least, the provision of electrical power, internet access, computers, and other multimedia technology for students in each school in Pakistan.

All of these recommendations highlight that there are big challenges ahead for education in general, and a huge lack of digital education in particular. When such a large proportion of the population of Pakistan, especially the female population, is deprived of the basic facilities of life and education, it is difficult to achieve any sustainable development, because SDG4 Quality Education and ESD are the foundation for improving people's lives and also for achieving all other SDGs.

REFERENCES

AfridiW. (2020). *Educating Fata*. Retrieved from https://www.the news.com.pk

Alexander, R. (2001). *Culture & pedagogy: the international comparison in primary education*. Wiley. Blackwell.

Ali, I. (2018). *Mainstreaming Pakistan's Federally Administered Teibal Areas. Reform Initiatives and Roadblocks*. Special Report 421. United States Institutive of Peace. https:// www.usip.org

Ayca, C., & Ilknur, R. (2022). Digitally competent Teacher. An examination of pre-service teachers' metaphor. *Journal of Digital Learning in Teacher Education, 38*(4).

Cochran-Smith, M. (2003). Teaching quality Matters. *Journal of Teacher Education*, *54*(2), 95–98. doi:10.1177/0022487102250283

Doyle, W. (1980). *Classroom Management*. Kappa Delta Pi.

Enelamericas. (2016). *Sustainable Development Goals: Our history and close relationship*. www.en-elamericas.com

Evans, L. S., & Gunn, A.A. (2012). It is not just the language: culture as an essential element in pre-service teacher education. *The Journal of Multiculturalism in Education, 7*(1).

FATA Development Indicators Household Survey 2013-14. (2015). *Bureau of Statistics – Planning and Development Department*. FATA Secretariat.

Haleem. (2022). Understanding the role of digital technologies in education: A review. Sustainable Operations and Computers, 3, 275-285. doi:10.1016/j.susoc.2022.05.004

Labor Force Survey. (2020-21). *Government of Pakistan, Ministry of Planning Development and Special initiatives*. Pakistan Bureau of Statistics.

Literacy/UNESCO UIS. (2022). Uis.unesco.org/ en/ topic/literacy

Mehsud, R. (2018). *Schools in Pakistan' Tribal Districts struggle to write the next chapter*. ARABNEWS. https:// www.arabnews.com/ 1423811/Pakistan

Muhammad, M. (2016). Education census 2015-16; 1,036 FATA schools, non functional. *Tribune, the Express*.

Nave'ed, S. (2018). Why do Pakistan's Federally Administered Tribal Areas have such a High Gender Gap in Education? Education plus development. Brookings.

Polter-Nelson, E. M., & O'Neil, J. K. (2019). Role of teachers on education for sustainable development. In Encyclopedia of sustainability in Higher Education. Springer.

Purhottan & Dhingra, A. (2017). Understanding the Indian tribal life and their issues. *International Journal of Advanced Research*, 5.

Rice, J. K. (2003). *Teacher Quality: Understanding the Effectiveness of Teacher Attributes. Economic policy institute*. Education.

Saed, A. (2018). "Ghosts schools" risk breeding militancy in Pakistan tribal areas. Conflict News. *The New Humanitarian*. www the new humanitarian.org.news/2018/01/25/breeding- militancy-pakistan-ghosts-schools-tribal-areas-risk-

Steven, B. (2010). Sociology: Understanding and changing the social world. Flatworld.

Sustainable Development Goals. (2020). *Take action for the sustainable goals-the United Nations*. https:// www.un.org,sustainable –dev

Tasshakkori, A., & Cresswell, J. W. (2007). The new era of Mixed methods. *Journal of Mixed Methods Research*, *1*(1), 3–7. doi:10.1177/2345678906293042

Wheeler, S. (2012). *E-Learning and Digital learning. Encyclopedia of the sciences of learning*. Springer.

Women from Pakistan tribal areas denied basic human rights. (2022). *ANI South Asia' leading multimedia News Agency*. Aninews.in/ news/ world/.

Zhang, Y., & Wildemuth, B.M. (2009). *Unstructured Interviews: Applications of social research methods questions in information and library science*. Libraries Unlimited.

Chapter 11
Updating the US K-12 Information Technology Curriculum

Cristofer G. Slotoroff
Vernon Township School District, USA

ABSTRACT

This chapter reviews recent research related to students' educational device use, online content consumption, and students' understanding of content providers' algorithmic targeting practices to make the case for a new information literacy content area that encompasses a comprehensive and responsive education initiative focused on maintaining students' autonomy and wellbeing. By examining the great extent to which online content providers' large-scale switch to algorithmic, responsive, individualized content provision proliferates, this chapter makes the case that students' (and teachers') lack of engagement in this regard makes for a crisis of sustainability. The chapter situates the need for systemic adaptation to this new reality as overdue and urgent.

INTRODUCTION

Information literacy is a critical component of contemporary K–12 education within the United States. Here, the widely-adopted 2010 Common Core Standards—the deeply influential (if also controversial) set of skills, knowledge, and understandings that has served as a touchstone for countless American schools' curricular initiatives—emphasized the importance of mastering informational texts (National Governors Association Center for Best Practices, Council of Chief State School Officers, 2010). Now, 12 years following the Common Core Standards' publication, substantively altered circumstances and conditions regarding the fundamental nature of information literacy necessitate the reevaluation of information literacy's treatment within US public schools. This action is fundamental to the sustainability of a progressive society that values personal autonomy, free discourse, and the right to know the extent to which one's digital experience is algorithmically influenced.

DOI: 10.4018/978-1-7998-5033-5.ch011

The circumstances and conditions that have changed are those focused on the ubiquitous role of the internet in nearly all Americans' lives (and in, of course, the lives of those throughout the world). Internet users no longer access and share a standardized online experience to the extent that they did in 2010. Today, users engage what this researcher calls the *Personally and Algorithmically Curated Internet Experience* (*PACIE*). Contemporary internet users' input is analyzed, aggregated, and evaluated according to often proprietary algorithms designed to optimize online entities' desired outcomes (Grandinetti & Bruinsma, 2022; Shin, 2020). The PACIE spans devices (e.g., computers, tablets, mobile phones, watches) and sectors (e.g., education, commerce, finance, socialization, healthcare). As algorithmically driven content provision becomes more personalized, Shin (2020) highlights (in the context of journalism) how important it is "to tackle the ethical and legal issues caused by utilizing data and algorithms to target users, such as fairness, accountability, transparency, and explainability (FATE)" (p. 542). As these issues remain actively debated and analyzed by adults across sectors and industries, school-aged children are access algorithmically driven content. It is now essential for schools to respond and adapt to this reality by instituting K–12 curricula focused on the PACIE.

As the PACIE permeates nearly every aspect of online decision-making—what to eat, what to wear, what to watch, where to go, how to arrive, what to know—it is critical to the sustainability of US public schools that the PACIE's ubiquitous permeation is treated as a distinct knowledge domain (e.g., English language arts, social studies, mathematics, science) in and of itself. The PACIE is worthy of purposeful K–12 academic focus alongside English language arts, social studies, mathematics, and science because the PACIE is effectively these four core subjects' combined manifestation: aggregated information culled from a wide range of users' input and characteristics—demographics, opinions, behaviors, and actions—before it is actionably pointed toward content providers' preferential outcomes.

The PACIE's evolutionary trajectory is, to this point, neither accidental nor complete. It is a purpose-built ecosystem in which user data has both relative and discrete value: relative, in that a wealth of users' input begets a personally curated, thus more relevant, online experience; discrete, in that a wealth of users' data—purchased for real money—yields leverage for companies and content providers in potential advertising revenue, website traffic, and content consumption. Teaching K–12 students to master this medium's intricacies requires researchers, policymakers, postgraduate teacher training programs, educational administrators, teachers, students, and students' families (among others) to rethink and ultimately reposition information literacy within US public schools' curricula as a responsive, continually updated endeavor that is both in the interest of students as individuals and in the interest of a progressive society.

RESEARCH QUESTIONS

This chapter explores three research questions:

- To what extent does the PACIE influence students' lives?
- To what extent are the US's K–12 schools positioned to educate students about the PACIE?
- To what extent do PACIE-focused education policies and practices targeting students' wellbeing fit into the US's current K–12 public education paradigm?

To answer these questions, this chapter synthesizes research focused on algorithms' pervasiveness in online content provision, ethical concerns surrounding online content algorithmically targeted toward children, educational technology implementation, and students' relationships with information literacy. The researcher approaches this chapter under the assumption that values such as transparency, social equity, and educational responsivity are meaningful virtues worth pursuing. With few exceptions (e.g., foundational theories or studies, landmark documents), the researcher's database search queries and subsequent chapter inclusions were limited to research published over the course of the past five years. This chronological constraint was adopted for two reasons. First, it aligns with this chapter's assumption that responsivity is a value worth pursuing. Second, it is an acknowledgement that the ongoing global COVID-19 Pandemic marks a significant change to educational technology research to the extent that one must prioritize recency (i.e., studies published just before and studies published since the COVID-19 Pandemic's onset) whenever possible.

THE PACIE'S INFLUENCE ON STUDENTS' LIVES

Students are already spending their time enmeshed within the PACIE. Thus, young Internet users are a coveted demographic for online content providers. It is well-known that large swaths of school-aged children in the US consume commensurately large swaths of content online; the case for PACIE-focused public education is underscored by the rate at which new or newly algorithmically driven platforms proliferate among school-aged users and the content they consume. In 2020, the social media app TikTok reported that "in the United States alone more than one-third of its daily 49 million users were under the age of 14" (Feller & Burroughs, 2021, p. 14). TikTok uses algorithms to curate content (Grandinetti & Bruinsma, 2022), showing videos to users based on proprietary algorithms. Researchers have called for scholarly papers focused on TikTok both because of its concurrent popularity and because of its capacity to algorithmically amplify flawed, incomplete, inaccurate, or hateful content on pertinent issues, such as those pertaining to public health or, perhaps, its own business interests (Zenone et al., 2021). On TikTok and on the other social media platforms that school-aged students continue to engage, this lattermost instance is especially concerning. Despite researchers' observations suggesting that "children are unable to recognize targeted online advertising as a marketing technique" (van Reijmersdal et al., 2017, p. 408), Instagram—"an app with over one billion active monthly users and counting" (p. 14)—revealed in 2021 its plans for a forthcoming, child-focused platform. Such a sector-wide focus on youth is in the interest of public health (Zenone et al., 2021), and in need of robust educational remediation.

With these use patterns and issues in mind, the essentiality of a PACIE-focused curriculum comes into relief when juxtaposing these apps' youthful focus with their young users' regard for the apps' value as a trusted, meaningful source of information. Contemporary college students seem to value social media for its utility as a news source. One study's survey of 5,259 college students found that 89% of respondents received news from social media within the past week, and 72% of respondents indicated that they utilized social media for news consumption on a daily basis (Head et al., 2019, p. 19). As for adults, though some evidence suggests that adults who rely primarily on social media for news consumption tend to show skepticism toward the veracity of the news (Kalogeropoulos et al., 2019, p. 3683), the lines that delineate *news* from *social media* are becoming more difficult to distinguish within the PACIE. Importantly, even the differences between social media platforms may not be as meaningful as users might believe. In a study focused on 22 Dutch participants between the ages of 16 and 26, Swart (2021) found that the participants regarded "Instagram, Facebook, Twitter, and WhatsApp" as "the most important gateways to news and journalism" (p. 4). Three of these four companies (all except Twitter) are, essentially, the same organization: Meta. Changing perceptions of trusted sources and fluid distinctions between content providers such as these require responsive education purposefully designed to prepare students to meet the PACIE's information literacy intricacies.

In the interest of social equity, social media platforms' staggering popularity in itself merits scrutiny. Too often, algorithms' use in high stakes situations—as in "who gets a job, a mortgage, or a loan, access to social services, admission to school or educational services" (Head et al., 2020)—is compromised by flaws or the absence of contextualizing data. Since the algorithms dictating the platforms' content distribution are proprietary, it is difficult to meaningfully vet companies' practices with fidelity. In response to users' observations or allegations of inequity, discrimination, or biased treatment of users' content, some have called for companies to provide researchers with independent tools for platforms' analysis (Zenone et al., 2021, p. 3). Others have expressed concerns that social media companies' "platforms have become a form of civic space. Because of this, platforms need to be held accountable about their biases, and they need to be more transparent about the rules that govern them" (Are, 2020, p. 744). Calls for increased algorithmic transparency will be greater in volume and in number following a K–12 education designed to cultivate a working understanding of the PACIE's manifestation.

THE MORAL CASE FOR TEACHING K–12 STUDENTS TO NAVIGATE THE PACIE

The moral case for explicitly teaching K–12 students to navigate the PACIE is based on two foundational educational premises. First: pursuing and acquiring an understanding of the phenomena constituting one's environment is preferable to ignorance of the phenomena. Second: US public education strives to educate students to make both self-interested decisions and selfless decisions designed to create a more equitable, progressive, and sustainable society.

When aligned to the first premise, the need for PACIE-focused education is evident if one considers the PACIE as an eminent conception school-aged children's reality. Put simply: the PACIE is where today's students spend a great deal of their time. When aligned to the second premise, students who better understand the PACIE are better able to leverage the perhaps incalculable benefits that artificial intelligence demonstrates or suggests as a technology: personalized learning opportunities, access to more relevant information, greater transparency in government, education, or health, and more robust and individualized technological innovation. Concurrently, better educated students are better equipped to counter the PACIE's most maligned and nefarious forces: misinformation, extremism, bigotry, hate speech, consumer manipulation, predation, abuse, and others.

These premises are aligned to those of extant K–12 curricula. The aims of long-canonized K–12 knowledge domains—such as literature and rhetoric, civics, mathematics, or biology—are not merely self-serving. Though these domains prepare students to succeed in postsecondary academic, professional, or entrepreneurial contexts, they also advance a concept of society: one that aspires to be egalitarian, progressive, and sustainable. A K–12 graduate who ably analyzes and authorial intents and landmark arguments, who makes informed decisions about representatives in government, who understands the arithmetic underpinning life's daily decisions, and as one who understands how the physical world manifests, is both better prepared to meet challenges in these areas and better positioned to positively contribute to society at large.

These K–12 knowledge domains are largely intrapersonal efforts while students are in school acquiring the requisite knowledge and skills necessary to demonstrate the mastery of these domains upon graduation. These domains' postsecondary practice, however, is interpersonal: in the adult world, a rhetorician's merits are evaluated in the context of others' arguments, one's choice to elect politicians in a representative democracy requires a sophisticated weighing of personal convictions against those in one's environs, one makes savvy personal finance decisions in the process of contributing to the economy, and one is ecologically conscious not for self-interest, but in the interest of one's perceived greater good.

Just as it is important to distinguish the moral educational premises underlying the need for PACIE-focused teaching and learning, it is equally important to distinguish an additional and foundational premise underlying this chapter's rendering of algorithms, machine learning, artificial intelligence, and the time that both children and adults spend online: none of the preceding sentence's foci are innately evil, problematic, or—in and of themselves—in need of remediation. Algorithms are nuanced, constantly changing, and complex. Grandinetti and Bruinsma (2022) warned against "narratives of determinism" when examining social media algorithms in particular, noting that they "did not *cause* a social landscape of mid(dis)information—our current moment is an ongoing part of decades of political strategies, global and local histories, economic shifts, and technological trajectories that embrace computational and data-driven ways of knowing" (p. 15).

In this context, it must be acknowledged that while the PACIE's yields are, by algorithms' nature, individualized and adaptive, its existence and its efficacy are responsive to societal wants and needs. The PACIE bears significant advantages when compared, for instance, to the depersonalized online experience. Given the option, online shoppers generally prefer to browse clothes they might purchase and wear. Music lovers would prefer that they enjoy the next song on a playlist. Single adults who use dating apps would hope, one supposes, to be matched with prospective partners with whom users are likely to be compatible. Just as readers have, for centuries, elected to purchase newspapers and magazines aligned to their worldviews, the PACIE helps Internet users to access preferential content and information online. Personalized, algorithmic content provision that uses machine learning can shrink the time that users spend searching for their desired results while increasing the time (and the quality of time) users spend engaging with these desired results. Curating users' online experiences within the PACIE is not necessarily a malevolent action. It is, as with other technologies, an innovation designed by its constructors in response to market effects: preferences, demands, and utility.

EXAMINING THE NATURE OF SCHOOL-AGED CHILDREN'S PACIE IN VIDEO CONTENT CONSUMPTION CONTEXTS

With these distinctions in mind, this chapter's call for PACIE-focused K–12 education is neither an alarmist's warning nor a Luddite's naïve request to sequester children from potentially objectionable content. This chapter is this author's contention that in the absence of PACIE-focused information literacy education, today's students are more likely to be unconsciously manipulated, less autonomous, less critical, and less susceptible of exercising agency in their postsecondary lives. This chapter's push for PACIE-focused education is the case for a robust and commensurate response to the emergence of algorithms' technological, scientific, social, economic, and political preponderance. A better understanding of the PACIE gives today's students a better chance to leverage its enormous power. That children stand to benefit from PACIE-focused education is this author's speculative supposition. More immediately and consequentially, however, it is this author's contention that—in the absence of PACIE-focused curricula—children are left without the opportunity to leverage long-accessible conduits for knowledge, context, and guidance: schools, and the educators who staff them.

One of the chief purposes of public education is to prepare students to navigate the world outside the school building's walls, and today's school-aged children in the United States spend a significant portion of their days within the PACIE consuming screen-based media. In 2019—before the onset of the COVID-19 pandemic's shift to remote learning—US children between the ages of eight- and 12-years-old spent almost five hours per day engaging with screen-based media, while teenagers were reported to "use an average of just under seven and a half hours' worth (7:22)—not including time spent using screens for school or homework" (Rideout & Robb, 2019, p. 3). While the nonacademic digital spaces that children navigate online have been shown to diversify over the course of their adolescence, the majority of their screen time from ages eight to 18 consists of video content consumption: eight- to 12-year-old children (i.e., *tweens*) spent 53% of their screen time consuming video content, while teenagers between 13 and 18 years old spent 39% of their screen time in this manner (p. 6). On YouTube alone, "children spend 1.39 hours each weekday and 1.47 hours each weekend day viewing YouTube videos" (Herodotou & Neumann, 2020, p. 72). These figures' scale suggests, at the very least, that a complementary education provided by a robust teaching and learning plan is in order. Responsive action—in the form of a broadened information literacy knowledge domain that includes PACIE-focused education as equal in scholastic focus to literature and rhetoric, civics, mathematics, and science—can help to contextualize and respond to students' staggering and individualized content consumption patterns.

Perhaps the foremost video content platform, YouTube, uses algorithms to drive content to particular users. These algorithms perform "an important organizing and gatekeeping function" (Schmitt et al., 2018, p. 781) for the site's content. While there are many websites and online services specializing in video content distribution, the scope of content available on YouTube is extremely vast (Hassinger et al., 2020), and both its enormous popularity and its use of algorithms to curate users' video content are noteworthy in the context of PACIE-focused education. Children's use of YouTube is difficult to definitively track, but around the world, "a recent report surveyed 3,154 families and showed that 80% of children aged 0-7 use YouTube, and 59% use YouTube Kids" (Neumann & Herodotou, 2020, p. 72). In the United Kingdom, at one time it was the highest rated downloadable app for children aged eight and under (Elias & Sulkin, 2017). This site is highlighted here not as a scapegoat or as a particularly malicious content platform, but as a function of its well-known deployment of algorithms, its ubiquity, and its consequentially available extant research that merits further analysis in this chapter's context.

A PACIE-focused information literacy curriculum can educate students to be critical of algorithmically curated video content consumed on YouTube. To be clear, neither YouTube's use of algorithms nor its school-aged users' video content consumption are inherently problematic, but each merits commensurate research, analysis, and education. When well-designed algorithms appropriately perform their desired functions for users in contexts like those YouTube deploys (e.g., to suggest further videos the user may also enjoy, to engage the user with a previously-viewed video's genre-specific predecessors, to lead users to discover previously unknown content creators the user may also enjoy), the platform's users may be satisfied to the extent that they are not cognizant of algorithmic content curation. Such undetected algorithmic curation spurs ethical debate: when algorithms drive extremist, conspiratorial, or hateful content to otherwise unsuspecting users, the extent to which YouTube does so intentionally or nefariously is unclear. Nonetheless, in either of these positive or negative algorithmically curated viewing circumstances, "as critical media scholars point out, social media platforms do not merely transmit content, but filter it on the basis of claiming to augment it, thereby making the content more relevant to its potential consumers" (O'Callaghan et al., 2015, p. 460). The extent to which such filtering by augmentation warrants a platform's accountability is debatable, and the extent to which this process could be construed as neutral or partisan in nature is equally so.

Since the scope of children's video consumption on YouTube and other video content platforms is ever-expanding and wildly variable, PACIE-focused information literacy curricula should not seek to dictate students' viewing patterns. This chapter does not suggest age restrictions to frame video content consumption, nor does this chapter suppose restrictions regarding the appropriateness of topics or genres regarding children's video content consumption. Even as school-aged children are inarguably consuming far more video content than they once did, "six hours of makeup tutorial videos on YouTube is different from six hours of Planet Earth" (Rideout & Robb, 2019, p. 25).

This chapter does, however, propose that a more robust, PACIE-focused education can prepare students to account for the abrupt fluctuations in tone, content, and sequence that may be encountered when viewing video content online. Though makeup tutorials and cinematic depictions of the natural world are likely harmless, YouTube is—as an algorithmically driven platform—equally capable of juxtaposing the harmless with the extreme without warning. Its algorithms can, for instance, favor makeup tutorials reinforcing stereotypes aligned with advertisers' profit-related goals (Bishop, 2018), or they can favor extremist perspectives targeting specific groups of people (Schmitt et al., 2018). Certainly, there are countless videos available on YouTube that are either harmless or greatly beneficial to young people: funny cat videos, accessible and kid-friendly entertainment, or topical historical videos. Accordingly, in advocating, designing, or implementing a PACIE-focused K–12 public education initiative, it is not the responsibility of educators or educational institutions to determine children's ability to access this content. It is educators' and educational institutions' responsibility to help their students to make decisions about what entities, agendas, practices, and technologies interact when platforms like YouTube curate their video content.

Preparing students in this regard—for widely unpredictable variations in algorithmically curated video content both within a platform and between platforms—is a new challenge for public education. To this point, K–12 information literacy education assumes the existence of contextualizing presentational elements that students can use to regard, evaluate, and analyze online content's veracity and its relevance. Students are taught to examine content according to characteristics better suited for academic scholarship or professional knowledge: the author of the content, the content's publisher, its publication, its originating locale, its date, its critical reception, its history. However, when a user watches a particular video that was suggested by YouTube's algorithm, the user is given a presentational template that offers an altogether different context: the content provider's username, the video's number of views, other users' comments on the video, and a selection of other algorithmically curated videos to watch. To school-aged viewers without an ample understanding of algorithmic content curation, the suggested video's mere presence can be construed as societal or depersonalized relevance (or legitimacy, or veracity) rather than the result of opaque, algorithmic decisions based on what YouTube can discern about the user. By the time K–12 students graduate and begin their postsecondary education, students struggle to accurately account for algorithmic influences. Head et al. (2020) detailed the changing notion of information literacy in this regard, advocating for a conception of the domain in which teachers and their assignments emphasize a command of content sources at large:

"It must be acknowledged that the information environment our students inhabit is not a cloister of scholarly knowledge. It more closely resembles an overgrown jungle where every resource must be tested for toxicity, and where students are stalked relentlessly, their data harvested as fodder for unknowable uses. We do a disservice to our students and to society by confining research assignments and information literacy instruction efforts to the walled garden of peer-reviewed scholarship, where truth is plucked from well-pruned sources and carefully packaged for instructors following explicit instructions. (p. 28)

In the absence of commensurate education prioritizing such instruction, and in consideration of the sheer amount of time that young people spend consuming personalized, algorithmically curated video content on platforms like YouTube, it is sobering to contemplate the extent to which proprietary algorithms have already been instrumental in shaping children's opinions, assumptions, and conceptions of the world around them.

Thus, robust PACIE-focused education must account for the changing nature of information literacy. It must account for the potential juxtaposition of the harmless with the harmful: "In the context of extremist content, algorithmic 'recommendation' could disguise ideological partisanship as they make content appear 'related'" (Schmitt et al., 2018, p. 781). There are already calls for information literacy-focused education seeking to make students more cognizant of the role that algorithms play in users' news and information preferences (Head et al., 2020), there are also wide-ranging surveys—spanning countries and continents—documenting the changing habits of children's online experiences (Livingstone et al., 2012; Rideout & Robb, 2019). It is time make the best practices, tools, and recommendations from these data actionable for teachers, administrators, and other school professionals. In this sense, teaching students to navigate the PACIE is to simply deploy a needs-based approach to public education: to *meet them where they are*, as the saying goes, but also *to take them further.* PACIE-focused education is both for the benefit of K–12 students' wellbeing and to the benefit of society.

AN EXPLORATION OF WELLBEING AS A VIRTUE WORTH PURSUING IN K–12 SCHOOLS

This chapter's call for PACIE-focused education is grounded in the belief that such education is to the benefit of K–12 students' wellbeing. This sense of wellbeing (i.e., *well-being*) is positioned within a conception of public education that values positive psychology as a worthwhile outcome. This conception of education goes further than skill mastery or knowledge acquisition, beyond public schools' longstanding mandate to "teach the tools of accomplishment" (Seligman et al., 2009, p. 293) by incorporating what Seligman et al. (2009) noted to be the desires of most students' parents: " 'Happiness', 'Confidence', 'Contentment', 'Balance', 'Good Stuff', 'Kindness', 'Health', 'Satisfaction', and the like" (p. 293). When decoupled from schools and rendered as a general concept, this chapter regards wellbeing within the larger context of subjective wellbeing. Diener (2000) likened wellbeing to "the good life" (p. 34), suggesting:

It is desirable for people themselves to think that they are living good lives. This subjective definition of quality of life is democratic in that it grants to each individual the right to decide whether his or her life is worthwhile. It is this approach to defining the good life that has come to be called 'subjective well-being' (SWB) and in colloquial terms is sometimes labeled 'happiness.' (p. 34)

These renderings of wellbeing function less as definitions and more as qualities that the term encompasses in each rendering's context: schools and psychology. This esotericism is not accidental. Perhaps the most important term in these preceding selections is *subjective*. What one considers to be a staple of personal wellbeing (e.g., daily prayer, meditation, walking through a nearby forest) can just as easily be construed as intrusive dogma or practices directly oppositional to one's own conception of the term. Seligman and Csikszentmihalyi (2000) acknowledge and embrace this subjectivity within the context of the positive psychology field, outlining it as one focused on:

Valued subjective experiences: well-being, contentment, and satisfaction (in the past); hope and optimism (for the future); and flow and happiness (in the present). At the individual level, it is about positive individual traits: the capacity for love and vocation, courage, interpersonal skill, aesthetic sensibility, perseverance, forgiveness, originality, future mindedness, spirituality, high talent, and wisdom. At the group level, it is about the civic virtues and the institutions that move individuals toward better citizenship: responsibility, nurturance, altruism, civility, moderation, tolerance, and work ethic. (p. 5)

These sentiments are considerably aligned with this chapter's foundational premises for public education. Like the pursuit of wellbeing, public education strives for both individuals' successes and a progressive society consisting of those who are, individually, successful. With the notable exceptions, perhaps, of "the capacity for love" and "spirituality" (if they are applied with undue orthodoxy), positive psychology (and, in turn, wellbeing itself) is already a canonized facet of K–12 public education within the United States.

These sentiments regarding wellbeing also align with this chapter's earlier acknowledgements of public education's traditional knowledge domains: those of literature and rhetoric, civics and society, mathematics, and scientific inquiry within the natural world. In this way, PACIE-focused K–12 public education that centralizes, prioritizes, and nurtures students' wellbeing as one of its stated goals should not be controversial. Neither wellbeing's innate abstraction nor its deep well of interpretive potential should suggest that it should remain at odds, or outside the auspices of a robust public education. Seligman et al. (2009) advocated for purposely teaching wellbeing. They identified three premises for doing so: "as an antidote to depression, as a vehicle for increasing life satisfaction, and as an aid to better learning and more creative thinking" (p. 295). These premises represent lofty ideals, but these ideals are already schools' responsibilities.

THE CASE FOR PACIE-FOCUSED K–12 EDUCATION THAT SEEKS TO IMPROVE STUDENTS' WELLBEING

There is a perpetually churning debate in US public schools regarding the extent to which school districts ought to incorporate explicitly values-oriented educational practices and policies like those proposed within this chapter. The case for PACIE-focused updates to K–12 information literacy education that seeks to improve students' wellbeing, however, falls well within the confines of American public education tradition. For example, physical education classes (frequently administered in conjunction with health-focused classes) have long been fixtures of American public schools. These classes are bolstered by the premise that students' physical health is, at least in part, the responsibility of the public education system. Certainly, parents' perspectives vary widely as to the specific role that schools (and the teachers, administrators, and other professionals who staff them) should play in teaching students about their bodies, let alone the appropriateness of scholastic evaluations centered on students' physical capabilities. The PACIE-focused education this chapter proposes docs not go as far as such classes: it does not prescribe worldviews or ideals as specific as, for instance, a student's timed mile run or a student's shooting percentage from the free throw line.

In this way, PACIE-focused education does not represent a radical departure from longstanding American ideas of education that transcends base information dissemination. PACIE-focused education should seek merely to build on what already takes place in schools: teaching and learning that takes into account the role that the Internet plays in students' present and future lives. The subjectivity of wellbeing should be, as the term suggests, interpretive according to local norms with the input and consent of local stakeholders. Students are already incurring formative, computer-centered experiences while they are in school. Indeed, one of the Common Core Standards' (2010) "College and Career Readiness Anchor Standards for Writing" was to "use technology, including the Internet, to produce and publish writing and to interact and collaborate with others" (National Governors Association Center for Best Practices and Council of Chief State School Officers, 2010, p. 63). In light of the PACIE's dramatic transformation of online experiences, as well as the staggering amount of time students spend within its confines, it hardly seems controversial to purposely educate students as to how it affects their wellbeing and their conception of the world around them. Right now, school districts' boards of education have increasingly become venues for heated discourse focused on educational content areas and practices spanning health classes (e.g., sexual and reproductive health, anatomy, consent and gender identity concepts), history courses (e.g., scholastic regard for Christopher Columbus's voyages, the US's treatment of marginalized peoples throughout the nation's history, the extent to which civics courses explicitly note political perspectives), and English language arts courses (e.g., canonization of particular authors, the degree to which diversity is reflected in curricular canons, the appropriateness of texts that address controversial or potentially traumatic subjects).

Though US parents' concerns and skepticism regarding values-oriented public education are longstanding, government-mandated (or, at the very least, government-encouraged or government-incentivized) public education initiatives focusing on students' character and students' values are not unprecedented. The deeply influential (if, again, equally controversial) Common Core Standards (National Governors Association Center for Best Practices, Council of Chief State School Officers, 2010) adopted well over a decade ago came as a result of states' collaboration in the educational sphere. Conceptually, Arthur (2005) observed that the government's role in promoting moral initiatives extends to the highest seats of power in Washington, D.C., as "The White House has even sponsored a series of Character Building Conferences at which those on both the right and left of the political spectrum have contributed ideas on how to improve the general character of American children" (p. 245). Though both the Common Core Standards and the bipartisan character education supporters Arthur noted also continue to garner skepticism, these (and other related) debates' ferocity should not be mistaken for an endorsement of past or present government entities' explicit instruction as to what to believe, desire, or feel in relation to oneself or society at large.

In the US, specific educational choices—as to what is, or what is not included in schools' and districts' curricula—continue to largely be decided at the local, rather than state or federal level. Individual courses' curricular documents or courses of study are primarily written by local educators according to the standards, understandings, or frameworks established by State-level entities. Nonetheless, in the midst of ongoing controversy surrounding health standards' misrepresentation in New Jersey, the Acting Education Commissioner was compelled to release a memo reiterating the fact that the State's Department of Education "does not review, approve, or actively endorse instructional materials such as sample lesson plans, textbooks, software, or videos in any content area" (Allen-McMillan, 2022, p. 1). PACIE-focused educational updates proposed in this chapter should not incur such public rancor.

DEFINING US K–12 SCHOOLS' ROLE IN EDUCATING STUDENTS ABOUT THE PACIE

To implement PACIE-focused curricular updates to information literacy in K–12 schools, this process's stakeholders must begin by recognizing and reflecting on past errors regarding educational technology initiatives. Many of the localized implementations that put schools' or districts' laptops into students' hands over the course of the past decades were implemented without students' agency (Lindh & Nolin, 2016), without clear measurements for success (Stone, 2017), without sincere teacher engagement (Gherardi, 2017), or within terms that positioned device use primarily in the context of financial investment (Hallman, 2019). Though many of these initiatives were hardware-driven (i.e., students were issued internet-equipped, laptop computers or tablets), PACIE-focused institutional initiatives aimed at improving information literacy can and should learn from available studies examining the successes and failures of such efforts. Today, in spite of the often-massive investments hardware-driven educational technology initiatives necessitated, schools' stated aims in issuing students technology were too often short-sighted, tying the success of an initiative to test scores or other transient factors. Tellingly, with regard to information literacy, schools' acceptable device use policies have hardly changed since the first versions of these policies were implemented in the 1990s (Sauers & Richardson, 2019).

A PACIE-focused information literacy curriculum can educate students as to how algorithms are already shaping younger users' opinions (Swart, 2021). There is ample context for this challenge: since the first years of a commercialized Internet, ethical concerns regarding marketing and advertising focused on children have been debated (Austin & Reed, 1999). Contemporary stakeholders must adjust their moral compass, tuned through the past 20+ years of research, to point their efforts toward the PACIE. Students must be aware of the means by which "recommender algorithms can help limit information overload" (Swart, 2021, p. 2) while also acknowledging the biases with which "these structures also limit user agency, taking automated decisions on what information to display and filter out" (p. 2). Students must be empowered by their teachers to rely on one another to raise awareness and, if necessary, circumvent algorithmic content curation, a practice they have independently adapted in college without institutional guidance in K–12 schools (Head et al., 2020). As social media companies specifically target younger users with algorithmically tailored recommendations and experiences (Feller and Burroughs, 2021), US public schools could comprise a frontline within a multi-tiered approach (alongside policymakers at the national, state, and local level) to confronting an unchecked PACIE experience for school-aged children.

Confronting the PACIE with educational intervention could allow for more robust discourse among more ideologically diverse groups. In the US, contemporary concerns among ideologically progressive and conservative education pundits focus on the fear that, at the expense of students' powers of self-determination, public schools are perpetuating a politically narrow conception of society. Perhaps their concerns are projections of a more familiar, digital narrowing in this regard? In one study, college students acknowledged their cognizance of the "filter bubbles" presented by their social media platforms (Head et al., 2020, p. 18). On Instagram, Fouquaert and Mechant (2021) found that "people appear to be unable to escape their filter bubble because of their ignorance of personalization mechanisms and their side effects, which in turn impedes the required change in critical attitudes, what we called the 'Algorithm

Paradox'" (pp. 17–18). Still, mere awareness of algorithms' role in driving content to users' devices may be insufficient (Bucher, 2017). A comprehensive education, however, that focuses on raising students' cognizance toward algorithms' influence has the benefit of drawing further attention to the myriad other ways in which decision making is impeded by subtle constraints both on- and offline.

CONCLUSION

Schools must consciously, intentionally teach students (and offer professional development to these students' teachers) to exist and to be happy within a life increasingly dominated by the PACIE. Schools would be wise to reject a curriculum that solely focuses on canonized, exclusively academic information in favor of one that produces, at minimum, an "algorithmic literacy" component of information literacy. Schools are well-positioned as instrumental agents in shaping adolescents' long-term relationships with their devices (Abdel Magid et al., 2021). A working understanding of algorithms' roles in students' content consumption is now an essential piece of these students' education within a free and productive society (Head et al., 2020). A PACIE-focused education could yield even more understanding of how "algorithms are becoming a ubiquitous part of contemporary life, understanding the affective dimensions—of how it makes people feel—seems crucial" (Bucher, 2017, p. 42). The more that is understood about how our own feelings are shaped by the artificial intelligence with which we interact, the more progress and ethical expertise with which we may deploy such intelligence (artificial and otherwise) with confidence.

In the interest of a sustainable, autonomous, and progressive society, today's students must be aware of algorithms' role in online content creation and consumption. Schools' viability depends on their ability to imbue their students with a level of information literacy that evolves at a pace commensurate with the sector's innovation and ubiquity. Without action, schools risk graduating an uninformed legion of consumers, rather than discerning students, who are unable to discern fact from fiction, person from nonperson, organic content from advertisement, and freedom from coercion. The stakes remain high: Already, there exist "embodied algorithms" (Lacković, 2020, p. 282), channeling users' desires into lifelike avatars that artificially inhabit a digital world. While these contemporary innovations are currently innocuous, this could change. To that end, Lacković (2020) concluded that "today they feed the desire for new socks and fancy tops, tomorrow it might be a new war" (p. 282). A responsive education that reflects the reality of one's lived experience is the only vehicle capable of transiting riders toward a desired destination. Today, students' lived experiences increasingly transpire within the PACIE.

The contemporary US public education system is already tasked with an educational scope that encompasses the mitigation of stressors adversely affecting students' wellbeing. When districts, schools, and their stakeholders implement mental health awareness initiatives, suicide prevention protocols, or proactive security drills to thwart potential school shooters, these measures are not strictly academic in nature. These measures are implemented under the premise that the education schools provide to students encompasses more than their proficiency in subject matter. Unless challenged, schools also implement these measures with the consent and the endorsement of the communities that fund them. Schools do not conduct assemblies focused on cyber bullying, peer pressure, or dating violence because assemblies on these topics yield higher standardized test scores. Schools conduct these assemblies because of their capacity to positively impact students' wellbeing.

Perhaps the most extensive argument for PACIE-focused K–12 education in US public schools is the argument for instilling—in an embodied, brick-and-mortar context—within students an appreciation and a mechanism for both transparency and accountability in the absence of these ideals' presence online. Public education is delivered to students according to similar principles as its representative government. From the federal to the local level, schools have (with some exceptions) elected schoolboards, who can be voted in and out according to regularly scheduled elections. Schoolboards are required to publicly declare their meeting schedules with reasonable notice, publicly publish their minutes, and publicly report to the taxpayers funding the school system exactly who and what receives these monies. In short: all school officials serve at the pleasure of their constituencies, and parents are permitted to pull their children from a school and place them elsewhere if they feel that the school's values do not align with their own.

When users engage the PACIE, however, users are—with or without lengthy, wordy, disclosure statements and end-user license agreements—often unwittingly offering their engagement to the content provider as a commodity to be used according to the provider's suitability. In short: content providers are not nearly accountable to their users to the extent that they are to their neighbors, their local officials, their teachers, or their schools. With this juxtaposition in mind, any parental wariness of school-based, values-centered education, manipulation, or indoctrination seems ironic in light of the PACIE's capacity to point unsuspecting or undiscerning users—children, students, teenagers—toward wholly unaccountable entities' outcomes that may or may not be geared toward purposes with which parents agree. Schools are already well-positioned to meet this challenge. With ample training, planning, and continued community dialogue, schools can leverage the accessibility and trust they are already given: by offering an education in which the PACIE's school-aged users are not easily-influenced consumers, but savvy students of information literacy.

REFERENCES

Abdel Magid, H. S., Milliren, C. E., Pettee Gabriel, K., & Nagata, J. M. (2021). Disentangling individual, school, and neighborhood effects on screen time among adolescents and young adults in the United States. *Preventive Medicine*, *142*, 106357. doi:10.1016/j.ypmed.2020.106357 PMID:33301823

Allen-McMillan, A. (2022). *A memo from the new jersey department of education: Clarification regarding 2020 new jersey student learning standards—Comprehensive health and physical education*. New Jersey Department of Education. https://www.nj.gov/education/broadcasts/2022/april/14/ClarificationRegarding2020NewJerseyStudentLearningStandards-CHPE.pdf

Are, C. (2020). How Instagram's algorithm is censoring women and vulnerable users but helping online abusers. *Feminist Media Studies*, *20*(5), 741–744. doi:10.1080/14680777.2020.1783805

Arthur, J. (2005). The re-emergence of character education in British education policy. *British Journal of Educational Studies*, *53*(3), 239–254. doi:10.1111/j.1467-8527.2005.00293.x

Austin, J., & Reed, M. (1999). Targeting children online: Internet advertising ethics issues. *Journal of Consumer Marketing*, *16*(6), 590–602. doi:10.1108/07363769910297579

Bishop, S. (2018). Anxiety, panic and self-optimization: Inequalities and the YouTube algorithm. *Convergence*, *24*(1), 69–84. doi:10.1177/1354856517736978

Bucher, T. (2017). The algorithmic imaginary: Exploring the ordinary affects of Facebook algorithms. *Information Communication and Society*, *20*(1), 30–44. doi:10.1080/1369118X.2016.1154086

Diener, E. (2000). Subjective well-being: The science of happiness and a proposal for a national index. *The American Psychologist*, *55*(1), 34–43. doi:10.1037/0003-066X.55.1.34 PMID:11392863

Elias, N., & Sulkin, I. (2017). YouTube viewers in diapers: An exploration of factors associated with amount of toddlers' online viewing. *Cyberpsychology (Brno)*, *11*(3), 3. Advance online publication. doi:10.5817/CP2017-3-2

Feller, G., & Burroughs, B. (2021). Branding kidfluencers: Regulating content and advertising on youtube. *Television & New Media*. Advance online publication. doi:10.1177/15274764211052882

Fouquaert, T., & Mechant, P. (2021). Making curation algorithms apparent: A case study of 'Instawareness' as a means to heighten awareness and understanding of Instagram's algorithm. *Information Communication and Society*, *0*(0), 1–21. doi:10.1080/1369118X.2021.1883707

Gherardi, S. (2017). Digitized and decoupled? Teacher sensemaking around educational technology in a model 1:1 program. *Mid-Western Educational Researcher*, *29*(2), 166–194.

Grandinetti, J., & Bruinsma, J. (2022). The Affective Algorithms of Conspiracy TikTok. *Journal of Broadcasting & Electronic Media*, 1–20. doi:10.1080/08838151.2022.2140806

Hallman, H. L. (2019). Personalized learning through 1:1 technology initiatives: Implications for teachers and teaching in neoliberal times. *Teaching Education*, *30*(3), 299–318. doi:10.1080/10476210.2018.1466874

Hassinger-Das, B., Dore, R. A., Aloisi, K., Hossain, M., Pearce, M., & Paterra, M. (2020). Children's reality status judgments of digital media: Implications for a covid-19 world and beyond. *Frontiers in Psychology*, *11*, 570068. doi:10.3389/fpsyg.2020.570068 PMID:33240158

Head, A. J., DeFrain, E., Fister, B., & MacMillan, M. (2019). Across the great divide: How today's college students engage with news. *First Monday*, *24*(8), 1–64. doi:10.5210/fm.v24i8.10166

Head, A. J., Fister, B., & MacMillan, M. (2020). *Information literacy in the age of algorithms: Student experiences with news and information, and the need for change. executive summary*. Project Information Literacy. https://eric.ed.gov/?id=ED605107

Kaiser, J., & Rauchfleisch, A. (2020). Birds of a Feather Get Recommended Together: Algorithmic Homophily in YouTube's Channel Recommendations in the United States and Germany. *Social Media + Society*, *6*(4), 2056305120969914. doi:10.1177/2056305120969914

Kalogeropoulos, A., Suiter, J., Udris, L., & Eisenegger, M. (2019). News media trust and news consumption: Factors related to trust in news in 35 countries. *International Journal of Communication*, *13*(0), 22.

Kern, M. L., Waters, L. E., Adler, A., & White, M. A. (2015). A multidimensional approach to measuring well-being in students: Application of the PERMA framework. *The Journal of Positive Psychology*, *10*(3), 262–271. doi:10.1080/17439760.2014.936962 PMID:25745508

Lacković, N. (2021). Postdigital living and algorithms of desire. *Postdigital Science and Education, 3*(2), 280–282. doi:10.100742438-020-00141-4

Lindh, M., & Nolin, J. (2016). Information we collect: Surveillance and privacy in the implementation of google apps for education. *European Educational Research Journal, 15*(6), 644–663. doi:10.1177/1474904116654917

Livingstone, S., Ólafsson, K., O'Neill, B., & Donoso, V. (2012, June). *Towards a better internet for children: Findings and recommendations from EU Kids Online to inform the CEO coalition*. The London School of Economics and Political Science. http://www.eukidsonline.net/

National Governors Association Center for Best Practices & Council of Chief State School Officers. (2010). *Common core state standards (English language arts)*. National Governors Association Center for Best Practices, Council of Chief State School Officers. http://www.corestandards.org/ELA-Literacy/

Neumann, M. M., & Herodotou, C. (2020). Young Children and YouTube: A global phenomenon. *Childhood Education, 96*(4), 72–77. doi:10.1080/00094056.2020.1796459

O'Callaghan, D., Greene, D., Conway, M., Carthy, J., & Cunningham, P. (2015). Down the (white) rabbit hole: The extreme right and online recommender systems. *Social Science Computer Review, 33*(4), 459–478. doi:10.1177/0894439314555329

Rideout, V., & Robb, M. B. (2019). *The Common Sense Census: Media Use by Tweens and Teens, 2019*. Common Sense Media. https://www.commonsensemedia.org/research/the-common-sense-census-media-use-by-tweens-and-teens-2019

Sauers, N. J., & Richardson, J. W. (2019). Leading the pack: Developing empowering responsible use policies. *Journal of Research on Technology in Education, 51*(1), 27–42. doi:10.1080/15391523.2018.1539644

Seligman, M. E. P., & Csikszentmihalyi, M. (2000). Positive psychology: An introduction. *The American Psychologist, 55*(1), 5–14. doi:10.1037/0003-066X.55.1.5 PMID:11392865

Seligman, M. E. P., Ernst, R. M., Gillham, J., Reivich, K., & Linkins, M. (2009). Positive education: Positive psychology and classroom interventions. *Oxford Review of Education, 35*(3), 293–311. doi:10.1080/03054980902934563

Shin, D. (2020). User perceptions of algorithmic decisions in the personalized AI system: Perceptual evaluation of fairness, accountability, transparency, and explainability. *Journal of Broadcasting & Electronic Media, 64*(4), 541–565. doi:10.1080/08838151.2020.1843357

Stone, J. A. (2017). The impact of technology exposure on student perceptions of a 1:1 program. *Education and Information Technologies, 22*(5), 2281–2309. doi:10.100710639-016-9541-6

Swart, J. (2021). Experiencing algorithms: How young people understand, feel about, and engage with algorithmic news selection on social media. *Social Media + Society, 7*(2). doi:10.1177/20563051211008828

Tedre, M., Toivonen, T., Kahila, J., Vartiainen, H., Valtonen, T., Jormanainen, I., & Pears, A. (2021). Teaching Machine Learning in K–12 Classroom: Pedagogical and Technological Trajectories for Artificial Intelligence Education. *IEEE Access : Practical Innovations, Open Solutions*, *9*, 110558–110572. doi:10.1109/ACCESS.2021.3097962

van Dijck, J. (2013). Youtube beyond technology and cultural form. In J. Teurlings & M. de Valck (Eds.), *After the Break: Television Theory Today* (pp. 147–160). Amsterdam University Press. doi:10.1515/9789048518678-010

van Reijmersdal, E. A., Rozendaal, E., Smink, N., van Noort, G., & Buijzen, M. (2017). Processes and effects of targeted online advertising among children. *International Journal of Advertising*, *36*(3), 396–414. doi:10.1080/02650487.2016.1196904

Waters, L., & White, M. (2015). Case Study of a School Wellbeing Initiative: Using Appreciative Inquiry to Support Positive Change. *International Journal of Wellbeing*, *5*(1), 1. Advance online publication. doi:10.5502/ijw.v5i1.2

Zenone, M., Ow, N., & Barbic, S. (2021). TikTok and public health: A proposed research agenda. *BMJ Global Health*, *6*(11), e007648. doi:10.1136/bmjgh-2021-007648 PMID:34819326

Chapter 12
Guidelines for Teachers on the Use of Digital Games on SDG-Relevant Topics in Geography Classes

Alexandra Budke
University of Cologne, Germany

ABSTRACT

The chapter is concerned with the use of digital games in educating about societal challenges connected to the Sustainable Development Goals (SDG) in geography classes. The first part of the chapter summarizes the potentials of the medium and answers the question of why bringing games into the classroom is worth the effort. Subsequently, the chapter offers guidelines to aid teachers in making this step, including guidance on how to choose the right game for the given purpose, how to integrate the game into the lesson, and most importantly, how to reflect on the playing experience with the students.

INTRODUCTION

The 17 Sustainable Development Goals (SDG)[1] formulated by the United Nations aim to achieve a systemic change of the global society in order to face current societal challenges and to create an ecologically and socially healthy, just world. Addressing the relevant societal issues and challenges in education is essential to raise empowered individuals who will implement the SDGs in the future. The issues and challenges, such as global food security, climate change, sustainable consumption, and production, are highly complex, and the contexts are often abstract.

As interactive media, digital games have unique potential for teaching complex SDG-relevant content in the classroom, such as the opportunity for explorative learning in complex contexts (Geithner & Menzel, 2016; Van Eck, 2006), practicing problem-solving (Gaber, 2007), and being introduced to other perspectives (Fromme et al., 2008). Many digital entertainment games already represent SDG-relevant topics and current societal issues such as climate change or resource conflicts, which are also addressed

DOI: 10.4018/978-1-7998-5033-5.ch012

in geography lessons. To benefit from games' potentials, digital games should be included in formal learning contexts (Medienberatung NRW, 2020, p. 21), as adolescents are considered to influenced by how the societal issues are presented, particularly as they are often in regular contact with this medium in their free time (MPFS, 2020, p. 54). As such, it is the responsibility of school teachers to build competence in dealing with this kind of medium, and in turn the games give them the opportunity to create more compelling and possibly more effective lessons on complex societal challenges.

The following guidelines aim to aid teachers to achieve the above. As our re-analysis of teacher interviews on political education in geography lessons has shown that digital games are not yet considered by teachers when planning and delivering education about SDG-relevant topics, guidelines such as ours may aid those educators who are open to teaching with this interactive, powerful, yet complex medium to make their first steps.

The guidelines are based on our research within the project DiSpielGeo. Within the project we, researchers from the Institute for Geography Education of the University of Cologne and from the Cologne Game Lab of TH Köln, conducted a range of studies on the potentials and limits of digital entertainment games for geography education on complex social and socio-ecological topics (Czauderna & Budke, 2020, 2021; Lux & Budke, 2020a, 2020b; Lux et al., in preparation). This research has been consultative and engaged with scientists working in the field of geography education and media education, game designers and game players. These studies focused mainly on strategy and simulation games, such as *SimCity*, *Cities: Skylines*, *Tropico 6*, and similar, which cover at least one of the societal topics of climate change, (sustainable) resource use, urban development and migration. Our studies consisted of analyses of their complexity, content, decision-making design and significance for political education, as well as of interviews with game designers and players. On the basis of these studies we derived practical guidelines for all involved use of geography-relevant games in the classroom. In our studies, we have worked out the advantages of digital games, as well as the possible disadvantages and challenges. This was a starting point for the guidelines, which aim to help teachers recognise the advantages and sensitise them to the challenges that should be taken into account when planning lessons with digital games. In addition, the game analysis revealed that the games differ in many characteristics. This has led to the formulation of guidelines to help take these differences into account when selecting games and using them in the classroom.

This chapter summarizes our research insights and gives an overview of the recommendations we derived. A detailed version is accessible online at www.dispielgeo.de. We do not claim these guidelines to be complete, but they can be used to get an initial overview of how to create geography classes with games. They include insights we could gain from our ground research on entertainment games that cover SDG-relevant, complex topics, but we are always keen on expanding them. Anyone is welcome to add to them with their experience and should not hesitate to contact us via our project website.

BACKGROUND: WHY USE DIGITAL GAMES IN CLASS TO TEACH ON SDG-RELEVANT TOPICS?

The approach of "game-based learning" has been developed and implemented in the classroom for many years. Games are used to encourage learning. The players interact with the systems according to certain rules and solve tasks in order to succeed in the game. New spaces for action and experience are created in which players can act and learn individually. With regard to digital games, it has long been known that they can increase player motivation (overview in Breitschaft, 2022) and contribute to knowledge acquisition (overview in Boyle et al., 2016).

When looking at the Learning objectives for achieving the SDGs published by UNESCO (2017), studies on digital strategy games show that five of the eight key competencies for sustainability can be promoted particularly well through the use of digital games in geography lessons. The competencies not discussed below have not yet been empirically studied in the context of digital games. Therefore, no results are available as to whether these can also be promoted through digital games.

UNSESCO (2017) formulates the promotion of “systems thinking competency” as a central goal of education for sustainable development. An analysis of 13 commercial strategy games conducted by us shows that the majority of the games analysed address at least two of the topics of climate change, migration and (sustainable) resource use simultaneously and place them in the context of urban and regional development (Lux & Budke, 2020a). The players can thus find out whilst playing the game what influence certain factors, such as actions in the area of use of resources, have on climate change. This allows them to experience “how systems are embedded within different domains” in the sense of the SDG goals of UNESCO (2017, p. 10). It was observed that central topics and curricular contents of geography lessons are included in these analysed games in an interconnected way (Lux & Budke, 2020a).

The detailed analysis shows that in 16 out of 18 games analysed, more than 10 different parameters or variables, including temperature, population growth and finances, are simultaneously influenced by the player actions (Lux & Budke, 2020b). In particularly demanding games such as Anno 2070 or Civilization VI, players even have to control more than 40 interrelated variables simultaneously. Many of the games studied show the effects of action decisions at different scale levels and thus correspond to the SDG goal of UNESCO (2017) that states it should be understood that “systems are embedded within different…scales” (p. 10). In the open-world simulation ECO, for example, each player can mine, harvest and build on local levels, which influences the region and ultimately causes global climate change. Overall, it can be stated that many strategy games model real-world issues as complex systems and are therefore suitable for teaching systems competence in the sense of Education for Sustainable Development (Lux & Budke, 2020b). However, this does not apply to all of the games studied and a minority of strategy and simulation games are less complex. The less complex games are mobile games like SimCity BuildIt and Pocket City as it is not possible for players in this case to keep track of a large number of factors that can be influenced on the small display. These games are deemed to be least suitable for engaging students in systemic thinking. The finding that commercial strategy games can teach systems thinking competency is also supported by studies by Adams (1998) and Manocchia (1999). Adams (1998), who has used SimCity in geography courses, saw the advantage of the game as general knowledge about the city as a complex system is taught using a clear example: “In regard to the growth of cities, computer modelling such as is possible in SimCity permits geographical teaching to combine the generality of a mathematical model with the complexity and individuality of a particular observation or example” (p. 51).

There are some studies that show that the “critical thinking competency” as another learning objective for achieving the SDGs developed by UNESCO (2017, p. 10) can also be achieved through digital strategy games. A meta-analysis of 14 studies on the efficacy of CBGs as an effective pedagogical tool shows that some studies demonstrate that after using the games, students were able to successfully critique and describe the games’ limitations (Breitschaft, 2022, p. 18). Nilsson and Jakobsson (2011), who used the city simulation game SimCity in class, found that some students recognised the limitations of the game mechanic and some criticised the fact that the rules in the game are based upon certain American or Western value systems. Kim and Shin (2016, p.48) also found, in relation to SimCity, that: “The participants critically evaluated whether theories that they learned in the urban geography course worked properly in SimCity." This is particularly important as the analysis by Lux and Budke (2020b) showed that the topics are presented realistically but not exhaustively in the games, so that relevant system elements and relationships are sometimes missing. This needs to be considered when using the game in an educational setting so that no misconceptions are transmitted to the players.

Typical for digital strategy games are "polytelic situations" in which decisions have to be made between several conflicting goals (Betsch et al., 2011, p. 142f.). In these cases, the students have to pursue different, mutually contradictory goals at the same time, such as developing an effective and cheap energy supply, for which they can build coal-fired power plants, and the simultaneous goal of reducing CO_2 emissions in order to stop climate change.

In fact, decisions are the essence of digital games and may explain their fascination. For example, Sid Meier, a famous game developer whose work includes the famous "SimCity games", said: "A game is a series of interesting decisions" (Meier cited in Adler, 2008, p. 28). Therefore, the learning objective for achieving the SDGs developed by UNESCO (2017), the "anticipatory competency", which includes "the abilities to understand and evaluate multiple futures" (p. 10) can be promoted very well through digital games. The possible effects of decisions players make in the game must be anticipated in order to be successful in the context of the game system.

In the language of game design, the polytelic situation initiates a "gameplay loop" (Salen & Zimmerman, 2003, p. 316; Czauderna & Guardiola, 2019), which models the players' actions in interaction with the game as a circular relationship between decision, action, and feedback from the game (Czauderna & Budke, 2020). This loop gives the players the opportunity to realise the effectiveness of their own decisions, i.e., to experience self-efficacy, as well as to get to know the consequences and complexity of their decisions and, ideally, to critically evaluate their own decisions and, if necessary, to repeat, adapt or revise them during the course of the game. These complex decisions are made in digital strategy games as part of a complex problem-solving process. Therefore, the SDG learning objective "integrated problem-solving competency" formulated by UNESCO (2017, p. 10) can be achieved very well through digital games. This was also confirmed in a study by Yang (2012) who used a city simulation game with students in class. The study showed that digital games can be more effective in improving students' problem solving competence than traditional teaching. Closely linked to the above is "strategic competency" as another SDG learning objective of UNESCO (2017). Sustainable solutions for the future can be explored in many digital games that address resource use, climate change and/or urban development by players (Lux & Budke, 2020a). "Interacting with a game requires a constant cycle of hypothesis formulation, testing, and revision" (van Eck, 2006, p. 20). However, only in a few of the collective solutions for these games can be developed together with other players, as in the game ECO. The majority of commercial strategy games analysed are single-player games and so do not offer this possibility (Lux & Budke, 2022a).

The literature review shows it is potentially possible to achieve goals that correspond to the ESD learning goals (UNESCO, 2017). However, whether these goals are actually achieved depends on the games used and the respective didactic embedding in the lesson, for which the following guidelines can be helpful.

GUIDELINES FOR THE USE OF DIGITAL GAMES IN CLASS

The following sections summarize the guidelines on the use of games in class that we have derived from our studies, and also include some practical advice that we have concluded from our experience.

Selection of Games

The first hurdle to overcome is selection of the right game to achieve the set learning goals. The vast choice of products available can be a challenge for teachers, particularly when they have no previous experience in teaching with games. Therefore, we want to give some guidance on this first step. The first choice to make is between the usage of serious or learning games and entertainment games. Though games for learning are already tailored for specific learning goals, various authors argue that such games are not the only valid choice for educational purposes. Commercial entertainment games have their own advantages, and we would like to encourage teachers to try these games. Our research has shown that entertainment games that center on social or socio-ecological, SDG-relevant challenges cover many aspects of geography curricula (Lux & Budke, 2020b). They do deviate from reality in many aspects, but even those deviations can be useful, as a discussion point for reflection in class and for fostering critical media literacy (Lux & Budke, 2020b; Lux, Budke & Guardiola, 2021; Van Eck, 2006). Strategy and simulation games are, according to our research (see Lux & Budke, 2020a), particularly geographically complex as they include, for example, various actors that are associated with the SDG-relevant issues such as climate change and a sustainable city development, as well as operating on multiple scale levels and incorporating complex cause-effect-relationships. In contrast, educational games that currently exist are often less motivating, less complex and offer less freedom of action (e.g., Shen et al., 2009), which is attributed to these games rarely being developed by experienced game developers, resulting in games that have boring game mechanics that are additional to the content, rather than merging the two in an engaging way. As such, we recommend to, at least, be open to the use of commercial games. In the following sections we have collected some criteria that will aid teachers choosing the right game for educating on SDG-relevant topics.

Regarding General Determining Factors, Considering Technical Preconditions, Topic, Age Appropriateness, and Accessibility!

General preconditions for game selection narrow the choice of games that can be used. The first decision to be made is the platform of the game, meaning computer or mobile devices. Generally, we recommend using computer games when it comes to teaching complex geographical topics, as they are usually more complex than mobile games (see Lux & Budke, 2020a, p. 28). Mobile games can be a valid choice as if they include sufficient geographical content and if the simplifications are reflected upon. Mobile games have the advantage of being easy to implement with the students' own hardware and they allow for more flexible playing times.

The next aspect to consider is appropriateness for the class and learning goal. This does not only involve the official age recommendation (for example by the "Pan-European Game Information" (PEGI) on https://pegi.info), but also the appropriateness of the content with regard to the curriculum. The game should at least cover some of the relevant aspects of a curricular topic. This does not mean that the game needs to be highly realistic in this aspect, as it is also valuable for media literacy and gaining subject knowledge to compare a game's simplifications with reality (Van Eck, 2006, p. 23). Additionally, some games assume a certain level of prior subject knowledge (for example, *Democracy* requires you to know what the GDP is), which in turn influences their suitability of a game for different grade levels. Information on this can be found in gameplay videos on platforms such as YouTube, or in game Wikis.

How much time it takes to encounter the societal topics in the game is also relevant to the feasibility for use in a class – is the game relevant from the start, or do players need to play for a number of hours before they need to make SDG-relevant decisions? For example, the main topic of *Fate of the World* is climate change, so pupils deal with it right away, while in *Civilization VI – Gathering Storm* it takes several hours until climate change becomes relevant, which makes the latter of these games more suitable for project weeks. To find out the relevance of a geographical topic in the game being considered you can use websites of game journals and trailers on YouTube or on game distribution platforms such as Steam, GOG or similar. You can also research whether a game is multiplayer (cooperative or competitive) or for single players on these platforms, which influences the extent of collaboration in class during play and may also be a factor in game selection.

Socio-Ecological Challenges and System Complexity

Aside from general factors to be considered, geographical content is the most important aspect to consider when choosing a game for use in a class. Games should at least partially represent the complexity of geographic systems, with their various actors, scale levels, and system relationships, an aspect that is also important to achieve the "systems thinking competency" as a goal in education for sustainable development formulated by UNSESCO (2017, p. 10).

We recommend choosing a game that represents at least two SDG-relevant societal topics, such as climate change and resource use in *ECO* or *Civilization VI – Gathering Storm* or city development, migration and resource use in *Tropico 6* (for an overview of topics in our game selection, see Lux & Budke, 2020b, p. 25). The inclusion of two or more topics enables depiction of interconnections between different social or socio-economical phenomena and resulting conflicting goals, which can then be discussed in class to build up system competence. Figure 1 shows an example of conflicting goals in the context of societal issues that we found in one of our game analyses (Lux & Budke, 2020b, p. 33), with the goals in this example being emission reduction for climate protection and ecological sustainability, which are in conflict with goals of both economic and population growth.

Figure 1. Selection of conflicting goals within the analyzed games
Lux and Budke (2020b, p. 33)

It is then important that legitimate positions to the chosen topic are represented (as recommended by Czauderna & Budke, 2020), as well as multiple perspectives on this issue. In games, this can be achieve, for example, by inclusion of different actors through whom the immanent conflicts become understandable, such as the political and interest groups in *Democracy* or *Tropico*. The games should also allow players to explore multiple paths to success, to enable them to try different approaches (Czauderna & Budke, 2020). As such, simulation and strategy games are a recommended genre, as overpowered roles incorporate in such games often give players the opportunity to experiment with different solutions.

Incorporating the Game Into Class

As we recommend the use of games that represent complex geographic systems (see Lux & Budke, 2020a), exploring the game intensively before bringing it into class is a required step. Otherwise, some potential may be lost if important aspects are overlooked in the discussion (Silseth, 2012), particularly if aspects are not brought up by students themselves (Peters & Vissers, 2004, p. 81), or if students' questions about the game cannot be answered. On the basis of this intensive engagement with the game, the lesson plan can be created and decisions can be made regarding the didactic placement of the game (introduction phase or elaboration phase) and about the technical integration (live gaming, playing together via projector, videos, or similar).

Decide on the Phase in Which the Game is Incorporated and in Which Way the Students Should Engage With the Game

Games can be used for both introducing a topic and for deepening the understanding of a topic. In the former, the game can be used to explore a topic (interactively) and to determine which aspects are important. For example, in the case of sustainable urban development, to find out what measures could be taken to make a city more sustainable. If used in the elaboration phase, the game should be used to test learned theories or deepen understanding of cause-effect-relationships. we strongly advise against using the game in an assessment phase. The performance in the game should not be evaluated, as this is contrary to the idea of play and negates many advantages of the medium, namely the experimentation without real consequences, the explorative learning, and the motivational effect.

To make full use of a games' potential, students should get the opportunity to play the games themselves, to enable them to explore different solution strategies to geographical problems on their own, and to share their own experiences in the debriefing phase. If the technical preconditions at school or the budget do not allow for individual gaming in class, it is an option to play the game together on one device using a projector. If there are no options to play any games or a specific game in class, there is the option of showing gameplay videos (for example on YouTube) in class and discussing game experiences (part of) the pupils made in their free time. This may mean that a lot of potential is lost, especially if students have not played the game(s) themselves in their free time, as first-hand experience, in every discipline, is particularly instructive (Montessori, 1949). However, this method can still provide a fruitful lesson if enough time is scheduled for the reflection.

Integrate the Game Into the Lesson Plan and Create Supplementary Material

It is crucial to set learning goals and establish the link to the curriculum. The lesson should start with a preparation for the problem or question that should be solved or explored in the game. Thus, it shall introduce the problem, activate the students' previous knowledge and evoke interest in the topic. For example, a lesson on city development that uses a city builder game (such as *Cities: Skylines* or *SimCity BuildIt*), could start with impressions from the city the students live in, to connect to the personal life of the pupils.

The gaming (or streaming) session should be connected to a precise task and the overall learning goal of the lesson. If for example the lesson is about learning about the causes of climate change, then the task for the playing session (e.g., with *ECO* or *Democracy 3 and 4*) could be to try out different political approaches in the game and note down how they influence climatic change. In case you can only include gameplay videos or play via beamer, there should be a task while watching nonetheless. We recommend that results from this phase be documented in writing as a basis for the reflection later on – for example, a table on the causes of climate change in the game. Then, we also recommend to collect the pupils' impressions on the gameplay session before starting with the reflection. An open discussion on what the students liked and didn't like about the game is a good option to get the discussion going.

Depending on the learning goals and the reflection that should take place, respective material for debriefing is required – for example if the lesson shall concern the complexity of city development, you may need informative texts or interviews with real actors in urban development.

Debriefing With Reflection

The most important task of teachers in the context of game-based learning is leading a content-related reflection. Discussing and reflecting on the gaming session triggers learning processes (Crookall, 2010; Kriz, 2010; Schwägele, 2021) meaning the process is fruitful for learning, even when the game deviates from reality or misses important content (Van Eck, 2006, p. 24), and it also strengthens the media competence of pupils (Medienberatung NRW, 2020, p. 21). The reflection stage is also important to achieve the "critical thinking competency" learning objective for reaching the SDGs developed by UNESCO (2017, p. 10) through the use of games. The limits of the game can be recognized by comparing it to reality outside the game. However, this stage must be guided by the teacher.

Both the group debriefing (as recommended by Peters & Vissers, 2004) and conversation about individual experiences (whose importance is stressed, e.g., by Lederman, 1992) are important part of the reflection process. The reflection can be placed at the end of a gaming session or in between. As an orientation on which parts of the game should be considered for a thorough and the most fruitful reflection, the model on our study on realism in games can be used (Figure 2) (see Lux et al., 2021, p. 3ff.).

Figure 2. Types of realism in games (inner square: internal realism; second square: external realism; outer square: perceived realism; dimensions: system, narrative, action, sensory)
Lux et al. (2021, p. 3)

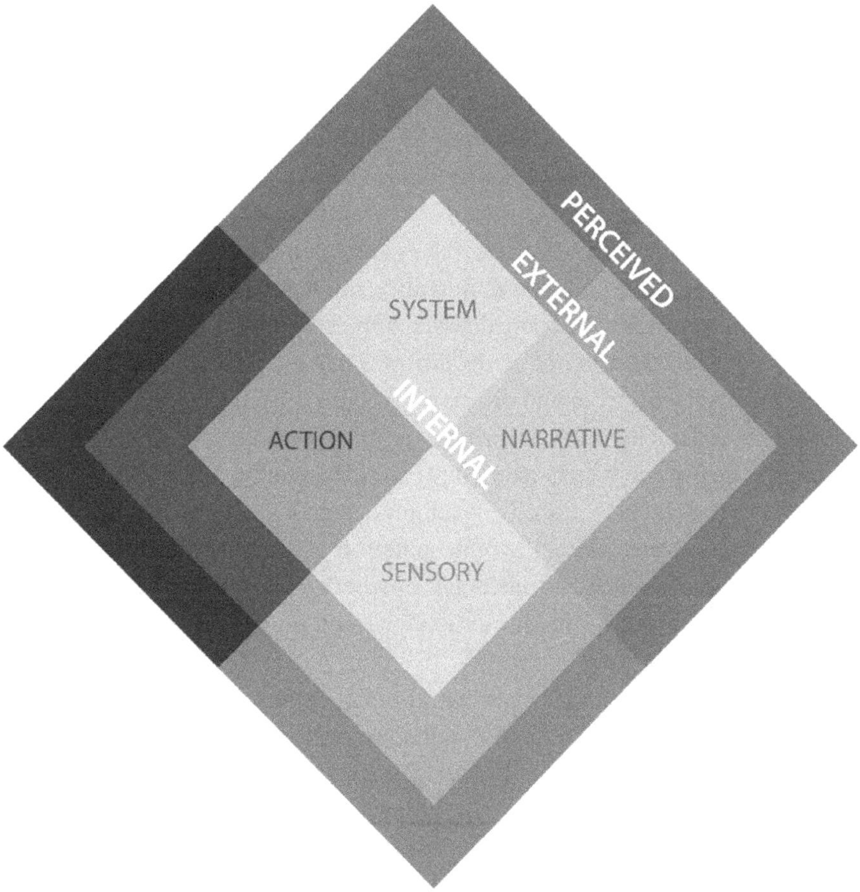

The model, developed on the basis of literature on game studies and our own analyses, shows that there are three layers of realism in games: An internal one, an external one, and a perceived one. The internal realism is concerned with the internal logic in the game. Questions that arise in the context of internal logic may be: How are the (human-environment-) systems with all their elements, actors and cause-effect-relationships designed so that it makes inherent sense; Are the effects of actions logical within the gameworld? Are the actors' actions and the story coherent?; How do the visuals support the worldbuilding? The external realism element is about the comparison with the real world outside the game, based on the current state of research. An example of this is determining how realistic the cause-effect-relationships are compared to the real-world system, whether all actors who are important in that context depicted in the game and which parts of the system are simplified. The outer layer of the model expresses how both internal and external realism are perceived by the player engaging with the game, and how their impression of the two may vary greatly and may not necessarily be what was intended by the game designers. In all three approaches to realism one can look at different dimensions: The systemic dimension, for example the climate system presented in a game; the narrative dimension, the story, and characters of the game; the dimension of action, mostly what the player can do within the game system and lastly, the sensory dimension, meaning everything connected to visuals and sounds. The three types of realism and their dimensions can give first clues on which parts of the game can be reflected upon in the debriefing phase. The parts we consider most important for a thorough reflection that promotes competencies in the context of SDG-relevant topics will be summarized in the following section.

Reflect Upon the Game System Itself

The first step of reflection on the game is the game system itself, so the representation and interconnections between topics within the game (see Figure 2, inner square, "system"). Understanding how the geographical system in the game works is the basis for a discussion on parallels and deviations from reality later on. The different parts of these systems are a good orientation exercise to determine which parts of a game to reflect upon in class. For one, the system elements could be focused upon. The game equivalent to actors and structures/ factors are, in reality, the virtual actors (players, non-player characters, virtual parties/interest groups), the controllable parameters (all variables that players can influence indirectly, such as the budget, the level of environmental damage, the number of inhabitants etc.) and the antagonistic factors (everything beyond the players' control, such as natural disasters or natural preconditions) (see Lux & Budke, 2020a, p. 6ff). For example, the actors could be the focus of reflection, by making the students determine which actors have an influence on a specific geographic issue in the game. For instance, the actors influencing city development in *Tropico* are the inhabitants, local political groups and political partner states. Then, the representation of these actors could be discussed, such as whether the city population is depicted as one mass, or whether they have differing needs and opinions, or whether there are interest groups. The discussion can then be used as a transition to a reflection on parallels and deviations to reality.

In real-world systems, processes, so the cause-and-effect-relations and interdependencies within the system, are also important (DGfG, 2020, p. 11). In games, particularly from the strategy and simulation genre, these can be found, too (see Lux & Budke, 2020a). Each action in a game has an influence on the virtual world. In the reflection phase you can, for example, explore how different parameters in the game are interconnected, meaning how changes in one variable (e.g., the number of traffic jams) affect other variables (e.g. the satisfaction of inhabitants and the greenhouse gas emissions), which then again influence the next. As different levels of scale are important to the subject of geography (DGfG, 2020, p. 11), it is also useful to reflect on how actions on one scale level in the game influence other scale levels. For example, how local measures can affect global climate change, how local city development influences the surrounding region or how international migration influences a city. These reflections on the in-game system are a good basis for the later stages of reflection, particularly when it comes to the comparison to reality.

It is also worth discuss players' approaches, solutions and strategies within the game. According to Charsky (2010), the full potential of a problem-based approach used in games can only be utilized in an educational context when the approaches of players are discussed with their teachers and peers in class. In the context of societal challenges, we particularly recommend reflecting upon players' strategies to deal with conflicting goals (such as those shown in Figure 1) that they encountered while solving social or socio-ecological issues. Questions to start a discussion could include the following: In which situations did you make the most conflicting decisions? Or, more precisely, In which decision-making situations did you need to weigh up ecological, economic, and social aspects? How did you decide the action you took and why?

During this phase, it may also be useful to consider exactly how decision-making works in the game. The decision-making in games is always based on a loop (Czauderna & Budke, 2020; Salen & Zimmerman, 2003). First, a problem/conflict/decision-making-situation occurs, then the player makes a decision, leading to an action taken, which in turn leads to a reaction by the game that is communicated via feedback, which then leads to new decision-making-situations and gives a basis for the next decision, while time modification and mediation of the choice of actions can assist in the decision-making. This process can also be reflected upon in class. Questions that can be posed could be: Which (geography-related) decision-making-situations did you find most interesting/ difficult and why?; What was the outcome of your choice (regarding the geographical issue)?; How did the game communicate the outcome to you?; Did others in class decide differently and why?; In hindsight, what do you think was the most beneficial strategy and why do you think so? Questions like these can also be used as an easy transition to the next step, which is the comparison to reality.

Reflect Upon the Parallels To and Deviations From Real-Life Systems

The next step in the debriefing process should consider the comparison to reality, which is crucial for making the connection to real-life societal issues and for preventing misinformation (see also Figure 2, second square). In an interview study with game designers, we found that intensive research (in the sense of information gathering) on societal issues is carried out when developing a game. However, this has rarely been undertaken with the help of scientific sources (Lux, Budke & Guardiola, 2021). On the one hand, this means that many aspects of the topics shown in common media are interwoven into the game, but on the other, excluding current scientific insights may lead to deviances from the current state of knowledge. Furthermore, we found that external realism, which aims to realistically depict aspects of real life, is often of lower priority than other forms of realism (ibid.). Of higher priority are internal realism, so game-internal logics that may have no connection to reality, and perceived realism, meaning that commonly believed concepts are depicted (even when they're wrong) to make the game content *seem* more realistic. First and foremost, game designers feel an obligation to entertain, and their awareness of their influence on the education of game players varies (Czauderna & Budke, 2021).

Debriefing on parallels and deviances of games from the real world can help to avoid the forming of misconceptions that could stem from these common practices, and it may strengthen the critical view that should be applied when dealing with information from any form of media. As Van Eck (2006) suggests, as a first step teachers can let the students discover for themselves the point at which their knowledge and the game content clash, to create a "cognitive disequilibrium" (p. 24). Then, we recommend providing material that looks at the social issues in question from a scientific perspective, as well as authentic material (e.g., newspaper articles, witness accounts/interviews). In this way, students can compare the game content and their own background knowledge to the state of research and current authentic sources.

During this phase of reflection, it is also helpful to consider the different forms of realism in games and discuss what kind of realism was emphasized most or least in the respective game. When you pick a certain situation in the game, it may, for example, be discussed as to whether the situation is internally realistic, so logically coherent, and/ or externally realistic, meaning that it could be like that in reality. Then, the class could determine which aspects of realism were emphasized: Was it the graphics and sounds? The actions that can be taken? The story? Or the geographical system with all its actors and factors? An overview of the different types of realism can be found in Lux et al. (2021).

Additionally, a further idea for debriefing could be to identify the strategies by which game designers deal with real societal issues. If an aspect is not externally represented realistically, how was it depicted? Was it completely left out? Or sugarcoated? Replaced with fictional content? For example, slavery in Anno 1800 appears in the story, but was, according to our designer interviews (Lux et al., 2021), completely left out of gameplay so as to not depict it as something players can have fun with. A discussion about such strategies may help to raise awareness that game content depends on the choice of its designers. Also, it may aid in identifying the political message of the designers that is interwoven in the game. Thus, a reflection on how designers deal with geographic topics could also counteract an ideological influence, in line with the Beutelsbach Consensus (Czauderna & Budke, 2021, p. 113). It might also be worthwhile explicitly discussing the tension between commercial intentions and constraints of the developers and publishers and political/ educational "side effects" or even political/ educational aspirations (ibid.). With such reflection, media literacy can be further promoted in a way that it is required to be fostered in school (e.g., Hobbs & Jensen, 2009; Medienberatung NRW, 2020).

Let the Players Reflect Upon Themselves

Whilst gaming, the pupils also learn something about themselves, at the very least about their personality in the game (and those of their fellow players), meaning their playing style. For example, they may learn about whether they rather seek or avoid conflicts in the game and why. If guided well, they may also learn about their (political) attitudes and moral concepts, for example whether they always try to build a sustainable city because this is an important topic to them in real life. We therefore recommend taking the time for self-reflection to promote personal growth.

As an incentive for discussion, it may be a good idea to use questions similar to those we posed in our study with players. They can be follow-up questions to the ones referring to the players' actions in the game. For example, the question "Why did you act in the game the way you did?" can be followed by "Would you act the same way in reality? Why/ why not?". As our interviews with players have shown, such questions mostly trigger reflection on their "gamer personality". When discussed in more depth, you may also trigger further insights into player's own personality, such as the political attitude that may influence the actions taken and the decisions made in the game. In our current study, it has become apparent that comparison to other players helps to position oneself and one's own actions. Often, for example, one's own playing style is compared with that of friends in our interviews. Such comparisons can therefore also be used in a class reflection, and particularly when incorporating questions that let the students' explore their own personality in more depth.

Reflect Upon the Medium of Games!

On the basis of the play experiences and previous reflection steps, a meta-reflection on the medium "game" can also be guided. Meta-reflection in this case means that a distanced view is taken on the medium as a whole and, in the context of the SDGs, particularly regarding the medium's suitability for learning about sustainability and the related topics. It is easiest to start with a critical view on the specific game used, and then to proceed with general considerations on the medium. Impulses for reflection could be:

- Do the students feel like the game in question did teach them about the societal topic considered, for example about the interconnections between city development and climate change or about the actors involved in sustainable resource use? Why/why not?
- Do they consider another game more suitable? Or another medium, such as textbooks, movies, etc.? Why?
- Do the students consider games, in general, a suitable medium for learning about societal topics? Why/why not?
- Which unique advantages and disadvantages of the medium (compared to other media) do the students see, particularly for the learning about current social challenges and phenomena?
- Which aspects do the students think they should look at critically when they play in their free time in the future?
- What could the intentions of the designers be, for example, in the way they present SDG-related topics?

Discussions like these may help to transfer the lessons learned from the game in question to the general medium of games and, as such, further complement the students' media competence.

The exact implementation and design of the reflection phase of a game can be seen, for example, in the teaching concept by Lux and Budke (2022), in which the mobile game SimCity BuildIt is used for the teaching of urban functions in the classroom.

CONCLUSION

The empirical results presented in Chapter two show that there is a wide range of digital games that address topics corresponding to the Sustainable Development Goals defined by the United Nations, which should be addressed in geography lessons. Topics such as sustainable resource use, climate change, sustainable urban development, sustainable industry and energy production are integrated into many digital games (overview in Lux & Budke, 2020b). These topics have also been successfully included in commercial games, as they are considered by responsible game designers to be particularly interesting for players due to their topicality and controversial nature (Lux et al., 2021). Therefore, in addition to serious games, certain commercial games are also suitable for use as learning media in geography lessons. The games that contain SDG-topics are often strategy games that focus on polytelic conflicts, which force players to make decisions about mutually exclusive goals. Numerous empirical studies show that the games are not only motivating for the players (overview in Breitschaft, 2022), but can also promote knowledge acquisition (overview in Boyle et al., 2016). In the context of Education for Sustainable Development (UNESCO, 2017), it is particularly interesting that through playing these games players can potentially achieve "systems thinking competency", "anticipatory competency", "Critical thinking competency", "integrated problem-solving competency" and "strategic competency. In the game system, players can try out the effects of sustainable and less sustainable decisions and get direct feedback on the success and the respective effects. It is particularly interesting that they can recognise the effects of decisions on very different areas of life such as housing, ecology, satisfaction of the residents, etc. with their respective interactions. However, whether the potentials of digital games described in the literature can actually be achieved depends on their precise integration into the classroom. In order to facilitate this process, "guidelines for the use of digital games in class" have been presented in this article, which address both the selection and integration of the game into the lesson as well as the reflection phase. Further key information about our research and publications can be found on our website: https://dispielgeo.de/.

In future, more research should be done to identify exactly which factors determine the successful acquisition of knowledge and skills when using digital games in geography lessons. It would also be useful to empirically investigate to what extent the ideas presented in the aforementioned guidelines contribute to achieving the goals of Education for Sustainable Development among the students. In any case, digital games have a great potential in this area, which should be used even more in school practice.

REFERENCES

Adams, P. C. (1998). Teaching and learning with SimCity 2000. *The Journal of Geography*, *97*(2), 47–55. doi:10.1080/00221349808978827

Adler, F. (2009). *Computerspiele als Lernmedium und ihr Einsatz in den Ingenieurwissenschaften. Erarbeitung eines Analyse- und Entwicklungsmodells* [Doctoral dissertation]. University of Augsburg.

Arnold, U., Söbke, H., & Reichelt, M. (2019). SimCity in Infrastructure Management Education. *Education Sciences*, *2019*(9), 209. doi:10.3390/educsci9030209

Bereitschaft, B. (2021). Commercial city building games as pedagogical tools: What have we learned? *Journal of Geography in Higher Education*, 1–27. doi:10.1080/03098265.2021.2007524

Betsch, T., Funke, J., & Plessner, H. (2011). *Denken- Urteilen, Entscheiden*. Problemlösen. doi:10.1007/978-3-642-12474-7

Charsky, D. (2010). Making a connection: Game genres, game characteristics, and teaching structures. In Gaming and Cognition. Theories and practice from the learning sciences. Information Science Reference (pp. 189-212). IGI Global.

Crookall, D. (2010). Serious games, debriefing, and simulation/gaming as a discipline. *Simulation & Gaming*, *41*(6), 898–920. doi:10.1177/1046878110390784

Czauderna, A., & Budke, A. (2020). How Digital Strategy and Management Games Can Facilitate the Practice of Dynamic Decision-Making. *Education Sciences*, *10*(4), 99. Advance online publication. doi:10.3390/educsci10040099

Czauderna, A., & Budke, A. (2021). Game Designer als Akteure der politischen Bildung. *MedienPädagogik: Zeitschrift für Theorie und Praxis der Medienbildung*, *38*, 94–116. doi:10.21240/mpaed/38/2021.01.25.X

Czauderna, A., & Guardiola, E. (2019). The Gameplay Loop Methodology as a Tool for Educational Game Design. *Electronic Journal of e-Learning*, *17*(3), 201-227. https://issuu.com/academic-conferences.org/docs/ejel-volume17-issue3-article682?mode=a_p

Fromme, J., Jörissen, B., & Unger, A (2008). Bildungspotenziale Digitaler Spiele Und Spielkulturen. *MedienPädagogik: Zeitschrift für Theorie Und Praxis Der Medienbildung, 15*, 1-23. doi:10.21240/mpaed/15_16/2008.12.22.X

Gaber, J. (2007). Simulating Planning: SimCity as a Pedagogical Tool. *Journal of Planning Education and Research*, *27*(2), 113–121. doi:10.1177/0739456X07305791

Geithner, S., & Menzel, D. (2016). Effectiveness of Learning Through Experience and Reflection in a Project Management Simulation. *Simulation & Gaming*, *47*(2), 228–256. doi:10.1177/1046878115624312

Hobbs, R., & Jensen, A. (2009). The Past, Present, and Future of Media Literacy Education. *The Journal of Media Literacy Education*, *1*(1), 1–11. doi:10.23860/jmle-1-1-1

Kim, M., & Shin, J. (2016). The pedagogical benefits of SimCity in urban geography education. *The Journal of Geography*, *115*(2), 39–50. doi:10.1080/00221341.2015.1061585

Kriz, W. C. (2010). A systemic-constructivist approach to the facilitation and debriefing of simulations and games. *Simulation & Gaming*, *41*(5), 663–680. doi:10.1177/1046878108319867

Lederman, L. C. (1992). Debriefing: Toward a systematic assessment of theory and practice. *Simulation & Gaming*, *23*(2), 145–160. doi:10.1177/1046878192232003

Lux, J.-D., & Budke, A. (2020a). Alles nur ein Spiel? Geographisches Fachwissen zu aktuellen gesellschaftlichen Herausforderungen in digitalen Spielen. *GW Unterricht*, *160*, 22–36. doi:10.1553/gw-unterricht160s22

Lux, J.-D., & Budke, A. (2020b). Playing with Complex Systems? The Potential to Gain Geographical System Competence through Digital Gaming. *Education Sciences*, *10*(5), 130. Advance online publication. doi:10.3390/educsci10050130

Lux, J.-D., & Budke, A. (2022). Die Funktion einer Stadt erleben. Mit Spielen fachliche und mediale Kompetenzen fördern. *Praxis Geographie. H.*, *3*, 11–15.

Lux, J.-D., Budke, A., & Guardiola, E. (2021). Games Versus Reality? How Game Designers Deal with Current Topics of Geography Education. Multimodal Technol. *Interact*, *5*(11), 70. Advance online publication. doi:10.3390/mti5110070

Manocchia, M. (1999). SimCity 2000 Software. *Teaching Sociology*, *27*(2), 212–215. doi:10.2307/1318710

Medienberatung, N. R. W. (2020). *Medienkompetenzrahmen NRW* (3rd ed.). Medienberatung NRW.

Montessori, M. (1949). *The absorbent mind.* Theosophical Publishing House.

MPFS (Medienpädagogischer Forschungsverbund Südwest). (2018). *JIM-Studie 2018 – Jugend, Information, Medien: Basisuntersuchung zum Medienumgang 12- bis 19-Jähriger.* https://www.mpfs.de/fileadmin/files/Studien/JIM/2018/Studie/JIM_2018_Gesamt.pdf

Nilsson, E. M., & Jakobsson, A. (2011). Simulated sustainable societies: Students' reflections on creating future cities in computer games. *Journal of Science Education and Technology*, *20*(1), 33–50. doi:10.100710956-010-9232-9

Peters, V. A. M., & Vissers, G. A. N. (2004). A simple classification model for debriefing simulation games. *Simulation & Gaming*, *35*(1), 70–84. doi:10.1177/1046878103253719

Salen, K., & Zimmerman, E. (2003). *Rules of Play: Game Design Fundamentals.* MIT Press.

Schwägele, S., Zürn, B., Lukosch, H. K., & Freese, M. (2021). Design of an Impulse-Debriefing-Spiral for Simulation Game Facilitation. *Simulation & Gaming*, *52*(3), 364–385. doi:10.1177/10468781211006752

Shen, C., Wang, H., & Ritterfeld, U. (2009). Serious Games and Seriously Fun Games. In U. Ritterfeld, M. Cody, & P. Vorderer (Eds.), *Serious games: Mechanisms and Effects* (pp. 48–61). Routledge.

Silseth, K. (2012). The multivoicedness of game play: Exploring the unfolding of a student's learning trajectory in a gaming context at school. *International Journal of Computer-Supported Collaborative Learning*, *7*(1), 6384. doi:10.100711412-011-9132-x

UNESCO. (2017). *Education for Sustainable Development Goals: learning objectives.* https://unesdoc.unesco.org/ark:/48223/pf0000247444

Van Eck, R. (2006). Digital game-based learning. It's not just the digital natives who are restless. *EDUCAUSE Review*, *41*(2), 55–63.

Yang, Y.-T. C. (2012). Building virtual cities, inspiring intelligent citizens: Digital games for developing students' problem solving and learning motivation. *Computers & Education*, *59*(2), 365–377. doi:10.1016/j.compedu.2012.01.012

ENDNOTE

1 https://sdgs.un.org/goals

Chapter 13
Promoting Education for Sustainable Development Using Blended Learning and Digital Tools:
Two University Courses, One Case Study

Helga Mayr
Universität Innsbruck, Austria

ABSTRACT

While online learning has become the new normal during the pandemic, experience shows the importance of face-to-face encounters with blended learning (BL) as a format that combines both. This chapter presents two interdisciplinary BL, project-based Master's courses. Both use the Sustainable Development Goals as a framework and design thinking as an approach, while one also uses digital tools beyond the digital media necessary for collaboration. After a brief introduction and consideration of the underlying concepts, the course and student reflections on their learning processes are described. The text concludes with considerations regarding the further development of the course.

INTRODUCTION

In the face of major global challenges such as the climate crisis, loss of biodiversity, social disparities, poverty, and health crises, accompanied by unprecedented dynamics of change driven by, among others, digitalization, we seek sustainable solutions. Education, especially education for sustainable development (ESD), is seen as a catalyst for the necessary societal transformation towards sustainable development (SD) (Stoltenberg & Michelsen, 2020; UN, 1992; UNESCO, 2020), by enabling and empowering people to participate in shaping a sustainable future. Digitalization, on the other hand – although it may increase efficiency aimed at conserving resources – is frequently associated with further growth or speed, as well as with maintaining a competitive mindset and practices that fuel an unsustainable development

DOI: 10.4018/978-1-7998-5033-5.ch013

(Ahel & Lingau, 2021; Stoltenberg & Michelsen, 2020), by exploiting natural resources or harming the environment and affected people. Apart from the damage that occurs along the whole life cycle of digital devices, the use of digital media enables the dissemination of fake news; may lead to health harms; and consolidates the power of large digital corporations and their access to data (Mayr & Madritsch, 2022).

Although the negative side effects of digitalization are well known and require urgent global solutions, they do not represent the focus of this paper. Instead, the author uses two specific interdisciplinary university courses at the University of Innsbruck to show how (E)SD, design thinking (DT), and blended learning (BL) can be brought together when designing courses aimed at breaking down major challenges related to (non-)SD and making them manageable for students.

Both courses use the Sustainable Development Goals (SDGs) as a guiding framework. Both follow a design thinking (DT) approach (Brown, 2016), that enables learners to iteratively research, define complex problems, co-creatively develop solutions (McDonald et al., 2018) and collaboratively implement them. Both course designs follow a critical-emancipatory, project-, problem- and solution-based understanding of ESD (Wals, 2011; Vare & Scott, 2007; Mayr & Oberrauch, 2022), and in both courses students are offered both analog and digital teaching-learning spaces in which to work on challenges related to SD in an interdisciplinary and participatory way, through the implementation of a real-world project.

In the past, both courses have had to be adapted to unprecedented developments and situations. The first course was originally designed and implemented as a pure face-to-face (F2F) course but had to be converted to a pure online course due to the pandemic in winter term 2020/21. The second course was originally designed as a BL course, but likewise had to be implemented as a pure online course due to the pandemic. In winter term 2021/22, both courses were finally implemented using a BL format. In doing so, the video conferencing program ZOOM and the digital whiteboard MIRO were used, additional to OLAT, the University's Learning Management System (LMS), which supports file exchange, information sharing, and different communication channels like email and Messenger apps. Using ZOOM and MIRO, students were able to cooperate and interactively collaborate within a virtual space. In one course, students used additional digital tools such as CoSpaces to create virtual realities, or the Locandy platform to develop hybrid scavenger hunts.

This paper describes the design and implementation of the two blended learning (BL) courses, based on theoretical frameworks such as ESD, BL, and DT. Although the focus of the article is not on empirics, an accompanying small research project provides first insights into students' perceived learning processes, as well as into their self-assessment regarding competence development. Moreover, available data helps to assess probable potentials and limits of the BL formats from a student's perspective.

BACKGROUND

In developing and implementing the two BL courses, the challenge was how to optimally integrate the underlying concepts of SD, ESD, digitalization/BL, and DT to most benefit students, given the current situation, uncertain future developments, and the requirements of the new working world. To aid understanding, the concepts underlying the course design are briefly introduced below.

Sustainable Development (SD)

The most common understanding of SD is derived from the Brundlandt report (UN, 1987, p.15) of the World Commission on Environment and Development. This relates to development that ensures that humanity "meets the needs of the present without compromising the ability of future generations to meet their own needs". It reflects a strongly anthropocentric understanding, that considers nature worthy of protection to be useful for humans, but not for the sake of nature itself. Since the publication of the Brundtland report, various models of sustainability have been developed, with more recent ones taking Earth's biophysical limits (Röckström et al., 2009) and minimum social standards (Raworth, 2015) into account. Given the human-made grand global challenges presiding, a strong understanding of sustainability that gives priority to the natural basis of life, should be the concept of choice and "pursued for medium to long-term strategic political planning" (Giannetti 2020). In the 2030 Agenda, the UN General Assembly recognizes that "social and economic development depends on the sustainable management of our planet's natural resources" (UN, 2015, p. 9), but still assumes economic growth, although "inclusive and sustainable" (UN, 2015, p.9), to be essential for human prosperity, without questioning the growth-driven economic system itself. Nor is nature ascribed an intrinsic value that should be protected for its own sake, and not merely as something to be used by humans, as the prevailing anthropocentric mindset conveys. In this sense, the SDGs are still based on a rather weak understanding of SD (Hickel, 2019; Bonnedahl et al., 2022), leading to the challenge to simultaneously minimize trade-offs and maximize synergies between the different goals and targets (Kroll et al., 2019). Nevertheless, the SDGs provide a good framework for sustainability activities in educational settings and beyond, because the 17 goals relate to both human wellbeing and a healthy planet, and are relevant, not only globally, but also nationally, regionally, and locally. The diversity of topics offers plenty of starting points for all stakeholders, such as governments, companies, organizations, institutions, and civil societies, along with opportunities for everyone to become active and contribute to achieving the goals. Moreover, dealing with the SDGs provides an opportunity to critically question and discuss sustainability concepts, as well as dilemmas and challenges associated with sustainability issues.

Education for Sustainable Development (ESD)

ESD not only aims at dealing with sustainability issues, but at empowering people to help in shaping a more sustainable world. Learning opportunities that support the development of key sustainability competencies such as interdisciplinary, critical, forward-looking thinking, problem-solving skills, and the ability to participate (Bormann & Rieckmann, 2020; Rieckmann, 2018, Wiek et al., 2011), enable learners to strengthen their sense of self-efficacy, as well as their ability to reflect and to develop relevant values, attitudes, and motivations (Rieckmann, 2018). Learners should have opportunities to network (Ahel & Lingau, 2021) and to participate in transdisciplinary and participatory learning processes that empower them to take part in shaping a sustainable present and future (Mayr & Oberrauch, 2022); reflect on their individual and collective learning processes in the context of SD; and to transfer learnings to different life worlds and the future. Project-based and problem solving-based learning deliver promising approaches that give students an opportunity to engage with real-world problems in the context of SD, and that in a critical, productive, creative, and effective way (Singer-Browdoski, 2016; Cörvers et al., 2016; Brundiers & Wiek, 2011). The experience of being able to participate in shaping a more sustainable society may strengthen their sense of self-efficacy (Rieckmann, 2018).

Design Thinking (DT)

DT is an approach that could facilitate affirmative experiences that meet the demand for a critically constructive ESD, as described above. Various definitions try to explain what DT means: a holistic concept that enables people to collaborate in multidisciplinary teams and to "enact positive, design-led change in the world, an approach to solve 'wicked problems'" (Rauth et al., 2010, p. 2); a mindset or a process (Panke 2019). Regardless of the definition, DT offers a learning space for students where they systematically start with exploring a problem space, move on to define specific challenges, and co-creatively develop various possible solutions, which are then tested at an early stage with potential users and relevant stakeholders (Beverland et al., 2015). The term "design thinking" evolved from the idea of approaching and solving problems like designers (Panke 2019), in an explorative, iterative, human-centered, collaborative, and co-creative way (Buhl et al., 2019; Brown, 2016). It is now increasingly applied to SD (Buhl et al., 2019; Maher et al., 2018, Brown, 2019). Although DT follows a predetermined process, it leaves room for creativity and critical analysis. Ideally, multidisciplinary teams collaborate (Meinel & von Thienen, 2016), so that as many different perspectives as possible are incorporated into the problem-finding and problem-solving processes.

Digitalization in Education (for SD) and Blended Learning

Digitalization may also support activities in the context of (E)SD, "serving as a lever and support for the Great Transformation towards sustainability" (WBGU, 2019, p.1). In contrast to digitization, the technical process of converting analog to digital information (Zhao et al., 2020), digitalization is seen much more comprehensively as a societal transformation process (von der Hede et al., 2017) providing new options for action and social and economic practices (Stalder, 2019; Gryl et al., 2020; Zhao et al., 2020, Mayr & Oberrauch, 2022). Given the fact that digitalization permeates all areas of life, appropriate educational processes that prepare for a responsible approach to the digital world are needed. These should focus on social and planetary responsibility, providing opportunities for participation, joint construction of knowledge, reflection on experiences, and on educational processes themselves (Stoltenberg & Michelsen, 2020).

Consequently, instead of unreflectively digitalizing learning processes for their own sake, the focus must shift to designing meaningful learning scenarios in the sense of ESD. Or, to put it another way, to developing a new understanding of learning or a new learning culture that adheres to both the paradigm of SD and digitalization. Using BL formats is one possible way of digitizing (university) teaching. Although there are different definitions of BL (Bowyer & Chambers, 2017; Vaughan, 2019), they have in common that BL combines F2F and online interactions. The interactions might, however, differ considerably regarding the degree of integration, ranging from a combination of F2F instruction with computer-mediated instruction, to a "thoughtful integration of classroom F2F learning with online learning experiences" (Garrison & Kanuka, 2004, p. 96), or, in a similar sense, "the organic integration of thoughtfully selected and complementary face-to-face and online approaches and technologies" (Garrison & Vaughan, 2008, p. 148). Mali and Lim (2021), point to studies showing positive effects of BL settings on student achievement, motivation, and engagement, but found that students prefer F2F instruction because it allows for better social interaction. Consequently, when designing BL courses, lecturers must pay attention to how they can support and facilitate social interaction.

Technology integration models such as SAMR[1] (Puentedura 2006), TIM[2] (Marcovitz et al., 2015), or PICRAT[3] (Kimmons et al., 2020), provide frameworks for systematically and thoughtfully designing educational processes using technology. Each of the models has its strengths and weaknesses (Kimmons et al., 2020), but by combining them with educational models that challenge students to "use technology in deep and meaningful ways" (Marcovitz et al., 2015, p. 1227), and that aim at supporting students in developing higher-order thinking skills (Puentedura, 2006), they help to improve and transform educational processes. In this sense, TPACK (Mishra et al., 2006, Shulman, 1986) may serve as an overarching concept in which considerations of the different technology integration models may be incorporated. TPACK tries to integrate Technology into the intersection of Pedagogical knowledge And Content Knowledge of teachers (Ledford, 2016, p. 8), and may encourage lecturers to reflect on "their role in improving their current pedagogy, technological infusion, and syllabus design to enhance student learning and teaching outcome" (Bokolo et al., 2020, p. 565).

Combination of Concepts

The fact that the underlying concepts ESD, digital education (DE), and DT have many parallels, offers an unique opportunity to think about and integrate them within the course design. These parallels are: All are future-oriented and aim at supporting the development of – or require – similar or partly identical competencies that promote an active and reflective approach to challenges and problems in a world characterized by complexity and uncertainty (Lexa, 2021; Schrüfer & Brendel, 2018; Birkelbach et al., 2019; Ahel & Lingau, 2021; WBGU, 2019, Mayr & Oberrauch, 2022; Panke, 2019; Rauth et al., 2010).

However, ESD is based on a normative concept of sustainability, whereas both DE and DT can be, and often are, viewed neutrally, without necessarily taking ethical requirements into account – or are even used to support non-sustainable practices. However, the parallels between the concepts offer an opportunity to combine them and to enrich ESD with the digital and the DT approach, to support the development of key sustainability competencies such as critical-reflective thinking, collaboration, participation, holistic and interdisciplinary thinking and integrated problem-solving, and that in a creative and innovative way (Mayr & Oberrauch, 2022; Schürfer & Brendel, 2018; Val et al., 2017). In educational settings, ESD and DE not only aim at the development of similar competencies that are useful for DT approaches but are based on the same constructivist understanding of learning (Schaumberg, 2018). DE, in the form of BL teaching-learning settings, offers an opportunity to make teaching-learning processes more flexible regarding time and space, more learner-oriented and communicative (Burbules, 2020). The author therefore calls for deliberately designing meaningful learning scenarios in the sense of ESD, using the DT approach and appropriate digital media, instead of unreflectively digitalizing learning processes for their own sake.

Design of the Courses: Integrating SD, ESD, DT, and DE in the Form of BL

When designing the courses, the lecturers aimed to integrate the different concepts (E)SD, DT and BL, and create a motivating, safe space for students, one that promoted creativity and getting into action. Moreover, the lecturers wanted to provide students with an opportunity to consciously perceive and reflect on their individual learning processes, regarding change in their conceptions and competencies. These considerations are shown in Figure 1.

Figure 1. Project-oriented learning process, based on the concept of a moderate active constructivism, using blended learning
Source: Mayr, adapted according to Erpenbeck et al. (2016, p. 12) and Riemeier (2007, p. 70)

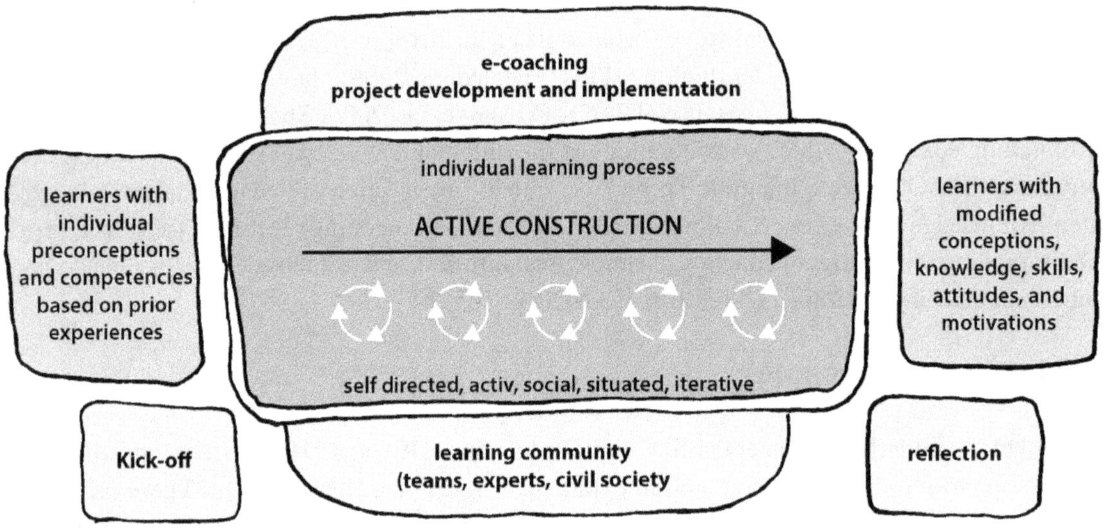

The BL format was intended to provide added value for students by enabling real-world encounters, as well as asynchronous and synchronous work phases and location-independent coaching in the virtual space. Digital media were supposed to scaffold students in developing and implementing their sustainability projects and give them an opportunity to practice an innovative way of working in both virtual and real spaces. The lecturers therefore selected them primarily regarding the extent to which they supported these processes and enabled students to co-creatively collaborate and organize their data, as well as themselves. The technology-integrating models mentioned above offered orientation and were used for cross-checking, challenging, and adapting course design and conscious selection of digital media.

Besides the university's Learning Management System (LMS) and additional communication channels like email or Messenger apps, the programs of choice were the video conference tool ZOOM and the virtual whiteboard MIRO, which allowed co-creative collaboration in the virtual space, as well as the ongoing visualization and documentation of the working process. For a better understanding, the course concepts are briefly presented below.

Practical Examples From Higher Education: Two Interdisciplinary University Courses

In the two courses #design.2030: Using Design Thinking (DT) to Achieve the Sustainable Development Goals (Course 1) and #design.2030: Digitalization and Sustainability – Innovative Digital Tools and Methods for a Better World (Course 2), participants should reach the following learning objectives. Students:

- Know and understand the human- and planet-centred design thinking mindset/approach, the process and tools, and are able to transfer this knowledge to meet challenges regarding sustainable development in the context of their studies, professional and private life
- Know respective methods and (digital) tools, and can critically reflect on them and situationally select and apply them
- Implement a project in the context of the Sustainable Development Goals and can discuss opportunities and limitations
- Strengthen key sustainability competencies and can reflect on their role as multipliers in the context of SD

Because of the great similarity of the two courses, this description refers primarily to the first course – differences will be mentioned only if necessary. In both courses, students enrolled in different master's degree studies participated. This fact enabled them to form heterogenous teams and to approach problems and solutions from multiple perspectives. In both courses, students dealt with challenges related to SD within the framework of the SDGs, in a critical, constructive, problem- and solution-oriented manner and using a DT mindset and approach. Students experienced a non-linear, iterative process following the Double Diamond Method shown in Figure 2, with "convergent and divergent modes of thinking employed in relation to the question being asked" (Clune & Lockrey, 2014, p. 71).

Figure 2. Double diamond
Source: Mayr

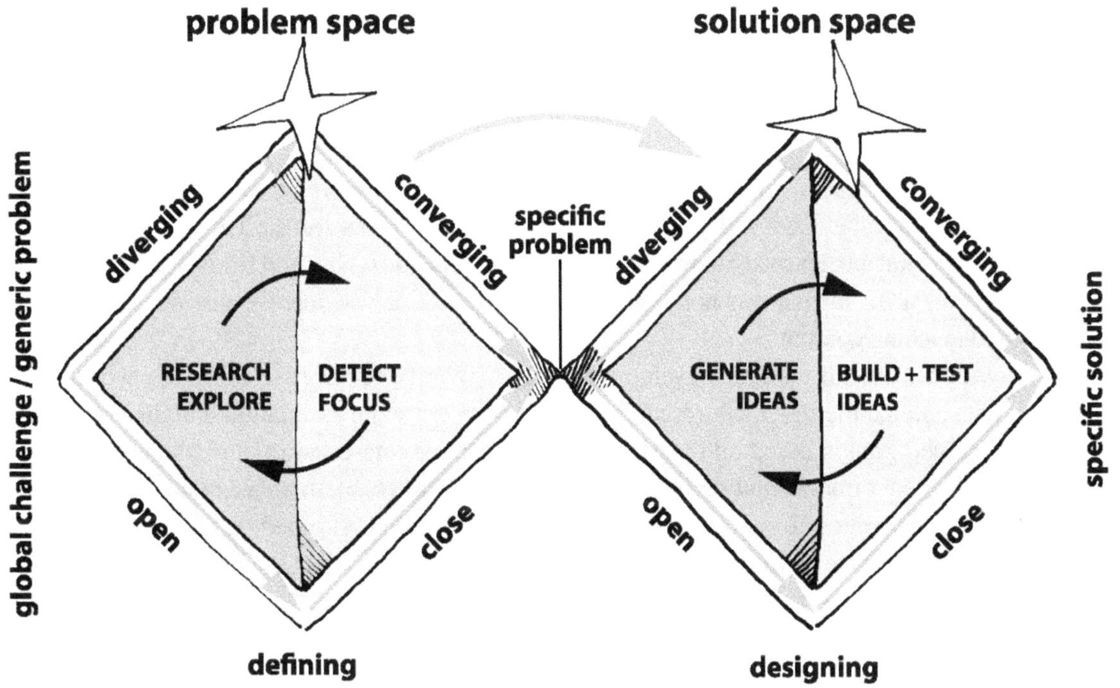

Figure 3 shows the course design and processes of Course #1, with alternate synchronous and asynchronous phases. Ongoing reflection phases allowed a critical-constructive confrontation with the individual and collective learning processes. The individual steps are briefly outlined.

Figure 3. Course processes
Source: Mayr, adapted according to Mayr and Oberrauch (2022)

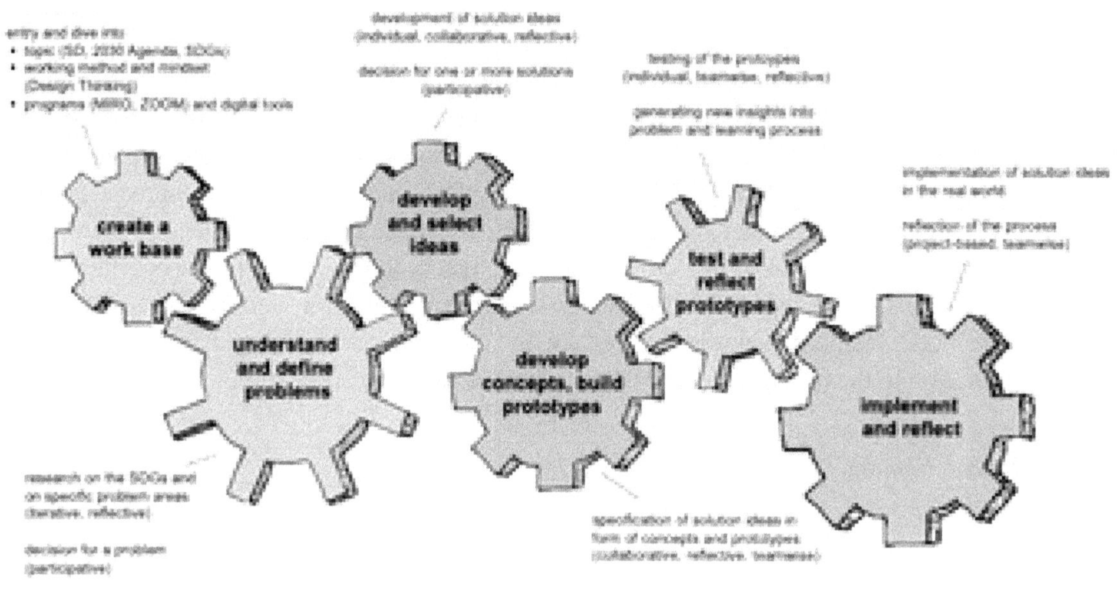

In the first step (1- create a working base), students not only got to know each other (virtually), but also the digital tools to be used, in addition to the University's LMS for the BL setting: ZOOM and MIRO. Moreover, students learned about the relevant concepts – DT, SD, and the SDGs. The organization in the form of a BL format was not explicitly addressed, as it was merely a means to an end, and not designated teaching content.

Starting with the overall task to "develop new and innovative services to make the world a better place", students entered the divergent research phase with a critical examination and discussion of the SDGs. They formed groups based on the SDGs they were most interested in, and planned their initial research to gain a better understanding of the SDGs and relevant problem areas, and later to be able to define individual challenges (2 - understanding and defining problems) based on the research findings. Selected challenges were then worked on in teams (3 - generate and select ideas, 4 - develop concepts and build prototypes, 5 - test and reflect prototypes, and 6 - implement and reflect).

Students' research processes were self-organized, and lecturers could be contacted for support if needed. The most extensive synchronous part of the course took place F2F in the form of a two-day workshop. Students started by reviewing their research findings, deriving key insights, and defining specific individual design challenges (2 - understanding and defining problems). They then evaluated the different challenges in a peer review process to decide which ones they would further pursue in teams. The method of choice for this was "Benny Hill sorting", which facilitated the identification of the most interesting and popular options in a "fast, high-energy" (Stickdorn et al., 2018, p. 184) and non-intimidating way, supported by music and with lots of fun. Although limited to the physical space, this again was a method that helped to create a safe space and relaxed atmosphere – a prerequisite for creative work. Moreover, it mixed design challenges (DC) and participants and, consequently, supported involvement as well as the development of co-ownership. Moreover, it helped students to let go of their own DCs (Stickdorn et al., 2018). Participants were free to decide which DC they would like to devote themselves to. The only limitation of choice was that students had to work in teams of at least 3, and at most 5. As a team, they reformulated the DC as needed and reflected on its importance and relevance (the "WHY"), as well as existing obstacles impeding solutions. These reflections helped to identify different areas of action for which to develop solutions.

Figure 4. Example of a design challenge, its relevance, and resistances
Source: Mayr

As shown in Figure 4, solutions could address different areas, such as reinforcing feeling good, raising awareness, or changing habits. The ideas that were developed in the next step (3 - generate and select ideas) therefore spread in various directions. The aim was to generate as many ideas as possible, to allow crazy ideas and to encourage new ways of thinking. Different methods are available for brainstorming ideas, although methods like 10 + 10 (Stickdorn et al., 2018), with alternating phases in which participants work alone and then exchange and build on each other's ideas, are recommended.

In the next step (4 - develop concepts and build prototypes), each team selected an idea or a bundle of ideas with which to create initial solutions, using a template that contained, among other things, the presentation of the solution from a target group's perspective. The students used the concept templates to present their ideas to members of other teams, asking for peer feedback that helped them to further develop their solution. After this iteration, in which new questions and ideas could emerge, and after a brief introduction to prototyping, its purpose, and methods, teams built "hands-on" prototypes of their solutions. Once again, new questions and ideas arose while working and, after a relatively short time, a first presentable prototype was available, which could be used for communicating and testing on the target group, as well as on experts. Prototyping in the physical space offered more possibilities than in the virtual space, both regarding the use of materials (such as cardboard, modelling clay or figurines) and group dynamics. (Even in the second course, which focused on the use of digital tools, it was not necessary to use the digital tool of choice at this stage.) Prototypes were still analog and had the quality of a "shitty first draft" – rough, but good enough to present to colleagues at the end of the two-day workshop, and later, self-organized, to members of the target group and experts. Feedback then helped the teams to further develop their ideas, or to decide to discard them because the solutions or the DC itself turned out not to fit. Prototypes were part of the ongoing iterative process, with repetitive research, ideation, and testing phases needed to further develop the projects before moving on to implementing them.

The process after peer feedback (6 - implement and reflect) within the workshop was highly self-organized and accompanied by two mandatory coaching sessions per team (with additional voluntary sessions available if needed). Students then presented their project process and outcome in a final session. Table 1 provides an overview of the projects implemented:

Table 1. Project overview

Course	Projects/Themes	Solutions
Course #1: contribute to the achievement of the SDGs with design thinking	Raising awareness of energy, green energy, and energy consumption	Podcast, Instagram campaign, poster
	Awareness 1: raising awareness of sustainability issues	Green table Green movie night
	Awareness 2: raising awareness of the SDGs	Interactive Instagram and poster campaign with specific tips related to each of the SDGs
	Waste: reducing waste at the campus, responsible consumption	Sustainable goodie-bags for students at the University of Innsbruck
Course #2 #design.2030: Digitalization and sustainability	Responsible consumption (fashion)	Scavenger hunt on slow fashion in Innsbruck, using Locandy
	Fostering empathy for animals	Scavenger hunt at the Alpine Zoo Innsbruck, using Locandy
	Climate-friendly everyday life	Virtual scenes about everyday decisions and their impact on climate change, using CoSpaces
	Learning garden	Virtual scenes that can be used to learn about gardening and sustainable nutrition, using CoSpaces

Finally, students reflected on and discussed their individual and collective learning processes in the last segment of the course. This unit was originally planned as a face-to-face event, to give students one more opportunity to meet in physical space and appreciate and celebrate their work accordingly. However, this had to be moved online due to the Covid-19 regulations in force. Because of this setting, students and faculty decided to meet in small groups for the reflection session. It was therefore possible to conduct focus group interviews and generate additional data answering the research questions outlined in the next chapter.

Research Design: Aim, Questions, Methods, and Participants

Research Aim and Questions

The research project accompanying the course aimed to assess their effect and impact regarding individual learning processes, and the coherence of the BL design applied. Specifically, the author was interested in answering the following research questions:

- How do students perceive their individual learning processes (Brandt et al., 2020)?
- What potentials and limitations do students see in the respective blended learning format and, in the 2nd course, in the use of digital tools for interventions that aim at fostering SD?
- What insights can be derived for the further development of the course?

Method

A written course reflection along guiding questions, as well as focus group discussions, provided qualitative data with which to answer these research questions. All data were transcribed and coded by the author using MAXQDA. All students delivered the written course reflection (N = 32) and most of the students (N = 28, 18/10) took part in the focus group interviews. The written course reflection delivered data on course decision and experience, as well as on the BL format, the individual learning process, and learning outcome. The structured focus group interviews (Brandt et al., 2020; Mayr & Oberrauch, 2022) focused on the understanding and reconstruction of learning processes and outcomes. Moreover, they included more specific questions and provided in-depth insights into participants' experience of the course in the virtual (WS 2020/21 N = 4) and the BL (WS 2021/22 N = 28) teaching-learning spaces, as well as information as to how students perceived their individual competence development. Finally, both data sources provided insights into how to further develop the course.

As in previous courses, a modified form of the PhotoVoice method (Wang & Burris, 1994; cf. Brandt et al., 2020) was used to elicit students' learning experiences, in which students described key moments of learning using photos, quotes, or objects (SS 2020: N= 9; WS 2020/21: N=20, WS 2021/22: n = 28). Data was analyzed using qualitative content analysis using MAXQDA Analytics Pro 2022 software. In a first step, codes were deducted from the categories of the reflection questionnaire and the focus group guide following Brandt et al., (2020). In a second step, additional categories and codes/subcodes were inductively generated based on students' answers. Categories covered "course experience", "learning outcomes" and "teaching and learning environment/BL". The coding followed the coding paradigm of the qualitative content analysis developed by Mayring (2014). As answers from the written course reflection could be traced back to individual students, these were pseudonymized by assigning a number – e.g., Student 1. The interviews were numbered, and in the case of quotations, the respective interview number was referred to in parentheses, e.g. (Interview1). The main findings are summarized in the results section below.

Results

In this section, the author provides results in the form of a general assessment of the course and the BL format, and, zooming in, key moments of learning, perceived competence development, as well as potentials and limitations of the blended learning format and the use of digital tools.

Overall Course Assessment

Results show:

- Students rated both courses very favorably and were satisfied with course design, organization and content, as well as with the digital media selected – supporting the findings on previous courses (Mayr & Oberrauch, 2022). From the student's perspective, course design was aligned with learning objectives.
- All but one student appreciated the BL format and recommended keeping it; that student would have preferred all sessions to be held F2F. All students agreed that it was important that the two-day workshop was held F2F. Most students would have preferred the final presentations to be F2F, basically for social reasons – to meet again and celebrate successes. All students found the online coaching appointments to be fine.

Key Moments of Learning

As key moments of learning, students describe experiences that relate to ways of thinking and working or, especially in Course #2, attitudes towards dealing with "new things". Here students explicitly reported having "aha experiences" when experimenting with digital tools that initially intimidated them.

Another aspect identified as a key learning in both courses concerned the approach to challenges or problems, e.g., breaking them down so that they became manageable, or viewing them from a positive perspective, shifting from problems towards solutions: "In addition, I was able to get to know various tools that helped me to see the problems with optimism and find solutions. Trial and error were certainly a big part of it, as well as great teamwork" (Student 2). "There we already prepared a first idea of a solution approach, which overall rather pointed out the negative aspects of fast fashion, etc. We then received feedback on this: Less condemnation of the negative, but more pointing out what you can do alternatively. And I think that's a message that should be integrated into life in general: get less upset about everything that's bad and instead look for better ways and solutions and point them out and pass them on" (Student 20). "The trial and error was great fun and showed what all is possible" (Student 25).

Fun was another keyword that some students mentioned, especially in the first course, addressing the need to create a safe space where, despite the gravity of the issues, lightness and joy are possible, encouraging creativity and innovation. "I was very surprised how quickly you can come up with a concrete project idea. Design thinking has supported me personally enormously and at the same time was great fun" (Student 10). "To be honest, I was even positively surprised by the relaxed course atmosphere. This once again confirmed my thesis that a relaxed atmosphere leads to more productivity. At first, I was skeptical about how the block sessions would go and if the day would be too long, but again I think we were always productive, in a good mood and had fun working and learning" (Student 11).

In Course #1, 6 (out of 14) students mentioned "Yes, but – yes, and" as one of the key learnings. This is the quintessence of an exercise that makes it possible to experience different modes, with "Yes, but" as the restrictive one which immediately evaluates ideas, hindering the creative process of developing many ideas, but beneficial when it comes to selecting them; and "Yes, and" as the opening one, which invites the generation of as many ideas as possible without filtering them. At different stages of the process, either one or the other mode is suitable. Moreover, people are more comfortable with either one mode or the other. Both should be considered accordingly, as Student 4 put it: "So that was my key moment, the "yes, but" and "yes, and", because I never gave much thought to the fact that you should perhaps also have phases when you need a lot of "yes, buts" and a lot of "yes, ands". And the time [for] the other will still come. I just never thought about that, and I noticed that it just makes you much more productive, much faster at solving problems."

Perceived Impact on Development of Competencies

Students were asked which competencies they felt they were able to strengthen or develop within the course, without giving them any further support regarding competence frameworks or naming explicit competences. Figure 5 shows the students' feedback. The more frequently mentioned terms appear larger and more centrally. Above all, working in a team, creativity, and, in the case of the 2nd course, digital skills, were mentioned most frequently by the students.

Figure 5. Word cloud: self-assessed competencies, no scaffolding provided
Source: Mayr

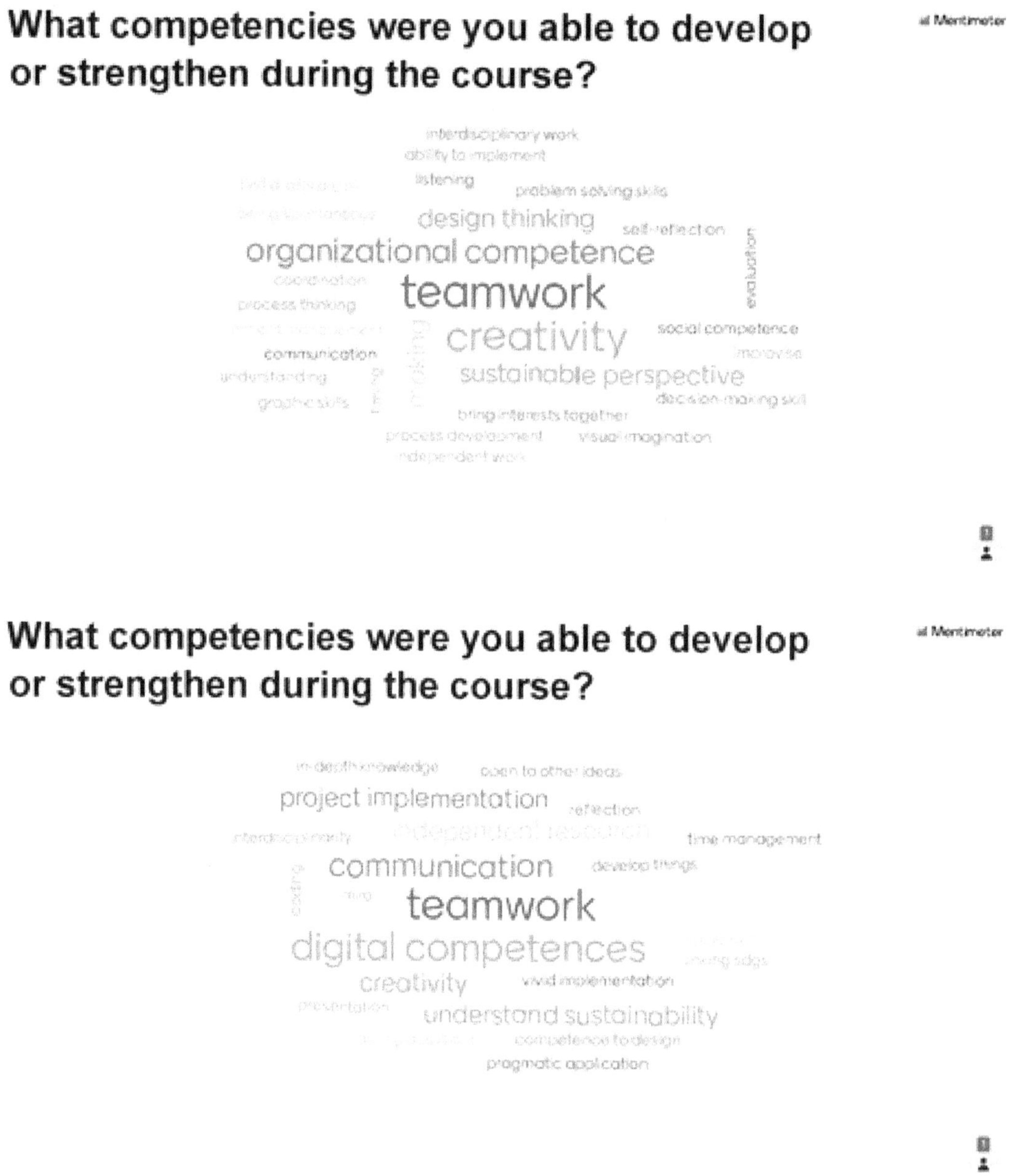

The key sustainability competencies shown in Figure 8 were then introduced. Students were asked to look at these and then self-assess which competencies they were able to develop or strengthen in the course.

Figure 6. (Key) sustainability competencies framework used for scaffolding self-assessment of students
Source: Mayr

Interpersonal competencies and digital skills scored highest for students in course #2, with 9 mentions out of 10, followed by cooperation and collaboration and problem-solving skills. In course #1, problem- solving and interpersonal competency were mentioned most often (6 out of 14), whereas other skills were addressed only once or twice.

In general, however, students found that the development of several of the mentioned key competencies were addressed in the course. "…critical thinking – that you must work together, cooperate, in the digital [space]; but also the problem-solving competency, because at the beginning we got some problem and then had to think about what the real problem [was], what we [could] do, what we [could] develop. But … then again, the self-competence – what can I as an individual do..." (Interview 1)

Potentials and Limitations of the Blended Learning Format and the Use of Digital Tools

Regarding course experiences, learning processes, and outcomes, students did not explicitly refer to BL on their own. For them, it had become "normal" in the 2nd year of the pandemic, and hardly played a role, both in general and regarding key learning experiences.

Students of both courses were then intentionally asked to reflect on the benefits and limitations of the BL format. Students from course #2 were also asked about the use of the selected digital tools. As mentioned above, students appreciated the BL format and suggested keeping it for subsequent university courses:

"In my opinion, the mixture of online and face-to-face courses was just right. It was very pleasant that the two initial days took place face-to-face. For the final event and for the feedback, the online setting was not disturbing, sometimes even practical, because you didn't have to go to the university for an hour. In this respect, the mixture is well done!" (Student 4). "The mixture of both was a really great thing for me since all other courses only took place in the virtual room. I think a mixture is great in itself – because I admittedly wouldn't feel like going to the university every day. I still wouldn't want to miss being present – that's why I think a 50/50 digital/presence mix is great" (Student 16).

"I found this to be very good! Online is flexible and time efficient. But the face-to-face days were by far the best part of this course. Super learned a lot in the two days! I would have liked it if the final presentations had also been face-to-face😉" (Student 18). "I would also stay with blended learning, especially because somehow everyone is now more used to the fact that you can participate in courses from anywhere and so everyone has the chance and if it's only a few days in presence you can always arrange that" (Student 1).

Overall, online teaching was assessed to be timesaving, location-independent and supportive of greater flexibility. This was offset, however, by certain disadvantages, in that attention, interaction, and collaboration suffered. And in return, the advantages of face-to-face teaching were mentioned, such as the opportunity for personal encounters and to perform "hands-on" work jointly. "I found the face-to-face time much more effective and exciting because you could work [in a more agile way] in the team. We also met several times online and face-to-face, and even in this small constellation, working face-to-face was more productive, positive, and relaxed. You could simply communicate faster, better, and more clearly; you knew when someone else wanted to talk, and you didn't have to wait for a stable Internet connection before you could talk" (Student 14).

"Where did I learn? As usual [with] Corona – a lot in front of the screen, because coaching sessions, kick-off and final presentation took place via Zoom. But most of all, I learned a lot at the university during the two days that took place face-to-face. There was a great exchange that could not have been replaced digitally" (Student 16).

Feedback relating to how students were able to engage in the online phases was informative. Some of them specifically stated that they did not speak up: "Since only one person can talk at a time online, I've often held back here" (Student 17). "I also find it difficult to get [in] a word without interrupting someone. Personally, that always stresses me out a lot, because sometimes I would like to contribute something, and then I feel like I'm on 'alert' for 15 minutes until I catch a good point to blabber on without interrupting anyone. That simply works better face-to-face, at least I personally find" (Student 16).

On the other hand, some students noted that they were used to online teaching and did not find it restrictive: "We've all gotten used to online teaching by now, and I didn't find it limiting in this course" (Student 20).

Students from course #2 were asked to assess the potential of the digital tools they learned about in the course. For them, the use of these tools primarily supports raising awareness. However, they see clear boundaries due to the risk of losing reference to reality – or, as one student put it during the presentation: "the tools are all good and well and might be suitable for education purposes, for raising awareness, or for a first encounter with SD. But that then one must go out into the real world and act."

LIMITATIONS

As with any research, there are limitations. In the current study, the results are based on the testimonies and written statements of a small number of participants, who self-assessed the impact course activities had on the development of their competencies. This was done without cross-checking them using instruments for assessing key competencies in sustainability (Redman et al., 2019) in a pre- and post-test procedure. No control group was available, and any changes that might have occurred in an individual or societal context, or because of other courses, were not considered. Moreover, the seminar was held at the time of the COVID-19 pandemic, when it was necessary to switch to online teaching after the two-day F2F workshop. Finally, participants specifically chose the course because they were interested in DT, SD and, for Course #2, in working with digital tools. Nevertheless, the results provide a good assessment of what the course can or cannot achieve and deliver useful suggestions for its further development.

SOLUTIONS AND RECOMMENDATIONS

Undeniably, both SD and digitalization are two key issues shaping life in the 21st century. However, these are often described as independent, unconnected features, neglecting the potential of digitization for promoting SD and ESD. Particularly regarding ESD, digital learning – as one aspect of digitalization in the context of SD – can support a more flexible teaching-learning process. It brings people together, regardless of their location, and enables co-creative development of (innovative) solutions – but does not replace real encounters. From the student's perspective, digital media/tools are merely seen as instruments with which to work. Students in both courses were concerned about these contributing to a more SD and appreciated the DT approach and the availability of appropriate digital media to facilitate organization, collaboration, and co-creation, or add value to the project. However, the core of the matter was, and is, implementation in the real world to shape a better present and future. In this context, DT was appreciated as an inspiring (new) way of thinking, approaching challenges, and acting. The results support the claim to create more opportunities for learners to engage in "'hands-on' collaboration, participation, interdisciplinary and holistic experimentation, and work based on real-world problems" (Mayr & Oberrauch, 2022), which might, but need not, be enriched by digital media. The challenge is to design BL scenarios that combine the potentials and advantages of digital learning, such as flexibility in terms of temporal and spatial independence, with those of the analog, such as enabling haptic experiences and social relationships (Mayr & Oberrauch, 2022).

CONCLUSION

The design of the two courses was intended to meet the demands outlined in "Solutions and Recommendations". Student feedback and lecturers' insights were, and will be, incorporated into further developing courses, using a DT approach. The results of the course evaluation can be seen as a validation of the basic course concept, which changed from the original F2F format (WS 19/20) to a BL format (WS 21/22) during the pandemic, when courses had to go completely online (SS 20, WS 20/21). In response to former participants' evaluations, students now implement real-world projects instead of participating in school workshops – and will continue to do so in future. Moreover, based on students' feedback and lecturer's reflection, the course architecture will continue to use BL, which is expected to be complemented by additional elements such as video tutorials for asynchronous teaching-learning phases. Finally, more focus will be placed on projects, so that they go beyond sensitization and raising awareness, towards activities that make a real and measurable contribution to the achievement of the SDGs.

REFERENCES

Ahel, O., & Lingenau, K. (2021). Digitale Ansätze zur Vermittlung der SDGs in der Hochschullehre im deutschsprachigen Raum. In L. W. Filho (Ed.), *Digitalisierung und Nachhaltigkeit* (pp. 129–146). doi:10.1007/978-3-662-61534-8_7

Birkelbach, L., Preglau, D., & Rammel, C. (2019). *White Paper BNE im Zeitalter der Digitalisierung. RCE Vienna.* RCE Vienna – Regional Centre of Expertise on Education for Sustainable Development.

Bonnedahl, K. J., Heikkurinen, P., & Paavola, J. (2022). Strongly sustainable development goals: Overcoming distances constraining responsible action. *Environmental Science & Policy*, *129*, 150–158. doi:10.1016/j.envsci.2022.01.004

Bormann, I., & Rieckmann, M. (2020). Lernende Hochschulen: Verankerung von Bildung für nachhaltige Entwicklung. In G. Bade, N. Henkel, & B. Reef (Eds.), *Politische Bildung: vielfältig – kontrovers – global. Festschrift für Bernd Overwien* (pp. 68–87). Wochenschau Verlag.

Bowyer, J. & Chambers, L. (2017). Evaluating blended learning: Bringing the elements together. *Research Matters, 23,* 17-26.

Brandt, J.-O., Bürgener, L., Redman, A., & Barth, M. (2020). *Educating Future Change Agents: Research Instruments applied in Case Studies on Teacher Education for Sustainable Development.* Lüneburg.

Brown, T. (2016). *Change by Design. Wie Design Thinking Organisationen verändert und zu mehr Innovationen führt.* Vahlen.

Brown, T. (2019). *Change by Design, Revised and Updated. How Design Thinking Transforms Organizations and Inspires Innovation.* Harper Collins Publ.

Brundiers, K., & Wiek, A. (2011). Educating Students in Real-world Sustainability Research: Vision and Implementation. *Innovative Higher Education*, *36*(2), 107–124. doi:10.100710755-010-9161-9

Buhl, A., Schmidt-Keilich, M., Muster, V., Blazejewski, S., Schrader, U., Harrach, Ch., Schäfer, M., & Süßbauer, E. (2019). Design thinking for sustainability: Why and how design thinking can foster sustainability-oriented innovation and development. *Journal of Cleaner Production*, *231*, 1248–1257. doi:10.1016/j.jclepro.2019.05.259

Burbules, N. C., Fan, G., & Repp, P. (2020). Five trends of education and technology in a sustainable future. *Geography and Sustainability*, *1*(2), 93–97. doi:10.1016/j.geosus.2020.05.001

Clune, S. J., & Lockrey, S. (2014). Developing environmental sustainability strategies, the Double Diamond method of LCA and design thinking: A case study from aged care. *Journal of Cleaner Production*, *85*, 67–82. doi:10.1016/j.jclepro.2014.02.003

Cörvers, R., Wiek, A., Kraker, J., Lang, D. J., & Martens, P. (2016). Problem-Based and Project-Based Learning for Sustainable Development. In H. Heinrichs, P. Martens, G. Michelsen, & A. Wiek (Eds.), *Sustainability Science. An Introduction* (pp. 349–358). Springer Netherland. doi:10.1007/978-94-017-7242-6_29

Erpenbeck, J., Sauter, S., & Sauter, W. (2016). *Social Workplace Learning. Kompetenzentwicklung im Arbeitsprozess und im Netz in der Enterprise 2.0*. Springer Gabler. Springer Fachmedien Wiesbaden. doi:10.1007/978-3-658-10499-3

Garrison, D. R., & Kanuka, H. (2004). Blended learning: Uncovering its transformative potential in higher education. *The Internet and Higher Education*, *7*(2), 95–105. doi:10.1016/j.iheduc.2004.02.001

Garrison, D. R. & Vaughan, N.D. (2008). *Blended Learning in Higher Education. Frameworks, Principles and Guidelines*. Jossey-Bass. A Wiley Imprint.

Giannetti, B. F., Agostinho, F., Almeida, C. M. V. B., Liu, G., Contreras, L. E. V., Vandecasteele, C., Coscieme, L., Sutton, P., & Poved, C. (2019). Insights on the United Nations Sustainable Development Goals scope: Are they aligned with a 'strong' sustainable development? *Journal of Cleaner Production*, *252*, 119574. doi:10.1016/j.jclepro.2019.119574

Hickel, J. (2019). The contradiction of the sustainable development goals: Growth versus ecology on a finite planet. *Sustainable Development*, *27*(5), 873–884. doi:10.1002d.1947

Kimmons, R., Graham, C. R., & West, R. E. (2020). The PICRAT model for technology integration in teacher preparation. *Contemporary Issues in Technology & Teacher Education*, *20*(1), 176–198.

Kroll, C., Warchold, A., & Pradhan, P. (2019). Sustainable Development Goals (SDGs): Are we successful in turning trade-offs into synergies? *Palgrave Communications*, *5*(1), 140. doi:10.105741599-019-0335-5

Ledford, D. M. (2016). *A professional learning framework to improve teacher practice in technology integration* [PhD dissertation]. Boise State University.

Mali, D., & Lim, H. (2021). How do students perceive face-to-face/blended learning as a result of the Covid-19 pandemic? *International Journal of Management Education*, *19*(3), 19. doi:10.1016/j.ijme.2021.100552

Mayr, H., & Madritsch, R. (2022). Mobile Endgeräte in der Bildung: ein Blick durch die ökologische, ökonomische und soziale Brille. In T. Hug (Ed.), Medien – Wissen – Bildung 2021: Ökologische Krisen und Ökologien in der Kritik (MWB 2021). Academic Press.

Mayr, H., & Oberrauch, A. (2022). Hochschulbildung für eine Nachhaltige Entwicklung – interdisziplinär, partizipativ, digital? In Bildung für nachhaltige Entwicklung und Digitalisierung als Beitrag für eine zukunftsorientierte Hochschulausbildung (pp. 67-82). Heidelberger Zentrum Bildung für nachhaltige Entwicklung.

Mayring, P. (2014). *Qualitative Content Analysis: Theoretical Foundation*. Basic Procedures and Software Solution.

McDonald, J. K., West, R. E., Rich, P. J., & Pfleger, I. (2018). "It's So Wonderful Having Different Majors Working Together": The Development of an Interdisciplinary Design Thinking Minor. *TechTrends*, *63*(4), 440–450. doi:10.100711528-018-0325-2

Meinel, C., & von Thienen, J. (2016). Design Thinking. *Informatik Spektrum*, *39*(4), 10–31. doi:10.100700287-016-0977-2

Mishra, P., & Koehler, M. J. (2006). Technological pedagogical content knowledge: A framework for teacher knowledge. *Teachers College Record*, *108*(6), 1017–1054. doi:10.1111/j.1467-9620.2006.00684.x

Rauth, I., Köppen, E., Jobst, B., & Meinel, C. (2010). Design Thinking: An Educational Model towards Creative Confidence. *DS-66-2: Proceedings of the 1st International Conference on Design Creativity (ICDC 2010).*

Raworth, K. (2015). *Doughnut Economics. Seven Ways to Think Like a 21st Century Economist.* Penguin Random House.

Redman, A., Barth, M., Wiek, A., & Timm, J.-M. (2019, May 29). (submitted to). Generating Generalizable Insights from Case Studies on Competencies-oriented Sustainability Education. *Draft. Gaia (Heidelberg).*

Rieckmann, M. (2018). Learning to transform the world: key competencies in Education for Sustainable Development. In A. Leicht, A. Heiss, & W. J. Byun (Eds.), *Issues and trends in education for sustainable development* (pp. 39–59). UNESCO.

Riemeier, T. (2007). Moderater Konstruktivismus. In Handbuch der Theorien in der biologiedidaktischen Forschung (pp. 69–79). Springer. doi:10.1007/978-3-540-68166-3_7

Röckström, J., Steffen, W., Noone, K., Persson, A., Chapin III, F.S., Lambin, E.F., Lenton, T.M., Scheffer, M., Folke, C., Schellnhuber, H.., Nykvist, B., de Wit, C. A., Hughes, T., van der Leeuw, S., Rodhe, H., Sörlin, S., Snyder, P.K., Costanza, R., Svedin, U., Falkenmark, M., … Foley, J. A. (2009). A safe operating space for humanity. *Nature, 461*, 472-475.

Schürfer, G., & Brendel, N. (2018). Globales Lernen im digitalen Zeitalter. In N. Brendel, G. Schrüfer, & I. Schwarz (Eds.), *Globales Lernen im digitalen Zeitalter* (pp. 9–33). Waxmann.

Shulman, L. (1986). Those who understand: Knowledge growth in teaching. *Educational Researcher*, *15*(2), 4–14. doi:10.3102/0013189X015002004

Singer-Brodowsky, M. (2016). *Studierende als Gestalter*innen einer Hochschulbildung für nachhaltige Entwicklung. Selbstorganisierte und problembasierte Nachhaltigkeitskurse und ihr Beitrag zur überfachlichen Kompetenzentwicklung Studierender. Umweltkommunikation, Band Nr. 8*. Berliner Wissenschaftsverlag.

Stickdorn, M., Hormess, M. E., Lawrence, A., & Schneider, J. (2018). *This is service design doing: applying service design thinking in the real world.* O'Reilly Media, Inc.

Stoltenberg, U., & Michelsen, G. (2020). Digitalisierung im Kontext von Bildung für Nachhaltige Entwicklung. In Nachhaltige Digitalisierung – eine noch zu bewältigende Zukunftsaufgabe (pp. 49-64). Hessische Landeszentrale für politische Bildung.

United Nations. (1987). *Report of the World Commission on Environment and Development: Our Common Future*. Author.

United Nations. (1992). Agenda 21. *United Nations Conference on Environment and Development.*

United Nations. (2015). *Agenda 2030. United Nations Conference on Environment and Development.*

United Nations Educational, Scientific and Cultural Organization. (2020). *Education for Sustainable Development. A roadmap*. UNESCO.

Val, E., Gonzalez, I., Iriarte, I. Beitia, A., Lasa, G. & Elkoro, M. (2017): A Design Thinking approach to introduce entrepreneurship education in European school curricula. *The Design Journal, 20*(1), 754-766.

Vare, P., & Scott, W. (2007). Learning for a Change: Exploring the Relationship between Education and Sustainable Development. *Journal of Education for Sustainable Development*, *1*(2), 191–198. doi:10.1177/097340820700100209

Vaughan, N. D. (2019). Foreword. In Handbook of Research on Blended Learning Pedagogies and Professional Development in Higher Education. IGI Global.

Wals, A. E. J. (2011). Learning Our Way to Sustainability. *Journal of Education for Sustainable Development*, *5*(2), 177–186. doi:10.1177/097340821100500208

WBGU – German Advisory Council on Global Change. (2019). *Towards Our Common Digital Future. Flagship Report*. WBGU.

Wiek, A., Withycombe, L., & Redman, C. L. (2011). Key competencies in sustainability: A reference framework for academic program development. *Sustainability Science*, *6*(2), 203–218. doi:10.100711625-011-0132-6

Zhao, M., Liao, H.-T., & Sun, S.-P. (2020). An Education Literature Review on Digitization, Digitalization, Datafication, and Digital Transformation. *Advances in Social Science, Education and Humanities Research*, *435*, 301–305. doi:10.2991/assehr.k.200428.065

KEY TERMS AND DEFINITIONS

Blended Learning: A method of teaching and a way of learning that integrates technology and combines (asynchronous and synchronous) online and face to face activities.

Design Thinking: A mindset, collaborative way of working that follows a structured, iterative process, provides a set of methods and leaves room for co-creative problem solving.

Education for Sustainable Development: A type of education that aims to empower people to shape the future.

ENDNOTES

1 SAMR = model that identifies four stages for using technology: to substitute traditional teaching tools and methods (Substitution), to functionally improve them (Augmentation), to significantly redesign tasks (Modification) and to finally create new, previously inconceivable tasks (Redefinition).

2 TIM = model that provides a description of the levels of technology integration in the form of a Technology Integration Matrix with 25 cells. It incorporates five interdependent characteristics of meaningful learning environments (active, collaborative, constructive, authentic, and goal-directed), which are associated with five levels of technology integration (entry, adoption, adaptation, infusion and transformation).

3 PICRAT = a model that considers the student's roles in using technology (Passive learning, Interactive Learning or Creative learning) as well as the impact of technology use on teacher pedagogy (Replacement, Amplification and Transformation).

Chapter 14
Digital Learning During COVID-19:
An Intersectional Perspective on Secondary Students' Motivation and Perceived Teacher Support

Marlene Kollmayer
University of Vienna, Austria

Selma Korlat Ikanovic
University of Vienna, Austria

Julia Holzer
University of Vienna, Austria

Elisabeth Rosa Pelikan
University of Vienna, Austria

Christiane Spiel
University of Vienna, Austria

Barbara Schober
University of Vienna, Austria

Marko Lüftenegger
University of Vienna, Austria

ABSTRACT

The spread of COVID-19 led to an interruption of physical school attendance for around 1.6 billion students worldwide. During the school closures, schools switched to digital teaching which created a unique situation for all students but especially for groups disadvantaged in the (virtual) classroom. The current study is theoretically based on the situated expectancy-value theory that argues that an individual's motivation is shaped by their social identities. Following the intersectionality framework, the impact of gender and first language on motivation is examined simultaneously. The chapter presents an empirical study of motivation and perceived teacher support for digital learning among 19,337 secondary school students from Austria, shortly after the first pandemic-induced school closures in spring 2020. Results show differences in perceived teacher support, competence beliefs, intrinsic value, and engagement regarding digital learning between students of different gender and first languages. Practical and theoretical implications of the study's findings are discussed.

DOI: 10.4018/978-1-7998-5033-5.ch014

INTRODUCTION

There have been calls for more digitalization in education over the last decade – especially given its game-changing potential for sustainability. Education for Sustainable Development aims to empower individuals of all ages and backgrounds to make informed decisions facilitating an equitable and environmentally sustainable society. To reach this goal, all individuals have to be provided with the necessary knowledge and skills, as well as the attitudes and values necessary to address sustainable development challenges. Digitalization in education has been proposed to be one key factor for creating transformative learning environments and learning outcomes that can lead to a more sustainable world, and also for enlarging the number of students getting access to Education for Sustainable Development. Digital education is assumed to improve important skills such as global awareness, problem solving and collaboration, to enable children from different parts of the word to connect to each other easily, and to open future job opportunities for young people. Therefore, schools need to build up the competences, skills, and attitudes necessary to take part in the process of digitalization.

The spread of COVID-19 led to temporary school closures in countries worldwide, which caused an interruption of physical school attendance for around 1.6 billion children and adolescents for several months (UNICEF, 2020). Despite the ongoing calls for more digitalization in education, most European school systems had employed face-to-face teaching as their standard method before COVID-19 and did not invest much time or effort in digitalization. During the school closures, schools all over the world switched to digital teaching and learning, often without being prepared for the accompanying challenges. Although digitalization is assumed to hold potential for supporting self-regulated, situated, and informal learning, this created a unique situation for all students and teachers, but especially for groups disadvantaged in the (virtual) classroom (UN, 2020). This might increase the "digital divide" between those who have the skills to use digital media productively and those who do not in early stages of educational careers. However, digitalization in education can only make a valuable contribution to empower people to actively shape the process of transforming towards sustainability when students with different social identities are equally promoted and supported.

This chapter deals with students' motivation for digital learning and analyses if there are individual differences in motivation that might lead to inequalities and thus hinder the potential of digital education for sustainability. First, the Situated Expectancy-Value Theory is introduced as the study's theoretical basis. Second, the chapter presents recent findings on individual differences in digital learning and explicates how intersectional perspectives can contribute to expanding our knowledge on digital education's potential for sustainability. Third, the chapter presents a large quantitative study conducted in Austria shortly after the first school closures due to the COVID-19 pandemic in spring 2020. The study investigates associations between students' competence beliefs, intrinsic value and learning engagement regarding digital learning as well as their perceived teacher support before analysing individual differences in these components. Following the intersectionality paradigm, students' age, gender and immigrant background are considered simultaneously. Based on the results of the study, directions for future research and recommendations to teachers and policymakers are derived.

THEORETICAL BACKGROUND

Developing the knowledge, skills, and attitudes necessary to use digital media productively requires students to be motivated for this challenge. One of the most influential theories for explaining human motivation is Expectancy-Value Theory (Wigfield & Eccles, 2000). Expectancy-Value Theory postulates that an individual will take up learning activities if they consider the task to be important (= value component) and if they believe that they can be successful in performing the task (= expectancy component). This quite general theoretical framework was recently updated with ideas from social cognition, developmental sciences, and sociocultural perspectives, now labeled Situated Expectancy-Value Theory (Eccles & Wigfield, 2020). In contrast to the original conceptualization, Situated Expectancy-Value Theory elaborates not only on how expectancy and value components of motivation interact in constituting an individual's achievement-related choices and performance, but also on the processes necessary to explain individual differences in task valuing and expectancies for success. In this sense, the Situated Expectancy-Value Theory argues that an individual's motivational beliefs are shaped by person characteristics like gender and immigrant background as these variables are connected with certain stereotypes and role expectations as well as socializers' beliefs and behaviors.

The intersectionality framework (Crenshaw, 1989), that originates from Black feminist scholarship, argues that the influence of relevant aspects of individuals' social identities (e.g., gender, race, class, sexual orientation, ability) should be examined simultaneously as power dynamics function in complex ways that cannot be adequately understood by considering these aspects independently. Therefore, the intersection of different social categories can lead to specific experiences of stereotyping and discrimination that go beyond the additive linkage of the effects of individual social categories. In recent approaches intersectionality is seen as a key framework to deconstruct and disrupt oppression in environmental and sustainability education (Maina-Okori et al., 2018).

Building on these theoretical considerations, the present chapter examines secondary school students' motivation for digital learning in spring 2020 – shortly after the first pandemic-induced school closures in Austria. On the one hand, associations of expectancy and value components of motivation and perceived teacher support were investigated, on the other hand, systematic variations of the various components of students' digital learning motivation depending on their age, gender and immigrant background were examined. In the present study, intrinsic value and learning engagement regarding digital learning represent the value component, whereas competence beliefs for digital learning represent the expectancy component. Intrinsic value is understood as the extent of enjoyment or positive affective evaluation of a learning activity (Wigfield & Eccles, 2000). Such enjoyment of learning for reasons within the activity itself rather than its consequences is a very desirable state. If the intrinsic value ascribed to a task is high, students learn by engaging in a pleasurable activity. That is why intrinsic value and learning engagement or flow – in the sense of full involvement or joyful absorption in an activity – are closely connected to each other and resemble the value component of motivation well. Competence beliefs – representing the expectancy component of motivation – indicate a student's sense of how good they are at certain tasks or in certain domains and thus how likely it is for them to succeed in this task or domain (Wigfield & Eccles, 2000). In addition, the study examined how students perceived their teachers' support for digital learning. In the Situated Expectancy-Value Theory and in educational research in general, socializers' beliefs and behaviors play a crucial role in shaping individual motivation. Moreover, schools represent organizations in which power is executed and in which adolescents' trajectories of growth and participation are shaped.

INDIVIDUAL DIFFERENCES IN DIGITAL LEARNING

Gender Differences in Digital Learning

Research and policy already pointed out the gender dimension of school closures due to COVID-19, especially in light of the so-called "gender digital gap" (IIEP-UNESCO, 2020; Nefesh-Clarke et al., 2020). Traditional gender stereotypes associate technical fields with masculinity (Kollmayer et al., 2018a) in Western societies, i.e., Europe and the US. Thus, information and communications technology (ICT) is often perceived as more suitable for boys than girls (Cooper, 2006). The gender digital gap begins in early childhood, when educators convey the stereotype that ICT is a male domain. Even parents of toddlers prefer toys that relate to technology and action for boys, and toys that encourage nurturance and beauty in girls (Kollmayer et al., 2018b). Moreover, boys are provided with more opportunities to do computing and sports by their parents, while girls are more encouraged to read and to interact with their peers (Eccles, 2009). Such gendered learning experiences can undermine girls' interest in ICT-related subjects as well as their confidence in their respective abilities. It is not surprising that by the time of adolescence, boys are more attracted to computers than girls (Volman & van Eck, 2001), report higher frequency of computer use and greater self-confidence in dealing with ICT (Colley & Comber, 2003), and generally display greater digital skills (Li & Kirkup, 2007).

Consequently, computers seem to be more relevant to boys' than girls' identities and self-images. When asked to spontaneously describe themselves, boys used ICT-related terms (e.g., "computer freak" or "I like computers") significantly more often than girls (Korlat et al., 2022). This can not only influence girls' use of computers but might also have consequences for girls' education and occupational aspirations, ultimately contributing to the "leaky pipeline" in science, technology, engineering, and mathematics and the continued horizontal gender segregation of work. The specific barriers and difficulties girls face in their experiences with ICT have led to concerns about gender equity in digital learning. It has been suggested that based on their higher perceived ability, comfort, and engagement with computers, boys may have an advantage over girls in the online classroom. Nevertheless, the results of studies investigating gender differences in digital learning are heterogeneous. On the one hand, boys have been shown to have a clear advantage over girls in confidence in their ICT abilities quite consistently from elementary school to university (for a review see Vekiri & Chronaki, 2008). On the other hand, a more recent meta-analysis revealed higher competence beliefs regarding learning in digital learning settings in female compared to male university students (Perkowski, 2013). During the COVID-19 pandemic, a current study conducted by the authors of this chapter indicates only small gender disparities in motivation for digital learning (Korlat et al., 2021). In general, gender differences in competence, attitudes, and motivation regarding digital learning seem to become less prevalent over time, which might indicate a narrowing of the gender digital gap (e.g., Vekiri, 2013).

Diverse and Intersectional Perspectives on Digital Learning

So far, almost all studies on gender differences in ICT (and in other domains), have simply compared boys and girls or men and women, sometimes including gender-role self-concept as an additional explanatory factor (Korlat et al., 2021). This is problematic as there is a growing percentage of gender-diverse or non-binary individuals, especially in adolescents. The percentage of those who are not cisgender varies between 0.1 and 2% of the population, depending on where the studies were held and on the specific inclusion criteria (Goodman et al., 2019). This percentage normally does not allow for including these individuals in quantitative studies due to the resulting small group sizes. However, examining motivational factors also in gender-diverse individuals is especially crucial as recent research found gender-diverse individuals to often suffer discrimination and exclusion, and have lower education attainment than those identifying as cisgender (Carpenter et al., 2020). A recent study from Finland even found non-binary lower secondary students to be the most worried to be left without support in remote learning settings due to COVID-19 (Oinas et al., 2022).

But of course, gender is not the only person-characteristic related to educational chances, motivation, and outcomes. Studies suggest that students with an immigrant background and especially those with non-German first languages also face specific challenges and discrimination in school (e.g., Khakpour, 2022). This is reflected by the fact that they are underrepresented in more demanding school types like grammar schools (AHS) and vocational high schools (Austrian Integration Fund, 2021), and achieve lower scores on the Program for International Student Assessment (PISA) in many participating countries (Entorf & Minoiu, 2005). With regard to digital learning, studies investigating differences between native students and students with an immigrant background and especially between students with different first languages are scare. However, it is known that students with an immigrant background more often visit schools with a lower socio-economic status (SES) than native students. Although student-computer ratios in high- and low-SES schools were found to be similar, students from low-SES schools were found to be affected by uneven human support networks and irregular home access to computers (Warschauer et al., 2004). In view of the fact that findings on this matter date back some time, it seems all the more relevant to take a look at the current situation, especially with regard to learning in times of COVID-19.

The present study aims to address some of the shortcomings of current research on individual differences in digital learning. Following the Situated Expectancy-Value Theory, secondary school students' motivation for digital learning is examined by focusing on their competence beliefs, intrinsic value and learning engagement regarding digital learning as well as their perceived teacher support. First, associations between the different components of students' digital learning motivation are examined to shed light on how achievement-related choices and performances are constituted in the domain of digital learning. Second, differences in student motivation between students of different age, gender – including gender diverse students – and between students with different first languages are investigated simultaneously to account for possible intersections between social categories in understanding individual differences in student motivation. While the intersectionality framework has been used widely in qualitative studies, only few quantitative studies have applied it so far (Bauer et al., 2021). However, research including the experiences of minority students is highly important to be able to better meet their educational needs and to ensure safe digital learning opportunities for all students in the future. Moreover, by also focusing on students' perceived teacher support, the chapter allows for insights on how power dynamics in schools might shape adolescents' motivation.

THE PRESENT STUDY

Participants and Procedure

The data used in this study was collected in April 2020 in Austria, as part of a larger research project investigating different aspects of learning during the COVID-19 pandemic with an online questionnaire. In Austria, schools stopped providing onsite learning on March 16, 2020, but had to ensure that education continued over the whole period of the closures. Schools were given autonomy in organizing and designing distance teaching, and remained open to provide childcare to students of parents with system-relevant professions or where necessary. However, only about 2% of students took up this option. To recruit participants, the link to the online questionnaire was distributed via manifold stakeholders such as school principals, school boards, and educational networks with the help of the Austrian Federal Ministry for Education, Science, and Research. Participation in the study was voluntarily and anonymous and students had to give active informed consent to be included in the dataset. The full sample consisted of 19,337 students. For this study, only data from students who indicated which language/s they speak at home was included. Students who stated that they only speak German at home form the group of the students with German first language, all other students form the group of students with non-German first languages. The subsample consisted of 19,025 secondary school students (M_{age} = 14.56, SD_{age} = 2.50, Range = 10–21; 61.4% girls, 37.8% boys, 0.5% gender-diverse students; 81.2% students with German first language, 17.8% students with non-German first languages) from all types of Austrian secondary schools.

Measures

Students answered questions about their competence beliefs, intrinsic value, learning engagement, and perceived teacher support regarding digital learning during the first school closure in spring 2020. Due to the novel circumstances related to the pandemic situation, existing scales had to be adapted and new items had to be developed to capture students' experiences during the school closures. To ensure the adapted or newly formulated items' content validity, all revisions were based on expert judgments. Moreover, all measures were piloted among adolescents of different ages with cognitive testing. Details on the measures, the complete set of items and the full data set can be found in Schober et al. (2020). Students were asked to answer the items with respect to the current situation and their corresponding digital learning experiences in mind. All items were rated on a five-point Likert scale ranging from 1 (strongly agree) to 5 (strongly disagree). To allow for easier interpretation, items were recoded so that higher values reflected higher agreement with the statements for all analyses.

Competence Beliefs

To assess students' competence beliefs regarding digital learning, three newly developed items were used (sample item: "Overall, I am managing e-learning pretty well.", Coefficient $\alpha = .712$).

Intrinsic Value

Three items adapted from the Scales for the Measurement of Motivational Regulation for Learning in University Students (SMR-LS) were used to assess students' Intrinsic Value (sample item: "Currently, I really enjoy studying and working for school", Coefficient $\alpha = .916$).

Learning Engagement

To measure students Learning Engagement, three items from the engagement subscale of the EPOCH Measure (sample item: "Currently when I am working on my schoolwork, I get completely absorbed in what I am doing", Coefficient $\alpha = .732$) were slightly adapted.

Perceived Teacher Support

To assess students' perceived teacher support for digital learning, three items concerning interactions with teachers were newly developed, (sample item: "Currently, my teachers help me with e-learning", Coefficient $\alpha = .746$).

Results

For interpreting the results, effect sizes are reported alongside statistical significance. According to Cohen's (1988) recommendations, *r*-values around .10 are interpreted as small effects, values around .30 as medium effects, and values > .50 as large effects. In case of η^2_p (partial eta square), values around .01 are interpreted as small, around .06 as medium, and > .14 as large effects.

Associations Between Components of Students' Motivation for Digital Learning

In a first step, simple bivariate correlations were used to examine associations between the different components of students' motivation for digital learning. While causation means that a change in one variable directly leads to a change in another variable, bivariate correlations analyse how much one variable will change when there is a change in another variable. For testing causality experimental or longitudinal designs are required. Cross-sectional research designs like ours can only demonstrate correlational links between variables. As expected, all different components of students' motivation for digital learning were statistically significantly correlated, see Table 1. The highest correlations were found between students' competence beliefs for digital learning and the intrinsic value they ascribed to digital learning and also between intrinsic value and learning engagement. Students' perceived teacher support showed the highest correlations with their competence beliefs, followed by intrinsic value and learning engagement.

Table 1. Bivariate correlations between components of students' digital learning motivation

	1.	2.	3.
1. Competence Beliefs			
2. Intrinsic Value	.499**		
3. Learning Engagement	.287**	.461**	
4. Teacher Support	.458**	.352**	.222**
Note: ** p<.01			

Individual Differences in Students' Motivation for Digital Learning

Second, four separate analyses of covariance (ANCOVAs) were conducted to examine differences in various aspects of digital learning motivation among adolescents of different gender and first languages from an intersectional perspective controlling for students' age. ANCOVA is a general linear model, which analyses whether the means of a dependent variable are equal across the different expressions of a categorical independent variable, while statistically controlling for the effects of one or more other continuous variables that is/are not of primary interest.

Digital learning competence beliefs, intrinsic value, engagement, and perceived support in digital learning served as the dependent variables. Gender (male/female/diverse) and first language (German/non-German) served as independent variables, which also allowed for analysing interactions between these two dimensions. The comparatively small group of gender-diverse students caused violations of the assumption of variance homogeneity, in turn leading to more conservative testing and thus possible underestimation of effects. Table 2 shows the descriptive statistics for digital learning competence beliefs, intrinsic value, engagement, and perceived support in digital learning by gender and first language.

Competence Beliefs

The analysis showed a statistically significant effect of age, $F(1, 19009) = 63.86$, $p <.001$, $\eta^2_p =.132$, indicating a negative relationship between age and competence beliefs regarding digital learning, $r = -.063$, $p <.001$. The main effect of gender was significant, $F(2, 19009) = 17.61$, $p <.001$, $\eta^2_p = .002$. Planned contrasts revealed that boys reported significantly lower competence beliefs than girls, $p =.002$, and diverse students reported significantly lower competence beliefs than boys, $p <.001$. The main effect of students' first language was also significant, $F(1, 19009) = 5.35$, $p =.021$, $\eta^2_p = .000$, whereby students with non-German first languages reported lower competence beliefs. There was no significant interaction effect of students' gender and first language.

Intrinsic Value

For intrinsic value, there was a statistically significant effect of age, $F(1, 19008) = 221{,}122$, $p < .001$, $\eta^2_p =.003$, indicating a negative relationship between age and intrinsic value of digital learning, $r = -.094$, $p <.001$. The main effect of gender was significant, $F(2, 19008) = 43.91$, $p < .001$, $\eta^2_p = 0.005$. Planned contrasts revealed that only the difference between boys' and girls' intrinsic value was significant, with boys reporting lower intrinsic value, $p < .001$, but no significant difference between boys and gender-diverse students, $p < .414$. The main effect of students' first language was also significant, $F(1, 19008) = 5.50$, $p = .019$, $\eta^2_p = 0.000$. Students with non-German first language reported slightly lower intrinsic value than students whose first language was German. The interaction effect of students' gender and native language on intrinsic value was also significant, $F(2, 19008) = 4.55$, $p = .011$, $\eta^2_p = 0.000$. In students whose first language was German, gender diverse students reported significantly lower intrinsic value than girls while there was no such difference in students with non-German first languages.

Learning Engagement

The results showed no statistically significant effect of age on learning engagement, $F(1, 18996) = 0.57$, $p = .451$. The main effect of gender was significant, $F(2, 18996) = 41.67$, $p < .001$, $\eta^2_p = .004$. Planned contrasts revealed that boys reported significantly lower learning engagement than girls, $p < .001$, but there was no significant difference between boys and gender-diverse students, $p < .396$. The main effect of students' first language was not significant, $F(1, 18996) = 3.27, p = .071$, and there was no significant interaction effect of students' gender and first language, $F(2, 18996) = 0.41, p = .643$.

Perceived Teacher Support

The analysis revealed a statistically significant effect of age, $F(1, 19009) = 609.04, p < .001, \eta^2_p = .031$, indicating a negative relationship between age and the intrinsic value of digital learning, $r = -.17, p < .001$. The main effect of gender was significant, $F(2, 19009) = 38.90, p < .001, \eta^2_p = 0.004$. Planned contrasts revealed that boys reported significantly lower perceived teacher support than girls, $p < .001$, and diverse students reported significantly lower perceived teacher support than boys, $p = .045$. The main effect of students' first language was not significant, $F(1, 19009) = 3.27, p = .071$, and there was no significant interaction effect of students' gender and first language, $F(2, 19009) = 0.41, p = .643$.

SOLUTIONS AND RECOMMENDATIONS

The main objective of this study was to investigate secondary school students' motivation for digital learning as experienced during the first school closure during the COVID-19 pandemic. This is of high relevance as the calls for more digitalization in education have long gone seemingly unheard – until the COVID-19 pandemic forced schools to switch to digital teaching and learning from one day to the next. Schools were not properly prepared for this challenge and teachers as well as students had to improvise a lot during the early stages of the pandemic-induced school closures. Research has shown that students' domain specific motivation and achievement is strongly related to their later educational and occupational choices. Therefore, it is of high importance to investigate, how motivated students were for digital learning when it suddenly became the standard modus operandi in schools. If digitalization in education is here to stay, it is crucial to know how students as its primary users perceive it and are affected by it.

The present research is theoretically based on the Expectancy-Value Theory that posits that individuals take up and follow through with learning activities if they consider them to be important and if they believe that they can be successful in performing them. This theory was recently expanded to the Situated Expectancy Value Theory that focusses more on individual differences in task valuing and expectancies for success by elaborating how person characteristics like gender and immigrant background are connected with certain stereotypes and role expectations. Following the intersectionality paradigm, the present study analysed effects of gender and immigrant background – person characteristics central to social identity formation – simultaneously. Moreover, considering the recent increase in adolescents identifying as gender non-binary, the authors did not just compare boys and girls but included gender diverse students in the analyses. This approach is necessary as digitalization in education is often seen as a key factor for more equity in education, but research on the motivation for digital learning in minority students is sparse – especially in the context of the rapid changes due to the COVID-19 pandemic.

The study's first objective was to examine associations between different expectancy and value components of digital learning motivation as well as their relation to perceived social support by teachers. In this study, intrinsic value and learning engagement represented the value component of motivation, and as expected were strongly associated: Students who enjoy digital learning are more likely to experience flow during digital learning tasks. Students' competence beliefs regarding digital learning represented the expectancy component of motivation. Interestingly, students' competence beliefs regarding digital learning were more strongly related to the intrinsic value they ascribed to digital learning than to learning engagement in this domain although both, intrinsic value and learning engagement represent facets of the value component of digital learning. Therefore, students who believe they can successfully master the challenges associated with digital learning are more likely to enjoy remote learning tasks than those who do not feel competent in this domain. Students' perceived teacher support for digital learning descriptively showed the highest correlations with their competence beliefs, followed by intrinsic value and learning engagement. This might be an indication that students who experience social support by their teachers during remote learning are more likely to feel prepared for the accompanying challenges. This might in turn lead to more positive attitudes toward digital learning and more engagement in this domain. However, this causal interpretation should be further examined using experimental methods. Nevertheless, the results suggest that teachers represent an important starting point for promoting students' digital learning motivation.

The second objective of the present study was to examine individual differences in the various digital learning components between students of different age, gender and immigrant background. There were age differences in students' competence beliefs, intrinsic value and perceived teacher support for digital learning, indicating that the motivational situation of young people develops unfavorably in the course of secondary school. This is in line with many studies from the last fifty years that find students' learning motivation to decrease during the teenage years and does not seem to be a specific feature of digital education (Schober et al., 2007). The findings demonstrate that changing the modus operandi of schools from on-site to digital learning does not automatically enhance student motivation. Teachers need to be better prepared for maintaining and fostering student motivation and lifelong learning competences in adolescence, e.g. during regular teacher education or via targeted training (Finsterwald et al. 2013). This is especially relevant in distance learning settings, where social aspects of learning do not happen automatically. Therefore, teachers have to be provided with tools and skills to offer social support – especially to students who have little support at home – and to promote social learning experiences between classmates using digital technologies.

Effective teaching requires knowledge and skills from many different domains. While teacher education often focuses on building teachers' expertise in their specific school subject matter and didactics, less emphasis is laid on motivational and learning psychology, and knowledge of technology. Moreover, many teachers who are still teaching were trained at a time when digital technology played no role in their studies at all. The model of technological pedagogical content knowledge (Mishra & Koehler, 2006) represents a helpful framework for integrating technology in teacher knowledge. In this model, content, pedagogy, and technology represent three main components of teacher knowledge that constitute effective teaching and have to be considered – including the interactions among and between them. There is no one-size-fits-all magic formula for successfully integrating technology in teaching. Therefore, efforts in this area have to be creatively designed and tailored to school subjects, age groups and classroom contexts.

The results of the present study revealed small gender differences in all examined components of digital learning motivation. Female students were found to show more favorable motivational patterns than male students and gender-diverse students. This is in line with studies finding higher competence beliefs regarding learning in digital settings in young women compared to young men (Perkowski, 2013). Moreover, this finding might also be connected school, learning and academic engagement being stereotyped as "feminine" (Heyder & Kessels, 2013). In addition, competence beliefs and perceived teacher support regarding digital learning were even lower in gender-diverse students than in male students, which highlights the importance of examining motivation not only in cisgender adolescents. Gender-diverse individuals were already found to suffer more discrimination and exclusion (Carpenter et al., 2020), and to be worried to be left without support in remote learning settings (Oinas et al., 2022) which might be associated with lower motivation for digital learning. Teachers need to be better prepared for teaching gender-diverse students to avoid unintended stereotyping and discrimination. Targeted interventions to promote gender sensitivity in teachers might be a solution as this topic is largely absent from regular teacher education (Kollmayer et al., 2020). However, it is important to mention that the reported gender differences from this study are small in size which is in line with authors arguing that gender differences in competence, attitudes, and motivation regarding digital learning are becoming less prevalent (e.g., Vekiri, 2013). Regarding differences between students with different first languages, there were very small differences in competence beliefs for and intrinsic value of digital learning to the detriment of students with non-German first languages. Moreover, the results showed a significant interaction between non-German first language and gender, in that gender-diverse students speaking German as their first language reported significantly lower intrinsic value than gender-diverse students non-German first language. However, these effects were in the close-to-zero range making it questionable if they can even be interpreted as relevant.

LIMITATIONS AND FUTURE RESEARCH DIRECTIONS

The present research investigated Austrian secondary school students' motivation for digital learning during the first school closures due to the COVID-19 pandemic, when for the first time ever all schools switched to digital education. Although this study has many strengths – like the large sample of students of different age, gender, native languages and from different school types – future research should focus more on the peculiarities of digital learning settings and examine which specific factors of digital education are associated with individual differences in students' motivation. Such findings are relevant to support schools and teachers in designing digital education in a way that motivates students of all ages, genders, origins and socio-economic backgrounds for digital learning. Especially regarding gender-diverse students, qualitative research could play an important role in finding out, what exactly reduces their motivation for digital learning. Moreover, future research should operationalize students' immigrant background more precisely. Students were simply asked for the language/s they speak at home and thus no differentiation between first- and second-generation immigrants is possible. Also, the sample did not contain enough students with non-German first languages to be able to examine the motivation for digital learning in different ethnic or cultural groups. In the 2019/20 school year, 27.4 percent of the students in Austria had a colloquial language other than German (Austrian Integration Fund, 2021), which shows that this group was underrepresented in our sample. In addition, students with low SES and consequently no or little access to digital devices are underrepresented in the sample due to the voluntary nature of the study and the recruitment process in the early days of the school closures. Future research should focus on these groups more as they are most likely the ones most at risk to suffer from the digital divide. With regard to the intersectionality framework, there are also some limitations to the present study. On the one hand, it is very likely that different ethnic or cultural groups are confronted with different stereotypes and discriminations, which was not considered in the study that only differentiated between students with German first language and students with non-German first languages. On the other hand, the study merely compared the motivation and perceived teacher support of different groups but did not explicitly consider the underlying power dynamics.

CONCLUSION

While digitalization in education is often seen as a key factor for creating learning environments and learning outcomes that support the societal transformation to a more equitable and sustainable world, not much is known about students' actual motivation for digital learning. Digital learning and especially emergency distance learning in a crisis such as COVID-19 poses challenges for schools, teachers and students in building the competences, skills, and attitudes necessary to take part in the process of digitalization. The present study demonstrates that students' competence beliefs, intrinsic value and learning engagement regarding digital learning are closely connected. Moreover, the results show that students' digital learning motivation is higher when they experience social support by teachers. Students' digital learning motivation decreases with age and is slightly higher in girls than in boys and gender-diverse students. Therefore, teacher education and training should be optimized to build the competences necessary for digital education that promotes motivation and competences for lifelong learning in all students and thus enables adolescents from all backgrounds to make informed decisions facilitating an equitable and environmentally sustainable society.

ACKNOWLEDGMENT

This research has been funded by the Vienna Science and Technology Fund (WWTF), the MEGA Bildungsstiftung, and the City of Vienna through project COV20-025.

REFERENCES

Austrian Integration Fund. (2021). *Bundesländer: Zahlen, Daten undFakten zu Migration und Integration 2021*. Bundeskanzleramt. Available online at https://www.integrationsfonds.at/fileadmin/user_upload/OEIF-BL-Broschuere_07012022_WEB.pdf

Bauer, G. R., Churchill, S. M., Mahendran, M., Walwyn, C., Lizotte, D., & Villa-Rueda, A. A. (2021). Intersectionality in quantitative research: A systematic review of its emergence and applications of theory and methods. *SSM - Population Health*, *14*, 100798. doi:10.1016/j.ssmph.2021.100798 PMID:33997247

Carpenter, C. S., Eppink, S. T., & Gonzales, G. (2020). Transgender status, gender identity, and socioeconomic outcomes in the United States. *Industrial & Labor Relations Review*, *73*(3), 573–599. doi:10.1177/0019793920902776

Cohen, J. (1988). *Statistical Power Analysis for the Behavioral Sciences*. Lawrence Erlbaum.

Colley, A., & Comber, C. (2003). Age and gender differences in computer use and attitudes among secondary school students: What has changed? *Educational Research*, *45*(2), 155–165. doi:10.1080/0013188032000103235

Cooper, J. (2006). The digital divide: The special case of gender. *Journal of Computer Assisted Learning*, *22*(5), 320–334. doi:10.1111/j.1365-2729.2006.00185.x

Crenshaw, K. (1989). Demarginalizing the intersection of race and sex: A Black feminist critique of antidiscrimination doctrine, feminist theory and antiracist politics. *University of Chicago Legal Forum*, (1).

Eccles, J. (2009). Who am I and what am I going to do with my life? Personal and collective identities as motivators of action. *Educational Psychologist*, *44*(2), 78–89. doi:10.1080/00461520902832368

Eccles, J. S., & Wigfield, A. (2020). From expectancy-value theory to situated expectancy-value theory: A developmental, social cognitive, and sociocultural perspective on motivation. *Contemporary Educational Psychology*, *61*, 101859. doi:10.1016/j.cedpsych.2020.101859

Entorf, H., & Minoiu, N. (2005). What a difference immigrant policy makes: A comparison of PISA scores in Europe and traditional countries of imimmigrant. *German Economic Review*, *6*(3), 355–376. doi:10.1111/j.1468-0475.2005.00137.x

Finsterwald, M., Wagner, P., Schober, B., Lüftenegger, M., & Spiel, C. (2013). Fostering lifelong learning–Evaluation of a teacher education program for professional teachers. *Teaching and Teacher Education*, *29*, 144–155. doi:10.1016/j.tate.2012.08.009

Goodman, M., Adams, N., Corneil, T., Kreukels, B., Motmans, J., & Coleman, E. (2019). Size and distribution of transgender and gender nonconforming populations: A narrative review. *Endocrinology and Metabolism Clinics*, *48*(2), 303–321. doi:10.1016/j.ecl.2019.01.001 PMID:31027541

Harris, J. C., & Patton, L. D. (2019). Un/doing intersectionality through higher education research. *The Journal of Higher Education*, *90*(3), 347–372. doi:10.1080/00221546.2018.1536936

Heyder, A., & Kessels, U. (2013). Is school feminine? Implicit gender stereotyping of school as a predictor of academic achievement. *Sex Roles*, *69*(11), 605–617. doi:10.100711199-013-0309-9

IIEP-UNESCO. (2020). *COVID-19 School Closures: Why Girls Are More at Risk*. Available online at: https://www.iiep.unesco.org/en/covid-19-school-closures-why-girls-are-more-risk-13406

Khakpour, N. (2022). *Deutsch-Können. Schulisch umkämpftes Artikulationsgeschehen*. Beltz.

Kollmayer, M., Schober, B., & Spiel, C. (2018a). Gender stereotypes in education: Development, consequences, and interventions. *European Journal of Developmental Psychology*, *15*(4), 361–377. doi:10.1080/17405629.2016.1193483

Kollmayer, M., Schultes, M.-T., Lüftenegger, M., Finsterwald, M., Spiel, C., & Schober, B. (2020). REFLECT – A Teacher Training Program to Promote Gender Equality in Schools. *Frontiers in Education, 5*, Article 136.

Kollmayer, M., Schultes, M. T., Schober, B., Hodosi, T., & Spiel, C. (2018b). Parents' judgments about the desirability of toys for their children: Associations with gender role attitudes, gender-typing of toys, and demographics. *Sex Roles*, *79*(5), 329–341. doi:10.100711199-017-0882-4 PMID:30147224

Korlat, S., Foerst, N. M., Schultes, M. T., Schober, B., Spiel, C., & Kollmayer, M. (2022). Gender role identity and gender intensification: Agency and communion in adolescents' spontaneous self-descriptions. *European Journal of Developmental Psychology*, *19*(1), 64–88. doi:10.1080/17405629.2020.1865143

Korlat, S., Kollmayer, M., Holzer, J., Lüftenegger, M., Pelikan, E. R., Schober, B., & Spiel, C. (2021). Gender Differences in Digital Learning During COVID-19: Competence Beliefs, Intrinsic Value, Learning Engagement, and Perceived Teacher Support. *Frontiers in Psychology*, *12*, 63776. doi:10.3389/fpsyg.2021.637776 PMID:33868109

Li, N., & Kirkup, G. (2007). Gender and cultural differences in Internet use: A study of China and the UK. *Computers & Education*, *48*(2), 301–317. doi:10.1016/j.compedu.2005.01.007

Maina-Okori, N. M., Koushik, J. R., & Wilson, A. (2018). Reimagining intersectionality in environmental and sustainability education: A critical literature review. *The Journal of Environmental Education*, *49*(4), 286–296. doi:10.1080/00958964.2017.1364215

Mishra, P., & Koehler, M. J. (2006). Technological pedagogical content knowledge: A framework for integrating technology in teacher knowledge. *Teachers College Record*, *108*(6), 1017–1054. doi:10.1111/j.1467-9620.2006.00684.x

Nefesh-Clarke, L., Orser, B., & Thomas, M. (2020). *COVID-19 Response Strategies, Addressing Digital Gender Divides*. https://www.g20-insights.org/policy_briefs/covid-19-response-strategies-addressing-digital-gender-divides/

Oinas, S., Hotulainen, R., Koivuhovi, S., Brunila, K., & Vainikainen, M. P. (2022). Remote learning experiences of girls, boys and non-binary students. *Computers & Education*, *183*, 104499. doi:10.1016/j.compedu.2022.104499

Perkowski, J. (2013). The role of gender in distance learning: A meta-analytic review of gender differences in academic performance and self-efficacy in distance learning. *Journal of Educational Technology Systems*, *41*(3), 267–278. doi:10.2190/ET.41.3.e

Schober, B., Finsterwald, M., Wagner, P., Lüftenegger, M., Aysner, M., & Spiel, C. (2007). TALK—A training program to encourage lifelong learning in school. *Zeitschrift für Psychologie. The Journal of Psychology*, *215*(3), 183–193.

Schober, B., Lüftenegger, M., & Spiel, C. (2020). *Learning Conditions During COVID-19 Pupils*. AUSSDA., doi:10.11587/VRQL3B

UN. (2020). *Education During COVID-19 and Beyond*. https://www.un.org/development/desa/dspd/wp-content/uploads/sites/22/2020/08/sg_policy_brief_covid-19_and_education_august_2020.pdf

UNICEF. (2020). *Keeping the World's Children Learning Through COVID-19*. https://www.unicef.org/coronavirus/keeping-worlds-children-learning-through-covid-19

Vekiri, I. (2013). Information science instruction and changes in girls' and boy's expectancy and value beliefs: In search of gender-equitable pedagogical practices. *Computers & Education*, *64*, 104–115. doi:10.1016/j.compedu.2013.01.011

Volman, M., & van Eck, E. (2001). Gender equity and information technology in education: The second decade. *Review of Educational Research*, *71*(4), 613–634. doi:10.3102/00346543071004613

Warschauer, M., Knobel, M., & Stone, L. (2004). Technology and equity in schooling: Deconstructing the digital divide. *Educational Policy*, *18*(4), 562–588. doi:10.1177/0895904804266469

Wigfield, A., & Eccles, J. S. (2000). Expectancy–value theory of achievement motivation. *Contemporary Educational Psychology*, *25*(1), 68–81. doi:10.1006/ceps.1999.1015 PMID:10620382

ADDITIONAL READING

Cooper, J. (2006). The digital divide: The special case of gender. *Journal of Computer Assisted Learning*, *22*(5), 320–334. doi:10.1111/j.1365-2729.2006.00185.x

Eccles, J. S., & Wigfield, A. (2020). From expectancy-value theory to situated expectancy-value theory: A developmental, social cognitive, and sociocultural perspective on motivation. *Contemporary Educational Psychology*, *61*, 101859. doi:10.1016/j.cedpsych.2020.101859

Finsterwald, M., Wagner, P., Schober, B., Lüftenegger, M., & Spiel, C. (2013). Fostering lifelong learning–Evaluation of a teacher education program for professional teachers. *Teaching and Teacher Education*, *29*, 144–155. doi:10.1016/j.tate.2012.08.009

Kollmayer, M., Schober, B., & Spiel, C. (2018). Gender stereotypes in education: Development, consequences, and interventions. *European Journal of Developmental Psychology*, *15*(4), 361–377. doi:10.1080/17405629.2016.1193483

Kollmayer M., Schultes M.-T., Lüftenegger M., Finsterwald M., Spiel C., & Schober B. (2020). REFLECT – A Teacher Training Program to Promote Gender Equality in Schools. *Frontiers in Education, 5*, Article 136.

Korlat, S., Kollmayer, M., Holzer, J., Lüftenegger, M., Pelikan, E. R., Schober, B., & Spiel, C. (2021). Gender Differences in Digital Learning During COVID-19: Competence Beliefs, Intrinsic Value, Learning Engagement, and Perceived Teacher Support. *Frontiers in Psychology*, *12*, 63776. doi:10.3389/fpsyg.2021.637776 PMID:33868109

Perkowski, J. (2013). The role of gender in distance learning: A meta-analytic review of gender differences in academic performance and self-efficacy in distance learning. *Journal of Educational Technology Systems*, *41*(3), 267–278. doi:10.2190/ET.41.3.e

Schober, B., Finsterwald, M., Wagner, P., Lüftenegger, M., Aysner, M., & Spiel, C. (2007). TALK—A training program to encourage lifelong learning in school. *Zeitschrift für Psychologie. The Journal of Psychology*, *215*(3), 183–193.

Warschauer, M., Knobel, M., & Stone, L. (2004). Technology and equity in schooling: Deconstructing the digital divide. *Educational Policy*, *18*(4), 562–588. doi:10.1177/0895904804266469

Wigfield, A., & Eccles, J. S. (2000). Expectancy–value theory of achievement motivation. *Contemporary Educational Psychology*, *25*(1), 68–81. doi:10.1006/ceps.1999.1015 PMID:10620382

APPENDIX

Table 2. Descriptive statistics of various aspects of students' digital learning motivation by gender and immigrant background

		Competence Beliefs			Intrinsic Value			Learning Engagement			Perceived Teacher Support		
Immigrant Background	**Gender**	*M*	*SD*	*N*	*M*	*SD*	*N*	*M*	*SD*	*N*	*M*	*SD*	*N*
Students with German native language	Female	4.16	0.672	9,613	2.92	1.150	9,613	3.28	0.916	9,608	4.18	0.764	9,614
	Male	4.05	0.717	5,980	2.69	1.118	5,981	3.13	0.937	5,977	4.07	0.836	5,980
	Diverse	4.14	0.682	61	2.38	1.110	61	3.03	0.967	61	3.74	1.026	61
	Total	4.12	0.715	15,654	2.83	1.143	15,655	3.22	0.927	15,646	4.14	0.796	15,655
Students with non-German native language	Female	4.01	0.801	2,102	2.90	1.196	2,110	3.41	0.917	2,109	4.07	0.810	2,111
	Male	4.11	0.732	1,204	2.78	1.178	1,215	3.23	0.997	1,213	4.00	0.907	1,215
	Diverse	3.79	0.917	33	2.81	1.304	35	3.16	1.159	35	3.90	0.942	35
	Total	3.63	0.996	3,339	2.85	1.192	3,360	3.35	0.953	3,357	4.04	0.849	3,361
Total	Female	3.73	0.944	11,715	2.92	1.158	11,723	3.30	0.918	11,717	4.16	0.774	11,725
	Male	4.14	0.690	7184	2.71	1.128	7,196	3.15	0.948	7,190	4.06	0.849	7,195
	Diverse	4.03	0.753	94	2.53	1.196	96	3.08	1.037	96	3.80	0.994	96
	Total	4.12	0.703	18,993	2.84	1.152	19,015	3.25	0.933	19,003	4.12	0.806	19,016

Chapter 15
Smart Energy, Smart Schools:
Project-Based Learning About Energy Transition and Digitalization

Nicole Raschke
TU Dresden, Germany

Lisa Wey
TU Dresden, Germany

Thomas Arendt
TU Dresden, Germany

ABSTRACT

This chapter presents the project "Smart Energy Smart Schools" (SENSOr), which develops project-oriented learning environments on the topic of energy in public school buildings. The project builds bridges between education for sustainable development and digitalization. In the chapter, three different educational modules, the environmental measuring station, the history of light sources, and the planetarium are dealt with in more detail. They show a useful connection between ESD and digitalization or digital media. Another focus is the evaluation of the first feedback from the students and teachers. This leads to the formulation of initial theses that can be derived from this. Finally, various opportunities and challenges that arose on an individual and institutional level during the implementation of the project are described.

INTRODUCTION

Topics of the energy transition confront society worldwide with complex challenges. Digitalization and new forms of connectivity promise smart solutions for the efficient usage of energy. Thus, not only technological, and institutional changes towards sustainable power sources are necessary, also new practices in dealing with energy in everyday life are becoming important. The explorative project "SENSOr - Smart Energy Smart Schools" brings together potentials of digitalization on the one hand and Education for

DOI: 10.4018/978-1-7998-5033-5.ch015

Sustainable Development (ESD) on the other hand. It aims to promote interest for the topics of energy transition, climate change and sustainability with the help of learning arrangements. This paper will discuss whether it successfully initiates this and triggers a potentially longer process. Thereby, the project uses the example of energy use in public school buildings in project-based learning environments and offers a contribution to a whole school approach (Mathie & Wals, 2022).

Based on theoretical considerations of transformative learning in the context of sustainable development and digitalization, the first chapter postulates central challenges that should be taken into account in conceptual considerations for designing learning opportunities. Subsequently, it is discussed, how the project SENSOr should meet the described challenges. The implementation of the project is concretised by using the example of three educational modules. These are representative for the usage and integration of digital tools in educational environments, as well as the promotion of new practices in everyday life for a sustainable transformation in the energy sector. The utilized questionnaire is briefly explained, and first feedbacks are evaluated. Ending with a discussion about the first preliminary theses, the opportunities and risks arising from educational practice are concerned.

THEORETICAL BACKGROUND

The need for a sustainable, future-oriented development is unquestioned and is described in the WBGU[1] report *"World in Transition"* (WBGU, 2011) as a comprehensive social transformation process. Especially in the confrontation with multiple crises, shaping social debates currently, it is postulated that education for sustainable development can have an important impact. Although many people are interested in sustainability and associate great chances to a sustainable future development, they have little faith in the achievability of the desired future (Grund & Brock, 2020). These insights are contradictory to a certain extent to the requirements of a social transformation process in which actors participate as responsible citizens in designing a sustainable development. The project on which this article is based addresses the issue and examines the chances and limitations of designing learning opportunities in the context of the energy transition.

ESD aims to empower people to think and act in a sustainable way which requires critical reflection on one's own actions and active participation in social decision-making processes (de Haan, 2008). Regarding this, learning opportunities should be designed to enable own experiences of self-efficacy (Bandura, 1977; Oberrauch et al., 2021), as well as encouragement. These actions demand reflection in the context of sustainability concepts. Research projects in the context of ESD have shown that proactive action and self-efficacy experiences have a great impact on students' sustainability-related awareness, interest formation and attitudes (e.g., Fisman, 2005; Malberg Dyg & Wistoft, 2018).

Changing social circumstances, like those found expression in or through digitalization, pose a challenge. In a culture of digitality (Stalder, 2016), all areas of life are digitally permeated and shaped. The WBGU (2019) also links digitalization and sustainability together and questions which framework could promote positive effects on resource consumption and environmental protection. This is also based on the demand that digitalization should be oriented towards a global transformation for sustainability. On the one hand, it can be stated that information and communication technologies undeniably make an important contribution to the global sustainability goals in the field of science, technology, and innovation. Thus, they represent a central instrument of sustainable development (Leal Filho et al., 2021). On the other hand, learning and education cannot be understood independently of the material and social relations in which they are embedded and which they (re-)produce (Allert et al., 2017, p. 156). The processes of experiencing, producing and reflecting on knowledge are also increasingly influenced and permeated by digitalization. The policy paper of the Higher Education Association for Geography Education shows how education and digitalization are interwoven in many ways (Dorsch et al., 2020).

In the context of ESD and digitalization, an educational practice of inquiry-based learning can offer a rewarding approach. The main reason for its effectiveness is geared towards pursuing individual questions in the learning process in self-selected methodological steps. Such learning is characterised by experiences, encounters and interactions that are individually and socially meaningful. Students actively shape and reflect the process of a research or learning project in terms of content and organisation. Thus, in the process of inquiry-based learning, students have the greatest possible degree of autonomy. It does not consist of building up a fund of handed-down, (supposedly) safe knowledge, but of a collaborative and participatory process of searching and finding, problematizing and seeing, wondering and inventing, researching and sharing (Huber, 2009). Therefore, inquiry-based learning can be considered a chance for ESD. It is linked to questioning and changing self- and world-relations by providing problem-oriented concrete spaces of experience and moments of reflection and contributing to the learners' ability to act. Occurring irritations, cognitive dissonances, and emotional experiences are accompanied by the teacher. This way both, teachers, and students, enter into dialogical and reflexive negotiations with each other (Getzin & Singer-Brodowski, 2016).

From the relationships described above, various challenges for designing learning environments can be identified at different levels. These mark central starting points in the project SENSOr. On an individual level, it is not only about learning as an extension of knowledge or development of skills, but more profoundly, about fundamental world and self-relations in social change. In this respect, the challenge is connected to how learning occasions can contribute to these procedures in the first place and how learning opportunities can be designed.

The main question on the institutional level is which conditions and structures could promote transformative learning in the sense of ESD and which are counterproductive. The main objects of this study are therefore the students and teachers in their individual development process. However, not only these are to be investigated but also the institutional framework conditions such as measures and strategies, possibilities for integrating project teaching or school timetables which can enable a constructive approach to existing challenges in the sense of ESD.

The advancing digitalization offers new ways of integrating ESD into everyday school life (Leal Filho et al., 2021). Geography appears to be the best subject to combine all the other disciplines in class. Working with geoinformation, for example, requires inter alia the general knowledge of physics, mathematics, informatics, history, and chemistry. Project SENSOr aims to entangle digitalization with ESD by offering educational modules, focussing on digital media, energy, and climate related topics. According to the OECD framework, competencies of acting sustainable are based on knowledge and skills inextricably intertwined with attitudes and values of everyone (OECD, 2016). By utilizing the school building as an example for sensor-based measurements and observations, students learn how to act sustainable within the given environment. Focussing on the energy consumption, they evaluate, the efficiency of daily used devices.

For evaluating these factors in the project SENSOr, a student-survey has been developed. The collected data will show whether an inquiry-oriented approach is a possibility to arouse the interest of the students in topics of energy consumption. Furthermore, the survey focuses on how they see themselves as active agents in the entire field (of action) of climate change and energy transition. On the one hand, the questionnaire offers students the chance of giving feedback to the project itself. On the other hand, it also looks at sustainability awareness and self-efficacy, which the project aims to promote. The questionnaire is performed after completing all educational modules on site. It targets three different levels: affective, cognitive, and conative. The affective level includes the students' opinions on feelings and attitudes. The cognitive one is about the knowledge and assessment. The last one examines the willingness or the possibilities to act. These are typical for measuring environmental consciousness (Oberrauch et al., 2021). Since this is to be promoted with the project SENSOr, the survey was structured accordingly.

PRESENTATION OF THE PROJECT SENSOR

SENSOr is an interdisciplinary project of the TU Dresden (project period 2020-2022), which is grant-aided by *The German Federal Environmental Foundation*. The project covers topics related to energy and its transition. It questions how these topics can be experienced by students and teachers in educational contexts, based on theoretical considerations of transformative ESD and digitalization. The aim of the explorative project is to critically question energy production and usage. In doing so, the project also investigates the functioning of ecosystems. These are closely related to the topic of energy, e.g., effects on the ecosystem through various forms of energy production or the storage of CO_2. The discussion is not only to be held together with students in the school community but also to derive possible measures for an energy-efficient everyday life. Through possible implementation, this could lead to a reduction in energy consumption (Ntanos et al., 2018).

The core task of the project is the development, testing, evaluation, and improvement of learning arrangements (also: educational modules) in the form of experiments and environmental measurements. The learning arrangements are project-based. They connect to existing disciplinary knowledge from different subjects such as geography, physics, or computer science. The educational modules are designed for grades 5 to 13. Depending on their age, the students can benefit from their previous knowledge of sustainability, energy or even programming skills. The project also takes up interdisciplinary and practical knowledge.

Even though educational modules are designed to be used in inquiry-based learning opportunities, they can be flexibly implemented in different ways. For example, subject-specific or in project-based arrangements. The modules are mostly developed based on inductive learning. As the students have to use examples (in the school building) to explain e.g., connections or effects, this should stimulate the students to think independently and encourage them to develop further questions of energy consumption, its production, and transition. For example, it could encourage students to question the energy supply at home: how is electricity generated or how does the photovoltaic system on the roof actually work? The students examine energy consumers, work and measure with various sensors and then evaluate the results obtained. The investigations can be carried out both analogue (e.g., reading the consumption figures) and digitally (CO_2-concentration measurement using sensors). In this way, the students gain new knowledge and ideally develop an awareness of physical quantities and the interactions between resources, climate and energy, as well as the associated possibilities for action in connection with energy consumption. The exemplary examination of the school building should raise consciousness for similar problems and possible actions in their everyday life. Results of this investigation could eventually be applied to the school building. This way, students experience self-efficacy and could become multipliers for the school community and the regional school environment. Scenarios like these are considered as the best case and a total success for the project.

The educational modules contain explanations on the content classification, educational design, methodical implementation, and optional material for the students and teachers. This way, they can be flexibly adapted and applied to the needs of different school situations and types of schools. To ensure that the materials stay available and can be used beyond the duration of the project, the educational modules will be preserved. Firstly, all materials will be published on the permanent project website (https://sensor.geo.tu-dresden.de/) under a Creative Commons licence (CC BY 4.0). A publication on other platforms is also planned. This allows open access, and the materials can be freely downloaded, adapted, and distributed for further usage. Secondly, a project seminar for teacher trainees on transformative ESD is being developed and was piloted in the winter semester of 2021/2022. Thirdly, teachers are trained and encouraged to implement the educational modules to create learning opportunities in study-groups and lessons. Although the modules were designed to be self-explanatory, individual trainings become necessary. They are performed on demand, especially when unavoidable adjustments to local conditions emerge.

Presentation of the Educational Modules

The modularised educational modules, each with a different pedagogical orientation are forming the core of the project SENSOr.

Figure 1. Overview modules (SENSOr website)

There are two different kinds of modules available. While the overview-modules are suitable to provide introduction points on topics like climate change, energy usage, sustainability, as well as, energy transition (see Figure 1), the experiment-based modules enable a more research-oriented approach. Latter modules cover more in-depth topics and related tools like the work with measurement devices for environmental data, sensors, microcontrollers, and physical experiments (see Figure 2).

Figure 2. Experimental modules (SENSOr website)

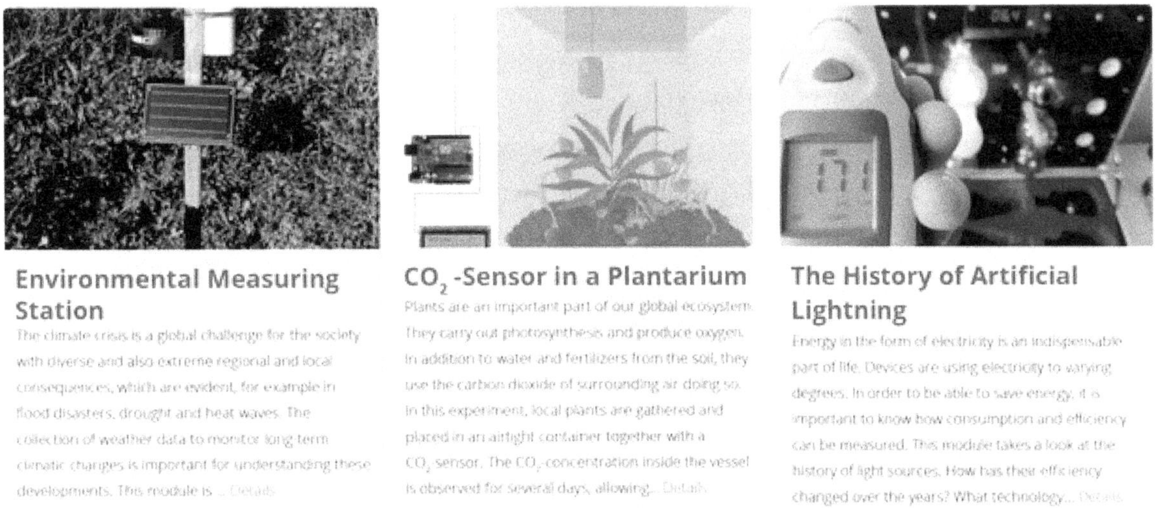

Thus, the overview modules offer the possibility to integrate the experimental modules into complex, thematic contexts. It is possible that these modules are picked by teachers or by the students based on their personal interests. If they, for example, choose to explore environmental factors and their interactions, it is very easy to link the overview module "Climate change" with the "Environmental Measuring Station" and the "CO_2-Sensor". These two are also linkable to the topic of energy and its transition since different types of energy production are emitting different amounts of greenhouse gases. Another variant might result in the usage of the overview module "Energy" together with the modules "Coal Power Plant", "Dye Solar Cell" and "The History of Artificial Lightning". This combination can stimulate an action-oriented examination of energy production and its consumption in the school building. In addition to the instructions and working materials for students, all modules contain also essential resources, course plans, and components for teachers.

The following, three experimental educational modules are presented as examples. These are meant to show how learning opportunities are designed and what possibilities are connected to them. The selected educational modules show in a special way how ESD, digitalization and energy transition are linked.

Educational Module "Environmental Measuring Station"

The educational module "Environmental Measuring Station" can be linked to global sustainability goals and focuses especially on ecological topics (UN, 2015). The connection to the energy issues does not seem to be clear at first. However, this becomes clear in the strategies that can be derived. These are briefly presented at the end of the module. The station (see Figure 3) collects data from three different environmental factors by using two separate sensors: precipitation, humidity, and temperature. In doing so, the data is collected in a database every minute. The module intends to read out the data manually or automatically at regular intervals. Afterwards, the students create diagrams of the collected data. These can be used to gain insights into the weather conditions of their own school. They can show different environmental influences, such as mild winters, hot summers, or extreme weather events. As part of an extracurricular study-group, the environmental measuring station could be expended with further devices, like anemometers, pyranometers, gas detectors or dust sensors.

Figure 3. Environmental measuring station

This module is an example of a useful combination of geoinformatics, digitalization and ESD in the project SENSOr. Among other things, it combines various perspectives of geographical education under the conditions of digitalization according to the policy paper mentioned above (Dorsch et al., 2020). This is, for example, the ability to represent, systematize and analyze geographical phenomena, structures, and processes by using digital geomedia. The students learn how and with which sensors data on environmental factors can be measured. They study data by creating their own diagrams. Therefore, they can explain and visualize observed weather phenomena with the help of their own data. Thus, this module has a supportive effect and invites to experience the topic of weather and climate change experimentally. In case of longer surveys, climate diagrams could be created for the school location. These could be compared with other official climate diagrams or contribute to the local measuring network of environmental data.

This way, students are sensitised to the topic of weather and (eventually) climate change. In addition to the measurable environmental factors, they learn how to visualize and evaluate data, as well as, how to work with sensors and microcontrollers. Students also learn to question the correctness of elaborated data critically and carry out an error analysis. This gives them the opportunity to derive strategies or measures related to weather phenomena from their own measurements. For example, one could be the regulation of the school heating system via the measured outdoor temperature, so energy resources do not have to be consumed unnecessarily. Another strategy could be the controlling of the watering of the school garden depending on the monitored precipitation amount.

Educational Module "The History of Artificial Lightning"

The educational module applies especially to the areas of environmental compatibility, economic efficiency, and security of supply. From a global perspective, it can be stated that the demand for energy is increasing worldwide and is related to the rising living standards and current trends such as digitalization. In this context, energy and energy supply are in the area of tension between technology, economy and society. In addition to technological advances, economic and social developments are also important. Regarding this statement, consumers also have an influence on how energy systems develop and how much energy is needed (Becker et al., 2021). It is important to understand how consumption and efficiency can be measured to use energy appropriately and effectively. Using the example of light bulbs, students are given the opportunity to distinguish between devices based on their efficiency-classes. They can also draw conclusions about their own usage behaviour in their everyday life and in the school environment.

This module looks at the technological achievements of the past 120 years. How has the efficiency of each technology changed over the years? What made the development in this sector necessary? The comparison of different types of lamps is used as an example to classify their evolution. The students study various materials and summarize essential information about the types. For example, the 120-year-old carbon-wire light bulb or the modern LED light. The different bulbs are installed in a demonstrator suitcase (see Figure 4). Students can read the consumed amount of power while measuring the irradiance of a light bulb by using a lux meter. Depending on the results, the students can draw comparisons between the different technologies.

Figure 4. Demonstrator suitcase

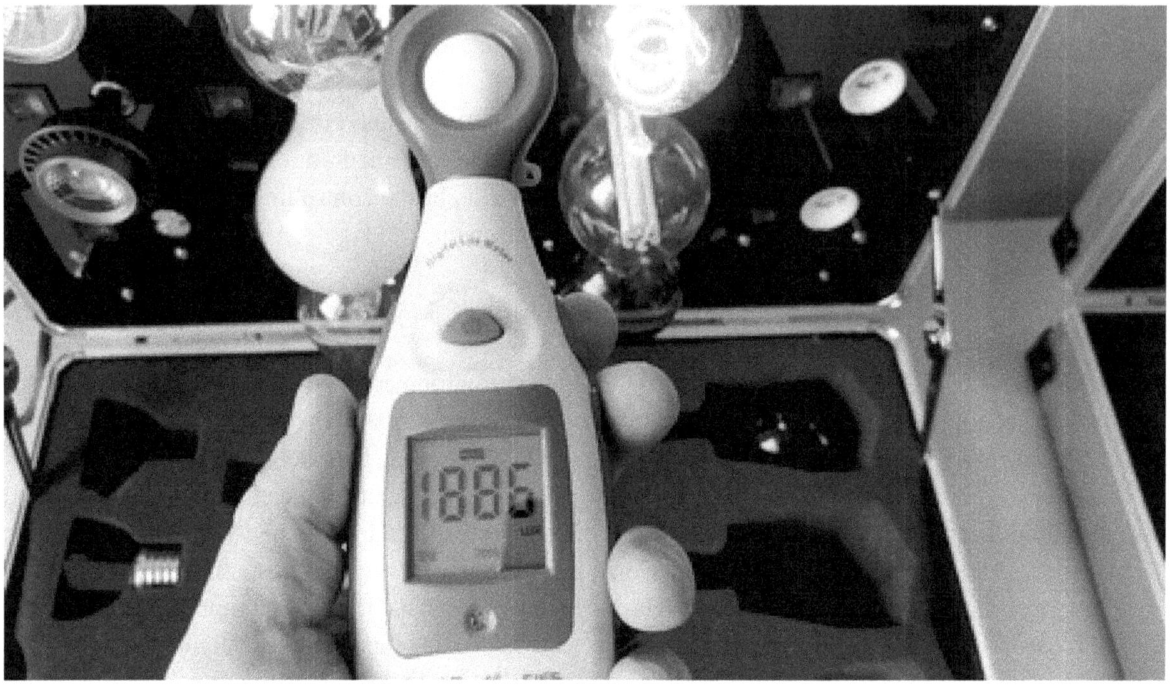

The focus of this experiment is on understanding physical terms in their everyday meaning. Units such as voltage, power, illuminance, and luminous flux are discussed and evaluated. This module is based on experimental learning and makes it possible to draw conclusions about the selection of suitable light sources through individual observations. Is the experimentation phase completed, the type, energy consumption and usage periods of the lamps should be known by every participant. It is possible to distinguish differences and rate used compartments in the school building easily. This is the entry point where students could actively influence the decision-makers around the school building and, thus, experience self-efficacy if their advices are implemented immediately.

Educational Module "CO_2 Sensor in a Planetarium"

Plants in all their biodiversity appear to be the most important part of the worldwide global carbon cycle. During daytime, they process carbon dioxide via photosynthesis into oxygen and carbon stored in their own cells creating biomass and growth. Everything needed to sustain is soil, air, fertilizers, water, and sunlight. This experiment will show how also local plants will perform such resource-conservations. For this purpose, an artificial 'ecosystem in a jar' will be created and a CO_2-sensor connected to an Arduino-microcontroller for measurement will be used (see Figure 5).

Figure 5. Planetarium with installed CO_2-sensor

In class the first step is to carefully gather tiny growing, hydrophilic (moisture-loving or swamp) plants, mosses and decorative elements including a little bit of soil. Microorganisms and insects such as springtails, woodlice, worms, and tiny bugs are part of the ecosystem and are highly recommended to be collected too. The gathering could be connected with excursions to nearby riverbanks and forests.

The second step is to prepare the planetarium itself. The bottom layer is the water-bearing reservoir. It needs to be filled with gravel and small stones in a recommended thickness of 2-4 cm. This is equal to the ground water layer on the earth. It drains the surface layer while providing water to the roots. The next one is a separator made of fiber, mesh, or non-rotting tissue. It is placed to prevent blending of the filter layer and the bottom layer. The filter layer consists of clean sand and activated carbon. To substitute the activated carbon, crushed charcoal can be used equally. The second layer should also be 2-4 cm high. Right above the two layers the soil can be placed. In case plants have already been collected, the soil where they originally grew in is perfectly suitable for our purpose. It contains enough animals and microorganisms to support the new ecosystem.

Once the plants and decorations (stones, branches, and moss) are in place, the CO_2-sensor is loosely placed in the container. The sensor will measure, store, and evaluate the number of CO_2-particles inside that hermetic environment. When the soil is humidified perfectly, and the experiment is placed on a bright spot it is expected that the CO_2-particles inside drop during daytime and slightly raise again in the night. Step by step it will be observed that the CO_2-level is reduced. This is the proof, that plants are indeed performing photosynthesis, help keeping the CO_2-level low and the air breathable.

The CO_2-sensor for the initial measurement, unfortunately, will not resist the humidity in a long-term observation. So, it needs to be removed from the container after two weeks. When sealed again, no maintenance is needed anymore. The amount of CO_2 will eventually become reduced to a point of equilibrium, where plants stop their growth because of missing carbon particles in the air. Over time the only available CO_2 is provided by the utilization of old plant material, biomass, and animal excrements. Some specimens will not be able to survive such conditions while others will adapt to their new environment. Similar experiments with plants in closed environments have sustained for over 60 years now. That's the reason this setup is considered as highly valuable to show processes of sustainable ecosystems.

EVALUATION OF THE PROJECT

Explanation of the Questionnaire

The project itself is evaluated using a method called Five Finger Feedback. Each finger represents a different aspect. For example, the thumb asks what the student liked, while the little finger asks what aspect of the project was neglected. Through open impulses, particularly successful or less successful implementations or suggestions for improvement are asked.

The four main items addressed by the project were used to formulate the questionnaire. These are energy transition, environmental protection, climate change, and the implementation of an extracurricular study-group for environmental research. The latter is one objective of the project SENSOr. Therefore, the item "extracurricular study-group" will be used to check the students' willingness to establish and participate. At least one question was formulated for each level (affective, cognitive, and conative), resulting in three to five questions per item. Table 1 shows some of the related questions. All the items and questions are carefully chosen to include and link aspects of self-efficacy according to Bandura (1997). Furthermore, it was given special attention to ask mainly closed questions with a four-point Likert-scale plus the additional response checkbox "I don't know".

Table 1. Items and levels of the questionnaire with related questions

	Environmental Protection	**Climate Change**	**Energy Transition**	**Extracurricular Study-Group**
Affective Level (students' opinion about feelings and attitudes)	It is important to me that others in my area are committed to environmental protection.	I am worried about climate change.	I think it is useful to avoid fossil energy sources (such as lignite or petroleum).	I consider a study-group as useful.
Cognitive Level (students' knowledge and assessment)	I know possibilities of contribution to environmental protection.	I know the causes of greenhouse gases.	I know how the energy transition is linked to climate change.	I have concrete ideas on what the study-group should deal with. Name examples:
Conative Level (students' willingness or possibilities to act)	I am actively committed to environmental protection.	I am willing to take action against climate change.	I am willing to save energy in my everyday life.	I would co-found a study-group.

An additional query of the topic “environmental protection” was included. This is designed to examine areas of life, which the students may already be engaged in. It also underlines the importance of this topic and determines the awareness of sustainability in everyday practices.

Project SENSOr sees itself as an explorative intervention study that investigates possibilities and limits of learning occasions on the topic of energy transition. This means that competences are not to be reproduced, but intended to promote the students’ interest. Items such as environmental awareness were included in the questionnaire to derive possible thesis. These can form the basis for future research. That is why it was decided not to use a pre-post design. Furthermore, a student-survey is influenced and relativised by various factors. These include, for example, the social desirability of the answer, answer tendencies to always say “yes” or “no”, answer refusals or answers that are given even though one has not formed an opinion on the question (Meier Kruker & Rauh, 2005).

Results

The current number of valid answers averaged 75 per question (41 female, 29 male, 5 no specification). Some responses count 95 valid answers per question (46 female, 42 male, 7 no specification). The reason for discrepancies is the insufficient validity of the given answers. Regarding the type and scope of the collected samples, it is not possible to make generalized statements. The results rather offer an exemplary insight into students’ point of view. The evaluation of the answers is presented in relation to the goals of the project. The main items are awareness, self-efficacy with consideration of the multiplier effect and the extracurricular study-group for environmental research.

Awareness

The awareness of the existence environmental crisis related issues can be derived among the questions focusing on areas of life for environmental protection. The survey shows that the areas of greatest interest are recycling and mobility. For example, over 70% of the girls and boys responded, that they are already actively involved in the area of *waste reduction / waste sorting*. In case of *recycling and reutilization*, it is also more than half of the girls and boys. Girls appear to be slightly more interested in *mobility, transport and travel* than boys. In general, the students’ introspection is that they are already involved in the areas mentioned above but all of them would like to become more engaged.

The majority of students stated that they are already involved in areas of *energy consumption, energy savings*, and almost a half are committed to *household electronics*. Similar to the areas about recycling and mobility they would like to do more. Just a few stated that these areas were not important to them at all. The question “I know how the energy transition is connected to the climate change” also illustrates the students’ awareness of environmentally relevant issues. Thus, the knowledge about the (often not obvious) connection becomes apparent. Here, most of the students agree or strongly agree.

Self-Efficacy/Multiplier Effect

The question “I am concerned about climate change” was (strongly) agreed by the vast majority. This means, that climate change is an important issue in the everyday life of the students. More than half of the students also stated that climate change lies in the responsibility of politics and everyone equally.

To support such thinking, self-efficacy experiences are beneficial and to be strived for (Oberrauch et al., 2021).

Figure 6. Answers to the question about commitment of others to environmental protection (N=95)

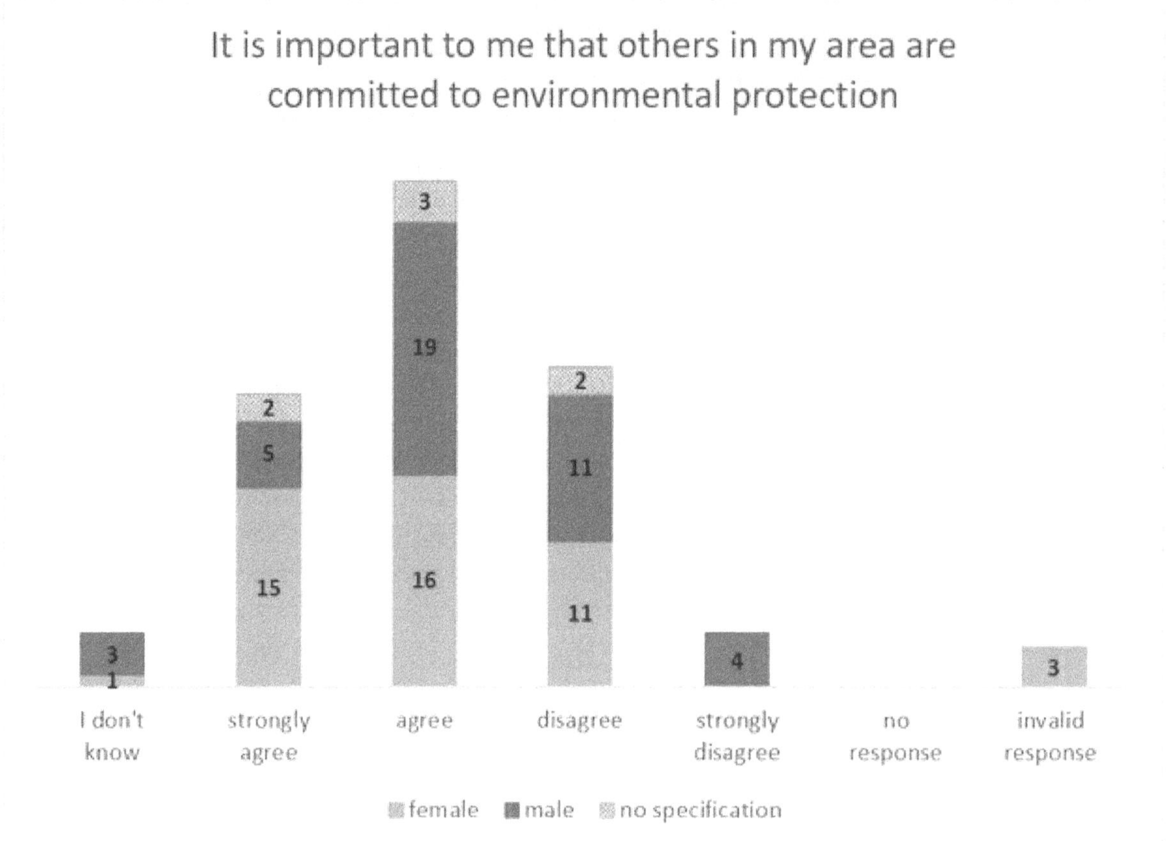

The following questions explore the willingness to do something about climate change or to save energy. They are examples of how students take action in everyday life and could act as multipliers. For the question "I am willing to save energy in my everyday life", nearly 80% (strongly) agreed. The question "I am willing to take action against climate change" was also (strongly) agreed by the majority of the students. A similar distribution of answers was also generated by the further question "It is important to me that others in my area are committed to environmental protection" (see Figure 6). Interpreting this figure, a slight gender difference is noticeable, how strongly boys and girls agree (or strongly disagree) to the commitment of others in their environment.

Extracurricular Study-Group for Environmental Research

Figure 7. Answers to the usefulness of a study-group (N=75)

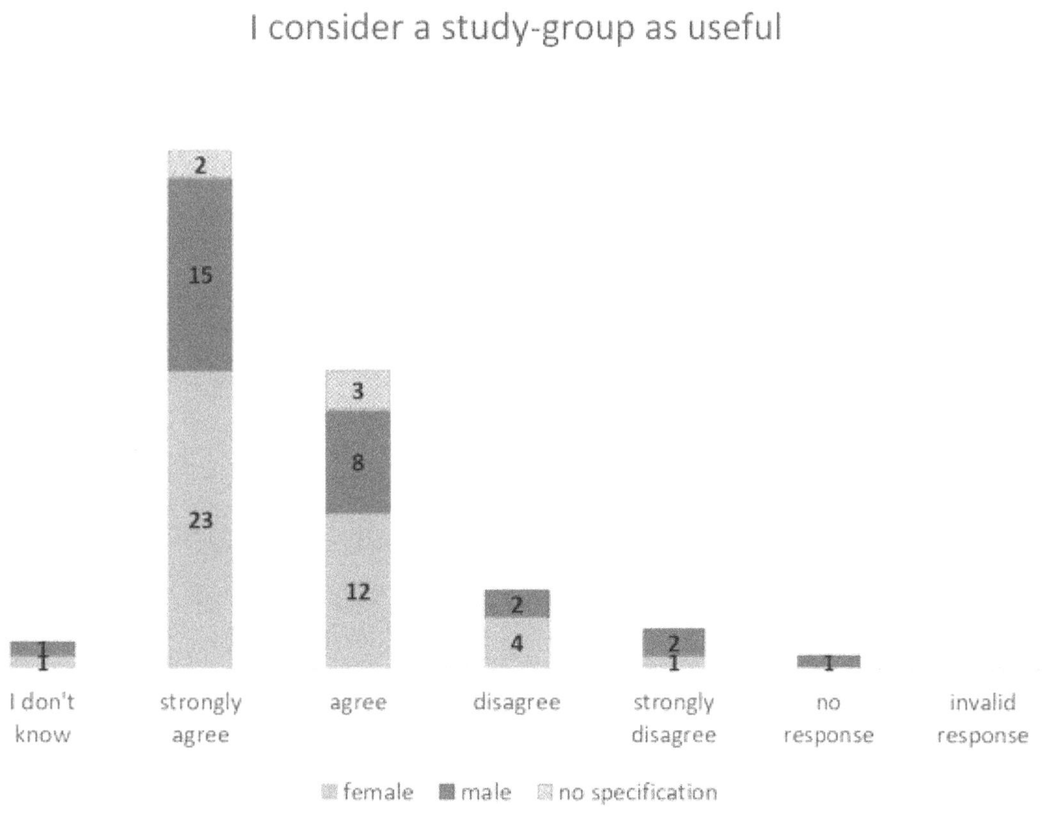

The project SENSOr aims to establish extracurricular study-groups for environmental research at cooperation schools. This way, contents of the project and energy related questions remain to be discussed in school, even after the project itself has been discontinued. The clear majority of the students consider such a study-group as useful at their own school. Over 80% of the students strongly agreed with this (see Figure 7).

Figure 8. Answers to the co-foundation of a study-group (N=75)

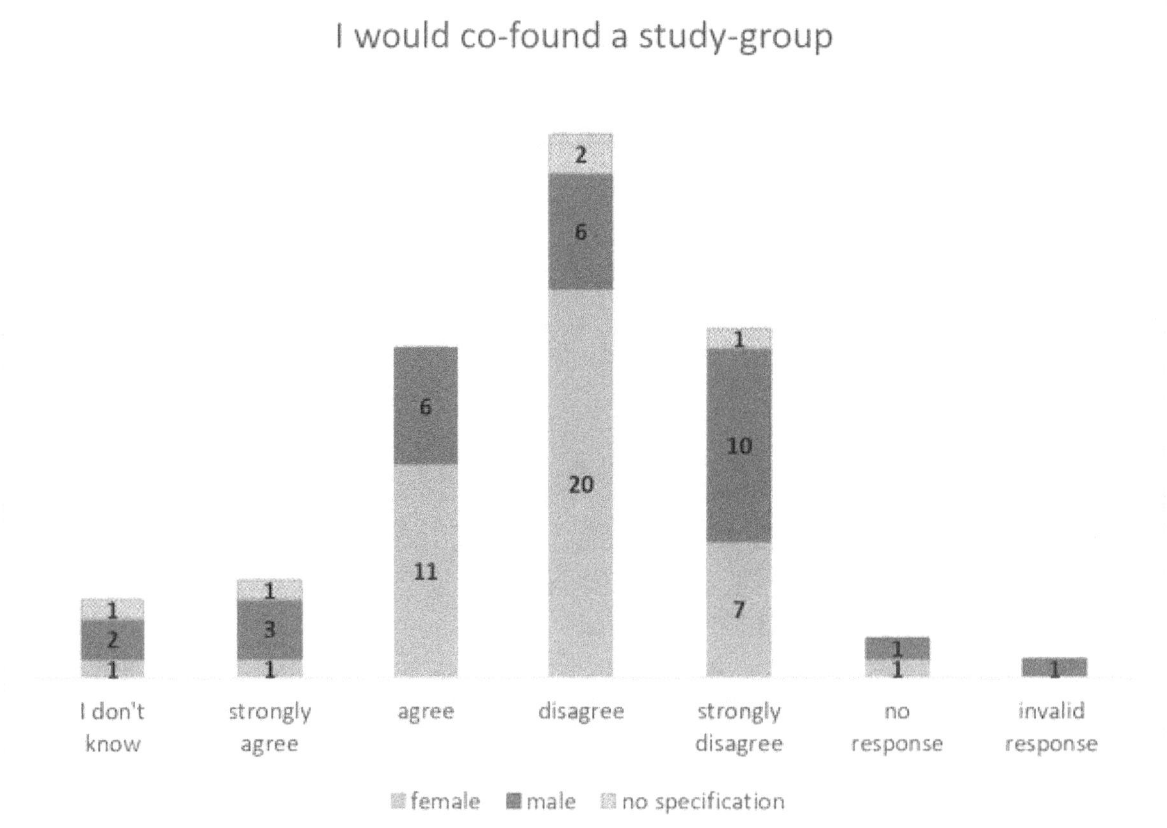

The opinion changes drastically when students are asked to become part of realizing such a group. Only about a third of the students intend to participate. The same applies to the question if they are willing to become one of its co-founders. Here, predominantly boys strongly agreed, while girls more disagreed (see Figure 8). According to an extracurricular study-group, there is a huge discrepancy between the assessment of the meaningfulness of that group and one's own willingness to act.

Project Evaluation in General

The Five Finger Feedback evaluated general reactions to the project concept. Most of the students liked the methodological approach and the implementation through inquiry-based learning. This shows that the methodology seems to be well chosen to bring this topic closer to the students. Some students did not find some of the different station topics so interesting, because they already knew the topic, for example. Nevertheless, most of them said that they enjoyed the lessons and liked them better than the "normal" ones.

The project can be considered a success, as many students stated that they took away a lot of new knowledge from the project, including how they can contribute to environmental protection. A lot of feedback also shows that the students want to pay more attention to and integrate different everyday aspects and behaviours in the future. Frequently mentioned aspects were recycling, buying regional products or saving energy.

Interim Conclusion

Even if the survey cannot be generalized exemplarily for other projects, the first results allow positive conclusions for this one. The students gave positive feedback on the methodology and approach of the project, which speaks for the success and further use of inquiry-based learning. The students show interest in the topics and a willingness to integrate sustainable behaviour in everyday life. In very few cases, a difference between genders can be identified. In the following, some theses are formulated that can be derived from the first evaluation:

Thesis 1: Students are aware of sustainability, climate change, and the energy transition.

Thesis 2: The issue of climate change is an important aspect of students' everyday lives.

Thesis 3: Inquiry-based learning is a good way to bring this topic closer to the students.

Thesis 4: There is a discrepancy between the interest and the active participation.

Thesis 5: A contribution to environmental protection (also from people in the area) is important for the students.

DISCUSSION

During the implementation of the project at the schools, different challenges arose at different levels. Based on various experiences and their documentation, these will be briefly explained here. The feedback so far shows that there is a general awareness of sustainability issues.

At the individual level of the students, it was noticeable, that the motivation and interest in the topic of energy and energy transition were initially almost non-existent. These findings can be taken from the Five Finger Feedback. Students indicate that they do not find the topic that exciting at first. Especially the extracurricular interest is missing. This becomes clear in the evaluation of the questions about the study-group. Here, a difference between boys and girls becomes particularly clear. While both genders find such a study-group useful, boys are more willing to found one. This could be related to gender issues in STEM subjects, where girls report significantly worse self-concepts and self-efficacy expectations or performance assessments than boys (Augustin-Dittmann, 2015). Although the students show equal interest in geographical topics, differences in the interests of the working methods can be identified. Girls prefer to work with texts or descriptive media, while boys like to work with maps, numbers/tables, diagrams, devices, etc. (Glade, 2015). If students associate a lot of technology with the extracurricular study-group, it could explain the distribution of answers.

It is worth mentioning that various studies show that GIS has the potential to design gender-inclusive geography lessons (Ditter & Siegmund, 2016; Glade, 2015). The study by Ditter & Siegmund (2016) *"Learning with digital satellite images - a gender-specific analysis"* states, that at the beginning of the project, girls were more reserved. However, during the project, they showed increasing interest as they became more technically proficient and more independent in handling these images. This possible gender issue or the discrepancy between interest and participation would be approaches for further research to question and investigate more closely. In the case of topics that are not obviously technical, far more initial engagement can be observed. The project SENSOr focuses on topics of energy, its transition and climate change, but to adapt the discrepancies, other areas of sustainability like transport or individual consumption could also be taken up. The obvious reference to technology topics could be attenuated this way.

While carrying out the project modules all students perceptible accepted the topic, even if it has a strong technical reference. Nevertheless, although the students found the topic not always that interesting, they accepted the intended learning occasions at all educational institutions. In particular, the students found the experimental work motivating and stimulating according to self-reporting through Five Finger Feedback. It corresponds with studies on students' interest (Hemmer & Hemmer, 2021). The students often answered the questionnaire that they liked the methodological approach. It can be concluded that inquiry-based learning is a good concept to bring the topic of energy closer to the students and stimulates further interest in the topic. For example, it was observed, that after the experiment "The History of Artificial Lightning", the students applied their findings directly to the school building. They chose to walk around the school counting outdated light sources and lamps. Then, they calculated the total energy consumption and researched the possibilities of modernization independently. Afterwards, a formal request to the headmaster of the school was formulated to replace the light sources in the gymnasium. It stated that an exchange of outdated fluorescent tubes onto LED lights will amortize within one single year of usage. Even though students haven't shown much confidence in their proposal, they were looking forward to being heard in the decision-making process of the school board. Now, one year later unfortunately none of the suggestions have been implemented by the school board yet (in this case the major of the city).

The findings of the project are also consistent with the study by Hoque et al. (2022). It was found that, among other things, project-based learning is a good way to teach energy topics to students. The study also found a discrepancy between the knowledge and the actual, sustainable actions of the students. Incorporating these topics into the curriculum at an early stage is mentioned as a way to overcome this obstacle. This is also accompanied by an increase in motivation, interest, and knowledge in relation to energy and sustainable development.

The evaluation of the questionnaire also showed that the students are willing to integrate sustainable behaviour in their everyday life. Assuming that they are not only willing to integrate these things, but also to implement them, as shown for example in the areas of life, the students could become multipliers for their living area. Conversations with friends or family members are often about significant and personally important issues. Questions about "what", "how" or "why" are usually clarified. This might encourage them to reflect and question their own behaviour. Especially, the question "It is important to me that others in my area are committed to environmental protection" makes it clear that the majority of the students pay attention to whether others in their area are committed to environmental protection. This shows that the students are aware of and question the behaviour of their social environment. Various studies reveal a statistical correlation between the behaviour of parents or closest friends and one's own behaviour. One's own behaviour usually adapts to that of others (Heitfeld & Reif, 2020; Hoque et al., 2022). The study by Ntanos et al. (2018) shows that when the school itself promotes sustainability, it helps to raise students' environmental awareness and integrate sustainable practices into their daily lives. It also states that school and family are key factors in enabling students to tackle future challenges in the energy sector.

At the institutional level, main challenges were to implement project-oriented, inquiry-based learning in the school system. For this purpose, project weeks are often planned that take place separately from the regular curriculum and have an extraordinary meaning. It is also common practice to offer project

work in peripheral phases, such as shortly before the end of the holidays. The choice of this period of time is inconvenient. The main reason is that the student's attention is not primarily focused on the project, but on the approaching vacations. Experiences made in the project can barely be memorized after the holidays. In addition, single lessons on the topics are often held in pre-chosen subjects in the project schools. Interdisciplinary teaching hardly ever takes place. Thus, the connections between geography, physics, and computer science are not sufficiently clear here either. During the project, another complicating factor revealed itself. This is the power of decision on physical conditions at schools, which lies with the school authorities. In Germany, the school authorities are often the owners of the schools, so they decide on the approval of changes to the school building. This fact means for example, that students may calculate the current energy consumption of the light sources and formulate a recommendation letter for the replacement of outdated light sources, but this must be approved by the school authorities, the mayor or the school board. If they reject the idea despite evident benefits such as decreasing costs, this not only leads to the preservation of the status quo, it also causes demotivation of students to deal with this topic any further. Therefore, implementing innovative, technical ideas from external projects, such as installing a solar equipment on the roof or changing the light sources in the school, is difficult without being backed by those who are in charge. Not only the school administration has to be involved, support from janitors, electricians, etc. is also needed for a successful implementation. Finally, the project also shows, that the implementation of innovative projects is only possible to a limited extent. According to the teachers, this is associated with considerably more planning effort, as entrenched school structures are often missing time, resources, and agility when it comes to change management. By designing suitable learning arrangements, the greatest flexibility of external partners is necessary for a successful cooperation.

CONCLUSION

The project SENSOr illustrates how ESD and digitalization can be linked through designing an inquiry-based learning environment that addresses energy and its transition. Through active and experimental learning opportunities that focus on experiences of self-efficacy and the use of digital technologies, the students develop interest towards energy topics. These topics are hidden and cannot be directly experienced in everyday life. At the same time, it is also about pointing out possibilities for action, reflecting on their global relevance and making them experiential in a concrete way. On an individual level of the students, it is shown that concepts of appropriately designed learning environments guided by this, stimulate further critical research. The conclusion is that project content needs to be presented in a more playful way to be more widely accepted by the students. However, structural and institutional challenges often stand in the way of transformative learning that is long-term and student-oriented. The greatest possible flexibility and openness of cooperation, formats and educational modules enables individualisation regarding school-specific situations. In this way, the needs of students and teachers can be considered.

ACKNOWLEDGMENT

This research was supported by *The German Federal Environmental Foundation* [35367/01]. The authors would like to thank former co-worker Robert Krüger for developing and providing the environmental measuring station from the project "Smart Rain" and for the informatics-expertise. They would also like to thank Tabea Langer for her assistance in the creation of the educational modules and for her knowledge in educational aspects.

REFERENCES

Allert, H., Asmussen, M., & Richter, C. (Eds.). (2017). Digitalität und Selbst: Interdisziplinäre Perspektiven auf Subjektivierungs- und Bildungsprozesse. Pädagogik.

Augustin-Dittmann, S. (2015). MINT und darüber hinaus. Gendersensibler Unterricht als Basis einer geschlechtergerechten Gesellschaft. In J. Wedl & A. Bartsch (Eds.), Teaching Gender? Zum reflektierten Umgang mit Geschlecht im Schulunterricht und in der Lehramtsausbildung (pp. 123-136). Transcript Verlag.

Bandura, A. (1977). Self-efficacy: Toward a unifying theory of behavioral change. *Psychological Review*, *84*(2), 191–215. doi:10.1037/0033-295X.84.2.191 PMID:847061

Bandura, A. (1997). *Self-Efficacy: The Exercise of Control*. Freeman.

Becker, S., Klagge, B., & Naumann, M. (2021). Einführung: Konzepte und Herausforderungen der Energiegeographie. In S. Becker, B. Klagge, & M. Naumann (Eds.), *Energiegeographie* (pp. 18–34). UTB. doi:10.36198/9783838553207

de Haan, G. (2008). Gestaltungskompetenz als Kompetenzkonzept der Bildung für nachhaltige Entwicklung. In I. Bormann & G. de Haan (Eds.), *Kompetenzen der Bildung für nachhaltige Entwicklung* (pp. 23–43). VS Verlag für Sozialwissenschaften. doi:10.1007/978-3-531-90832-8_4

Ditter, R., & Siegmund, A. (2016). Lernen mit digitalen Satellitenbildern – eine genderspezifische Analyse. *GWU*, *142/143*, 162-173.

Dorsch, C., Gryl, I., Hermes, A., Jekel, T., Lehner, M., Meyer, C., Pettig, F., Pokraka, J., Schrüfer, G., & Schulze, U. (2020). *Der Beitrag des Fachs Geographie zur Bildung in einer durch Digitalisierung und Mediatisierung geprägten Welt.* https://geographiedidaktik.org/download/positionspapier-des-hgd-geographische-bildung-und-digitalisierung/?wpdmdl=1185&r efresh=624e93489ea191649316680

Fisman, L. (2005). The Effects of Local Learning on Environmental Awareness in Children: An Empirical Investigation. *The Journal of Environmental Education*, *36*(3), 39–50. doi:10.3200/JOEE.36.3.39-50

Getzin, S., & Singer-Brodowski, M. (2016). Transformatives Lernen in einer Degrowth-Gesellschaft. *Journal of Science-Society Interfaces*, *1*(1), 33–46. doi:10.5167/uzh-135963

Glade, N. (2015). Einsatz von Geoinformationssystemen im Geographieunterricht. Chancen für einen geschlechtergerechten Unterricht. In J. Wedl & A. Bartsch (Eds.), Teaching Gender? Zum reflektierten Umgang mit Geschlecht im Schulunterricht und in der Lehramtsausbildung (pp. 215-234). Transcript Verlag.

Grund, J., & Brock, A. (2020). Education for Sustainable Development in Germany: Not Just Desired but Also Effective for Transformative Action. *Sustainability,* 12(7), 28-38. doi:10.3390/su12072838

Heitfeld, M., & Reif, A. (2020, August). *Transformation gestalten lernen. Mit Bildung und transformativem Engagement gesellschaftliche Strukturen verändern.* https://germanwatch.org/sites/default/files/Transformation%20gestalten%20lernen-1.pdf

Hemmer, I., & Hemmer, M. (2021). Das Interesse von Schülerinnen und Schülern an geographischen Themen, Regionen und Arbeitsweisen – ein Bundeslandvergleich zwischen Bayern und Nordrhein-Westfalen. *Zeitschrift für Geographiedidaktik, 49*(1), 3–24.

Hoque, F., Yasin, R. M., & Sopian, K. (2022). Revisiting Education for Sustainable Development: Methods to Inspire Secondary School Students toward Renewable Energy. *Sustainability, 14*(14), 8296. doi:10.3390u14148296

Huber, L. (2009). Warum Forschendes Lernen nötig und möglich ist. In L. Huber, J. Hellmer, & F. Schneider (Eds.), *Forschendes Lernen im Studium* (pp. 9–35). Universitätsverlag Webler.

Leal Filho, W., Wolf, F., & Pohlmann, J. (2021). Digitalisierung und Nachhaltigkeit durch internationale Ansätze – Beispiele der HAW Hamburg. In W. Leal Filho (Ed.), *Digitalisierung und Nachhaltigkeit* (pp. 1–22). Springer Berlin Heidelberg. doi:10.1007/978-3-662-61534-8_1

Malberg Dyg, P., & Wistoft, K. (2018). Wellbeing in school gardens – the case of the Gardens for Bellies food and environmental education program. *Environmental Education Research, 24*(8), 1177–1191. doi:10.1080/13504622.2018.1434869

Mathie, R. G., & Wals, A. E. J. (2022). *Whole school approaches to sustainability. Exemplary practices from around the world* (2nd ed.). Wageningen University, Education & Learning Sciences. doi:10.18174/572267

Meier Kruker, V., & Rauh, J. (2005). *Arbeitsmethoden der Humangeographie*. WBG.

Ntanos, S., Kyriakopoulos, G. L., Arabatzis, G., Palios, V., & Chalikias, M. (2018). Environmental bevahior of Secondary Education Students: A Case Study at Central Greece. *Sustainability, 10*(5), 1663. doi:10.3390u10051663

Oberrauch, A., Mayr, H., Nikitin, I., Bügler, T., Kosler, T., & Vollmer, C. (2021). "I Wanted a Profession That Makes a Difference"—An Online Survey of First-Year Students' Study Choice Motives and Sustainability-Related Attributes. *Sustainability, 13*(15), 8273. doi:10.3390u13158273

OECD. (2016). *Global competency for an inclusive world.* https://gisigpl.files.wordpress.com/2017/12/global-competency-for-an-inclusive-world.pdf

Stalder, F. (2016). Kultur der Digitalität (3rd ed.). Originalausgabe.

UN. (2015). *Resolution adopted by the General Assembly on 25 September 2015.* https://www.un.org/ga/search/view_doc.asp?symbol=A/RES/70/1&Lang=E

WBGU. (2019). *Unsere gemeinsame digitale Zukunft*. WBGU.

WBGU (Wissenschaftlicher Beirat der Bundesregierung Globale Umweltveränderungen). (2011). *Welt im Wandel: Gesellschaftsvertrag für eine Große Transformation*. WBGU.

ENDNOTE

1 German Advisory Council on Global Change.

Chapter 16
Sustainability Online?
Actors, Hierarchies, and Communication Patterns in Collaborative Development of Open Educational Resources

Jana Dlouhá
Charles University, Czech Republic

Eduard Petiška
Charles University, Czech Republic

Marie Pospíšilová
Charles University, Czech Republic

Jiří Dlouhý
Charles University, Czech Republic

ABSTRACT

The concept of ESD is innovative, aiming to catalyse changes in the way we learn; in this context, new teaching/learning approaches and ESD pedagogies have been widely discussed in the literature. Digital media may also change the learning process if different actors including students are involved in co-creating learning content. The question raised in this chapter is whether these changes in the "metabolism" of information could contribute to the transformations foreseen by ESD, and how. The authors focus on open educational resources (OER) used in higher education, specifically wiki systems, and explore mutual relationships/hierarchies of actors involved in its development. In a case study, they discuss whether competences to collaboratively develop OER may support ESD competences, what the opportunities/limitations of this synergy are, and offer a framework to reflect academic writing processes from sustainability point of view.

DOI: 10.4018/978-1-7998-5033-5.ch016

INTRODUCTION

There is common understanding that sustainable development (SD) cannot be achieved without educational input, and education systems should be reoriented towards this goal at all levels of education. The concept of Education for Sustainable Development (ESD) evolved particularly during the UN Decade of Education for SD when its principles were outlined (Tilbury, 2009). There is ongoing discussion on pedagogical approaches that would translate these principles into practice in higher education (Lozano et al., 2019). The sustainability perspective focuses on competences that have a normative dimension (Rodríguez Aboytes, 2020) with the aim both to support learners' critical perspectives, capacity for anticipating change, and to develop the ability to implement these changes in practice. To have a real impact and meet the Sustainable Development Goals, these changes need to take place on a personal, community and societal level (Boström et al., 2018) pointing unequivocally towards the transformative learning dimension in ESD.

In the ESD discourse, competences are considered to be the basis of sustainability literacy: the ability to describe, analyse, plan and solve sustainability issues in different contexts, using knowledge and information. Michelsen and Adomssent (2007) also emphasise the formative role of this approach in terms of the impact on learner development. In further expert discussions, core competences for sustainability have been identified (Wiek et al., 2011) providing a foundation for defining competences for the implementation of the SDGs (UNESCO, 2017). An important component of sustainability transformation are action competences, which according to Jensen and Schnack (1997) are based on students' self-awareness and ability to identify what needs to change and work together to bring this about. Education in general re-orients towards a competence-based system that then underpins decision-making and action in the context of policy development (Dlouhá, 2014). The recognition of these imperatives then drives curriculum development and requires re-organization of higher education in practice (Brundiers et al., 2021).

In contrast to the intense discussion on sustainability pedagogies, the "genres" of the written text have not yet been reflected in depth. The texts used for educational purposes are specific - they "didactically" transform knowledge (cf. Riemann et al., 2020) to meet the needs of the target group of learners, thus addressing specific learning objectives which may in themselves be innovative. This is an opportunity for ESD where learners are supposed not only to read and learn from the texts but also to use the information as a basis for action. Moreover, as the SD terrain is highly uncertain, the learner should be able to critically assess and identify texts relevant for this action, select evidence as a basis for decisions, and to develop one's own arguments that "translate" information into strategies for practice. Other sustainability competences (such as self-awareness and normative competence) are needed to align the questions posed by learners, and arguments to answer these questions, with sustainability values (Henderson et al., 2021).

In general, the ability to learn critically from texts is essential at all levels, but especially in higher education (HE). Here we deal with the *educational resources* for use of which general reading literacy is needed. Our focus is on *digital educational resources,* some of which may be particularly appropriate for developing writing literacy as is the case with the Open Educational Resources (OER); they provide students with the opportunity to participate in the writing process. These resources offer opportunities for pedagogical innovation - *OER enabled pedagogies* are students-centred and interactive (DeRosa, 2017), involving constructivist approaches which are otherwise missing at HE level (Scarff Seatter, 2017) but are necessary for understanding and building capacity to take action in a multi-dimensional sustainability context (Evans, 2020). OER also support varied, self-regulated learning with a decentralised organisational structure (in contrast to the standardised, directed learning in a centralised environment offered by traditional resources), with holistic (as opposed to only cognitive) learning outcomes (Huitt, 2017). Open digital environments, such as wiki, may be useful for ESD where the development of texts is based on dialogue among disciplinary experts and with those active in practice: multiple actors enter the process of writing and guarantee quality of the outcome.

The questions which we strive to address in this chapter are the following: whether and how may SD-relevant OER represent an opportunity to meet a broad range of ESD learning objectives at HE level, and what is the potential of digital media, specifically wiki, with regards to ESD competence development? In this regard, we try to describe/understand 1) wiki texts as a specific educational genre characterised by the process of creation, 2) the actors involved in this writing process and its publishing, 3) the quality of the outcome, and particularly 4) the competences associated with academic writing in comparison with key sustainability competences.

ESD Principles

To answer the research questions posed above, sustainability competences at HE level are described in the three dimensions of learning as outlined by UNECE (2011):

1. A holistic approach, which seeks integrative thinking and practice;
2. Envisioning change, which explores alternative futures, learns from the past and inspires engagement in the present;
3. Achieving transformation, which serves to change in the way people learn and in the systems that support learning.

These dimensions also represent a general framework for analysing educational texts. While ESD pedagogies aim to develop competences for action, background educational materials (texts) are less equipped for this task. The classical texts provide evidence for argumentation and decision, some of them also offer information needed for action; the use of these arguments in sustainability-oriented action is usually left to the learner while the teacher may (or may not) provide the necessary guidance. In the context of praxis, the learner is thus expected to act towards the (normatively set) goals that are "external" to the knowledge discourse delivered by the teacher through texts (cf. Shephard et al., 2019). We argue here that the learning environment itself may support development of action competences, besides offering knowledge - and that digital resources in particular can be instrumental in this role: they may have specific functions also within the ESD framework.

Role of Digital Media (Wiki Systems) in ESD

To see how development of sustainability competences could be supported by the learning environment, we analyse online educational resources, OER with a specific focus on Wiki systems, often known as "wiki" – a type of "collaborative software" that enables multiple users to simultaneously contribute to content. We attempt to better understand the innovations wiki systems may bring to the processes of learning, specifically the potential to develop collaborative writing competences. However, we do not compare digital media with classical (written) texts as this is not a focus of our analysis.

Wiki is the best solution for open "mass collaboration" as the other software enabling collaboration such as GoogleDocs have a limited number of users. The idea and concept of wiki is old, yet MediaWiki software is still the most widespread (in terms of unique visitors) wiki system in the history of the internet. It started in 1995 as WikiWikiWeb, a collaborative database to facilitate the exchange of ideas among programmers (Wikipedia Contributors, 2022). Wiki systems however became popular only due to the success of Wikipedia which was launched in 2001 on its own domain, wikipedia.com. Since 2002 it has run on MediaWiki software which is optimised to efficiently handle large projects that can have terabytes of content and hundreds of thousands of hits per second. In this environment, thousands of users can easily work on editing one page and we can see their history of editing. Due to this feature and also the fact that MediaWiki is internationally compatible (its interface is available in over 300 languages), Wikipedia is the most famous project resulting in the largest encyclopaedia in human history. But there are many other projects based on MediaWiki software, such as language versions of Wikipedia, its other "sister projects" (Wikinews, Wikimedia Commons or Wikisource and the newest Wikipedia project – Wikidata) - and many educational applications of MediaWiki software not directly connected with Wikipedia.

This evolution suggests that although the concept of the wiki system is almost as old as the web itself, it is still the most often used MediaWiki software. Wiki systems are often used as OER, but not every OER is a wiki system (and vice versa). The basic properties of most wiki systems can be defined as follows (Petiška et al., 2021):

Openness Both in Reading and Editing: Although each system is designed differently and so openness varies accordingly. The accessibility of the resources and transparency of the educational outcomes (if published openly), and opportunities for its assessment all enrich the learning process. However, wiki systems can be also relatively closed and hidden from the public (e.g., wiki systems used in companies).

Collaborative Editing: The ability to collaborate on text creation is one of the main benefits of wiki systems in education as it supports collaboration competency.

Hypertext (Redirection to Related Links): The idea of hypertext in practice brings an opportunity for cross-referencing. Interdisciplinary sustainability themes are better understandable if different disciplinary perspectives are simply accessible.

Version Control: It is possible to trace the history of the page and restore old versions. For educational purposes, the option to trace the history of the writing process allows teachers to provide guidance in its different stages (clarifying research questions, developing the structure, review of resources etc.) and is useful also for assessment (cf. Zahradník, 2009).

Due to their specific properties, wikis serve in education not only as an open resource for learning (OER), but also allow students to contribute to the pool of knowledge. According to Wiley and Hilton (2018), creation of supplementary learning resources may enrich the learning process. Being interdisciplinary, they transfer existing knowledge into new contexts, and provide an opportunities to update content (especially in the sustainability field, new information and concepts evolve rapidly). The process of resources development provides opportunities for a change in communication practices between teachers and students and consequently underpin deep learning approaches (Dlouhá, 2015); in the long term, students' efforts contribute to future students' learning.

CASE STUDY: WIKI RESOURCES USED IN UNIVERSITY TEACHING/LEARNING

Wiki has been used in Charles University since 2005 by the authorial team, thus providing us with the opportunity to link theory and practice. It was established as a knowledge base "Enviwiki" where environmental themes are continuously developed and updated with the goal of communicating expert knowledge to teachers at lower levels of education, and serve as an interface between different disciplines. The open online environment has enabled the involvement of students in developing information (wiki pages). With the aim of supporting students' active approach to knowledge generation this tool has been used in university courses with different disciplinary backgrounds. Based on this experience, a method of teaching with wiki at higher education was developed (Dlouhá et al., 2012) and continuously reflected upon to better understand the innovations that wikis bring to the processes of learning (Dlouhá et al., 2015). Over a decade of efforts culminated in an applied research project on criteria for quality assessment of wikis which are used as a resource and also a tool for learning (Petiška et al., 2021).

Wikis are perceived here as a specific genre characterised by the process of its creation, among others. To identify its specific role in education we present: 1) an overview of wiki systems used in Charles University, 2) an analysis of actors that enter this process, and their roles, 3) the criteria for quality of the wiki resources, 4) comparison of the key sustainability competences with those competences that are associated with academic writing. To answer the above-mentioned research questions, we use the methodology outlined in each chapter introduction.

Overview of Wiki Systems Used in Charles University

Wikis used for educational purposes in Charles University, Prague were identified by reviewing the webpages of all faculties and institutes; Table 1 briefly describes its content.

Table 1. Characteristics of the functional wiki OERs at Charles University (CU)

Project and OER	Who Is Responsible	Brief Description	Level of Openness
Enviwiki	Charles University Environment Centre	An electronic platform dedicated to environmental education and sustainable development issues.	Open to read and edit without registration.
WikiSkripta	1st Faculty of Medicine, CU & MEFANET network of medical faculties	A space for the cooperative creation and storage of medical teaching materials. WikiSkripta was created for students and teachers of all medical faculties in the Czech Republic and Slovakia.	Open to read and edit without registration.
WikiSofia	Faculty of Arts, CU	A portal for creating, storing and retrieving study materials in the humanities.	Open to read and edit, registration required for editing.
Students Write Wikipedia	Wikimedia Foundation	Czech project that works with universities to create and improve scholarly encyclopaedic texts on the Czech Wikipedia.	Open to read and edit without registration.
WikiLibrary	The Library Community	A project for sharing and creating learning materials in the field of library and information science. It serves all those interested in these fields, especially university students and teachers from relevant disciplines.	Open to read and edit, registration required for editing.

Source: webpages of the respective OER.

The wiki pages have been created by students (with guidance by teachers), and their content can be described as academic essays. The arguments are based on citations of primary and secondary resources. The texts (after approval) serve as a supplementary teaching material for different disciplines, mainly for tertiary education.

Actors and Their Roles

An actor analysis was carried out in 2019, and was based upon semi-structured interviews with the main representatives of the respective OER. The question was how these actors contributed to the establishment of the main characteristics of this genre; the responses were recorded, transcribed and coded. This qualitative analysis identified categories of actors (see Table 2) and their different roles in the studied wiki projects. From the overview in Table 1, the only OER targeting students interested in environmental topics is Enviwiki. This resource is maintained by the authorial team, and their responses were used in analysis as a reference point.

It was observed that the principle of collective development of the OER in a wiki environment requires the inclusive involvement of different actors within the editorial team and distribution of responsibilities between team members. The diversity of roles within this team ensures the quality of the outcome: the texts and the resource as a whole. Some of these roles may be performed by students - usually they develop texts that are part of their learning assignments. Students' involvement is however not only outcome-oriented: from a pedagogical perspective the learning process associated with competence development is important. The specifics of students' involvement were reflected in the interviews as follows:

The motivation to contribute is the reward system of intrinsic motivation. The perceived benefits of being involved is closely associated with the lack of barriers (ease of publishing) which makes the writing process smooth, with a visible result.

This motivation is supported by community specifics. The editorial team with multiple actor roles guarantees the content and formal aspects of the OER - mutual trust and cooperation is needed. To attract new members, or at least not to lose extant members of the team, the social environment is actively cultivated and the *person* is in the centre of attention. The community may apply a peer teaching method (student-student interaction), and other opportunities for supporting cooperation and developing relevant competences that should be acquired during HE. To ensure constructive relationships, communication skills are actively taught - in the WikiSkripta project it is considered to be a major educational benefit.

Due to its openness (of both actors and the digital learning environment), the observed wiki projects offer teaching/learning methods that differ from those applied in the usual education system. Students are thus required to step out of habitual ways of thinking (WikiSkripta respondent).

Table 2. Overview of (potential or extant) roles in the OER editorial team

Initiator, project leader	This is someone who initiates the project – very often an individual with a strong vision concerning the use of a wiki, and simultaneously with an academic background and management/communication abilities. S/he is aware of the benefits of the wiki environment, usually in terms of active involvement of students in the writing process so that they develop important academic competences, in addition to understanding the theme. The strong role of this leader was observed in all analysed projects. This leadership role is however often associated with the overall management of the project, including financial aspects, advocacy in relation to university representatives, and organising students' involvement (including development of rules for this involvement). A lot of voluntary work is associated with this role unless the project receives regular support from the university - financial and moral. However, this university support must provide sufficient freedom for decision-making concerning the overall design of the OER, and relevant publication processes.
Ambassador - "driver"	The ambassador, a role typical for Wikipedia projects, is in charge of communicating the benefits of the project to the academic community; s/he advocates also for the involvement of students and teachers in writing texts, explains principles of wiki, and supports the writing process by providing technical advice. In some cases, ambassadors are students interested in the project. They sometimes also identify the student needs (in terms of missing educational materials), and organise for these "blind spots" to be filled in by original texts written by the students. The ambassador is not needed if university teachers are already involved in the Wikipedia community. However, the ambassador rarely has sufficient influence to resolve potential conflicts resulting from their different approaches.
Leader of the writing process (teacher)	This is the role of content guarantor which is usually played by the university teacher and/or someone in charge of assessing the quality of the text. However, for university teachers, use of wiki represents pedagogical innovation, and they rarely have the capacity to invest into innovating their teaching methods. Thus, they usually do not have sufficient motivation for wiki development (unless there are missing educational materials that could be supplemented by students). Support by an ambassador, mentor or someone from the editorial team with technical skills may be necessary for explaining how to use the electronic environment (wiki) and guide the writing process . The academic leader might not be involved in the publication processes at all – these may be overseen by someone from the editorial team.
Students – contributors	Students are responsible for the quality of the content they produce; however, their involvement does not usually include updating the text after publishing – unless the project sustains the team over time, and/or its members are paid for their work (one of the projects financed text development). When a strong community of interest is built, students continue writing/updating articles beyond their assignments just to stay involved in the community.
Editorial team	This team may include different roles if the project is sufficiently supported (the team has adequate capacities in terms of a number of team members who can divide responsibilities). One of the successful projects has developed a hierarchy of roles so that those with an experience proceed along a "career" progression and their work is acknowledged in resulting "hierarchy" . If the project is not sufficiently supported and the editor is a single person, this arrangement does not allow for regular revision and update of all the published texts.
Mentor	A mentor is someone who guides students through the writing process. This person should have writing skills, knowledge of the theme, and be able to provide technical advice. A mentor role was missing in most of the observed projects – this role was delivered by other actors. If a community is well developed, this community itself plays the role of mentor with members providing support to each other and newcomers.
Reviewer	The review process to ensure the quality of the text, and the reviewer's role, is unique for this genre. In well-developed projects with large-scale involvement of students and teachers, the role of reviewer is played by the whole community (as in the case of Wikipedia). In medical wiki (WikiSkripta) for example, the community as collective reviewer has been more efficient than expert review: collectively they discovered mistakes in printed educational materials which were referred to in wiki. In another project, student-student peer review was required (which contributed to the learning process but did not really guarantee the quality). In reality, however, the role of reviewer is played mostly by the university teachers involved while some of the projects seek external (paid) reviewers.
Technical support	To ensure technical functionality, an administrator with technical skills is needed. In smaller teams this role is usually performed by someone who also holds other roles.

Continued on following page

Table 2. Continued

Communication, PR	As these projects represent substantial pedagogical innovation (which is not always welcomed in academia), communicating its benefits is essential for its growth/sustainability. This communication can be provided by different team members, for example the Wikipedia management team is involved in PR, while some of the other projects have been presented at academic conferences by the project initiator. In the case of successful projects, the benefits are shared directly within the community of students and more teachers are attracted. However institutional support is however required in this case.
Experts from other disciplines and lay people	Actors beyond disciplinary boundaries contributed only in the ESD-oriented resource (Enviwiki) which was explicitly interdisciplinary. Other resources did not allow for "lay" contributions.
Community	In successful projects, the role of community (of those who contribute) is very important. A well-developed community then: ● ensures relevance of the texts for study purposes and provides direction for selection of the texts to be written on a self-regulation principle (demand or offer-driven); ● safeguards the growth of the community as the members generate interest among students and students also attract teachers; ● rewards the members for their work (in terms of providing a prominent position in the team, delivering awards, and organising community celebrations); ● guarantees quality - all of the members have certain expertise and collective responsibility (with specific roles within the team). A "critical mass" of team members can replace expert authority.
Quality guarantor	In the observed projects, different mechanisms to the ensure quality of the content and usability of the whole resource were in place. These include the regular review process ensured by the university teachers and/or involving an external reviewer. Some of the texts thus received a "seal of quality". In projects with large teams, quality is guaranteed by the community, not by an expert – this is the 2.0 approach to writing. The community role in quality assurance is based on the quantity of its members – more people with partial knowledge are more likely to spot an error. Rules to ensure formal qualities of the whole resource (its structure, coverage, hyperlinks that stress interdisciplinarity) are established by the initiator (as rules of contributing to wiki) and further ensured by the editorial team. In one of the projects (Enviwiki), a general Methodology of text development in an open internet environment exists. (Dlouhá et al., 2012).

Source: authorial team research.

In general, different roles are played by the actors within the editorial team, but their communication is usually non-hierarchical. Where hierarchies in roles exist, they are sometimes similar to Wikipedia, defined partly by the technology (access rights). But in well-functioning projects, these hierarchies are considered to be the main barrier to communication, and effort is made to define the roles equitably. Respectability of the team members is built upon their expertise and does not lead to achieving a powerful position.

Instead of building hierarchies, community aspects are stressed – involvement in the community is also one of the motivational factors; community-based wiki projects are more likely to be self-sustained over time through cooperation of senior-junior team members. Projects which rely on student duties (to produce assignments) or provide financial rewards (paid authors/editors) are less successful and sustainable in the long term.

Besides actors, also the role of technology is important. Technology is active against violation (spam) – it identifies the creation of new articles and notifies the team if someone outside the community contributes. Moreover, technology may provide some important information in relation to users, for example a high ranking in google search indicates the interest of readers.

In general, due to a wide range of actor roles necessary to ensure quality of the resource, wikis often face substantial difficulties. The team of actors is fully functional only in the WikiSkripta which is sufficiently supported by the university; the other projects lack this support and rely mostly on the voluntary work of enthusiastic contributors and editors, sometimes students. Some of the projects have

In contrast to traditional resources, none of these formal criteria of OER quality (alone or in combination) reliably assess the resource - there is nothing like a "respected publisher" guaranteeing the process. On the contrary, guaranteeing quality in wikis is related to one of its main characteristics which is openness. Wikis are open not only for reading but also for editing and there are mechanisms to ensure their quality within the writing process. In an academic environment, educational wikis are usually not as open as Wikipedia, providing a space for teachers to control its content.

The ongoing discussion about the quality of the OER is however often focused on the quality of the content (Atenas & Havemann, 2014), especially concerning anonymous OER such as Wikipedia. At the same time, some of these aspects are subjective, for example in assessing the appropriateness of the resource for different study purposes (as perceived by students). In any case, a transparent quality assurance of the resource would significantly support the meaningful use of OER in higher education.

Comparison of the ESD and Academic Writing Competences Supported by Wiki

This analysis aims to outline the specific functions and opportunities provided by wikis with regards to the sustainability relevant-learning outcomes: competences. First, we use a framework of key competences for SDGs (UNESCO, 2017) in three learning dimensions (mentioned above), and apply it to the competences achieved within the reading/writing process. A theoretical description of these competences was provided by Deane, et al. (2008) and adjusted in line with the authors' experience with the learning outcomes in the wiki environment. This reflection on how the texts (educational materials) can contribute to the ESD learning objectives is summarised in Tables 4-6.

Holistic Approach

A holistic educational approach is based upon integrative thinking, inclusivity, and dealing with complexities (UNECE, 2011) – relevant learning objectives see Table 4.

Table 4. Key sustainability competences relevant for holistic approach in ESD, and their relationship with competences for reading/writing

Key Sustainability Competences	OER Relevant Reading/Writing Competences (Sustainability Focus)
Self-awareness competency (SA): the ability to reflect on one's own role in the local community and (global) society…	Reflecting on personal values, developing one's own perspective in the process of reading/writing, comparing personal viewpoint with systemic perspective.
Systems thinking competency (ST): the abilities to recognize and understand relationships; to analyse complex systems; ... and to deal with uncertainty.	Reading texts with different disciplinary backgrounds, considering the text's purpose in the context of practice, building upon the texts in the process of writing.
Collaboration competency (C): the abilities to learn from others; … to deal with conflicts in a group; and to facilitate collaborative and participatory problem solving.	Involving different actors in the writing process / being involved in a team and working with co-authors.

Source: UNESCO (2017), Deane et al. (2008), Dlouhá et al. (2015)

only temporary financial support from grants and struggle with continuity. These limitations often lead to a reduction and/or cumulation of the roles of actors, thus restricting readiness for action of the whole team. In result, educational materials in the wiki are produced in a standard, rather than innovative process. Updating the resource is then also a problem which limits its usability over time. A successfully growing resource requires a corresponding growth of capacities – personal and institutional.

Criteria for Quality Assurance

The quality of the OER is a main factor of its wider usability. In previous studies (Petiška et al., 2020, 2021) we arrived at the conclusion that OER quality is strongly connected with the selection of the resources and information cited in the text. However, no specific quality criteria are universally accepted by the most important actors: creators and also users of the OER. Therefore, it is always necessary to assess a concrete resource in context of its development/use. The issue of OER quality can be divided into two areas:

1. Formal attributes relevant for the OER environment;
2. Content.

Regarding formal attributes, we can define the criteria as follows (see Table 3). It should be noted that while a resource may meet the formal quality criteria, it may not contain quality texts for study.

Table 3. Criteria by which it is possible to evaluate the formal attributes of the texts published as OER (wiki)

Criteria	Description
Copyright	Copyright alone cannot be considered as a guarantee of content quality. Thanks to its rules for further use, however, it is possible to recognise whether the source is an OER.
Authorship	Indicating the authorship of the original text is a criterion that is important for assessing the text based on the respectability of the author. In wikis, authorship is usually collective; however, some of the wikis display the author, others allow the author to be traced in the history of the page.
Date of publication	Marking the date of publication or update is important for evaluating the novelty of the text. In wikis, this can be traced in the history of the page.
Proper citations	Proper citation and quality of resources that were used in the creation of OER can be considered as another indicator of quality for evaluating the text, as in printed resources.
Reviews	Reviews are an important indicator of the text quality. In wikis, reviewers usually correct the text directly, then comparing different versions of the text is possible and the reviewer's changes can consequently be traced. Also the comments for example on the discussion page of the text could be used for assessment.
Quality labelling	This criterion shows whether the quality of a published text is labelled by the editorial team, i.e. whether higher quality materials are distinguished from lower quality ones by e.g. a quality seal, practised by some of educational wikis.
Ethical writing processes	This criterion examines whether the OER follows ethical principles, i.e. whether it contains materials that violate legal or ethical rules - this is to be overseen by the teacher.

Source: Dlouhá et al. (2015)

From a holistic point of view, *texts* should be transdisciplinary: in a digital environment they highlight relationships between disciplines through hyperlinks so that it is easy to switch from one discipline or discourse to another. Holistic *education* should address cognitive, socio-emotional and behavioural domains of learning, which also is a pre-requisite for balanced learner engagement (cf. Dlouhá et al., 2019). In the wiki environment, associated competences are developed collaboratively, within the editorial team where relationships are often built on community principles. The non-hierarchical nature of their work in an open online environment requires specific collaboration competency, one of the most important ESD learning objectives.

Future Oriented Approach

Considering alternative futures is one of the primary goals in ESD (UNECE, 2011) while the associated learning objectives may be derived from the principles of sustainability science (Barth, Michelsen, 2013) – such as the ability to find scientifically grounded solutions in a normative framework of decision-making and action (learning objectives see Table 5).

Table 5. Sustainability competences relevant for future-oriented learning, and their relationship with competences for reading/writing

Key Sustainability Competences	OER Relevant Reading/Writing Competences (Sustainability Focus)
Anticipatory competency (A): the abilities to understand and evaluate multiple futures – possible, probable and desirable; to create one's own visions for the future; … and to deal with risks and changes.	Brainstorming, considering alternatives in a sustainability value framework. Employing imagination and creativity to hypothesise on desirable futures or possible solutions.
Normative competency (N): the abilities to understand and reflect on the norms and values that underlie one's actions; and to negotiate sustainability values, principles, goals, and targets …	"Decision-making" & "action" within the writing process: reviewing resources with a focus on the normative aspects of the anticipated future.

Source: UNESCO (2017), Deane et al. (2008), Dlouhá et al. (2015)

The future not only happens but is shaped by our efforts – it is a normative concept that entails many uncertainties in its achievement. Future-oriented texts are in principle innovative, exploring and/or opening new fields of knowledge and practice. Digital media can offer alternatives and inspiration, while the learning environment itself helps effective learning in a landscape of uncertainties.

Transformative Approach

To achieve transformation, action competences applied in praxis are a prerequisite (cf. Henderson, Dlouhá, 2021) – learning objectives identified in this context see Table 6.

Table 6. Sustainability competences relevant for transformative learning and sustainability action, and their relationship with competences for reading/writing

Key Sustainability Competences	Relevant Reading/Writing Competence (Sustainability Focus)
Critical thinking competency (CT): the ability to question norms, practices and opinions; to reflect on one's values, perceptions and actions; and to take a position in the sustainability discourse.	Reading competence: critically selecting resources, finding one's own way through the complex information landscape with respect to quality of information, understanding differences in a transdisciplinary framework.
Strategic competency (S): the abilities to collectively develop and implement innovative actions that further sustainability at the local level and further afield	Posing unique research questions, considering alternatives that appeared during brainstorming processes, identifying strategic priorities.
Integrated problem-solving competency (IPS): the overarching ability to apply different problem-solving frameworks to complex sustainability problems and develop viable, inclusive and equitable solution options …	Analysing alternatives, developing justified arguments, reflecting the context of transformation, considering conditions for success, designing evidence-based strategy for action.

Source: UNESCO (2017), Deane et al. (2008), Dlouhá et al. (2015)

Transformative competence is associated with transformative action which may be practiced within the academic writing process in a wiki environment. The resulting texts should be not only well-structured, clear and meaningful, but also galvanise values-based change; this may require innovative pedagogical approaches. In the sustainability field, developing self-awareness to realise authentic action is a prerequisite (cf. Dlouhá et al., 2021).

Even if teaching/learning with wikis provides opportunities to develop sustainability competences, it is usually difficult to evaluate whether, how and to what extent they were developed. This difficulty with assessing competences is typical for (higher) education in general (Brundiers et al., 2021). A wiki environment can however provide additional opportunities for assessment: the teacher can trace the history of the page, and students can reflect on the learning process in its discussion.

POTENTIAL ROLE OF WIKIS IN ESD (DISCUSSION AND CONCLUSIONS)

In the case study presented in this chapter we described digital resources (OER, specifically wiki) and reflected on the opportunities this genre provides in the sustainability context. This experience was limited to several Czech university courses with different disciplinary backgrounds which is a limitation to broader generalisation. The description of the learning processes and its results (competence development) was compared to similar experiences with other wikis (representatives of which were addressed in structured interviews), which increases the validity of the research. These results however depend on the learning context and environment, especially its social aspects.

In general, the authors argue that wiki systems can provide unique opportunities for ESD competence development if combined with appropriate learning approaches. In contrast to the printed educational materials which require reading literacy, wiki supports a more active approach as it is developed collaboratively. In this regard, a change has been observed in the way these online educational resources (OER) are produced, used and how their quality is assessed.

Digital media, in particular those that are co-produced by learners (in our case, university students), provide an environment to develop action competence: the ability to design new research questions, review

existing knowledge in order to find answers, and write a focused, well-argued text, possibly with a potential practical impact. We can thus see that action competence is closely associated with the competences necessary for academic writing which are among the core HE learning objectives. Sustainability oriented themes infuse this writing process with values and support decision-making in practice.

Recommendation

It has been illustrated that research and writing is an academic action itself. It results in a text that follows academic criteria; in the sustainability field the text provides a ground for action: it offers alternatives, arguments, information and pertinent methods. The academic text is thus the result of learning but also underpins transformative practice. It is recommended that development of writing reading/literacy on HE level is redefined with regards to the imperatives of sustainability - not only to include standard writing competences, but also to find one's way in a complex, uncertain information environment, cooperate with other actors and be directed towards change by sustainability values. To practise these competences, digital media such as wiki may provide unique opportunities. Of course, attention and space for testing and reflection of innovative pedagogical approaches is essential to ensure the best use of these opportunities, an areas which is rather neglected in higher education (Lozano et al., 2019).

FURTHER RESEARCH DIRECTIONS

There is an ongoing change in the field of research - as scientific knowledge is generated under new circumstances and with different objectives, the way in which it is communicated, to whom and how it is transferred, is also changing. We can infer that transformation of (higher) education follows closely, especially in the sustainability framework where values and uncertainties play a prominent role. Besides changing pedagogical approaches, this transformation is also manifested in the educational "text" itself - its form and purpose are changing, i.e., why, how and for whom has it been "written". This "text" is still based on verified and scientifically established information but is developed and used in a novel way. Also the quality criteria are changing: for educational purposes, the texts that have been recognised by "educational authorities" (expert books, textbooks, etc.) are recommended, but also those that students spontaneously use and that serve, for example, for interdisciplinary communication (Wikipedia and other wikis) need to be taken into account. They offer the possibility to choose from multiple ways of generating and utilising knowledge that may have implications for the design of university courses, setting learning objectives, assessment of students and many other aspects of HE.

Digital media provide a specific learning environment the educational potential of which has not been yet sufficiently discussed as an opportunity for ESD, and for educational innovation in general. On a more theoretical level, OER with quality content may represent a particular "genre" which is characterised by specific processes of text development, publishing and quality assurance which are non-hierarchical, interactive and based on community principles. Although this chapter illustrated some of these features, many questions about establishment of this genre on academic level remain unanswered.

ACKNOWLEDGMENT

The research was supported from Cooperatio project (Charles University) and the project "The use of regional case studies of sustainable development in university teaching and for the creation of Open Educational Resources" (TD020400) funded by the Technology Agency of the Czech Republic.

We would like to express our gratitude to Laura Henderson for the proof-reading the text.

REFERENCES

Atenas, J., & Havemann, L. (2014). Questions of quality in repositories of open educational resources: A literature review. *Research in Learning Technology*, *22*(1). doi:10.3402/rlt.v22.20889

Barth, M., & Michelsen, G. (2013). Learning for change: An educational contribution to sustainability science. *Sustainability Science*, *8*(1), 103–119. doi:10.100711625-012-0181-5

Boström, M., Andersson, E., Berg, M., Gustafsson, K., Gustavsson, E., Hysing, E., Lidskog, R., Löfmarck, E., Ojala, M., Olsson, J., Singleton, B., Svenberg, S., Uggla, Y., & Öhman, J. (2018). Conditions for Transformative Learning for Sustainable Development: A Theoretical Review and Approach. *Sustainability*, *10*(12), 4479. doi:10.3390u10124479

Brundiers, K., Barth, M., Cebrián, G., Cohen, M., Diaz, L., Doucette-Remington, S., Dripps, W., Habron, G., Harré, N., Jarchow, M., Losch, K., Michel, J., Mochizuki, Y., Rieckmann, M., Parnell, R., Walker, P., & Zint, M. (2021). Key competencies in sustainability in higher education—Toward an agreed-upon reference framework. *Sustainability Science*, *16*(1), 13–29. doi:10.100711625-020-00838-2

Deane, P., Odendahl, N., Quinlan, T., Fowles, M., Welsh, C., & Bivens-Tatum, J. (2008). Cognitive Models of Writing: Writing Proficiency as a Complex Integrated Skill. *ETS Research Report Series*, *2008*(2), i–36. doi:10.1002/j.2333-8504.2008.tb02141.x

DeRosa, R., & Robinson, S. (2017). From OER to Open Pedagogy: Harnessing the Power of Open. In Open: The Philosophy and Practices that are Revolutionizing Education and Science (pp. 115–124). Ubiquity Press. doi:10.5334/bbc.i

Dlouhá, Heras, Mulà, Salgado, & Henderson. (2019). Competences to Address SDGs in Higher Education—A Reflection on the Equilibrium between Systemic and Personal Approaches to Achieve Transformative Action. *Sustainability*, *11*(13), 3664. doi:10.3390u11133664

Dlouhá, J., Braniš, M., Dlouhý, J., Jančaříková, K., Jančařík, A., & Šauer, P. (2012). *Metodika tvorby textů v otevřeném internetovém prostoru – Enviwiki* [Methodology of text development in an open internet space]. https://enviwiki.cz/wiki/Metodika_tvorby_text%c5%af_v_otev%c5%99en%c3%a9m_internetov%c3%a9m_prostoru

Dlouhá, J., & Burandt, S. (2015). Design and evaluation of learning processes in an international sustainability oriented study programme. In search of a new educational quality and assessment method. *Journal of Cleaner Production*, *106*, 247–258. doi:10.1016/j.jclepro.2014.09.096

Dlouhá, J., & Dlouhý, J. (2014). Higher education for sustainability – a change of education genre? *Envigogika, 9*(1). doi:10.14712/18023061.440

Dlouhá, J., Henderson, L., Kroufek, R., Jančaříková, K., & Neprašová, S. (2021). Vzdělání k udržitelné spotřebě a životnímu stylu – cíle a výstupy [Education for sustainable consumption and lifestyle change—Educational goals and outcomes]. *Envigogika, 16*(1). doi:10.14712/18023061.619

Dlouhá, J., Petiška, E., Dlouhý, J., & Kapitulčinová, D. (2015). Možnosti a rizika využití otevřených vzdělávacích zdrojů v environmentálních oborech na vysokoškolské úrovni v ČR: Kritéria pro posouzení kvality [Opportunities and Risks of the Use of Open Education Resources in Environmental Disciplines at University Level in the Czech Republic: A Criteria for Assessing Quality]. *Envigogika, 10*(4). doi:10.14712/18023061.503

Evans, N., & Ferreira, J.-A. (2020). What does the research evidence base tell us about the use and impact of sustainability pedagogies in initial teacher education? *Environmental Education Research, 26*(1), 27–42. doi:10.1080/13504622.2019.1703908

Henderson, L., & Dlouhá, J. (2021). Myšlení budoucnosti a potřebnost transformativního přístupu ve vzdělávání [Future thinking and the need for a transformative approach in education]. *Envigogika, 16*(1). doi:10.14712/18023061.621

Henderson, L., Kuříková, M., & Kroufek, R. (2021). Syntéza kreativního učení a vzdělávání pro udržitelný rozvoj v České republice [Synthesis of Creative Learning and Education for Sustainable Development in the Czech Republic]. *Envigogika, 16*(2). doi:10.14712/18023061.628

Huitt, W. G., & Monetti, D. M. (2017). Openness and the Transformation of Education and Schooling. In Open: The Philosophy and Practices that are Revolutionizing Education and Science (pp. 43–65). Ubiquity Press. doi:10.5334/bbc.d

Jensen, B. B., & Schnack, K. (1997). The Action Competence Approach in Environmental Education. *Environmental Education Research, 3*(2), 163–178. doi:10.1080/1350462970030205

Lozano, R., Barreiro-Gen, M., Lozano, F., & Sammalisto, K. (2019). Teaching Sustainability in European Higher Education Institutions: Assessing the Connections between Competences and Pedagogical Approaches. *Sustainability, 11*(6), 1602. doi:10.3390u11061602

Michelsen, G., & Adomssent, M. (2007). Education for sustainable development strategies in German universities. *From cosmetic reform to meaningful integration: Implementing education for sustainable Development in Higher Education Institutes—The state of affairs in Six European countries*, 21–24.

Petiška, E., Korhoňová, L., Pospíšilová, M., & Dlouhý, J. (2020). Use and evaluation of the quality of open educational resources in the context of universities: The situation at Charles University. *Envigogika, 15*(1). doi:10.14712/18023061.607

Petiška, E., Pospíšilová, M., Dlouhý, J., Korhoňová, L., & Dlouha, J. (2021). Metodika zajištění kvality otevřených vzdělávacích zdrojů pro vysokoškolské vzdělávání [Quality Assurance Methodology for Open Educational Resources for Higher Education]. *Envigogika, 16*(2). doi:10.14712/18023061.634

Riemann, T., Kreß, A., Roth, L., Klipfel, S., Metternich, J., & Grell, P. (2020). Agile Implementation of Virtual Reality in Learning Factories. *Procedia Manufacturing*, *45*, 1–6. doi:10.1016/j.promfg.2020.04.029

Rodríguez Aboytes, J. G., & Barth, M. (2020). Transformative learning in the field of sustainability: A systematic literature review (1999-2019). *International Journal of Sustainability in Higher Education*, *21*(5), 993–1013. doi:10.1108/IJSHE-05-2019-0168

Scarff Seatter, C., & Ceulemans, K. (2017). Teaching Sustainability in Higher Education: Pedagogical Styles that Make a Difference. *Canadian Journal of Higher Education*, *47*(2), 47–70. doi:10.47678/cjhe.v47i2.186284

Shephard, K., Rieckmann, M., & Barth, M. (2019). Seeking sustainability competence and capability in the ESD and HESD literature: An international philosophical hermeneutic analysis. *Environmental Education Research*, *25*(4), 532–547. doi:10.1080/13504622.2018.1490947

Tilbury, D., & Mulà, I. (2009). *A Review of education for sustainable development policies from a cultural diversity and intercultural dialogue perspective: Identifying opportunities for future action—UNESCO Digital Library*. https://unesdoc.unesco.org/ark:/48223/pf0000211750

UNECE. (2011). *Learning for the future: Competences in Education for Sustainable Development. ECE/CEP/AC.13/2011/6*. UNECE. https://unece.org/fileadmin/DAM/env/esd/ESD_Publications/Competences_Publication.pdf

UNESCO. (2017). *Education for Sustainable Development Goals: Learning objectives—UNESCO Digital Library*. https://unesdoc.unesco.org/ark:/48223/pf0000247444

Wiek, A., Withycombe, L., & Redman, C. L. (2011). Key competencies in sustainability: A reference framework for academic program development. *Sustainability Science*, *6*(2), 203–218. doi:10.100711625-011-0132-6

Wikipedia Contributors. (2022). WikiWikiWeb. In *Wikipedia*. https://en.wikipedia.org/w/index.php?title=WikiWikiWeb&oldid=1092639361

Wiley, D., & Hilton, J. L. III. (2018). Defining OER-Enabled Pedagogy. *The International Review of Research in Open and Distributed Learning*, *19*(4). doi:10.19173/irrodl.v19i4.3601

Zahradník, M., & Pachmanová, L. (2009). Příklad využití wiki-prostředí v environmentálním vzdělávání na vysoké škole: Hodnocení kurzu Organizace a řízení ochrany životního prostředí [Example of using wiki-software in environmental education at university: evaluation of the course Management of Environmental Protection]. *Envigogika*, *4*(3). doi:10.14712/18023061.46

ADDITIONAL READING

Cottafava, D., Cavaglià, G., & Corazza, L. (2019). Education of sustainable development goals through students' active engagement: A transformative learning experience. *Sustainability Accounting. Management and Policy Journal*, *10*(3), 521–544. doi:10.1108/SAMPJ-05-2018-0152

Enviwiki Contributors. (2023). *Enviwiki*. https://www.enviwiki.cz/wiki/Hlavn%C3%AD_strana

Petiška, E. (2020). *Otevřené vzdělávací zdroje v kontextu environmentálních studií* [Open Educational Resources in the Context of Environmental Studies] [Unpublished doctoral dissertation]. Univerzita Karlova.

VCSEWiki Contributors. (2021). *VCSEwiki*. https://vcsewiki.czp.cuni.cz/wiki/Main_Page

Wals, A. E. (2019). Sustainability-oriented ecologies of learning: A response to systemic global dysfunction. In *Ecologies for Learning and Practice* (pp. 61–78). Routledge. doi:10.4324/9781351020268-5

WikiSkripta Contributors. (2023). *WikiSkripta*. https://www.wikiskripta.eu/w/Home

WikiSofia Contributors. (2023). *Wikisofia.* https://wikisofia.cz/wiki/Hlavn%C3%AD_strana

Chapter 17
Will Social Media Replace Face-to-Face Interactions in International Collaboration Discussions?

Martin Dür
University of Innsbruck, Austria

Lars Keller
University of Innsbruck, Austria

ABSTRACT

Within the education-research cooperation AustrIndia-4QOL, 102 teenagers from Austria and India jointly conducted research on the topics 'quality of life' and 'sustainability'. While the collaboration was mainly carried out via social media, some of the teenagers took part in an additional one-week face-to-face collaboration. This chapter offers insights into the effects of the collaboration on students' concepts of the quality of life perceptions of teenagers from different socio-cultural backgrounds and on their awareness of the importance and impact of environmental aspects on quality of life and their willingness to act towards more sustainable lifestyles. Social media enables learning experiences that cannot be facilitated within classical educational settings and should therefore be afforded greater attention in formal education. However, examination of the AustrIndia-4QOL project shows that social media collaborations have their own limitations and that the total removal of the opportunity for live face-to-face interactions is questionable.

DOI: 10.4018/978-1-7998-5033-5.ch017

INTRODUCTION

There is widespread agreement that further human development on this planet will ultimately depend upon the willingness and capacity of individuals as well as societies to undertake a fundamental transformation towards sustainability (IPCC, 2021; Kubisch et al., 2021; UN, 2021; UNEP, 2021; UNESCO, 2022). To enable humans to take action for sustainability, education has to undergo a profound, if not revolutionary, change. It is hoped that Education for Sustainable Development (ESD) will be the key enabler for achieving all Sustainable Development Goals (SDGs) and that it will play the most important role in providing learners with the required competencies (Schank & Rieckmann, 2019; Stoltenberg & Michelsen, 2020; UNESCO, 2022).

Nowadays, all these issues are strongly linked with the question of whether the use of digital media will help assist this learning revolution. After all, digital media is not only predicted to improve traditional learning settings, but also to completely redefine them. The possibilities for self-regulated and informal learning with the help of digital media supports a constructivist understanding of learning, and offers opportunities for networking and cooperating with other learners (Brendel & Schrüfer, 2018). Participation in societal processes as well as initiating and questioning them is another benefit (Kanwischer, 2014). The use of digital media in this capacity can make a valuable contribution for achieving the competencies mentioned in various competency frameworks for ESD (Lozano et al., 2017; Rieckmann & Barth, 2022; UNESCO, 2017; Wiek et al., 2015).

Research studies exploring the effects of social media in education settings frequently emphasize positive effects (e.g., Greenhow & Galvin, 2020) and Dron and Anderson's claim that such learning is transformed and has a more socio-constructivist approach (Dron & Anderson, 2014). Critical voices, however, propose that discussions via social media run the danger of remaining superficial because a lower quantity of information tends to be exchanged between participants in comparison with the quantity transferred in face-to-face discussions (Jeong, 2013). Kirschner feels that, in general, the structure of social media sites does not support the exchange of different opinions and perspectives since these tools are mainly used for self-presentation and due to algorithms people are primarily connected with other people who share similar interests and opinions (Kirschner, 2015).

The education-research-collaboration "AustrIndia-4QOL" (Teenagers from Austria and India perform research on Quality of Life) gives us the opportunity to compare the effects of social media and face-to-face discussions. This article examines how far an international collaboration of 56 teenagers from India and 46 teenagers from Austria leads to an increase of students' awareness of the importance of environmental aspects for quality of life (QOL) as well as to an increase in their willingness to act toward more sustainable lifestyles.

Within the project, one group of students took part in a collaboration restricted to social media (Social Media Group) and another group, who took part in a collaboration via social media and face-to-face collaboration (Face-to-Face Group). This provides the opportunity to compare the effectiveness of both learning settings and leads to the following research hypotheses:

1. An international collaboration based on social media influences students' concepts of the QOL perceptions of teenagers from different socio-cultural backgrounds.
2. An international collaboration based on social media increases teenagers' awareness of the importance of environmental aspects for QOL.

3. An international collaboration based on social media and face-to-face collaboration promotes an even greater increase in teenagers' awareness of the importance of environmental aspects for QOL.
4. An international collaboration based on social media increases teenagers' willingness to act toward more sustainable lifestyles.
5. An international collaboration based on social media and face-to-face collaboration promotes an even greater increase in teenagers' willingness to act towards more sustainable lifestyles.

The results from this project offer insights into the effectiveness of a moderate constructivist learning approach, enabling learners to question their deep-rooted individual lifestyle concepts, and thus, into how to translate the extensive theoretical foundation on competences for sustainable development into pedagogical practice. The outcome of the AustrIndia-4QOL project demonstrates very clearly learners' difficulties in questioning their lifestyle concepts and shows that international collaboration between the Global North and the Global South may lead to unintended and unexpected effects.

THE SEARCH FOR EFFECTIVE EDUCATIONAL APPROACHES FOR ESD

To support further human development within the planetary boundaries, far reaching changes in human lifestyles are needed. To achieve this goal, in 2015 the United Nations agreed upon 17 SDGs to be reached by 2030 (Agenda 2030). Of the 17 SDGs, goal number four (Quality Education) is specifically dedicated to the subject of education, but the importance of education is stressed within several other goals as well, and education is acknowledged to be a key for achieving a sustainable future. To reach this goal education and learning have to be refocused so that "everyone has the opportunity to acquire the knowledge, skills, values and attitudes that empower them to contribute to sustainable development", and education and learning have to be strengthened "in all agendas, programs and activities that promote sustainable development" (UNESCO, 2018).

Therefore, the focus of ESD must be the acquisition of competences deemed essential for the active and reflective participation of individuals in the process of transforming a society moving toward sustainability (Stoltenberg & Michelsen, 2020). There is an urgent need for more learner-centered, participative, action-oriented and transformative pedagogy, which ultimately empowers and motivates learners to act (Olsson et al., 2016; Schank & Rieckmann, 2019; UNESCO, 2022). This means "a shift from teaching to learning" (UNESCO, 2017, p. 7), and a widespread change toward a more constructivist understanding of learning. Only then will it be possible for young people to acquire the competences for self-determined and responsible participation in our modern, increasingly interconnected and multilayered global societies (Schank & Rieckmann, 2019; UNESCO, 2022).

The tricky question regarding which competences are actually required is still debated. When looking at the far-reaching similarities between often mentioned lists of competences in the literature, the ability to collaborate with others is frequently mentioned (Lozano et al., 2017; Rieckmann & Barth, 2022; UNESCO, 2017; Wiek et al., 2015). Collaborative efforts are reported to be required to take into account that sustainability challenges manifesting on local levels are linked to regional, national or even global levels (Stoltenberg & Michelsen, 2020).

Due to the extreme complexity and interconnection of sustainability challenges, no simple and clear-cut answers exist. Beyond that, in a pluralist society, solution approaches should always be negotiated between different interest groups within the framework of their respective norms, perspectives, and values (Wals, 2015). According to the UNESCO, collaboration competence includes "the abilities to learn from others; to understand and respect the needs, perspectives and actions of others (empathy); to understand, relate to and be sensitive to others (empathic leadership); to deal with conflicts in a group; and to facilitate collaborative and participatory problem solving" (UNESCO, 2017, p. 10). By assuming that pluralism and heterogeneity is more promising as compared to singularity and homogeneity, it is particularly interesting when individuals with different ideas, perspectives, and values work together. Dissonances, in particular, can provide the basis for creative solutions desperately required for a societal transformation toward sustainability. International collaborations appear to be one such promising approach for a learning setting. By jointly searching for solution approaches with learners from different socio-cultural backgrounds, individuals are confronted with different perspectives. This may lead to the critically questioning of existing concepts and to developing them further (Greenhow & Galvin, 2020).

Today's technological advancements offer new opportunities for implementing international collaborations without the typical disadvantages of classical "study abroad programs". These programs not only require enormous financial and organizational efforts, but, due to traveling, have negative environmental impacts (Kimmerle et al., 2015). If it were possible to design social media collaborations that were as enriching for participants as actual face-to-face collaborations, this would have considerable potential for international collaboration in formal education.

Previous research about the potential of social media has often been referred to as under-theorized (Kimmerle et al., 2015). Furthermore, Clark et al.'s (2009) conclusion that the potential benefits of social media for formal education were not recognized by either teachers or learners, and that social media was therefore not implemented in an appropriate fashion in formal education, may still hold a grain of truth. Until now, new technologies tend to be used in classrooms to reproduce traditional learning approaches instead of creating completely new ways of learning (Eckstein, 2022). Learning with social media could easily be in line with social constructivist learning, where knowledge is created collaboratively and in social contexts (Brendel & Schrüfer, 2018; Kimmerle et al., 2015) and where emotions, values, and attitudes play important roles (Greenhow & Galvin, 2020). Accessibility without limitations in time and space (Dron & Anderson, 2014) and the possibility of building worldwide networks might even provide learners with opportunities for gaining totally different perspectives (Brendel & Schrüfer, 2018). Let us also add to the mix the promise expressed in numerous studies that learning via social media often increases learners motivation (Greenhow & Galvin, 2020).

Despite these potential benefits, critical perspectives have also been raised. Critiques frequently refer to social media collaborations as lacking in depth with regard to the extent of information exchanged and debated (Jeong, 2013). Kirschner (2015) also questions the suitability of social media sites for controversial discussions in learning contexts. According to him, comments on social media are overwhelmingly used for personal marketing with a tendency towards narcissism which "might not be the right tool for discussion and argumentation for knowledge construction" (Kirschner, 2015, p. 622). Furthermore, algorithms support connections between users with similar perspectives (within bubbles) rather than supporting a variety of viewpoints. Generally, the linear structure of discussion boards on social media sites technically inhibits real debate. Authentic debating depends on making claims and providing justifications for these claims (Kirschner, 2015).

In international collaborations, particular attention is necessary when participants from the Global North and the Global South are interacting. Research shows that students from the Global North are rarely capable of reflecting critically on their own socially constructed method of valuation. Thus, when conducting an international collaboration, the equality of both partners has to be a central aspect (Höhnle, 2014). "Reciprocity, equality and mutuality" (Martin & Griffiths, 2012, p. 923) has to form the basis.

In designing the learning-settings for the AustrIndia-4QOL project, these recommendations were on the forefront of researchers' minds. The aims of the survey presented in this paper were on the one hand to test whether an international collaboration of high school students from Austria and India influences the students' concepts of the QOL perceptions of their project counterparts. On the other hand, it was evaluated if this international collaboration has positive effects on the students' awareness of the importance of environmental aspects for QOL as well as on their willingness to act toward more sustainable lifestyles. The overarching topic QOL was chosen to make the students aware of their personal concerns and also of their personal responsibilities. Today's young people, as future adults, will have a major say in their choice of QOL-concepts which will determine to what extent inter- and intra-generational justice and the transformation toward sustainability will succeed (Hauff & Jörg, 2017). Additionally, their future QOL will depend on the success of sustainable development (Helne & Hirvilammi, 2015; UNESCO, 2021).

IMPLEMENTATION OF AN INTERNATIONAL COLLABORATION IN THE CONTEXT OF ESD

Study Design

The international collaboration within AustrIndia-4QOL's project had two distinct phases, each of which lasted three months. Interrupted by various school holidays, the collaboration occurred between September 2015 and September 2016. The specific program sequence of these project phases will be described in detail below (see also Dür & Keller, 2019). This sequence was conducted twice within the AustrIndia-4QOL project. Each time, one school class from Austria and one from India collaborated. Great attention was paid to the fact that the students from both schools were able to bring their ideas and contributions to the project, to support cooperation on an equal footing.

In the respective starts of the project, the students had to produce short videos on their smartphones to introduce their school, their hometown, their local leisure opportunities and so on. The videos were uploaded to a closed group on the Facebook platform and commented on by their foreign collaborators. Facebook was chosen because of its easy accessibility for all project participants, and because all students had already had some experiences on this platform when the project started. Furthermore, the students could work with their own smartphones, and so were not dependent on the access to laptops.

In this stage of the project, a video conference via Skype was also held so students could see each other and introduce themselves virtually.

A moderate constructivist learning exercise came next. For this task, students jointly carried out research about the QOL-perceptions of teenagers their age. The students in Austria and India developed ten closed questions each. Through a voting process, 15 of these questions were chosen for a questionnaire. Before administrating the instrument, students shared their outcome expectations for each question in their research diaries. During the following week, each student in Austria and India interviewed other teenagers using the jointly developed questionnaire. The completed questionnaires were reviewed by both classes, and results were shared on Facebook. Based on these results, working in pairs, the students created diagrams (Figure 1) with the help of Excel software and added their interpretations of the data.

The diagrams and interpretations were shared as well as commented on via Facebook. A video conference via Skype provided an additional opportunity to discuss some of the results in greater detail.

Figure 1. Selected results from a survey administered by the students to teenagers of their age in Austria and India

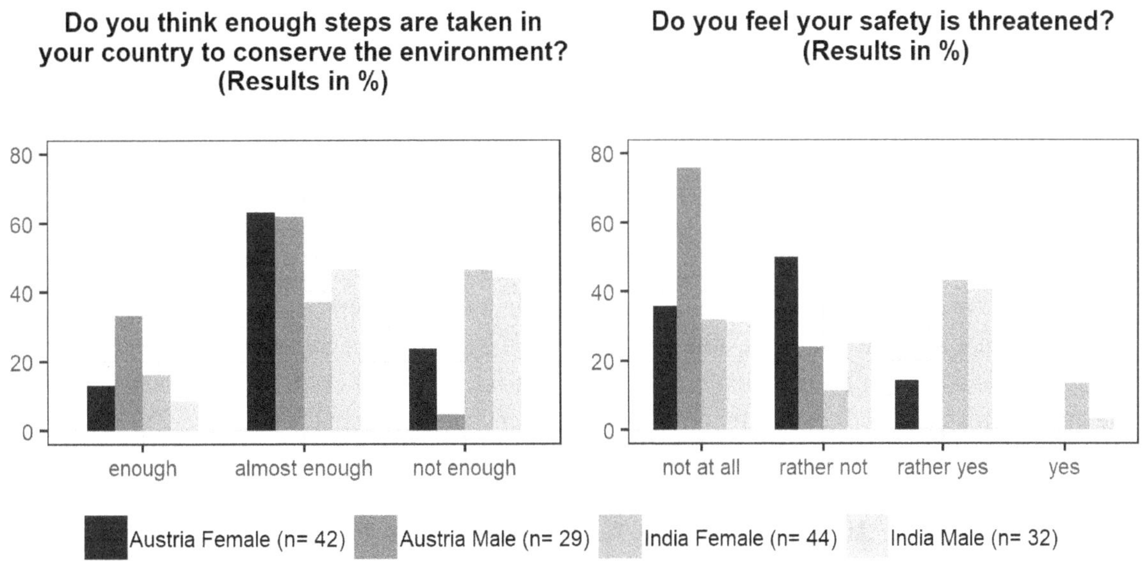

The second project phase again adopted a moderate constructivist learning approach. The students, once more working in pairs, selected a specific topic of interest to them related to QOL, and their vision of sustainable development on the planet. They formulated research questions to guide their inquiries on the internet and wrote short papers about their findings. Examples of issues students focused on were waste treatment, sustainable energy supply, gender equality, food waste, and the pressure on biodiversity in the seas due to human activities. The abstracts of these research papers were uploaded on Facebook and commented upon by the other students.

A jointly created final statement by students concluded the collaboration within the AustrIndia-4QOL project. In this statement, the students shared specific goals that should be achieved to secure a high quality of life for all people on this planet now and in future. Students developed their initial statements in small groups and then uploaded these statements on Facebook. The final statement was developed based on debating and expanding on several of the initial statements until an overarching one was approved by all participants. The goals were also translated into action steps that should be taken on the global, national, and individual levels.

At the end of the social media collaboration, ten Indian students were able to travel to Austria to visit their research colleagues and join a one-week actual face-to-face experience, including workshops. For the remainder of this article, this group is called "Face-to-Face Group" whereas students who were only able to take part in the social media collaboration will be referred to as the "Social Media Group"

Study Sample

The AustrIndia-4QOL project included high school students from the Day Star School (DSS) in Manali, India, and the Gymnasium Schillerstrasse (GYS) in Feldkirch, Austria. All of the participants were aged 16 or thereabouts. From the outset, the project was developed in continuous consultation with representatives from the DSS to moderate Eurocentric views. At both schools the classes taking part in the AustrIndia-4QOL project were selected by the school administrators based on organizational criteria. Before starting the project, general information was presented to the students and their participation was voluntary.

In financial terms the Austrian families of the involved students from the state operated GYS could be described mainly as middle-class.

The DSS is an English-speaking, privately-operated school whose ethos is to actively accept students from different ethnic / cultural backgrounds in their region. While the majority of these students come from families who may be described as being financially well-off, approximately 20% are able to attend this school due to sponsorship by external donors from India and Europe.

The ten Indian students who were able to take part in the face-to-face experience all originated from the upper-middle class of their region but had different religious and caste backgrounds. The Indian caste system still influences daily life in this region. Their families were able to cover the costs of the trip to Austria. For all of the ten Indian students, as well as their accompanying teacher, it was their first journey outside their own country. They were hosted by the families of their Austrian project partners. Living together with the Austrian families allowed for direct insights into their lifestyles, which proved to be important.

Data Collection and Data Analysis

Teenagers from Austria (n=201) and India (n=190) took part in a pre-test at the beginning of the AustrIndia-4QOL project. From this initial group, one class of each school was randomly chosen to serve as a control group without any special educational intervention. Two other classes from both the Austrian and Indian schools participated in the social media collaboration on the topics of quality of life and sustainability. With these three school classes from both countries a post-test was conducted at the end of the project. Additionally, the students kept a research diary in which they noted their insights as a consequence of the collaboration.

The pre- and post-tests included freewriting about QOL, and a survey with several open and closed questions. For the freewriting sessions the students were given ten minutes during which to spontaneously write down whatever came up to their minds concerning the issue "Quality of Life". For the analysis on the effects of the international collaboration on participants' QOL concepts, seven questions focused on students' awareness of the importance of environmental aspects for QOL, and nine on students' willingness to act toward more sustainable lifestyles. The questionnaire was tested with other students as part of a pilot stage of the project. Teachers from both schools provided feedback to adapt the questions to students' realities in both countries.

A qualitative content-analysis was conducted to analyze the students' freewritings and open-ended survey questions. The coding was done independently by two researchers. A three-point Likert scale was used to transform the responses of each student into a numerical value. If, for example, environmental aspects were not considered as important for QOL, the students' responses were scored as "zero". If some environmental aspects were mentioned, a score of "one" was assigned. If environmental aspects were mentioned extensively, a score of "two" was assigned. The answers to the closed questions as well as to ranking questions (e.g. "Choose the three most important …") were also transformed into numerical values between "zero" and "two". For the seven questions regarding students' awareness of the importance of environmental aspects for QOL, a numerical maximum of 14 was possible, for the nine questions regarding the students' willingness to act toward more sustainable lifestyles the maximum was 18. For the purpose of analysis for this chapter, however, we focus on the percentage score each student y achieved in the pre- and post-test.

Statistical analyses were conducted with the software "RStudio". A Mann-Whitney-Wilcoxon rank-sum test was used to test for statistically significant differences between pre- and post-tests as well as between different project groups. Spearman's ρ was calculated to examine correlations. For deeper insights into students' concepts, illustrative quotes are provided. To achieve better coherency, obvious grammar and spelling mistakes in students' quotes were corrected. Austrian students' quotes were translated into English by the authors.

RESULTS AND DISCUSSION

Impact of Social Media Collaboration About Quality-of-Life Perceptions of Teenagers From Different Socio-Cultural Backgrounds

As indicated earlier, students jointly developed a survey including a variety of questions on QOL. Among others, personal safety, the protection of the environment, religion, family matters, and plans for the future were topics they selected for this purpose. In addition to the analyzing and interpretating the data they collected, students also reflected on the results they had anticipated and compared the actual survey results. The students' comments in their research diaries show that quite a few of them became aware of stereotypes they had had in their mind beforehand.

My experience with this project was exciting. I loved to talk to the Austrians. First, I thought talking to them would be like talking to aliens, and it would be difficult. But the total opposite was true. . . . I understood that Austrians and Indians have more or less the same way of thinking. They have their faults, we have our faults. (Male student from India)

Doing the project AustrIndia-4QOL was a really good experience. I became aware of some differences between the students from India and Austria. I also found out more about the Indians, and what is in their mind. I also got to know myself and even my friends better. I found that Austrian students do not believe in religion, but Indians do. (Female student from India)

It was very interesting to see what the Indian students think. It was especially interesting to see that not all clichés turned out to be true. For example: A lot of people think that in India nobody is interested in protecting the environment, but the results from the questionnaire showed a completely different picture. Other exiting results were delivered with the help of the question about the future perspectives of the Indian students. My assumption that Indians are rather conservative and only see themselves with their own family was completely taken apart. Most of them see themselves working or at the university. (Male student from Austria)

I got completely disillusioned about the "typical Indian". I thought that Indians are very much into traditions, and that they do a lot of farming. But the impression I got through to our research project was one of an Indian who does not help his mother at home but sits in front of a computer and is posting selfies of himself and his friends on Facebook all the time. I was very surprised that high tech is of such great importance for them. (Female student from Austria)

These statements show that the collaboration via social media had a great impact on the students' concepts about QOL perceptions of teenagers from different socio-cultural backgrounds. Even if students generalized in inappropriate manners and even created new clichés, these revised perspectives were more realistic when compared to their original views. All in all, the collaboration in the AustrIndia-4QOL project shows an effect on students' concepts that probably would not have been changed in a classic educational setting which tends to perpetuate clichés.

Teenagers' Awareness of the Importance of Environmental Aspects for Quality of Life

The analyses of the seven questions focused on students' awareness of the importance of environmental aspects for QOL in the pre-test identified statistically significant differences for the two groups of students (Table 1). The average awareness of the importance of environmental aspects for QOL of the Austrian students turned out to be significantly higher ($p < 0.001$) as compared to the awareness of the Indian students.

Interestingly, however, environmental aspects were hardly identified as relevant for QOL. In the pre-test freewriting, only 10.8% of the Austrian and 9.6% of the Indian students actually mentioned environmental aspects. Instead, their perception of QOL was dominated by social (68.7% of the Austrian and 71.5% of the Indian students) as well as economic aspects (62% of the Austrian and 45.2% of the Indian students). This is in line with results from a survey conducted by Oberrauch et al. (2014) with students from Austria, Germany, and Italy around the same age. Examining data from other pre-test questions, however, shows that the students were aware of current global environmental challenges, even though only very few connected these challenges with their own lives. Moreover, they mainly expected the consequences of these challenges to happen in the distant future.

In our region, we don't notice how far climate change has already progressed. We still have many natural areas and so are not confronted with this problem. (Female student from Austria; translated)

Of course, some day all of us will encounter environmental problems. But in Austria we are fortunate that, at the moment, no relevant problems occur. (Male student from Austria; translated)

At the moment, I do not see the impact of ecological problems. But maybe in the future there will be an impact. (Male student from India)

Ecological problems will have a direct effect on humans in the future as new diseases will occur. There can be water and food scarcity. (Female student from India)

The lack of concern over more immediate impacts may result in students believing that changes in their behaviors are not necessary and/or can be postponed.

Comparing pre- and post-test results suggests increasing students' awareness of the importance of environmental aspects on QOL is not easy to achieve. This is consistent with findings from other studies suggesting that deep-rooted beliefs are hardly changed by learners (Persson et al., 2019). A Mann-Whitney-Wilcoxon rank-sum test indicates only insignificant changes for the Social-Media Group. This is in contrast to the awareness of the Austrian and Indicant students in the Face-to-Face Group which differed significantly from pre to post-test (Table 1, Figure 2). Therefore, research hypotheses 2 has to be rejected, while research hypotheses 3 can be confirmed.

Table 1. Teenagers' awareness of the importance of environmental aspects for quality of life

	Number of Teenagers (Female/Male)	Awareness Pre-Test in Percentage of Maximum Value	Awareness Post-Test in Percentage of Maximum Value	Change Between Pre- and Post-Test in Percentage Points (*p*-Value)	Correlation Coefficient - Spearman's ρ
Control Group AT	20 (10 / 10)	28.50	28.71	0.21 (0.601)	−0.867
Control Group IN	31 (17 / 14)	22.86	21.98	−0.88 (0.657)	−0.614
Social Media Group AT	24 (12 / 12)	29.05	30.60	1.55 (0.321)	−0.418
Social Media Group IN	46 (29 / 17)	19.63	19.91	0.28 (0.536)	−0.609
Face-To-Face Group AT	22 (14 / 8)	37.27	43.77	**6.50* (0.049)**	−0.594
Face-To-Face Group IN	10 (7 / 3)	19.00	29.28	**10.28* (0.032)**	−0.587

AT = Austrian teenagers
IN = Indian teenagers
*Statistically significant on a 95% confidence level according to a Mann–Whitney–Wilcoxon rank-sum test (p-value).
Spearman's ρ: Correlation between the individual's awareness in the pre-test and increase in awareness.
Source: adopted from Dür and Keller (2019)

Figure 2. Change of the participating teenagers' awareness of the importance of environmental aspects for QOL between pre- and post- test in percentage points

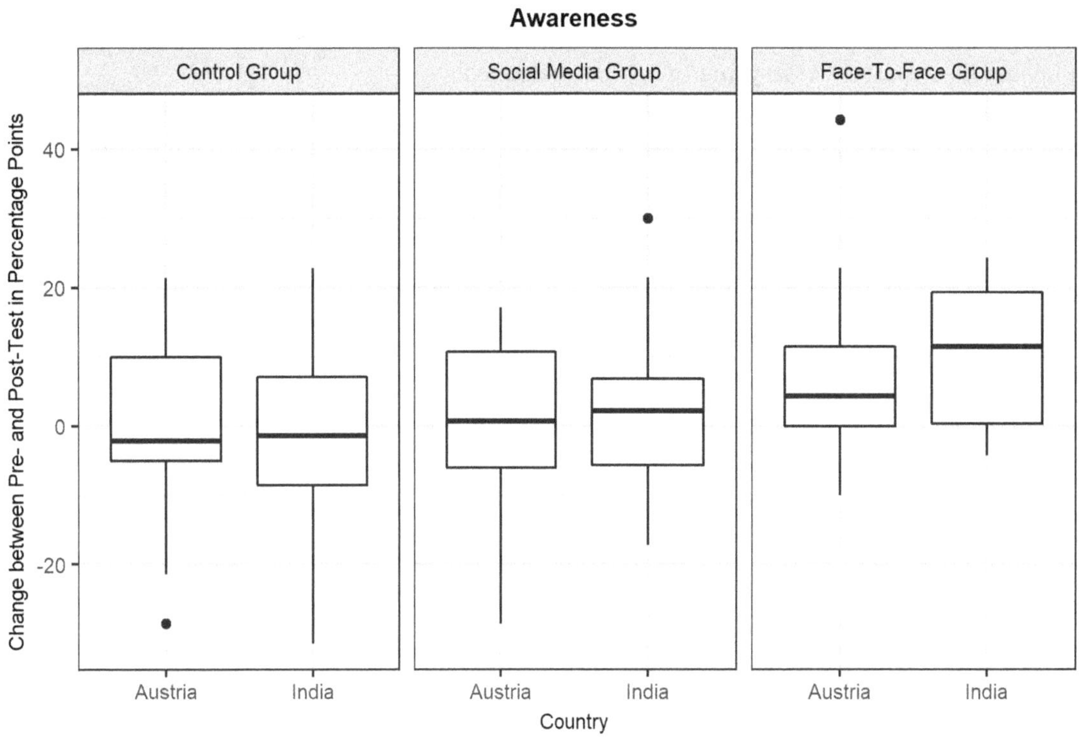

Focusing on solely on the effect size measured at the group level, however, is limiting. An analysis of the freewritings in the post-test of the Face-to-Face group provides more comprehensive insights into teenagers' perspectives.

Having a high quality of life does not mean having money, luxury, machines, well developed infrastructure, but being happy in what you have and enjoy it. We should enjoy the beautiful nature rather than disturbing the nature and the ecosystem. (Female student from India)

Thinking about major challenges like climate change, gender equality, water supply and water treatment and the need for energy. Once we are able to solve these problems, surely, we will be able to have a better quality of life! (Female student from India)

In my opinion, the topic environment plays one of the most important roles when it comes to quality of life. From waste separation, waste-water treatment, and regular cleaning activities up to clean air. (Female student from Austria; translated)

The students from India made me aware of how important it is to protect the environment. Natural resources are important and I as a human being want to preserve nature in order to be able to enjoy myself in nature in the future. (Female student from Austria; translated)

A qualitative analysis of students' freewriting on the importance of the environment on QOL in the post-test helps to explain the differences between the students of the Social Media and Face-to-Face groups as the following results show.

The intensive in-depth discussions during the face-to-face workshops may be responsible for the fact that 53% of the students of the face-to-face group explicitly referred to information they received from students of the other country, and, in the case of the Indian students, also the personal experiences they had during their stay in Austria, observing the lifestyles of the families they stayed with. This is in contrast to the students in the social media group. Though most emphasized that they obtained new insights into the topic of sustainability as a result of participating in the project, only 21% of them explicitly referred to information from their project counterparts.

Examining individual students' responses leads to further insights. The correlation coefficient (Spearman's ρ) between individual's awareness of the importance of the environment to QOL at the pre-test and the increase in awareness was negative for all groups This suggests that students with high levels of awareness at the pre-test were less able to further increase this awareness when compared to students' whose awareness was lower at the beginning of the project.

Teenagers' Willingness to Act Toward More Sustainable Lifestyles

An analysis of the nine questions focused on students' willingness to act toward more sustainable lifestyles in the pre-test suggests that a high percentage of students were already reaching or getting close to the maximum of the scale possible at the beginning of the project, and there are only small deviations between the different group of students (Table 2). Qualitative data are consistent with these quantitative findings. In their responses to the open-ended questions in the survey, students from all survey groups mentioned several different actions (recycling waste, using public transport instead of private cars etc.) that can be taken to protect the environment. Some students also emphasized specific actions they already take.

Personally, we can change many things. We can recycle waste and be careful that we are not throwing rubbish everywhere. I think we will have a direct impact on our personal quality of life, since there may be many diseases because of pollution. These are personal responsibilities. Before blaming other countries, we should try to maintain our own surroundings. Most important is to manage waste and to recycle it. (Female student from India)

We, as the humans are the only ones responsible for climate change by polluting with industries and automobiles. We should prefer the use of buses and bicycles instead of cars. These things are possible, but everyone must be a part of it and also contribute. If everyone contributes, this earth will also be changed, and we can save the lives of animals and people and save the earth. The earth can only be saved for tomorrow by actions today. (Female student from India)

Personally, one can help to protect the environment by not throwing away waste and by producing less waste. For me, this seems very important because the future of our planet is up to us. Of course, we will not be alive anymore, but other people would suffer, and therefore we should consider these small details and think of our future children. (Female student from Austria; translated)

Of course, everyone is responsible for the environment. Even with small steps, e.g., saving electricity, separating waste correctly, not wasting water and the use of public transport it is possible to contribute to a better future. I, myself, try to consider these measures because I think if this is done by everyone, we will be able to take a big step forward. (Female student from Austria; translated)

Examining responses to the survey's closed-ended questions allows for further insights into the teenagers' willingness to act toward more sustainable lifestyles: 68% of the Austrian and 73% of the Indian students stated their willingness ("rather imaginable for me", "imaginable for me" or "I want to realize this consequently in the future, or I realize this already") to reduce their consumption of meat. Supporting politicians who are willing to act for more social justice and act in favor of the environment was imaginable for 74% of the Austrian students and 70% of the Indian students, even if this leads to higher tax burdens and less personal freedom. In comparison, a substantial change in individual mobility behavior seems to be more difficult, especially for the Austrian teenagers: Although 78% of the Austrian students (vs 83% of the Indian students) stated their willingness to reduce the use of a private car even if this is less convenient, only 38% of them (vs 70% of the Indian students) were willing to renounce the ownership of an own private car.

There is of course the question of how far students' willingness to act sustainably will translate into action. This is reflected in students' descriptions of their shopping habits. For example, 43% of the Austrian and 53% of the Indian students reported considering (rather often, often, by each purchase) environmental criteria (transport route, way of production) in their purchase decisions. However, the price of products (75% of the Austrian students and 68% of the Indian students) and, in case of the Indian students, fashion trends (83% of the Indian students compared with 40% of the Austrian students) influenced their individual purchasing behavior to a greater extent.

Comparing the students' willingness to act toward more sustainable lifestyles in the pre- and post-test by conducting a Mann-Whitney-Wilcoxon rank-sum test identified only one significant change for the Austrian students from the Face-to-Face Group (Table 2). In general, it can also be seen that the effect of the project on the students' willingness to act was limited (boxplot in Figure 3). While research hypotheses 4 has to be rejected, research hypotheses 5 can neither be simply verified nor can it be rejected. Although not statistically significant, the decreased willingness to act of the Indian students in all project groups must be highlighted. Based on statements participants wrote at the beginning and at the end of the face-to-face experience (see Dür & Keller, 2018), it appears that in the case of the Indian students, the experience in Austria led to an increased desire for a stronger economic development in their own country as well as for greater global justice. As such, global (in)justices may receive greater attention as a result of collaborations between individuals in the Global North and Global South (Martin & Griffiths, 2012).

The developed countries are mainly to blame for the ecological problems like climate change, the pollution of seas, etc. In my opinion, the developed countries should change their standard of living as they have a high standard of living. The developing countries have a low standard of living, so if there is a balance, we could have a good global justice. (Female student from India)

They [the western countries] have developed due to their industries, which have caused a lot of carbon dioxide emissions. And now, due to climate change it is difficult for the developing countries which are dependent on their industries. . . . Thus, we need to promote global justice for the developing countries so that they can match up with the other countries and help in making the world a better place to live. (Male student from India)

Table 2. Teenagers' willing to act toward more sustainable lifestyles

	Number of Teenagers (Female/ Male)	Willingness to Act Pre-Test in Percentage of Maximum Value	Willingness to Act Post-Test in Percentage of Maximum Value	Change Between Pre- and Post-Test in Percentage Points (p-Value)	Correlation coefficient - Spearman's ρ
Control Group AT	20 (10 / 10)	64.17	65.50	1.33 (0.363)	−0.476
Control Group IN	31 (17 / 14)	60.68	58.17	−2.51 (0.199)	−0.350
Social Media Group AT	24 (12 / 12)	59.21	61.44	2.23 (0.184)	−0.432
Social Media Group IN	46 (29 / 17)	61.96	60.89	−1.07 (0.705)	−0.668
Face-To-Face Group AT	22 (14 / 8)	63.99	69.14	**5.15 * (0.023)**	−0.324
Face-To-Face Group IN	10 (7 / 3)	62.22	60.33	−1.89 (0.878)	−0.863

AT = Austrian teenagers
IN = Indian teenagers
* Statistically significant on a 95% confidence level according to a Mann–Whitney–Wilcoxon rank-sum test (p-value).
Spearman's ρ: Correlation between the individual's awareness in the pre-test and increase in awareness.
Source: adopted from Dür and Keller (2019)

The correlation coefficient (Spearman's ρ) between students' willingness to act toward more sustainable lifestyles in the pre-test and their increase in willingness to act was negative for all project groups. This suggests that students who expressed a high willingness to act at the pre-test were less able to further increase their willingness to act, as compared to students whose willingness to act was lower initially.

Figure 3. Change of participating teenagers' willingness to act towards more sustainable lifestyles

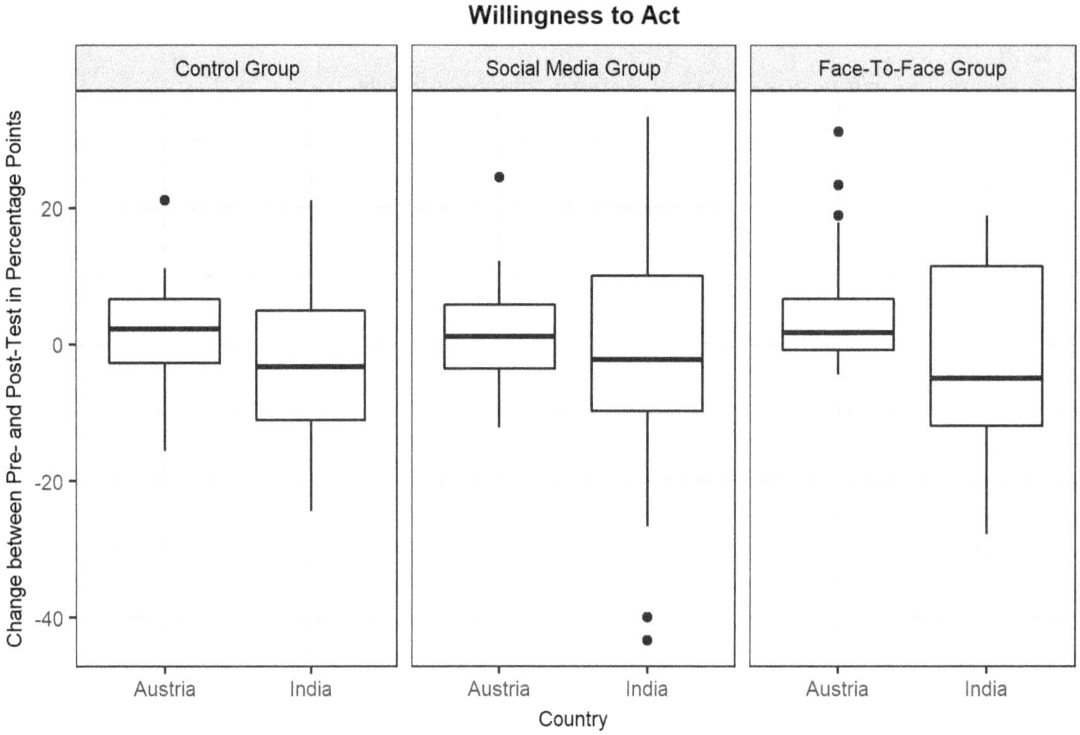

LIMITATIONS AND FUTURE RESEARCH DIRECTIONS

An educational intervention like the AustrIndia-4QOL project requires a lot of organizational efforts and considerable concessions by school administrators and others. It is difficult to implement such interventions and therefore, associated studies with a large sample size to meet statistical power requirements. To minimize the limitations of a small sample size, the classes that took part in this project were selected solely based on organizational constraints by the respective school administrators. However, the selection of the ten Indian students who participated in the Face-to-Face Group does not meet these requirements. In this case, students' personal motivation, the financial background of their families and their access to a passport were the decisive factors. There were more Indian students interested in coming to Austria but financial constraints and missing documents for passport applications made it impossible for them to take part. The biggest challenge for the organization of the face-to-face collaboration was to persuade the authorities to grant the Indian students travel visas.

The use of social media in a formal learning setting was new for all participants. As a result, the intervention may have benefited students who prefer learning through social interaction and who are best able to use social media as a learning tool. This is one reason, the Facebook platform was chosen. All students had some experiences with this platform in advance of the project.

The success of a collaboration via social media is dependent on students' access to a device like a smartphone or computer and the availability of a stable internet connection. The limited access to a device with reliable internet connectivity turned out to be a challenge for Indian students. The students also tended to rely on their smartphones for the assignments.

To improve the quality of personal exchanges between the project participants regular real time communication via the social media platform Skype were planned. However, due to the time difference between Austria and India, it turned out to be difficult to find a common time slot and Indian students had to be prepared to stay longer at school. The limited data capacity of the internet connection at both schools presented a further challenge and the video conferences were interrupted several times.

The introduction of their schools, their hometowns etc. with the help of short videos led to a lively exchange between students on Facebook. This was also true for the joint creation of the questionnaire as well as for the exchange about the data that were collected and analyzed. During this project phase the students were dependent on the information from the other side for their assignment and were therefore actively engaged on Facebook. The students' notes in their research diaries show that this project phase influenced students' concepts about the QOL-perceptions of teenagers from the other country.

The limitations of collaboration via social media only became apparent in the second phase of the project. It was very difficult to engage in intensive debates about complex issues through Facebook (Jeong, 2013). The teachers had to remind the students that simply selecting the like button on Facebook does not contribute to an exchange of knowledge and perspectives. Compared to the intensive exchange during project phase one, the debates via social media in project phase two often remained superficial and the students mainly worked on their chosen topics on their own, instead of exchanging their ideas with others.

In contrast, the face-to-face collaboration between the 22 students from Austria and 10 students from India, led to in-depth and emotional discussions between the participants, including being confronted with many different opinions (Dür & Keller, 2018).

Further research for using social media in international learning settings is needed to overcome the described deficits. In particular, the outcomes of different learning settings have to be examined to find suitable ways for more intensive discussions about complex topics.

CONCLUSION

Insights from the AustrIndia-4QOL project, for the most part, confirm the overall difficulty in achieving changes to learners' deep-rooted concepts within an educational setting. In addition, the data also provide evidence that an international collaboration that included face-to-face workshops and living experiences can have a slightly greater impact on students' concepts as compared to collaborations solely restricted to social media.

Even though it was not statistically significant, the results of the AustrIndia-4QOL project suggest that a collaboration between participants from the Global North and the Global South may have unintended effects. In the case of the Indian students, the collaboration with students from one of the wealthiest countries in the world (i.e., Austria) led to a lower willingness to act toward more sustainable lifestyles. The desire for higher living-standards overruled existing concerns about associated, negative consequences.

Nonetheless we suggest that social media offer new possibilities for formal education and especially international collaborations to support learning. Reports in schoolbooks about the living conditions in different parts of the world can be replaced by virtual, personal social media interactions with individuals from all over the world. This way, far more realistic insights are possible, and stereotypes can be examined and questioned. An intensive exchange over Facebook was facilitated through jointly performed research about teenagers' QOL perceptions whereas discussions about more complex issues turned out to be difficult and merely scratched the surface when an assignment could be completed by students on their own. In the latter case, students had to be kept motivated by the teachers to post comments. It is therefore not surprising that complex concepts were hardly affected.

The face-to-face discussions about similar topics resulted in a very different outcome. Discussions between students in workshop settings often continued after the end of the official learning experience. As a result, a high percentage of students in the face-to-face group explicitly referred to information they learned from their project counterparts at the end of the project.

The relatively easy and cheap implementation of social media collaborations as compared to the difficulties and hurdles of international face-to-face interactions call for further research to test and improve the effectiveness of social media collaborations in innovative ways as well as with different groups of students. The evaluation of AustrIndia-4QOL indicates that the value of face-to-face collaborations should not be underestimated, even now, when social media has become so much a part of teenagers' daily lives.

REFERENCES

Clark, W., Logan, K., Luckin, R., Mee, A., & Oliver, M. (2009). Beyond Web 2.0: Mapping the technology landscapes of young learners: Beyond Web 2.0. *Journal of Computer Assisted Learning*, *25*(1), 56–69. doi:10.1111/j.1365-2729.2008.00305.x

Dron, J., & Anderson, T. (2014). *Teaching Crowds: Learning and Social Media*. Athabasca University Press. doi:10.15215/aupress/9781927356807.01

Dür, M., & Keller, L. (2018). Education for Sustainable Development through International Collaboration. A Case Study on Concepts and Conceptual Change of School-Students from India and Austria on Gender Equality and Sustainable Growth. *Education Sciences*, *8*(4), 187. doi:10.3390/educsci8040187

Dür, M., & Keller, L. (2019). Research Collaboration of Austrian and Indian Teenagers in the Context of Education for Sustainable Development. *Sustainability*, *11*(18), 1–17. doi:10.3390u11185094

Eckstein, V. (2022). Stolpersteine für die (geographische) Bildung in der Digitalität. *GW-Unterricht*, *1*, 5–16. doi:10.1553/gw-unterricht167s5

Globales Lernen im digitalen Zeitalter. (2018). InBrendel, N., & Schrüfer, G. (Eds.), *Globales Lernen im digitalen Zeitalter* (Vol. 11, pp. 9–33). Waxmann.

Greenhow, C., & Galvin, S. (2020). Teaching with social media: Evidence-based strategies for making remote higher education less remote. *Information and Learning Sciences*, *121*(7/8), 513–524. doi:10.1108/ILS-04-2020-0138

Hauff, M., & Jörg, A. (2017). *Nachhaltiges Wachstum* (2nd ed.). Walter de Gruyter. doi:10.1515/9783110532845

Helne, T., & Hirvilammi, T. (2015). Wellbeing and Sustainability: A Relational Approach: Wellbeing and Sustainability. *Sustainable Development*, *23*(3), 167–175. doi:10.1002d.1581

Höhnle, S. (2014). *Online-gestützte Projekte im Kontext Globalen Lernens im Geographieunterricht: Empirische Rekonstruktion internationaler Schülerperspektiven* (Vol. 53). HGD-Hochschulverband für Geographiedidaktik.

IPCC. (2021). *The Physical Science Basis. Working Group I Contribution to the IPCC Sixth Assessment Report*. IPCC.

Jeong, H. (2013). Verbal data analysis for understanding interactions. In C. E. Hmelo-Silver, C. A. Chinn, C. K. K. Chan, & A. O'Donnell (Eds.), *The international handbook of collaborative learning* (pp. 168–183). Routledge.

Kanwischer, D. (2014). Digitale Geomedien und Gesellschaft. Zum veränderten Status geographischen Wissens in der Bildung. *Geographische Rundschau*, *6*, 12–17.

Kimmerle, J., Moskaliuk, J., Oeberst, A., & Cress, U. (2015). Learning and Collective Knowledge Construction With Social Media: A Process-Oriented Perspective. *Educational Psychologist*, *50*(2), 120–137. doi:10.1080/00461520.2015.1036273 PMID:26246643

Kirschner, P. A. (2015). Facebook as learning platform: Argumentation superhighway or dead-end street? *Computers in Human Behavior*, *53*, 621–625. doi:10.1016/j.chb.2015.03.011

Kubisch, S., Parth, S., Deisenrieder, V., Oberauer, K., Stötter, J., & Keller, L. (2021). From Transdisciplinary Research to Transdisciplinary Education—The Role of Schools in Contributing to Community Well-Being and Sustainable Development. *Sustainability*, *13*(1), 306. doi:10.3390u13010306

Lozano, R., Merrill, M., Sammalisto, K., Ceulemans, K., & Lozano, F. (2017). Connecting Competences and Pedagogical Approaches for Sustainable Development in Higher Education: A Literature Review and Framework Proposal. *Sustainability, 9*(1889), 1–15. doi:10.3390/su9101889

Martin, F., & Griffiths, H. (2012). Power and representation: A postcolonial reading of global partnerships and teacher development through North—South study visits. *British Educational Research Journal*, *38*(6), 907–927. doi:10.1080/01411926.2011.600438

Oberrauch, A., Keller, L., Sanin, P., & Riede, M. (2014). Lebensqualitätsvorstellungen von Jugendlichen im Kontext des Leitbilds nachhaltiger Entwicklung. *Mitteilungen der Österreichischen Geographischen Gesellschaft*, *156*, 221–248. doi:10.1553/moegg156s221

Olsson, D., Gericke, N., & Chang Rundgren, S.-N. (2016). The effect of implementation of education for sustainable development in Swedish compulsory schools – Assessing pupils' sustainability consciousness. *Environmental Education Research*, *22*(2), 176–202. doi:10.1080/13504622.2015.1005057

Persson, M., Andersson, K., Zetterberg, P., Ekman, J., & Lundin, S. (2019). Does Deliberative Education Increase Civic Competence? Results from a Field Experiment. *Journal of Experimental Political Science*, 1–10. doi:10.1017/XPS.2019.29

Rieckmann, M., & Barth, M. (2022). Educators' Competence Frameworks in Education for Sustainable Development. In P. Vare, N. Lausselet, & M. Rieckmann (Eds.), *Competences in Education for Sustainable Development. Critical Perspectives* (pp. 19–26). Springer International Publishing. doi:10.1007/978-3-030-91055-6_3

Schank, C., & Rieckmann, M. (2019). Socio-economically Substantiated Education for Sustainable Development: Development of Competencies and Value Orientations Between Individual Responsibility and Structural Transformation. *Journal of Education for Sustainable Development, 13*(1), 67–91. doi:10.1177/0973408219844849

Stoltenberg, U., & Michelsen, G. (2020). Digitalisierung im Kontext von Bildung für eine nachhaltige Entwicklung. In M. Hauff von & A. Reller (Eds.), Nachhaltige Digitalisierung – eine noch zu bewältigende Zukunftsaufgabe (pp. 49–64). Hessische Landeszentrale für politische Bildung.

UN. (2021). *The 17 goals*. https://sdgs.un.org/goals

UNEP. (2021). *State of Finance for Nature*. https://www.unep.org/resources/state-finance-nature

UNESCO. (2017). *Education for sustainable development goals: Learning objectives*. UNESCO Publishing. https://www.unesco.at/fileadmin/Redaktion/Publikationen/Publikations-Dokumente/2017_Education_for_SDG.pdf

UNESCO. (2018). *Global Action Programme on Education for Sustainable Development*. https://en.unesco.org/gap

UNESCO. (2021). *ESD for 2030 toolbox: Priority action areas*. https://en.unesco.org/themes/education-sustainable-development/toolbox/priorities

UNESCO. (2022). *Education for sustainable development*. https://www.unesco.org/en/education/sustainable-development

Wals, A. E. J. (2015). *Beyond unreasonable doubt: Education and learning for socio-ecological sustainability in the anthropocene*. Wageningen University.

Wiek, A., Bernstein, M., Foley, R., Cohen, M., Forrest, N., Kuzdas, C., Kay, B., & Withycombe Keeler, L. (2015). Operationalising Competencies in Higher Education for Sustainable Development. In M. Barth, G. Michelsen, M. Rieckmann, & I. Thomas (Eds.), *Handbook of Higher Education for Sustainable Development* (pp. 241–260). Routledge.

KEY TERMS AND DEFINITIONS

Constructivism: Learning theories that have been developed since the end of the 1970s. According to these learning theories, knowledge cannot simply passed on from teachers to learners. Instead, learning is seen as an active, social, self-determined and learner centered process.

Freewriting: A flowing writing technique in which everything that comes spontaneously into one's mind is written down (also known as 'stream of consciousness'). The participants try to write continuously during a certain amount of time without breaks in between. Only the overall topic is shared at the beginning.

Global North and Global South: A classification of countries in terms of economic development and wealth. While wealthier countries are mostly located in the Northern Hemisphere, poorer countries are mainly located in the Southern Hemisphere.

Moderate-Constructivism: In contrast to radical constructivism, which assumes that everything perceived is only constructed, moderate-constructivism is a more pragmatic approach. Thereby, the presumption is that a certain amount of instruction is needed for learning. This includes the creation of suitable learning settings as well as critical feedbacks for learners.

Quality of Life: The belief that humans' well-being depends on material as well as on immaterial components.

Compilation of References

Abdel Magid, H. S., Milliren, C. E., Pettee Gabriel, K., & Nagata, J. M. (2021). Disentangling individual, school, and neighborhood effects on screen time among adolescents and young adults in the United States. *Preventive Medicine*, *142*, 106357. doi:10.1016/j.ypmed.2020.106357 PMID:33301823

Adam, N. A., & Alarifi, G. (2021). Innovation practices for the survival of small and medium enterprises (SMEs) in the COVID-19 times: The role of external support. *Journal of Innovation and Entrepreneurship*, *10*(15), 1–22. doi:10.118613731-021-00156-6 PMID:34075328

Adams, P. C. (1998). Teaching and learning with SimCity 2000. *The Journal of Geography*, *97*(2), 47–55. doi:10.1080/00221349808978827

Adegboye, D., Williams, F., Collishaw, S., Shelton, K., Langley, K., Hobson, C., Burley, D., & van Goozen, S. (2021). Understanding why the COVID-19 pandemic-related lockdown increases mental health difficulties in vulnerable young students. *JCPP Advances*, *1*(1), e12005. doi:10.1111/jcv2.12005 PMID:34485985

Adler, F. (2009). *Computerspiele als Lernmedium und ihr Einsatz in den Ingenieurwissenschaften. Erarbeitung eines Analyse- und Entwicklungsmodells* [Doctoral dissertation]. University of Augsburg.

Adorno, T. W. (1971). *Erziehung zur Mündigkeit. Vorträge und Gespräche mit Hellmut Becker*. Suhrkamp.

AfridiW. (2020). *Educating Fata*. Retrieved from https://www.the news.com.pk

Agustriyana, D., Ramadhan, N., Oktavien, S., & Sofyandi, H. R. (2021). Keeping Business in SMEs in the Midst of the COVID-19 Pandemic. *Journal of Devotion Dharma Laksana Serving the Nation*, *3*(2), 93–99.

Ahel, O., & Lingenau, K. (2021). Digitale Ansätze zur Vermittlung der SDGs in der Hochschullehre im deutschsprachigen Raum. In L. W. Filho (Ed.), *Digitalisierung und Nachhaltigkeit* (pp. 129–146). doi:10.1007/978-3-662-61534-8_7

Alemu, B. M. (2017). Transforming Educational Practices of Ethiopia into Development and the Knowledge Society through Information and Communication Technology. *American Educational Research Journal*, *5*(1), 1–14.

Alexander, R. (2001). *Culture & pedagogy: the international comparison in primary education*. Wiley. Blackwell.

Ali, I. (2018). *Mainstreaming Pakistan's Federally Administered Teibal Areas. Reform Initiatives and Roadblocks*. Special Report 421. United States Institutive of Peace. https:// www.usip.org

Allen, M., Webb, A. W., & Matthews, C. E. (2016). Adaptive teaching in STEM: Characteristics for effectiveness. *Theory into Practice*, *55*(3), 217–224. doi:10.1080/00405841.2016.1173994

Allen McMillan, A. (2022). *A memo from the new jersey department of education: Clarification regarding 2020 new jersey student learning standards—Comprehensive health and physical education.* New Jersey Department of Education. https://www.nj.gov/education/broadcasts/2022/april/14/ClarificationRegarding2020NewJerseyStudentLearningStandards-CHPE.pdf

Allert, H., Asmussen, M., & Richter, C. (Eds.). (2017). Digitalität und Selbst: Interdisziplinäre Perspektiven auf Subjektivierungs- und Bildungsprozesse. Pädagogik.

Al-Mubaraki, H. M. (2015). The Importance of business incubation in developing countries: Case study approach. *International Journal of Foresight and Innovation Policy*, *10*(1), 17–28. doi:10.1504/IJFIP.2015.070054

Amoore, L. (2020). *Cloud ethics: Algorithms and the attributes of ourselves and others.* Duke UP.

Andrews, D. R. (1995). Subjective Reactions to Two Regional Pronunciations of Great Russian: A Matched-Guise Study. *Canadian Slavonic Papers*, *37*(1–2), 89–106. doi:10.1080/00085006.1995.11092083

Anis, M., & Anwar, C. (2020). Self-organized learning environment teaching strategy for ELT in Merdeka Belajar concept for high school students in Indonesia. [Journal of English Educators Society]. *JEES*, *5*(2), 199–204. doi:10.21070/jees.v5i2.869

Are, C. (2020). How Instagram's algorithm is censoring women and vulnerable users but helping online abusers. *Feminist Media Studies*, *20*(5), 741–744. doi:10.1080/14680777.2020.1783805

Arnold, U., Söbke, H., & Reichelt, M. (2019). SimCity in Infrastructure Management Education. *Education Sciences*, *2019*(9), 209. doi:10.3390/educsci9030209

Arthur, J. (2005). The re-emergence of character education in British education policy. *British Journal of Educational Studies*, *53*(3), 239–254. doi:10.1111/j.1467-8527.2005.00293.x

Assefa, T. (2017). Educational Technology Implementation in Ethiopian High Schools: Benefits and Challenges of the Instructional Plasma TV. In A. Marcus-Quinn & T. Hourigan (Eds.), *Handbook on Digital Learning for K-12 Schools.* Springer International Publishing. doi:10.1007/978-3-319-33808-8_25

Astari, N. (2021). A Literature Review: Digital Marketing Trends in Indonesia During the COVID-19 Pandemic. *CHANNEL: Jurnal Komunikasi*, *9*(2), 125–134. doi:10.12928/channel.v9i2.20836

Atenas, J., & Havemann, L. (2014). Questions of quality in repositories of open educational resources: A literature review. *Research in Learning Technology*, *22*(1). doi:10.3402/rlt.v22.20889

Augustin-Dittmann, S. (2015). MINT und darüber hinaus. Gendersensibler Unterricht als Basis einer geschlechtergerechten Gesellschaft. In J. Wedl & A. Bartsch (Eds.), Teaching Gender? Zum reflektierten Umgang mit Geschlecht im Schulunterricht und in der Lehramtsausbildung (pp. 123-136). Transcript Verlag.

Austin, J., & Reed, M. (1999). Targeting children online: Internet advertising ethics issues. *Journal of Consumer Marketing*, *16*(6), 590–602. doi:10.1108/07363769910297579

Austrian Integration Fund. (2021). *Bundesländer: Zahlen, Daten undFakten zu Migration und Integration 2021.* Bundeskanzleramt. Available online at https://www.integrationsfonds.at/fileadmin/user_upload/OEIF-BL-Broschuere_07012022_WEB.pdf

Ayca, C., & Ilknur, R. (2022). Digitally competent Teacher. An examination of pre-service teachers' metaphor. *Journal of Digital Learning in Teacher Education, 38*(4).

Bandura, A. (1977). Self-efficacy: Toward a unifying theory of behavioral change. *Psychological Review*, *84*(2), 191–215. doi:10.1037/0033-295X.84.2.191 PMID:847061

Bandura, A. (1997). *Self-Efficacy: The Exercise of Control*. Freeman.

Barth, M. (2007). *Gestaltungskompetenz durch Neue Medien? Die Rolle des Lernens mit Neuen Medien in der Bildung für eine nachhaltige Entwicklung*. Berliner Wissenschaftsverlag.

Barth, M., & Michelsen, G. (2013). Learning for change: An educational contribution to sustainability. *Science Sustain Science*, *8*(1), 103–119. doi:10.100711625-012-0181-5

Barth, M., & Rieckmann, M. (2016). State of the art in research on higher education for sustainable development. In M. Barth, G. Michelsen, M. Rieckmann, & I. Thomas (Eds.), *Routledge Handbook of Higher Education for Sustainable Development* (pp. 100–113). Routledge.

Bates, R., Brenner, B., Schmid, E., Steiner, G., & Vogel, S. (2022). Towards meta-competences in higher education for tackling complex real-world problems - a cross disciplinary review. *International Journal of Sustainability in Higher Education*, *24*(1), 290–308. doi:10.1108/IJSHE-06-2021-0243

Bauer, G. R., Churchill, S. M., Mahendran, M., Walwyn, C., Lizotte, D., & Villa-Rueda, A. A. (2021). Intersectionality in quantitative research: A systematic review of its emergence and applications of theory and methods. *SSM - Population Health*, *14*, 100798. doi:10.1016/j.ssmph.2021.100798 PMID:33997247

Becker, S., Klagge, B., & Naumann, M. (2021). Einführung: Konzepte und Herausforderungen der Energiegeographie. In S. Becker, B. Klagge, & M. Naumann (Eds.), *Energiegeographie* (pp. 18–34). UTB. doi:10.36198/9783838553207

Behailu, A. (2021). Higher Education Students' Social Media Literacy in Ethiopia: A Case of Bahir Dar University. *The Journal of Media Literacy Education*, *13*(3), 86–96.

Benjamin, R. (2019). Race after technology: Abolitionist tools for the new Jim Code. *Polity*.

Bento, F., Giglio Bottino, A., Cerchiareto Pereira, F., Forastieri de Almeida, J., & Gomes Rodrigues, F. (2021). Resilience in higher education: A complex perspective to lecturers' adaptive processes in response to the COVID-19 pandemic. *Education Sciences*, *11*(9), 492. doi:10.3390/educsci11090492

Bereitschaft, B. (2021). Commercial city building games as pedagogical tools: What have we learned? *Journal of Geography in Higher Education*, •••, 1–27. doi:10.1080/03098265.2021.2007524

Betsch, T., Funke, J., & Plessner, H. (2011). *Denken- Urteilen, Entscheiden*. Problemlösen. doi:10.1007/978-3-642-12474-7

Biasutti, M., Makrakis, V., Concina, E., & Frate, S. (2018). Educating academic staff to reorient curricula in ESD. *International Journal of Sustainability in Higher Education*, *19*(1), 179-196. doi:10.1108/IJSHE-11-2016-0214

Bilali, H. E., Ben Hassen, T., Baya Chatti, C., Abouabdillah, A., & Alaoui, S. B. (2021). Exploring Household Food Dynamics During the COVID-19 Pandemic in Morocco. *Frontiers in Nutrition*, *8*, 724803. doi:10.3389/fnut.2021.724803 PMID:34646850

Bird, S. E. (2003). *The audience in everyday life: Living in a media world*. Routledge.

Birkelbach, L., Preglau, D., & Rammel, C. (2019). *White Paper BNE im Zeitalter der Digitalisierung. RCE Vienna*. RCE Vienna – Regional Centre of Expertise on Education for Sustainable Development.

Birkelbach, L., Preglau, D., & Rammel, Ch. (2019). *BNE im Zeitalter der Digitalisierung*. Regional Centre of Expertise on Education for Sustainable Development Wien. openscience4sustainability.at.

Bishop, S. (2018). Anxiety, panic and self-optimization: Inequalities and the YouTube algorithm. *Convergence*, *24*(1), 69–84. doi:10.1177/1354856517736978

Bjork, C. (2005). *Indonesian education: Teachers, schools, and central bureaucracy*. Routledge. doi:10.4324/9780203959015

Blesia, J. U., Iek, M., Ratang, W., & Hutajulu, H. (2021). Developing an Entrepreneurship Model to Increase Students' Entrepreneurial Skills: An Action Research Project in a Higher Education Institution in Indonesia. *Systemic Practice and Action Research*, *34*(1), 53–70. doi:10.100711213-019-09506-8

Boehn, D., & Hamann, B. (2011). Approaches to sustainability. Examples from geography textbook analysis in Germany. *European Journal of Geography*, *2*(1). http://www.eu-rogeographyjournal.eu/articles/2_1_APPROACHES%20TO%20SUSTAINABILITY_BOEHN_HAMANN.pdf

Bojie, F. (2020). Promoting Geography for Sustainability. *Geography and Sustainability*, *2020*(1), 1–7.

Boltanski, L., & Esquerre, A. (2017). *Enrichissement: Une critique de la merchandise*. Gallimard.

Bonnedahl, K. J., Heikkurinen, P., & Paavola, J. (2022). Strongly sustainable development goals: Overcoming distances constraining responsible action. *Environmental Science & Policy*, *129*, 150–158. doi:10.1016/j.envsci.2022.01.004

Bormann, I., & Rieckmann, M. (2020). Lernende Hochschulen: Verankerung von Bildung für nachhaltige Entwicklung. In G. Bade, N. Henkel, & B. Reef (Eds.), *Politische Bildung: vielfältig – kontrovers – global. Festschrift für Bernd Overwien* (pp. 68–87). Wochenschau Verlag.

Boström, M., Andersson, E., Berg, M., Gustafsson, K., Gustavsson, E., Hysing, E., Lidskog, R., Löfmarck, E., Ojala, M., Olsson, J., Singleton, B., Svenberg, S., Uggla, Y., & Öhman, J. (2018). Conditions for Transformative Learning for Sustainable Development: A Theoretical Review and Approach. *Sustainability*, *10*(12), 4479. doi:10.3390u10124479

Bowyer, J. & Chambers, L. (2017). Evaluating blended learning: Bringing the elements together. *Research Matters, 23,* 17-26.

Brandt, J.-O., Bürgener, L., Redman, A., & Barth, M. (2020). *Educating Future Change Agents: Research Instruments applied in Case Studies on Teacher Education for Sustainable Development.* Lüneburg.

Bröckling, U. (2007). *Das unternehmerische Selbst: Soziologie einer Subjektivierungsform* [The entrepreneurial self: Sociology of a form of subjectivation]. Suhrkamp.

Brown, T. (2016). *Change by Design. Wie Design Thinking Organisationen verändert und zu mehr Innovationen führt.* Vahlen.

Brown, T. (2019). *Change by Design, Revised and Updated. How Design Thinking Transforms Organizations and Inspires Innovation.* Harper Collins Publ.

Brundiers, K., Barth, M., Cebrián, G., Cohen, M., Diaz, L., Doucette-Remington, S., Dripps, W., Habron, G., Harré, N., Jarchow, M., Losch, K., Michel, J., Mochizuki, Y., Rieckmann, M., Parnell, R., Walker, P., & Zint, M. (2021). Key competencies in sustainability in higher education—Toward an agreed-upon reference framework. *Sustainability Science*, *16*(1), 13–29. doi:10.100711625-020-00838-2

Brundiers, K., & Wiek, A. (2011). Educating Students in Real-world Sustainability Research: Vision and Implementation. *Innovative Higher Education*, *36*(2), 107–124. doi:10.100710755-010-9161-9

Bucher, T. (2017). The algorithmic imaginary: Exploring the ordinary affects of Facebook algorithms. *Information Communication and Society*, *20*(1), 30–44. doi:10.1080/1369118X.2016.1154086

Buckingham, D. (2020). Epilogue: Rethinking digital literacy: Media education in the age of digital capitalism. *Digital Education Review*, (37), 230–239. doi:10.1344/der.2020.37.230-239

Buckingham, D. (2021, May 12). *Media literacy and media education in the age of digital capitalism* [Paper Presentation]. *4th International Conference on Literacy and Contemporary Society*, Cyprus.

Budiman, A., Samani, M., & Setyawan, W. H. (2021). The Development of Direct-Contextual Learning: A New Model on Higher Education. *International Journal of Higher Education*, *10*(2), 15–26. doi:10.5430/ijhe.v10n2p15

Buhl, A., Schmidt-Keilich, M., Muster, V., Blazejewski, S., Schrader, U., Harrach, Ch., Schäfer, M., & Süßbauer, E. (2019). Design thinking for sustainability: Why and how design thinking can foster sustainability-oriented innovation and development. *Journal of Cleaner Production*, *231*, 1248–1257. doi:10.1016/j.jclepro.2019.05.259

Burbules, N. C., Fan, G., & Repp, P. (2020). Five trends of education and technology in a sustainable future. *Geography and Sustainability*, *1*(2), 93–97. doi:10.1016/j.geosus.2020.05.001

Burton, P., Bwalya, M., & Sihubwa, S. (2022). *Zambia Kids Online: A Global Kids online study*. Save the Children.

Cabrera, D., & Cabrera, L. (2012). *Thinking at every desk: Four simple skills to transform your classroom. Norton books in education*. W.W. Norton & Company.

Calma, J. (2020). Apple ditching chargers saves costs but not the planet. *The Verge*. https://www.theverge.com/2020/10/16/21519466/apple-iphone-12-chargers-airpods-greenhouse-gas-emissions-e-waste

Çam, Ş. S., & Erdamar Koç, G. (2021). Technological pedagogical content knowledge practices in higher education: First impressions of preservice teachers. *Technology. Knowledge and Learning*, *26*(1), 123–153. doi:10.100710758-019-09430-9

Caniglia, G., Jaeger, C., Schernhammer, E., Steiner, G., Russo, F., Renn, J., Schlosser, P., & Laubichler, M. D. (2021). Covid-19 heralds a new epistemology of science for the public good. *History and Philosophy of the Life Sciences*, *43*(2), 59. doi:10.100740656-021-00413-7 PMID:33864155

Caniglia, G., John, B., Bellina, L., Lang, D., & Laubichler, M. (2018). Digital Technologies for Transnational Collaboration: A Glocal Approach from Sustainability Education.

Caniglia, G., John, B., Kohler, M., Bellina, L., Wiek, A., Rojas, C., Laubichler, M. D., & Lang, D. (2016). An experience-based learning framework. *International Journal of Sustainability in Higher Education*, *17*(6), 827–852. doi:10.1108/IJSHE-04-2015-0065

Caniglia, G., Luederitz, C., Groß, M., Muhr, M., John, B., Withycombe Keeler, L., von Wehrden, H., Laubichler, M., Wiek, A., & Lang, D. (2017). Transnational collaboration for sustainability in higher education: Lessons from a systematic review. *Journal of Cleaner Production*, *168*, 764–779. doi:10.1016/j.jclepro.2017.07.256

Carpenter, C. S., Eppink, S. T., & Gonzales, G. (2020). Transgender status, gender identity, and socioeconomic outcomes in the United States. *Industrial & Labor Relations Review*, *73*(3), 573–599. doi:10.1177/0019793920902776

Chang, M. C., Al-Samarrai, S., Ragatz, A. B., Shaeffer, S., De Ree, J., & Stevenson, R. (2013). *Teacher reform in Indonesia: The role of politics and evidence in policymaking*. World Bank Publications.

Charsky, D. (2010). Making a connection: Game genres, game characteristics, and teaching structures. In Gaming and Cognition. Theories and practice from the learning sciences. Information Science Reference (pp. 189-212). IGI Global.

Cieslewicz, K., Lang, D., & Barth, M. (2022). Der europäische Weg. In: Ökologisches Wirtschaften, 37(1), 8–9. doi:10.14512/OEW370108

Claramita, M. (2016). Revealing "Tut Wuri Handayani": A student-centered learning approach-by Ki Hajar Dewantara from the early 20th century: A literature review. *Jurnal Pendidikan Kedokteran Indonesia*, *5*(1), 14. doi:10.22146/jpki.25295

Clark, I., Nae, N., & Arimoto, M. (2020). *Education for sustainable development and the "Whole Person" curriculum in Japan*. ORE. doi:10.1093/acrefore/9780190264093.013.935

Clark, W., Logan, K., Luckin, R., Mee, A., & Oliver, M. (2009). Beyond Web 2.0: Mapping the technology landscapes of young learners: Beyond Web 2.0. *Journal of Computer Assisted Learning*, *25*(1), 56–69. doi:10.1111/j.1365-2729.2008.00305.x

Clifford, C. (2022). How Google plans to use 100% carbon-free energy in its data centers by 2030. *CNBC*. https://www.cnbc.com/2022/04/13/google-data-center-goal-100percent-green-energy-by-2030.html

Clune, S. J., & Lockrey, S. (2014). Developing environmental sustainability strategies, the Double Diamond method of LCA and design thinking: A case study from aged care. *Journal of Cleaner Production*, *85*, 67–82. doi:10.1016/j.jclepro.2014.02.003

Cochran-Smith, M. (2003). Teaching quality Matters. *Journal of Teacher Education*, *54*(2), 95–98. doi:10.1177/0022487102250283

Cohen, J. (1988). *Statistical Power Analysis for the Behavioral Sciences*. Lawrence Erlbaum.

Colao, A., Piscitelli, P., Pulimeno, M., Colazzo, S., Miani, A., & Giannini, S. (2020). Rethinking the role of the school after COVID-19. *The Lancet. Public Health*, *5*(7), e370. doi:10.1016/S2468-2667(20)30124-9 PMID:32464100

Colley, A., & Comber, C. (2003). Age and gender differences in computer use and attitudes among secondary school students: What has changed? *Educational Research*, *45*(2), 155–165. doi:10.1080/0013188032000103235

Collins, P. H. (1990). *Black feminist thought: Knowledge, consciousness, and the politics of empowerment*. Hyman.

Combes, B. P. (2005). The United Nations decade of education for sustainable development (2005–2014): Learning to live together sustainably. *Applied Environmental Education and Communication*, *4*(3), 215–219. doi:10.1080/15330150591004571

Cooper, J. (2006). The digital divide: The special case of gender. *Journal of Computer Assisted Learning*, *22*(5), 320–334. doi:10.1111/j.1365-2729.2006.00185.x

Corbacho, A. M., Minini, L., Pereyra, M., González-Fernández, A. E., Echániz, R., Repetto, L., Cruz, P., Fernández-Damonte, V., Lorieto, A., & Basile, M. (2021). Interdisciplinary higher education with a focus on academic motivation and teamwork diversity. *International Journal of Educational Research Open*, *2*, 100062. doi:10.1016/j.ijedro.2021.100062

Cörvers, R., Wiek, A., Kraker, J., Lang, D. J., & Martens, P. (2016). Problem-Based and Project-Based Learning for Sustainable Development. In H. Heinrichs, P. Martens, G. Michelsen, & A. Wiek (Eds.), *Sustainability Science. An Introduction* (pp. 349–358). Springer Netherland. doi:10.1007/978-94-017-7242-6_29

Costanza-Chock, S. (2020). *Design justice: Community-led practices to build the worlds we need*. MIT Press. doi:10.7551/mitpress/12255.001.0001

Crenshaw, K. (1989). Demarginalizing the intersection of race and sex: A Black feminist critique of antidiscrimination doctrine, feminist theory and antiracist politics. *University of Chicago Legal Forum*, (1).

Crookall, D. (2010). Serious games, debriefing, and simulation/gaming as a discipline. *Simulation & Gaming*, *41*(6), 898–920. doi:10.1177/1046878110390784

Curwen, M. S., Ardell, A., MacGillivray, L., & Lambert, R. (2018). Systems Thinking in a Second Grade Curriculum: Students Engaged to Address a Statewide Drought. *Frontiers in Education*, *3*, 90. doi:10.3389/feduc.2018.00090

Cusumano, M. A., Gawer, A., & Yoffie, D. B. (2019). *The Business of Platforms: Strategy in the Age of Digital Competition, Innovation, and Power*. Harper Business.

Czauderna, A., & Guardiola, E. (2019). The Gameplay Loop Methodology as a Tool for Educational Game Design. *Electronic Journal of e-Learning*, *17*(3), 201-227. https://issuu.com/academic-conferences.org/docs/ejel-volume17-issue3-article682?mode=a_p

Czauderna, A., & Budke, A. (2020). How Digital Strategy and Management Games Can Facilitate the Practice of Dynamic Decision-Making. *Education Sciences*, *10*(4), 99. Advance online publication. doi:10.3390/educsci10040099

Czauderna, A., & Budke, A. (2021). Game Designer als Akteure der politischen Bildung. *MedienPädagogik: Zeitschrift für Theorie und Praxis der Medienbildung*, *38*, 94–116. doi:10.21240/mpaed/38/2021.01.25.X

D'Ignazio, C., & Klein, L. F. (2020). *Data Feminism*. MIT Press. doi:10.7551/mitpress/11805.001.0001

Daniels, J. (2009). *Cyber racism: White supremacy online and the new attack on civil rights*. Rowman & Littlefield.

de Haan, G. (2008). Gestaltungskompetenz als Kompetenzkonzept der Bildung für nachhaltige Entwicklung. In I. Bormann & G. de Haan (Eds.), *Kompetenzen der Bildung für nachhaltige Entwicklung* (pp. 23–43). VS Verlag für Sozialwissenschaften. doi:10.1007/978-3-531-90832-8_4

Deane, P., Odendahl, N., Quinlan, T., Fowles, M., Welsh, C., & Bivens-Tatum, J. (2008). Cognitive Models of Writing: Writing Proficiency as a Complex Integrated Skill. *ETS Research Report Series*, *2008*(2), i–36. doi:10.1002/j.2333-8504.2008.tb02141.x

Delors, J., Mufti, I. A., Amagi, I., Carneiro, R., Bronislaw, C., Gorham, W., Kornhauser, A., Manley, M., Quero, P. M., Savane, M.-A., Singh, K., Stavenhagen, R., Suhr, M. W., & Nanzhao, Z. (1996). *Learning: The treasure within: Report to Unesco of the International Commission on Education for the 21st century*. UNESCO.

DeRosa, R., & Robinson, S. (2017). From OER to Open Pedagogy: Harnessing the Power of Open. In Open: The Philosophy and Practices that are Revolutionizing Education and Science (pp. 115–124). Ubiquity Press. doi:10.5334/bbc.i

Dewantara, K. H. (1962). *Karja Ki Hadja Dewantara. Bagian Pertama: Pendidikan* (M. L. P. T. Siswa, Ed.; 1st ed.).

DGfG (Deutsche Gesellschaft für Geographie) (2020). *Bildungsstandards im Fach Geographie für den mittleren Schulabschluss [Educational standards in the subject of geography for the middle school graduation]*. DGfG.

Diana, H. L. (2020). Collaborative Strategy Between Universities, Industry and Government: A Conceptual Review in Efforts to Improve Educational Innovation and Learning Creativity in Higher Education. *Proceedings of the National Conference on Management Economics and Accounting*. Master Program in Accounting, Faculty of Economics, Universitas Islam Indonesia, Yogyakarta.

Diener, E. (2000). Subjective well-being: The science of happiness and a proposal for a national index. *The American Psychologist*, *55*(1), 34–43. doi:10.1037/0003-066X.55.1.34 PMID:11392863

Ditter, R., & Siegmund, A. (2016). Lernen mit digitalen Satellitenbildern – eine genderspezifische Analyse. *GWU*, *142/143*, 162-173.

Dlouhá, J., Braniš, M., Dlouhý, J., Jančaříková, K., Jančařík, A., & Šauer, P. (2012). *Metodika tvorby textů v otevřeném internetovém prostoru – Enviwiki* [Methodology of text development in an open internet space]. https://enviwiki.cz/wiki/Metodika_tvorby_text%c5%af_v_otev%c5%99en%c3%a9m_internetov%c3%a9m_prostoru

Dlouhá, Heras, Mulà, Salgado, & Henderson. (2019). Competences to Address SDGs in Higher Education—A Reflection on the Equilibrium between Systemic and Personal Approaches to Achieve Transformative Action. *Sustainability, 11*(13), 3664. doi:10.3390u11133664

Dlouhá, J., & Burandt, S. (2015). Design and evaluation of learning processes in an international sustainability oriented study programme. In search of a new educational quality and assessment method. *Journal of Cleaner Production, 106*, 247–258. doi:10.1016/j.jclepro.2014.09.096

Dlouhá, J., & Dlouhý, J. (2014). Higher education for sustainability – a change of education genre? *Envigogika, 9*(1). doi:10.14712/18023061.440

Dlouhá, J., Henderson, L., Kroufek, R., Jančaříková, K., & Neprašová, S. (2021). Vzdělání k udržitelné spotřebě a životnímu stylu – cíle a výstupy [Education for sustainable consumption and lifestyle change—Educational goals and outcomes]. *Envigogika, 16*(1). doi:10.14712/18023061.619

Dlouhá, J., Petiška, E., Dlouhý, J., & Kapitulčinová, D. (2015). Možnosti a rizika využití otevřených vzdělávacích zdrojů v environmentálních oborech na vysokoškolské úrovni v ČR: Kritéria pro posouzení kvality [Opportunities and Risks of the Use of Open Education Resources in Environmental Disciplines at University Level in the Czech Republic: A Criteria for Assessing Quality]. *Envigogika, 10*(4). doi:10.14712/18023061.503

Döbeli Honegger, B. (2017). Mehr als 0 und 1. Schule in einer digitalisierten Welt. 2. Auflage, Bern.

Dolata, U., & Schrape, J. F. (2022). Platform Architectures. The Structuration of Platform Companies on the Internet. SSRN *Electronic Journal*. doi:10.2139/ssrn.4018396

Dorsch, C. (2022). *Mündigkeit und Digitalität: E-Portfolioarbeit in der geographischen Lehrkräftebildung (= Praxis Neue Kulturgeographie, 16) [Maturity and Digitality: E-Portfolio in geography teacher education (= Praxis of New Cultural Geography, 16)]*. Lit.

Dorsch, C., Gryl, I., Hermes, A., Jekel, T., Lehner, M., Meyer, C., Pettig, F., Pokraka, J., Schrüfer, G., & Schulze, U. (2020). *Der Beitrag des Fachs Geographie zur Bildung in einer durch Digitalisierung und Mediatisierung geprägten Welt*. https://geographiedidaktik.org/download/positionspapier-des-hgd-geographische-bildung-und-digitalisierung/?wpdmdl=1185&refresh=624e93489ea191649316680

Doyle, W. (1980). *Classroom Management*. Kappa Delta Pi.

Dron, J., & Anderson, T. (2014). *Teaching Crowds: Learning and Social Media*. Athabasca University Press. doi:10.15215/aupress/9781927356807.01

Dür, M., & Keller, L. (2018). Education for Sustainable Development through International Collaboration. A Case Study on Concepts and Conceptual Change of School-Students from India and Austria on Gender Equality and Sustainable Growth. *Education Sciences, 8*(4), 187. doi:10.3390/educsci8040187

Dür, M., & Keller, L. (2019). Research Collaboration of Austrian and Indian Teenagers in the Context of Education for Sustainable Development. *Sustainability, 11*(18), 1–17. doi:10.3390u11185094

Dwivedi, Y. K., Hughes, L., Baabdullah, A. M., & Wamba, S. F. (2022). Metaverse beyond the hype: Multidisciplinary perspectives on emerging challenges, opportunities, and agenda for research, practice and policy. *International Journal of Information Management*, *66*, 102542. doi:10.1016/j.ijinfomgt.2022.102542

Eccles, J. (2009). Who am I and what am I going to do with my life? Personal and collective identities as motivators of action. *Educational Psychologist*, *44*(2), 78–89. doi:10.1080/00461520902832368

Eccles, J. S., & Wigfield, A. (2020). From expectancy-value theory to situated expectancy-value theory: A developmental, social cognitive, and sociocultural perspective on motivation. *Contemporary Educational Psychology*, *61*, 101859. doi:10.1016/j.cedpsych.2020.101859

Eckstein, V. (2022). Stolpersteine für die (geographische) Bildung in der Digitalität. *GW-Unterricht*, *1*, 5–16. doi:10.1553/gw-unterricht167s5

Elias, N., & Sulkin, I. (2017). YouTube viewers in diapers: An exploration of factors associated with amount of toddlers' online viewing. *Cyberpsychology (Brno)*, *11*(3), 3. Advance online publication. doi:10.5817/CP2017-3-2

Emrich, C. (2015). *Nachhaltigkeits-Marketing-Management. Konzept, Strategien, Beispiele* [Sustainability Marketing Management. Concept, strategies, examples]. De Gryter. doi:10.1515/9783110376302

Enelamericas. (2016). *Sustainable Development Goals: Our history and close relationship*. www.enelamericas.com

Entorf, H., & Minoiu, N. (2005). What a difference immigrant policy makes: A comparison of PISA scores in Europe and traditional countries of imimmigrant. *German Economic Review*, *6*(3), 355–376. doi:10.1111/j.1468-0475.2005.00137.x

Erpenbeck, J., Sauter, S., & Sauter, W. (2016). *Social Workplace Learning. Kompetenzentwicklung im Arbeitsprozess und im Netz in der Enterprise 2.0*. Springer Gabler. Springer Fachmedien Wiesbaden. doi:10.1007/978-3-658-10499-3

Eshete, A. (2003). Women in Faculties of Teacher Training Institutions in Ethiopia. Addis Ababa: UNESCO International Institute for Capacity Building in Africa .

Evans, L. S., & Gunn, A.A. (2012). It is not just the language: culture as an essential element in pre- service teacher education. *The Journal of Multiculturalism in Education, 7*(1).

Evans, P. C., & Gawer, A. (2016). *The Rise of the Platform Enterprise: A Global Survey*. The CGE. https://www.thecge.net/app/uploads/2016/01/PDF-WEB-Platform-Survey_01_12.pdf

Evans, N., & Ferreira, J.-A. (2020). What does the research evidence base tell us about the use and impact of sustainability pedagogies in initial teacher education? *Environmental Education Research*, *26*(1), 27–42. doi:10.1080/13504622.2019.1703908

Fargher, M. (2019). The Role of Geography and Geospatial Technologies. In González R. D., Donert, K. and Koutsopoulos, K. (eds.), Geospatial Technologies in Geography Education. Cham: Springer Nature Switzerland AG

Farrugia, D. (2020). Youth, work and global capitalism: New directions. *Journal of Youth Studies*, 1–16. doi:10.1080/13676261.2020.1729965

FATA Development Indicators Household Survey 2013-14. (2015). *Bureau of Statistics – Planning and Development Department*. FATA Secretariat.

FDRE (The Federal Democratic Republic of Ethiopia). (2016). *The National Information and Communication Technology (ICT) Policy and Strategy: Final Draft. Addis Ababa Genet Zewde (2018). No One Left Behind: Redesigning the Ethiopian Education System*. Mega Publishing and Distribution PLC.

Feierabend, S., Rathgeb, Th., & Reuter, Th. (2018). Jugend, Information, Medien. Ergebnisse der JIM-Studie 2018. In: Media Perspektiven.

Feller, G., & Burroughs, B. (2021). Branding kidfluencers: Regulating content and advertising on youtube. *Television & New Media*. Advance online publication. doi:10.1177/15274764211052882

Ferede, B., Elen, J., Van Petegem, W., Hunde, A. B., & Goeman, K. (2022). Determinants of instructors' educational ICT use in Ethiopian higher education. *Education and Information Technologies*, *27*(1), 917–936. doi:10.100710639-021-10606-z PMID:34230802

Finsterwald, M., Wagner, P., Schober, B., Lüftenegger, M., & Spiel, C. (2013). Fostering lifelong learning–Evaluation of a teacher education program for professional teachers. *Teaching and Teacher Education*, *29*, 144–155. doi:10.1016/j.tate.2012.08.009

Fischer, G. (2011). Understanding, fostering, and supporting cultures of participation. *Interaction*, *18*(3), 42–53. doi:10.1145/1962438.1962450

Fisman, L. (2005). The Effects of Local Learning on Environmental Awareness in Children: An Empirical Investigation. *The Journal of Environmental Education*, *36*(3), 39–50. doi:10.3200/JOEE.36.3.39-50

Foucault, M. (1975). *Discipline and punish: The birth of the prison*. Vintage.

Fouquaert, T., & Mechant, P. (2021). Making curation algorithms apparent: A case study of 'Instawareness' as a means to heighten awareness and understanding of Instagram's algorithm. *Information Communication and Society*, *0*(0), 1–21. doi:10.1080/1369118X.2021.1883707

Franc, S., & Bilas, V. (2016). Financing Sustainable Development: The Role of the European Union. *Global Journal of Business Social Sciences Review*, *4*(4), 79–86. doi:10.35609/gjbssr.2016.4.4(9)

Fredriksson, U. N., Kusanagi, K., Gougoulakis, P., Matsuda, Y., & Kitamura, Y. (2020). A comparative study of curriculums for education for sustainable development (ESD) in Sweden and Japan. *Sustainability*, *12*(3), 1123. doi:10.3390u12031123

Fridayani, H. D., Iqbal, M., & Atmojo, M. E. (2021). Cloud Kitchen: Strategy for Indonesian Culinary Business (SMEs) Growth During and Post Pandemic Era. *Management Research and Behavior Journal*, *1*(2), 41–46.

Fromme, J., Jörissen, B., & Unger, A (2008). Bildungspotenziale Digitaler Spiele Und Spielkulturen. *MedienPädagogik: Zeitschrift für Theorie Und Praxis Der Medienbildung, 15*, 1-23. doi:10.21240/mpaed/15_16/2008.12.22.X

Gaber, J. (2007). Simulating Planning: SimCity as a Pedagogical Tool. *Journal of Planning Education and Research*, *27*(2), 113–121. doi:10.1177/0739456X07305791

Gandolfo, R., & Hamilton, M. (2022). How China will censor the metaverse. *SupChina*. https://supchina.com/2022/04/13/how-china-will-censor-the-metaverse/

Garrison, D. R. & Vaughan, N.D. (2008). *Blended Learning in Higher Education. Frameworks, Principles and Guidelines.* Jossey-Bass. A Wiley Imprint.

Garrison, D. R., Anderson, T., & Archer, W. (2000). Critical inquiry in a text-based environment: Computer conferencing in higher education model. *The Internet and Higher Education*, *2*(2-3), 87–105. doi:10.1016/S1096-7516(00)00016-6

Garrison, D. R., & Kanuka, H. (2004). Blended learning: Uncovering its transformative potential in higher education. *The Internet and Higher Education*, *7*(2), 95–105. doi:10.1016/j.iheduc.2004.02.001

Gawer, A. (2021). Digital platforms' boundaries: The interplay of firm scope, platform sides, and digital interfaces. *Long Range Planning*, *54*(5), 102045. doi:10.1016/j.lrp.2020.102045

Geithner, S., & Menzel, D. (2016). Effectiveness of Learning Through Experience and Reflection in a Project Management Simulation. *Simulation & Gaming*, *47*(2), 228–256. doi:10.1177/1046878115624312

George, J., George, T., & Moquin, R. (2021). I can't breathe: How digital video becomes an emancipatory technology. *Proceedings of the 54th Hawaii International Conference on System Sciences*. https://scholarspace.manoa.hawaii.edu/server/api/core/bitstreams/515c6a80-29f7-4731-94a3-f856f55b39ea/content

Getzin, S., & Singer-Brodowski, M. (2016). Transformatives Lernen in einer Degrowth-Gesellschaft. *Journal of Science-Society Interfaces*, *1*(1), 33–46. doi:10.5167/uzh-135963

Gherardi, S. (2017). Digitized and decoupled? Teacher sensemaking around educational technology in a model 1:1 program. *Mid-Western Educational Researcher*, *29*(2), 166–194.

Giannetti, B. F., Agostinho, F., Almeida, C. M. V. B., Liu, G., Contreras, L. E. V., Vandecasteele, C., Coscieme, L., Sutton, P., & Poved, C. (2019). Insights on the United Nations Sustainable Development Goals scope: Are they aligned with a 'strong' sustainable development? *Journal of Cleaner Production*, *252*, 119574. doi:10.1016/j.jclepro.2019.119574

Gilbert, T. K., Dean, S., Zick, T., & Lambert, N. (2022). *Choices, Risks, and Reward Reports: Charting Public Policy for Reinforcement Learning Systems*. University of California.

Giroux, H. (n.d.). Teachers as transformative intellectuals. Symposium on understanding quality education. *Conference on Re-envisioning Quality Education*. http://www.afed.itacec.org/document/henry_giroux_2_ok.pdf

Giroux, H. (1988). *Teachers as intellectuals*. Bergin & Garvey.

Giroux, H. A., & Mclaren, P. (1996). Teacher education and the politics of engagement: The case for democratic schooling. In P. Leistyna, A. Woodrum, & S. A. Sherblom (Eds.), *Breaking free: The transformative power of critical pedagogy* (pp. 301–331). Harvard Educational Review.

Glade, N. (2015). Einsatz von Geoinformationssystemen im Geographieunterricht. Chancen für einen geschlechtergerechten Unterricht. In J. Wedl & A. Bartsch (Eds.), Teaching Gender? Zum reflektierten Umgang mit Geschlecht im Schulunterricht und in der Lehramtsausbildung (pp. 215-234). Transcript Verlag.

Goffman, E. (1959). *The presentation of self in everyday life*. Doubleday.

Goleman, D., & Senge, P. M. (2015). *The triple focus: A new approach to education*. More Than Sound.

Goodhart, D. (2017). *The road to somewhere: The populist revolt and the future of politics*. Hurst & Company.

Goodman, M., Adams, N., Corneil, T., Kreukels, B., Motmans, J., & Coleman, E. (2019). Size and distribution of transgender and gender nonconforming populations: A narrative review. *Endocrinology and Metabolism Clinics*, *48*(2), 303–321. doi:10.1016/j.ecl.2019.01.001 PMID:31027541

Grandinetti, J., & Bruinsma, J. (2022). The Affective Algorithms of Conspiracy TikTok. *Journal of Broadcasting & Electronic Media*, 1–20. doi:10.1080/08838151.2022.2140806

Greenhow, C., & Galvin, S. (2020). Teaching with social media: Evidence-based strategies for making remote higher education less remote. *Information and Learning Sciences*, *121*(7/8), 513–524. doi:10.1108/ILS-04-2020-0138

Grund, J., & Brock, A. (2020). Education for Sustainable Development in Germany: Not Just Desired but Also Effective for Transformative Action. *Sustainability*, 12(7), 28-38. doi:10.3390/su12072838

Grunwald, A. (2018). *Der unterlegene Mensch. Die Zukunft der Menschheit im Angesicht von Algorithmen, künstlicher Intelligenz und Robotern*. Riva.

Gryl, I., & Jekel, T. (2012). Re-centering geoinformation in secondary education: Toward a spatial citizenship approach. *Cartographica*, *47*(1), 18–28. doi:10.3138/carto.47.1.18

Gryl, I., Schlottmann, A., & Kanwischer, D. (2016). Mensch:Umwelt:System. Zur Einbettung naturwissenschaftlichen Lernens. [Human:Environment:System. On the embedding of science learning] In K.-H. Otto (Ed.), *Geographie und naturwissenschaftliche Bildung – Der Beitrag des Fachs für Schule, Lernlabor und Hochschule* [Geography and science education – The subject's contribution to school, learning lab and university]. (pp. 188–205). Monsenstein und Vannerdat.

Guo, Y., Zhang, Y., Boulaksil, Y., Qian, Y., & Allaoui, H. (2022). Modelling and analysis of online ride-sharing platforms– A sustainability perspective. *European Journal of Operational Research*. doi:10.1016/j.ejor.2022.04.035

Guzmán-Valenzuela, C., Gómez-González, C., Rojas-Murphy Tagle, A., & Lorca-Vyhmeister, A. (2021). Learning analytics in higher education: A preponderance of analytics but very little learning? *International Journal of Educational Technology in Higher Education*, *18*(1), 1–19. doi:10.118641239-021-00258-x PMID:34778523

Haleem. (2022). Understanding the role of digital technologies in education: A review. Sustainable Operations and Computers, 3, 275-285. doi:10.1016/j.susoc.2022.05.004

Hallman, H. L. (2019). Personalized learning through 1:1 technology initiatives: Implications for teachers and teaching in neoliberal times. *Teaching Education*, *30*(3), 299–318. doi:10.1080/10476210.2018.1466874

Hare, H. (2007). ICT in Education in Ethiopia, https://documents1.worldbank.org/curated/en/995541468256142802/pdf/463910BRI0Box31ia010ICTed0Survey111.pdf (accessed on 23 March, 2022)

HaroonM. (2022). *YouTube, The Great Radicalizer? Auditing and Mitigating Ideological Biases in YouTube Recommendations*. Arxiv. https://arxiv.org/abs/2203.10666v2

Harris, J. C., & Patton, L. D. (2019). Un/doing intersectionality through higher education research. *The Journal of Higher Education*, *90*(3), 347–372. doi:10.1080/00221546.2018.1536936

Harrison, D. (2010). Teacher Factors Influencing Classroom ICT Use. In *Sara Hennessy et al., Developing Use of ICT to Enhance Teaching and Learning in East African Schools: A Review of the Literature*. University of Cambridge and DFID.

Hasanat, M. W., Hoque, A., Shikha, F. A., Anwar, M., Hamid, A. B. A., & Tat, H. H. (2020). The impact of coronavirus (COVID-19) on E-business in Malaysia. *Asian Journal of Multidisciplinary Studies*, *3*(1), 85–90.

Hasse, J. (2006). Bildung für Nachhaltigkeit statt Umweltbildung? Starke Rhetorik – schwache Perspektiven. [Education for sustainability instead of environmental education? Strong rhetoric – weak perspectives] In B. Hiller & M. Lange (Eds.), *Bildung für nachhaltige Entwicklung. Perspektiven für die Umweltbildung (= Vorträge und Studien. Zentrum für Umweltforschung der Westfälischen Wilhelms-Universität, 16)* [Education for Sustainable Development. Perspectives for Environmental Education (= Lectures and Studies. Centre for Environmental Research of the Westphalian Wilhelms University, 16)]. (pp. 29–43). Zentrum für Umweltforschung.

Hassinger-Das, B., Dore, R. A., Aloisi, K., Hossain, M., Pearce, M., & Paterra, M. (2020). Children's reality status judgments of digital media: Implications for a covid-19 world and beyond. *Frontiers in Psychology*, *11*, 570068. doi:10.3389/fpsyg.2020.570068 PMID:33240158

Haubrich, H., Reinfried, S., & Schleicher, Y. (2007). Lucerne Declaration on Geographical Education for Sustainable Development. In S. Reinfried, Y. Schleicher, & A. Rempfler (Eds.), *Geographical Views on Education for Sustainable Development (= Geographiedidaktische Forschungen, 42)* [Geography education research, 42]. (pp. 243–250). HGD.

Hauff, M., & Jörg, A. (2017). *Nachhaltiges Wachstum* (2nd ed.). Walter de Gruyter. doi:10.1515/9783110532845

Head, A. J., Fister, B., & MacMillan, M. (2020). *Information literacy in the age of algorithms: Student experiences with news and information, and the need for change. executive summary*. Project Information Literacy. https://eric.ed.gov/?id=ED605107

Head, A. J., DeFrain, E., Fister, B., & MacMillan, M. (2019). Across the great divide: How today's college students engage with news. *First Monday*, *24*(8), 1–64. doi:10.5210/fm.v24i8.10166

Heitfeld, M., & Reif, A. (2020, August). *Transformation gestalten lernen. Mit Bildung und transformativem Engagement gesellschaftliche Strukturen verändern.* https://germanwatch.org/sites/default/files/Transformation%20gestalten%20lernen-1.pdf

Helne, T., & Hirvilammi, T. (2015). Wellbeing and Sustainability: A Relational Approach: Wellbeing and Sustainability. *Sustainable Development*, *23*(3), 167–175. doi:10.1002d.1581

Hemmer, I., & Hemmer, M. (2021). Das Interesse von Schülerinnen und Schülern an geographischen Themen, Regionen und Arbeitsweisen – ein Bundeslandvergleich zwischen Bayern und Nordrhein-Westfalen. *Zeitschrift für Geographiedidaktik*, *49*(1), 3–24.

Henderson, L., & Dlouhá, J. (2021). Myšlení budoucnosti a potřebnost transformativního přístupu ve vzdělávání [Future thinking and the need for a transformative approach in education]. *Envigogika*, *16*(1). doi:10.14712/18023061.621

Henderson, L., Kuříková, M., & Kroufek, R. (2021). Syntéza kreativního učení a vzdělávání pro udržitelný rozvoj v České republice [Synthesis of Creative Learning and Education for Sustainable Development in the Czech Republic]. *Envigogika*, *16*(2). doi:10.14712/18023061.628

Henrich, J. (2016). *The secret of our success: How culture is driving human evolution, domesticating our species, and making us smarter*. Princeton University Press. https://www.degruyter.com/isbn/9781400873296, doi:10.1515/9781400873296

Herrington, G. (2021). Update to limits to growth: Comparing the World3 model with empirical data. *Journal of Industrial Ecology*, *25*(3), 614–626. doi:10.1111/jiec.13084

Heyder, A., & Kessels, U. (2013). Is school feminine? Implicit gender stereotyping of school as a predictor of academic achievement. *Sex Roles*, *69*(11), 605–617. doi:10.100711199-013-0309-9

HGD. (2020). *Der Beitrag des Fachs Geographie zur Bildung in einer durch Digitalisierung und Mediatisierung geprägten Welt. Positionspapier des Hochschulverbands für Geographiedidaktik (HGD) e.V. [The contribution of the subject of geography to education in a world shaped by digitalisation and mediatisation. Position paper of the Association for Geography Education (HGD) e.V.]* Geographie Didaktik. https://geographiedidaktik.org/download/der-beitrag-des-fachs-geographie-zur-bildung-in-einer-durch-digitalisierung-und-mediatisierung-gepraegten-welt/

Hickel, J. (2019). The contradiction of the sustainable development goals: Growth versus ecology on a finite planet. *Sustainable Development*, *27*(5), 873–884. doi:10.1002d.1947

Hintermann, C., Bergmeister, F., Kessel, V., Pichler, H., & Raithofer, D. (2018). Hybride Identitaten im Kopf. Nachlese zur Abschlussveranstaltung des Sparkling Science Projekts MiDENTITY [Hybrid identities on the mind. Follow-up to the closing event of the Sparkling Science project MiDENTITY]. *GW-Unterricht*, *1*(151), 59–62. doi:10.1553/gw-unterricht151s59

Hobbs, R., & Jensen, A. (2009). The Past, Present, and Future of Media Literacy Education. *The Journal of Media Literacy Education*, *1*(1), 1–11. doi:10.23860/jmle-1-1-1

Höhnle, S. (2014). *Online-gestützte Projekte im Kontext Globalen Lernens im Geographieunterricht. Empirische Rekonstruktion internationaler Schülerperspektiven* (Vol. 53). HGD-Hochschulverband für Geographiedidaktik.

Hollingshead, A., & Carr-Chellman, D. (2019, Feb). Engaging learners in online environments utilizing Universal Design for Learning principles. *eLearn Magazine.* https://elearnmag.acm.org/featured.cfm?aid=3310383

Hone, K. S., & El Said, G. R. (2016). Exploring the factors affecting MOOC retention: A survey study. *Computers & Education*, *98*, 157–168. doi:10.1016/j.compedu.2016.03.016

Hopkins, Ch., Michelsen, G., Salite, I., Siegmund, A., Wagner, D., Yokoi, A., Fischer, D., Kohl, K., Razak, D., & Tilleczek, K. (2020). Sustainability as a Purpose on the Path of Learning. In: *Humanistic Futures of Learning. Perspectives from UNESCO Chairs and UNITWIN Networks* (pp. 58–62). UNESCO.

Hoque, F., Yasin, R. M., & Sopian, K. (2022). Revisiting Education for Sustainable Development: Methods to Inspire Secondary School Students toward Renewable Energy. *Sustainability*, *14*(14), 8296. doi:10.3390u14148296

Huber, L. (2009). Warum Forschendes Lernen nötig und möglich ist. In L. Huber, J. Hellmer, & F. Schneider (Eds.), *Forschendes Lernen im Studium* (pp. 9–35). Universitätsverlag Webler.

Huckle, J., & Sterling, S. (1999). *Education for sustainability: An invitation to join a debate.* https://john.huckle.org.uk/download/2106/Education%20for%20Sustainability,%20an%20invitation%20to%20join%20a%20debate.doc

Huitt, W. G., & Monetti, D. M. (2017). Openness and the Transformation of Education and Schooling. In Open: The Philosophy and Practices that are Revolutionizing Education and Science (pp. 43–65). Ubiquity Press. doi:10.5334/bbc.d

IIEP-UNESCO. (2020). *COVID-19 School Closures: Why Girls Are More at Risk.* Available online at: https://www.iiep.unesco.org/en/covid-19-school-closures-why-girls-are-more-risk-13406

ILO. (2021). *Digitalization in Teaching and Education in Ethiopia, Kenya, Malawi, Rwanda and the United Republic of Tanzania: Digitalization, the Future of Work and the Teaching Profession Project, A Synthesis Report.* International Labour Office.

Imara, K., & Altinay, F. (2021). Integrating Education for Sustainable Development Competencies in Teacher Education. *Sustainability*, *13*(22), 12555. doi:10.3390u132212555

Indiana University. (2022). *New social media tools help public assess viral posts, check for bots.* IU News. https://news.iu.edu/stories/2022/07/iub/releases/27-social-media-tools-bots-viral-posts.html

Indrawati, S. M., & Kuncoro, A. (2021). Improving competitiveness through vocational and higher education: Indonesia's vision for human capital development in 2019–2024. *Bulletin of Indonesian Economic Studies*, *57*(1), 29–59. doi:10.1080/00074918.2021.1909692

IPCC. (2021). *The Physical Science Basis. Working Group I Contribution to the IPCC Sixth Assessment Report.* IPCC.

Irawan, A. P., Supriyatna, E., Widjaja, I., & Lin, L. L. C. (2021). The Implementation of Basic Principles of Financial Management to Improve Higher Education Reputation. In *International Conference on Economics, Business, Social, and Humanities (ICEBSH 2021)* (pp. 1510-1514). Atlantis Press. 10.2991/assehr.k.210805.238

Ivascu, L., Cirjaliu, B., & Draghici, A. (2016). Business Model for the University-industry Collaboration in Open Innovation. *Procedia Economics and Finance*, *39*, 674–678. doi:10.1016/S2212-5671(16)30288-X

Jaeggi, R. (2014). *Kritik von Lebensformen* [Critique of life forms]. Suhrkamp.

Jang, C. I. (2020). *Teachers' Beliefs and Practices of ICT Use in Secondary Schools in Addis Ababa, Ethiopia.* [Thesis Submitted for the Degree of Doctor of Philosophy to the School of International Development of the University of East Anglia].

Jannah, C. (2019). *Merdeka Belajar: Kebijakan Lompat-lompat ala Nadiem Makarim,* Muslimahnews. https://www.muslimahnews.com/2019/12/23/merdeka-belajar-kebijakan-lompat-lompat-ala-nadiem-makarim/

Jensen, B. B., & Schnack, K. (1997). The Action Competence Approach in Environmental Education. *Environmental Education Research*, *3*(2), 163–178. doi:10.1080/1350462970030205

Jeong, H. (2013). Verbal data analysis for understanding interactions. In C. E. Hmelo-Silver, C. A. Chinn, C. K. K. Chan, & A. O'Donnell (Eds.), *The international handbook of collaborative learning* (pp. 168–183). Routledge.

John, B., Caniglia, G., Bellina, L., J. Lang, D., & Laubichler, M. (2017). The Global Curriculum: A Practical Guide to Teaching and Learning in an Interconnected World tredition.

Jonassen, D. (2008). *Meaningful Learning with Technology*. Pearson, Merrill Prentice Hall.

Jorissen, B., & Marotzki, W. (2009). *Medienbildung – Eine Einführung: Theorie – Methoden – Analysen* [Media Education - An introduction: theory - methods – analyses]. UTB. doi:10.36198/9783838531892

Kaczinski, A., Hennig-Thurau, Th. & Sattler, H. (2019). *Wie Deutschland soziale Medien nutzt und was das für unsere Gesellschaft bedeutet.* Social Media & Society Report.

Kaiser, J., & Rauchfleisch, A. (2020). Birds of a Feather Get Recommended Together: Algorithmic Homophily in YouTube's Channel Recommendations in the United States and Germany. *Social Media + Society*, *6*(4), 2056305120969914. doi:10.1177/2056305120969914

Kalogeropoulos, A., Suiter, J., Udris, L., & Eisenegger, M. (2019). News media trust and news consumption: Factors related to trust in news in 35 countries. *International Journal of Communication*, *13*(0), 22.

Kanwischer, D. (2014). Digitale Geomedien und Gesellschaft. Zum veränderten Status geographischen Wissens in der Bildung. *Geographische Rundschau*, *6*, 12–17.

Kanwischer, D., & Schlottmann, A. (2017). Virale Raumkonstruktionen – Soziale Medien und Mündigkeit im Kontext gesellschaftswissenschaftlicher Medienbildung [Viral constructions of space – social media and maturity in the context of social science media education]. *Zeitschrift für Didaktik der Gesellschaftswissenschaften*, *8*(2), 60–78. doi:10.46499/979.1232

Kaplan, M., & Larkin, E. (2021). Building community: Intergenerational projects with young children. In M. Renck Jalongo & P. A. Crawford (Eds.), *Intergenerational Bonds. Educating the Young Child, 18*. Springer., doi:10.1007/978-3-030-81965-1_12

Karantalis, N., Koukopoulos, D. (2022). Utilizing digital storytelling as a tool for teaching literature through constructivist learning theory. *SN Soc Sci, 2*, 109. doi:10.1007/s43545-022-00412-w

Kemendikbud. (2019). *Merdeka Belajar: Pokok-Pokok Kebijakan Merdeka Belajar.* Jakarta: Makalah Rapat Koordinasi Kepala Dinas Pendidikan Seluruh Indonesia.

Kenya Ministry of Education. (2019). *A policy framework for reforming education and training for sustainable development in Kenya: Towards realizing quality, relevant and inclusive education and training for sustainable development.* Republic of Kenya.

Kern, M. L., Waters, L. E., Adler, A., & White, M. A. (2015). A multidimensional approach to measuring well-being in students: Application of the PERMA framework. *The Journal of Positive Psychology*, *10*(3), 262–271. doi:10.1080/17439760.2014.936962 PMID:25745508

Kersting, P. (2015). Ein kritischer Überblick systemtheoretisch geprägter Ansätze in der Geographie [A critical overview of system theoretical approaches in geography]. In I. Gryl, A. Schlottmann, & D. Kanwischer (Eds.): Mensch:Umwelt:System. Theoretische Grundlagen und praktische Beispiele für den Geographieunterricht [Human:Environment:System. Theoretical foundations and practical examples for geography education] (43-60). Lit.

Ketelle, D. (2017). Introduction to the special issue: What is storytelling in the higher education classroom? *Storytelling, Self, Society*, *13*(2), 143–150. doi:10.13110torselfsoci.13.2.0143

Ketter, E., & Avraham, E. (2021). # StayHome today so we can# TravelTomorrow: Tourism destinations' digital marketing strategies during the Covid-19 pandemic. *Journal of Travel & Tourism Marketing*, *38*(8), 819–832. doi:10.1080/10548408.2021.1921670

Khakpour, N. (2022). *Deutsch-Können. Schulisch umkämpftes Artikulationsgeschehen.* Beltz.

Khan, N., Sarwar, A., Chen, T. B., & Khan, S. (2022). Connecting digital literacy in higher education to the 21st century workforce. Knowledge Management & E-Learning. *International Journal (Toronto, Ont.)*, 46–61. doi:10.34105/j.kmel.2022.14.004

Kim, M., & Shin, J. (2016). The pedagogical benefits of SimCity in urban geography education. *The Journal of Geography*, *115*(2), 39–50. doi:10.1080/00221341.2015.1061585

Kimmerle, J., Moskaliuk, J., Oeberst, A., & Cress, U. (2015). Learning and Collective Knowledge Construction With Social Media: A Process-Oriented Perspective. *Educational Psychologist*, *50*(2), 120–137. doi:10.1080/00461520.2015.1036273 PMID:26246643

Kimmons, R., Graham, C. R., & West, R. E. (2020). The PICRAT model for technology integration in teacher preparation. *Contemporary Issues in Technology & Teacher Education*, *20*(1), 176–198.

Kim, S.-W., & Bogale, G. (2014). Does Satellite Program Satisfy Ethiopian Secondary School Education? In *International Conference e-Learning 2014*, (p. 79–86).

Kirkpatrick, C. E., & Lee, S. (2022). Comparisons to picture-perfect motherhood: How Instagram's idealized portrayals of motherhood affect new mothers' well-being. *Computers in Human Behavior*, *107417*, 107417. doi:10.1016/j.chb.2022.107417

Kirschner, P. A. (2015). Facebook as learning platform: Argumentation superhighway or dead-end street? *Computers in Human Behavior*, *53*, 621–625. doi:10.1016/j.chb.2015.03.011

Kitchenham, H. (2008). One-to-One Computing and Teacher Transformation. In *Hansson, T. Handbook of Research on Digital Information Technologies: Innovations, Methods, and Ethical Issues*. Information Science Reference. doi:10.4018/978-1-59904-970-0.ch007

Kjell, O. N. (2011). Sustainable well-being: A potential synergy between sustainability and well-being research. *Review of General Psychology*, *15*(3), 255–266. doi:10.1037/a0024603

Klafki, W. (2007). *Neue Studien zur Bildungstheorie und Didaktik: Zeitgemäße Allgemeinbildung und kritisch-konstruktive Didaktik [New studies in educational theory and didactics: Contemporary general education and critical-constructive didactics]*. Beltz.

KMK – Kultusministerkonferenz (2016). Bildung in der digitalen Welt. *Beschluss der Kultusministerkonferenz vom 8.12.2016.*

Kolb, D. A. (1984). *Experiential learning: Experience as the source of learning and development*. Prentice-Hall.

Kollmayer, M., Schultes, M.-T., Lüftenegger, M., Finsterwald, M., Spiel, C., & Schober, B. (2020). REFLECT – A Teacher Training Program to Promote Gender Equality in Schools. *Frontiers in Education, 5*, Article 136.

Kollmayer, M., Schober, B., & Spiel, C. (2018a). Gender stereotypes in education: Development, consequences, and interventions. *European Journal of Developmental Psychology, 15*(4), 361–377. doi:10.1080/17405629.2016.1193483

Kollmayer, M., Schultes, M. T., Schober, B., Hodosi, T., & Spiel, C. (2018b). Parents' judgments about the desirability of toys for their children: Associations with gender role attitudes, gender-typing of toys, and demographics. *Sex Roles, 79*(5), 329–341. doi:10.100711199-017-0882-4 PMID:30147224

Költzsch, T. (2022). Apple soll klimafeindliche Gruppierungen unterstützen [Apple is said to support anti-climate groups]. *Golem.de*. https://www.golem.de/news/greenwashing-apple-soll-klimafeindliche-gruppierungen-unterstuetzen-2206-165818.html

Korlat, S., Foerst, N. M., Schultes, M. T., Schober, B., Spiel, C., & Kollmayer, M. (2022). Gender role identity and gender intensification: Agency and communion in adolescents' spontaneous self-descriptions. *European Journal of Developmental Psychology, 19*(1), 64–88. doi:10.1080/17405629.2020.1865143

Korlat, S., Kollmayer, M., Holzer, J., Lüftenegger, M., Pelikan, E. R., Schober, B., & Spiel, C. (2021). Gender Differences in Digital Learning During COVID-19: Competence Beliefs, Intrinsic Value, Learning Engagement, and Perceived Teacher Support. *Frontiers in Psychology, 12*, 63776. doi:10.3389/fpsyg.2021.637776 PMID:33868109

Krings, T. (2008). Politische Ökologie. Grundlagen und Arbeitsfelder eines geographischen Ansatzes der Mensch-Umwelt-Forschung [Political Ecology. Basics and fields of a geographical approach of human-environment research]. *Geographische Rundschau, 60*(12), 4–9.

Kriz, W. C. (2010). A systemic-constructivist approach to the facilitation and debriefing of simulations and games. *Simulation & Gaming, 41*(5), 663–680. doi:10.1177/1046878108319867

Kroll, C., Warchold, A., & Pradhan, P. (2019). Sustainable Development Goals (SDGs): Are we successful in turning trade-offs into synergies? *Palgrave Communications, 5*(1), 140. doi:10.105741599-019-0335-5

Kubisch, S., Parth, S., Deisenrieder, V., Oberauer, K., Stötter, J., & Keller, L. (2021). From Transdisciplinary Research to Transdisciplinary Education—The Role of Schools in Contributing to Community Well-Being and Sustainable Development. *Sustainability, 13*(1), 306. doi:10.3390u13010306

Kusanagi, K. (2021). Indonesia ni okeru sogo gakushu to ESD—Sogo karikyuramu to kankyo kyoiku puroguramu Adiwiyata no jissen. *Musashi University In-service Education Bulletin, 35*, 203–211.

Kusanagi, K. N. (2020). Education for sustainable development and the implementation of "tokkatsu" in Indonesia. In *International Conference on Social Studies and Environmental Issues (ICOSSEI 2019)* (pp. 69–74). Atlantis Press. 10.2991/assehr.k.200214.013

Kusanagi, K., & Suratno, T. (2020). Kodomo no manabi wo chushin to shita jyugyo kenkyu to manabi no kyodotai zukuri. *Tokyo Future University Bulletin, 14*, 63–68.

Kuşay, Y. (2019). Digital storytelling as a part of participatory culture in communication and public relation practices. In R. Yilmaz, N. Erdem, & F. Resuloglu (Eds.), *Handbook of Research on Transmedia Storytelling and Narrative Strategies* (pp. 271–291). IGI Global. doi:10.4018/978-1-5225-5357-1.ch014

Labor Force Survey. (2020-21). *Government of Pakistan, Ministry of Planning Development and Special initiatives.* Pakistan Bureau of Statistics.

Lacković, N. (2021). Postdigital living and algorithms of desire. *Postdigital Science and Education*, *3*(2), 280–282. doi:10.100742438-020-00141-4

Lange, St. & Santarius, T. (2018): Smarte Grüne Welt? Digitalisierung zwischen Überwachung. *Konsum und Nachhaltigkeit. oekom Verlag.*

Le Tendre, G. K. (1999). Community-building activities in Japanese schools: Alternative paradigms of the democratic school. *Comparative Education Review*, *43*(3), 283–310. doi:10.1086/447564

Leal Filho, W., Wolf, F., & Pohlmann, J. (2021). Digitalisierung und Nachhaltigkeit durch internationale Ansätze – Beispiele der HAW Hamburg. In W. Leal Filho (Ed.), *Digitalisierung und Nachhaltigkeit* (pp. 1–22). Springer Berlin Heidelberg. doi:10.1007/978-3-662-61534-8_1

Lederman, L. C. (1992). Debriefing: Toward a systematic assessment of theory and practice. *Simulation & Gaming*, *23*(2), 145–160. doi:10.1177/1046878192232003

Ledford, D. M. (2016). *A professional learning framework to improve teacher practice in technology integration* [PhD dissertation]. Boise State University.

Lehner. (n.d). Widersprüche und Ambivalenzen als Impulse für eine Bildung für Nachhaltige Entwicklung. [Contradictions and ambivalences as impulses for an education for sustainability]. *GW Unterricht.*

Lewis, C., Perry, R., & Friedkin, S. (2009). Lesson study as action research. In *The SAGE handbook of educational action research* (pp. 142–154). Sage Publications Ltd. doi:10.4135/9780857021021.n14

Li, N., & Kirkup, G. (2007). Gender and cultural differences in Internet use: A study of China and the UK. *Computers & Education*, *48*(2), 301–317. doi:10.1016/j.compedu.2005.01.007

Linden, G., Smith, B., & York, J. (2003). Amazon.com recommendations: Item-to-item collaborative filtering. *IEEE Internet Computing*, *7*(1), 76–80. doi:10.1109/MIC.2003.1167344

Lindh, M., & Nolin, J. (2016). Information we collect: Surveillance and privacy in the implementation of google apps for education. *European Educational Research Journal*, *15*(6), 644–663. doi:10.1177/1474904116654917

Literacy/UNESCO UIS. (2022). Uis.unesco.org/ en/ topic/literacy

Liu, Z., Deng, Z., Zhu, B., Ciais, P., Davis, S. J., Tan, J., Andrew, R. M., Boucher, O., Arous, S. B., Canadell, J. G., Dou, X., Friedlingstein, P., Gentine, P., Guo, R., Hong, C., Jackson, R. B., Kammen, D. M., Ke, P., Le Quéré, C, & Schellnhuber, H. J. (2022). Global patterns of daily CO2 emissions reductions in the first year of COVID-19. *Nature Geoscience*, *15*(8), 615–620. Advance online publication. doi:10.103841561-022-00965-8

Livingstone, S., Ólafsson, K., O'Neill, B., & Donoso, V. (2012, June). *Towards a better internet for children: Findings and recommendations from EU Kids Online to inform the CEO coalition.* The London School of Economics and Political Science. http://www.eukidsonline.net/

Lott, Y. (2019). Weniger Arbeit, mehr Freizeit? [Less work, more leisure time?]. *WSI Report*, (47), 1–16.

Lozano, R., Merrill, M., Sammalisto, K., Ceulemans, K., & Lozano, F. (2017). Connecting Competences and Pedagogical Approaches for Sustainable Development in Higher Education: A Literature Review and Framework Proposal. *Sustainability, 9*(1889), 1–15. doi:10.3390/su9101889

Lozano, R., Barreiro-Gen, M., Lozano, F., & Sammalisto, K. (2019). Teaching Sustainability in European Higher Education Institutions: Assessing the Connections between Competences and Pedagogical Approaches. *Sustainability*, *11*(6), 1602. doi:10.3390u11061602

Luhmann, N. (2018). Soziale Systeme: Grundriß einer allgemeinen Theorie (17. Auflage). Suhrkamp-Taschenbuch Wissenschaft: Vol. 666. Suhrkamp.

Lunch, N., & Lunch, C. (2006). *Insights into participatory video: A handbook for the field.* Insight.

Lux, J.-D., & Budke, A. (2020a). Alles nur ein Spiel? Geographisches Fachwissen zu aktuellen gesellschaftlichen Herausforderungen in digitalen Spielen. *GW Unterricht*, *160*, 22–36. doi:10.1553/gw-unterricht160s22

Lux, J.-D., & Budke, A. (2020b). Playing with Complex Systems? The Potential to Gain Geographical System Competence through Digital Gaming. *Education Sciences*, *10*(5), 130. Advance online publication. doi:10.3390/educsci10050130

Lux, J.-D., & Budke, A. (2022). Die Funktion einer Stadt erleben. Mit Spielen fachliche und mediale Kompetenzen fördern. *Praxis Geographie. H.*, *3*, 11–15.

Lux, J.-D., Budke, A., & Guardiola, E. (2021). Games Versus Reality? How Game Designers Deal with Current Topics of Geography Education. Multimodal Technol. *Interact*, *5*(11), 70. Advance online publication. doi:10.3390/mti5110070

Macgilchrist, F. (2019). Digitale Bildungsmedien im Diskurs. In: Aus Politik und Zeitgeschichte: Bildung und Digitalisierung. (Vol. 69). Bildung und Digitalisierung.

Maftuna, G. (2022). Methodology of Organizing Problem Lessons in Higher Education. *International Journal of Culture and Modernity*, *14*, 72–77.

Maina-Okori, N. M., Koushik, J. R., & Wilson, A. (2018). Reimagining intersectionality in environmental and sustainability education: A critical literature review. *The Journal of Environmental Education*, *49*(4), 286–296. doi:10.1080/00958964.2017.1364215

Makrakis, V. (2014a). ICTs as transformative enabling tools in education. In R. Huang, Kinshuk, & J. Price (Eds.), ICT in Education in Global Context (pp. 101-119). Springer Verlag.

Makrakis, V. (2017a). Developing and validating a sustainability justice instrument to transform curriculum, Learning and Teaching. *9th International Conference in Open & Distance Learning – November 2017, Athens, Greece–Proceedings*. https://eproceedings.epublishing.ekt.gr/index.php/openedu/article/viewFile/1368/1303

Makrakis, V. (2018). *From STEM to STEAM and to STREAM enabled through meaningful critical reflective learning.* Paper presented at the 2nd International Conference on Innovating STEM Education. 24-28 June 2018, Deutsch School Athens.

Makrakis, V., & Kostoulas-Makrakis, N. (2012b). The challenges of ICTs to online climate change education for sustainable development: The ExConTra learning paradigm. In S. A. Anwar (Ed), *Proceedings of the 5th Conference on eLearning Excellence in the Middle East - Sustainable Innovation in Education* (pp. 594–605). Hamdan Bin Mohammed e-University.

Makrakis, V. (2006). *Preparing United Arab Emirates teachers for building a sustainable society, E-Media Publications.* University of Crete.

Makrakis, V. (2014b). Transforming university curricula towards sustainability: A Euro-Mediterranean initiative. In K. Tomas & H. Muga (Eds.), *Handbook of research on pedagogical innovations for sustainable development* (pp. 619–640). IGI Global. doi:10.4018/978-1-4666-5856-1.ch032

Makrakis, V. (2017b). Unlocking the potentiality and actuality of ICTs in developing sustainable–justice curricula and society. *Knowledge Cultures*, *5*(2), 103–122. doi:10.22381/KC5220177

Makrakis, V., & Kostoulas-Makrakis, N. (2012a). Course curricular design and development of the M.Sc. programme in the field of ICT in education for sustainable development. *Journal of Teacher Education for Sustainability*, *14*(2), 5–40. doi:10.2478/v10099-012-0007-7

Makrakis, V., & Kostoulas-Makrakis, N. (2017). Paradigm shift in higher education teaching and learning: Practices towards education for sustainability. In G. Mickelsen & P. J. Wells (Eds.), *A Decade of Progress on Education for Sustainable Development Reflections from the UNESCO Chairs Programme* (pp. 94–102). UNESCO.

Makrakis, V., & Kostoulas-Makrakis, N. (2020). The quest for meaningful learning. In *Humanistic Futures of Learning. Perspectives from UNESCO Chairs and UNITWIN networks* (pp. 143–147). UNESCO.

Malberg Dyg, P., & Wistoft, K. (2018). Wellbeing in school gardens – the case of the Gardens for Bellies food and environmental education program. *Environmental Education Research*, *24*(8), 1177–1191. doi:10.1080/13504622.2018.1434869

Mali, D., & Lim, H. (2021). How do students perceive face-to-face/blended learning as a result of the Covid-19 pandemic? *International Journal of Management Education*, *19*(3), 19. doi:10.1016/j.ijme.2021.100552

Manocchia, M. (1999). SimCity 2000 Software. *Teaching Sociology*, *27*(2), 212–215. doi:10.2307/1318710

Mansell, R. (1982). The 'new dominant paradigm' in communication: Transformation versus adaptation. *Canadian Journal of Communication*, *8*(3), 42–60. doi:10.22230/cjc.1982v8n3a278

Martha, A. S. D., Junus, K., Santoso, H. B., & Suhartanto, H. (2021). Assessing Undergraduate Students' e-Learning Competencies: A Case Study of Higher Education Context in Indonesia. *Education Sciences*, *11*(4), 189. doi:10.3390/educsci11040189

Martin, F., & Griffiths, H. (2012). Power and representation: A postcolonial reading of global partnerships and teacher development through North—South study visits. *British Educational Research Journal*, *38*(6), 907–927. doi:10.1080/01411926.2011.600438

Massey, D. (1998). Power geometries and the politics of space-time. Hettner Lectures, University of Heidelberg.

Mathie, R. G., & Wals, A. E. J. (2022). *Whole school approaches to sustainability. Exemplary practices from around the world* (2nd ed.). Wageningen University, Education & Learning Sciences. doi:10.18174/572267

Mayr, H., & Madritsch, R. (2022). Mobile Endgeräte in der Bildung: ein Blick durch die ökologische, ökonomische und soziale Brille. In T. Hug (Ed.), Medien – Wissen – Bildung 2021: Ökologische Krisen und Ökologien in der Kritik (MWB 2021). Academic Press.

Mayr, H., & Oberrauch, A. (2022). Hochschulbildung für eine Nachhaltige Entwicklung – interdisziplinär, partizipativ, digital? In Bildung für nachhaltige Entwicklung und Digitalisierung als Beitrag für eine zukunftsorientierte Hochschulausbildung (pp. 67-82). Heidelberger Zentrum Bildung für nachhaltige Entwicklung.

Mayring, P. (2014). *Qualitative Content Analysis: Theoretical Foundation.* Basic Procedures and Software Solution.

McDonald, J. K., West, R. E., Rich, P. J., & Pfleger, I. (2018). "It's So Wonderful Having Different Majors Working Together": The Development of an Interdisciplinary Design Thinking Minor. *TechTrends*, *63*(4), 440–450. doi:10.100711528-018-0325-2

McLuhan, M. (1964). *Understanding media: The extensions of man* (2nd ed.). Mentor.

Meadows, D. H. (Ed.). (1972). *A Potomac Associates book. The limits to growth: A report for the club of rome's project on the predicament of mankind*. Earth Island Limited.

Medienberatung, N. R. W. (2020). *Medienkompetenzrahmen NRW* (3rd ed.). Medienberatung NRW.

Mehsud, R. (2018). *Schools in Pakistan' Tribal Districts struggle to write the next chapter*. ARABNEWS. https:// www.arabnews.com/ 1423811/Pakistan

Meier Kruker, V., & Rauh, J. (2005). *Arbeitsmethoden der Humangeographie*. WBG.

Meinel, C., & von Thienen, J. (2016). Design Thinking. *Informatik Spektrum*, *39*(4), 10–31. doi:10.100700287-016-0977-2

Merkle, J. (2021). Reisen für „Likes". Wie Instagram den Tourismus verändert. *Geographische Rundschau*, *2021*(1), 16–20.

Michelsen, G., & Adomssent, M. (2007). Education for sustainable development strategies in German universities. *From cosmetic reform to meaningful integration: Implementing education for sustainable Development in Higher Education Institutes—The state of affairs in Six European countries*, 21–24.

Milson, A., Kerski, J., & Demirci, A. (2012). The world at their fingertips. GIS in secondary education. In A. Milson, J. Kerski, & A. Demirci (Eds.), *International Perspectives on Teaching and Learning with GIS in Secondary Schools* (pp. 1–11). Springer. doi:10.1007/978-94-007-2120-3_1

Ministry of Education. (2017). *Culture, Sports, Science and Technology (MEXT)*. Basic Education in Japan. https://www.eduport.mext.go.jp/epsite/wp-content/uploads/2021/03/educa2017_pamphlet.pdf

Ministry of Education. (2019). Culture, Sports, Science and Technology (MEXT). *The Ministry of Education, Culture, Sports, Science and Technology (MEXT) website*. http://www.mext.go.jp/a_menu/shotou/new-cs/1383986.htm#section4

Miranda, S. M., Young, A., & Yetgin, E. (2016). Are social media emancipatory or hegemonic? Societal effects of mass media digitization. *Management Information Systems Quarterly*, *40*(2), 303–329. doi:10.25300/MISQ/2016/40.2.02

Mishra, P., & Koehler, M. J. (2006). Technological pedagogical content knowledge: A new framework for teacher knowledge. *Teachers College Record*, *108*(6), 1017–1054. doi:10.1111/j.1467-9620.2006.00684.x

Mitchell, K. (2018). *Making Workers: Radical Geographies of Education*. Pluto Press.

Mochizuki, Y., & Fadeeva, Z. (2010). Competences for sustainable development and sustainability: Significance and challenges for ESD. *Int. J. Sustain. High. Educ.*, *1*, 391–403. doi:10.118640723-021-00081-x

MOE (Ministry of Education). (2018). Ethiopian Education Development Roadmap (2018-30): An Integrated Executive Summary. Addis Ababa: Education Strategy Center (ESC)

Mohring, K., & Brendel, N. (in press). Erkenntnisse aus einer körpersensiblen Lehre mit und zu dem digitalen Medium VR – Potentiale für eine nachhaltigkeitsbezogene geographische Bildung. [Findings from a body-sensitive teaching with and about the digital medium VR – Potentials for a sustainability-related geographical education] In F. Pettig & I. Gryl (Eds.), *Geographische Bildung in einer Kultur der Digitalität* [Geographical education in a culture of digitality]. Springer.

Mondejar, M. E., Avtar, R., Diaz, H. L. B., Dubey, R. K., Esteban, J., Gómez-Morales, A., Hallam, B., Mbungu, N. T., Okolo, C. C., Prasad, K. A., She, Q., & Garcia-Segura, S. (2021). Digitalization to achieve sustainable development goals: Steps towards a Smart Green Planet. *The Science of the Total Environment*, *794*, 148539. doi:10.1016/j.scitotenv.2021.148539 PMID:34323742

MONE. (2007). *Reforming teachers: Towards educational equality and quality*. Ministry of National Education.

Montessori, M. (1949). *The absorbent mind*. Theosophical Publishing House.

Moore, D. T. (2010). Forms and issues in experiential learning. In D. M. Qualters (Ed.), *New Directions for Teaching and Learning* (pp. 3–13). Wiley.

Moore, J. (2005). Seven recommendations for creating sustainability education at the university level: A guide for change agents. *International Journal of Sustainability in Higher Education*, *6*(4), 326–333. doi:10.1108/14676370510623829

MPFS (Medienpädagogischer Forschungsverbund Südwest). (2018). *JIM-Studie 2018 – Jugend, Information, Medien: Basisuntersuchung zum Medienumgang 12- bis 19-Jähriger*. https://www.mpfs.de/fileadmin/files/Studien/JIM/2018/Studie/JIM_2018_Gesamt.pdf

Muhammad, M. (2016). Education census 2015-16; 1,036 FATA schools, non functional. *Tribune, the Express*.

Mühlmann, K., Satalkina, L., Zenk, L., & Steiner, G. (2022). Transition, Innovation and Sustainability Environments, TISE: A Showcase of Education Geared Towards Societal Challenges and Future Orientation. In M. E. Auer, H. Hortsch, O. Michler, & T. Köhler (Eds.), *Lecture Notes in Networks and Systems. Mobility for Smart Cities and Regional Development - Challenges for Higher Education* (Vol. 390, pp. 879–887). Springer International Publishing. doi:10.1007/978-3-030-93907-6_94

Musolin, M., & Nisa', K. (2021). Pendidikan Masa Pandemik Covid 19: Implementasi Konsep Tri Pusat Pendidikan Ki Hajar Dewantara. *Edukatif: Jurnal Ilmu Pendidikan*, *3*(6), 4134–4144. doi:10.31004/edukatif.v3i6.1316

Nager, I. T. (2022). *Die faire Maus. [The fair mouse]* https://www.nager-it.de/maus

National Governors Association Center for Best Practices & Council of Chief State School Officers. (2010). *Common core state standards (English language arts)*. National Governors Association Center for Best Practices, Council of Chief State School Officers. http://www.corestandards.org/ELA-Literacy/

Nave'ed, S. (2018). Why do Pakistan's Federally Administered Tribal Areas have such a High Gender Gap in Education? Education plus development. Brookings.

Nedelkoska, L., Diodato, D., & Neffke, F. (2018). Is Our Human Capital General Enough to Withstand the Current Wave of Technological Change? Pachauri, R. K., & Meyer, L. (Eds.). (2015). Climate change 2014: Synthesis report: [longer report]. Intergovernmental Panel on Climate Change.

Nefesh-Clarke, L., Orser, B., & Thomas, M. (2020). *COVID-19 Response Strategies, Addressing Digital Gender Divides*. https://www.g20-insights.org/policy_briefs/covid-19-response-strategies-addressing-digital-gender-divides/

Neumann, M. M., & Herodotou, C. (2020). Young Children and YouTube: A global phenomenon. *Childhood Education*, *96*(4), 72–77. doi:10.1080/00094056.2020.1796459

Nieborg, D. B., & Poell, T. (2018). The platformization of cultural production: Theorizing the contingent cultural commodity. *New Media & Society*, *20*(11), 4275–4292. doi:10.1177/1461444818769694

Nielsen, M. L., Laursen, C. S., & Dyreborg, J. (2022). Who takes care of safety and health among young workers? Responsibilization of OSH in the platform economy. *Safety Science*, *149*, 105674. doi:10.1016/j.ssci.2022.105674

Nilsson, E. M., & Jakobsson, A. (2011). Simulated sustainable societies: Students' reflections on creating future cities in computer games. *Journal of Science Education and Technology*, *20*(1), 33–50. doi:10.100710956-010-9232-9

Novitasari, A. T., Wijayanti, R., & Sholeh, Y. (2021). Socialization of Souvenir Craft Marketing Strategy Using Online Media in the Era of the COVID-19 Virus Pandemic. *Journal of Community Service*, *4*(2), 190–196.

Ntanos, S., Kyriakopoulos, G. L., Arabatzis, G., Palios, V., & Chalikias, M. (2018). Environmental bevahior of Secondary Education Students: A Case Study at Central Greece. *Sustainability*, *10*(5), 1663. doi:10.3390u10051663

O'Callaghan, D., Greene, D., Conway, M., Carthy, J., & Cunningham, P. (2015). Down the (white) rabbit hole: The extreme right and online recommender systems. *Social Science Computer Review*, *33*(4), 459–478. doi:10.1177/0894439314555329

O'Neil, C. (2016). *Weapons of math destruction: How Big Data increases inequality and threatens democracy*. Crown.

Oberrauch, A., Keller, L., Sanin, P., & Riede, M. (2014). Lebensqualitätsvorstellungen von Jugendlichen im Kontext des Leitbilds nachhaltiger Entwicklung. *Mitteilungen der Österreichischen Geographischen Gesellschaft*, *156*, 221–248. doi:10.1553/moegg156s221

Oberrauch, A., Mayr, H., Nikitin, I., Bügler, T., Kosler, T., & Vollmer, C. (2021). "I Wanted a Profession That Makes a Difference"—An Online Survey of First-Year Students' Study Choice Motives and Sustainability-Related Attributes. *Sustainability*, *13*(15), 8273. doi:10.3390u13158273

OECD. (2016). *Global competency for an inclusive world*. https://gisigpl.files.wordpress.com/2017/12/global-competency-for-an-inclusive-world.pdf

Oinas, S., Hotulainen, R., Koivuhovi, S., Brunila, K., & Vainikainen, M. P. (2022). Remote learning experiences of girls, boys and non-binary students. *Computers & Education*, *183*, 104499. doi:10.1016/j.compedu.2022.104499

Ollivaud, P. (2021). Investing in competences and skills and reforming the labour market to create better jobs in Indonesia. *OECD Economics Department Working Papers*. No. 1670, OECD Publishing, Paris, doi:10.1787/18151973

Olsson, D., Gericke, N., & Chang Rundgren, S.-N. (2016). The effect of implementation of education for sustainable development in Swedish compulsory schools – Assessing pupils' sustainability consciousness. *Environmental Education Research*, *22*(2), 176–202. doi:10.1080/13504622.2015.1005057

Papadopoulos, T., Gunasekaran, A., Dubey, R., Altay, N., Childe, S., & Fosso-Wamba, S. (2017). The role of big data in explaining disaster resilience for sustainability. *Journal of Cleaner Production*, *142*, 1108–1118. doi:10.1016/j.jclepro.2016.03.059

Parrisius, A. (2019). Stromfresser Internet. Was unser Digitalkonsum an Energie kostet [Internet as an energy guzzler. What our digital consumption costs in energy]. *Tagesspiegel*. https://www.tagesspiegel.de/wirtschaft/stromfresser-internet-wie-viel-strom-wir-im-einzelnen-verbrauchen/25182828-2.html

Paul, J. (in press). Socially Hyped Locations. *Wochenschau*.

Pavlova, M. (2013). Towards using transformative education as a benchmark for clarifying differences and similarities between environmental education and education for sustainable development. *Environmental Education Research*, *19*(5), 656–672. doi:10.1080/13504622.2012.736476

Pedersen, C. L. (2019). Is Silicon Valley Diverse Enough to Resist Reduction? *Journal of Design and Science*.

Perkowski, J. (2013). The role of gender in distance learning: A meta-analytic review of gender differences in academic performance and self-efficacy in distance learning. *Journal of Educational Technology Systems*, *41*(3), 267–278. doi:10.2190/ET.41.3.e

Perrotta, C., Gulson, K. N., Williamson, B., & Witzenberger, K. (2020). Automation, APIs and the distributed labour of platform pedagogies in Google Classroom. *Critical Studies in Education*, *62*(1), 97–113. doi:10.1080/17508487.2020.1855597

Persson, M., Andersson, K., Zetterberg, P., Ekman, J., & Lundin, S. (2019). Does Deliberative Education Increase Civic Competence? Results from a Field Experiment. *Journal of Experimental Political Science*, 1–10. doi:10.1017/XPS.2019.29

Peters, V. A. M., & Vissers, G. A. N. (2004). A simple classification model for debriefing simulation games. *Simulation & Gaming*, *35*(1), 70–84. doi:10.1177/1046878103253719

Petiška, E., Korhoňová, L., Pospíšilová, M., & Dlouhý, J. (2020). Use and evaluation of the quality of open educational resources in the context of universities: The situation at Charles University. *Envigogika*, *15*(1). doi:10.14712/18023061.607

Petiška, E., Pospíšilová, M., Dlouhý, J., Korhoňová, L., & Dlouha, J. (2021). Metodika zajištění kvality otevřených vzdělávacích zdrojů pro vysokoškolské vzdělávání [Quality Assurance Methodology for Open Educational Resources for Higher Education]. *Envigogika*, *16*(2). doi:10.14712/18023061.634

Pettig, F. (2021). Transformative Lernangebote kritisch-reflexiv gestalten. Fachdidaktische Orientierungen einer emanzipatorischen BNE [Designing transformative learning opportunities critically and reflectively. Subject didactic orientations of an emancipatory ESD]. *GW Unterricht*, *162*(2), 5–17. doi:10.1553/gw-unterricht162s5

Pettig, F., & Gryl, I. (in press). Diskursive Orientierungen geographischer Bildung in digitalen Kulturen. [Discursive orientations of geographical education in digital cultures] In F. Pettig & I. Gryl (Eds.), *Geographische Bildung in einer Kultur der Digitalität* [Geographical education in a culture of digitality]. Springer.

Podgoršek, S. (2020). The Changing Role of the Teacher in ICT-Supported Foreign Language Instruction: A Multiple-Case Study. In *Eva Podovšovnik, Examining the Roles of Teachers and Students in Mastering New Technologies*. IGI Global. doi:10.4018/978-1-7998-2104-5.ch018

Politische Ökologie. (2018). Smartopia. Geht Digitalisierung auch nachhaltig? 36.

Polter-Nelson, E. M., & O'Neil, J. K. (2019). Role of teachers on education for sustainable development. In Encyclopedia of sustainability in Higher Education. Springer.

Posch, A., & Scholz, R. W. (2006). Transdisciplinary case studies for sustainability learning. *International Journal of Sustainability in Higher Education*, *7*(3). doi:10.1108/ijshe.2006.24907caa.001

Posch, A., & Steiner, G. (2006). Integrating research and teaching on innovation for sustainable development. *International Journal of Sustainability in Higher Education*, *7*(3), 276–292. doi:10.1108/14676370610677847

Postman, N. (1992). *Technopoly: The surrender of culture to technology*. Alfred A. Knopf.

Postman, N., & Weingarter, C. (1971). *Teaching as a subversive activity*. Delta.

Pucer, P., Vičič, Š. G., & Žvanut, B. (2020). ICT Adoption among Higher Education Teachers: A Case Study of a University in the Awareness/Exploration Stage of Blended Learning Adoption. In *Eva Podovšovnik, Examining the Roles of Teachers and Students in Mastering New Technologies*. IGI Global. doi:10.4018/978-1-7998-2104-5.ch016

Puentedura, R. R. (2009). SAMR: First steps. *Hippasus*. http://hippasus.com/resources/tte/

Purba, J.H., Fathiah, R. & Steven, S. 2021. The impact of covid-19 pandemic on the tourism sector in indonesia. *Jurnal Aplikasi Ekonomi Akuntansi dan Bisnis, 3*(1), 389 - 401. DOI:. doi:10.37641/riset.v3i1.82

Purhottan & Dhingra, A. (2017). Understanding the Indian tribal life and their issues. *International Journal of Advanced Research, 5*.

Purnama, S., Bangun, C. S., Panjaitan, A. R. S., & Sampoerna, S. T. (2022). The Effect Of Digitalization On Culinary MSMEs On Increasing Sales Turnover During COVID 19 Pandemic. [ATT]. *Artist Transactions on Technopreneurship, 4*(1), 59–68. doi:10.34306/att.v4i1.228

Purwanti, E. (2021). Preparing the implementation of merdeka belajar–kampus merdeka policy in higher education institutions. *In 4th International Conference on Sustainable Innovation 2020–Social, Humanity, and Education, Atlantis Press. (ICoSIHESS 2020).* ACM. 10.2991/assehr.k.210120.149

Quebral, N. (1988). *Development communication.* UPLB College of Agriculture.

Rauth, I., Köppen, E., Jobst, B., & Meinel, C. (2010). Design Thinking: An Educational Model towards Creative Confidence. *DS-66-2: Proceedings of the 1st International Conference on Design Creativity (ICDC 2010).*

Raworth, K. (2015). *Doughnut Economics. Seven Ways to Think Like a 21st Century Economist.* Penguin Random House.

Raza, H., Saputra, J., & Muhammad, Z. (2022). The effect of the implementation of financial accounting standards on MSMEs. *Accounting, 8*(2), 209–216. doi:10.5267/j.ac.2021.6.018

Reckwitz, A. (2019). Die Gesellschaft der Singularitäten. *edition suhrkamp.*

Redman, A., Barth, M., Wiek, A., & Timm, J.-M. (2019, May 29). (submitted to). Generating Generalizable Insights from Case Studies on Competencies-oriented Sustainability Education. *Draft. Gaia (Heidelberg).*

Rice, J. K. (2003). *Teacher Quality: Understanding the Effectiveness of Teacher Attributes. Economic policy institute.* Education.

Richter, U. M., Veerabhatla, S., & Zasiekina, L. (2021). Managing and facilitating student learning in teams in higher education. In *Cases on Active Blended Learning in Higher Education* (pp. 149–171). IGI Global. doi:10.4018/978-1-7998-7856-8.ch008

Rideout, V., & Robb, M. B. (2019). *The Common Sense Census: Media Use by Tweens and Teens, 2019.* Common Sense Media. https://www.commonsensemedia.org/research/the-common-sense-census-media-use-by-tweens-and-teens-2019

Ridsdale, C., Rothwell, J., Smit, M., Bliemel, M., Irvine, D., Kelley, D., Matwin, S., Wuetherick, B. & Ali-Hassan, H. (2015). Strategies and Best Practices for Data Literacy Education. *Knowledge Synthesis Report.*

Rieckmann, M. (2018). Learning to transform the world: key competencies in Education for Sustainable Development. In A. Leicht, A. Heiss, & W. J. Byun (Eds.), *Issues and trends in education for sustainable development* (pp. 39–59). UNESCO.

Rieckmann, M. (2018). Learning to transform the world: Key competencies in education for sustainable development. *Issues and Trends in Education for Sustainable Development, 39*, 39–59.

Rieckmann, M., & Barth, M. (2022). Educators' Competence Frameworks in Education for Sustainable Development. In P. Vare, N. Lausselet, & M. Rieckmann (Eds.), *Competences in Education for Sustainable Development. Critical Perspectives* (pp. 19–26). Springer International Publishing. doi:10.1007/978-3-030-91055-6_3

Riemann, T., Kreß, A., Roth, L., Klipfel, S., Metternich, J., & Grell, P. (2020). Agile Implementation of Virtual Reality in Learning Factories. *Procedia Manufacturing*, *45*, 1–6. doi:10.1016/j.promfg.2020.04.029

Riemeier, T. (2007). Moderater Konstruktivismus. In Handbuch der Theorien in der biologiedidaktischen Forschung (pp. 69–79). Springer. doi:10.1007/978-3-540-68166-3_7

Risopoulos-Pichler, F., Daghofer, F., & Steiner, G. (2020). Competences for Solving Complex Problems: A Cross-Sectional Survey on Higher Education for Sustainability Learning and Transdisciplinarity. *Sustainability*, *12*(15), 6016. doi:10.3390u12156016

Röckström, J., Steffen, W., Noone, K., Persson, A., Chapin III, F.S., Lambin, E.F., Lenton, T.M., Scheffer, M., Folke, C., Schellnhuber, H.., Nykvist, B., de Wit, C. A., Hughes, T., van der Leeuw, S., Rodhe, H., Sörlin, S., Snyder, P.K., Costanza, R., Svedin, U., Falkenmark, M., … Foley, J. A. (2009). A safe operating space for humanity. *Nature, 461*, 472-475.

Rodríguez Aboytes, J. G., & Barth, M. (2020). Transformative learning in the field of sustainability: A systematic literature review (1999-2019). *International Journal of Sustainability in Higher Education*, *21*(5), 993–1013. doi:10.1108/IJSHE-05-2019-0168

Rogers, E. (1976). Communication and development: The passing of the dominant paradigm. *Communication Research*, *3*(2), 213–240. doi:10.1177/009365027600300207

Rolf, A. (2018). *Weltmacht Vereinigte Daten. Die Digitalisierung und Big Data verstehen.* Metropolis.

Rolf, S., O'Reilly, J., & Meryon, M. (2022). Towards privatized social and employment protections in the platform economy? Evidence from the UK courier sector. *Research Policy*, *51*(5), 104492. doi:10.1016/j.respol.2022.104492

Rosser, A. (2022). Higher Education in Indonesia: The political economy of institution-level Governance. *Journal of Contemporary Asia*, 1–26.

Ruchi, T., Suresh, V., Zubkov, S. A., & Shariq, M. (2020). ICT Skills for Sustainable Development Goal 4. In W. Leal Filh (Eds.), *Quality Education, Encyclopedia of the UN Sustainable Development Goals*. Springer Nature Switzerland AG.

Sadowski, J. (2020). The Internet of Landlords: Digital Platforms and New Mechanisms of Rentier Capitalism. *Antipode*, *52*(2), 562–580. doi:10.1111/anti.12595

Saed, A. (2018). "Ghosts schools" risk breeding militancy in Pakistan tribal areas. Conflict News. *The New Humanitarian.* www the new humanitarian.org.news/2018/01/25/breeding- militancy-pakistan-ghosts-schools-tribal-areas-risk-

Saka, B. (2014). Petty commodity production in the neoliberal phase of global capitalism. *Research in Rural Sociology and Development*, *20*, 93–113. doi:10.1108/S1057-192220140000020004

Salen, K., & Zimmerman, E. (2003). *Rules of Play: Game Design Fundamentals.* MIT Press.

Sánchez-Carracedo, F., Moreno-Pino, F. M., Romero-Portillo, D., & Sureda, B. (2021). Education for sustainable development in Spanish university education degrees. *Sustainability*, *13*(3), 1467. doi:10.3390u13031467

Satalkina, L., Zenk, L., Mühlmann, K., & Steiner, G. (2022). Beyond Simple: Entrepreneurship as a Driver for Societal Change. In M. E. Auer, H. Hortsch, O. Michler, & T. Köhler (Eds.), *Mobility for Smart Cities and Regional Development—Challenges for Higher Education* (Vol. 390, pp. 888–896). Springer International Publishing. doi:10.1007/978-3-030-93907-6_95

Sato, N. (2003). *Inside Japanese classrooms: The heart of education.* Routledge. doi:10.4324/9780203465707

Sauers, N. J., & Richardson, J. W. (2019). Leading the pack: Developing empowering responsible use policies. *Journal of Research on Technology in Education*, *51*(1), 27–42. doi:10.1080/15391523.2018.1539644

Scarff Seatter, C., & Ceulemans, K. (2017). Teaching Sustainability in Higher Education: Pedagogical Styles that Make a Difference. *Canadian Journal of Higher Education*, *47*(2), 47–70. doi:10.47678/cjhe.v47i2.186284

Schank, C., & Rieckmann, M. (2019). Socio-economically Substantiated Education for Sustainable Development: Development of Competencies and Value Orientations Between Individual Responsibility and Structural Transformation. *Journal of Education for Sustainable Development*, *13*(1), 67–91. doi:10.1177/0973408219844849

Scheller, H. (2019). “Digitalpakt Schule.” Föderale Kulturhoheit zulasten der Zukunftsfähigkeit des Bildungswesens? In: Aus Politik und Zeitgeschichte: Bildung und Digitalisierung. (Vol. 69).

Schernhammer, E., Weitzer, J., Laubichler, M. D., Birmann, B. M., Bertau, M., Zenk, L., Caniglia, G., Jäger, C. C., & Steiner, G. (2022). Correlates of COVID-19 vaccine hesitancy in Austria: Trust and the government. *Journal of Public Health (Oxford, England)*, *44*(1), e106–e116. doi:10.1093/pubmed/fdab122 PMID:33948665

Schober, B., Finsterwald, M., Wagner, P., Lüftenegger, M., Aysner, M., & Spiel, C. (2007). TALK—A training program to encourage lifelong learning in school. *Zeitschrift für Psychologie. The Journal of Psychology*, *215*(3), 183–193.

Schober, B., Lüftenegger, M., & Spiel, C. (2020). *Learning Conditions During COVID-19 Pupils*. AUSSDA., doi:10.11587/VRQL3B

Scholz, R. W., Beckedahl, M., Noller, S., & Renn, O. (2021). DiDaT Weißbuch. Nomos Verlagsgesellschaft mbH & Co. KG. doi:10.5771/9783748924111

Scholz, R. W., & Binder, C. R. (2011). *Environmental literacy in science and society: From knowledge to decisions*. Cambridge University Press. doi:10.1017/CBO9780511921520

Scholz, R. W., & Steiner, G. (2015a). The real type and ideal type of transdisciplinary processes: Part II—what constraints and obstacles do we meet in practice? *Sustainability Science*, *10*(4), 653–671. doi:10.100711625-015-0327-3

Scholz, R. W., & Steiner, G. (2015b). The real type and ideal type of transdisciplinary processes: Part I—theoretical foundations. *Sustainability Science*, *10*(4), 527–544. doi:10.100711625-015-0326-4

Scholz, R., Bartelsman, E., Diefenbach, S., Franke, L., Grunwald, A., Helbing, D., Hill, R., Hilty, L., Höjer, M., Klauser, S., Montag, C., Parycek, P., Prote, J., Renn, O., Reichel, A., Schuh, G., Steiner, G., & Viale Pereira, G. (2001). [Gerald], & Viale Pereira, G. (2018). Unintended Side Effects of the Digital Transition: European Scientists' Messages from a Proposition-Based Expert Round Table. *Sustainability (New Rochelle, N.Y.)*, *10*(6), 2001. Advance online publication. doi:10.3390u10062001

Schuilenburg, M., & Peeters, R. (2020). *The Algorithmic Society*. Routledge. doi:10.4324/9780429261404

SchüllerK.BuschP.HindingerC. (2019): Future Skills: Ein Framework für Data Literacy – Kompetenzrahmen und Forschungsbericht. Arbeitspapier Nr. 47. Berlin: Hochschulforum Digitalisierung. doi:10.5281/zenodo.3349

Schulze, U., & Gryl, I. (2022). Geographische Bildung in der digitalen Welt. Die digitale Transformation im Fokus der Geographiedidaktik - Theorie, Empirie, Praxis. [Geographical education in the digital world. The digital transformation in the focus of geography didactics - theory, empiricism, practice] In V. Frederking & R. Romeike (Eds.), *Fachliche Bildung im Zeichen von Digitalisierung, Big Data und KI* [Professional education under the sign of digitalisation, big data and AI]. (pp. 143–173). Waxmann.

Schürfer, G., & Brendel, N. (2018). Globales Lernen im digitalen Zeitalter. In N. Brendel, G. Schrüfer, & I. Schwarz (Eds.), *Globales Lernen im digitalen Zeitalter* (pp. 9–33). Waxmann.

Schwägele, S., Zürn, B., Lukosch, H. K., & Freese, M. (2021). Design of an Impulse-Debriefing-Spiral for Simulation Game Facilitation. *Simulation & Gaming*, *52*(3), 364–385. doi:10.1177/10468781211006752

Seligman, M. E. P., & Csikszentmihalyi, M. (2000). Positive psychology: An introduction. *The American Psychologist*, *55*(1), 5–14. doi:10.1037/0003-066X.55.1.5 PMID:11392865

Seligman, M. E. P., Ernst, R. M., Gillham, J., Reivich, K., & Linkins, M. (2009). Positive education: Positive psychology and classroom interventions. *Oxford Review of Education*, *35*(3), 293–311. doi:10.1080/03054980902934563

Setyowati, D. L., Paramita, S., Ifroh, R. H., Asrianti, T., Fitriani, E., & Rahman, W. (2021). Work readiness during COVID-19 among taxibike online drivers in Samarinda, Indonesia. *International Journal of Public Health Science*, *10*(13), 617. doi:10.11591/ijphs.v10i3.20870

Sharma, M. (2017). Teacher in a Digital Era. *Global Journal of Computer Science and Technology (G)*, *17*(3).

Shen, C., Wang, H., & Ritterfeld, U. (2009). Serious Games and Seriously Fun Games. In U. Ritterfeld, M. Cody, & P. Vorderer (Eds.), *Serious games: Mechanisms and Effects* (pp. 48–61). Routledge.

Shephard, K., Rieckmann, M., & Barth, M. (2019). Seeking sustainability competence and capability in the ESD and HESD literature: An international philosophical hermeneutic analysis. *Environmental Education Research*, *25*(4), 532–547. doi:10.1080/13504622.2018.1490947

Shin, D. (2020). User perceptions of algorithmic decisions in the personalized AI system: Perceptual evaluation of fairness, accountability, transparency, and explainability. *Journal of Broadcasting & Electronic Media*, *64*(4), 541–565. doi:10.1080/08838151.2020.1843357

Shulman, L. (1986). Those who understand: Knowledge growth in teaching. *Educational Researcher*, *15*(2), 4–14. doi:10.3102/0013189X015002004

Silseth, K. (2012). The multivoicedness of game play: Exploring the unfolding of a student's learning trajectory in a gaming context at school. *International Journal of Computer-Supported Collaborative Learning*, *7*(1), 6384. doi:10.100711412-011-9132-x

Silverstone, R. (1992). *Consuming technologies: Media and information in domestic spaces*. Psychology Press.

Singer-Brodowsky, M. (2016). *Studierende als Gestalter*innen einer Hochschulbildung für nachhaltige Entwicklung. Selbstorganisierte und problembasierte Nachhaltigkeitskurse und ihr Beitrag zur überfachlichen Kompetenzentwicklung Studierender. Umweltkommunikation, Band Nr. 8*. Berliner Wissenschaftsverlag.

Skog, D. A., Wimelius, H., & Sandberg, J. (2018). Digital Disruption. *Business & Information Systems Engineering*, *60*(5), 431–437. doi:10.100712599-018-0550-4

Skouge, J., & Ra, K. (2009). Digital storytelling in teacher education: Creating transformations through narrative. *Educational Perspectives*, *42*(1&2), 54–60.

Smith, B., & Linden, G. (2017). Two Decades of Recommender Systems at Amazon.com. *IEEE Internet Computing*, *21*(3), 12–18. doi:10.1109/MIC.2017.72

Stalder, F. (2016). Kultur der Digitalität (3rd ed.). Originalausgabe.

Stalder, F. (2016): Kultur der Digitalität. *edition suhrkamp*.

Stalder, F. (2017). The digital condition. *Polity*.

Steiner, G. (2013). Competences for Complex Real-World Problems: Toward an Integrative Framework. *Working Paper 2013-0002, Weatherhead Center for International Affairs*. Harvard University.

Steiner, G. (2023). *Turning digital vulnerability spaces into innovation niches. Results from the Transdisciplinary USA Expert Round Table Series on sustainable digital transformation.* Working Paper.

Steiner, G., & Laws, D. (2006). How appropriate are two established concepts from higher education for solving complex real-world problems? *International Journal of Sustainability in Higher Education*, *7*(3), 322–340. doi:10.1108/14676370610677874

Sterling, S. (2004). Higher education, sustainability and the role of systemic thinking. In P. B. Corcoran & A. E. J. Wals (Eds.), *Higher education and the challenge of sustainability: problematics, promise, and practice* (pp. 49–70). Kluwer Academic Publishers. doi:10.1007/0-306-48515-X_5

Steven, B. (2010). Sociology: Understanding and changing the social world. Flatworld.

Stickdorn, M., Hormess, M. E., Lawrence, A., & Schneider, J. (2018). *This is service design doing: applying service design thinking in the real world.* O'Reilly Media, Inc.

Stoll, C. (1996). *Die Wüste Internet. Geisterfahrten auf der Datenautobahn.* Fischer.

Stoltenberg, U., & Michelsen, G. (1999): Lernen nach der Agenda 21: Überlegungen zu einem Bildungskonzept für eine nachhaltige Entwicklung. In: NNA-Berichte, 12. Jg., H.1.

Stoltenberg, U., & Michelsen, G. (2020). Digitalisierung im Kontext von Bildung für eine nachhaltige Entwicklung. In M. Hauff von & A. Reller (Eds.), Nachhaltige Digitalisierung – eine noch zu bewältigende Zukunftsaufgabe (pp. 49–64). Hessische Landeszentrale für politische Bildung.

Stoltenberg, U., & Michelsen, G. (2020). Digitalisierung im Kontext von Bildung für Nachhaltige Entwicklung. In Nachhaltige Digitalisierung – eine noch zu bewältigende Zukunftsaufgabe (pp. 49-64). Hessische Landeszentrale für politische Bildung.

Stoltenberg, U. (2007). Gesellschaftliches Lernen und Partizipation. In: H. Jonuschat, E. Baranek, M. Behrendt, K. Dietz, B. Schlussmeier, H. Walk, & A. Zehm (Eds.), *Partizipation und Nachhaltigkeit – Vom Leitbild zur Umsetzung. Ergebnisse sozial-ökologischer Forschung. oekom Verlag.*

Stoltenberg, U., & Fischer, D. (2018). Bildung für eine nachhaltige Entwicklung in Deutschland: vom Projekt zur Struktur? In: *Perspektive wechseln. In: Jahrbuch Bildung für nachhaltige Entwicklung.* Forum Umweltbildung Vienna.

Stoltenberg, U., & Michelsen, G. (2020). Digitalisierung im Kontext von Bildung für eine nachhaltige Entwicklung. In: M. von Hauff & A. Reller (Eds.): *Nachhaltige Digitalisierung – eine noch zu bewältigende Zukunftsaufgabe Wiesbaden.*

Stone, J. A. (2017). The impact of technology exposure on student perceptions of a 1:1 program. *Education and Information Technologies*, *22*(5), 2281–2309. doi:10.100710639-016-9541-6

Strickland, E. (2022). Are You Still Using Real Data to Train Your AI? *IEEE Spectrum.* https://spectrum.ieee.org/synthetic-data-ai

Strotmann, C., Baur, V., Börnert, N., & Gerwin, P. (2022). Generation and prevention of food waste in the German food service sector in the COVID-19 pandemic–Digital approaches to encounter the pandemic related crisis. *Socio-Economic Planning Sciences*, *82*, 101104. doi:10.1016/j.seps.2021.101104 PMID:35721382

Sugiyama, M., Deguchi, H., Ema, A., Kishimoto, A., Mori, J., Shiroyama, H., & Scholz, R. (2017). Unintended Side Effects of Digital Transition: Perspectives of Japanese Experts. *Sustainability*, *9*(12), 2193. doi:10.3390u9122193

Sühlmann-Saul, F. & Rammler, St. (2018): Der blinde Fleck der Digitalisierung. *oekom Verlag.*

Sukmawati, D., & Maryanti, R. (2022). Development of education and economic circulation in supporting local potential as community empowerment efforts amid the Covid-19 pandemic. *Indonesian Journal of Multidiciplinary Research, 1*(2), 235–250. doi:10.17509/ijomr.v1i2.37598

Sundberg, L. T., & Holmström, J. (2022). Towards 'Lightweight' Artificial Intelligence: A Typology of AI Service Platforms. *AMCIS 2022 Proceedings.* AMC. https://aisel.aisnet.org/amcis2022/sig_odis/sig_odis/13

Suryahadi, A., Al Izzati, R., & Suryadarma, D. (2020). The Impact of COVID-19 Outbreak on Poverty: An Estimation for Indonesia (Draft). *SMERU Working Paper,* 1–20. https://smeru.or.id/en/content/impact-COVID-19-outbreak-poverty-estimation-indonesia

Susilawati, E., Khaira, I., & Pratama, I. (2021). Antecedents to student loyalty in Indonesian higher education institutions: The mediating role of technology innovation. *Educational Sciences: Theory and Practice, 21*(3), 40–56.

Sustainable Development Goals. (2020). *Take action for the sustainable goals-the United Nations.* https://www.un.org,sustainable –dev

Swart, J. (2021). Experiencing algorithms: How young people understand, feel about, and engage with algorithmic news selection on social media. *Social Media + Society, 7*(2). doi:10.1177/20563051211008828

Tanaka, H. (2017). Current state and future prospects of education for sustainable development (ESD) in Japan. *Educational Studies in Japan, 11*(0), 15–28. doi:10.7571/esjkyoiku.11.15

Tanaka, S. (2019). Tokkatsu plus in Egypt: Extending the tokkatsu concept. In *Tokkatsu: The Japanese educational model of holistic education* (pp. 225–250). World Scientific. doi:10.1142/9789813232679_0017

Tan, J. P. L., Choo, S. S., Kang, T., & Liem, G. A. D. (2017). Educating for twenty-first century competencies and future-ready learners: Research perspectives from Singapore. *Asia Pacific Journal of Education, 37*(4), 425–436. doi:10.1080/02188791.2017.1405475

Tasshakkori, A., & Cresswell, J. W. (2007). The new era of Mixed methods. *Journal of Mixed Methods Research, 1*(1), 3–7. doi:10.1177/2345678906293042

Tedre, M., Toivonen, T., Kahila, J., Vartiainen, H., Valtonen, T., Jormanainen, I., & Pears, A. (2021). Teaching Machine Learning in K–12 Classroom: Pedagogical and Technological Trajectories for Artificial Intelligence Education. *IEEE Access : Practical Innovations, Open Solutions, 9,* 110558–110572. doi:10.1109/ACCESS.2021.3097962

Tilbury, D., & Mulà, I. (2009). *A Review of education for sustainable development policies from a cultural diversity and intercultural dialogue perspective: Identifying opportunities for future action—UNESCO Digital Library.* https://unesdoc.unesco.org/ark:/48223/pf0000211750

Tjoa, A., & Simon, T. (2016). The Role of ICT to Achieve the UN Sustainable Development Goals (SDG). *6th IFIP World Information Technology Forum (WITFOR),* (pp.3-13).

Toffler, A. (2022). *Future Shock. Random House Publishing Group.* EBook Central. https://ebookcentral.proquest.com/lib/kxp/detail.action?docID=6829200

Trespalacios, J., Snelson, C., Lowenthal, P. R., Uribe-Flórez, L., & Perkins, R. (2021). Community and connectedness in online higher education: A scoping review of the literature. *Distance Education, 42*(1), 5–21. doi:10.1080/01587919.2020.1869524

Tristananda, P. W. (2018). Membumikan education for sustainable development (ESD) di Indonesia dalam menghadapi isu–isu global. *Purwadita: Jurnal Agama dan Budaya, 2*(2), 42–49.

Tsuneyoshi, R. (Ed.). (2012). *The World of Tokkatsu.* Tsune Lab. http://www.p.u.-tokyo.ac.jp/~tsunelab/tokkatsu/

Tsuneyoshi, R., & Nukaga, M. (2021). *Shin gurōbaru jidai ni idomu Nihon no kyōiku: Tabunka shakai o kangaeru hikaku kyōikugaku no shiza* [Japanese education in the new global era: A comparative education perspective on a multicultural society]. Tokyo University Press.

Tsuneyoshi, R., Sugita, H., Kusanagi, K., & Takahashi, F. (Eds.). (2019). *Tokkatsu: The Japanese educational model of holistic education.* World Scientific. doi:10.1142/10781

TWI2050. (2019). The Digital Revolution and Sustainable Development: Opportunities and Challenges. *Report Prepared by The World in 2050 Initiative. International Institute for Applied Systems Analysis (IIASA),* Laxenburg, Austria. www.twi2050.org

U.S. Department of Education. (2010). *Evaluation of evidence-based practices in online learning*. USDE. www.ed.gov/about/offices/list/opepd/ppss/reports.html

UN. (2015). *Resolution adopted by the General Assembly on 25 September 2015.* https://www.un.org/ga/search/view_doc.asp?symbol=A/RES/70/1&Lang=E

UN. (2020). *Education During COVID-19 and Beyond.* https://www.un.org/development/desa/dspd/wp-content/uploads/sites/22/2020/08/sg_policy_brief_covid-19_and_education_augu st_2020.pdf

UN. (2021). *The 17 goals.* https://sdgs.un.org/goals

UNECE. (2011). *Learning for the future: Competences in Education for Sustainable Development. ECE/CEP/AC.13/2011/6.* UNECE. https://unece.org/fileadmin/DAM/env/esd/ESD_Publications/Competences_Publication.pdf

UNEP. (2021). *State of Finance for Nature*. https://www.unep.org/resources/state-finance-nature

UNESCO (2018). A Global Framework of Reference on Digital Literacy Skills for Indicator 4.4.2. *Information Paper No. 51*. UNESCO.

Unesco (2018). *Progress on Education for Sustainable development and Global Citizenship*. UNESCO.

UNESCO. (2015b). *Rethinking education: Towards a global common good?* UNESCO.

UNESCO. (2016). *Incheon Declaration and Framework for Action for the Implementation of Sustainable Development Goal 4: Ensure Inclusive and Equitable Quality Education and Promote Lifelong Learning Opportunities For All.* UNESCO.

UNESCO. (2017). *Education for Sustainable Development Goals. Learning Objectives.* UNESCO. https://www.unesco.de/sites/default/files/2018-08/unesco_education_for_sustainable_development_goals.pdf

UNESCO. (2017). *Education for Sustainable Development Goals: learning objectives.* https://unesdoc.unesco.org/ark:/48223/pf0000247444

UNESCO. (2017). *Education for sustainable development goals: Learning objectives.* UNESCO Publishing. https://www.unesco.at/fileadmin/Redaktion/Publikationen/Publikations-Dokumente/2017_Education_for_SDG.pdf

UNESCO. (2017). *Education for Sustainable Development Goals: Learning objectives—UNESCO Digital Library.* https://unesdoc.unesco.org/ark:/48223/pf0000247444

UNESCO. (2018). *Global Action Programme on Education for Sustainable Development*. https://en.unesco.org/gap

UNESCO. (2018). *Issues and Trends in Education for Sustainable Development*. UNESCO.

UNESCO. (2021). *ESD for 2030 toolbox: Priority action areas*. https://en.unesco.org/themes/education-sustainable-development/toolbox/priorities

UNESCO. (2022). *Education for sustainable development*. https://www.unesco.org/en/education/sustainable-development

UNICEF. (2020). *Keeping the World's Children Learning Through COVID-19*. https://www.unicef.org/coronavirus/keeping-worlds-children-learning-through-covid-19

United Nations (2015): Transforming our World: The 2030 Agenda for Sustainable Development. UN.

United Nations Educational, Scientific and Cultural Organization. (2020). *Education for Sustainable Development. A roadmap*. UNESCO.

United Nations. (1987). *Report of the World Commission on Environment and Development: Our Common Future*. Author.

United Nations. (1992). Agenda 21. *United Nations Conference on Environment and Development.*

United Nations. (2015). *Agenda 2030. United Nations Conference on Environment and Development.*

Val, E., Gonzalez, I., Iriarte, I. Beitia, A., Lasa, G. & Elkoro, M. (2017): A Design Thinking approach to introduce entrepreneurship education in European school curricula. *The Design Journal, 20*(1), 754-766.

van Dijck, J. (2020). Governing digital societies: Private platforms, public values. *Computer Law & Security Review, 36*, 105377.. doi:10.1016/j.clsr.2019.105377

van Dijck, J. (2013). Youtube beyond technology and cultural form. In J. Teurlings & M. de Valck (Eds.), *After the Break: Television Theory Today* (pp. 147–160). Amsterdam University Press. doi:10.1515/9789048518678-010

van Dijck, J., de Winkel, T., & Schäfer, M. T. (2021). Deplatformization and the governance of the platform ecosystem. *New Media & Society, 23*(9). doi:10.1177/14614448211045662

van Dijck, J., Poell, T., & de Waal, M. (2018). *The Platform Society: Public Values in a Connective World*. Oxford University Press. doi:10.1093/oso/9780190889760.001.0001

Van Eck, R. (2006). Digital game-based learning. It's not just the digital natives who are restless. *EDUCAUSE Review, 41*(2), 55–63.

van Reijmersdal, E. A., Rozendaal, E., Smink, N., van Noort, G., & Buijzen, M. (2017). Processes and effects of targeted online advertising among children. *International Journal of Advertising, 36*(3), 396–414. doi:10.1080/02650487.2016.1196904

Vare, P., Lausselet, N., & Rieckmann, M. (2022): *Competences in Education for Sustainable Development.* Springer International Publishing.

Vare, P., & Scott, W. (2007). Learning for a Change: Exploring the Relationship between Education and Sustainable Development. *Journal of Education for Sustainable Development, 1*(2), 191–198. doi:10.1177/097340820700100209

Vaughan, N. D. (2019). Foreword. In Handbook of Research on Blended Learning Pedagogies and Professional Development in Higher Education. IGI Global.

VBW - Vereinigung der bayerischen Wirtschaft e.V. (2018). *Digitae Souveränität und Bildung*. White paper

Vekiri, I. (2013). Information science instruction and changes in girls' and boy's expectancy and value beliefs: In search of gender-equitable pedagogical practices. *Computers & Education*, *64*, 104–115. doi:10.1016/j.compedu.2013.01.011

Viale Pereira, G., Estevez, E., Cardona, D., Chesñevar, C., Collazzo-Yelpo, P., Cunha, M. A., Diniz, E. H., Ferraresi, A. A., Fischer, F. M., Cardinelle Oliveira Garcia, F., Joia, L. A., Luciano, E. M., de Albuquerque, J. P., Quandt, C. O., Sánchez Rios, R., Sánchez, A., Da Damião Silva, E., Silva-Junior, J. S., & Scholz, R. W. (2020). South American Expert Roundtable: Increasing Adaptive Governance Capacity for Coping with Unintended Side Effects of Digital Transformation. *Sustainability*, *12*(2), 718. doi:10.3390u12020718

Viberg, O., Mavroudi, A., Khalil, M., & Bälter, O. (2020). Validating an Instrument to Measure Teachers' Preparedness to Use Digital Technology in their Teaching. *Nordic Journal of Digital Literacy*, *15*(1), 38–54. doi:10.18261/issn.1891-943x-2020-01-04

Volman, M., & van Eck, E. (2001). Gender equity and information technology in education: The second decade. *Review of Educational Research*, *71*(4), 613–634. doi:10.3102/00346543071004613

Wagiran, W., Suharjana, S., Nurtanto, M., & Mutohhari, F. (2022). Determining the e-learning readiness of higher education students: A study during the COVID-19 pandemic. *Heliyon*, *8*(10), e11160. doi:10.1016/j.heliyon.2022.e11160 PMID:36276754

Wajdi MF, Mangifera L, Isa M. 2020. Strategy for strengthening business incubators in developing small and medium enterprises. *Competitiveness Journal of resource management economics. 22*(2): 101-107.

Wals, A. E. J. (2011). Learning Our Way to Sustainability. *Journal of Education for Sustainable Development*, *5*(2), 177–186. doi:10.1177/097340821100500208

Wals, A. E. J. (2015). *Beyond unreasonable doubt: Education and learning for socio-ecological sustainability in the anthropocene*. Wageningen University.

Waltner, E.-M., Rieß, W., & Mischo, C. (2019). Development and validation of an instrument for measuring student sustainability competencies. *Sustainability*, *11*(6), 1717. doi:10.3390u11061717

Wardenga, U. (2002). Alte und neue Raumkonzepte für den Geographieunterricht [Old and new spatial concepts for geography education]. *Geographie heute, 23*(200), 8-11.

Warschauer, M., Knobel, M., & Stone, L. (2004). Technology and equity in schooling: Deconstructing the digital divide. *Educational Policy*, *18*(4), 562–588. doi:10.1177/0895904804266469

Waters, L., & White, M. (2015). Case Study of a School Wellbeing Initiative: Using Appreciative Inquiry to Support Positive Change. *International Journal of Wellbeing*, *5*(1), 1. Advance online publication. doi:10.5502/ijw.v5i1.2

Watson, S., Fulton, K. A., Carpio, C., & Boonsaeng, T. (2022). Virtual Student Teamwork in Higher Education: Is There a Secret Recipe for Productivity? *American Journal of Distance Education*, 1–13. doi:10.1080/08923647.2022.2143700

WBGU – German Advisory Council on Global Change (2011). *World in Transition. A Social Contract for Sustainability*. WGBU. https://www.wbgu.de/fileadmin/user_upload/wbgu/publikationen/hauptgutachten/hg2011/pdf/wbgu_jg2011_en.pdf

WBGU – German Advisory Council on Global Change (2019). *Towards our Common Digital Future*. WBGU. https://www.wbgu.de/en/publications/publication/towards-our-common-digital-future

WBGU – German Advisory Council on Global Change. (2019). *Towards Our Common Digital Future. Flagship Report*. WBGU.

WBGU (Wissenschaftlicher Beirat der Bundesregierung Globale Umweltveränderungen). (2011). *Welt im Wandel: Gesellschaftsvertrag für eine Große Transformation*. WBGU.

WBGU. (2019). *Unsere gemeinsame digitale Zukunft*. WBGU.

Wehler, H.-U. (1987). *Deutsche Gesellschaftsgeschichte. Erster Band Vom Feudalismus des alten Reiches bis zur defensiven Modernisierung der Reformära. 1700-1815*. C.H. Beck.

Weiser, A., van Deest, J., & Barth, M. (2022): Transformation verstehen lernen: Nachhaltigkeitsbildung und Data Literacy Education in der Studieneingangsphase. In: Weselek, J., Kohler, F. & Siegmund, A. (Hrsg., 2022): Digitale Bildung für nachhaltige Entwicklung. Springer.

Weitzer, J., Birmann, B. M., Steffelbauer, I., Bertau, M., Zenk, L., Caniglia, G., Laubichler, M. D., Steiner, G., & Schernhammer, E. S. (2022). Willingness to receive an annual COVID-19 booster vaccine in the German-speaking D-A-CH region in Europe: A cross-sectional study. The Lancet Regional Health. *Europe*, *18*, 100414. doi:10.1016/j.lanepe.2022.100414 PMID:35651957

Weitzer, J., Laubichler, M. D., Birmann, B. M., Bertau, M., Zenk, L., Caniglia, G., Jäger, C. C., & Steiner, G [Gerald], & Schernhammer, E. (. (2021). Comment on Alley, S.J., et al. As the Pandemic Progresses, How Does Willingness to Vaccinate against COVID-19 Evolve? Int. J. Environ. Res. Public Health 2021, 18, 797. *International Journal of Environmental Research and Public Health*, *18*(6). doi:10.3390/ijerph18062809 PMID:33801986

Weitzer, J., Papantoniou, K., Seidel, S., Klösch, G., Caniglia, G., Laubichler, M., Bertau, M., Birmann, B. M., Jäger, C. C., Zenk, L., Steiner, G., & Schernhammer, E. (2021). Working from home, quality of life, and perceived productivity during the first 50-day COVID-19 mitigation measures in Austria: A cross-sectional study. *International Archives of Occupational and Environmental Health*, *94*(8), 1823–1837. doi:10.100700420-021-01692-0 PMID:33877416

Weizenbaum, J. (1976). *Computer Power and Human Reason*. W.H. Freeman and Company.

Werlen, B. (1993). *Society, action, and space: An alternative human geography*. Routledge.

Wheeler, S. (2012). *E-Learning and Digital learning. Encyclopedia of the sciences of learning*. Springer.

Wiek, A., Keeler, L., & Redman, C. (2011): Key Competencies in Sustainability: A Reference Framework for Academic Program Development. In: Sustainability Science. 6. doi:10.100711625-011-0132-6

Wiek, A., Bernstein, M., Foley, R., Cohen, M., Forrest, N., Kuzdas, C., Kay, B., & Withycombe Keeler, L. (2015). Operationalising Competencies in Higher Education for Sustainable Development. In M. Barth, G. Michelsen, M. Rieckmann, & I. Thomas (Eds.), *Handbook of Higher Education for Sustainable Development* (pp. 241–260). Routledge.

Wigfield, A., & Eccles, J. S. (2000). Expectancy–value theory of achievement motivation. *Contemporary Educational Psychology*, *25*(1), 68–81. doi:10.1006/ceps.1999.1015 PMID:10620382

Wikipedia Contributors. (2022). WikiWikiWeb. In *Wikipedia*. https://en.wikipedia.org/w/index.php?title=WikiWikiWeb&oldid=1092639361

Wiley, D., & Hilton, J. L. III. (2018). Defining OER-Enabled Pedagogy. *The International Review of Research in Open and Distributed Learning*, *19*(4). doi:10.19173/irrodl.v19i4.3601

Wiliyanto, R., Mahirah, A., & Firmansyah, F. I. (2022). Determining the Promotion Strategy of MSME Fashion and Souvenirs with the Market Basket Analysis Method. *INISTA: Journal of Informatics, Information Systems. Software Engineering and Applications*, *4*(2), 46–54. doi:10.20895/insta.v4i2.559

Wilson, D. J., & Serisier, T. (2010). Video activism and the ambiguities of counter-surveillance. *Surveillance & Society*, *8*(2), 166–180. doi:10.24908s.v8i2.3484

Wölbert, C. (2014). Apple ist ganz groß im Greenwashing [Apple is big on greenwashing]. *Heise online*. https://www.heise.de/mac-and-i/meldung/Kommentar-Apple-ist-ganz-gross-im-Greenwashing-2253419.html

Women from Pakistan tribal areas denied basic human rights. (2022). *ANI South Asia' leading multimedia News Agency*. Aninews.in/ news/ world/.

Wood, S., & Joicus, R. (2014). Beyond fun and games: Using an iPad as a tool for critical response. *The Reading Teacher*, *68*(2), 129–133. doi:10.1002/trtr.1309

Wurdinger, D. D., & Carlson, J. A. (2010). *Teaching for experiential learning: Five approaches that work*. Rowman & Littlefield Education.

Yang, Y.-T. C. (2012). Building virtual cities, inspiring intelligent citizens: Digital games for developing students' problem solving and learning motivation. *Computers & Education*, *59*(2), 365–377. doi:10.1016/j.compedu.2012.01.012

Yigezu, M. (2021). Digitalization in Teaching and Education in Ethiopia. In *ILO, Digitalization, the Future of Work and the Teaching Profession Project, Background Report*. International Labour Office.

Zahradník, M., & Pachmanová, L. (2009). Příklad využití wiki-prostředí v environmentálním vzdělávání na vysoké škole: Hodnocení kurzu Organizace a řízení ochrany životního prostředí [Example of using wiki-software in environmental education at university: evaluation of the course Management of Environmental Protection]. *Envigogika*, *4*(3). doi:10.14712/18023061.46

Zenone, M., Ow, N., & Barbic, S. (2021). TikTok and public health: A proposed research agenda. *BMJ Global Health*, *6*(11), e007648. doi:10.1136/bmjgh-2021-007648 PMID:34819326

Zhang, Y., & Wildemuth, B.M. (2009). *Unstructured Interviews: Applications of social research methods questions in information and library science*. Libraries Unlimited.

Zhang, X., & Tavitiyaman, P. (2022). Sustainability courses in hospitality and tourism higher education: Perspectives from industry practitioners and students. *Journal of Hospitality, Leisure, Sport and Tourism Education*, *31*, 100393. doi:10.1016/j.jhlste.2022.100393

Zhao, M., Liao, H.-T., & Sun, S.-P. (2020). An Education Literature Review on Digitization, Digitalization, Datafication, and Digital Transformation. *Advances in Social Science, Education and Humanities Research*, *435*, 301–305. doi:10.2991/assehr.k.200428.065

Zhu, M., Bonk, C. J., & Sari, A. R. (2018). Instructor experiences designing MOOCs in higher education: Pedagogical, resource, and logistical considerations and challenges. *Online Learning*, *22*(4), 203–241. doi:10.24059/olj.v22i4.1495

Zscheischler, J., Brunsch, R., Rogga, S., & Scholz, R. W. (2022). Perceived risks and vulnerabilities of employing digitalization and digital data in agriculture – Socially robust orientations from a transdisciplinary process. *Journal of Cleaner Production*, *358*, 132034. doi:10.1016/j.jclepro.2022.132034

About the Contributors

Lars Keller is Full Professor for Education for Sustainable Development at Universität Innsbruck, Austria. Leader of the research team Education and Communication for Sustainable Development, leader of various scientific research projects in Climate Change Education and ESD, publications of books and research articles in renowned journals, editor of journal GW-Unterricht (Education in geography and economics), various awards for scientific work (e.g. Hans Bobek Award of the Austrian Geographical Society, Austrian Sustainability Award), Consultant for the Austrian Federal Ministry for Education, leader of SDG4 in Uninetz Austria.

Gerd Michelsen studied economics at the Universities of Kiel and Freiburg i. Br., Professor for Environmental and Sustainability Communication at Leuphana University Lueneburg from 1995 to 2013, then Senior Professor for Sustainability Research. From 2005 to 2021 holder of the UNESCO Chair "Higher Education for Sustainable Development" at Leuphana University Lueneburg. Main research interests: sustainable development, (higher) education for sustainable development, sustainability communication; various voluntary activities at national and international level.

Martin Dür is a lecturer at the University College of Teacher Education Tyrol as well as at the Institute of Geography at the University of Innsbruck where he is part of the Research Team of Education and Communication for Sustainable Development. Beside this he is in charge of several project in which secondary high school students from Austria collaborate with peers from different parts of the world (mainly from the Global South) and jointly conduct research in order to develope a more sustainable lifestyle. A collaboration of students from Austria and India was awarded by the Austrian Ministry for Agriculture, Environment and Water Management. For the Austrian Ministry of Education he works as an appraiser for teaching materials.

Syamsul Bachri is an associate professor of disaster risk management at the geography department, social science faculty, state university of Malang, Indonesia. He is recently appointed vice dean of research, innovation, and community engagement. Before, he was the head of the master's and doctoral geography education study program. He graduated with his Ph.D. from the Department of Geography at Innsbruck University Austria, and he continues researching geography related to disaster management and sustainable development. His primary expertise is in human-environment systems interaction with the complex condition at local to regional scales. In addition, he also engages research in sustainable education.

* * *

Muhammad Tanveer Afzal has MSc in Mathematics and PhD in Education. He is working as Assistant Professor in Science Education Department at Faculty of Education, Allama Iqbal Open University, Islamabad, Pakistan. He has been performing duties as a faculty coordinator and resource person for Mphil and PhD programs. He has many national and international research publications to his name. He has visited university of Leicester, UK under HEC International Research. His areas of interest are, ICT in Education, Mathematics Education, Assessment and Evaluation in Education. He has achieved status of Associate Fellow of Higher Education against UK Professional Standards Framework for Teaching and learning.

Martin Bertau is Professor of Chemical Technology, Freiberg University of Mining and Technology, Germany.

Alexandra Budke is Professor of Human Geography and Geography Education at the Institute for Geography Education at the University of Cologne. Her research focuses on argumentation, civic education, digital media, intercultural learning, language-sensitive teaching and education for sustainable development. She completed her habilitation on ideological education in geography teaching in the GDR (2010, Humboldt University Berlin). She passed the first and second state examinations in order to be able to work as a teacher at the Gymnasium for Geography and French (2004). She wrote her PhD on Erasmus students' perceptions of their own country and Germany (2002, University of Osnabrück).

Guido Caniglia's work aims to shape epistemological and theoretical frameworks that contribute to ongoing scientific developments. Guido studies how experimental and theoretical practices contribute to producing evidence and knowledge about complex phenomena of transformation, especially purposeful transformations towards sustainability in our contemporary world. Guido previously held a Marie-Curie post-doctoral fellowship in the Faculty of Sustainability at Leuphana University of Lüneburg. He earned a PhD in Philosophy from the University of Florence (Italy) in 2010 while working in different academic communities mostly in Italy, Germany, Spain, and the United States. In January 2016 Guido obtained a second PhD, this time in Biology, from the Center for Biology and Society at Arizona State University (USA). Since November 2018, Guido is the Scientific Director of the Konrad Lorenz Institute for Evolution and Cognition Research in Klosterneuburg, Austria.

Jana Dlouhá is a researcher in Charles University Environment Centre; editor in chief of Envigogika journal; founder and coordinator of the Regional Centre of Expertise Czechia; 2nd vice chairman of the Czech Commission for UNESCO; ex vice-president and current member of the Advisory Board of the international network of higher education institutions COPERNICIS Alliance. Concerned with transformative education and educational transformation in the light of sustainable development; interests span from digital media, open education resources (co-founder of the Enviwiki and VCSEWiki knowledge base), to social learning and participatory approaches in public dialogue (mapping actors and decision-making processes on regional level). Involved in national and international networks and projects of cooperation with universities, NGOs and other social actors.

Jiří Dlouhý has been working for 30 year as a researcher in the Environmental Center of Charles University, he is deputy director. He is also chairman of Society for Sustainable Living, one of Czech environmental NGOs. His specialization is environmental education and education for sustainable development, especially the use of open educational resources in ESD. He is a member of the Board of the European Environmental Bureau, representing Czech Republic there.

Inga Gryl is professor for Primary Social and Science Education at the Institute for Geography at University of Duisburg-Essen. Her research interests are situated in the fields of education and digitalization, transformative geographical education, education for sustainable development and innovativeness in school. She is part of several national and curriculum initiatives to promote an emancipatory education in a culture of digitality.

Jehad Halawani is a Doctoral Student of Learning Technologies Design Research and International Education at George Mason University, VA. She is also the Presidential Scholar of the Center for International Education. Her research focuses on designing professional development and learning opportunities for in-service teachers using the Problem-Based Learning (PBL) framework to promote effective teaching practices, the use of PBL in the classroom, and Future-Ready Learning and Teaching.

Julia Holzer is a postdoctoral researcher at the Department of Developmental and Educational Psychology at the University of Vienna. Her research focuses on well-being, motivation and equity in the educational context.

Marlene Kollmayer is a postdoctoral researcher at the Department of Developmental and Educational Psychology at the University of Vienna. Her research focuses on gender stereotypes and their role in educational careers.

Selma Korlat earned her doctorate degree in Psychology in 2021. She is a postdoctoral researcher at the Department of Developmental and Educational Psychology at the University of Vienna. Her research focuses on stereotypes and their effects on performance, academic success, and motivation. She likes podcasts and jogging.

Nelly Kostoulas-Makrakis is a Professor of Education for Sustainable Development and Teaching Methodology in the Primary Teacher Education Department at the University of Crete, Greece and the focal point for the Earth Charter. She got her Ph.D from the University of Stockholm, Sweden. Her main teaching and research interests focus on education for sustainable development pedagogy. She is the author of three books and several articles in international journals and has participated in many international projects dealing with education for sustainable development.

Kanako N. Kusanagi is an Assistant Professor at the Center for Advanced School Education and Evidence-based Research, Graduate School of Education, The University of Tokyo. She specializes in comparative education and sociology of education, mainly focusing on international education transfer and the professional development of teachers. She is the author of Lesson Study as Pedagogic Transfer (2022), published by Springer and the co-author of Tokkatsu: The Japanese Educational Model of Holistic Education (2019), published by World Scientific.

Manfred Laubichler is Global Futures Professor and President's Professor of Theoretical Biology and History of Biology. He is Director of the School of Complex Adaptive Systems and the Global Bio-social Complexity Initiative at Arizona State University. His work focuses on evolutionary novelties from genomes to knowledge systems, the structure of evolutionary theory and the evolution of knowledge. His undergraduate training was in zoology, philosophy and mathematics at the University of Vienna (Austria) and his graduate training was in biology at Yale and in History/History of Science at Princeton. He is external professor at the Santa Fe Institute and, visiting scholar at the Max Planck Institute for the History of Science in Berlin, Germany, and external faculty member at the Complexity Science Hub Vienna. He is also an elected fellow of the American Association for the Advancement of Science, a former fellow of the WIssenschaftskolleg zu Berlin and Vice Chair of the Global Climate Forum.

Marko Lüftenegger is an Associate Professor for Developmental and Educational Psychology of the School Age at the University of Vienna. His main research focus is on emotion, motivation and self-regulated learning in educational contexts, teacher burnout and the evaluation of intervention programs in educational contexts.

Vassilios Makrakis is a Professor of ICT in Education for Sustainable Development (ESD) at the University of Crete, Greece and Frederick University, Cyprus. He is also a UNESCO Chair holder in the theme of ICT in ESD at the University of Crete. His expertise is on climate change education, sustainability policy, virtual learning, ICT-enabled ESD. Prof. Makrakis has published 5 books and more than 200 scientific articles in the field of ICT and ESD. He has coordinated more than 10 European-funded projects in the Middle East, South East Asia and South Africa.

Helga Mayr studied International Economic and Business Studies at the University of Innsbruck and at Tulane University, New Orleans/USA as well as Business Education at the University of Innsbruck where she finished both with a Diploma's degree. She taught at several vocational schools in Austria, worked in the field of school quality management and for the local education authority in the fields of health promotion in schools and education for sustainable development (ESD), among others. Since 2019, she coordinates the area of ESD at the University College of Teacher Education Tyrol/Austria. She is a lecturer at the University of Innsbruck, facilitates workshops and develops teaching materials. In the course of her doctoral thesis she deals with the design thinking approach in the context of education for sustainable development (with and without digital media).

Khalida Nasreen has Master in English Literature and MPhil in Education. She belongs to Taunsa Shareef and is working as teacher in tribal area of Dera Ghazi Khan, Punjab, Pakistan. She has worked on research articles and currently she is also working on many research projects in the field of education.

Elisabeth Pelikan is a university assistant and doctoral candidate at the Department of Developmental and Educational Psychology at the University of Vienna. Her research focuses on self-regulated learning and motivation in educational contexts.

Eduard Petiška has a Ph.D. (2015-2020) at Charles University, Faculty of Humanities and Environment Center. The thesis focused on Open educational resources (OER) in the context of environmental disciplines. Researcher and Research assistant at Charles University, Environment Center (2013 – 2022). Specialist and lecturer in Open educational resources (OER) and wiki systems at the Central Library (2017-2019). From 2020 managing partner of Sciencecom Agency focused on science communication.

Marie Pospíšilová is currently a member of the Department of Gender and Sociology, Institute of Sociology of the Czech Academy of Sciences, Prague, Czech Republic. Her expertise is in qualitative methodology and data analysis, gender inequalities, gender in the environmental sphere and digital interaction and communication.

Anton Rahmadi is an Associate Professor at the University of Mulawarman, East Kalimantan, Indonesia. His research field is on the antioxidant properties of foods and industrial downstream for the food products developed in the lab. His team develops an attachment to more than 300 food-based Small and Medium Enterprises (SMEs), giving consultation on factory layout, food product formulation, product certification, to digital marketing of the products. He was invited to be a national consultant for SMEs in Indonesia in 2022. This article is an example of a consultative framework that his team applies for SMEs in Indonesia, integrating laboratory work into the local industry.

Nicole Raschke is a junior professor of geography education and environmental communication at Technische Universität Dresden (Germany). Her research focuses on education for sustainable development, outdoor education and digitalization in geography education.

Eva Schernhammer is an alumna of the Medical University of Vienna (MD 1992), who conducted several years of clinical work at the SMZ-Süd (formerly Kaiser-Franz-Josef Hospital) in Vienna, with a focus on oncology, before she became full-time faculty at Harvard Medical School/HSPH in 2003. Since 2015, she is Professor of Epidemiology and Head of the Department of Epidemiology at the Medical University of Vienna, while maintaining active research programs at Harvard. In addition to her MD (Medical University of Vienna, 1992) and Doctor of Public Health, Epidemiology (DrPH, 2003 Harvard School of Public Health), she also holds an MPH (Harvard School of Public Health, 2000) and MSc (Psychology, University of Vienna, 2003). In 2005, Dr. Eva Schernhammer received her Habilitation in Public Health/Social Medicine from the Medical University of Vienna.

Barbara Schober is Professor for Psychological Research on Education and Transfer at the University of Vienna. Her research focuses on self-regulation, motivation and well being in educational contexts as well as on the implementation of interventions.

Maxim Shatkin received his Candidate of Sciences in Philosophy degree (PhD) from Saratov State University in 2004. In 2017 he received his master's degree in Theology, defending his thesis on the theological analysis of genetic experiments. Since 2018, he has been working at Povolzhsky Institute of Management named after P.A. Stolypin, a branch of Russian Academy of National Economy and Public Administration. His research concerns the trends in the transformation of higher education under digitalization and platformization of society.

Cris Slotoroff is the Supervisor of Humanities for the Vernon Township School District in Vernon Township, New Jersey, USA. For 12 years, Cris taught English Language Arts to students in grades 9–12 in New Jersey, focusing primarily on AP Language & Composition instruction. His research primarily focuses on changes to students' and teachers' regard for communication, autonomy, and socialization in the era of mobile technology's ubiquity. In this regard, Cris seeks to create a more informed teacher workforce and a more empowered student populace that collectively lead happier, more autonomous lives.

Christiane Spiel is emer. professor for Bildung-psychology and evaluation at the University of Vienna, Faculty of Psychology, Department of Developmental and Educational Psychology. Her research focuses on self-regulated learning, gender stereotypes, evaluation, implementation and the transfer of scientific knowledge in policy and practice.

Ilja Steffelbauer studied history and ancient history at the University of Vienna and Athens. His work within his original disciplines ranged from the topography and institutional history of ancient Attica to ephemeral films as sources for the urban history of Vienna, with publications on the social history of warfare, global history, and environmental history. At the Institute of Social and Economic History of the University of Vienna he focused on teacher education and was editor in chief of the journal "Historische Sozialkunde" for history and political education. Switching his career focus to science management and project administration in science he has worked for the Institute for Social and Cultural Anthropology of the University of Vienna and now for the Faculty of Business and Globalization at the University of Continuing Education, Krems. He continues to be active in continuing education for teachers and publishes on the history of warfare, food history and social evolution.

Gerald Steiner is a Full Professor of Organizational Communication and Innovation, Head of the Department for Knowledge and Communication Management, Dean of Faculty of Business and Globalization. He is a former Schumpeter Professor (Schumpeter Fellowship) and Visiting Scholar at Harvard University's Weatherhead Center for International Affairs (WCFIA). Before, he was an Associate Professor of Systemic and Sustainability Management at the Institute of Systems Sciences, Innovation and Sustainability Research at the University of Graz. He was also one of four founding members of this institute; subsequently he chaired the curriculum development working group. Further, he teaches applied innovation processes at the School of Industrial Design in Graz. Gerald Steiner received his Venia Legendi in "Systemic and Sustainability Management" ("Habilitation") in 2009. Over the past decades he has developed and codirected several graduate school curricula and teaches numerous graduate level seminars and courses both nationally and internationally.

Ute Stoltenberg was professor of education for sustainable development and sustainability science at Leuphana University Lueneburg, Germany. Since 1995, she has been involved in shaping the concept of education for sustainable development in theory and practice, for different areas of education (kindergarten, school, teacher education, non-formal education, university) but also in its significance for municipal and regional development. Fundamental to this were research projects with the participation of practical partners. She participates in international UNESCO networks and activities and is committed to the implementation of ESD at national level.

Kate Maloney Williams, MSc, is a PhD Candidate in International Education Policy at the University of Maryland, College Park. Her research interests lie in the intersection between new literacies, digital pedagogy, ICT4E, and education in emergencies. Currently, she provides research and evaluation support to the Teaching and Learning Transformation Center at the University of Maryland, College Park and is a consultant to UNICEF. She also holds a MSc in Media, Communication & International Development from The London School of Economics and a Graduate Certificate in Digital Literacy Education from the University of Rhode Island. She has provided technical assistance on several aid projects and been a lecturer at Loyola University Maryland.

Lukas Zenk works as an Associate Professor for Innovation and Network Research and the Deputy Head of Research at the Department of Knowledge and Communication Management, Danube University Krems. In his applied research projects, he investigates how people collaboratively solve complex problems and how creative and innovative processes can be supported. Currently, he leads the applied project "Organizational Improvisation" (www.improvisation.science) and developed the one-week university modules "Business Improvisation", "Lego Serious Play" and "Cognition and Creativity". Furthermore, he works as a network partner at Beratergruppe Neuwaldegg and founded the company The Lightbox Network () to innovate and consult organizations. He co-created the method Designing. Events (www.designing.events), co-developed the web app Collective Pictures (), and co-founded the improvisational theater company Quintessenz in Vienna. His innovative lectures, talks, and research projects in Networks, Innovation, and Improvisation have earned him several awards.

Index

ADVANCED RESEARCH. INCLUSIVE & AFFORDABLE.

IGI Global e-Book Collection

- **Flexible Purchasing Options** (Perpetual, Subscription, EBA, etc.)
- Multi-Year Agreements with **No Price Increases** Guaranteed
- **No Additional Charge** for Multi-User Licensing
- No Maintenance, Hosting, or Archiving Fees
- Continually Enhanced & Innovated **Accessibility Compliance Features** (WCAG)

Handbook of Research on Digital Transformation, Industry Use Cases, and the Impact of Disruptive Technologies
ISBN: 9781799877127
EISBN: 9781799877141

Handbook of Research on New Investigations in Artificial Life, AI, and Machine Learning
ISBN: 9781799886860
EISBN: 9781799886877

Handbook of Research on Future of Work and Education
ISBN: 9781799882756
EISBN: 9781799882770

Research Anthology on Physical and Intellectual Disabilities in an Inclusive Society (4 Vols.)
ISBN: 9781668435427
EISBN: 9781668435434

Innovative Economic, Social, and Environmental Practices for Progressing Future Sustainability
ISBN: 9781799895909
EISBN: 9781799895923

Applied Guide for Event Study Research in Supply Chain Management
ISBN: 9781799889694
EISBN: 9781799889717

Mental Health and Wellness in Healthcare Workers
ISBN: 9781799888130
EISBN: 9781799888147

Clean Technologies and Sustainable Development in Civil Engineering
ISBN: 9781799898108
EISBN: 9781799898122

Request More Information, or Recommend the IGI Global e-Book Collection to Your Institution's Librarian

www.ingramcontent.com/pod-product-compliance
Lightning Source LLC
LaVergne TN
LVHW080637011026
849160LV00014B/1243